PUBLIC EXPENDITURES AND POLICY ANALYSIS

****

PUBLIC EXPENDITURES AND POLICY ANALYSIS

****

Edited by

ROBERT H. HAVEMAN
Grinnell College

and

JULIUS MARGOLIS
Fels Institute
University of Pennsylvania

MARKHAM PUBLISHING COMPANY / CHICAGO

MARKHAM ECONOMICS SERIES

Julius Margolis, Editor

ARROW, *Essays in the Theory of Risk-Bearing*

BOWLES *and* KENDRICK *in Collaboration with* TAYLOR *and* ROBERTS, *Notes and Problems in Microeconomic Theory*

BUCHANAN, *Cost and Choice: An Inquiry in Economic Theory*

HARBERGER, *Project Evaluation: Collected Papers*

HAVEMAN *and* MARGOLIS, *eds., Public Expenditures and Policy Analysis*

KLEIN, *An Essay on the Theory of Economic Prediction*

TOBIN, *Essays in Economics: Volume I, Macroeconomics*

WAGNER, *The Public Economy*

FIFTH PRINTING JANUARY 1973

PRINTED IN U.S.A.

LIBRARY OF CONGRESS CATALOG CARD NUMBER: 76-111985

PAPERBACK STANDARD BOOK NUMBER: 8410-2007-8
HARDCOVER STANDARD BOOK NUMBER: 8410-2013-2

CONTENTS

PART FOUR THE PLANNING–PROGRAMING–BUDGETING SYSTEM: A CRITIQUE AND SOME RECOMMENDATIONS

PART FIVE POLICY ANALYSIS IN FEDERAL PROGRAMS: SOME LESSONS AND NEXT STEPS

PREFACE

The purpose of this book is to assemble several of the major contributions to the recent literature of public expenditure economics in one readily accessible volume. It provides a much needed source of theoretical and applied material as the long-neglected expenditure side of the public budget receives increased attention in the curricula of economics and political science departments and schools of business and public administration. The essays included in this volume are appropriate for use in public finance and policy analysis courses in all of these areas.

Many of these essays first appeared in publications of the Joint Economic Committee of the U.S. Congress. During 1968 and 1969, the Subcommittee on Economy in Government of the Joint Economic Committee undertook a major study of federal expenditure policy and the role of economic analysis in the public decision process. This study culminated in the publication by the Subcommittee of a 3-volume compendium entitled *The Analysis and Evaluation of Public Expenditures: The PPB System.* While on leave from Grinnell College, Professor Haveman coordinated this study and edited the papers in the Subcommittee compendium. The choice of papers from the Subcommittee study to be included in this volume rested with Professor Margolis. Several excellent papers were excluded because of duplication and the desirability of having a broad range of concerns as well as depth of analysis represented in this volume. It should be noted that several of the essays in this volume have been substantially altered, revised, and consolidated since their appearance in the Joint Economic Committee study.

We would like to thank all of the authors represented in this volume for their cooperation in revising and editing the papers and in meeting rather tight deadlines. The efforts of Senator William Proxmire in focusing the attention of the Subcommittee on the role of economic analysis in improving government efficiency are also acknowledged. Without his initiative, the study would not have been undertaken and many of these essays would not have been written. Finally, we are grateful to Mrs. Anne McAfee for her most helpful clerical and typing assistance and to John Stark, Executive Director of the Joint Economic Committee staff, for his support.

February 1970

Robert H. Haveman
Julius Margolis

INTRODUCTION

PUBLIC EXPENDITURES AND POLICY ANALYSIS: AN OVERVIEW

Robert H. Haveman

PUBLIC EXPENDITURE ECONOMICS: A NEGLECTED DISCIPLINE

Until the late 1950s or early 1960s, public expenditure analysis was not generally recognized as a distinct field of economic inquiry. The literature of economics which focused on matters of public choice, the application of economic criteria to public spending alternatives, and the values created or destroyed by government expenditures was limited in both coverage and sophistication. Although concern with the economics of public spending was formally included in the field of public finance, economists specializing in this field were more fascinated with taxation matters than with the expenditure of public monies. Similarly, public finance courses seldom treated the economics of public spending in the depth accorded the analysis of taxation. The expenditure side of the public budget was discussed with brevity, and then descriptively rather than analytically. Although there was no lack of concern about the provision of public services, there was little significant application of economic analysis to the design and scale of services.

In public finance literature, theorizing about the economic effects of taxation developed simultaneously with neo-classical economics early in the century. By 1950, the basic issues concerning the resource allocation, growth, and incidence effects of different taxes had been debated and generally resolved in the literature of economics. Moreover, substantive empirical work on the efficiency and distributional effects of alternative tax structures had been undertaken. However, theorizing about public expenditures was in short supply and empirical analysis of a rigorous sort was undeveloped. With good reason, public finance prior to the late 1950s was widely interpreted as the economics of taxation.[1]

In part, the neglect of public expenditure analysis was due to a lack of readily accessible information about the composition and incidence of expenditure programs. Although most citizens and businesses file a tax return showing not only the amount given up but also the income and expenses which determine the taxes paid, most public outputs are given away with no trace of the beneficiaries or their characteristics. Typically, there is not even a market transaction whose terms could provide some information. Economic analysis and research rather naturally gravitated to the areas where information and data is readily available.

The lack of appropriability which characterizes many public expenditures is a second reason for the tardy development of a distinct field of study in this area. When a public expenditure produces a public good whose value accrues to all whether or not they desire it, explicit analysis of the distributional impact, economic efficiency, or individual behavior response generated by the expenditure is extremely difficult. Until recent years, expenditures for such nonappropriable outputs dominated public budgets. The problem of nonappropriability does not afflict the tax side of the budget. The sacrifice entailed by the raising of public revenue is duly recorded and attributed to each individual. Taxes, therefore, are visible and painful; the benefits of public expenditures are less visible and often intangible.[2]

Moreover, even when public outputs are appropriable, a multitude of difficulties surround estimates of the values to be attached to them. In most cases, it is some form of market failure which stimulated public provision of the output in the first place; where market failure is present, observed prices are either nonexistent or poor indicators of economic values. And, it must be admitted, the development of appropriate willingness-to-pay values by which to appraise the worth of public outputs is a difficult and treacherous undertaking.

Finally, the structure of institutions which surrounds public expenditure decisions has also contributed to the slow development of public expenditure economics. An individual decision on tax policy typically involves a large sum of money and affects the vast majority of citizens. Conversely, decisions on individual public expenditures usually involve relatively small sums of money and directly affect only limited groups of citizens. Moreover, at the federal level, tax policy is handled by a single executive agency and a pair of Congressional committees; expenditure decisions are divided among 30 or so agencies and substantive program decisions are made by several Congressional committees.

The neglect of public expenditure analysis by economists has been reflected in federal government practice. Prior to the late 1950s, it was the rare government expenditure program whose benefits and costs were evaluated either before its establishment or while in progress. Although isolated analyses were undertaken during this period, usually in the Bureau of the Budget, there was no systematic effort to appraise the relative worth of expenditure options or to base public spending decisions on analysis.

This situation can be contrasted to the application of analysis to federal revenue policy. In the period before 1960, the Department of Treasury began to establish staff capability to analyze the economic effects of federal revenue alternatives on a regular basis. Similarly, fiscal and monetary policy analysis was undertaken at the Treasury, the Federal Reserve Board, and the Council of Economic Advisers. Although the quality of these analyses has increased over the last decade or two, they did exist in the 1940s and 1950s and they did influence federal tax and monetary-fiscal policy.

Economic analysis did not often influence decisions on federal expenditure programs during this period, with one notable exception. Because of the Flood Control Act of 1936, the U.S. Army Corps of Engineers was required to evaluate the benefits and costs of all water resource projects "to whomsoever they accrue." Although the early analytical work in this area has been criticized for lack of conceptual and empirical sophistication, it did stimulate efforts by both economists and decisionmakers to apply the logic of economics to public expenditure decisions.

THE DEVELOPMENT OF PUBLIC EXPENDITURE ECONOMICS

Since the mid-1950s, the theory and practice of public expenditure economics have changed radically. Both the economics literature and college and university curricula now reflect a concern with the effect of public expenditures on the size and composition of the nation's output, the allocation of its resources, and the distribution of its income. Similarly, the practice of governmental budgeting and decisionmaking has begun to recognize the importance of applying analysis to expenditure decisions. The economic analysis of taxation policy has become supplemented by serious efforts to evaluate and appraise public expenditure alternatives.

These developments in the economics profession and in government were reinforced by changes in the curricula of schools of business, public administration, and engineering. In schools of business, application of economic criteria and the techniques of systems analysis and operations research to private management decisions was transferred to the public sector and its decisions. Similarly, public administration curricula began to reflect a concern for policy analysis and systematic decisionmaking, although at a less sophisticated level than the business schools. Perhaps most significantly, schools of engineering came to recognize that efficient public facility planning must be guided by the *value* of inputs and outputs in addition to physical and engineering relationships, and that in project design, economic optima may not coincide with engineering optima.

A number of factors have contributed to the recent emergence of public expenditure economics as a significant field of study. Although many of the influences are complex and obscure, a few are sufficiently clear to warrant special comment.

Economic theory provided a major contribution through developments in welfare economics; often highly refined but always suggestive. These studies helped clarify the conditions under which government should intervene in the market economy and provided guidance for the choice of instruments to accomplish social objectives. The notions of collective consumption, externalities, and community welfare have been defined with precision. That these phenomena had implications for the economic role of the state came to be generally recognized by economists.

In the early 1950s, many of the loose ends of the early contributions of welfare theory were tied together in an important study by W. Baumol, *Welfare Economics and the Theory of the State*.[3] Although Baumol was pessimistic about the ultimate ability of economic analysis to establish definitively the relationship between public decisions and social welfare, his work made discussions of private market failure and its causes a legitimate enterprise. More important, it legitimized the search for criteria that isolate those public decisions which increase society's economic welfare from those which do not.

By the end of the 1950s, Francis Bator could write with authority on the "failures of the market." Moreover, a large literature had been developed, and through it, analytical concensus was attained. In this literature, the characteristics of free market operation were examined, those structural conditions which cause social costs and gains to diverge from their private counterparts were clarified, the characteristics of public goods were defined, and the reasons why markets fail to produce them were identified. These contributions isolated the circumstances in which the private market economy would fail to provide certain worthwhile outputs and would overproduce or underproduce others. Market power, decreasing costs, immobilities, lack of knowledge and their ruinous effiects on the efficient operation of the private economy became part-and-parcel of realistic economic analysis. By 1960, "market failure" possessed significance which it did not previously have.

Concurrent with these developments in welfare economics was a general relaxation of the traditional free enterprise presumption which had long dominated economic thought. Economists found it increasingly uncomfortable to assume that the basic structure of the economy was that of free competition in which government activities represented only a minor aberration from universal private decisionmaking. Recognition that neoclassical analysis was unable to explain the behavior of markets dominated by oligopoly, advertising, and administered prices, contributed to the altered viewpoint. Similarly, the rapid postwar growth of the public sector, both absolutely and relative to the private sector, fostered a revision of the earlier presumption. With 20 percent of the nation's gross national product accounted for by government purchases of goods and services, and 8 to 10 percent of the nation's final output regularly devoted to the military budget, it became difficult to pass off the public sector as a minor flaw in an otherwise smoothly functioning market system.

Related to the contributions of theoretical welfare economics was an applied and empirical line of development. If public expenditures are necessary to attain certain worthwhile collective objectives—to correct for market failure—how can those public decisions which contribute to society's economic welfare be separated from those that do not? Even if we knew that governments should intervene under certain conditions, what rules should guide their behavior? Efforts to find a functional and theoretically correct answer to these questions resulted in the development of an economic criterion for evaluating public expenditure alternatives. The early benefit-cost efforts by water resources agencies encouraged economists interested in applying a public sector efficiency criterion to focus on this program area.[4] These studies in turn stimulated additional research efforts which extended quantitative and systematic analysis to public decisions in all areas of the Federal budget. These later studies incorporated many of the techniques developed in the operations research and systems analysis literature. Through these efforts, appropriate methods were developed for measuring the benefits and costs of a wide variety of public expenditures and an economic criterion—maximum net benefits—became widely accepted.

One further factor influencing the development of public expenditure economics should be mentioned. In the 1950s and 1960s, a concern, quite unrelated to public finance matters, caught the interest of economists. During this period, the field of economic development and growth, focusing on the low-income problems of the less developed nations, grew rapidly. In the search for meaningful instruments of national economic planning, the appropriate criteria for public sector choice were widely discussed in this literature. Those concerned with development policy required just those concepts formulated in the public expenditure literature—social benefits and costs, the public discount rate, the valuing of public outputs, and the nature of the efficiency criterion. Because of the convergence of these two quite separate concerns, progress in developing the concepts and methods of public expenditure analysis occurred which would not otherwise have done so.[5]

Simultaneous with these developments in theoretical and applied economics and, in part, because of them, there was agitation among decisionmakers within the federal government for improved policy analysis. The 1950s and 1960s witnessed an enormous demand for government programs to produce a wide range of outputs which until that time had either not been produced or had been produced in the private sector. With the resources to meet these demands severely constrained, many public decisionmakers sought an economic criterion to aid them in choosing efficiently among the available alternatives. As public sector expenditures and programs expanded rapidly during this period, it became increasingly recognized that effective choice required more and better knowledge of the economic effects of public expenditures.

Because of all of these factors, the flow of policy analysis increased rapidly in the 1960s. Pioneering studies in the areas of natural resources, health, education, and pollution were added to the literature. Under the sponsorship of the RAND Corporation, the techniques of systematic analysis were applied to national defense planning decisions. Resources for the Future, Inc. and The Brookings Institution provided the auspices for major breakthroughs in the analysis of natural resource and domestic programs. In these studies, analysts isolated the relevant policy alternatives in a program area and, to the extent possible, estimated the economic costs and gains expected from each.

Where the conceptual problems of defining the output and establishing its value could be solved, analysts calculated ratios of benefits to costs for alternative programs or for the components of programs. If a project or program demonstrated a benefit-cost ratio which exceeded 1, there was a prima facie presumption that the undertaking was an economic one—that the value of the output which it produced exceeded the value of the inputs which it drew away from other uses.

In those cases in which the program output was difficult to define or measure or where the output could not be valued, analysts performed what is called cost-effectiveness analysis. In this form of analysis, the task involves searching for the lowest cost means of attaining an explicit objective rather than evaluating both benefits and costs, and searching for that optimally designed project with the greatest surplus of benefits over costs.

Benefit-cost analysis has been applied to public expenditures for natural resources development and, to a more limited extent, transportation and human resource investments. Investments in the national defense and space programs have been subjected to cost-effectiveness analysis. In these programs, the good produced is a public good in which everyone automatically benefits once the good is produced. Quantitative estimation of the benefits of such expenditures is not possible and cost-effectiveness analysis replaces benefit-cost analysis as the appropriate instrument of evaluation.

SOME BASIC NOTIONS IN PUBLIC EXPENDITURE ANALYSIS[6]

The basic theme which runs through economic or policy analysis is that of economic efficiency, broadly defined. Considered most simply, economic efficiency is achieved when the value of what is produced by any set of resources exceeds by as much as possible the value of the resources used; or when the least valuable set of resources is utilized in producing any particular worthwhile output. Both benefit-cost and cost-effectiveness analyses apply this economic efficiency principle to public expenditure choices.

The first task in applying benefit-cost analysis to a proposed undertaking is to isolate the full set of impacts, both favorable and unfavorable, which it generates. The favorable effects can be labelled outputs and the unfavorable ones inputs. It should be emphasized that this concept of inputs and outputs is broader than that typically considered in business decisions. For business firms, outputs and inputs are salable and quantifiable objects—shoes, labor, capital, and so on. While public expenditures often produce such outputs and absorb such inputs, their total input and output impact also includes side effects and less easily quantified impacts than typical business firm decisions.

Consider a labor retraining program as an example. The output of such a program surely includes the added productivity of the workers which are trained. This added productivity is quantifiable and salable, like the output of a private sector business. Consider the many private schools which train secretaries, musicians, mechanics, and so on. However, the output of a retraining program also includes the gains which accrue to the society in general because of the changed behavior of the newly-trained people. Having been trained, these workers are now less likely to be unemployed (contributing to the ghetto and low-income problems), and are more likely to provide stable homes and a better education for their children. Because these side effects or spillovers contribute to community welfare, they must also be included in the output category and attributed to the decision.

One of the most elusive of these unsalable outputs results when something is created which automatically gives satisfaction to all people in the society as soon as it is produced. Such outputs are called "public goods." National defense and a successful moon shot are examples of such public goods. A man's shirt or his car or U.S. Steel's factory do not have this characteristic.[7]

Once the full set of inputs and outputs attributable to a public decision is isolated, the next step in benefit-cost analysis is to attach a value or price to each input and output. The price which is attached should represent the value which society places on the input or the output. If measured in dollars, the value of the inputs is the amount which would have to be paid to all of the people adversely affected by the decision, just to compensate them for the dissatisfaction which they incurred. Similarly, the value of the outputs is the amount which those people who gained from the decision would be willing to pay rather than go without the output. Once these values are placed on inputs and outputs, they become known as *costs* and *benefits*.

While valuing the inputs and outputs of a public expenditure is the most difficult task of benefit-cost analysis, a market economy such as that of the United States can provide substantial guidance in assigning values. In fact, if the market system is running smoothly and is a competitive system, observed prices can be directly applied to many of the inputs and outputs of public decisions. This is possible if these inputs and outputs are bought or sold by the government or if they are closely reated to items traded in the private economy. In a competitive market economy, the ratios of the observed prices of outputs represent the relative value to society of the goods or services produced, and the ratios of the observed prices of inputs represent the relative costs of these goods and the values which these resources would have produced if they had not been diverted.[8]

Having transformed the inputs and outputs of a public expenditure into costs and benefits, the final step of policy analysis is the establishment of a criterion by which to appraise the economic worth of the undertaking. In planning a program or designing a project, the criterion consistent with maximizing the value of the nation's output is the *maximum net benefits criterion.*[9] According to this criterion, the optimum size or design of a project or program is that for which the excess of benefits over costs is as great as possible. Stated alternatively, if net benefits are not maximized, resources can be added or subtracted, or the design can be changed so as to increase the value of net benefits.

If all the projects and programs in the government's "wish list" were designed on the basis of the maximum net benefits criterion, there would still be a problem of choice. With a limited budget, the government can choose only a portion of the items in this list. In making this choice, the maximum net benefits criterion will again lead to an efficient decision. By allocating his budget according to this rule, the public decisionmaker can be confident that, given available knowledge, the dollars which he spends will produce the largest possible economic gain to the society.

While the basic benefit-cost formulation is a straightforward maximizing problem, there are a number of complex considerations which confront the analyst as he applies this criterion to public expenditure decisions. These can be mentioned only briefly in this overview.

Externalities An externality is an indirect side effect or spillover impact which results from a decision. Not typically considered a direct benefit or cost, externalities either inflict harm on someone without compensating him for it, or confer gain on someone without demanding payment. In accurately analyzing public expenditure decisions, all externalities, good and bad, must be taken into account.

For example, consider the proposal to construct and operate a large dam which will prevent downstream flooding on a river. The analysis of this proposal will obviously include as benefits the value of the flood damage which will be averted, the power which will be produced, the water supply which will be created, and the recreation which will be provided. As costs, the analysis will account for the value of the resources which are required to build and operate the installation. However, if flooding the river valley to form the reservoir pool irreparably destroys natural landscape and scenic views, an external cost is imposed on society. The scenic effects are no less real than, say, the flood control effects but because the scenic effects are not included among the objectives of the agency, they are "external consequences." Comprehensive benefit-cost analysis must also attribute a value to such externalities.

The range of external impacts which can and do spill over from public expenditure decisions is wide. Among them are physical interdependence effects, population migration effects, impacts on local employment, regional saving and investment rates, effects which induce discontinuous changes in technology or foreclose options which may be of value in the future, impacts on human attitudes and tastes, effects on the international balance-of-payments position, and impacts on state and local government budgets. The analyst and decisionmaker must be sensitive to these impacts and, wherever possible, implement his analysis so as to insure that they are discovered and taken into account.

Secondary Impacts In analyzing a public decision from a national perspective, the basic question is: What is the value of the net gain to the nation which will be generated by the expenditure? From a national point of view, some of the impacts generated by a public expenditure are not legitimately included in the estimates of benefits or costs so defined. These are termed "transfer" or "secondary" impacts and must be distinguished from "real" impacts.

Secondary impacts are those effects which a public expenditure decision has on the prices of and demands for certain inputs and outputs in the economy as the primary gainers or losers from a public project change their spending patterns because of the increases or decreases in their incomes. For example, if the government builds a park which attracts large numbers of recreationists, a businessman might well find it profitable to locate a restaurant opposite the park entrance. Should the profits of the restaurant be counted as a benefit attributable to the construction of the park? In a smoothly functioning market economy, the answer is *no*. The profits created by the altered spending decisions of the beneficiaries of the park (the park users) will be offset by decreased profits experienced elsewhere in the economy because of the decreased spending of those who bear the cost of the park (the taxpayers). Consequently, the construction of the park generates positive secondary impacts in the region in which it is located; those impacts are matched by negative secondary effects elsewhere in the economy. The gain conferred on one person is offset by a simultaneous loss for someone else. On balance, there has been no real consumption or production effect on the economy through this secondary impact mechanism—only an income transfer from secondary losers to secondary gainers.[10]

Careful public expenditure analysis must insure that these secondary impacts are treated uniformly on both the benefit and cost sides of the ledger. If the analyst chooses to count secondary benefits while ignoring the offsetting secondary costs, the evaluation will be seriously biased. This must be emphasized because of the visibility and concentration of secondary benefits relative to secondary costs. The profits of the restaurant across from the park are highly visible and readily brought to the attention of the public agency; the secondary losses due to the reduced expenditures of taxpayers are dispersed throughout the economy and there is no mechanism by which they can be brought to bear on any public agency.

Present Values Many public expenditures to which benefit-cost analysis is applied are longlived investments. The outputs of these projects accrue over several years and they require inputs as long as they are producing. Because today's appraisal of the value of inputs and outputs depends on when in the future they will occur, it is important that a consistent mode of accounting for these future effects be determined.

The procedure ordinarily adopted to account for the effect of time on values is called *discounting*. Through discounting analysis, all future benefits and costs are transformed into dollars of present worth. This is done by applying a formula which adjusts dollars of future gains and costs based on the society's appraisal of the dollar value today relative to a dollar not expected until tomorrow. For example, if optimal investment of $100 today would yield $108 next year, then $108 expected next year is worth only about $100 today. In this case, the interest rate is 8 percent. It represents society's evaluation of the effect of time on values. When the appropriate interest rate (r) is incorporated into the discounting equation, the present value of a future stream of benefits (or costs) can be calculated by adding up each of the future year's benefits (or costs) after each has been adjusted by r percent per year because of the lapse of time.

Consider a public investment which will produce outputs for 25 years. It will require an initial cost of $5 million and an annual cost of $.1 million for operation and repair for each year of its life. The investment will yield $.6 million of annual benefits in each of the 25 years. Table 1 shows the influence of various interest or discount rates (0, 3, 5, and 10 percent) on the evaluation of this investment. From the table, it is apparent that the size of the discount rate is crucial in placing future benefits and costs on a present-value basis. With a zero discount rate (no discounting), benefits are evaluated at twice the costs;[11] at an interest rate of 5 percent, benefits are only 1.3 times the costs; at an interest rate of 10 percent, costs exceed benefits by nearly $.5 million.

In economics literature, the appropriate concept and size of the public discount rate has long been debated. Because of imperfections in the market economy, many interest rates and capital productivities can be observed. Most economists now agree that the interest rate which should be used in public sector evaluation is that opportunity cost rate implicit in the

Table 1
The Effect of Discounting on the Evaluation of a Typical Investment, Using Discount Rates of 0, 3, 5, and 10 percent
[Dollar amounts in thousands]

	Interest rate (in percent)			
	0%	3%	5%	10%
Value today of total benefits	$15,000	$10,448	$8,456	$5,442
Value today of total costs	$ 7,500	$ 6,741	$6,409	$5,906
Benefit-cost ratio	2.00	1.45	1.32	0.92
Value today of excess of benefits over costs	$ 7,500	$ 3,707	$2,047	–$468

private sector spending which is displaced because of the public expenditure. The application of this principle implies that a discount rate of 8–10 percent should currently be applied in evaluating public expenditures.[12]

Non-Efficiency Objectives We have argued that efficient public choice should be guided by benefit and cost calculations in which inputs and outputs are valued by the prices which a competitive market system would assign to them. Benefit estimates would equal the total willingness to pay of beneficiaries, and costs would be the opportunity costs borne by the community because of the expenditure. Public expenditure decisions based upon these calculations would generate an efficient allocation of national resources.

It must be emphasized, however, that the prices which are used as instruments of valuation have a very particular meaning. While the market system's price generating process captures many of the tastes of the citizens of a society, there are a number of society's values which are excluded. Observed prices depend on the pattern of market demands in the private economy which, in turn, depend on the way in which society's income is distributed. If the existing income distribution is not optimal (and, presumably, it is not), it is difficult to claim that these prices have absolute normative significance. While the economic efficiency goal would likely be served by public sector reliance on benefits and costs calculated from observed prices, the goal of equity or income redistribution—also a legitimate social goal—would be given no weight in the decision process. The question is: How should these nonefficiency goals be accounted for in public sector decisionmaking?

One answer given to this question is based on the recognition that observed market prices fail to distinguish among the beneficiaries and cost-bearers of a public decision—a dollar's worth of benefits is a dollar's worth of benefits, no matter who gets them. If society has an equity goal, this approach notes, the characteristics of the people who receive the benefits and bear the costs do make a difference. Society has made the judgment that increments of income to some people (the poor, blacks, those living in region x) are of more collective value than increments to other people. Using this logic, it is argued that the government should place different weights on dollars of benefit or cost, depending on who gets them or who bears them. Because these weights represent a value judgment about how society's income ought to be distributed, they should be decided by the political process and consistently applied in evaluating public expenditures.

While all observers agree that information on the characteristics of the beneficiaries and the cost-bearers is pertinent to public expenditure decisions and should be presented to the decisionmaker, many object to the weighting procedure as a means of accounting for nonefficiency objectives. A number of reservations to this procedure have been offered:

- If all benefit and cost estimates were weighted with "equity weights" prior to presentation to the decisionmaker, he would not be able to readily discern the relative portions of efficiency (or national output) and equity (or income redistribution) benefits generated by an expenditure. It is important that the efficiency and equity impacts be kept separate so that the decisionmaker can alter the relative importance given each of these goals in moving from programs undertaken primarily for efficiency reasons (to correct for market failures, such as externalities, public goods, and information inadequacies) to programs whose primary objective is to redistribute income.
- Obtaining accurate data on the distributional impact of public expenditures is terribly difficult. Not only must the distribution of the benefits be ascertained, but also the distribution of the costs to taxpayers and real resource suppliers. Because of the difficulty of accurately estimating these patterns with existing knowledge, it is not yet appropriate to incorporate equity weights into formal benefit and cost estimates.
- The ability of Congress, a transient grouping of individuals, to publicly generate an optimal set of equity weights which would not oscillate wildly over time is doubtful. A rational planning process requires stability in the parameters with which it operates.

THE PPB SYSTEM AND ITS PERFORMANCE

The past decade has witnessed a significant upsurge in the application of economic criteria to public expenditures by government agencies. This has reversed the serious neglect of analysis and the rational planning of expenditures prior to the 1960s. Clearly, the tardy establishment of a planning and analytic capability in the federal government is related to the slow development of the field of public expenditure analysis among economists.

Recent efforts to introduce systematic analysis into the public decision process began in the Department of Defense. The story of its introduction there is by now well-known and documented. Under the leadership of Secretary McNamara and his Comptroller, Charles Hitch, an Office of Systems Analysis was established and headed by an Assistant Secretary. Applying cost-effectiveness concepts and analytical tools developed at the RAND Corporation and similar research centers, the systems analysis staff was able to furnish the Secretary with the kind of performance and cost information essential for a rational choice among alternatives.

The asserted success of this effort stimulated the judgment that quantitative analysis could and should also be applied to civilian programs. This judgment was reinforced by the fact that water resources expenditures had been subject to benefit-cost evaluation since the decade of the 1930s.

On August 25, 1965, President Johnson signed an Executive Order establishing a comprehensive Planning-Programing-Budgeting (PPB) System throughout the federal government. In his words, this system would enable public decisionmakers to:

(1) Identify our national goals with precision and on a continuing basis;
(2) Choose among those goals the ones that are most urgent;
(3) Search for alternative means of reaching those goals most effectively at the least cost;
(4) Inform ourselves not merely on next year's costs, but on the second, and third, and subsequent years' costs of our programs;
(5) Measure the performance of our programs to insure a dollar's worth of service for each dollar spent.

The Bureau of the Budget was assigned responsibility for implementing this system and for assisting agencies to develop methods of analysis and an analytic staff. The PPB System was to be the vehicle for generating open, explicit, and comprehensive economic evaluation of all programs and establishing a decision process in which choices would be based on the results of analysis.

It has been nearly five years since the inception of the PPB System. Numerous assertions have been made concerning both the wisdom and the efficacy of the effort. Failures have been documented and well publicized. Successes have also been claimed. Some who fancy themselves "generalists" have viewed efforts to apply sound and systematic thinking about benefits and costs as a narrow "specialist" enterprise. Others, whose traditional power over the federal budget requires the absence of an open and informed decision process, have viewed it as a threat to their influence.

From the outset, the PPB System encountered serious obstacles which have impeded improvements in the public decision process. They include the following:

- The failure of many agency heads to demand program analysis or to use it in decisionmaking when it was available;
- The lack of interest in (and sometimes opposition to) the system by important congressional committees and Congressmen;
- The failure of much legislation to clearly stipulate program objectives and to provide funds for the collection of follow-up data and other appraisal information;
- The existence of private interest groups which anticipate that hard and quantitative program evaluation will endanger the size or existence of expenditures which benefit them;
- The constraints on substantive and time-consuming policy analysis

imposed by the annual budget cycle and process to which the PPB System is tied;
• A serious scarcity of analytical personnel in the PPB offices of civilian agencies;
• A basic resistance by many federal employees to economic analysis and the difficult job of program evaluation;
• The lack of professional agreement on certain basic analytical issues, such as the size of the appropriate public discount rate, the development of shadow prices when outputs are not marketed, and the evaluation of expenditures with multiple objectives.
• The lack of adequate data from which to develop measures of the benefits of outputs and costs of inputs.

While advocates of the PPB System recognize the seriousness of these impediments, they assert that the system has significantly improved the decision process. Decisions have been based on better information and analysis. Parties to the political bargaining process have been forced to focus on the inputs and outputs and the benefits and costs of alternative programs. However, even the most enthusiastic admit that substantial progress toward the goal of a rational, consistent, and economic budgetary process has yet to be made.

THE STRUCTURE OF THIS VOLUME AND ITS GOALS

The papers included in this volume form a comprehensive study of public expenditure economics. The theory of public expenditure analysis is surveyed. Current federal government practice of evaluating program alternatives is described and critiqued. Conceptual problems in applying economic analysis to public expenditures are discussed and the institutional factors which affect the government's ability to implement effective public expenditure decisions are described.

In Part One, the economic basis for public expenditures and other governmental action is explored. These papers analyze the appropriate economic functions of government and the optimal devision of national resources between the public and private sectors. They discuss the need for collective action when market failure is present and detail the alternative public sector responses for adjusting the private sector outcome. The final paper in this section discusses public sector responsibility for adjusting the distribution of income and analyzes a number of criteria for evaluating attempts to redistribute income through public expenditure policy.

The papers in Part Two focus on institutional arrangements which affect the ability of the federal government to implement efficient public expenditure policy. The first paper in this section argues that sound decisionmaking requires careful and explicit consideration of the incentives, penalties, and rewards which are created by public programs. Because program success requires appropriate responses of those affected by an expenditure, sound program design must take account of the structure of incentives. Additional institutional considerations surrounding public expenditure policy are discussed in the other papers in this section. These include analyses of (1) the complex political process surrounding expenditure decisions in which the interplay of a diverse set of interest groups with varying motivations determines the character of decisions; (2) the inflexibility of the federal budget which limits the effectiveness of policy analysis; and (3) the extent to which our present knowledge of the distributional impacts of public expenditures falls short of the information needed to make informed equity decisions.

In Part Three, several of the most basic analytical and empirical problems encountered in estimating the benefits and costs of public expenditure alternatives are analyzed. These include (1) the valuation of benefits and costs when there are no observable market values or when the government has objectives in addition to economic efficiency; (2) the correct concept and size of the public rate of discount; (3) the appropriate treatment of risk and uncertainty; and (4) the application of benefit-cost analysis when there are unemployed resources. These papers discuss both the nature and the causes of these analytical problems and, in most cases, suggest improvements in the practice of federal government expenditure evaluation.

Part Four contains an evaluation of the Planning-Programing-Budgeting System and its component parts. The first paper presents the current position of the Bureau of the Budget on the status of the PPB System and its plans for improving the system's structure and performance. Other papers in this section critique the performance of the PPB System and offer suggestions for modification in both its structure and its operation in the legislative and executive branches. These papers have been prepared either by individuals who have been intimately involved in the federal government budgetary process or in implementing the PPB System.

The papers collected in Part Five deal with the unresolved issues, the problem areas, and next steps for policy analysis and program evaluation in selected functional areas of the federal budget. They have been prepared by analysts knowledgeable in the implementation of policy analysis in these areas. In most cases these authors have been directly responsible for the implementation of economic analysis in the agencies concerned.

All of the papers in this volume were prepared initially for the Subcommittee on Economy in Government of the Joint Economic Committee. In June 1969, the Subcommittee published a three-volume study entitled "The Analysis and Evaluation of Public Expenditures: The PPB

System," which contained over 25 papers in addition to those in this volume. The objective of the Committee study was to focus the attention of the Congress, the new administration, and social scientists on the need for quantitative policy analysis in the formation of federal expenditure decisions. It hoped to stimulate research required to apply welfare economics to public policy decisions and to emphasize the need for traditional college and university curricula to reflect the growing importance of public expenditure economics. This volume shares those objectives and seeks, in addition, to provide a readily accessible body of literature to be used in both graduate and undergraduate economics curricula, in schools of business, public administration, and engineering, and in training programs for government analysts.

NOTES

[1] The dominance of the revenue side in the public finance literature is illustrated by a casual survey of the *Index of Economic Journals* from 1950 to 1959. Of a total of 450–500 articles published in the field of "Public Finance" and included in the subfields of "Public Expenditure" and "Taxation and Other Revenue," only 52, or about 10 percent, treated the expenditure side of the public budget.

[2] Whereas the ultimate effect of taxes on the allocation of resources, economic growth, and income distribution is elusive and difficult to measure, the initial or first-round impacts are relatively easy to discern.

[3] Cambridge: Harvard University Press, 1952.

[4] See, for example, O. Eckstein, *Water Resources Development: The Economics of Project Evaluation* (Cambridge: Harvard University Press, 1958); R. McKean, *Efficiency in Government Through Systems Analysis* (New York: John Wiley & Sons, 1958); J. V. Krutilla and O. Eckstein, *Multiple-Purpose River Development* (Baltimore: Johns Hopkins Press, 1958).

[5] While its impact is more difficult to trace, the private sector–public sector debate stimulated by J. K. Galbraith's *The Affluent Society* (Boston: Houghton Mifflin Co., 1958) could also be added to the list of factors contributing to the increased concern by economists with public expenditures and their effects. Indeed, Galbraith's plea for a larger public sector was based on a judgment that the "outputs" generated by the next public dollar spent have a greater value than those produced by the next dollar spent by private consumers or businesses. Both his critics and supporters recognized that additional knowledge of the benefits and costs of public expenditures was necessary to test both Galbraith's social imbalance assertion and its opposite.

[6] For a more advanced discussion of the conceptual issues of public expenditure analysis, see A. R. Prest and R. Turvey, "Cost-Benefit Analysis: A Survey," *Economic Journal,* December, 1965, pp. 683–735, also reprinted in *Surveys of Economic Theory,* Vol. III: Resource Allocation (New York: Macmillan and St. Martin's Press, 1966).

[7] It should be noted that some of these "private goods" often have localized effects on others—"I find some shades of orange shirts distasteful." Even though these

"externalities" may give rise to imperfections in the market, they are typically not sufficiently extensive to form the basis for public action.

[8] While a strong claim can be made for the guidance which the market system provides in valuing the inputs and outputs of public programs, a few reservations should be noted. First, some observed prices in a market economy are badly distorted and must themselves be adjusted in order to represent social values. Where monopoly is present, observed prices will be too high; where unemployment is present, observed wage rates will overstate the social cost of employing a worker; where buyers or sellers operate without full knowledge or where resources are immobile or where there are unaccounted-for spillovers caused by private sector activities, market observations must be appropriately adjusted to compensate for the imperfection.

A second difficulty of observed prices is that in a market economy these prices depend upon the prevailing tastes and preferences of consumers. Clearly the legitimacy of these preferences can be questioned as a guide for social policy. The existence of a massive advertising industry supported by private sector businesses undermines any absolute normative significance which might be attached to these prices.

[9] It should be noted that in applying the criterion, all of the benefits and costs should be placed on a common time basis. This is discussed in the section on *Present Values.*

[10] The income transfer character of secondary impacts is illustrated by the government's construction of waterways. Because of the waterway, the real cost of shipping by barge is reduced (a real benefit) and traffic shifts from the railroad to barge lines. Railroads lose revenues and profits; barge lines gain revenues and profits. The increased profits of barge lines is a secondary benefit representing a transfer of profits from railroads who have experienced a secondary loss. The stockholders of barge lines have gained and the stockholders of railroads have lost, but society as a whole is likely to show no net loss or gain due to these secondary impacts if transportation markets are competitive. It should be emphasized, however, that if there are certain real imperfections in the operation of the market system—regional unemployment, lack of competition, immobilities, economies of scale—secondary impacts may signify real economic gains (or losses). The analyst must carefully consider the market conditions in those sectors affected by the public decision.

[11] With a zero interest rate, the annual benefits and costs are simply added up with no adjustment. Thus, the $15 million of benefits shown in the table represent the product of $.6 million of benefits per year times 25 years.

[12] See U.S. Congress, Joint Economic Committee, Report of the Subcommittee on Economy in Government, "Economic Analysis of Public Investment Decisions: Interest Rate Policy and Discounting Analysis," 1968.

PART ONE

The Economic Basis of Public Expenditures

****

CHAPTER 1

THE PUBLIC SECTOR AND THE PUBLIC INTEREST

Peter O. Steiner

INTRODUCTION

If one starts at any point and place in history—say the United States in 1970—it is clear that the society has decided that there exist certain activities that are legitimately performed by governments. Many activities are by long tradition provided by various levels of government and are paid for by using the police powers of the state to raise funds. Others are left to the private sector. Without wishing to disparage the importance of the debate about the proper dividing line between private and public sectors, the fact is there is a large, relatively stable and broadly uncontroversial governmental "sector" of this economy, and of every other economy in the world.

In order to focus on certain critical issues I shall suppress some real distinctions and create some arbitrary ones. The most important simplification is to treat "government" as a single cohesive force, thus neglecting intergovernmental transfers as well as conflicts of authority and philosophy among federal, state, and local governments. The most important complication is to pretend that the theory of public expenditure policy is in reality two very different sets of propositions. One of these may be called the theory of the marginal public expenditure. It takes as given the legitimacy of government activity, and is concerned with choicemaking of the public decisionmaker between competing demands for his limited resources. The other set of propositions may be called the theory of the public interest, and concerns the way in which demands for public activity arise, are articulated, and are legitimatized. It is this latter that I wish to discuss in this paper.

Peter O. Steiner is Professor of Economics and Law at the University of Michigan.

This paper is a modification and abridgement of a larger study published by The Brookings Institution [43]. Research underlying that study has been supported by The Brookings Institution, by the Graduate School of the University of Wisconsin, and by the Cook Foundation of the University of Michigan Law School. [Bracketed numbers refer to sources listed in the References found at the end of the chapter.]

This is a separation of convenience, not of fact. For example, every marginal decision to expand some public program into a new area implies a legitimate public purpose in that area; thus proposed discrete extensions often pose the questions of public interest. Similarly, making a marginal decision requires rationally knowing what aspects of the public interest are being served.

There is one decisive reason for treating the theories separately. It is, simply, that as of this date the available theories are of very different levels of adequacy in the two cases. For the marginal decision a well-developed, highly articulated and largely uncontroversial set of theories exists and awaits implementation into practice. In contrast, with respect to the nature of the public interest, it is we theorists who are the primitives in the sophisticated world of public decisionmakers. It is the theorists who know how to choose between two public housing proposals but not whether public housing is right and proper; while the bureaucrats and Senators have less difficulty deciding when public housing is required than in choosing between alternative schemes of public housing.

Definition of the public interest is genuinely difficult because the notion embodies at least two implicit distinctions. One is between collective action and individual action, the second between public (that is, governmental) action and private action. Each is important. It is necessary to ask what it is that persuades or requires members of a group to seek a collective solution to some problem rather than to rely solely on individual action. It is also necessary to ask whether collective desires merit public support, public indifference, or public hostility. Finally, if collective desires are in some sense legitimatized the question remains as to what form of collective action is to be chosen. There is no simple dichotomy between individual private activities and collective public action. Instead there are various kinds of collectivities—clubs, unions, churches, political parties, as well as governments; various degrees of public involvement from outright prohibition of certain activities, to taxes or subsidies, to direct public provision of services.

The *desire* for collective action, which underlies many demands for public provision of goods and services, may arise any time a group feels it cannot achieve its objectives unaided. But mere demands (however genuine) are not enough. Aid to the needy aged (or unattractive prostitutes) may be the only effective device by which this portion of the population may be assured a subsistence level of living; price supports may provide farmers (or retail grocers, or racetrack touts) with protection against excessive competition that they could not achieve without Government action; a program to place a man on the moon by 1970 (or to build a tunnel under Lake Michigan, or to commit genocide) can be visualized only as a collective program. Each of these activities transcends individual solution and thus requires collective solution or no solution, but that per se does not render it a legitimate activity of government. Most will find some of these proposed activities meritorious but some objectionable as spheres of public action.

Moreover, the required use of collective action is not only not sufficient to define public activities, it is not strictly *necessary*. We may have governments provide education, housing, transportation, and recreation even though private alternatives exist. Such a choice might rest upon considerations of efficiency but it might also reflect captious preference or even prejudice. What leads men to choose public provision from among alternative means of meeting particular ends?

Casual observation suggests that the public interest may be served by providing or encouraging provision of a variety of goods or services, and by nonprovision or discouragement of others. Let me loosely define these goods and services as vested with the public interest, or as *public goods*. Let us first look more closely at the nature of public goods.

THE NATURE OF PUBLIC GOODS

Serving the public interest may take many forms, among them providing of goods, subsidizing their private provision, passing laws that impede or prohibit their provision or constrain the form in which they are provided. Because of the focus of this compendium, I shall limit attention to policies that involve public expenditures. But it should be remembered that an important policy issue always concerns choice among alternative available means.

The goods and services provided by public expenditures or encouraged by public policies can be described and classified in a number of different ways. Though we speak of a single category, "public goods," any review of actual public policies shows great diversity and variety. Some kinds of public goods are provided publicly or not at all because there exist no reasonable private alternative ways of providing them. This can happen (as in the case of national parks, national defense, or space research) because there exists no private mechanism to pay for the provision of these goods, or it can happen (as in the case of sewage disposal or justice) because compulsory use of the goods by all is required to permit its enjoyment by any group. Other public goods, such as public housing or public education, may be functionally similar to available private alternatives, but be qualitatively different in ways that society somehow prefers. Still other public goods may differ from private ones in no way other than in the distribution of beneficiaries and costs.

If the proper domain of public expenditure policy is public goods, their definition becomes vital. The concept has been defined in many ways, and for diverse purposes, and it is not surprising that definitions motivated by purposes other than ours—understanding the rationale and process of public expenditure policy—are not wholly satisfactory.

"A *public good* is any good or service which is *de facto* provided for or subsidized through Government budget finance" (Birdsall [5], p. 235).[1] This definition is neat but unhelpful. It is deficient in that it provides no guidance as to what attributes of a potential good or service a policymaker should look to in deciding whether to provide the goods. In this definition "publicness" is an act of congressional designation, not of any characteristics of the good or service.

In many ways, it would be desirable to have an intrinsic definition based upon technical characteristics of goods or services. One such definition of public goods is of the perfect collective consumption good. An impressive array of economists have so defined public goods including Samuelson [39], Strotz [45], Bowen [7], Breton [9], and most recently Dorfman [14]. Hear Dorfman:

> "There are certain goods that have the peculiarity that once they are available no one can be precluded from enjoying them whether he contributed to their provision or not. These are the public goods. Law and order is an example, and there are many others too familiar to make further exemplification worthwhile. Their essential characteristic is that they are enjoyed but not consumed [and that their benefits are derived] without any act of appropriation" ([14], p. 4).

This kind of very narrow definition was designed to demonstrate that there may be a type of activity that is socially desirable but that will not be achieved by the unaided private market. It serves well the purpose of showing the existence of public goods. It can prove a hindrance, however, if it leads to the view that such goods are *the only* class of goods which Government can legitimately provide. In fact, examples are hard to find, not ubiquitous, and the great bulk of (nondefense) public expenditures are for goods and services that do not meet the definition. Roads, schools, welfare payments, recreational facilities, housing, public power, irrigation (among others) are important classes of public expenditures that some can be precluded from enjoying, that can be consumed in whole or in part, and that technically can be made subject to user charges. The perfect collective consumption good, while sufficient to justify public expenditure, is neither necessary nor does it embrace much of what public expenditure policy concerns. What it does do is to identify certain characteristics such as nonconsumption, nonappropriation, and the existence of externalities that may give a good public goods aspect.

Externalities are very important, as has been recognized for a long time. Wicksell (himself citing earlier authority) put it eloquently in 1896:

> "If the community or at any rate a sizable part of it has an interest in a particular utility accruing to an individual, then it would clearly be unreasonable to allow the creation of that more general utility to depend solely upon that individual: he might not value the state activity highly enough to make the sacrifice of paying the required fee or charge, or else ignorance may cause him or poverty force him to do without the service. Herein lies the chief justification of the modern demands for free or very cheap process of law, elementary education, and medical care, certain public health measures, and so forth."[2]

While they are important, it would be easy to follow externalities too far. Few goods fail to have some elements of externality in the sense of some benefits or costs that do not require an act of appropriation. But if few goods fail to meet this test it cannot provide guidance as to which goods ought to be candidates for public provision, nor to explain which goods are publicly provided.

Let me venture a definition of my own: *any publicly induced or provided collective good* is a public good. A "collective good" in my definition is not necessarily a collective consumption good. Collective goods arise whenever some segment of the public collectively wants and is prepared to pay for a different bundle of goods and services than the unhampered market will produce. A collective good thus requires (1) an appreciable difference in either quantity or quality between it and the alternative the private market would produce, and (2) a viable demand for the difference.

Collective goods may be privately or publicly provided. Co-ops, unions, vigilante organizations, country clubs, carpools, and trade associations are all examples of private organizations that arise in response to collective demands for private collective goods or services. When the coordinating mechanism for providing a collective good invokes the powers of the state I define the good as a public good. In this definition there is the requirement that a public good must meet the tests of being a collective good. Public provision by itself does not create public goods. This definition is virtually implicit in the discussions of Head [20], Musgrave [33], Olson [35], Weisbrod [50] and Margolis [30]. It provides something of a framework for considering various sources of public goods, as we shall see just below.

A most important aspect of this definition is that it makes "publicness" not an all-or-nothing attribute of a good, but an attribute that may apply merely to particular aspects of a good. While there are cases (for example, national defense) in which the choice is between public provision and no provision, and why we thus argue that the good is entirely a public good, the more common situation is for goods to provide a variety of services only some of which have the attributes of collective goods. When the aspects that are thus of collective interest become sufficiently important, we may be led to public provision either of those aspects, or of the entire good (including its noncollective aspects). Thus provision of smog control or river purification attacks a particular externality of private production. In contrast public housing provides individuals with services they would otherwise have purchased privately, along with the peculiarly public services that public housing is supposed to entail.

Such mixed goods test and stretch definitions. "Public education" and "public housing" reflect both quantitative and qualitative differences from the privately produced or producible goods, "private housing" and "private education." If the differences are intended and desired, the differences constitute public goods in my definition.

This somewhat vague and embracing notion of public goods can be filled out by a more detailed classification of different types of public goods.

A CLASSIFICATION OF PUBLIC GOODS

I have (in effect) defined the vector of public goods as a vector of differences between the goods and services the private economy is motivated to provide and the goods and services the "public" wants, is willing to pay for, and expects its government to assist it in achieving.[3] This is, to an important degree, a normative definition, and much of the debate about the appropriate elements of the public goods vector is a normative debate. But there is a positive aspect as well: What is it about particular goods and services that makes them candidates for public consideration? What is it that makes certain activities the traditional province of governments?

It seems worthwhile to distinguish three types of public goods: (1) Those arising from intrinsic (perhaps technical) characteristics of specific goods that result in externalities that are not effectively marketed; (2) those arising from imperfections in the market mechanisms (rather than in the nature of the goods or services themselves); (3) those arising not from specific goods or services but from aspects concerning the quality or nature of the environment. These become increasingly elusive as we proceed from (1) to (3), but it is impossible to capture the flavor of actual government expenditure programs without all of them.

Public Goods Arising from Nonmarketable Services of Particular Goods

A discrepancy between public wants and private supplies often arises from externalities (or as they are alternatively called, spillover or third-party effects). Any time provision of a good or service provides side effects whose value is not reflected in the prices of the outputs sold or the resources used, external economies or diseconomies are produced. There can be many reasons for such externalities: Private producers may use resources they do not consider scarce, or produce byproducts that they do not consider valuable because they cannot control and market them. Familiar examples are discharges of noxious wastes into water or air, downstream navigational or flood control consequences of a private power dam, civic beautification or uglification incident upon building of private golf courses, factories, or slaughterhouses. Because some of the resources used or outputs produced are not correctly valued by the market there is every reason to expect the market to misuse them. Thus collective concern and public action may be required on simple efficiency grounds to allocate resources in accord with "true" valuations.

Whether the existence of such externalities (which must surely be present to some extent in every good) justifies public notice and action depends upon the benefits to be achieved measured against the costs of interference. Different people will have divergent views of the costs of interference, but debate as to what the cutoff level should be is a different matter than debates about the nature and size of the externalities.

The perfect collective consumption good is really an extreme case of externalities: all of the output is regarded as individually unmarketable; all of the benefits are external. The outputs of those goods from which one cannot be excluded as a consumer—and thus for which one cannot be compelled to pay his share of the cost of provision—play a large role in the thinking of those who have been concerned with deriving a legitimate role for public activity. Defense, public health, law and order, hurricane watches, are familiar examples. It is common to list a few examples (and not press them very hard) and then say, "there are many other examples." This is close to fraudulent. If excludability implies no one can conceivably be excluded, the list of such goods is short indeed. One need not police the ghetto, nor defend Alaska. Television signals can be scrambled so as to exclude buyers who will not pay for the unscrambler. Movies, concerts, hospitals, and colleges all use walls to exclude those who will not meet the requirements placed upon their use.

Collective goods may arise because it would be relatively costly to exclude free riders rather than because it is impossible. If at any moment this cost is above a certain level there may be no effective supply of the good privately provided. But in other cases the cost of exclusion may be annoying rather than prohibitive and potential consumers may urge public action merely to avoid bearing the costs. Put differently, the cost of arranging exclusion may be an avoidable externality.

Implicit in this discussion is an important attribute of the public collective good: the willingness to appeal to the police power of the state. One can slide in imperceptible steps from situations where there is no viable alternative means of providing the good, to cases where the alternative seems unnecessarily costly, to cases where the alternative while not very costly is simply judged to be less desirable, to cases where the alternative differs only in who pays for it.

There is real purpose in downgrading the distinction between *inability* and *unwillingness* to provide a good privately. If there is to be a practical definition of specific collection consumption goods and services, it seems difficult to escape the view that a judgment is required about reasons for turning to the political process and the coercive power of the state, rather than dealing with the second best solution. These reasons must be judged meritorious by the social decision process. *If this is so, collective consumption goods are defined by the exercise of legitimate governmental decision processes as much as they define them.*

Among the positive issues that underlie the normative debate about whether a particular collective good ought to be publicly provided are (1) whether private market alternatives to public provision are impossible, impractical, merely costly or simply unwanted; (2) why the market solution is unsatisfactory to members of the group and to society as a whole; and (3) the identity of the group of beneficiaries. The last deserves a bit of comment.

A collective good need not provide joint benefits to all of a society's members, only to some subgroup. But which group? The larger the group the more persuasive its demand for public action is likely to be, or (put differently) the less willing will its members be to accept a costly alternative. There are bases other than size for weighing the merits of the demands of any group, and these may vary over time. Domestic producers of goods subject to foreign competition, farmers, labor unions, small businessmen, and minority groups are among the identifiable groups that have asked and received special treatment. Today, for example, we seem more responsive to the demands of the underprivileged than the wealthy; a half century ago it was clearly otherwise.

One reason many collective consumption goods lead to demands for public provision is because the potential willingness to pay of different consumers cannot be tapped by private suppliers. Weisbrod [50], in an important paper, suggests a further source of values for which there is no market: option demands.[4] Some examples: I value Yellowstone Park being there, though I hope I never have to visit it again; I value the Everglades because I may want to visit them (but probably will not); I value the existence of a first-rate tuberculosis sanatorium, though in all probability I shall never need its services. Were any of these threatened with extinction I should be the loser, but there is no market whereby my willingness to pay for the option of being able to use them can be translated into revenue to the providers.[5]

Weisbrod's most suggestive example concerns the standby availability of transport. How much is it worth to the New York–Washington air travelers to have a good rail alternative in case of snow or strike? Suppose it is worth enough to justify the rail service, but that the railroad has no way of being reimbursed by those whose option demands are critical to continuation of the services. In these circumstances, the public good may be provided by the government's insistence that the railroad's passenger service be maintained with or without subsidy. In this view governments may not have been irrational in trying to preserve passenger train service even in the face of inability of the carriers to find user charges that will repay the marginal costs.

Public Goods Arising from Market Imperfections

There can be in practice no sharp distinction between market failure caused by technical characteristics of particular goods, and market failure caused by market imperfections. Inability to handle externalities, for example, may be regarded as a shortcoming of existing markets rather than as the absence of markets for specific services. But a distinction suggests additional sources of unsatisfactory private market performance that generate demand for public collective action. Efficient markets frequently suppose adequate information, sufficient competition, timely adjustment, and modest transaction costs. The absence of any of these may create motives to replace market determination by nonmarket provision, or to supplement markets with ancillary public goods.

Information Suppose all conditions for ideal resource allocation are satisfied except that market signals are systematically not read or are misperceived by economic actors. An allocation of goods and resources will occur, but it will, in general, differ from the allocation that would occur without ignorance or misinformation. Information may be a collective good (and thus generate a demand for its public provision) because even if there is a well-articulated private desire to have information, there may be no effective market in which to buy it efficiently.[6] It may be a public good in addition because the externalities of misinformed traders may be judged to be socially undesirable.

Time Lags If resources respond to market signals surely but slowly, the market process may prove an expensive way to achieve resource shifts. If physicists are in short supply, their price may be expected to rise and this may motivate additional youngsters to undertake education leading to careers as physicists. Since education is a slow process, existing physicists may earn high rents over long periods due to the long supply lags. It may well be that public policy can increase the supply of physicists more quickly and more cheaply by fellowships, by research grants, etc.[7] than the unaided market. If increases in supply of physicists, but not increased incomes of existing physicists, are desired results, then such programs supply public goods.

There is a large and growing literature that is concerned with the extent and causes of factor immobility. Education is but one of the sources; others include unemployment rates, prejudice, institutional barriers such as seniority and pension laws and state laws affecting eligibility for relief. Whenever markets work to reallocate resources sufficiently slowly, there may be a collective demand to supplement the market mechanism, or to replace it. Retraining programs, moving allowances, public employment services and even attacks on prejudice may be public goods if they serve to reduce the lags that the market economy accepts.

Monopoly Power Noncompetitive imperfections need little comment here. Public activities to encourage or compel competitive behavior, or to replace monopolistic private by public provisions are further sources of public goods.

Transaction Costs We have seen that an important aspect of collective goods concerns the inability of the market to translate potential willingness to pay into revenues. Related is the situation where the private market is technically able to collect revenues, but at a high cost. Collection of user tolls on interurban roads and urban bridges may or may not be both feasible and efficient, but intraurban toll roads would surely involve even larger collection costs and time losses. Prohibitive transaction costs of collecting revenues for intraurban toll roads give to high-speed roads attributes of public goods. Metering costs may be justified for high unit value commodities such as gas and electricity, but not for sewage (and, in some high population density areas, for water).

Where these high transaction costs inhere in the particular service they are simply an externality; where they reflect the institutional arrangements of the market they are a potential additional source of collective concern. The higher cost of attempting to gear a pricing system to an individual's willingness to pay is a repeated source of turning away from the market. For many goods, willingness to pay may be regarded as rising at least proportionally with income. Most private services are not provided on a basis that reflects income, because of the enormous costs of administration that such pricing would entail. If such a basis of payment is appropriate, reliance on the income tax, and thus on state provision, may appear desirable.

Public Goods Arising because of Concern with the Quality of the Environment

To this point public goods have been discussed in terms of market failure; failure either because of the absence or the imperfections of private markets. This is the grand tradition of classical economics. But even perfectly functioning markets for *all* goods and services would not eliminate the desire for market interference. Men may choose to reject the market solutions to allocative problems with respect to the distribution of income, the nature or quality of goods produced, or the patterns of consumption that markets produce.

The most compelling examples of collective public goods have always seemed to me to be national defense, law and order, and public health. What is their particular appeal? Is it that they are collective consumption goods? So is television. It is not in the specific planes, rockets, soldiers, policemen, vaccines, or nurses that are their elements—each of which can be readily provided as private goods to private users—but rather in the fact that they are part of and condition the *environment* of the society. Even the criminal who detests the legal framework is affected by it. Looked at this way they suggest other things that affect the environment and thus create externalities not linked to particular goods: for example, the literacy rate, the level of unemployment, the crime rate, the rate of technological progress, and importantly, the pattern of distribution of income and wealth.

Distribution of Income[8] Accept this assertion: it is fully feasible to charge users for use of parks and playgrounds, to charge parents for school bus service and school lunches, to charge fishermen for fishing privileges. Suppose in each of these cases that there is sufficient willingness to pay and ability to collect so as to assure private provision of parks, playgrounds, school buses, school lunches, and fishing opportunities. Should these functions be left to private provision?

To answer this question we must decide whether we are concerned merely with the distribution of income or instead with the pattern of consumption. When we provide subsidized public housing to the urban poor do we desire to provide more or better housing to users who would be excluded by private provision (or who would exclude themselves) or do we simply choose to increase their share of national consumption and use public housing instead of a cash income supplement for some obscure reason? (One might use indirect means, for example, in order not to impair the feelings of self-respect of the recipients.)

It is sometimes argued that purely redistributional objectives which reflect a dissatisfaction with the initial situation of ownership of wealth and resources ought to be satisfied by income transfers rather than by provision of goods and services in order not to distort resource allocation. This familiar argument is unpersuasive if one regards as legitimate a desire of a society to interfere with the *pattern of consumption* that would result from market determinations. A society may choose to affect jointly both income distribution and the pattern of consumption. Provision of housing, education, milk, and recreation for underprivileged children may be public goods because of the externalities which children so treated bestow upon others. Public policies designed to provide aid for small business, for the family farm, for the needy aged, and for the slum child all reflect rejection of market determination, rather than denial of the possibility of market determination.

It is, of course, not clear that all actual interferences reflect a positive intention both to redistribute income *and* to change consumption patterns. In the United Kingdom (by way of contrast to the United States), fishing rights are sold, and it is an upper class form of recreation. On the other hand, virtually all Scottish golf courses are subsidized municipal ones, and in Scotland golf (but not fishing) is a working class recreation. But if some consumption distortions are fortuitous, others are intended.

Nature and Quality of Output For some goods and services the quality and nature of the goods produced is of public concern, quite independent of any distributional considerations. Often the nature of the goods or service is affected by who provides it—for better or for worse. Government newspapers differ from private ones, public television and radio from commercial broadcasting, a system of public schools from a private school system, private research and development from public. In some of these examples both kinds of goods may coexist, in others an exclusive choice is made. But in all cases a choice among qualitatively different outputs may and can be made; the qualitative difference of public from private constitutes a public good or a public bad.

Public Goods: A Summary View

I have stressed the pluralistic nature of the sources of collective demands, as arising from technical characteristics of particular goods, from market imperfections and failures, and also from other divergences between collective and individual values. This time is long since past when we need to define public goods merely in order to establish the *prima facie* case for some public interference with private markets; instead we seek a framework to structure debate about whether particular activities merit inclusion in the public sector.

It seems to me worth identifying in each case what is the alleged source of collective concern. Does it depend upon a major qualitative difference between public and private provision, or does it merely seek some incremental output, perhaps by considering a particular neglected externality? In this distinction often lies an important policy choice between public provision on the one hand or a less fundamental public restructuring of private incentives. Similarly one wants an indication of whether public concern is specific to the particular good or service or is of a general environmental type. There are more ways to reduce overall unemployment than there are ways to retrain Appalachian miners. Again the relevant alternatives are affected by what are the real objects of policy. A frequent issue concerns whether redistributional policies achieved by provision of specific goods and services are intended to bring about changes in consumption patterns or do so incidentally.

Next, having established the basis of *collective* concern, it is worth establishing the basis of *public* concern. Who are the alleged beneficiaries, and what is their claim to recognition? What is the "second best" that they face if their claims are rejected?

I believe that defining as specifically as one can the vector of differences between a private good and its public alternative to be a critical part of the public decisionmaking process. Neither *de facto* definitions (such as Birdsall's), nor neat but narrow ones (such as that of the perfect collection consumption good) prove very helpful for the critical problem of defining the scope of the public sector.

SOURCES OF A PUBLIC INTEREST: ALTERNATIVE VIEWS

To convert a collective interest of some group into the public interest requires a distinct act of legitimization. How does it occur? Views differ both with respect to what it is that is aggregated, and with reference to the requisite degree of consensus.

My dominant reaction to rereading the discussion among economists about the "public interest" is surprise at its defensive tone, as if we are somehow disloyal when we find a role for extramarket forces in the economy. Perhaps because economists have felt defensive, much of the economic discussion has revolved not around the issue of how to define the public interest, but rather how to demonstrate that there is a *de minimis* role of government activity that clearly benefits everybody. Much of welfare economics consists of such a possibility theorem. Possibility theorems are fine in their own way. If, however, they are misinterpreted they may greatly limit the scope of the phenomenon whose possibility they are concerned to establish. This has, I believe, been the problem and the fate of formal welfare economics. To document this view or to discuss the alternatives in any detail involves technical issues best avoided in this paper.[9] But it is possible to identify a variety of different points of view and the different implications that they may lead to.

The Point of View of Individual Utility

Those who hold this view consider the public interest of a society as being simply an appropriate aggregate of the private interests of the individuals who comprise the society. Each individual is assumed to seek his own utility (or satisfaction) by pursuing all avenues open to him. Assume as a rough distinction that he draws satisfaction from the consumption of two kinds of goods, private goods and collective goods. (He may, of course, derive utility not only from his own consumption but from the status of others, rejoicing in either their good fortune or their bad.) Let us distinguish initially the individual's wants reflected by his tastes and preferences and his effective demands, determined by his utility function *and* the constraints, such as income, that bind him.

For private goods there is a market through which individuals can make their effective demands for goods felt, and in the context of an enterprise system whenever the aggregate of such individual demands warrant there is incentive for private producers to meet these demands. Collective goods differ in that (as we have seen) private markets fail to respond to real effective demands; thus *collective action* is required to satisfy *individual demands*. The devices of government can provide the form of collective action that substitutes for private markets in channeling resources to meet the aggregate of individual demands. (So far as the individual's utility depends upon others' consumption, it is likely to be outside of his individual ability to do much about; thus here is further motive for looking to the government.) In this attractively symmetrical view, government activity permits individuals better to achieve their individual objectives.

These assumptions have settled an issue of principle (that there may be a legitimate role of government) without having answered the practical question of which public goods the society should provide. Granted that individuals have demands for collective goods, how should individual preferences be aggregated to determine whether the aggregate welfare is sufficient to justify the total cost? Is this answer affected by the system of taxes used to raise the funds? These are among the critical questions of welfare economics.

A simple and uncontroversial solution is available in cases where unanimity prevails. Clearly, if some quantity of a particular new public good had the happy property that for every individual it added at least as much to his utility as his contribution to its cost detracted from his utility, such a good would be desirable. A totally *de minimis* view of the public interest would limit it to cases that fit this requirement. It is *de minimis* because, while it is conceivable that there are goods that satisfy this criterion, there cannot be many. In a many-person economy, if even one person had less use for the public good than his contribution to its costs no positive quantity of output would achieve unanimous consent.

Most public activities imply (often intentionally) a redistribution of income which leaves some individuals worse off and some better. Whatever the merit of establishing *at least* the quantity that might achieve unanimous consent as desirable, any implication that exactly that quantity is desirable seems quite unwarranted. Few economists, welfare or other, are content to rule out any change merely because it has redistributional consequences. To do so invests the initial distribution of society's resources with an overriding sanctity. Nor can we avoid this difficulty by assuming that an individual's utility function includes as an argument preferences about the distribution of income. For, unless an implied redistribution were to be regarded as desirable by everyone, there would be no unanimous consent to it.

The struggle of formal welfare economics to escape this dilemma has been tortured and fruitless. The Kaldor-Hicks "compensation principle" wherein a change that benefited some but not all was justified if the gainers *could* compensate the losers even if they *did not* only encounters technical ambiguities[10] but implies an inherent neutrality toward redistributional consequences.

Neither an I impressed with the argument that we ought to be neutral toward redistribution in allocational decisions, on the ground that redistribution of income can be accomplished directly if it is desired. The inertia of social change is such that this would overweight the current distribution of income, and would serve in practice to limit the possibilities for redistribution.

Clearly we would be paralyzed by an operating rule that said: "provide no public good if it changes the distribution of income." But if we permit redistributions there is no reason why we cannot regard some as desirable and others as undesirable.

Clearly some reckoning of redistribution gains and losses is required if all proposals are not to be rejected. If one insists on basing decisions on individual utility functions this implies either assigning weights to the utility of individuals or being able and willing to measure and compare individual utilities. Making interpersonal comparisons is potentially unattractive,[11] unless it is itself subject to well-defined rules of procedure. Such rules might be formulated. For example, one may take a strict majoritarian view. But there is nothing inherently just or appealing about a rule that leads to the median effective demand of the society being dominant: indeed, without protections of minorities it would seem offensive to most people.

The major objection to a utility-consensus view of social welfare functions is that it is nonoperational and does not seem to provide guidance to the decisions of real societies. Certainly we *do* take decisions with less than unanimous consent. Certainly too, many public goods provide benefits in excess of their contributions only to very small minorities of the society, but with the evident acquiescence of sizable majorities. One can argue that, *ex post,* individuals are thus revealed to value the benefits which accrue primarily to others. But this rationalization leads us back to a *de facto* definition: whatever the Government does is revealed to be desired by the people.

Thus if formal welfare economics does not go beyond individual utility functions, it fails either because it justifies too little or because it justifies too much of public expenditure. Viewed from the vantage point of welfare economics, public decisions about public goods appear to be impossible to make.[12] Fortunately, other economic views are possible: economists are saved the humiliation of abandoning as barren a fertile field. It is the wasteland of welfare economics, not the reality of public decisionmaking that is the mirage.

A partial escape from the wasteland can come from a pluralistic view of the individual. Suppose that each individual in addition to his personal evaluation of any proposed activity will also view it from the point of view of any one of a number of groups he belongs to, be it social club or trade union.[13] If he is willing to be bound by the consensus view of the members of the group, there is a much greater possibility of consensus, first because a significant clustering of views is likely to emerge, and second because logrolling between groups can create collections of activities that command dominant majorities. Suppose individuals are prepared to accept and to be taxed for things they consider socially worthwhile, such as (say) foreign aid, wars on poverty, and higher pay for Senators, even though they cost many individuals more in income foregone than they contribute to that individual's utility. They accept them as part of a package which they find adds to their own utility on an all-or-nothing basis.

The view that social choices may rest on collective values arrived at by caucus rather than by simple aggregation is more than an escape from the general impossibility of deriving a social welfare function from individual values. It has positive merit in that it embraces a view of the individual which many find descriptively accurate and analytically helpful. In this view an individual functions in a pluralistic sense with loyalties, commitments, and valuations at many levels: to himself, his family, his church, his neighborhood, his employer—and possibly also to his race, religion, class, country, and political party. The pluralistic view is the heart of sociology, social anthropology, and much of economics. If it is accepted it suggests that individuals will be prepared to act on collective issues without inevitably tracing back to the explicit question: "What's in it for me?" They may ask instead: "What's in it for the Negro?" or the farmer, workingman, etc. If they do, they invite an analysis of the views of political pressure groups, which usually have highly articulate spokesmen and well-defined programs they are seeking to enact.

The Point of View of Willingness to Pay

The difficulties of deriving an aggregate preference ordering based on individual utilities arise from the incommensurability of individual's utility indexes. Without unanimity of views or well-defined rules for assigning weights, consistent decisions become impossible to make.

A second view is to ask not how much an individual values a given collective good, but how much he is willing to be taxed to provide it. The differences between this view and the previous one may seem small but they may make a substantial difference in one's view of the scope of the public interest. In the first place a shift from every individual having a positive preference for some activity, to his being willing to tolerate it, is practically quite substantial, as the well-known political literature on the use of veto power makes clear. Second, the metric of value of the activity has been shifted from the inherently unmeasurable "utility," to the discernible, and interpersonally comparable, willingness of individuals to pay. To be sure we pay a price for this, in that an individual's willingness to pay reflects the *status quo,* and particularly his income and wealth. We must therefore, be all the more wary about distributional biases toward the *status quo*.

When applied to the collective consumption good this approach leads to the so-called *pure theory of public expenditure*. This theory has a long life and is well articulated by Bowen [7] and Samuelson [38].[14] In barest essence the argument is that since demands of different individuals for a collective good are complementary rather than competitive we can add the willingness to pay of different individuals and if the aggregate sum exceeds the costs, the good is worth producing. For all quantities for which this is true, there exists a tax policy which would collect levels of taxes sufficient to cover marginal costs, and still leave all citizens satisfied.

Appeal to the "existence of tax policy such that . . ." sounds very much like the compensation principle once again. And it is subject to a similar objection. If the tax structure is not (or should not be) malleable, there is no bliss in this solution. At independently determined tax rates some taxpayers are getting more than they are willing to pay for and are being coerced to provide what others want. If these others' needs are in some sense more meritorious than those of the reluctant taxpayers, this may be appropriate, but there is then no automatic stopping point. One cannot escape the distributional question, unless one insists on regarding it as irrelevant. If the collective good involves aid to the needy aged, one may take a different view of the effects of the coercion than if it involves providing a civic yacht harbor.

Nor (in my view) are these difficulties with the optimal solution merely symptoms of imperfections in the taxing schema. Citizens have social values about appropriate tax policies too. Suppose we are building a public playground to be used by underprivileged children. If A is a rich misanthrope and B a poor Samaritan, there is no compelling reason why B should carry more of the tax burden, even though he may be willing to do so.

Notwithstanding these and other difficulties, some have argued that this approach offers the following rule as a usable rough guideline to public decisionmaking: if, in aggregate, effective demands exceed cost, the service should be provided whether or not payment is exacted. Unfortunately this opens the door to game strategic behavior. Suppose payment proportional to demand is not to be required. Any group that knows it will not be asked to pay more than a fixed share can exaggerate its valuation of a service it desires. If (on the other hand) proportional payment is to be required, every group will have an incentive to understate its real valuation as long as others value the service enough to get it provided.

The Point of View of an Aggregate Social Welfare Function

Society is necessarily made up of individuals, but it need be no simple aggregate of them. In looking at their behavior it may be that the interdependencies between people and their interactions are more important than the individual value structures. Nations, races, even football teams, acquire personalities and modes of behavior. While a search for collective values has until recently been more congenial to political scientists and sociologists than to economists, an increasing number of economists are moving toward the view that individuals voluntarily yield certain coercive power to a government which is somehow charged to discover, articulate and implement social priorities, or collective wants.

This (collective) view is broader than, not necessarily competitive with, the previous ones. It may be that social priorities are indeed arrived at by some aggregation process. But there are other possibilities as well. Political theory has long been concerned with the legitimacy of government and with the nature of the social contract among citizens or between a government and its citizens.

In this view a collectivity, *society* may be fruitfully viewed as an independent entity possessing its own value orderings. In Rothenberg's view [36], if I understand it, social valuation as opposed to solely individual valuation is an existent reality. This view has the great pragmatic value that it invites the search for revealed social priorities without insisting on a single source of them. If priorities with respect to income distribution (for example) are established, and consented to by the citizens, then the distributional consequences of particular public decisions become "benefits" or "costs" instead of barriers to either clear thinking or clear action. The formidable measurement issues—of quantifying the benefits, and assessing the costs—remain, but a major hurdle has been crossed. In this view one is aggregating not across individual utility, nor willingness to pay, but rather across individual political influence and tolerance. In so doing we vest to some extent the existing distribution of political power and influence, but possibly it can be argued that this is more nearly the result of a social contract than is the distribution of wealth.[15] The degree of consent that is required is whatever the political process demands.

Personally, I find this view of the problem both congenial and fruitful. It does not dispense with the individual and individual values, for one must ask how the political process articulates the public interest, but it does recognize that most individuals have a large range of things they will accept without opting out of the system, and will vent their approval or disapproval in some sort of orderly political process. It does not lead, inherently, to either a minimal or maximal role for government. It does not exclude distributional questions from policy, nor does it vest the existing distribution of income with a special status. What it lacks is any clear indication that one situation is superior to another in a wholly unambiguous sense. This does not mean that whatever society does is desired, rather it means that particular public decisions can be shown to be valid only in terms of particular value judgments. It tends to pose issues of public policy in terms of whether society does in fact hold certain value judgments rather than in terms of the demonstrable inherent legitimacy of certain activities. Some will regard this as retrogress. I am not so inclined. Economists have long sought a calculus of consent, but in the search have found it easier to derive a lower bound to public activities than to define their proper domain. If we are fruitfully to discuss public expenditure policy we must be prepared to go beyond this.

The central issue in this debate does not concern the logical correctness of looking at social choices on the one hand as an aggregation of individual values or on the other as a two-step procedure in which we first agree (some way, any way) on collective values and then use them to make social choices. Any perfectly understood aggregate behavior can be decomposed into its disaggregated elements. It is instead a matter of research strategy. Are we likely to achieve greater insight one way or the other? If there is stability in aggregate social values then basing policy on such aggregate values is likely to work. My own view is that at this stage in the development of our science there is more insight and less bias in the third view of the public interest than in either of the others. Many will disagree.

If one accepts the notion that aggregate social views must be discovered there remain two important questions to discuss. First, how these views get articulated and, second, how competing objectives get reconciled. It is convenient to treat them in reverse order.

THE PROBLEM OF WEIGHTING

It is increasingly the practice to treat the public interest (or "social welfare") as a function with several arguments. For example following Marglin [28] we might write:

$$U = U(Z_1, Z_2, Z_3, \ldots Z_n)$$

where the Z's are different aspects of the public interest such as economic efficiency (or contribution to national income) the pattern of income distribution, the rate of economic growth, balance of payments equilibrium, economic stability, national security, and freedom. Whether one considers these as different aspects of a one dimensional index of utility, or as different dimensions of a multi-dimensional concept is more than a semantic issue. If for example Z_1 and Z_2 are readily comparable in terms of a cardinal measure of their contribution to utility (e.g., market value of electric power and market value of irrigation water) they can easily be elements of a scalar measure of welfare. Their relative weights are given by the common yardstick used for measuring them. If on the other hand Z_1 and Z_2 represent efficiency and freedom each of which (let us suppose) may be meaningfully defined and ordinally measured we may have no simple yardstick for comparing them. Thus the problem of trade-offs between these "separate dimensions" of a public interest vector remains to be solved. Because noncomparability, or difficulties in comparison are a feature of many public choice problems, it seems to me convenient to regard the public interest as genuinely multidimensional, and thus to consider explicitly conflicts among objectives.

The number of dimensions and their definition is a matter of analytic and operational convenience. Because there are many different sources of a public (as distinct from private) interest there will be many forms of a proximate contribution to public welfare. Whether it makes sense to combine different effects into a single dimension or to treat them as separate dimensions of the public interest depends upon whether one believes there is an acceptable cardinal measure of their contribution to public welfare. If so it makes sense to combine; if not, it makes sense to keep them separate.

With a one dimensional objective there is a simple decision rule. If (for example) one is concerned solely with contribution to national income it is conceptually easy to choose between a dam in Oregon and a retraining program in West Virginia. But if one cares as well about who gets the income, such a simple rule can become simplistic. Given multiple objectives, it is inevitable that individual proposed actions will affect more than a single dimension. Inevitably also the objectives will often conflict. The definition of a multidimensional objective function neither creates nor resolves the conflicts, instead it identifies them.

The central aspects of choosing policies when faced with multiple objectives are how to define an appropriate measure of each objective, and how to resolve conflicts among objectives.

A very simple, indeed trivial, theorem says that if weights are left unspecified, any policy A may in general be made to appear less or more desirable after the fact that an alternative B (which may easily be "not A"), by specifying which objective is implicitly the important one. This theorem is important only because it is so frequently neglected.

Many forms of "implicit" weighting exist in practice. It is almost routine in lay discourse to argue that because a proposed policy advances *some* object of social policy, it is desirable: "The war on poverty will improve the distribution of income." Or to argue that because it retards some other objects it is undesirable: "The war on poverty extends the role of government and thus reduces individual freedom." Neither of these statements tells us whether the war on poverty is desirable.

Somewhat subtler is the implicit neglect of certain objectives by assuming the dominance of others. Much of the economist's traditional emphasis on efficiency has had the effect of giving it a very high weight relative to growth or distribution. Interestingly, Joseph Schumpeter, always treated as a giant with respect to his theories of development and cycles, is still regarded as a crank with respect to his views on monopoly, because he challenged orthodoxy by arguing that static efficiency considerations are overweighted relative to growth.

If objectives are genuinely multidimensional and not immediately comparable, some solution to the weighting problem is implicit or explicit in *any* choice, and that solution reflects someone's value judgment. Put formally, we now accept in principle that the choice of weights is itself an important dimension of the public interest. This choice is sometimes treated as a prior decision which controls public expenditure decisions (or at least should), and sometimes as a concurrent or joint decision—as an inseparable part of the process of choice.

Weight Selection Viewed as a Prior Decision

Several widely divergent views of the public decision process have in common a view that important aspects of the weighting decision should be regarded by the decisionmaker as given to him. Two of these virtually assume lexicographic ordering of certain objectives. In lexicographic ordering, objective "1" is dominant, but in case two choices are equivalent in terms of objective "1," choice is made upon the basis of objective "2," etc. (Listing in alphabetical order is the best known lexicographic procedure.)

One view of this kind is that efficiency, as measured by private market allocations, is the dominant criterion; if a project is efficient in this sense, it (or some substitute) is worth undertaking; otherwise not. Once a project is so legitimized, the decisionmaker is welcome to examine other, secondary objectives in project selection or design. This appears to me to be the view of McKean [27], Harberger [18], and Mishan [32] when they insist that the correct (really the only correct) discount rate for discounting future benefits and costs and for assessing the opportunity costs of public funds is some specified measure of the marginal productivities of capital in the private sector.[16] This view "solves" the weighting problem of assumption and makes many otherwise difficult decisions easy. Those who hold this view are repeatedly appalled at the obvious outrages performed by the public sector, and the apparent acquiescence therein of otherwise sensible men.

A different but no less arbitrary lexicographic view is that public budgets for particular activities reflect dominant social choices, and that while efficient allocation of the funds within such budgets is appropriate, efficiency considerations do not reflect sensibly on the size of the budget.[17]

While neither of these forms of solution-by-assumption of the weighting problem is likely to prove literally satisfactory in all situations, either might provide insight into how the public decisionmakers regard their actions as constrained by a society's underlying consensus view of key issues they face.

An alternative to taking weights as inherently given is to regard them as an explicit prior decision. It is conceivable to imagine the political system having a procedure whereby we decide upon and then announce a fixed set of weights that will be controlling in choosing among income, income distribution, and so on. No one suggests this is the procedure used, although both Chenery [12] and Marglin [29] urge this as a real possibility for economic planners.[18] Chenery, for example, suggests the planners announce a national income equivalent to balance-of-payments effects, thus making for a fixed tradeoff.[19]

Eckstein [16], Haveman [19] and Weisbrod [51] among others, while more or less accepting the view that weighting decisions are relatively stable and pre-existing, do not wish to assume them nor to expect political leaders to articulate them. Instead they suggest attempting to infer the weights by an analysis of past choices. Eckstein [16] suggests we look at an issue such as differential tax rates in which a decision on distribution is at the heart of congressional intent in order to discover implied values Congressmen hold. Haveman [19] applies this approach to evaluating water resource investments with respect to a multidimensional objective. These approaches are suggestive, even if one is unwilling to go all the way and take congressional actions as perfectly revealing social consensus.

Weisbrod deals with a two-dimensional objective function covering efficiency and income distribution. He suggests that every example of choice of a less efficient over a more efficient alternative implies a minimum implicit weight to the redistribution that is involved. His hope is that analysis of many decisions would reveal a weighting scheme. The advantage of this procedure is the potentially large sample available. The hazard is that any irrational choices, any misestimates of efficiency, and any nonincluded objectives would all be imputed as distributional benefits. But the real test of Weisbrod's suggestion will depend upon whether it produces a clear and consistent pattern of implicit values. To my knowledge, it has not been tested as yet.

Yet another approach to weighting of objectives is to regard certain objectives as constraints. Suppose we would like to attain one objective, with the constraint that we cannot concentrate on that objective until certain other basic goals have been secured, at least to a minimum extent. Initially, then, these latter goals assume high priority, for we cannot turn our major attention to the former objectives without having satisfied the latter. Once the latter goals have been satisfied, they can be given shadow prices which reflect the price paid in assuring their achievement. This is often a useful (as well as a traditional) approach to allocational problems. It may, however, prove difficult to define which objectives are genuinely to be regarded as constraining.

Weights as the Outcome of Political Process

The discussion above treated the appropriate weighting scheme as a preexisting condition for the decision process. Dahl and Lindblom [13], Braybrooke and Lindblom [8], and Maass [25], Major [26], Banfield [2], Eckstein [16] among many others regard weights as generated by the process of decision. In this view the political process addresses weighting problems not abstractly but as a case-by-case confrontation. In each case need for a decision about what to do forces a discussion, or compromise, or struggle between competing objectives. To Maass, the essence of the *legislative* process is the making of choices between conflicting objectives. The decisions will be made upon the basis of the information (or prejudices) available, and the scope for the analyst in affecting the decision will be reasonably to identify the choices. Eckstein expresses the strong view (to which I find no academic dissent) that administrators and project analysts should not arrogate the weighting process and bury the choices within a single measure of benefit.

This whole area strikes an analyst as untidy. It is clear that choices among objectives must be made, and that the political process must somehow make them. But we appear to be undecided about whether it does so within narrowly confined limits of underlying consensus, or with substantial discretion. Is the alternative to the invisible hand the responsible arm or the visible paw? Perhaps more important is the source of such political discretion as exists; is it simply variance in underlying views, is it ignorance or indifference on the part of the citizen, or is it an explicit delegation of authority by the electorate? Answers to these questions critically affect subsequent research strategy. Banfield [2] appears to espouse the nihilistic view that discretion arises from such deep underlying ignorance and/or indifference that there are no effective limits on the wondrous ways of politicians. At the opposite extreme, if one assumes that politics is a mere veil that masks a variety of different underlying views, a key to understanding the outcome is to study the variance of underlying views. Downs [15] and to a lesser extent, Lindblom, embody this view. It has important precursors in an older political science literature on interest groups.[20]

What is particularly disturbing is that I can find virtually no disposition on the part either of economists or political scientists to engage in an empirical study of the decision process that will resolve these areas of debate. The large literature is almost entirely theoretical and assertive. Yet, survey data about public attitudes on issues exist and provide some sort of a base. Similar data about *ex-post* public reaction to political decisions and procedures might be developed. In fact we now ask such evaluative questions but only about things like a major war or the overall evaluation of a president or a party. Even to say more would take me further along the road than I care to go to design a study of how decisions are reached and the extent to which they are responsive to public opinion. Such a study seems worth somebody's undertaking; it seems more promising than another decade of assertions in resolving our differences.

ARTICULATION OF THE PUBLIC INTEREST

There are divergent views about how the political structure articulates social priorities and the extent to which *process* determines outcome. It is helpful to start with a dichotomous classification that overstates differences in points of view. In one view the political process is a market-like mechanism that coalesces views that inhere in the members of the society. Here the political process is a facilitating and implementing one, not inherently a formative one. An efficient government, like an efficient market, quickly and accurately translates inherent preferences into explicit consensus. Just as a market may perform a mapping function (since people discover their preferences best by confronting real alternatives) so an efficient government serves to help people discover as well as fulfill their their collective preferences. In principle (though, of course, not necessarily in practice) one should be able to simulate such a process, and simply add a government sector to a general equilibrium model of the society. Government (in this view) is a decisionmaker only in the limited sense of a reactor and processor of signals it receives. A properly functioning government will arrive at an optimal decision set without exercise of independent judgment.

The second view is that while individual social preferences clearly exist and play a role, they are sufficiently inchoate, ambiguous, or conflicting that the political process is required to forge a public interest and it does so with substantial discretionary choice. Without knowledge of the motives of the governors, and of the political process itself, there is no indicated solution, nor accurate prediction of governmental action. In this view, to create a government sector it must be given objectives, procedures, and decisionmakers. However, the way in which individual's preferences constrain or otherwise affect public decisionmakers must be made explicit.

The differences between the approaches are important not only in terms of the information each requires in order to permit prediction of outcomes, but in whether comparative static analysis is possible or must be replaced by a genuinely dynamic model of political decisions. I limit myself to a few dicta here, and refer the interested reader to the fuller discussion in [43].

The Government as a Quasi-market

In all market-type analyses of the political process, voting is the means by which individual values are translated into action decisions. Bowen's pioneer article [7] is of this type. If we assume that the tax burden of any public expenditure on each individual is known to him, and if we assume everyone votes under simple majority rule we can predict the outcome of elections.

Abstracting from the effect of the tax structure on political choices, it is clear that so far as we can reduce preference to a single dimension, it is the median preference that dictates the outcome of majoritarian voting. The result thus depends wholly upon the pattern and variance of voters' preferences and the structure of taxes. The result may, but need not, yield the pure theory of public expenditure solution. That is based upon aggregate willingness to pay and thus, if tax burdens are equal, it depends upon the mean rather than the median willingness to pay. Bowen believes that the institutional facts are such that median and mean will tend to coincide because voters' preferences are symmetrically distributed. I know of no evidence with which to confirm this conjecture. Bowen does not suggest that a referendum on each proposed decision actually is the decision procedure, but rather that it is a decision procedure that might be used, and that perhaps roughly is represented by the institutions of democratic government.

A much more elaborate but broadly similar theory is presented by Downs [15] to whom government consists of men who like the emoluments and perquisites of their jobs and whose goal is reelection or reappointment by elected officials. The government is thus motivated to maximize its political support. The government is interested in a citizen's vote, not his welfare; it must, however, cater to his view of welfare to get his vote. Were it not for uncertainty, Downs' model would be fully mechanistic and predictable.[21]

A less mechanistic model is offered by Maass. He offers an explanation that to a major degree is a two-stage political market theory. In the first stage the voters choose "men, who in their personal capacity, and in virtue of their character, are fitted to discharge the task of deliberation and discussion at the parliamentary stage."[22] In the second stage, these officials are held accountable for their political acts by the need to seek periodic reelection.

Maass' model gives rather more freedom to the politician than does

Downs': officials are not worrying about the probability of reelection in every move, only in their overall performance. At the very least they are only constrained to be aware of their constituents' sensibilities. Indeed if they regard their mandate as sufficiently general they have the need as well as the opportunity to crystalize their constituents' values. Here Maass verges into a creative or formative view of government and the definition of public interest.

Market theories can be criticized from within or from outside the market framework. Most critics of the votes-as-market-signals approach to analysis of the political process have sought a more substantial discretionary role of government; we shall consider these just below. Within the market-analogy framework, Arrow [1], Black [6] and Buchanan [11] have questioned the ability of such a system to translate inherent preferences into rational social priorities, and the efficiency of such a quasi-market system.

Arrow's well-known demonstration of the paradox of collective choice is so simply illustrated that it bears repeating.

Individual	*Individual's preference ordering*
I	A→C→B
II	C→B→A
III	B→A→C

Even if each of the individuals has no difficulty ordering his preferences among three competing possibilities—A, B, and C—there may be no clear collective preference. In the example clearly two-thirds prefer A to C, and two-thirds prefer C to B. Thus, if they first choose between B and C and then between A and C, A will command a majority. But two-thirds prefer B to A and a different order of choice can produce any one of the choices.[23] Black [6] and Rothenberg [37] among others have explored the theoretic consequences of alternative voting and balloting schemes in producing outcomes, and both discover a purely political dimension to the politics of consent. To this we shall return.

Buchanan [11] in a paper stimulated by Arrow, identifies some important weaknesses in the market analogy. He accepts the voting process as analogous to the market mechanism, but is wary about drawing welfare implications from the analogy. Buchanan believes in the efficiency of decentralized market decisions and is concerned lest the loose analogy with voting give a similar blessing to voters' decisions. He notes:

(1) Voting involves an extra dimension of uncertainty: consequences follow the collective vote, not the individual vote; therefore, the voter may

not really vote his own best interests because he underestimates the possibility of the decision impinging on him. Indeed since in a collective vote there is a diffusion of responsibility for the collective decision, the individual may act in the mass as he would never act individually. A man may vote for prohibition, for capital punishment, or for a war policy while at the same he would not abstain from alcohol, invoke the death sentence, or opt for military service for himself or his son.

(2) In voting, the individual is influenced by his sense of participation in social choice. A vote for open housing need not imply willingness to live in a racially mixed neighborhood: indeed many of the most ardent supporters of such laws have exercised their option to move further away from integrated neighborhoods. Men may be willing to do collectively unto others what they would not do individually nor consent to have done to them unless done to all.[24]

(3) In voting, the individual is often faced with indivisible votes for mutually exclusive choices. He cannot make marginal choices, or influence very much the definition of candidate or choices. Often he votes for candidates some of whose policies he disapproves. Thus the mandate of a winning candidate is readily misinterpreted.

(4) Minority votes are wasted, whereas even minority preferences exert influences in the market. If fear of wasting their votes leads voters to vote for their second choices, even actual votes for candidates may fail to reflect the strength of the support their views have.[25] Nonvoting, an alternative form of expression, is not often easily interpreted.

(5) Typically, voting provides equality of influence of individuals, instead of reflecting command over resources. Bowen is wrong: the weighting of individual choices is different in the marketplace and the polling booth. Buchanan here goes well beyond the point that it would require some remarkable coincidences to assure that the distribution of political and economic influence were perfectly correlated. He adopts (I think) a view of Frank Knight's [22] that market votes are in some sense superior to political votes.[26]

These critiques by Arrow and Buchanan serve to warn against too quick acceptance of an analogy of the political process with the market process. The practical question is whether the two situations are sufficiently similar that the economist's techniques of analysis and his theorems about market behavior can be applied directly and fruitfully to political decision-making. My own answer after reading in the political-market literature is "No." I certainly believe that individual citizen voters both influence and constrain political choices; but they do so within limits sufficiently broad that attention to choices *within the limits* needs, deserves, and repays analysis.

The important issue is, of course: how large are the limits? In the political choice arena, the limits seem to me sufficiently large that we cannot merely pay attention to voters' preferences. All of the following contribute to a substantial discretionary role of government: the variance in individuals' views; the fact that voters choose infrequently and among bundles of policies; the fact that many views are not held so strongly that a political leader who violates them is at once anathema; that many voters' preferences are inchoate, uncertain, and subject to change; that pressure groups can and do negotiate with governments; and finally that political leaders can, in fact, lead their followers on many issues. If these things are true, the choice set of the government while constrained by voters' preferences may be far from singular.

Government as an Organic Chooser of Ends

Dorfman [14] presents a suggestive model of the public sector that is close to the market analogy models while yet explicitly introducing governmental choice.[27] He returns to an older view of the world in which individual views are oriented to and expressed by socioeconomic pressure groups. The government is in a sense a coalition of such blocs that cooperate in order to provide public goods. The constraint of coalition requires that no group be sufficiently badly treated that it is motivated to withdraw its support. In Dorfman's terminology each group has a potential voters' surplus: the excess of its self-perceived benefits from provision of the public good over the group's contribution to its provision. The imposed constraint is that this voters' surplus must be nonnegative for each group. But the government has multiple possibilities beyond this since it can weight the interests of the different groups unequally. Dorfman notes that the differences in political parties constitute, in effect, different weighting schemes, and members of the party in power have substantial freedom to pursue their own preferences, and to compete for the right to govern by catering to those groups that can generate sufficient support to keep them in power.

What is refreshing in this formulation is first the explicit statement of the constraint; second, the recognition of Governors as a group with ends of its own and some ability to pursue them; and third, the recognition of intermediate groups as a focus for articulating and coalescing individual values. What the behavioral implications of this view are, are in dispute. Dorfman believes that the need to satisfy all (or most) groups imposes a downward pressure on public expenditure; I suspect that this same need is more likely to lead to logrolling and expenditure increases than to limit expenditures.

A more direct view of governmental search procedures can be represented by work of Maass [25] and Major [26]. Here the legislative process is centrally concerned to discover what agreement on objectives can be reached. Partly this is a matter of bringing together elected spokesmen for individuals and groups, but more basically it is a genuine search. The process of discussion is critically involved in a mapping function—it poses issues that permit both legislators and their constituents to discover their views about objectives. It may thus permit (via compromise and persuasion) the development of agreement on public objectives, which can serve for a time as the social objective function. This view continues to disquiet many economists, for it leaves a large element of slack within the governmental decision process that is not readily understood in terms of inputs into governmental decisions. Thus we are limited in our ability to predict Government decisions.

Rothenberg [37] has an enormously elaborate model whose purpose is to remove this element of slack. Unfortunately it defies concise description. To quote his summary, in part, "The legislative process is seen as an n-person, nonzero sum, repeated cooperative game of strategy, for which no general solution exists . . . unfortunately, manipulation of the model to elucidate its complications is beyond the scope of the present paper." I confess to being skeptical. Game theory, here as elsewhere, seems to me to provide a vocabulary for discussing a multiplicity of outcomes rather than proving a tool for predicting particular outcomes.

One aspect of Rothenberg's model picks up a strand that has characterized the work of Duncan Black [6] over two decades: the influence of the institutional rules of legislative decision on the outcome of the decision process. I shall neglect this fascinating literature only because the chief question this paper addresses is the choice of policies within a relatively fixed institutional framework, not with the influence on choices of changes in the institutional framework.

Banfield [2], like Maass and Black, is a political scientist, but unlike them he is profoundly skeptical of the utility of the type of analysis that characterizes economics: the solution of constrained maximization problems. His central point is that in the articulation of social values, the techniques of economics do not merely fail to predict behavior (because we need more information about individuals' values, or the nature of the constraints, etc.) but rather that they are inherently biased and are bound to mispredict. As I understand Banfield's view, the alternating and intertwined activities of discussion, of struggle, and of arbitration, constitute the heart of the decision process and exhibit such variance in possible outcomes that they dominate the problem of explaining political behavior. To neglect these in favor of the inputs into the political hopper is to neglect the major sources of variance in favor of the minor ones. In effect he argues that the limits placed on decisionmakers by individual preferences are so wide as to be of no real interest.

Banfield's view might be expected to lead him toward the Black and

Rothenberg analyses of process, or toward the literature by Schelling [40], and others on the strategy of conflict, or perhaps toward the organizational theorists. Here too, however, Banfield is pessimistic almost to the point of nihilism. His pessimism seems to me extreme, but it underlines the absence as yet of a compellingly effective set of predictive theories. Banfield's view that politics and thus also the prediction of its outcomes, is an art rather than a science, may prove right; at this stage neither the economists nor the bulk of the political scientists seem prepared to abandon the search for an explanation of public decisionmaking.

Evaluation of Alternative Views

This extended discussion of alternative views as to the nature of and means of articulation of the public interest clearly reveals no consensus. Indeed it is relatively easy to demonstrate why each approach is deficient. While one of these theories may with slight changes prove adequate, it is more likely we will have to await a more profound insight. It seems to me of prime importance to distinguish between the present inadequacy of our theories, and the presence of a phenomenon. Things need not be understood to exist; substantial agreement on certain social priorities may exist despite our inability (at any point in time) adequately to derive them from basic principles. Suppose we are today unable to *derive* from individual values a consistent set of social valuations that enable us to say "there is a clear collective demand for this activity." Are we constrained to act as if it does not exist, or to settle for the logic of the lowest common demoninator of acceptable action, that which will command unanimous consent? The answer seems to me to be "No." To answer otherwise would make us prisoners of our ignorance. It is less elegant, but not less scientific, to take as a starting point for evaluating social actions, the revealed objectives of society instead of the derived ones.

Let me put the matter more strongly. Suppose one could prove that in some fundamental sense the prediction of social values is impossible from basic information about individuals and their political representatives. Would it then be necessary to quit the analysis of public decisionmaking? I think not. One might take the nature of social valuations as revealed by past actions and assume that such preferences have some stability. In other words it might be possible to infer dominant collective social priorities from social actions and the repudiation or nonrepudiation of them by the electorate.[28]

In the United States today it is hard to avoid a strong presumption in favor of believing there is a strong collective preference for certain public goods such as public aid to education, for improved highways, for redistribution of income in favor of the elderly, and in favor of farmers. Are these only today's choices of today's individuals or are they a reliable indicator of how Americans are likely to feel next year or even 10 years hence? I think there is evidence of stability in some choices, and gradual change in others. In any period there are highly debatable issues that get resolved and stay resolved for generations, not unanimously, but sufficiently that legislators of each party are content to let them lie. Today the debates about minimum wages, and social security (even medicare), seem remote and (in this sense) resolved. We may ask about the appropriate level of the programs, but their existence is not likely to be subject to any serious challenge. On the other hand, I would not argue very strongly in favor of the presumption of similar preferences for or against integrated housing or schools, for foreign aid of nonaligned or Eastern countries, for domestic gun control, or for international disarmament. At any time some issues are genuinely unresolved, for others the degree of consensus is uncertain.

Evidence on these matters is available even in the absence of analytic solution. Not only do elections provide some information about revealed preferences but enormous quantities of attitudinal information can be collected by the techniques of survey research. As theorists, we tend to denigrate stability and regularity in the absence of comprehensive theory. We should not. Men successfully and repeatedly circumnavigated the globe using navigational theories now regarded as naive and wrong. Today we can predict with enormous accuracy the tides along the Bay of Fundy but we do not begin to understand their differences from place to place. Closer to home, we can more accurately predict the aggregate effects of a tax cut, than the incidence of it.

In arguing so I do not mean to minimize or disparage the progress of the purely theoretical debate. Even our failures are more promising now, and we have come a long way beyond the emptiness of the new welfare economics. Most encouraging is the genuine joint dialogue among social scientists of different fields as well as different persuasions.

CONCLUDING COMMENTS: THE ROLE OF EFFICIENCY

Economists traditionally place major emphasis on the efficient allocation of resources, and much of the public interest debate is also so phrased. This is particularly, but not exclusively, the case when dealing with the portion of the debate concerning the discount rate. In this paper I have stressed a multi-dimensional objective function rather than one involving only efficiency. Economists who disagree with this approach are not likely to do so on the grounds that efficient use of resources is the only sensible objective of social policy, nor on the grounds that efficient use of resources will never conflict with other objectives. Instead they may argue first, that any worthwhile objectives can be incorporated within an efficiency framework by an appropriate set of measurements of benefits and costs. Thus efficiency can embrace maximizing a utility function that may have several arguments. Or they may argue, second, that objectives like income redistribution not conveniently and conventionally included within the efficiency framework can and should be satisfied by lump sum taxes and transfers that do not serve to distort resource allocation.

Since either one of these arguments is, if correct, sufficient, the case for efficiency seems powerful and it has many adherents. Nevertheless, many economists, including this one, do not find these arguments persuasive.

The first argument has already been discussed at some length and constitutes a highly important question of research strategy: if there is a multi-dimensional objective structure, can it effectively be compressed into a single dimension by assignment of a measure of benefits? My view is that while it is possible so to compress it, it is not desirable to do so because it leads to submerging real issues behind a facade of faulty measurements. Bias can run either way: by overvaluing intangibles (see for example the characteristically shoddy imputation of secondary benefits), or by neglecting as benefits those differences in the vector of public and private goods that are not readily measured. There is, of course, no inherently correct answer to the question of what is the best form of response to difficulties in accurate measurement. I would rather measure only what I have confidence in measuring with some accuracy and leave "incommensurables" to be decided by explicit choice. It may be easy to choose between defense and education at a given time even though it is hard to express a price that equilibrates them.[29] If one does not use a uniform system of valuations (and I am arguing that one need not) there is a danger that one will make some inconsistent decisions. But if one uses badly biased data there is a danger of making consistent but faulty decisions. As has been said in another connection, it may be better to be vaguely right than precisely wrong.

The second defense of efficiency fails to prove compelling if one believes that appropriate lump sum transfers cannot be made, that they cannot be made without high transaction costs, or that they will not be made. These are factual questions but I have no real doubt about the facts. It might for example be possible to achieve indirectly for under-privileged urban residents what direct public action is today providing via urban redevelopment, and other poverty programs. But it is unlikely that in a political context the same results would have been achieved. The current effort to replace a myriad of welfare programs by a negative income tax provides a contemporary test of how easy or difficult it will prove to achieve by taxes or transfers what might otherwise be provided by direct public action. Whether for good or for ill it is frequently easier to do things one way than another. To limit the public policymaker to allocationally neutral tools constrains him, and thus changes the nature of the results he achieves. Whether the change is (as I believe) large or whether it is small is a factual matter on which one day we may have facts.

Obviously the question "What is the public interest?" has no simple answer. Indeed, asking the question invites the sort of smile reserved for small children and benign idiots. Let me end this discussion by some wholly personal assertions. There is a role for measurement, a role for analysis and some need for explicit decisionmaking. We do our decisionmakers a disservice if we blur the roles. One such blurring occurs if we submerge real decisionmaking among competing objectives into a mere measurement problem by giving the advice: "assign benefits and costs and then pick the optimal set of projects." This provides too little help. One of the economist's most potent functions is honestly to identify what can be accurately measured and compared and what (on the other hand) involves such heroics of assumption that actual measurements are but concealed preferences. The advantage of articulating real choices over assigning measures that appear to obviate them is to make the decision explicit and subject to review. But having identified the scope for explicit choice does not mean public administrators have unconstrained choice. Within particular dimensions, departures from the efficient solution ought to be identified and justified.

Clearly all sorts of decisions do get made and not all of them are sensible. My conception of the analyst's role is to force an articulation of the proximate objectives served and of the conflicts between such objectives. I should be willing to regard open decisions so arrived at by elected (or otherwise responsible) public officials as a reasonable approximation to the collective values that we call the public interest. I think at present that we conceal so many issues and conflicts, both among objectives and among alternative means, that we increase the discretion of the policymaker beyond that necessary or desirable.

NOTES

[1] Simliar is Musgrave's definition of public goods as those produced under public management ([33], p. 42). It should be noted that Musgrave recognized the need for a more complex classification, which he provides.

[2] Knut Wicksell, "A New Principle of Just Taxation." Reprinted in [34].

[3] The identity of who the "public" is, is deferred for the moment.

[4] Millard F. Long [24] has recently challenged Weisbrod's concept.

[5] Option demands are in a sense much like consumers surplus: they arise because the price charged for the good or service is below the maximum each buyer would be willing to pay. Thus the option to buy at a low future price has present value. Weisbrod's insight, I think, is that option demands are a significant source of demand for public action.

[6] Stigler [44] provides a conceptual analysis of the costs and benefits of obtaining information. Telser [46] deals with the problem of buying information in the form of advertising as a joint product with news, entertainment, etc.

[7] A Department of Health, Education, and Welfare study [49] supplies some evidence on the incentive effects of subsidies to scientists and other academic personnel.

[8] See Freeman [17] for a recent effort to work out the implications of income distribution for public investment planning. See also the papers by Freeman and Burton Weisbrod in this volume.

[9] They are discussed in [43].

[10] Scitovsky [41] demonstrated an inconsistency in the principle in the case in which price changes occurred: Baumol [4], Little [23], and Kennedy [21] questioned the use of potential compensation.

[11] Banfield ([2], p. 11) suggests the following as an extreme parable about a society that can make accurate interpersonal comparisons of the subjective states of individuals A and B:

> "If A's preference is for putting B into a gas chamber, then 'bliss for the whole universe' is served by his putting him there, provided only that B's loss of satisfaction at being put there is less than A's at putting him there. Even if B claims that his loss of satisfaction will be at least as great as A's gain of it, the just and equitable society will tell him that he is mistaken and put him there anyway in the 'good cause of adding more to the rest of mankind's (that is to say, A's) well-being.' If perchance A and his friends constitute 51 percent of the population and B and his friends only 49 percent, the matter will be simple indeed."

[12] This is, of course, a conclusion of Arrow's "General Possibility Theorem": "If we exclude the possibility of interpersonal comparisons of utility, then the only methods of passing from individual tastes to social preferences which will be satisfactory and which will be defined for a wide range of sets of individual orderings are either imposed or dictatorial" ([1], p. 59). For discussion and criticism of this famous proposition, see especially: Little [23], and Tullock [48].

[13] See Truman [47] for an extended discussion of groups in the political process.

[14] A better historian of thought might define it as the Sax-Wicksell-Lindahl-Musgrave-Bowen-Samuelson . . . tradition, to recognize the apparently valid theorem that no one ever has an original idea. Samuelson is diligent in identifying his predecessors and Musgrave provides admirable summaries of earlier views. In an earlier day theories of this type were called voluntary exchange theories.

[15] Buchanan and Tullock [10] develop an ingenious "economic theory of constitutions" in which individuals find it advantageous to agree in advance to certain rules even though they may work to the individual's disadvantage on occasion.

[16] The discussion of the discount rate as an implicit weighting scheme involves technical issues best omitted from this paper. They are discussed in [43]. See also the paper by William Baumol in this volume.

[17] A paper of my own [42] is a good example of use of this approach.

[18] See also the paper by Myrick Freeman in this volume.

[19] One is not limited in principle to linear relationships. Chenery's tradeoff at time t could be a variable function of the size and sign of balance of payments disequilibrium at time t.

[20] An admirable summary with an extended bibliography is found in Truman [47].

[21] Uncertainty creates some scope for leadership, and for errors that give politics an interesting dynamics. It is not possible to pursue them now. See Downs [15], esp. chapters 5–8.

[22] The words are Barker's [3], quoted with evident approval by Maass [25], p. 569.

[23] The theorem proved is that transitivity in all individual orderings is not sufficient to assure a collectively transitive set of choices.

[24] Margolis and Marglin offer yet a different view of this problem. A man may be willing to pay his share of a joint venture only if he can force his reluctant neighbors to do the same [31]. In this view a vote is an offer to sign a social contract if enough others also sign.

[25] This phenomenon may be found in the market too. If buyers can be persuaded to accept second best, their true preferences may not be effective.

[26] Knight points out that individuals may be unequally constrained by voting from utilizing their "normally available capacities for action." Evidently Knight feels that unequal constraints are more unfair than unequal initial distributions of wealth.

[27] See also the paper by Dorfman and Henry Jacoby in this volume.

[28] See Birdsall [5] for such an attempt.

[29] Obviously once the dividing line between them is set, an implicit (shadow) price exists. But the price may be very different a few years hence. In any case I am arguing that it may be easier to make the decision (and thus imply the price) than in some objective sense to assign the price and thus determine the decision. Only at a purely formal level are these equivalent.

REFERENCES

[1] Arrow, Kenneth J., *Social Choice and Individual Values,* second edition, New York: John Wiley & Sons, 1963.

[2] Banfield, Edward C., " 'Economic' Analysis of 'Political' Phenomena: A Political Scientist's Critique," Harvard Seminar on Political-Economic Decisions, March 1967 (ditto).

[3] Barker, Ernest, *Reflections on Government,* London: Oxford University Press, 1942.

[4] Baumol, William J., *Welfare Economics and the Theory of the State,* second edition, London: G. Bell & Sons, 1965.

[5] Birdsall, William C., "A Study of the Demand for Public Goods," in Richard A. Musgrave, editor, *Essays in Fiscal Federalism,* Washington: The Brookings Institution, 1965, pp. 235–292.

[6] Black, Duncan, *The Theory of Committees and Elections,* Cambridge: Cambridge University Press, 1958.

[7] Bowen, Howard R., "The Interpretation of Voting in the Allocation of Economic Resources," *Quarterly Journal of Economics,* 58:27–48, November 1943.

[8] Braybrooke and Lindblom, *A Strategy of Decision,* New York: 1963.

[9] Breton, Albert, "A Theory of the Demand for Public Goods, *Canadian Journal of Economics and Political Science,* 32:455–467, November 1966.

[10] Buchanan, James M., "Individual Choice in Voting and the Market," *Journal of Political Economy,* 62:334–343, August 1954.

[11] Buchanan, James M., and Gordon Tullock, *The Calculus of Consent,* Ann Arbor: University of Michigan Press, 1962.

[12] Chenery, Hollis B., "The Application of Investment Criteria," *Quarterly Journal of Economics,* 67:76–96, February 1953.

[13] Dahl, Robert A., and Charles E. Lindblom, *Politics, Economics, and Welfare,* New York: Harper & Row, 1953.

[14] Dorfman, Robert, "General Equilibrium with Public Goods," presented to International Economics Association Conference on Public Economics, September 1966 (in press).

[15] Downs, Anthony, *An Economic Theory of Democracy,* New York: Harper & Row, 1957.

[16] Eckstein, Otto, "A Survey of the Theory of Public Expenditure Criteria," in James M. Buchanan, editor, *Public Finances: Needs, Sources and Utilization,* National Bureau of Economic Research, Princeton: Princeton University Press, 1961.

[17] Freeman, A. Myrick, III, "Income Distribution and Planning for Public Investment," *American Economic Review,* 57:495–508, June 1967.

[18] Harberger, Arnold C., "Survey of Literature on Cost-Benefit Analysis for Industrial Project Evaluation," *Inter-Regional Symposium in Industrial Project Evaluation,* sponsored by the Economic and Social Council of the United Nations, Committee for Industrial Development, Prague: October 1965 (mimeograph).

[19] Haveman, Robert H., *Water Resource Investment and the Public Interest,* Nashville: Vanderbilt University Press, 1965.

[20] Head, J. G., "Public Goods and Public Policy," *Public Finance,* 17:197–220, No. 3, 1962.

[21] Kennedy, Charles F., "The Economic Welfare Function and Dr. Little's Criterion," *Review of Economic Studies,* 20:137–142, No. 2, 1953.

[22] Knight, Frank H., "The Meaning of Freedom," in C. M. Perry, editor, *The Philosophy of American Democracy,* Chicago: 1943.

[23] Little, Ian Malcolm David, *A Critique of Welfare Economics,* second edition, Oxford: Oxford University Press, 1957.

[24] Long, Millard F., "Collective-Consumption Services of Individual-Consumption Goods: Comment," *Quarterly Journal of Economics,* 81:351–352, May 1967.

[25] Maass, Arthur, "System Design and the Political Process: A General Statement," in *Design of Water-Resource Systems,* Cambridge, Mass.: Harvard University Press, 1962, pp. 565–604.

[26] Major, David C., *Decision-Making for Public Investment in Water Resource Development in the United States,* Harvard University, Graduate School of Public Administration, Harvard Water Program, August 1965 (mimeograph).

[27] McKean, Roland N., *Efficiency in Government through Systems Analysis, with Emphasis on Water Resource Development,* New York: John Wiley & Sons, 1958.

[28] Marglin, Stephen A., "Objectives of Water-Resource Development: A General Statement," in *Design of Water-Resource Systems,* Cambridge, Mass.: Harvard University Press, 1962, pp. 17–87.

[29] ———, *Public Investment Criteria,* Cambridge, Mass.: Massachusetts Institute of Technology Press, 1967.

[30] Margolis, Julius, "Secondary Benefits, External Economies, and the Justification of Public Investment," *Review of Economics and Statistics,* 39:228–291, August 1957.

[31] ———, "The Structure of Government and Public Investment," *American Economic Review, Papers and Proceedings,* 54:236–242, May 1964, with discussion, pp. 250–257, *ibid.*

[32] Mishan, E. J., "Criteria for Public Investment: Some Simplifying Suggestions," *Journal of Political Economy,* 75:139–146, April 1967.

[33] Musgrave, Richard A., *The Theory of Public Finance,* New York: McGraw-Hill, 1959.

[34] ———, and Alan T. Peacock, *Classics in the Theory of Public Finance,* New York: Macmillan, 1958.

[35] Olson, Mancur, Jr., *The Logic of Collective Action,* Cambridge, Mass.: Harvard University Press, 1965.

[36] Rothenberg, Jerome, *The Measurement of Social Welfare,* Englewood Cliffs: Prentice-Hall, 1961.

[37] ———, "A Model of Economic and Political Decision Making," Harvard Seminar on Political-Economic Decisions, March 1967 (ditto).

[38] Samuelson, Paul A., "Diagrammatic Exposition of a Theory of Public Expenditure," *Review of Economics and Statistics,* 37:350–356, November 1955.

[39] ———, "The Pure Theory of Public Expenditure," *Review of Economics and Statistics,* 36:387–389, November 1954.

[40] Schelling, Thomas C., *The Strategy of Conflict,* Cambridge, Mass.: Harvard University Press, 1960.

[41] Scitovsky, Tibor, "A Note on Welfare Propositions in Economics," *Review of Economic Studies,* 9:77–88, November 1941.

[42] Steiner, Peter O., "Choosing Among Alternative Public Investments in the Water Resource Field," *American Economic Review,* 49:893–916, December 1959.

[43] ———, "Public Expenditure Budgeting," The Brookings Institution, 1969.

[44] Stigler, George J., "Economics of Information," *Journal of Political Economy,* 69:213–225, June 1961.

[45] Strotz, Robert H., "Two Propositions Related to Public Goods," *Review of Economics and Statistics,* 40:329–331, November 1958.

[46] Telser, Lester G., "How Much Does It Pay Whom to Advertise?" *American Economic Review,* 51:194–205, May 1961.

[47] Truman, David B., *The Governmental Process,* New York: 1962.

[48] Tullock, Gordon, "The General Irrelevance of the General Impossibility Theorem," *Quarterly Journal of Economics,* 81:256–270, May 1967.

[49] United States, Department of Health, Education, and Welfare, *A Survey of Federal Programs in Higher Education,* 1962.

[50] Weisbrod, Burton A., "Collective-Consumption Services of Individual-Consumption Goods," *Quarterly Journal of Economics,* 78:471–477, August 1964.

[51] ———, "Income-Redistribution Effects and Benefit-Cost Analysis of Government Expenditure Programs," in Samuel B. Chase, Jr., editor, *Problems in Public Expenditure Analysis,* Washington: The Brookings Institution, 1968.

CHAPTER 2

THE ORGANIZATION OF ECONOMIC ACTIVITY: ISSUES PERTINENT TO THE CHOICE OF MARKET VERSUS NONMARKET ALLOCATION

Kenneth J. Arrow

INTRODUCTION

The concept of public goods has been developed through a process of successive refinement over a long period of time. Yet surprisingly enough there does not seem to exist anywhere in the literature a clear general definition of this concept or the more general one of "externality." The accounts given are usually either very general and discursive, difficult of interpretation in specific contexts, or else they are rigorous accounts of very special situations. What exactly is the relation between externalities and such concepts as "appropriability" or "exclusion"?

Also, there is considerable ambiguity in the purpose of the analysis of externalities. The best developed part of the theory relates to only a single question: the statement of a set of conditions, as weak as possible, which insure that a competitive equilibrium exists and is Pareto efficient.[1] Then the denial of any of these hypotheses is presumably a sufficient condition for considering resort to non-market channels of resource allocation—usually thought of as government expenditures, taxes, and subsidies.

At a second level the analysis of externalities should lead to criteria for nonmarket allocation. We are tempted to set forth these criteria in terms analogous to the profit-and-loss statements of private business; in this form, we are led to benefit-cost analysis. There are, moreover, two possible aims for benefit-cost analysis; one, more ambitious but theoretically simpler, is specification of the nonmarket actions which will restore Pareto efficiency; the second involves the recognition that the instruments available to the government or other nonmarket forces are scarce resources for one reason or another, so that all that can be achieved is a "second-best."

Other concepts that seem to cluster closely to the concept of public

Kenneth J. Arrow is Professor of Economics at Harvard University and is associated with the Project on Efficiency of Decisionmaking in Economic Systems at that institution.

goods are those of "increasing returns" and "market failure." These are related to Pareto inefficiency on the one hand and to the existence and optimality of competitive equilibrium on the other; sometimes the discussions in the literature do not adequately distinguish these two aspects. I contend that market failure is a more general category than externality; and both differ from increasing returns in a basic sense, since market failures in general and externalities in particular are relative to the mode of economic organization, while increasing returns are essentially a technological phenomenon.

Current writing has helped bring out the point that market failure is not absolute; it is better to consider a broader category, that of transaction costs, which in general impede and in particular cases completely block the formation of markets. It is usually though not always emphasized that transaction costs are costs of running the economic system. An incentive for vertical integration is replacement of the costs of buying and selling on the market by the costs of intrafirm transfers; the existence of vertical integration may suggest that the costs of operating competitive markets are not zero, as is usually assumed in our theoretical analysis.

Monetary theory, unlike value theory, is heavily dependent on the assumption of positive transaction costs; the recurrent complaint about the difficulty of integrating these two branches of theory is certainly governed by the contradictory assumptions made about transaction costs. The creation of money is in many respects an example of a public good.

The identification of transaction costs in different contexts and under different systems of resource allocation should be a major item on the research agenda of the theory of public goods and indeed of the theory of resource allocation in general. Only the most rudimentary suggestions are made here. The "exclusion principle" is a limiting case of one kind of transaction cost, but another type, the costliness of the information needed to enter and participate in any market, has been little remarked. Information is closely related on the one hand to communication and on the other to uncertainty.

Given the existence of Pareto inefficiency in a free market equilibrium, there is a pressure in the market to overcome it by some sort of departure from the free market; i.e., some form of collective action. This need not be undertaken by the government. I suggest that in fact there is a wide variety of social institutions, in particular generally accepted social norms of behavior, which serve in some means as compensation for failure or limitation of the market, though each in turn involves transaction costs of its own. The question also arises how the behavior of individual economic agents in a social institution (especially in voting) is related to their behavior on the market. A good deal of theoretical literature has arisen in recent years which seeks to describe political behavior as analogous to economic, and we may hope for a general theory of socioeconomic equilibrium. But it must always be kept in mind that the contexts of choice are radically different, particularly when the hypotheses of perfectly costless action and information are relaxed. It is not accidental that economic analysis has been successful only in certain limited areas.

COMPETITIVE EQUILIBRIUM AND PARETO EFFICIENCY

A quick review of the familiar theorems on the role of perfectly competitive equilibrium in the efficient allocation of resources will be useful. Perfectly competitive equilbrium has its usual meaning: households, possessed of initial resources, including possibly claims to the profits of firms, choose consumption bundles to maximize utility at a given set of prices; firms choose production bundles so as to maximize profits at the same set of prices; the chosen production and consumption bundles must be consistent with each other in the sense that aggregate production plus initial resources must equal aggregate consumption. The key points in the definition are the parametric role[2] of the prices for each individual and the identity of prices for all individuals. Implicit are the assumptions that all prices can be known by all individuals and that the act of charging prices is not itself a consumer of resources.

A number of additional assumptions are made at different points in the theory of equilibrium, but most are clearly factually valid in the usual contexts and need not be mentioned. The two hypotheses frequently not valid are (C), the convexity of household indifference maps and firm production possibility sets,[3] and (M), the universality of markets. While the exact meaning of the last assumption will be explored later at some length, for the present purposes we mean that the consumption bundle which determines the utility of an individual is the same as that which he purchases at given prices subject to his budget constraint, and that the set of production bundles among which a firm chooses is a given range independent of decisions made by other agents in the economy.

The relations between Pareto efficiency and competitive equilibrium are set forth in the following two theorems:

1. *If (M) holds, a competitive equilibrium is Pareto-efficient.* This theorem is true even if (C) does not hold.

2. *If (C) and (M) hold, then any Pareto-efficient allocation can be achieved as a competitive equilibrium by a suitable reallocation of initial resources.*

When the assumptions of proposition 2 are valid, then the case for the competitive price system is strongest. Any complaints about its operation can be reduced to complaints about the distribution of income, which should then be rectified by lump-sum transfers. Of course, as Pareto already emphasized, the proposition provides no basis for accepting the results of the market in the absence of accepted levels of income equality.

The central role of competitive equilibrium both as a normative guide and as at least partially descriptive of the real world raises an analytically difficult question: does a competitive equilibrium necessarily exist?

3. *If (C) holds, then there exists a competitive equilibrium.* This theorem is true even if (M) does not hold.

If both (C) and (M) hold, we have a fairly complete and simple picture of the achievement of desirable goals, subject always to the major qualification of the achievement of a desirable income distribution. The price system itself determines the income distribution only in the sense of preserving the status quo. Even if costless lump-sum transfers are possible, there is needed a collective mechanism reallocating income if the status quo is not regarded as satisfactory.

Of course (C) is not a necessary condition for the existence of a competitive equilibrium, only a sufficient one. From proposition 1, it is possible to have an equilibrium and therefore efficient allocation without convexity (when (M) holds). However, in view of the central role of (C) in these theorems, the implications in relaxing this hypothesis have been examined intensively in recent years by Farrell (1959), Rothenberg (1960), Aumann (1966), and Starr (1969). Their conclusions may be summarized as follows: Let (C′) be the weakened convexity assumption that there are no indivisibilities large relative to the economy.

4. *Propositions 2 and 3 remain approximately true if (C) is replaced by (C′).*

Thus, the only nonconvexities that are important for the present purposes are increasing returns over a range large relative to the economy. In those circumstances, a competitive equilibrium cannot exist.

The price system, for all its virtues, is only one conceivable form of arranging trade, even in a system of private property. Bargaining can assume extremely general forms. Under the assumptions (C′) and (M), we are assured that not everyone can be made better off by a bargain not derived from the price system; but the question arises whether some members of the economy will not find it in their interest and within their power to depart from the perfectly competitive price system. For example, both Knight (1921, pp. 190–194) and Samuelson (1967, p. 120) have noted that it would pay all the firms in a given industry to form a monopoly. But in fact it can be argued that unrestricted bargaining can only settle down to a resource allocation which could also be achieved as a perfectly competitive equilibrium, at least if the bargaining itself is costless and each agent is small compared to the entire economy. This line of argument originated with Edgeworth (1881, pp. 20–43) and has been developed recently by Shubik (1959), Debreu and Scarf (1963), and Aumann (1964).

More precisely, it is easy to show:

5. *If (M) holds and a competitive equilibrium prevails, then no set of economic agents will find any resource allocation which they can accomplish by themselves (without trade with the other agents) which they will all prefer to that prevailing under the equilibrium.*

Proposition 5 holds for any number of agents. A deeper proposition is the following converse:

6. *If (C′) and (M) hold, and if the resources of any economic agent are small compared with the total of the economy, then, given any allocation not approximately achievable as a competitive equilibrium, there will be some set of agents and some resource allocation they can achieve without any trade with others which each one will prefer to the given allocation.*

These two propositions, taken together, strongly suggest that when all the relevant hypotheses hold, (*a*) a competitive equilibrium, if achieved, will not be upset by bargaining even if permitted, and (*b*) for any bargain not achievable by a competitive equilibrium there is a set of agents who would benefit by change to another bargain which they have the full power to enforce.

The argument that a set of firms can form a monopoly overlooks the possibility that the consumers can also form a coalition, threaten not to buy, and seek mutually advantageous deals with a subset of the firms; such deals are possible since the monopoly allocation violates some marginal equivalences.

In real life, monopolizing cartels are possible for a reason not so far introduced into the analysis: bargaining costs between producers and consumers are high, those among producers low—a point made most emphatically by Adam Smith (1937, p. 128); "People of the same trade seldom meet together, even for merriment or diversion, but the conversation ends in a conspiracy against the public, or in some contrivance to raise prices." *It is not the presence of bargaining costs per se but their bias that is relevant.* If all bargaining costs are high, but competitive pricing and the markets are cheap, then we expect the perfectly competitive equilibrium to obtain, yielding an allocation identical with that under costless bargaining. But if bargaining costs are biased, then some bargains other than the competitive equilibrium can be arrived at which will not be upset by still other bargains if the latter but not the former are costly.

Finally, in this review of the elements of competitive equilibrium theory, let me repeat the obvious and well-known fact that in a world where time is relevant, the commodities which enter into the equilibrium system include those with future dates. In fact, the bulk of meaningful future transactions cannot be carried out on any existing present market, so that assumption (M), the universality of markets, is not valid.

EXTERNALITIES ILLUSTRATED

After this long[4] excursus into the present state of the theory of equilibrium and optimality, it is time to discuss some of the standard concepts of externality, market failure, and public goods generally. The clarification of these concepts is a long historical process, not yet concluded, in which the classic contributions of Knight (1924), Young (1913, pp. 676–684), and Robertson (1924) have in more recent times been enriched by those of Meade (1952), Scitovsky (1954), Coase (1960), Buchanan and Stubblebine (1962), and Demsetz (1966). The concept of externality and the extent to which it causes nonoptimal market behavior will be discussed here in terms of a simple model.

Consider a pure exchange economy. Let x_{ik} be the amount of the kth commodity consumed by the ith individual ($i = 1, \ldots, n;\ k = 1, \ldots, m$) and $\bar{x}_k$ be the amount of the kth commodity available. Suppose in general that the utility of the ith individual is a function of the consumption of all individuals (not all types of consumption for all individuals need actually enter into any given individual's utility function); the utility of the ith individual is $U_i(x_{11}, \ldots, x_{mn})$. We have the obvious constraints:

$$\sum_i x_{ik} \leqq \bar{x}_k \tag{1}$$

Introduce the following definitions:

$$x_{jik} = x_{ik}. \tag{2}$$

With this notation a Pareto-efficient allocation is a vector maximum of the utility functions $U_j(x_{j11}, \ldots, x_{jmn})$, subject to the constraints (1) and (2). Because of the notation used, the variables appearing in the utility function relating to the jth individual are proper to him alone and appear in no one else's utility function. If we understand now that there are n^2m commodities, indexed by the triple subscript jik, then the Pareto-efficiency problem has a thoroughly classical form. There are n^2m prices, p_{jik}, attached to the constraints (2), plus m prices, q_k, corresponding to constraints (1). Following the maximization procedure formally, we see, much as in Samuelson (1954), that Pareto efficiency is characterized by the conditions:

$$\lambda_j(\partial U_j/\partial x_{ik}) = p_{jik}, \tag{3}$$

and

$$\sum_j p_{jik} = q_k, \tag{4}$$

where λ_j is the reciprocal of the marginal utility of income for individual j. (These statements ignore corner conditions, which can easily be supplied.)

Condition (4) can be given the following economic interpretation: Imagine each individual i to be a producer with m production processes, indexed by the pair (i,k). Process (i,k). has one input, namely commodity k, and n outputs, indexed by the triple (j,i,k). In other words, what we ordinarily call individual i's consumption is regarded as the production of joint outputs, one for each individual whose utility is affected by individual i's consumption.

The point of this exercise is to show that by suitable and indeed not unnatural reinterpretation of the commodity space, externalities can be regarded as ordinary commodities, and all the formal theory of competitive equilibrium is valid, including its optimality.

It is not the mere fact that one man's consumption enters into another man's utility that causes the failure of the market to achieve efficiency. There are two relevant factors which cannot be discovered by inspection of the utility structures of the individual. One, much explored in the literature, is the appropriability of the commodities which represent the external repercussions; the other, less stressed, is the fact that markets for externalities usually involve small numbers of buyers and sellers.

The first point, Musgrave's "exclusion principle," (1959, p. 86) is so well known as to need little elaboration. Pricing demands the possibility of excluding nonbuyers from the use of the product, and this exclusion may be technically impossible or may require the use of considerable resources. Pollution is the key example; the supply of clean air or water to each individual would have to be treated as a separate commodity, and it would have to be possible in principle to supply to one and not the other (though the final equilibrium would involve equal supply to all). But this is technically impossible.

The second point comes out clearly in our case. Each commodity (j,i,k) has precisely one buyer and one seller. Even if a competitive equilibrium could be defined, there would be no force driving the system to it; we are in the realm of imperfectly competitive equilibrium.

In my view, the standard lighthouse example is best analyzed as a problem of small numbers rather than of the difficulty of exclusion, though both elements are present. To simplify matters, I will abstract from uncertainty so that the lighthouse keeper knows exactly when each ship will need its services, and also abstract from indivisibility (since the light is either on or off). Assume further that only one ship will be within range of the lighthouse at any moment. Then exclusion is perfectly possible; the lighthouse need only shut off its light when a nonpaying ship is coming into range. But there would be only one buyer and one seller and no competitive forces to drive the two into a competitive equilibrium. If in addition the costs of bargaining are high, then it may be most efficient to offer the service free.

If, as is typical, markets for the externalities do not exist, then the allocation from the point of view of the "buyer" is determined by a rationing process. We can determine a shadow price for the buyer; this will differ from the price, zero, received by the seller. Hence, formally, the failure of markets for externalities to exist can also be described as a difference of prices between buyer and seller.

In the example analyzed, the externalities related to particular named individuals; individual i's utility function depended on what a particular individual, j, possessed. The case where it is only the total amount of some commodity (e.g., handsome houses) in other people's hands that matters is a special case, which yields rather simpler results. In this case, $\partial U_j/\partial x_{ik}$ is independent of i for $i \neq j$, and hence, by (3), p_{jik} is independent of i for $i \neq j$. Let,

$$p_{iik} = p_{ik},\ p_{jik} = \bar{p}_{jk} \text{ for } i \neq j.$$

Then (4) becomes,

$$p_{ik} + \sum_{j \neq i} \bar{p}_{jk} = q_k,$$

or,

$$(p_{ik} - \bar{p}_{ik}) + \sum_{j} \bar{p}_{jk} = q_k,$$

from which it follows that the difference, $p_{ik} - \bar{p}_{ik}$, is independent of i. There are two kinds of shadow prices, a price $\bar{p}_{ik}$, the price that individual i is willing to pay for an increase in the stock of commodity k in any other individual's hands, and the premium, $p_{ik} - \bar{p}_{ik}$, he is willing to pay to have the commodity in his possession rather than someone else's. At the optimum, this premium for private possession must be the same for all individuals.

Other types of externalities are associated with several commodities simultaneously and do not involve named individuals, as in the case of neighborhood effects, where an individual's utility depends both on others' behavior (e.g., esthetic, criminal) and on their location.

There is one deep problem in the intepretation of externalities which can only be signaled here. What aspects of others' behavior to we çonsider as affecting a utility function? If we take a hard-boiled revealed preference attitude, then if an individual expends resources in supporting legislation regulating another's behavior, it must be assumed that that behavior affects his utility. Yet in the cases that students of criminal law call "crimes without victims," such as homosexuality or drug-taking, there is no direct relation between the parties. Do we have to extend the concept of externality to all matters that an individual cares about? Or, in the spirit of John Stuart Mill, is there a second-order value judgment which excludes some of these preferences from the formation of social policy as being illegitimate infringements of individual freedom?

MARKET FAILURE

The problem of externalities is thus a special case of a more general phenomenon, the failure of markets to exist. Not all examples of market failure can fruitfully be described as externalities. Two very important examples have already been alluded to; markets for many forms of risk-bearing and for most future transactions do not exist and their absence is surely suggestive of inefficiency.

Previous discussion has suggested two possible causes for market failures: (1) inability to exclude; (2) lack of necessary information to permit market transactions to be concluded.

The failure of futures markets cannot be directly explained in these terms. Exclusion is no more a problem in the future than in the present. Any contract to be executed in the future is necessarily contingent on some events (for example, that the two agents are still both in business), but there must be many cases where no informational difficulty is presented. The absence of futures markets may be ascribed to a third possibility: (3) supply and demand are equated at zero; the highest price at which anyone would buy is below the lowest price at which anyone would sell.

This third case of market failure, unlike the first two, is by itself in no way presumptive of inefficiency. However, it may usually be assumed that its occurrence is the result of failures of the first two types on complementary markets. Specifically, the demand for future steel may be low because of uncertainties of all types; sales and technological uncertainty for the buyer's firm, prices and existence of competing goods, and the quality specification of the steel. If, however, adequate markets for risk-bearing existed, the uncertainties could be removed, and the demand for future steel would rise.

TRANSACTION COSTS

Market failure has been presented as absolute, but in fact the situation is more complex than this. A more general formulation is that of transaction costs, which are attached to any market and indeed to any mode of resource allocation. Market failure is the particular case where transaction costs are so high that the existence of the market is no longer worthwhile. The distinction between transaction costs and production costs is that the former can be varied by a chance in the mode of resource allocation, while the latter depend only on the technology and tastes, and would be the same in all economic systems.

The discussions in the preceding sections suggest two sources of transaction costs. (1) exclusion costs; (2) costs of communication and information, including both the supplying and the learning of the terms on which transactions can be carried out. An additional source is (3) the costs of disequlibrium; in any complex system, the market or authoritative allocation, even under perfect information, it takes time to compute the optimal allocation, and either transactions take place which are inconsistent with the final equilibrium or they are delayed until the computation are completed (see T. Marschak, 1959).

These costs vary from system to system; thus, one of the advantages of a price system over either bargaining or some form of authoritative allocation is usually stated to be the economy in costs of information and communication. But the costs of transmitting and especially of receiving a large number of price signals may be high; thus, there is a tendency not to differentiate prices as much as would be desirable from the efficiency viewpoint; for example, the same price is charged for peak and offpeak usage of transportation or electricity.

In a price system, transaction costs drive a wedge between buyer's and seller's prices and thereby give rise to welfare losses as in the usual analysis. Removal of these welfare losses by changing to another system (for example, governmental allocation on benefit-cost critera) must be weighed against any possible increase in transaction costs (for example, the need for elaborate and perhaps impossible studies to determine demand functions without the benefit of observing a market).

The welfare implications of transaction costs would exist even if they were proportional to the size of the transaction, but in fact they typically exhibit increasing returns. The cost of acquiring a piece of information, for example, a price, is independent of the scale of use to which it will be put.

COLLECTIVE ACTION: THE POLITICAL PROCESS

The state may frequently have a special role to play in resource allocation because, by its nature, it has a monopoly of coercive power, and coercive power can be used to economize on transaction costs. The most important use of coercion in the economic context is the collection of taxes; others are regulatory legislation and eminent domain proceedings.

The state is not an entity but rather a system of individual agents, a widely extensive system in the case of a democracy. It is appealing and fruitful to analyze its behavior in resource allocation in a manner analogous to that of the price system. Since the same agents appear in the two systems, it becomes equally natural to assume they have the same motives. Hotelling (1929, pp. 54–55) and Schumpeter (1942, ch. XXII) had sketched such politicoeconomic models, and von Neumann and Morgenstern's monumental work is certainly based on the idea that all social phenomena are governed by essentially the same motives as economics. The elaboration of more or less complete models of the political process along the lines of economic theory is more recent, the most prominent contributors being Black (1958), Downs (1957), Buchanan and Tullock (1962), and Rothenberg (1965).

I confine myself here to a few critical remarks on the possibilities of such theories. These are not intended to be negative but to suggest problems that have to be faced and are raised by some points in the preceding discussion.

1. If we take the allocative process to be governed by majority voting, then, as we well know, there are considerable possibilities of paradox. The possible intransitivity of majority voting was already pointed out by Condorcet (1785). If, instead of assuming that each individual votes according to his preferences it is assumed that they bargain freely before voting (vote-selling), the paradox appears in another form, a variant of the bargaining problems already noted in section 2. If a majority could do what it wanted, then it would be optimal to win with a bare majority and take everything; but any such bargain can always be broken up by another proposed majority.

Tullock (1967) has recently argued convincingly that if the distribution of opinions on social issues is fairly uniform and if the dimensionality of the space of social issues is much less than the number of individuals, then majority voting on a sincere basis will be transitive. The argument is not, however applicable to income distribution, for such a policy has as many dimensions as there are individuals, so that the dimensionality of the issue space is equal to the number of individuals.

This last observation raises an interesting question. Why, in fact, in democratic systems has there been so little demand for income redistribution? The current discussion of a negative income tax is the first serious attempt at a purely redistributive policy. Hagström (1938) presented a mathematical model predicting on the basis of a self-interest model for voters that democracy would inevitably lead to radical egalitarianism.

2. Political policy is not made by voters, not even in the sense that they choose the vector of political actions which best suits them. It is in fact made by representatives in one form or another. Political representation is an outstanding example of the principal-agent relation. This means that the link between individual utility functions and social action is tenuous, though by no means completely absent. Representatives are no more a random sample of their constituents than physicians are of their patients.

Indeed, the question can be raised: to what extent is the voter, when acting in that capacity, a principal or an agent? To some extent, certainly, the voter is cast in a role in which he feels some obligation to consider the social good, not just his own. It is in fact somewhat hard to explain otherwise why an individual votes at all in a large election, since the probability that his vote will be decisive is so negligible.

COLLECTIVE ACTION: SOCIAL NORMS

It is a mistake to limit collective action to State action; many other departures from the anonymous atomism of the price system are observed regularly. Indeed, firms of any complexity are illustrations of collective action, the internal allocation of their resources being directed by authoritative and hierarchical controls.

I want, however, to conclude by calling attention to a less visible form of social action: norms of social behavior, including ethical and moral codes. I suggest as one possible interpretation that they are reactions of society to compensate for market failures. It is useful for individuals to have some trust in each other's word. In the absence of trust, it would become very costly to arrange for alternative sanctions and guarantees, and many opportunities for mutually beneficial cooperation would have to be foregone. Banfield (1958) has argued that lack of trust is indeed one of the causes of economic underdevelopment.

It is difficult to conceive of buying trust in any direct way (though it can happen indirectly, for example, a trusted employee will be paid more as being more valuable); indeed, there seems to be some inconsistency in the very concept. Nonmarket action might take the form of a mutual agreement. But the arrangement of these agreements and especially their continued extension to new individuals entering the social fabric can be costly. As an alternative, society may proceed by internalization of these norms to the achievement of the desired agreement on an unconscious level.

There is a whole set of customs and norms which might be similarly interpreted as agreements to improve the efficiency of the economic system (in the broad sense of satisfaction of individual values) by providing commodities to which the price system is inapplicable.

These social conventions may be adaptive in their origins, but they can become retrogressive. An agreement is costly to reach and therefore costly to modify; and the costs of modification may be especially large for unconscious agreements. Thus, codes of professional ethics, which arise out of the principal-agent relation and afford protection to the principals, can serve also as a cloak for monopoly by the agents.

NOTES

[1] A competitive equilibrium is defined below. An allocation of resources through the workings of the economic system is said to be Pareto efficient if there is no other allocation which would make every individual in the economy better off.

[2] By "parametric role" is meant that each household and firm takes the market prices as given, not alterable by its consumption or production decisions.

[3] For households, "convexity" means that if we consider two different bundles of consumption, a third bundle defined by averaging the first two commodity by commodity is not inferior in the household's preferences to both of the first two. For a firm, "convexity" means that if we consider two different specifications of inputs and outputs, either of which is possible to the firm (in that the inputs suffice to produce the outputs), then a third specification defined by averaging the inputs and outputs of the first two is also possible for the firm to carry out.

[4] The extended version of this paper which appeared in the Compendium of the Joint Economic Committee contained sections on Imperfectly Competitive Equilibrium and Risk and Information.

REFERENCES

Aumann, R. J. 1964. Markets with a continuum of traders. *Econometrica* 32:39–50.

Aumann, R. J. 1966. The existence of competitive equilibria in markets with a continuum of traders. *Econometrica* 34:1–17.

Banfield, E. C. 1958. *The Moral Basis of a Backward Society*. The Free Press.

Black, D. 1958. *The Theory of Committees and Elections*. Cambridge, U.K.: Cambridge University Press.

Buchanan, J. and W. C. Stubblebine. 1962. Externality. *Economica* 29:371–384.

Buchanan, J. and G. Tullock. 1962. *The Calculus of Consent*. Ann Arbor, Michigan: University of Michigan Press.

Coase, R. H. 1960. The problem of social cost. *Journal of Law and Economics* 3:1–44.

Condorcet, Marquis de. 1785. *Essai sur l'application de l'analyse à la probabilitié des décisions rendues à la pluralité des voix*. Paris.

Demsetz, H. 1966. Some aspects of property rights. *Journal of Law Economics* 9:61–70.

Downs, A. 1957. *An Economic Theory of Democracy*. New York: Harper.

Hagström, K. G. 1938. A mathematical note on democracy. *Econometrica* 6:381–383.

Hotelling, H. 1929. Stability in competition. *Economic Journal* 39:41–57.

Knight, F. H. 1921. *Risk, Uncertainty, and Profit*. Boston and New York: Houghton-Mifflin. Reprinted by London School of Economics and Political Science, 1948.

Knight, F. H. 1924. Some fallacies in the interpretation of social cost. *Quarterly Journal of Economics* 38:582–606.

Marschak, T. 1959. Centralization and decentralization in economic organizations. *Econometrica* 27:399–430.

Meade, J. E. 1952. External economies and diseconomies in a competitive situation. *Economic Journal* 62:54–67.

Musgrave, R. A. 1959. *The Theory of Public Finance: A Study in Public Economy*. New York: McGraw-Hill Book Company.

von Neumann, J., and O. Morgenstern. 1944. *Theory of Games and Economic Behavior*. Princeton, N.J.: Princeton University Press. Second edition, 1947.

Robertson, D. H. 1924. Those empty boxes. *Econonic Journal* 34:16–30.

Rothenberg, J. 1960. Non-convexity, aggregation, and Pareto optimality. *Journal of Political Economy* 68:435–468.

Rothenberg, J. 1965. A model of economic and political decision-making. In J. Margolis (ed.) *The Public Economy of Urban Communities*. Washington, D.C.: Resources for the Future.

Samuelson, P. A. 1954. The pure theory of public expenditures, *Review of Economic Statistics* 36:387–389.

Samuelson, P. A. 1967. The monopolistic competition revolution. In R. E. Kuenne (ed.) *Monopolistic Competition Theory: Studies in Impact*. New York, London, and Sydney: Wiley, pp. 105–138.

Schumpeter, J. 1942. *Capitalism, Socialism, and Democracy*. New York: Harper. Third Edition, 1950.

Scitovsky, T. 1954. Two concepts of external economies. *Journal of Political Economy* 62:143–151

Shapley, L. S., and M. Shubik. 1967. Ownership and the production function. *Quarterly Journal of Economics* 81:88–111.

Shubik, M. 1959. Edgeworth market games. In A. W. Tucker and R. D. Luce (eds.) *Contributions to the Theory of Games IV. Annals of Mathematics Study*. Princeton, New Jersey: Princeton University Press, 40:267–278.

Smith, A. 1937. *An Enquiry Concerning the Causes of the Wealth of Nations.* New York: Modern Library.

Starr, R. 1969. Quasi-equilibria in markets with nonconvex preferences. *Econometrica* 37:25–38.

Tullock, G. 1967. *Toward a Mathematics of Politics.* Ann Arbor, Michigan: University of Michigan Press.

Young, A. A. 1913. Pigou's Wealth and Welfare. *Quarterly Journal of Economics* 27:672–686.

CHAPTER 3

EXTERNALITIES, INFORMATION AND ALTERNATIVE COLLECTIVE ACTION

Otto A. Davis and Morton I. Kamien

INTRODUCTION

Awareness that an action often entails subsidiary as well as direct consequences is commonplace. In choosing an occupation we consider not only the direct monetary remunerations involved, but also the associated security, power, and prestige. When purchasing apparel we take into account its attractiveness as well as the protection and comfort which it affords. In using drugs, we should be acutely conscious of their possibly harmful side effects as well as of their direct curative powers. When purchasing a house, we are likely to take into account not only the size and age but also the quality of the neighborhood in which it is located, its proximity to good schools, and the possible availability of public transportation.

In everyday parlance we refer to these secondary attributes of products or actions as "side-effects," "fringe-benefits," or "occupational disease." Our concern with these matters is not wasted on the advertising industry which promotes many products by stressing their desirable side-benefits. Witness the number of advertisements that allude to the masculinity, femininity, youthfulness, and glamour that are to be derived from the use of this or that product. Indeed, some products and occupations have become better known by their side effects than by their direct benefits.

Of course, concern with secondary consequences is not solely confined to the advertising industry. Regard for side-effects finds expression in the selection of products or occupations and the amounts we are willing to pay or sacrifice to avoid or incur them. For example, a desire to live in a "better" neighborhood manifests itself by a willingness to pay more for a house in the preferred neighborhood than for a comparable house elsewhere. Likewise, a strong preference for a relatively secure occupation is satisfied by a willingness to sacrifice potentially higher monetary gains in other occupations. Businessmen find it profitable to be responsive to these desires of consumers. Though the primary function of an automobile is

Otto A. Davis is Professor of Managerial Economics, Northwestern University. Morton I. Kamien is Professor of Economics at Carnegie-Mellon University.

transportation, manufacturers provide a wide variety of models to satisfy the secondary features desired by purchasers. Drug producers attempt to develop new drugs that possess the same beneficial properties as existing ones while reducing undesirable side-effects. Moreover, the responsiveness of producers is spurred by the knowledge that competitors will cater to the preferences of customers. For this reason, competition among producers is thought to be desirable. Similarly, competition among buyers assures that goods and services will be allocated in conformity with the relative desires and abilities of the participants to pay.

From the above account, one might be tempted to conclude that a freely competitive economy should provide the goods and services desired by consumers in such a way as to preclude the possibility that another allocative mechanism (such as government) might be judged to be more appropriate for given situations. Given certain conditions and a plausible criterion, one of the major contributions of modern economic theory is the confirmation of this conclusion. Yet, even the most casual observation of the real world discloses that our society often takes recourse to collective governmental action for the provision of certain goods and services. It might be supposed, therefore, that modern economic theory must be either wrong or irrelevant for the real world. While there probably is considerable sympathy for such a conclusion in some circles, it is taken here to be an obviously incorrect deduction. An alternative explanation of this apparent divergence between theory and reality is that collective decisions are necessarily bad and that governments act in a nonsensical manner. That conclusion is also rejected here. Of course, the denial of this alternative does not imply that governments always make the wisest or best decisions since it is clearly possible that governmental decision process can be improved and that we should do what we can to improve them. Yet another explanation of the apparent divergence between theory and reality (accepted here), is that the conditions or assumptions which are the basis for the conclusion regarding the efficiency of a market system are not always satisfied in reality. According to this viewpoint, it is advantageous to study certain aspects of economic theory because it produces insight into situations where market systems cannot be expected to work very well. The existence of such situations raises the problem of selecting the proper institutional arrangements for the performance of specific activities. Although solutions to these problems that would elicit a consensus are not currently available, there is nonetheless advantage in knowing where markets might, and where they might not, work tolerably well.

The purpose of this essay is to present and amplify the major conclusion of modern welfare economics which may be viewed as a theorem concerning the allocation of resources by a market mechanism. Particular attention will be paid to certain of the assumptions upon which this theorem is based. Examples will be used to help make the major points clear. The question of selecting proper criteria for institutional choice will be addressed. Perhaps the outcome of the discussion will be a better understanding of some of the issues and difficulties involved in selecting institutional mechanisms capable of attaining an acceptable allocation of limited resources.

THE CRITERION, THE MARKET AND OPTIMALITY

To talk meaningfully about selection among alternatives, one must have in mind a method of ordering or weighing the various possibilities. Economists employ the notion of efficiency or (to use the more technical term), the concept of Pareto optimality, for weighing different allocative mechanisms. An allocation of resources is inefficient or non-optimal if it is possible to make at least one member of society better off without making any other member worse off via a reallocation. An allocation is Pareto optimal if it is impossible to better someone's condition without simultaneously worsening another's, via reallocation. It is worth noting that this criterion of efficiency or Pareto optimality need not lead to an unambiguous ordering of alternative allocations since (theoretically), there exists an infinity of positions which are Pareto optimal. Still, there is good reason to insist (within the limits of practicality), that all solutions be efficient since, by definition, a non-Pareto optimal solution permits bettering someone's condition without worsening things for anyone else. The qualifying phrase "within the limits of practicality" here denotes that, although the theoretical possibility of improving at least one person's position without inflicting harm on anyone else must be admitted whenever the situation is not Pareto optimal, the practical means of actually accomplishing such an improvement need not be at all obvious to frail human minds. An allocative mechanism is deemed desirable if it leads to Pareto optimal allocations of resources.

The notion of Pareto optimality probably would be neither interesting nor useful were it not for some of the developments of modern welfare economics. The most important of these can be regarded as one of the fundamental theorems of economics. It can be stated informally as follows: Given certain assumptions about the technology, the availability of information, the characteristics of goods and services, and the absence of monopoly power, there exists a set of market prices which, responded to by profit-maximizing firms and utility-maximizing consumers, will result in the attainment of a Pareto optimum position for the economic system. The theorem is a powerful argument for the organization of our society so that resource allocation proceeds via the mechanism of competitive markets. If the assumptions of the theorem were universally satisfied, then government could limit itself largely to programs aimed at the attainment of desirable income distribution and be quite certain that competition would cause the system to be efficient.

There is little need to review in detail the entire set of assumptions upon which the above theorem rests. Indeed, economists have long been searching for a minimal set of assumptions which are sufficient for markets to attain Pareto optimality, and it is doubtful that the end of the search is anywhere in sight. Accordingly, it is appropriate to focus here only on those which seem to cause the great difficulties in the real world. Fortunately or unfortunately, it will be seen that these difficulties appear to be interrelated in ways that are not always obvious.

Consider the technology first. A strong assumption here is that all firms have convex production possibility sets. This supposition means that there cannot be increasing returns to scale. Or, it must *not* be true that ever larger firms can produce the same product at a lower per unit cost than relatively smaller ones.

A second consideration is the availability of information. Producers are assumed to have complete knowledge about the available technology. Consumers are supposed to know whether particular goods and services are available, and their characteristics. Finally, both producers and consumers are presumed to know the relevant set of prices.

The third condition concerns the characteristics of goods and services that the economic system is supposed to produce. Not only are there supposed to be no "public" goods—e.g., goods such as radio waves or television signals which can be "used" by one listener or viewer via reception, without diminishing their availability to others—but the consumption of other goods and services (called "private" goods) by any one decision unit is not supposed to directly affect other decision units. Thus, although the "side effects" mentioned in the introduction are allowed, there is presumed an absence of what economists call non-pecuniary externalities. One should note that the presence of externalities is not sufficient cause for the market to avoid optimality, but such a presence means that attainment of optimality by the market mechanism cannot be guaranteed.

A fourth condition worth noting is the absence of monopoly power. It is the *competitive* market that, under certain circumstances, is capable of attaining Pareto optimality. Since there will be little further discussion of monopoly in this essay, we mention at this point that monopoly is often related to the other conditions under consideration. For example, it is acknowledged that one of the difficulties associated with increasing returns is the emergence of monopoly. Likewise, initial monopoly power can sometimes be maintained because technological knowledge is not always available to all and, even when it can be made available, there may be barriers to its transmission and assimilation.

All this assumes that markets either do or can be made to exist for all goods. Unfortunately, this does not always seem to be the case.

In the remainder of this essay, we concentrate upon the dual considerations of information and externality with an emphasis upon the latter. The discussion will be testimony to the fact that all of these matters are interwoven and cannot always be separated.

PROBLEMS OF INFORMATION

Traditionally, theoretical discussions have assumed that participants in the economic system have complete knowledge; there has, however, been a widespread awareness that this assumption is not fully satisfied. Some recent works have taken cognizance of the fact that information is both scarce and costly. Obviously, some kinds of information are more easily acquired than other types and recognition of this continuum of costs is helpful in any attempt to understand the functioning of the market. Imagine a consumer faced with the problem of selecting a detergent. In the terminology of marketing, such a purchase is called a "repeat sale" which emphasizes the fact that the consumer purchases this type of product on a weekly or monthly basis. Detergents and items purchased often, offer a minimal informational problem for the consumer. There is little cost in "trying out" various brands until one, with characteristics most suited for the individual task at hand, is found. Advertising often gives information about the product's properties, such as its cleaning power or sudsiness. Even here, however, it is clear that laws which promote truth in advertising can help the market perform its proper function; without such regulations advertising might not be a reliable source of information.

Items which are not purchased very often, such as consumer durables, offer a more difficult informational problem. Clearly, it is not always practical for the consumer to learn the characteristics of the brands in this class of products by simply trying out various items until one is identified which has the desired properties. Occasionally, relatively expensive items that are easily transported and sufficiently complex, are available to potential customers for a trial period during which they can discover some of the characteristics of the product. When this practice is followed, however, salesmen seldom desire to make it easy for the customer to make systematic comparisons among available brands. Hence, other sources of information must be relied upon. Clearly, an important channel is informal and casual conversation in which experiences with various brands are related from one person to another. Another source, again, is advertising. Regulations designed to prevent misleading claims from being made are even more important for this class of goods than for those cited before, because absence of frequent and periodic purchases makes it more difficult for the customer to gain comparative information from his own experience. Still another source is independent "testing laboratories" such as Consumer's Union. Several points are relevant here. Any serious or casual reader of Consumer's Reports knows that for every major product, with the possible exception of automobiles, the information that can be presented is so scarce and model specific (with many models not being examined), that there is simply not enough information for careful comparison and selection among the models that might be available. This statement is not, of course, intended as a criticism of the management of Consumer's Union.

Despite the existence of various sources of information, there is reason to suppose that the amount available is less than optimal. The reason is that knowledge of the characteristics of a product is analogous to a public good. Once the characteristics are known, then the "consumption" of this knowledge by one shopper does not diminish the availability or usefulness of that knowledge for any other shopper. All of the well-known difficulties of trying to market a useful public good are relevant here. Although there are obvious costs associated with the production of information about a product's characteristics, the producer of that knowledge cannot hope to recoup anything approximating its value to the consumer. Moreover, even if it were possible for him to do so—and it is not possible since the information can be transmitted easily from one person to another —it does not follow that he *should* do it, since the optimal conditions require that the transmission take place at a marginal cost trivially close to zero. This means that the private producer of information is not motivated to produce as much as it would be socially optimal to provide, both in the quality of information produced and the range of models covered among the various products.

The preceding point should not be mistaken for criticism of the provision of this class of goods, mainly durables, by the private sector. Even the governmental supply of this class of goods would not alter in any basic way the problem under consideration. What is suggested, however, is that a certin kind of governmental regulation can serve to improve the functioning of an otherwise unregulated market. Producers are certainly in a better position than anyone else to know the characteristics of their products. It would appear to be relatively simple to have groups of people who are familiar with the various products, and aware of the characteristics one should consider in making a purchase, draw up a list of these features for each product category. Manufacturers would then be responsible for making this information available to their dealers and they, in turn, could be required to furnish the information to prospective purchasers. Claims about products could be checked in the way that advertising is now regulated. Note that this proposal differs from the existing situation where producers are motivated to furnish the public only information favorable to their product. No one would claim, of course, that information concerning all of the relevant characteristics can be made available. Even the manufacturer may not know, for example, the expected life of the new kind of machine.

There is another class of goods and services where the informational problems can be substantially greater than those discussed above. The salient features of this class are: (1) Information about the relevant characteristics, even when it is available, is difficult to understand, interpret, and evaluate without the benefit of special training; (2) the consequences of an incorrect choice can be serious to the extent that there is an order of magnitude difference in terms of real costs between this and previous cases. Probably, some drugs are the best example of a product category belonging to this class. The usual incentives of the market place operate here as elsewhere in the sense that consumers are willing to pay more, *ceteris paribus,* for a drug that is safer. Consequently, manufacturers should have an incentive to produce safer drugs. The obvious informational difficulty here, however, is the very problem of identifying which drug is safer. It is difficult to consider seriously the possibility of consumers having to use various drugs in order to determine experimentally both their curative powers and their safety when possible side effects may not be immediate and may be irreversible. While private "testing laboratories" might be relied upon for information, with all the difficulties previously discussed about this kind of institution, it is easy to see why our society has made the collective decision that the Food and Drug Administration should regulate this market. Thus, given that a drug is on the market, one can be certain that manufacturers have tried, at least minimally, to determine the side effects and associated dangers. Of course, given the difficulties associated with the attempt to make such a determination, there can be no certainty that harmful side effects are absent, as illustrated by the Thalidomide case of a few years ago. This particular case happened under the additional safeguard, which society has imposed, of allowing certain drugs to be used only when a prescription certifies that one is under the care of a physician. One rationale for allowing certain drugs to be sold only under prescription is, of course, informational costs. Supposedly, the physician has the necessary information at his finger tips and can exercise his professional judgment in administering any drug which is known to have undesirable side effects for some (unidentified) portion of the population. There is little need to mention that the arrangement does not work perfectly, but one of the authors has been pointedly reminded several times of the imperfection when, suffering a serious attack of asthma in a strange town, he visited local physicians who were uninformed of the available range of drugs and also had to be advised about the particular drug which had the properties most desirable to be prescribed for the given condition. In addition, some practices of physicians are not designed to stimulate price competition among drug manufacturers, so that the market is certainly non-competitive and may be monopolistic. The cost of monopoly in the present arrangement must be weighed against the lower information cost it affords.

PROBLEMS ASSOCIATED WITH EXTERNALITIES

All the preceding difficulties, associated with the acquisition of a commodity and the institutional arrangements which have been or might be designed to deal with them bear, for the greater part only, upon the purchaser. It is plausible, as the next step, to inquire about the possible effects of the purchase and consumption of certain products upon persons or decision units that were not parties to the exchanges. Effects upon those not associated with specified purchases or activities, are called externalities. Alternative terms are spillovers, external effects, or social effects. While the literature distinguishes many kinds of externalities, it is necessary for the purposes of this essay to identify only two types: technological (or non-pecuniary) and pecuniary externalities.

Let us first deal with the concept of the pecuniary externality. When deciding whether or not to purchase an item, an individual will ordinarily take into account his own desire for the item, its price, and his budgetary situation. Rarely, and generally only in the case of a monopsony, does the individual consider that his decision to purchase can contribute to—maybe even increase—the demand for that product and thereby cause its price to rise. Usually, this disregard is justified, for the individual's purchase of a commodity is such a small fraction of the total amount sold, that his decision has a negligible impact upon price. Whenever an individual's decision does effect price, not only he, but also all other purchasers bear the resulting increase or decrease. This change in price, caused by individual decisions, is termed a pecuniary externality. If the individual decision causes the price to rise—the usual case associated with an increase in demand—then the phenomenon is a pecuniary external diseconomy to other consumers. Whenever the decision causes the price to fall—as illustrated by the decision to join a group travel arrangement which is not yet at capacity—the phenomenon is termed a pecuniary external economy to other consumers. Of course, by symmetry, a pecuniary external diseconomy to consumers is a pecuniary external economy to sellers, and a pecuniary external economy to consumers is a diseconomy to sellers.

The important point to note is that pecuniary externalities, be they economies or diseconomies, pose no problem for the market economy. Indeed, they are the central ingredient of the market place. Changing demands cause prices to rise and fall; these fluctuations provide the essential signals for the market place to ration the available goods and services efficiently.

Technological externalities are quite another matter. These refer to more or less direct effects, other than price changes, that one decision unit might impose on another. Technological externalities can, and in many instances do, prevent the market mechanism from functioning efficiently i.e. giving rise to a Pareto optimal allocation. In these instances, there exists a possibility for action to improve society's well-being, i.e. bettering one citizen's lot but not at another's expense. Some examples may serve to illustrate the issue here.

Since both of the authors resided in Pittsburgh, it may be appropriate to begin with an example relating to steel manufacture. For expository purpose, imagine that Pittsburgh does not have a smoke control ordinance. Then, according to the production process employed, more or less smoke may be discharged into the atmosphere as a by-product of steel manufacture. Insofar as the producer is interested in profits (most manufacturers are), there is an incentive to choose that method of production which is most profitable without regard for the associated level of smoke discharge. The manufacturer may regard smoke disposal as another resource which contributes to the production of steel. The justification for conceiving of disposal as a resouce is that reduction in smoke discharge can only be achieved by adopting an alternative (and more expensive), production method which emits less smoke, or by using the same process with the addition of smoke control devices. Either alternative involves the use of additional resources such as labor and capital. These additional resources are not free; since there is no charge for the emission of smoke into the atmosphere, there is little if any motivation to limit the use of the resource which might be called smoke disposal.

Although the discharge of smoke into the atmosphere might be viewed as a free resource by the firm, it is certainly not without consequence to those residing within adjoining communities. Not only does smoke cause more rapid deterioration of the exteriors of buildings and certain kinds of equipment—which will certainly mean that compensatory resources will have to be spent in more intensive cleaning, maintenance and repair—it also contributes to smog creation—which probably has a direct, though not yet fully documented, effect upon the health of some residents in the community. In other words, to the community at large the discharge of smoke into the atmosphere is not a free resource. Economists call the situation, in which the firm does not bear the full costs of its actions, an instance where private costs diverge from social costs. The essential point to notice about the situation as outlined here, is that—without some kind of institutional change—the steel producer has nothing more than possible humanitarian concerns as a counterbalance to his profit interests, to make him recognize that smoke discharge imposes costs upon his neighbors.

Of course, industrial smoke is not the only cause of smog. One of the most oft-mentioned contributors today is the automobile. To comprehend the nature of the relevant motivations, imagine the situation prior to the regulation requiring installation of smog control devices in all new cars. It is obvious that if consumers demand and are willing to pay for smog control devices, the automobile industry would develop and sell these devices in much the same way that it supplies other optional equipment. Moreover, competition among manufacturers, foreign and domestic, would assure improvement of these devices over time. Thus, all that would be required (technical difficulties aside), to call forth a supply of smog control devices is the potential of profits. Unfortunately, there may not be any foreseeable profits.

Imagine, for the sake of argument, that the auto industry had developed an effective smog control device that it offers as optional equipment for all new cars. A person deciding whether or not to order this optional equipment might reason as follows: Suppose I purchase the smog control devices for my new car, and everyone else also purchases them, then we will have less smog in the city. But, since my car adds only a negligible amount to the smog problem, it follows that if everyone else purchases a device and I do not, smog will be diminished by almost exactly the same amount and I will have saved the cost of the device. Hence, if everyone else purchases a device, I will be better off if I do not get one installed on my car. Suppose now that no one else purchases a device. Obviously, there will be a smog problem. However, if I do purchase a device, the problem will not be noticeably better and I will be out the money which I paid for the smog control device. Thus, if no one else purchases, I should not purchase either. Obviously, the analysis is the same if some of the other people purchase and some do not, for my contribution to smog is negligible. Conclusion: I will be better off, no matter what other people do, if I do not purchase a smog control device.

Since all potential new car buyers will reason roughly as the representative individual does, there will be a zero demand for smog control devices. In the absence of some kind of regulation or collective decision, the automobile manufacturers will have no motivation to develop and market smog control devices. This conclusion holds even if—and it is an if—everyone would be better off when all cars were equipped with smog control devices. For each prospective purchaser of a device, the benefits from his purchase are widely dispersed while the costs accrue to him. The technological externality associated with the exhaust of a car can prevent the unregulated market from leading the system to a Pareto optimum.

For the final example of this section, consider the problem of the pollution of Lake Erie. Biologists tell us that Lake Erie is dying and that it has "aged" 15,000 years in the past half century. It was long believed that Lake Erie's pollution was caused largely by the dumping of raw sewage and industrial wastes into the lake. A major source of the raw sewage is antiquated sewage systems, some of which are combined sanitary and storm sewers so that the overflow runs directly into the lake during periods of rain. For the moment, imagine that the entire pollution problem is caused by the raw sewage so that treatment—designed to remove organic material which otherwise is digested in the lake via biological process that depletes its dissolved oxygen content—could solve the problem. The now familiar dilemma would act to frustrate a pure market solution. Each municipality or sewage district would reap only a fraction of the benefits of its own efforts at treating sewage, but would bear the full costs of that treatment. Employing the same reasoning as the customer considering the purchase of a smog control device, each would come to the rational decision to continue to allow raw sewage to flow into the lake even though all muncipalities together might be better off if each installed treating devices. Thus, the technological externality reflected in reverse by failure to receive the full benefit of one's expenditure for treatment—the fact that the decision-making entity does not bear the full costs of its decision to forego treatment and allow a flow of raw sewage—results in failure of the pure market solution unless a financial incentive to come to the opposite decision is offered by a higher level of government.

In actuality, the pollution of Lake Erie is a much more complex phenomenon than indicated by the above discussion. Even after treatment to remove indigestible solids and to break down organic material so that the sewage is discharged as mostly inorganic products, the residual inorganic matter contains large amounts of nitrate and phosphate which, instead of being swept harmlessly to the sea, tend to remain in the lake long enough to fertilize monstrous growths of algae which use up to an estimated eighteen times as much oxygen as the present flow of organic matter from inadequate sewage plants. Thus the standard treatment of sewage, primarily aimed at organic matter, is not likely to solve the problem even if such treatment were undertaken.

It might be suggested that one of the "essential" nutrients such as the phosphate should be removed from the waste so that the algae would not grow. Unfortunately some two-thirds of the phosphorus in municipal waste, which is roughly three-quarters of the total wastes, stems from detergents. If the housewife or commercial laundry knew that the detergents they use contribute importantly to the pollution of the lake, which they probably do not know, would there be any incentive to economize on the use of detergents or to demand a new kind that contained less phosphorus? Again, the familiar dilemma appears. Even if they were aware of contributing to pollution, each could rationalize that their own contribution was negligible, so that the rational decision would be to ignore the entire situation. Thus the manufacturers of detergents would have no incentive to try to develop products which contain less phosphorus, the municipal sewage systems would have no more incentive than in the previous instance to remove the material, with the result that the pure market solution would be to continue pollution of the lake. Again the existence of this technological externality—the fact that those causing the pollution do not bear the full costs of their actions—can cause the market mechanism to generate an allocation of resources which is not Pareto optimal.

THE POSSIBILITY OF A SOLUTION

The preceding illustrations indicate that the existence of technological externalities can necessitate modifications to claims of the unregulated market mechanism's efficiency. It must be admitted that the problems created by technological externalities are most perplexing. Only a few years ago, economists may have thought that an adequate solution was available, but the consensus has now vanished. Instead, one finds that a variety of solutions have been suggested by various persons—many are not economists—and a goodly number of these have even been tried or implemented in certain situations.

The belief that a universal solution might be found is present in many discussions and analyses of technological externalities in the literature. Thus, proposals are often treated as if they are supposed to the "the" solution to the problem of technological externalities. Unfortunately, this belief has not yet been justified and it may be that there is no simple and universally acceptable solution to the problem. Perhaps, at least for the foreseeable future, our society has no alternative but to seek pragmatic solutions to the problem.

Accordingly, it is necessary to examine many of the suggested solutions to the problem. The remainder of this essay is devoted to the description of some proposed solutions. It is desirable, of course, to make the point of view adopted in this discussion, explicit. Specifically, we view the situation as one which can be conceptually accommodated to cost-benefit analysis. All of the proposals have associated costs and benefits. The trick is to identify which is most suitable for a given situation. It is hoped that the following discussion will be useful for this purpose.

SOLUTION BY PROHIBITION

When one is convinced that collective action is necessary to correct the abuses caused by a technological externality, the first impulse is to simply prohibit the action giving rise to it. After all, if creation of the externality is prohibited, will not the market system then bring the economy to a Pareto optimal position?

Although this course of action may seem appealing at first, it takes little thought to realize that simple prohibition of activities that create technological externalities is a poor approach. Obviously, one could not seriously propose that car owners stop driving, that steel manufacturers stop producing, or that municipalities stop disposing of their sewage. Some might conclude, however, that we should have perfectly clean water or perfectly clean air, so that full treatment of effluents is needed. That conclusion, however, misses the fundamental point. Optimality does not call for the complete elimination of externalities. Instead, optimality requires that externalities be present in the "right amount." Some examples may help clarify this point.

Consider the case of water pollution. Natural biological processes in both lakes and streams give them a certain capability of cleansing themselves. If absolutely no untreated wastes are allowed to flow into these waters, this natural capability will not be used. From an economic standpoint, however, this natural capability is a resource available for use in the production of desired goods and services. In establishing the desired level of water quality, the benefits of cleaner water must be balanced against the costs of attaining it. Moreover, the assimilative capacity of a body of water can always be used up to the point at which objectionable side effects occur.

Air pollution affords a similar example. It would be prohibitively expensive to prevent any contaminants whatsoever from escaping into the air. Further, there is no reason not to use the natural absorbic capacity of the atmosphere. Air pollution is said to occur when this capacity is exceeded.

The above examples should illustrate that strict prohibition of whatever causes a technological externality is almost certain to prevent attainment of Pareto optimality. An appropriate level of externality, not necessarily equal to zero, is needed. So, in the case of water pollution a Pareto optimal solution may in fact mean some deterioration of water quality in certain streams and possibly complete deterioration of water quality in other streams.

SOLUTION BY DIRECTIVE

Having seen that the crux of the problem is to get just the right amount of technological externality, it is tempting to suggest that the government decide how much of it should be produced. This procedure would involve, for example, governmental determination of the extent to which municipalities bordering Lake Erie should treat their sewage in terms of, say, the percentage of organic matter removed, phosphorous content, and setting an absolute quantity limit above which sewage would have to be completely purified. Similarly, in the air pollution example the government would have to specify just how much smoke a factory could emit.

There are several difficulties with this procedure. First, as already noted there is the problem of determining just how much of the externality is desirable. This question is related to the problem of determining the overall quality standard. In principle this could be done by careful weighing of costs and benefits. To be specific, consider again the example of the pollution of Lake Erie. Suppose that it would cost 50 billion dollars per year in operating costs alone to process the sewage to an extent that pollution in the lake would diminish from present levels. Although the benefits to be derived from an unpolluted Lake Erie may be substantial, it is rather doubtful that they would be valued at anything near 50 billion dollars per year. The costs in this case would simply outweigh the benefits. Hence, the rational decision would be to tolerate an even higher level of pollution and not increase the level of sewage processing. On the other hand, imagine that all the sewage could be processed with an increase in annual expenditures of only five dollars. Clearly, the yearly benefits from an unpolluted lake would exceed this figure, so that the quality standard should be set to cause total sewage treatment. In between these extremes, however, the computations become very difficult. The difficulties of determining the benefits associated with various degrees of pollution are almost insurmountable. Consequently, there must be a great deal of arbitrariness in setting the overall standard. Another problem, overlooked in the above discussion, is the absence of complete understanding of lake ecology; there is still some uncertainty about the effects of treatment upon pollution.

Even if the overall standard could be determined despite the stated difficulties, other difficulties would remain. The overall standard must be translated into directives for each of the entities that emit pollutants. In principle, the directives should cause the marginal effectiveness of the last dollar spent upon the processing of wastes to be equalized for each of the pollutors. In practice, the marginal effectiveness of dollars spent for treating wastes cannot be determined accurately for any given pollutor because it depends upon the policies pursued by other pollutors. Thus, a degree of arbitrariness results at this level too.

In the case of air pollution, implementation of the procedure is even more difficult, although the same principles are involved. The overall standard should still be determined by weighing and comparing the benefits and the costs of different alternatives. However, the degree of arbitrariness is greater because even less is known about the relationship between the level of air pollution and the health of the residents, than about stream ecology. Also, there is the complication that in most urban areas the amount of pollutants which can be released into the atmosphere for any given standard depends upon weather conditions and prevailing winds.

The above comments are not intended to convey that the control of externalities by directives is to be dismissed as being obviously inappropriate. Our intention is to point out some of the difficulties associated with the procedure. We might also add that this procedure also involves administrative costs of policing the directives, which cannot be ignored in its evaluation.

SOLUTION BY VOLUNTARY ACTION

Some argue that collective action is not needed to correct the market solution when there are technological externalities. It has often been pointed out that there is motivation for private parties to act to correct the situation by a variety of methods. Two methods frequently discussed are bribes and merger.

Consider again the example of a steel producer, unchecked by a smoke control ordinance, discharging smoke into the atmosphere. The previous discussion indicated that this situation potentially gives rise to a divergence between private and social cost or between the private and social benefit of steel production. To avoid the adverse effects of smoke discharge, the community might resort to bribing the steel producer to decrease or discontinue altogether the discharge of smoke. The rationale for this behavior is that as long as the amount of the bribe needed to induce the steel manufacturer to reduce smoke discharge is less than the damage inflicted on the community, then the community will be better off by paying the bribe. Of course, the community acting rationally in its own interest would never proffer a bribe that exceeded the value of the damage inflicted via smoke discharge. The steel producer should (in turn), accept or reject the bribe in accordance with his best interests. Therefore, if the bribe exceeded the amount he would have to spend on means to reduce smoke discharge, he should accept the bribe and effect the desired reduction; if the costs were too great, he should not. In any case, a quantitative measure of the damage suffered by the community from smoke would have been presented to the manufacturer in a way as to make him cognizant of this figure when deciding how much smoke to discharge. Moreover, whatever the final level of smoke discharge, that level would be Pareto optimal if there were such a thing as perfect bargaining. One can reason as follows: Acceptance of the bribe by the manufacturer indicates that he is at least as well off as before, while payment of the bribe by the community indicates that it is at least as well off as before. Consequently, the situation is improved. If the bargaining were perfect, any departure from the agreed-upon position would only improve the position of one of the parties at the expense of the other. It is also true that rejection of the bribe by the manufacturer, under perfect bargaining, leads to a Pareto optimal solution. By rejecting the bribe, the manufacturer would disclose that the value of this resource (release of smoke into the air) is of greater value to him than to the community.

The method of avoiding a divergence between private and social cost described above is purely voluntary and leads, when bargaining is perfect, to a Pareto optimal allocation of resources. In the absence of distributional considerations, it would, therefore, appear to be the ideal way in which to resolve problems. Unfortunately, bargaining is not perfect and there are several impediments to its widespread use. The first difficulty is associated with the valuation of smoke damage suffered by the community. The most direct way of estimating the damage is to ask each member of the community how much he would be willing to contribute to the bribe to be offered the manufacturer. In principle, each individual should be willing to contribute the amount he would have to expend to avoid the damage from smoke by other means. Unfortunately, the individual would realize that if he contributes nothing towards the bribe but others contribute positive amounts and smoke abatement is effected, he will reap the benefits of smoke abatement at no cost to himself. If all members of the community adopt this attitude, no bribe will be offered and the scheme will fail. In other words, the fact that the benefit from smoke abatement is distributed to many individuals impedes the realization of the necessary collective action by the community. The second difficulty with the bribe procedure is that it requires that the community know all the available methods for manufacturing steel, as these are related to smoke control, and the associated costs so that they might prevent the manufacturer from cheating. Suppose (to illustrate the point), that after the bribe has been accepted by the manufacturer, the demand for steel rises and output increases. The producer can now argue legitimately that a larger bribe is required for him to maintain the previously agreed upon level of smoke discharge. Unless the community is completely knowledgeable about steel-making technology, it cannot be sure that the manufacturer is not expanding his output more than would be optimal for him in the absence of the bribe. Thus, a seemingly ideal scheme for avoidance of a divergence between private and social cost is marred by difficulties in implementation.

Another voluntary scheme for internalizing non-pecuniary externalities, free of some of the implementation difficulties mentioned, is the merger of the involved entities whenever merger is a feasible possibility. To illustrate how this procedure might work, consider the following situation: A firm discharges wastes which are harmful to fish life into a stream. Assume, further, that a fishery operates downstream from the firm. In the absence of any governmental regulation, the upstream firm will discharge waste into the stream without regard to the damage—smaller catches or tainted fish—inflicted on the fishery. Were the firm and the fishery to merge under a single ownership, it would be in the consolidated firm's best interest to take account of the losses incurred by its downstream subsidiary as a consequence of the actions of its upstream plant. The consolidated firm should balance the cost of disposing of waste at the upstream plant by other means than discharge into the stream, against the costs incurred by the downstream fishery as a result of waste discharge into the stream, if it is to maximize the combined profit from the two operations. Since, in this example, Pareto optimality corresponds to joint profit maximization by the two entities, merger will assure a Pareto optimal allocation of the resource in question—viz. the stream. It might also be noted that the profit of the consolidated firm will always be at least as great as the combined profits of the two firms operating in isolation. The reason for this is that the merged firm always has the option of adopting the operating policies of the two firms working independently. The difference between the profits of the consolidated firm and the combined profits of the individual firms reflects the loss to society from the presence of a non-pecuniary externality.

Two difficulties with the merger solution can be pointed out. The first is the practical consideration that the entities have to be firms. The second difficulty is that merger is feasible only when the number of entities involved is small. As a number of decisionmaking units entering the consolidation increases, the chances of effecting the merger decline. This is because it becomes increasingly more difficult to persuade potential participants that it is in their best interest to join the coalition as the number of participants increases. Individual units may find it profitable to postpone entry into the coalition in order to extract a larger portion of the joint profits from the merged entity. A more practical consideration involves the increase in the difficulties of coordination and computation with the number of participants; it becomes increasingly difficult for the merged entity to actually realize the potential gains. Yet another difficulty is that of a merged entity becoming big enough to cause a distortion in the allocation of resources via monopoly or monopsony power. In this case, the losses from the presence of non-pecuniary externalities have to be weighed against the losses to society from the resource allocation distortions engendered by imperfectly competitive markets.

SOLUTION BY TAXES AND SUBSIDIES

If voluntary arrangements among the entities effected by non-pecuniary externalities are impractical or not forthcoming, collective governmental action might be justified. In economics literature, the classic form of government intervention in this situation is the payment of a subsidy to units whose actions confer external economies upon other units, and the levying of taxes upon those entities whose actions confer external diseconomies upon other units. In essence, the idea is to encourage those activities that contribute to the "common good" and discourage those that detract from the "common good."

To illustrate how this scheme might work, consider again the example of an upstream firm and a downstream fishery. Suppose that the waste discharged into the stream by the firm provides food for fish in the stream and is therefore *beneficial* to the fishery. Since, by hypothesis, voluntary negotiation by the parties involved is ruled out here, the fishery has no way of communicating the magnitude of the benefits it derives from the firm's discharge of waste into the stream. Consequently, the amount of food provided to the fish may not be ideal. In this case, a government subsidy to the firm for the discharge of waste can in principle be devised to achieve the desired result. Likewise, if (as in our earlier description of the situation) the waste discharged is harmful to fish life, then in principle a tax can be imposed on the firm that reflects the damage imposed on the fishery.

We have stressed the "in principle" nature of these conclusions because of the immense informational requirements necessary for the implementation of this scheme. A little reflection will make it apparent that the governmental agency imposing a tax or offering a subsidy will need to know the production technologies of all the entities involved. In effect, the governmental agency will have to solve the same problem that the directors of the merged firm solve. They would have to know the effect upon fish life which the discharge of waste caused so that a tax or subsidy could be imposed that would result in just the right amount of waste discharge. Instead of issuing orders regarding the quantities of each product that every subsidiary should produce to maximize joint profits (a practice that the executives of the merged firm might follow), the agency would attempt to achieve the same results under this scheme by determining the "proper" tax or subsidy. Suffice it to say the information available to the directors of the merged firm is rarely available to an outside governmental agency. Bits of this information may of course be available and it might be possible—at a cost—to obtain additional information.

The amount of information required also depends on the nature of the productive technologies involved. Less information is required by the agency for the successful implementation of a tax-subsidy scheme if the underlying productive technologies are separable or additive, than if they are not. For example, if the cost of producing the upstream firm's product and the cost of waste treatment are additive, then the tax on waste discharge simply depends on the amount of waste discharge. However, if these costs are not additive, then the tax must vary not only in accordance with the level of waste discharge, but also with the amount of the firm's primary product. Of course, the informational requirements mount enormously as the number of involved economic entities increases. Despite all these difficulties, an attempt to achieve optimal resource allocation by taxes and subsidies might be justified if the losses to society from the presence of non-pecuniary externalities is large enough. In essence, what has to be balanced in this situation is the cost of acquiring the needed information against the losses to society if nothing is done or another imperfect policy is followed.

SOLUTION BY REGULATION

Another collective action which is often suggested is governmental regulation. For example, the official governmental response to the fact that cars contribute to the air pullution in our cities has been to reduce the range of consumer choice by simply requiring that all new cars be equipped with devices designed to reduce the level of pollutants in the exhaust gases. This regulation obviously permits an escape from the dilemma described earlier where a rational calculation would cause the consumer to refrain from purchasing a control device.

Regulation also has implementation difficulties associated with it. In the case of automobiles, for example, there is uncertainty as to whether the devices will be effective in reducing the discharge of pollutants, especially as the cars grow old. There are also problems of enforcement. For instance, there is speculation that if the devices are effective and pollutants are kept in the engine instead of being spewed into the atmosphere, then the life of the engine might be shortened and repairs will have to be made more frequently. These are costs of the regulation which, along with the costs of the devices, have to be weighed against possible benefits that are rather difficult to compute. If the devices do have the anticipated effect upon engines, then each owner has an incentive to take action that will render the devices ineffective and thereby increase the life of the engine and reduce his repair bills. Certainly, the owner cannot be expected to keep the device in good working order, or to repair it when it breaks, since this action would not be in his own self-interest. Consequently, the regulation cannot be expected to be successful in reducing air pollution, even if the devices work, unless it is accompanied by the practice of periodically inspecting all cars and requiring that the devices be maintained in good working order.

This discussion should indicate that solution by regulation is not as simple as it first seems. The administrative costs of enforcing the regulations are relevant and cannot be overlooked. Neither should the fact that a regulatory solution is necessarily inflexible be ignored. This point can also be better understood by recourse to the prior example. Many of our nation's motor vehicles are operated for a considerable portion of their life in non-urban areas where air pollution is not considered a problem. Ideally, vehicles operating in these areas should not be required to have smog control devices so that the natural ability of the atmosphere to accommodate a certain level of pollutants could be utilized. Obviously, it is impossible to design regulations which would accomplish this ideal due to the very mobility of motor vehicles and the population. Solution by regulation is inherently incapable of bringing the system to a Pareto optimal solution for many externalities, because regulations are inherently inflexible.

SOLUTION BY PAYMENT

One of the obvious ways of trying to accommodate the market system to the presence of technological externalities is to provide a financial incentive for the desired actions to be taken. In the pollution of Lake Erie, for example, one of the problems supposedly is caused by Cleveland's archaic sewage system which combines storm and sanitary sewers. The limited capacity of the treatment facilities for anything beyond modest rainfall causes raw sewage to flow directly into the lake. Although it certainly contributes to the pollution of Lake Erie, the citizens of Cleveland do not bear the full cost of their archaic sewage system since persons residing outside of Cleveland desire use of the lake too. Other people, therefore, bear part of the costs of pollution, including that portion of the pollution which stems from Cleveland's sewage system. Of course, what is true for Cleveland is also true for many other cities and towns in the lake area.

Because each entity does not bear the full costs of its own contribution to pollution, none have enough incentive to remedy the situation. A possible remedial policy is for a higher level of government—e.g., the federal government—to provide the proper incentive. A federal subsidy for the capital costs of improving the sewage facilities might do the trick.

The major drawback of this policy is its crudeness. It does not easily provide proper coordination for all of the relevant units in the relevant system. Another limitation of this policy is that it is suited only to those kinds of externalities where capital costs are the only really significant block to the improvement of the situation.

SOLUTION BY ACTION

Sometimes, there are simple and direct actions which can be taken to ameliorate the effects of an externality. Probably the clearest example involves fishing. Consider a lake or stream where many people come to fish. Beyond some level of activity, the future fish population is endangered. Thus, when a fisherman makes a catch, he can affect the future population of fish and thus lower the pleasure and profits of fishermen in the future. The individual fisherman, of course, has no incentive to consider the effect his own activity has upon others. In extreme cases, of course, the fish population could be exhausted.

An immediate remedy for this situation is for the government to continually stock the lake or river so that the fish population is never diminished to the danger point. The externality is then more or less eliminated by this direct action. Needless to say, there are drawbacks to this policy—not the least is its limited applicability.

CONCLUDING REMARKS

It should be obvious by now that there is a whole menu of policies which can be formed to deal with problems caused by technological externalities. None of these policies, at our present level of knowledge, appears to be perfect. Nor do we believe that any one clearly dominates all others as the best of the imperfect lot for dealing with each and every technological externality. Thus, it is argued here that policies must be designed with particular situations in mind and that what is best for dealing with one externality may be inappropriate for another. Accordingly, it is appropriate to conclude this essay with the seemingly suitable procedure for policy selection.

The tools of cost-benefit analysis appear to provide the proper perspective. In a given situation, the policymaker should consider the problem and imagine the application of the alternative approaches to it. The principle of selection is simple. Each measure of policy (including that of doing nothing) will have costs and benefits associated with it. The policymaker should select that measure for implementation which produces the greatest net benefits.

CHAPTER 4

UNCERTAINTY AND THE NEED FOR COLLECTIVE ACTION

Richard Zeckhauser

INTRODUCTION

In a perfectly competitive world it is well known that the free working of the market mechanism will lead to an efficient outcome, a Pareto optimum.[1] The neoclassical model of perfect competition requires perfect knowledge; there can be no uncertainty. The presence of uncertainty, a lack of knowledge of which state of nature will obtain in the future, makes the model inoperative. Ostensibly some corrective action will be required if an efficient outcome is still to be achieved. As with other forms of market breakdown such as externalities, public goods and declining marginal cost industries, some form of collective action might be an appropriate way to seek a remedy.

CONTINGENT CLAIMS MARKETS

A number of recent papers have shown that the presence of uncertainty need not prevent the free-market mechanism from achieving an efficient outcome. It may be possible to expand the class of traded goods to include what are sometimes called contingent claims. A contingent claim is a right to a variable amount of a commodity, the amount to depend upon the state of nature which obtains. In real life, quite frequently, a positive amount of the good is received only in the event of a single state. An insurance policy is a good example of a contingent claim. Typically it pays the face value of the policy should the state "death of the insured" prevail. Similarly, a lottery ticket is a contingent claim. It might give one the right to $10,000 should the number 904521 be drawn.

Contingent claims markets need not lead to efficiency. Transactions costs on these markets are far from negligible. The result is that the market price of a contingent claim may far exceed its actuarial value. Even if these markets were actuarially fair, other factors might prevent the

Richard Zeckhauser is Assistant Professor of Economics at Harvard University.

Helpful comments on this paper by Professors Robert Edelstein, Robert Haveman, Howard Raiffa and Thomas Schelling are acknowledged.

achievement of a Pareto optimum. If there are substantial disagreements on probabilities or if probabilities are difficult to estimate, the free-market mechanism will not in general lead to an efficient outcome. However, the primary difficulty is not that existing contingent claims markets do not function effectively, but rather that these markets are established in but few areas. Many goods are difficult to trade on a contingent basis for reasons that will be elaborated later. In some instances it is impossible to make trades before the state of nature is known or at least a great deal of information has become available. This limits the risk-sharing advantages of trades of contingent claims. Once contingent claims trades have been made, incentive structures change, and the trading individuals may take actions that affect the probabilities that different states occur. For example, the individual who has insured his car may drive somewhat less carefully. On a realistic basis we cannot expect contingent claims markets to achieve optimality in a world with uncertainty. This paper examines the role of collective action, with the government as the likely agent, in overcoming the inefficiencies that uncertainty engenders.

Varieties of Uncertainty

Most of us are accustomed to look at uncertainities from the standpoint of the individual. Will there be good times? Will I prosper? Will a hurricane destroy my home? Will I be disabled in an accident? To the individual these questions may appear to be structurally similar. To the government they may appear very different. If I am lucky in the first instance then so is everyone else. A hurricane will affect others, but hardly the whole country. An accident on the other hand is likely to involve just me or perhaps a few others. The government is concerned with all citizens and would likely see these uncertainties in very different ways. The actions that it might or should take with respect to them might vary as well.

COLLECTIVE PROVISION WITH INDIVIDUAL'S PREFERENCES UNCERTAIN[2]

An individual will rarely be able to determine exactly his future level of demand for a good. This demand will depend upon the evolution of his preferences something that he may not be able to predict accurately. This need not reflect an inability to know his own future mind. Rather, events over which the individual has little control may significantly affect his future preferences. An individual would have to know whether his house would catch fire to predict his demand for firefighting services. He would have to know whether he would be involved in an accident before he could estimate his need for hospital accident emergency room.

In normal circumstances, the inability of individuals to predict their future demands for goods is not of great consequence. A good is supplied to the market, and is consumed according to the individuals' preferences at that time. Only if action must be taken at present to insure an efficient level of provision for the good is it important to make accurate predictions. Thus, for example, if there is a significant leadtime for production, it will be most useful to be able to predict aggregate demand with some accuracy.

This section considers situations in which individuals who are unable to predict their individual portions of future total demand may find it useful to make some decisions on the collective provision of a good before preferences become known. For the most part it is concerned with goods which by their very nature make accurate prediction of future preferences impossible. At best, for such goods, it will be possible to attach some probability assessment to possible sets of preferences for the individual. The acronym PIP derived from probabilistic individual preferences is used to refer to the goods of this nature. Most frequently, the probabilities attached to these sets of preferences will be determined subjectively rather than objectively. For the present purposes, this distinction is not of importance.

Option Values

Consider a community that must decide whether to supply itself with a PIP good, perhaps a supply of plasma at a blood bank, or a fire engine to protect its homes. Following conventional efficiency dictates, the community should estimate future levels of demand for the good and decide whether perfect price discrimination against future consumers would yield sufficient returns to enable discounted revenues to cover discounted expected costs. If the decision is negative, we are told that the community should not provide itself with the good. This stipulation holds whether or not consumption by one individual reduces the amount available to be consumed by another, whether or not the good has any aspects of a collective-consumption good.

Many PIP goods serve a preventive purpose; for example, programs to deter crime or to immunize against disease. If such goods are provided, it may never be known who are the major beneficiaries, who would have been the victims of the crime or the sufferers from the disease. For such goods, discriminatory pricing questions could only be asked on a hypothetical basis. If you have been identified as a future target of a mugging or a future victim of polio, how much would you pay to prevent the unfortunate happening from taking place?

In an article dealing with commodities "the purchase of which is infrequent and uncertain," commodities which are in effect PIP goods,

Burton A. Weisbrod argued that even if there will be perfect price discrimination, the option values of potential consumers would influence the decision whether such commodites should be provided. He states, "If these consumers behave as 'economic men,' they will be willing to pay something for the option to consume the commodity in the future."[3]

The key question for Weisbrod, then, is, What will be the magnitude of these option values? The amount that an "economic man" will pay for the right to consume a commodity in the future will depend upon the price that he will be charged for the commodity. The discriminatory price of a good for an individual is the maximum price that he would pay for the good, an amount just short of the one at which he would refuse to purchase. As a consequence, if an economic man will be faced with perfect price discrimination, should he be interested in consuming the good, he will be indifferent whether or not he purchases it. He will not be able to reap any consumer's surplus at the time of purchase; the availability of the good will in no way be able to increase his welfare. His option value to keep the purchase available will be zero. I disagree with Weisbrod and assert that in this regard the conventional efficiency dictate is not called into question.

Risk Spreading

The option value, discriminatory price approach to the allocation decision problem is not sufficiently rich. It overlooks some important considerations, one of which is the risk-spreading property of PIP goods. Every potential consumer of a PIP good is in an uncertain situation. He does not know whether he will wish to consume the good in the future. The value in use of many of these goods can be very high.[4] If the actual consumer is to be faced with perfect price discrimination, then each potential consumer is in the position of having some probability of incurring a substantial charge.

However, it may not be necessary to charge the actual consumers even a small fraction of their discriminable price. The community of potential consumers as a whole can agree to share the costs of making the good available, with little or no additional cost to be borne by the actual consumers. In this way, each individual will bear a small certain cost rather than run the risk of a much larger, but considerably less probable cost. If the individuals in the community are risk averters, this indirect form of risk sharing may be of value to them.

The possibility of risk sharing introduces a new consideration to the question as to whether the good should be provided. Let me illustrate with the fire engine example. Consider a community of 100 identical individuals, with identical utility functions for wealth, log (w), each with a house they value at $10,000, and each with a nonhouse wealth of $10,000. Every year one house, no more, no less, burns down. The community must decide whether to get a super fire engine that stops all fires instantaneously. The rental on the fire engine is \$12,000 per year in comparison to the \$10,000 that the individual whose house starts burning would pay for the services of the engine. (If the income effect for housing were positive, this would somewhat reduce the \$10,000 figure, and conversely.)[5] Following conventional efficiency dictates, the community would compare the amount that could be secured for the good through perfect price discrimination with the cost of provision. It would decide not to rent the engine.

However, the individuals within the community are risk averters. They would be willing to pay a premium to reduce the variance in their payoffs. If they share the costs of providing the engine, they can accomplish this. Let x represent the certainty equivalent dollar value for the lottery that gives the individual's payoff in the absence of the fire engine. We have, $\log(x) = .99 \cdot \log(20{,}000) + .01 \cdot \log(10{,}000)$. This gives, $x = 19{,}861.85$, and $20{,}000 - x = 138.15$. To avoid one chance in 100 of a \$10,000 loss, each individual in the community would be willing to pay \$138.15. This amount can be looked at as the individual's option value for the right to consume at zero cost the fire engine's services at any time during a 1-year period. The sum of the individuals' option values would be \$13,815, an amount well in excess of the rental price.

What, then, of the decision not to rent the engine? Each individual would rather pay his share of the rental rather than be faced by the lottery that confronts him if the fire engine is not rented. If the only alternative to renting the engine is to let the houses burn and have individuals suffer the losses, then the engine should be rented, and the rental cost shared equally. This will involve a loss in efficiency with regard to resource use, but there will be a more than compensating gain because, unlike the costs of a fire, the costs of fire control can be spread among all the members of the community.

But another, more attractive alternative may be available. It may be possible to spread the cost of the fires through an insurance pool in the community. If each individual agreed to pay one-hundredth of all fire losses in the year, his annual cost would be \$100. This would give him a considerable saving over paying his share of the engine rental cost. If there are no institutional constraints to prevent the operation of an insurance plan, then so long as administrative costs are not prohibitive (below \$2,000 in this example), this alternative will be the most attractive.

The Community Insurance Decision When the Size of Loss Is Variable

The assumption that a single house will burn each year is certainly unrealistic. There may be major conflagrations, and even if house burnings are independent events, there will be some variance in the number of houses burned each year. The fire engine has the advantage that it eliminates all such variance in total cost to the community. This improves its attractiveness relative to an insurance scheme. If there is significant variance in the number of houses that burn each year, the community might choose the fire engine over the community-wide insurance plan even though the latter would have a lower expected cost per individual.

The limiting case of complete contagion would have the only possible fires in the community destroy all houses, the annual probability of such a catastrophe being one in 100. In this case the insurance plan would serve no risk-spreading purpose. The lottery for each individual's payoff would be the same as the one in the absence of insurance. Following the analysis above, the fire engine should be rented.

Assume that there were no fire engines. We observed that a risk-spreading plan in a community will be the more effective the less positive correlation there is between significant losses for its individual members. This observation may be of import if each individual will be charged a proportional premium above his share of community losses if an insurance plan is instituted, if, for example, there are administrative costs that are some fixed percentage of total reimbursed losses. The individuals might find it desirable to establish an insurance plan that would reimburse losses if one or two houses were lost in a year, but not if a great many had burned.

By way of illustration, assume that there are but four possibilities. The number of houses that burn in the community with the probabilities of occurrence are: 0, .75; 1, .15; 10, .07; 50, .003. The expected number of houses burned is one. Our community would find it desirable to reimburse losses from single-house fires if the premium over fair actuarial value were not more than 38.1 percent. It would be worth while to insure losses in 10 house fires as well if the premium were less than 33.9 percent. Only if the premium fell below 17.2 percent would the community wish to include losses from 50 house fires in its insurance plan.

Utilities of Anticipation Versus Utilities of Use

There are some special characteristics of goods the future consumers of which are unknown that render the actuarial model of decision inadequate. The lottery model is essentially static. The decisionmaker is assumed to act as if the probabilistic outcome is to be determined immediately when his decision is made. Pleasure or pain derived from anticipation or anxiety over the outcome of the lottery does not enter into the model. But these feelings are not imaginary. We cannot afford to neglect these real and potentially significant utilities of sensation. They must be considered in addition to the familiar (what might be called) utilities of use.

Many individuals would gladly incur significant costs so that they could live in a community with a museum or symphony even though they are unlikely to make use of these cultural advantages. A shopper might pay to have a wide selection of goods available even though she knows she will probably choose her purchases from among a very few. We have in effect what might be called a utility of variety. Consumers like and get a positive utility from the fact that goods are kept available. From what we can observe, the amount that these individuals would pay to keep these facilities available is well in excess of the expected value to them, the probability they use them times the difference between the price they will be charged and the discriminatory price that they could be charged. For most individuals the discriminatory price would be low enough so that risk considerations do not play a major role. It would seem that another factor is present. It is what we might think of as the utility of knowing you can use something even though it is unlikely that you will use it. It is a utility that is defined independently of the use itself. In this way it is quite different from the actuarial aspects of payments for PIP goods (or those that Weisbrod discusses). This distinction is reinforced to the extent that payments for utilities of variety are independent of the prices that will be charged for the goods or the probabilities that they will be consumed.

Misestimation of Probabilities

There is the possibility that some individuals may misestimate the probability that they will wish to consume some good or service in the future. If there were a consistent bias toward overestimation, individuals would be willing to pay more than fair actuarial value to keep the good available. The converse is of course true.

This raises what might be more of a philosophical than an economic question. If individuals calculate their option values on an actuarial basis using expected consumers' surplus, and if they overestimate probabilities of use, should we correct for this bias? Let us say that the head of a community asks each individual how much he would pay to keep a museum available. Assume that the community head knows from experience that on the average individuals will overestimate the probability of future visits to the museum and will thus arrive at somewhat inflated option values. Has he done something useful if he deflates these values when he decides whether to provide the museum?

A number of considerations must be weighed in arriving at our answer. If all utilities are in use rather than anticipation, we would argue that the community head should modify the stated option values to reflect accurate probability estimates. If utility in anticipation is a meaningful concept, the question is more difficult and will depend on the specific parameters of specific cases.

Will individuals learn that their probability estimates were too high, that they made a mistake? We would surely agree that the more likely they are to find out, the more desirable it is to correct their misestimates. It is by no means clear by what means an individual would discover that his subjective probability estimate for an unlikely, nonreplicated event was in error. The less danger there is of becoming informed, the more blissful is ignorance. Taking the argument to the extreme, we might even argue that we should provide a little-used museum if we can convince community members that they are fairly likely to visit it. If the pleasures in anticipation are sufficient, the provision of the museum could yield positive utility to each individual who shares in the cost of making it available. This will result in a real, though unanimously favored, misallocation of resources.

This is tricky material. This brief discussion is hardly adequate. The primary present purpose is to point out that in some instances there are benefits to be gained from fleshing out the conventional skeletal framework for expected utility calculations.

PIP GOODS, INSURANCE, AND MARKETS FOR CONTINGENT CLAIMS

Prospective and Retrospective Benefits

In our discussion thus far we have found a number of relationships and similarities between insurance mechanisms and PIP goods. An insurance policy gives one claim to future resources should some prespecified event occur. One takes out the policy because it provides an expected positive benefit. It cannot be known in advance whether one will actually benefit from having the insurance policy. Generally, in retrospect, one will not prove to have benefited. The events that we insure against usually have a low probability of occurrence. When one shares in the provision of a PIP goods so as to be included as a potential consumer, one is in a similar position. There may only be a small chance of benefiting from the consumption of the good, but the benefit may be sufficient to make the premium (sharing in its provision) worth while.

Quite frequently, PIP goods are provided by a political unit of a nonvoluntary contribution basis. In insurance, the equivalent arrangement is some form of mandatory policy. The social security system is a good example of a nonvoluntary contribution, risk-sharing arrangement implemented by a political unit. At present, there are discussions in progress within the federal government on a mandatory flood insurance program for those holding property on the flood plain. This type of provision, whether for PIP goods or insurance, can be justified on efficiency grounds only if the gains of some individuals, as measured by the excess of expected consumer's surplus over share of provision cost, more than outweighs the losses of these who would not join voluntarily.

An insurance policy may provide a nonactuarial benefit that in some sense is parallel to the utility of variety that is associated with PIP goods. It is a utility that is not directly connected with the use of the goods or the money that is received should the insured against event occur. It is the pleasurable sensation that is derived from knowing that one has protected one's self (or one's family) in case an unfortunate contingency should arise.

Thomas Schelling kindly suggested the following demonstration of the value of this "peace of mind," what we might call a utility of security. A man with a medical ailment is fully aware of the seriousness of his condition, but does not know whether it will exclude him from life insurance. He asks his wife to find out and to pay the premium if his life can be insured. We would likely agree that she may be doing something useful if she can deceive her husband should he be uninsurable, and convince him that his life can be insured.

Insurance and Markets for Contingent Claims

When one takes out an insurance policy, one sacrifices current assets in exchange for a contingent claim to be paid, if at all, in the future. An insurance policy represents a trade in a contingent claims market, that is restricted in two ways. (1) In an open contingent claims market, future as well as present payments can be used to purchase contingent claims. This restriction will not be of consequence if there are perfect capital markets and if borrowing and lending rates are identical. (2) In an unrestricted contingent claims market, one can exchange a contingent as well as a certain claim for a contingent claim.

If one wished to take out medical disability insurance, rather than pay some fixed amount, it might be far preferable to agree to pay an appropriate fixed percentage of future income that would result in the same expected payment. Carrying this reasoning one step further, it would likely be even better if one could work out an arrangement under which the percentage was higher the higher was future income.

An arrangement like this one might be worked out if the federal government decides to provide financial assistance to individuals seeking higher education. To fund this program the government could charge these individuals a percentage of future income, or better yet, a variable percentage that increased with income. This repayment could be transmitted easily along with normal income tax collections.

There may be situations in which contingent claims markets or insurance are not available but where good substitutes can be found. A farmer who cannot find a future market in the particular commodity which he produces can in effect insure his price if he can sell short a related or derivative commodity which will have parallel price movements. In financial markets it is often possible to secure a form of insurance through arbitrage-type operations; for example, one can sell short in a stock for which one holds convertible bonds. Some situations call for more inventive action. An individual who cannot buy storm insurance on his home in a hurricane belt might cover himself by investing in a roof repair company. In all these situations, the object is to diversify. The extensive literature on the subject of diversification is of consequence because perfect insurance and contingent claims markets do not exist. To the extent that balanced portfolios can be secured, a suitable substitute for these markets can be found.

If contingent claims markets are restricted and if opportunities for complete diversification are not available, there will be distortionary effects on many economic variables. This is particularly true where intertemporal allocations are concerned.

UNCERTAINTY AND INTERTEMPORAL RESOURCE TRANSFERS

The transfer of resources from present to future, what is commonly called savings, is both an intertemporal shift and a shift from a period in which income is known to one in which income is an uncertain variable. The greater is uncertainty about future income, expected income constant, the more a risk-averse individual will wish to transfer to the future. With fair and perfect contingent claims markets, uncertain incomes will not be of consequence. The risk-averting individual will be able to insure that he receives the expected value of his future income.[6] There will be no additional transfers in response to risk considerations. The absence of complete, perfect, and actuarially fair contingent claims markets makes transfers to the future greater than they would be in a perfect world with all desirable markets established. Considering this factor alone, the level of savings in society will be supraoptimal.

The question as to whether the freely arrived at rate of savings will be socially optimal has recently received much attention in the theoretical literature. Other essays in this volume discuss it in relation to the appropriate rate of discount for social projects and to the responsibility of the government to provide for the future. To the extent that they neglect the influence of uncertainty in our imperfect world of incomplete markets, their answers for discount rates should be raised and those for provision for the future diminished.[7]

COLLECTIVE PROVISION OF PIP GOODS, INSURANCE AND CONTINGENT CLAIMS MARKETS

Pip Goods

Throughout this paper, I have discussed, with good reason, community or collective provision of these goods or trading arrangements. There are at least three factors that might make it best to provide PIP goods on a collective basis. (1) If the probability is small that any one individual will consume a good in a given short period of time, and if it must be kept continually available, there will be considerable waste if each individual provides for himself. We find it efficient to store plasma in a common pool in blood banks rather than have each individual keep a personal supply. (2) PIP goods possess aspects of collective-consumption goods and for the conventional reasons are best provided on a collective basis. For example, the consumption of the services of a fire engine by one individual in no way reduces the amount that is available to be consumed by another.[8] An essential collective-consumption element of some PIP goods is that it is desirable to keep an inventory available. Thus, in our plasma example, the good itself is of the private consumption variety, but the existence of a stockpile upon which any member can draw has collective-consumption aspects, consumption of the "good" by one individual does not reduce the amount available to be consumed by another. (3) If PIP goods are provided on a collective basis, the costs of provision can be shared, and the as yet unknown consumers need not be charged any great amounts. In this way some useful risk spreading can be accomplished.

Equity Considerations

On an equity basis, we might object to the collective provision of collective-consumption goods that are not enjoyed equally by all contributors (assuming equal incomes and contributions to provision). It might seem that such an objection would apply with a vengeance to PIP goods, but such is not the case. Collective provision of PIP goods can only be called inequitable if on a prospective basis it is clear that some community members will have a higher expected benefit. Even then, there might be disagreement.

Final judgment may depend whether higher probabilities of use or higher values in use are the primary explanation of higher expected benefits for some individuals. If the former, it might be relevant to know why the probabilities are higher, whether they depended upon conscious choices. On an equity basis, we would be more likely to object to a subsidized public facility to treat those injured skiing than to a subsidized public facility to treat those who suffer from a particular inherited illness, even though we may be better able to predict who will be the beneficiaries of the latter.

The lessons of equity considerations in situations of uncertainty have not been thoroughly enumerated. These lessons may be applicable to the most basic of philosophical considerations. If we state that society should establish a mechanism that insures individuals against unfavorable outcomes in the lottery of genetic inheritance, against the possibility that they will have low capabilities and little opportunity to earn in a competitive factor market, is our statement based on considerations of equity or on considerations of efficiency? Is it not possible that we would have all agreed in advance to such a scheme, that the insurance mechanism gets us to the ex ante contract curve? These questions and others that relate in similar fashion to such matters as the desirability of nonfault compensation of accident victims, the justness of racial differences in income, or the obligation of the developed countries to aid the underdeveloped world merit further consideration. They are touched upon in the section that follows.

Insurance and Contingent Claims Markets

For reasons similar to those relevant for PIP goods, it may be desirable to provide contingent claims markets, and their somewhat restricted offshoots, insurance markets, on a collective basis. To provide such a market is to provide a mechanism that has many of the characteristics of a collective-consumption good. The use of the mechanism by one individual not only does not reduce the amount available to another, it is likely to increase the utility in use of the mechanism for them. Each additional consumer (trader) extends the market and makes it more perfect, thus providing a benefit for all other consumers.

We would suspect that in the absence of some form of collective provision, markets for trades in contingent goods will not be established in many desirable areas. Those markets that are established we would fear to be insufficiently extensive. Unlike most markets, it is essential to have many parties to single trades. The marginal costs of accommodating addition users are likely to be low in comparison to the fixed costs of starting and maintaining the market. Efficiency considerations would dictate that transactions costs be kept low, and that the market be supported by charges assessed independently of use or the frequency of use. It is hard to see how a private entrepreneur would go about setting up a market with such features.

There are, of course, privately supplied mechanisms that approximate mechanisms for contingent goods. The best example is insurance companies. To make ends meet and then some, insurance companies find it necessary to charge amounts considerably over fair actuarial value. We would speculate that the excess charge over actuarial value is well above the nonactuarial costs of including another individual in the insurance pool. This is inefficient. It is equivalent to charging more than marginal cost to a man who uses a public park. I have not been able to find any abundance of privately provided mechanisms that would call into question my contentions relating to the provision of markets for contingent goods.

I have argued above that the government may see fit to provide PIP goods, particularly in those instances in which adequate insurance mechanisms are not available. At times the government may participate directly in the provision of insurance protection. At present governments engage in many programs of this nature, including crop insurance, unemployment and disability insurance, and social security. Recently it has been proposed that the federal government provide insurance to high-risk ghetto businesses, and to those who might suffer from certain types of natural disasters.

The government need not limit itself to conventional insurance services. It may identify areas in which individuals would have purchased insurance if only mechanisms had been available. The question is what to do if the would-have-been-insured-against misfortunes have already occurred.

Governments generally step in to aid disaster areas. This form of relief can be justified on efficiency grounds quite apart from humanitarian or altruistic considerations. Disasters take tremendous tolls of public and private property. Public property is rarely protected by insurance. Disasters are highly unlikely events. As such, transactions costs to provide insurance would be quite significant in comparison to actuarial costs. It may be efficient for the government to operate as if an implicit arrangement had been reached that all will pitch in to help after an unfortunate occurrence, rather than collect premiums to be paid to the losers in case of disaster. Without any explicit agreement, the government can serve as an insurer. It collects premiums in its general tax funds and pays out claims as needed.

Aid to depressed areas can be viewed in a similar light. In the 1920's all areas of the country, including then coal-rich Appalachia, might have agreed to an assistance scheme to those areas of the country that turned out to be depressed in the sixties. The federal government might carry out such assistance now on the efficiency argument that on an expected value basis this arrangement would have been desirable if only it could have been formulated in advance.

A similar argument can be made for assistance to people who are handicapped to some extent, perhaps because of inadequate intelligence or physical disability. Is it not the case that if none of us knew our future position in society that we would have agreed to a redistribution scheme from the more to the less fortunate? Contracts of this nature can never be made. By the time parties reach the age at which they could consent the die has already been cast. Ivy League men know that they are the blessed. Ghetto dropouts are aware of the bleakness of their future. However, as unidentified fetuses not knowing which they would be, these two groups might have agreed to a massive redistribution scheme. Arguments in favor of radically progressive tax schemes can be made on this basis as well. If only the agreements were drawn before the state of nature was revealed or at least substantially hinted at, all would have agreed to a substantial redistribution of income.

The principle here is a most simple one. If at some time during the play of a game it becomes clear that all players would have agreed to a particular rule in advance, then invoke that rule. This dictate is particularly important in the situations here, because, for the most part, these rules cannot be agreed upon ahead of time.

TRADES IN CONTINGENT GOODS AND INCENTIVES—AN INCOME TAX EXAMPLE

Unfortunately, trades in contingent goods that have a risk-sharing objective may reduce incentives for individual effort. Consider a completely levelling income tax scheme. In a community of n individuals, an additional dollar earned by any individual will yield him but $1/n$ of a dollar in extra income. If n is large, there will be no financial incentive to work.

The incentives problem can be examined with an income tax example. A group of individuals wants to develop an optimal tax scheme. They are able to contract before any of them know their earning capabilities. The possible wages are 1, 2, 3, and 4 dollars per hour. One quarter of the individuals earn each wage rate. The probability, p_i, that an individual receives wage rate w_i is thus ¼ for all i.

Each of the individuals has a utility function in each 100-hour period. As arguments it has two variables: after-tax income, z; and leisure hours, x. The utility function, assumed to be common to all is

$$U(z, x) = z^{\frac{1}{2}}x^{\frac{1}{2}}.$$

Each individual is allowed to follow his individual preferences to decide how many hours, h, he wishes to work leaving him with 100-h hours of leisure. It is this area of free decision that gives rise to incentives considerations. An individual's before tax income, y, equals his wage rate times the number of hours he works,

$$y = wh.$$

The individuals contract on a tax scheme $T(y)$ that tells the amount of taxes an individual must pay on a given before-tax income. After-tax income for an individual whose wage is w and works h hours is

$$z = wh - T(wh).$$

The tax scheme that maximizes expected utility is the one that maximizes

$$\sum_i p_i U(w_i h_i - T(w_i h_i), 100 - h_i),$$

subject to the constraint that

$$\sum_i p_i T(w_i h_i) = 0.$$

To simplify the search task, I considered only quadratic tax schemes. These schemes are sufficiently diverse in shape to allow a close approximation to the optimal scheme of general form.

The optimal quadratic tax scheme, the one that maximizes expected utility, is

$$T(y) = -.0007y^2 + .372y - 30.125.$$

The shape of this tax function is rather interesting. The marginal tax rate continually falls over the relevant range although the average tax rate is rising. This tax scheme is progressive on an average though not on a

Table 4.1
Values for the Optimal Scheme

Wage rate	1	2	3	4
Leisure	72.178	58.500	53.316	50.347
Before-tax income	27.822	83.000	140.052	198.614
After-tax income	48.139	87.072	131.809	182.468
Average tax rate	−.730	−.049	.059	.081
Marginal tax rate	.343	.256	.176	.094

marginal basis. At first glance this may seem a bit perplexing, but the explanation is quite evident. The large negative constant in the tax scheme represents a lump sum payment that each individual receives. This provides the progressivity. The decreasing marginal rate insures that high income people will maintain the incentive to work. Table 4.1 gives the outcome with the optimal scheme.

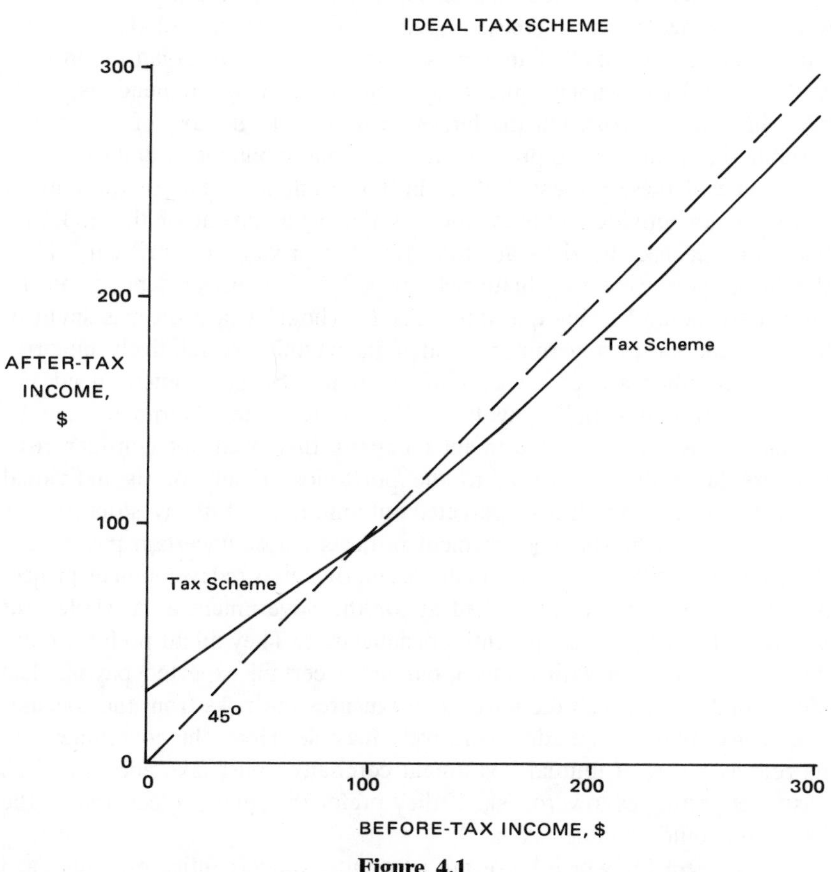

Figure 4.1

Figure 4.1 illustrates the ideal tax scheme. This result is only suggestive of the type of outcome that can be achieved with this type of analysis. It is interesting however, that with no special consideration of the problems of the poor or the lowly skilled, it produces results remarkably like those of the negative income tax at the bottom end of the income scale.[9]

THE GOVERNMENT'S ATTITUDE TOWARD RISK

In many instances a government will be in a position to insure individual's risks with very little risk to itself. This will be the case, for example, with disability insurance. The number of people disabled is a predictable figure with fairly little variance. However, in many instances there will be significant positive correlation among the losses of a great number of individuals. Natural disasters can create losses ranging into the hundreds of millions of dollars. In periods of economic slack, unemployment compensation and welfare payments may increase significantly. Research and development efforts like that for the SST may be so risky that even an organization such as the federal government must take cognizance of the tremendous variability in potential cost. On the largest scale of all, the cost of a war is a variable that is difficult to predict within the many billions of dollars.

Some of these projects fall to the government as part of the natural course of its activities. Others, such as the development of the SST, are taken on because the risks are too great for private entrepreneurs. How should the government evaluate risky payoffs? The answer depends on the answer to the underlying question risky to whom? If a project is small in terms of the entire government, and if its payoffs are relatively uncorrelated with other aspects of national income, the government need not consider variability in its payoff. In this context the government can be thought of as a mutual investment company that need not consider risks that are large in comparison to the portfolios of any of its individual investors but very small once parceled out among all of its investors.

There may be some government projects whose uncertain payoffs are directed to specific groups. A small speculative area redevelopment project may be a small risk when looked at for the government as a whole, but substantially risky for the potential beneficiaries. They might prefer a more conservative project with a lower but more certain expected payoff. The ideal situation in which the government insures the risks from the speculative project may not be administratively feasible. Here, the government, in its role as a sort of mutual investment company, must take account of its customers attitudes toward risk. If they prefer the safer project, that is the one that should be undertaken.

A project for which there are substantial uncertainties presents each affected individual with an uncertain set of benefits and costs. It presents him, in effect, with a lottery on net payoffs (benefits minus costs). The efficiency-oriented government should evaluate the payoffs from uncertain projects in terms of the certainty equivalents of those who pay for and receive its benefits. A certainty equivalent of a lottery for an individual is the "for sure" amount that would afford him a utility equal to the expected utility he would reap from the uncertain payoffs provided by the lottery. It is the greatest amount that he would pay (if negative) or the least amount that he would accept (if positive) rather than participate in the lottery of payoffs that the project would present to him. If the sum of the affected individuals' certainty equivalents is positive, the project should be undertaken.[10]

With this efficiency approach, it need not be the case that the government will undertake projects that yield positive expected benefits nor reject projects whose expected benefits are negative. A project that produces substantial benefits in times of general well-being will be much less attractive to individuals, will have lower certainty equivalents, than one whose payoffs are negatively correlated with other aspects of income. The latter type of project, for example dikes for flood control, viewed in isolation is a creator of risks. However, when viewed together with all other payoffs it helps to create what in effect is a more balanced portfolio for the entire nation. As such, it is even to be preferred to a certain payoff equal to its expected value.

In some cases, the direct payoffs from a project itself may not vary greatly, but the project may be responsible for variations in other payoffs. The unexpectedly high cost of the Vietnam war has had the effect of making the nation forgo much needed domestic social welfare projects. If Congress attempts to hold the federal budget relatively constant, uncertainties on costs will make their risky aspect felt indirectly through substantial fluctuations in other benefits. If Congress lets the budget swing in response to fluctuating costs, variations in tax rates or the size of the government debt will be the way the risk is transmitted to the individual.

THE GOVERNMENT AS A SOURCE OF INFORMATION

The acquisition of information may enable us to ameliorate the effects of uncertainty, it may permit us to make informed predictions about future states of nature. We can then change our actions in response to these predictions so as to increase our expected payoffs. Accurate weather forecasting enables farmers to plant and reap at appropriate times. Perceptive forecasts of economic conditions enable corporations to make wise investment and production decisions. Information is a superb example of a public good. Its consumption by one individual in no way reduces the amount that is available to be consumed by another. (In certain competitive situations its value in use, though not its quantity, may be reduced.) As a public good, information is efficiently provided at zero marginal cost. It is natural then that information provision should often be handled by the government.

In actuality, not only does the government provide ordinary forecasting and information provision services, but it also carries out testing and grading operations that would be costly and expensive for the individual consumer. In the absence, let us say, of federal grading of meat, quality would be highly undertain and the market would function less well. The FDA tests new drugs and makes the results available to all. The argument for government action here is that of economies of scale. It is much more efficient to have a single organization provide the information rather than have everyone provide it for himself.

THE GOVERNMENT AS AN ECONOMIC AGENT

Most of the discussion above relates to the role of the government in overcoming the market imperfections that are created by the presence of uncertainty. In recent years, the federal government has come to play a conscious economic role in our society. The primary goal of this participation is to maintain the economy along a full employment, low inflation growth path. Ideally the government acts as a stabilizing force, curbing demand when inflation is a danger, stimulating the economy when it shows a bit of slack. There can be much debate about the effectiveness of these actions, but one thing is clear, the government's role is to keep the economy from swinging wildly.

It would be incorrect to conclude that the advantage from reducing these swings is primarily one of reduction of risk. The consequences of excess and inadequate demand are undesirable. However, the method in which the government achieves this stabilization may be through a form of uncertainty reduction. As Keynes emphasized, convergent expectations can control the business cycle. If all businessmen independently would like to invest heavily, but all thought that others would not, a slack economy would be the self-fulfilling fear. The converse would be the case if all thought heavy spending would be the order of the day. However, if the government assures everyone that it will step in to keep things on an even keel, then galloping or collapsing expectations are not likely to ever take over. The promise (or threat) of government participation might be enough to prevent the very conditions in which the government promises to participate. If everyone believes in the exceptional fiscal and monetary skills of the government, they may never get a severe test.

CONCLUSION

In recent years, there has been an impressive expansion of knowledge on the subject of uncertainty in economics. For the most part the role of the government in a world of uncertainty has not been stressed. This paper has attempted to show that the presence of uncertainty creates special obligations and possibilities for collective or governmental action.

NOTES

[1] A Pareto optimum is a situation in which it is impossible to increase the welfare of any individual without decreasing the welfare of some other individual. A situation that is not Pareto optimal is inefficient in the sense that we could find another situation (one which might be called Pareto superior to the first) which was better for at least one individual and worse for none.

[2] Part of this section has appeared in the *American Economic Review, Papers and Proceedings,* May, 1969. It is taken from the author's manuscript, *Microeconomic Interdependence.*

[3] "Collective-Consumption Services of Individual Consumption Goods." *The Quarterly Journal of Economics,* LXXVIII (August 1964), p. 472.

[4] This is particularly true of goods in this class which are primarily used to avoid or ameliorate unfortunate occurrences. Many goods with such a purpose fall into the class of PIP goods.

The expected time until a highly unlikely loss is incurred is great. All losses or expenses in this essay are assumed to be discounted. With uncertain occurrence time, the discounting process is complicated.

[5] Income-type effects can be important if PIP goods are of exceptional value in use. For example, condition X has a 0.8 chance of being fatal. The discriminable amount an X-sufferer would pay for treatment B which would reduce this probability to 0 might not be much greater than that for treatment A (assuming B unavailable) which would merely reduce it to 0.4. If there were one unknown sufferer in a large community the result would be much different. The total discriminable payments from all members to make treatment A available to the unfortunate member would be approximately twice that for treatment B.

Where specific goods, such as houses, make up the potential losses to be prevented or insured, the amount that would be paid at the higher, before-loss income is the relevant amount for efficiency calculations.

[6] Contingent claims markets will not be actuarially fair unless some individuals are risk neutral, or if there is zero correlation among individuals' incomes.

[7] This section greatly simplifies a complex problem. In the author's *Studies in Interdependence,* the effects of restricted contingent claims markets are considered at greater length.

[8] In the unlikely event that the demand periods for the services overlap, there will be the congestion problem that is frequently associated with "nearly-collective goods."

[9] The mathematics of this example has been omitted here. Other simulations have been run for other utility functions and distribution of earning opportunities without achieving markedly different results. This example is considered in another context in the *American Economic Review, Papers and Proceedings,* May, 1970, "Ideal Government Responsiveness and an Optimal Income Tax."

This same type of analysis can be applied to other related problems, such as the optimal plan for car insurance. The optimal result usually involves some form of limited risk sharing; it involves a tradeoff between risk sharing and the maintaining of incentives.

[10] This is a gross simplification. It neglects distributional considerations, and assumes that the project does not compete with others that also offer net positive benefits. Certainty equivalents defined at present incorporate discounting considerations.

CHAPTER 5

COLLECTIVE ACTION AND THE DISTRIBUTION OF INCOME: A CONCEPTUAL APPROACH

Burton A. Weisbrod

INTRODUCTION

The public sector is generally conceived by economists as being concerned with three conceptually distinct functions: (1) income redistribution, (2) allocative efficiency, and (3) economic stabilization.[1] This essay focuses on the first function although, as will be explained below, the three are interrelated. The principal point of view is that of the federal government, but since state and local governmental units also act with respect to at least the first two functions, much of what is said will apply to all government levels.

The paper is divided into three parts. First is a discussion of the ways in which governmental activities affect—intentionally and unintentionally—the distribution of income in the society. Second is an examination of types of redistributional programs and of criteria for judging their desirability. Third is an analysis of conflicts among some of those criteria and of the resulting difficulty in choosing among alternative programs having a redistributional component. Overall, the objective of this paper is an improved understanding of why income redistribution is a goal of public policy, what alternative means exist for bringing about such a redistribution, and what problems exist in choosing among the alternative means.

Emphasis throughout is on the problems associated with the "benefits" side of the redistributional process—that is, with helping the "needy." Much of what is said, however, will apply, *mutatis mutandis,* to the problems of deciding who should pay for these benefits and in what manner the required sums should be obtained. Moreover, it is assumed explicitly that income redistributions are intended to aid persons at the lower tail of the distribution of economic well-being—that is, to deal with "poverty."[2]

Burton A. Weisbrod is Professor of Economics and Staff Member, Institute for Research on Poverty at the University of Wisconsin.

The author acknowledges the helpful suggestions of W. Lee Hansen, Robert Haveman, Allen Kelley, M. Jack Lefcowitz, T. R. Marmor, and participants in the University of Wisconsin's Workshop on the Economics of Human Resources.

INCOME DISTRIBUTION AND THE ECONOMIC GOALS OF GOVERNMENT

This secion takes up each of the three economic roles of government, examining, first, why government is concerned with the distribution of income, and, then, how governmental activities in the allocative and stabilization spheres impinge on the income-distribution role.

Income Redistribution as a Goal

The income distribution in the United States depends largely on the outcome of forces operating through the private market. At its most efficient "best," the private market rewards people in accordance with their contribution to marketable output which, in turn, reflects consumer preferences and incomes. This implies that persons whose productivity, in value terms, is low will earn little—regardless of whether the low productivity is attributable to lack of effort, lack of skill, or low demand for the skill.

The market rewards output, not effort. People who lack education and training, persons with limited intellectual ability or poor health, people producing goods and services for which the supply is so large relative to demand that very low prices result—all of these are likely to earn little. By contrast, those with greater ability, more and better education and training, and having skills that are in relatively short supply will tend to earn more, perhaps even when working shorter hours and under more attractive conditions. As consumer preferences change—partly in response to development of new products—and as technological advances alter production techniques, demand for workers with certain skills rise, and for those with others skills, fall. Given the absence of rapid supply shifts, earnings will behave similarly, as will the rewards to owners of capital equipment, land and other natural resources, the demand for which shifts.

This is all to note the degree to which incomes determined in the private market depend on changeable forces over which the individual has, at best, limited control. Thus, it is understandable that the levels of rewards offered by the market, and changes—particularly sharp drops—in those levels, have become relevant for social policy.

But the discussion above has assumed that the private market was functioning efficiently, actually rewarding those whose social contribution was large. Such a smoothly functioning system is, however, not the rule. The benefits from some activities, for example, in basic research, may be so broadly diffused that the individuals producing them cannot capture the bulk of their contribution to society. In addition, discrimination—against black, Puerto Ricans, Mexican-Americans, particular religious groups, etc.

—has the effect of not fully rewarding people for their actual productivity, or not permitting them to obtain jobs in which their productivity would be maximized. Consequently, the resulting income distribution may be both inequitable and "inefficient"—that is, reflective of an inefficient use of resources.[3] For both reasons, social action to influence the distribution of income has a rationale.

Whatever the forces contributing to the existing distribution of income, there may be dissatisfaction with that distribution and, hence, attempts to alter it. The federal government is generally the most effective governmental level to undertake redistributions because the opportunities to circumvent federal actions are most limited. By contrast, attempts by individual state or local governments to help certain people are likely to produce incentive effects resulting in an influx of the categories of persons to be assisted, while at the same time resulting in an exodus of persons and businesses who must pay for the aid being provided others.

The reference above to discrimination in the labor market suggests what should now be made explicit: collective (governmental) attention to the distribution of income need not involve merely the size distribution of income. There may also be concern about the distribution of income between whites and nonwhites, the distribution among geographic regions (witness recent efforts to develop Appalachia), and the distribution among age groups.

The public sector's concern about the distribution of income should not be limited to the consequences of the *private* sector's concentration on efficiency and its essential disregard of income-distributional considerations. The public sector itself, as we shall see, is a significant contributor to undesired income redistributions. These occur as government pursues its other goals of allocative efficiency and economic stability. That is, governmental activities, whatever their avowed objective, frequently if not inevitably affect individuals' income levels differently.

This observation is important for two reasons. One is that insofar as governmental activities designed to alter the allocation of resources—for example, highway and water resource programs—also have unintended side effects on the distribution of income, wise governmental policy should consider these effects when judging and designing such programs. The other is that since such "resource-allocation" programs actually do affect the distribution of income, they might be utilized deliberately for this purpose. The point is that a change in the income distribution—that is, in the absolute or relative positions of particular people or groups—is achievable in a variety of ways which include taking advantage of the redistributional "side effects" of programs that are normally regarded not as income-redistributional but as resource allocative.

Allocative Efficiency as a Goal

When government attempts to influence the production of particular goods and services—housing, highways, dams, schools, rivers and harbors, air traffic control systems, etc.—even though the motivation may be to enhance allocative efficiency, the fact is that these activities do affect the distribution of income, sometimes in subtle though powerful ways. Increased spending on highway construction is likely to send upward the price of cement companies' securities, as rising profits are expected. The automobile industry and its employees would also benefit, but officials of commercial airlines are likely to be less than enthusiastic. Water-resources projects in the arid Southwest enhance land productivity in that region; but even if it were shown that such projects were efficient for the economy as a whole, it would remain true that agricultural producers and workers in other regions would be hurt by this new competition.

This essay, concentrating on the rationale for governmental concern about the income distribution, is not the place to delve deeply into the justification for governmental activity as a provider of goods and services or as an influence on the level and forms of private provision of particular goods and services. Justifications have been offered—involving the provision of "collective-consumption" goods (such as national defense), for which consumption by one person does not reduce the consumption opportunities available to others, or involving, more generally, goods such that external effects are significant and are not taken into account by private decisionmakers (anti air and water pollution activities illustrate most clearly this type of commodity.)[4]

When "allocative efficiency" is being considered, whether with respect to private or governmental activities, it is vital to understand how that term is defined—particularly in the context of our attempt to examine the rationale for governmental attempts to alter the distribution of income. The key point is that there is no single "efficient" allocation of the economy's resources; instead, there is an efficient allocation corresponding to each initial distribution of income. This is so because the income distribution affects consumer demand patterns and resource-owners' supply patterns which, in turn, determine the pattern of production that will maximize the economic welfare of the society, given those demand and supply patterns. The efficient allocation of society's resources is not defined in abstraction from the distribution of income. What is efficient for the economy to produce with one income distribution may be quite inefficient if the distribution of income were altered.

It has been pointed out above that when the government alters its purchases or production of goods and services, it benefits (or hurts) particular groups of people and in this way it alters the distribution of real income. Whether the government's primary objective in undertaking a given program is redistribution, increased allocative efficiency, or economic stabilization is immaterial; one effect of a change in either the composition or level of government spending is a change in the income distribution.[5]

These distributional effects extend beyond the initial impact. More is involved than simply whose land is made more productive by a government-financed flood control project or who saves time and expense by traveling on a new segment of interstate highway. For in addition to the distributional impact of these real benefits from the projects, there are many secondary effects that are income redistributional in character. Property values near the new highway will leap as opportunities are sought to construct new motels, restaurants, and automobile service stations. These increases in land values have their counterparts, however, in the decreases occurring elsewhere, particularly along the roads from which traffic is being diverted. Urban renewal projects bring about similar pecuniary or income-redistributional results. Not only are property owners affected—with some gaining and others losing—but residents, too, feel the consequences. Some receive relocation subsidies although they planned to move even without them; and others suffer because a reduced supply of housing units pushes rents upward, at least temporarily.

Beyond the direct and the secondary distributional effects of a program, additional distributional effects will be felt through the respending process. Those whose incomes have increased may well have marginal expenditure patterns different from those whose incomes have decreased. As a result, the respending effects, operating through the conventional economic "multiplier" process, will bring about further distributional changes.[6]

So far our attention has focused largely on governmental *expenditures,* but, of course, decisions regarding the method of *financing* governmental services also affect the distribution of real income in the society. A benefit-principle of taxation assumes implicitly that government provision of goods and services should be financed in such a way as to leave unchanged the distribution of income (somehow-defined).[7] The ability-to-pay principle, by contrast, explicitly contemplates income redistribution, although whether a redistribution actually occurs depends on how the benefits of the governmental goods and services are divided among income groups. If benefits are correlated positively with ability to pay—as may be the case with many publicly-provided services such as interstate highways, waterway improvements, and art museums—then adoption of the "ability" principle of taxation is equivalent to adoption of the benefit principle. Unfortunately, little is known at present about how the benefits of public services are divided among persons at various levels of ability to pay.[8]

Economic Stabilization as a Goal

The stabilization efforts of government involve changes in tax revenues, expenditure levels, and/or in monetary variables that alter interest rates and credit terms. Whenever tax revenues are altered by adding or abolishing taxes, raising or lowering tax rates, or adding or eliminating deductions, exemptions, or exclusions, the result is that particular groups of persons benefit or are hurt. There is no escaping this fact and, indeed, it is sufficiently evident that lengthy debates on the merit of proposed redistributions inevitably accompany consideration of legislative change in taxes.

When and insofar as fiscal policy for economic stability involves changes in expenditure levels the income distributional consequences are also powerful. These consequences are possibly somewhat less evident to the society in general, because changes in the level of any one expenditure program are likely to have a pronounced effect on only a small segment of the population. At any rate, the fact remains that different people benefit from government expenditures on elementary-secondary education, higher education, medicare, medicaid, interstate highways, water resources, and urban renewal. Thus, the distribution of *real* income—of the economic well-being of various people—is inevitably affected by government efforts to stabilize the economy by varying expenditure levels. The point is that when fiscal policy is being utilized for stabilization, it is not an amorphous category of "expenditures," that is varied, but expenditures on specific programs, each of which affects some persons more than others and in different ways.

To summarize this section: Income redistribution is only one of the three primary economic goals of government; yet as the government seeks to achieve the other goals of efficiency in the allocation of resources and employment stability of the economy, its actions inevitably affect the income distribution. Thus, governmental concern about the distribution of income reflects—or, at least, it ought to reflect—both the undesirable distributional outcome of private sector activities—for that sector is preoccupied with efficiency and profits, not with distributional consequences—and also any undesirable side effects of the government's own activities in pursuit of the goals of economic efficiency and stability.

If income is to be redistributed, two questions must be answered: (1) *what* (and how much of a) redistribution should be brought about—that is, to whom and from whom should the redistribution be made—and (2) *how* should the redistribution be brought about—that is, what method should be used? These are perfectly analogous to the questions involved in ordinary production decisions by a firm: (1) What (and how much) should the firm produce, and (2) what technique of production should it employ? These questions are not really independent, in either the production or the redistribution context. The answer to question 1 depends partly on costs which, in turn, depend on the choice of production or redistribution technique (question 2). And the answer to question 2 depends in part on the type of commodity or redistributional program that is being considered (question 1). Thus, in principle these questions should be dealt with simultaneously.

The emphasis of this paper, however, is on questions of the second type. Granted that a tentative decision has been made to redistribute from group A to group B, and to provide a given level of benefits (in some form) to group A, which redistributive technique—among the alternatives available—should be used?

If a number of criteria are deemed relevant to program selection—and this is doubtless the case—the problem is, first, to identify the criteria; second, to develop operational measures of how fully each criterion is met by any particuar program; and, third, to determine the relative importance of each criterion—that is, the weights that should be attached to a given level of achievement of each criterion. These weights imply normative judgments regarding what is "desirable" public policy in the income distribution area. The summation of these weighted criteria-measures would give a "score" for each redistributional technique, the highest score determining the technique to be used.

Once the highest score technique for bringing about a given redistribution has been determined—a most difficult task—the desirability of that redistribution may be called into question. It might be decided that the best program available for producing a given redistribution is so poor that plans for the particular redistribution should simply be dropped. Some other redistribution, involving groupings other than A and B (though perhaps overlapping with them), might be preferable. In other words, while the A-B redistribution might be thought preferable to one involving groups C and D, the best technique available for the latter might be considerably better, and so the C-D redistribution might be chosen. This would be analogous to a case involving some ordinary commodities in which one commodity was more valuable than another (at the margin) but the cost was so much greater that it was deemed best (more efficient) to produce the less-valuable good.

The tasks of (1) stating decision criteria for choosing among redistributional programs, of (2) devising operational measures, and of then (3) determining weights, constitute a large order. The emphasis in this paper is on the first step, and although there is some attention to the second step, the paper stops short of tackling the third.

CRITERIA FOR CHOOSING AMONG ALTERNATIVE MEANS FOR REDISTRIBUTING INCOME

A number of alternative approaches exist for a government that desires to alter the distribution of income. In general the alternatives involve programs to transfer money, to transfer income *in kind,* or to enhance earning power for the group to be aided. Transfers in money form may take such diverse forms as a "negative income tax"—which might be addressed to all low-income persons—or agricultural price supports—which are available only to farmers. The money-transfer program may allow the recipient to spend the added income as he wishes (negative income tax) or it might constrain the use (rent supplements). Transfers in kind occur via distribution of surplus food or subsidies for production or consumption of specific goods such as public housing. Redistributions can also take forms aimed not at expanding consumption opportunities directly—as the programs mentioned above do—but aimed at increasing the individual's productive capacity and earning power, and in this way increasing his consumption opportunities indirectly. Education and training programs are the principal means by which this approach is currently being pursued.

We turn now to the criteria by which the desirability of any particular approach can be judged. Since a number of avenues are available for influencing the income distribution, the first step in choosing intelligently among them is the specification of standards or norms.[9] The following is a list and discussion of six such standards. It is not a logically exhaustive list. Hopefully, however, it is one that can be supported widely as a basis for program choice. The emphasis here is on the "transfer" side of the tax-transfer process, although much of what is said can be applied also to the tax portion of the redistributional mechanism.[10]

1. *Administrative cost* One consideration relevant to program selection is the cost of its administration. A family allowance, for example, involving systematic payments to all families with dependent children,[11] requires smaller administrative costs per dollar of benefits than does a conventional welfare program with its elaborate machinery for determining eligibility, preventing cheating and monitoring beneficiary behavior. To be sure, a principal reason for the divergence of administrative cost is that the welfare programs are intended to make a great effort to assist only the very needy, and clearly it is more costly to identify them than, for example, simply to identify a family with a dependent child.

Implied by this last statement is a second criterion for program selection—that the "deserving," and only the deserving should be aided. To this we turn next.

2. *Target efficiency* By this term I mean the degree to which the actual redistribution coincides with the desired redistribution. For example, a manpower retraining program may be intended to benefit the hard-core unemployed—those who cannot find regular employment even under full-employment conditions—but as it is actually administered it may (1) miss many in the hard-core group, while at the same time it (2) aids a number of less needy persons. Some would argue that these effects detract from the desirability of the program. Similarly, insofar as other antipoverty programs turn out to benefit the nonpoor while bypassing many of the poor, they may be regarded as inefficient means of redistributing income.

Two issues are involved, having to do with the accuracy of the program in assisting *only* the "target" group, and the comprehensiveness of the program in assisting *all* of that group. The first matter—the degree to which a program intended to benefit a low-income group A also benefits a higher income group B—might be termed the program's *vertical target efficiency* (or, more simply, vertical efficiency). The second is the degree to which a program intended to benefit group A reaches all members of this group. This concept of comprehensiveness may be termed the program's *horizontal target efficiency* (horizontal efficiency).

The vertical efficiency of a program might be defined as the ratio of benefits received by the intended beneficiaries to total benefits. A ratio of unity would thus indicate that all resources of the program are being devoted to the target group and none to any other group.

Horizontal efficiency may be defined in the two dimensions: (1) as the ratio of the number of beneficiaries in the target group to the total number of persons in the target group, and (2), as the ratio of benefits going to the target group to the total benefits "needed" by that group. Whereas the vertical concept involves the reaping of benefits by persons outside the target group, the horizontal concept involves the absence of "adequate" benefits to some or all persons within the target group. The concept of horizontal efficiency is related to the equity norm of equal treatment of equals,[12] for the lower is the value of ratio 1 the smaller is the proportion of the target group that is being treated. But the horizontal efficiency concept is also related to the equity norm of adequacy, for the lower the value of ratio 2, the smaller is the proportion of the target-group *problem* that is being treated. All persons in the target group might be treated equally but inadequately. Only in the limiting case in which (1) everyone in the target group received benefits, and (2) the benefits were at an adequate level, would full horizontal efficiency—in both dimensions—be achieved.

Governmental efforts to redistribute income—whether by transferring money, income-in-kind, or investment opportunities for raising earning power—often fail to reach all of those whom it is desired to aid (or tax), and aid (or tax) others unintentionally.[13] A desire to assist the "poor" may become operational in a program that disqualifies some of the poor on grounds of an inadequate period of residency. At the same time the program, if based on current income alone, may provide aid to persons whose low income is temporary or who possess considerable wealth (net worth) even though having very limited income.[14]

Governments sometimes provide goods and services at subsidized or even zero prices in an effort to raise the real income of certain persons. But the actual beneficiaries are frequently not the same as the intended beneficiaries. The provision of medical attention in a "free" clinic does, no doubt, benefit many of the poor. Yet the frequently long waiting time required discriminates against the "working poor"—those for whom the opportunity cost of waiting is high because it involves the loss of work time and earnings.[15] (This is the horizontal efficiency criterion.) At the same time, the clinic may be utilized by some persons outside the target group—some of the nonpoor—those for whom the opportunity cost of waiting is low, because they forgo little by waiting.

In a recent study of the distribution of public higher education subsidies in California, W. Lee Hansen and I discovered that the amount of subsidy actually received is correlated positively with the level of parental income of students.[16] A key factor is the presence of a very low, heavily subsidized tuition rate—which applies to all students, regardless of their ability to pay. Students from higher-income families benefit most from this subsidy because they are more likely than their lower-income counterparts to go to college, are more likely to go to a high cost (high public subsidy) school, and are more likely to remain in college until graduation. Thus, a public higher-education system that many feel is, or at least should be, a means of redistributing economic opportunity in favor of children of the poor is having quite the opposite effects, in the aggregate. That is, public higher education performs rather badly by the vertical efficiency criterion. To be sure, the public subsidies are permitting some low-income students to attend college when they would otherwise be unable financially to do so, but many of the poor receive little or no subsidy through the higher education system—thus causing the program also to perform badly by the horizontal efficiency criterion—at the same time that many nonpoor reap the largest subsidies.

The vertical efficiency criterion poses a thorny problem of the importance of distributional as compared with efficiency goals of government tax-expenditure policy. The question is whether a program such as compensatory education for the disadvantaged or retraining for the hard-core unemployed—which are aimed at particular kinds of people—should count any benefits (outputs) that accrue to persons not in the target group, and, if so, whether these benefits should be given the same weight per dollar as benefits to the intended beneficiaries. The importance of this issue is indicated in a recent study by Thomas Ribich of a number of compensatory education programs.[17] He argues that since many children from poor families will not grow up to become poor adults, compensatory education, considered only *as an anti-poverty device,* need not be provided to *all* poor children. Whatever other arguments may be made in favor of added government spending on education in general or on education specifically for poor children, the point is that some of it will be provided to the nonneedy. The issue, then, is how to weigh the benefits from compensatory education programs that accrue to the needy versus the nonneedy.

Vertical efficiency may be desired for either or both of two reasons. For one, taxpayers may have a psychological aversion to seeing nonneedy persons receiving benefits. For another, vertical efficiency can be viewed as a proxy for cost effectiveness in the sense that the greater is the vertical efficiency ratio the smaller is the cost per unit of benefit to the target group. Thus, as between two programs that bring equal benefits to a given target group the program having the higher vertical efficiency ratio, *ceteris paribus*, will be the least costly.

This latter interpretation implies, however, that benefits to nontarget persons should be given a weight of zero, and this is a questionable procedure. Even though the benefits to nontarget persons are agreed to be valueless from the standpoint of redistributional programs, they may represent real benefits which can be justified on other than redistributional grounds—for example, allocative efficiency. For example, a compensatory education program that is aimed at reducing the future prevalence of poverty among today's poor children may increase learning and subsequent labor market productivity of some who would not be poor even in the absence of compensatory education; this increase in productivity, while possibly valueless with respect to the redistributional goal, is quite relevant to the overall benefit-cost evaluation of the program—an evaluation that ought to reflect allocative efficiency as well as distributional-equity goals of government economic policy.[18] This leads to the conclusion that some "unintended" benefits of a redistributional program should receive a positive weight—when they contribute to nondistributional goals.[19]

Another objection to giving a weight of zero to those benefits from redistributional programs that accrue to the nontarget groups, relates to the observation above that there may be an aversion to seeing windfall gains to the "undeserving." Thus such unintended benefits to the nontarget group should receive a weight not of zero but of less than zero. This aversion is especially likely to be expressed when pure transfer programs are involved, for then it is clear that benefits to nontarget persons are unlikely to be justifiable on allocative efficiency grounds. Thus, one of the objections to the various negative-income-taxation (NIT) plans for transferring income to the poor is that in order to provide a meaningful floor on income and to avoid very high "tax" rates on incremental income—reductions in NIT payments per additional dollar of the unit's income—it is necessary that sizable payments go to persons who clearly are not poor.[20] This fact would be disclosed, of course, by the vertical efficiency ratio, though possibly not in a fully satisfactory manner.

3. *Allocative efficiency* At issue here are the effects of the redistributional scheme on the allocation of resources. Principally involved are the effects on incentives of those who benefit from the redistribution and of those who are made worse off by it. Conceptually, incentive effects are avoidable by the utilization of "lump sum" transfers to the target group and lump-sum taxes on those who are to finance the transfers. The essence of the lump-sum taxes and transfers is that, while leaving some persons richer and some poorer, no one could avoid the tax or increase the benefit he receives by altering his behavior.[21] Thus, no incentives would be established for resource suppliers or consumers to alter their behavior except as a consequence of having more (or less) income.

The fact is that incentive effects cannot, in practice, be avoided. We have discovered no way to tax or to subsidize without producing incentives to avoid paying the taxes and to qualify for receipt of the subsidies. Thus, the current controversy over negative income tax or other schemes to help the poor centers largely on the (unknown) magnitude (but not the direction) of incentive effects on the recipients who, as a consequence of an income guarantee, might decide to work less, or to have more children. Whether such consequences are "bad" is obviously a value judgment, but they appear to be fairly widely deplored in our society at this time. The negative income tax experiment now underway in New Jersey—designed and administered jointly by Mathematica, Inc. and the University of Wisconsin's Institute for Research on Poverty—has as its principal research objective the assessment of work-incentive effects of various levels of income guarantees.[22]

Another form of incentive effect—one that is believed to be caused by AFDC (aid for families of dependent children) transfer programs—is the breakup of families. In some states a low-income or unemployed father can increase his family's income by deserting it, thereby permitting the family to qualify for AFDC payments. The quantitative significance of this behavior is not known, but such an incentive exists, and was a factor leading to the adoption by more than 20 states of an AFDC–UP (unemployed parent) program under which a family with an unemployed father could qualify for welfare aid.

For decades, economists have generally faulted the agricultural price support programs because of their adverse incentive effects. Since the subsidies even though joined with land-use diversion programs, are available only to farmers, the effect is to establish incentives to remain in farming. Thus, the movement of capital, land, and labor out of agriculture and into more productive activities has been slowed.

Because we are unable to devise redistributional devices that produce no incentive effects at all, all redistributional programs fall short of the ideal, but, clearly, some are better than others. Most welfare programs are especially weak in this respect, because welfare recipients who increase their earnings are frequently penalized by cuts in welfare payments that are as large, and sometimes even larger, than their additional earnings.[23] By contrast, manpower training programs produce an incentive to take advantage of new skills and thereby to increase earnings.

As the manpower-training program illustration makes clear, allocative-efficiency effects are not limited to pure transfer programs. Whenever the redistributional technique involves the use of real resources (e.g., in manpower training or highway construction) rather than simply transfers, the question arises of whether and to what extent the resources are being used in an economically efficient manner—efficient in the sense that the value of outputs (better trained men, new roads) exceed the costs of production. If the equity effects of a particular program are sufficiently favorable, it may be worthwhile to sacrifice some economic efficiency, but in any event, account needs to be taken of both types of program consequences.

4. *Nondemeaning benefits* This criterion reflects the norm that benefits should not be provided in a manner that tends to stigmatize or to destroy self-respect. This criterion can be said to reflect a concern not only about how much income people have, but also as to what they must do to qualify for a redistributional aid program, and in what manner the aid is provided. Receipt of a check with the imprint, "Department of Welfare," might, by this standard, be regarded by recipients as inferior to an equal amount of money received from some other agency "for services rendered." A price-support program, in which a subsidy is paid as an above-market price for a product, would, in this context, be preferred, at least by recipients, to an outright cash dole.

Even when it is agreed that a particular redistributional program is demeaning to its beneficiaries, there may not be concensus that this is undesirable. "The degree of stigma associated with a program may be viewed as one means of rationing government program utilization."[24] In addition, the stigma may be desired (by taxpayers) because of its incentive effect, encouraging recipients to move out of the needy category.

At the same time it is worth considering that what taxpayers regard as demeaning or stigmatizing may not be so regarded by beneficiaries. Recent research has disclosed that welfare programs—which seem to be quite demeaning in their requirements, particularly for proving an individual's eligibility—are not regarded by recipients as especially demeaning.[25]

5. *Consumer versus taxpayer sovereignty* Some would argue that if the distribution of income is viewed as unsatisfactory, then taxes and transfers should be made in money form, thereby permitting each taxed person to decide how to reduce his spending, and permitting each transfer recipient to decide for himself what to do with his added purchasing power. This is the principle of consumer sovereignty, embodying the liberal ethic of freedom of choice. Given the consumer's set of preferences he can maximize his economic welfare if the tax he pays or the transfer he receives occurs in an unconstrained form. (In fact, this is a necessary condition for efficiency in the consumer sector.)

If consumer sovereignty is extended to all consumers, the beneficiaries of an income-redistributional program would be free to do as they wished with their added income. Those who make the payments, however, may be willing to give up income only if their sacrifices produce added purchasing power that is used in particular ways—"wisely"—by the recipients. Of course, conflicts can and do arise over the meaning of wisely, and so taxpayers may wish to constrain the freedom of recipients in the uses to which their increased income may be put. Thus, "taxpayer sovereignty" may supersede consumer sovereignty. When this occurs, a rather strong value judgment is implied regarding who knows best what a consumer ought to have—the individual himself or someone else? Traditional liberalism has opted for the former—as has modern theoretical welfare economics[26]—but for reasons discussed below, actual redistributive policy has often followed another course.[27]

Nowhere is this issue of who should decide how additional income should be spent seen more clearly than in current debate over governmental antipoverty policy. The case for a negative income tax, a children's allowance, or a guaranteed income rests firmly (though not entirely) on the foundation of freedom of choice—consumer sovereignty. By contrast, programs to provide goods and services for the poor—public housing, compensatory education, medical care clinics, or training programs—suggest taxpayers' preferences for minimum standards in consumption of housing, health services, and education, but apparently not in clothing, entertainment, or automobile transportation. It is not my objective here to urge one or the other of these viewpoints, consumer versus taxpayer sovereignty; rather it is to note that the choice between them is rooted in a value judgment regarding who ought to determine the pattern of consumption by beneficiaries of a public program.

The issue of transfers in kind versus transfers in cash (or, better perhaps, constrained versus unconstrained transfers) may be viewed from another perspective—allocative efficiency. If consumption of goods and services produces external economies (favorable effects on outsiders) while consumption of other goods produces external diseconomies (unfavorable effects on outsiders), it is both understandable and economically efficient that consumption of the former class of goods be encouraged (e.g., subsidized) while consumption of the latter class of goods is discouraged (e.g., taxed).

Taxpayers' interest in providing better housing for the poor may thus be explainable as a response to the external diseconomies that slum housing causes for outside parties—fires, crime, personal despair.[28] Similarly, the interest in providing better health care for the poor may be justified as at least partially a response to external diseconomies—in particular to the dangers that contagious disease may spread.[29]

6. *Flexibility over time*[30] Redistributive programs are seldom once-and-for-all events; they are continuing efforts. As such, their effects need to be examined over a "suitable" time period. The length of this period is itself a policy variable which is manifest in discussions about the intergeneration consequences of various antipoverty programs and about the likelihood that a program will contribute to increased self-sufficiency and decreased dependency. The point to be emphasized here, however, is this: Even if the program were fully in accord with the criteria of desirability at a given point in time, there remains the question of whether it will remain satisfactory as conditions change. For example, as technological advances have increased economies of scale in agriculture, price supports have increasingly benefited not the small, low-income family farmer, but the large, profitable corporate farm enterprises. (The extent to which price supports for one crop, cotton, are benefiting primarily the largest producers is documented in a recent study by James Bonnen.)[31] Perhaps such programs are less justifiable with the passage of time, but once instituted they are politically difficult to eliminate. It is important, therefore, that redistributional programs be flexible and adaptable to new conditions, either through an automatic mechanism that brings about needed shifts or a more responsive political system.

POLICY CHOICES

Two principal types of problems arise in applying the six criteria presented above. One is the lack of information as to how well any specific redistributional program will work, in terms of each criterion. Second is the conflict among criteria.

Consider first, the information problem. With regard to criterion 3, the incentive issue, how substantial are the likely work-disincentive effects of a negative income tax for the poor? How large are the external diseconomies resulting from the greater fire hazards in slums? Regarding criterion 5 (consumer sovereignty and taxpayer sovereignty), to what extent is there a difference between the uses to which poor people would put additional income if they had it, and the uses to which the nonpoor wish to allocate additional income?

Turning to the target efficiency criterion (2): How much of the benefits of a program will accrue to the intended beneficiaries and how many of the intended beneficiaries will receive little or no help? While the answer to this question is frequently unavailable because the matter has not been studied, a contributing factor is that it is often not entirely clear precisely whom the program aims to benefit. The issue is how one moves from a conceptual definition of the "needy" (or "deserving," or "poor") to an operational definition. For example, recent analyses of the "poor" population of the United States have disclosed rather different numbers of poor families and different characteristics of those families, depending on which operational definition of poverty is used—e.g., at least $3,000 annual income per family,[32] at least $3,000 of combined annual income and annuity value of net worth,[33] or a variable minimum annual income that depends on family size and rural versus urban location.[34] When wealth as well as income is taken into account there is a particularly striking effect on the prevalence of poverty among the aged; although the proportion of poor families among all families headed by a person 65 years or over remains high, it drops from 47 to 32 percent.[35]

The point is that before a determination can be made as to the target efficiency of a project the target group must be defined operationally, not merely conceptually. And our operational measures are always far from perfect. Thus, programs to help the poor have to struggle with the facts that low income in a single year does not "really" constitute poverty, that actual money income is likely to be greater than reported money income,[36] and that total income, including nonmoney income, often exceeds money income considerably. Yet reported money income for a single year may be the firmest information available for determining program eligibility and for defining operationally the target group for a program.

The choice of a precise specification of the target group may also have implications for the decision criteria discussed above. Aid in a form that is demeaning to one group may not be to another. Aid in a form that produces significant efficiency (incentive) effects for one group may not do so for another. Aid that would be spent in a specific way by one group may be spent quite differently by another. (This is germane to the consumer sovereignty/taxpayer sovereignty criterion.)

Having pointed up a few of the informational requirements for applying our six criteria in making choices among alternative governmental redistributional programs, we can now raise additional questions: (1) Do these decision criteria conflict? (2) Whether they do or not, if programs are differentially good according to each criterion, how much weight should be given to each criterion in order to come up with an overall "mark" or a ranking for each alternative redistributional program?

The decision criteria surely do conflict. Before investigating some of the conflicts, however, a brief digression will be useful in order to consider the case for lump-sum taxes and transfers as an ideal. In the tradition of modern theoretical welfare economics, such taxes and transfers have appeal because they cannot be avoided. Thus, they would produce no incentive effects and no changes in the market allocation of resources other than those which resulted from the fact that some people were better off financially and others worse off. But whether such a system would be desirable even if it were feasible is not clear. For its justification rests on the premises that the allocation of resources was efficient to begin with, and that no incentive effects are desirable. In an economy with widespread deviations from perfect competition in both output and input markets, and with numerous federal, state, and local taxes and subsidies that also produce deviations between marginal production costs and market prices, there is little reason to believe that the economy is organized in a near perfectly efficient manner prior to any income redistributional program that is being considered. Consequently, it is difficult to accept the proposition that redistributions of income should be made only through lump-sum taxes and transfers.[37]

This issue of the economic efficiency (incentive effects) of alternative courses of government action has been debated for decades in the context of efficient tax policy—in particular, regarding the choice of "direct" (income) taxation versus "indirect" (commodity) taxation.[38] Regardless of the reason for collecting revenue—whether to redistribute income or to finance a national defense force or for any other purpose—the basic efficiency argument is that taxes should be levied in a manner that minimizes their misallocative effects in the economy. As the analysis and debate developed it became clear that all of the taxes that are actually utilized—as contrasted with the theoretical lump-sum variety—do produce incentive effects. The income tax, for example, distorts the choice between work and leisure by taxing income from the former but not enjoyment from the latter. Moreover, given the preexisting distortions of relative prices, an additional "distorting" incentive effect might actually improve the allocative efficiency of the economy.[39] The choice of a redistributional mechanism that minimizes all incentive effects is not necessarily desirable. Lump-sum taxes and transfers, even if implementable, may not be suitable norms.

Whether lump sum or another form of redistribution is considered, it is likely that an effort will be required to identify the target group and devise a mechanism for aiding it. The conflict between the desire to minimize administrative costs (criterion 1), and to maximize vertical and horizontal target efficiency (criteria 2a and 2b) immediately develops. In order to achieve 2a—that is, to limit benefits to the target group—it is likely either that some members of the group will be missed—which conflicts with 2b—or that large administrative costs will be required, which conflicts with 1. In general, it appears that to perform well by any of these criteria requires a sacrifice in at least one of the other two.

It has been implied by the discussion above of criterion 3, incentive effects, that a redistributional program should avoid producing "adverse" incentive effects. One might argue that the program ought not to provide an incentive to escape poverty, for example, by a mechanism that involves high resource costs when a lower cost alternative does, or at least, could exist. Thus, it might be argued that if it is more costly in resources to alleviate poverty through compensatory education programs than by, say, cash transfers, then the latter mechanism should be used.[40] To provide an incentive for the poor to utilize compensatory education programs would be undesirable—because it would represent an inefficient allocation of resources.

Such an adverse (allocatively inefficient) incentive effect can be avoided, but to do so could conflict with the objective of avoiding demeaning forms of redistributional programs. Even if a compensatory education, manpower retraining or Job Corps program were not efficient in the sense of raising earning power by as much as the (marginal) cost of the program, they might raise incomes in a more self-respecting (less demeaning) manner than would a pure transfer-payment program. The point is that a program of investment in increased labor productivity—through training, education, relocation, etc.—might score weakly in terms of allocative efficiency while earning a high mark for its contribution to the recipients' self-respect.[41]

Of possibly greater significance is the conflict between the criteria of non-demeaning benefits and of vertical target efficiency. If all of the benefits of a redistributional program—especially a transfer program—go to the target group, such as the poor, the benefits are quite likely to be viewed as demeaning. If only poor people (or say, poor farmers) receive aid, then anyone who receives that aid is clearly identifiable—by himself and by others—as being poor. If, however, benefits go partly to the non-poor, then receipt of a benefit is likely to be less demeaning, for the (target group) recipients would not need to think of themselves as recipients of poverty aid, and outsiders would not be able to distinguish easily the poor from the non-poor recipients of the program's benefits.

Thus, the very process of pursuing the criterion of non-demeaning benefits tends to lead to the choice of redistributional programs that perform badly by the vertical efficiency criterion. For, by design, the tendency for well-targeted redistributions to be demeaning can be offset by deliberate non-targeting—by redistributing to some of the non-needy. The appeal of agricultural price supports may be understood in this context, as may programs to develop depressed regions such as Appalachia. While proportionately more farmers and residents of Appalachia are poor than is the case for the Nation as a whole, it is nonetheless true that the majorities of both groups are not poor, using government yardsticks. Similarly, a Headstart program of compensatory education for the disadvantaged (the target group) is likely to be more appealing (less demeaning) if the groups include non-disadvantaged as well as disadvantaged youngsters.[42] Broadening the group of participants, however, runs directly into conflict with the vertical efficiency criterion and also with the horizontal efficiency criterion insofar as a budget constraint necessitates the exclusion of some members of the target group in order to accommodate some outsiders.

Another illustration of the conflict between the objectives of vertical efficiency and nondemeaning benefits involves public higher education. There is in this country a well established system of private higher education, but costs of attendance have been too high to permit large numbers of youth from low income families to attend. Partially in response to the essentially income-distributional objective of broadening access to higher education, state supported colleges and universities have been established. The criterion of vertical efficiency would dictate that public subsidies in higher education be restricted to the needy.[43] Either the nonneedy would be excluded from the state universities, or else the nonneedy would have to pay a larger tuition, thereby losing some or all of the public subsidy.[44]

In practice, publicly supported institutions of higher education have neither prohibited entrance by the nonneedy nor have they charged differential tuition rates according to ability-to-pay.[45] They have preferred, instead to keep tuition as low as possible for all students, regardless of ability to pay. As a result, large subsidies have gone to the affluent via the higher education system. As noted earlier, a study of public higher education in California revealed that the affluent benefited disproportionately from the public subsidies because they were more likely to attend a public college, more likely to attend a high-subsidy school and more likely to remain until graduation.[46] The following table shows the estimated distribution of subsidies by level of family income. The difference between the pattern indicated and the pattern that would exist if vertical efficiency were being maximized —all subsidies going to the poor—is obviously great.

A number of justifications could be offered for this vertical ineffi-

	California families without children in California public higher education	California families with children in California public higher education—children in—		
		Junior college	State college	University of California
Average income	$7,900	$8,800	$10,000	$12,000
Average subsidy	0	$1,050	$ 3,810	$ 4,870
Subsidy as percent of income	0	12	31	41

Source: W. Lee Hansen and Burton A. Weisbrod, *Benefits, Costs, and Finance of Public Higher Education* (Chicago: Markham Publishing Co., 1969), ch. IV.

ciency. Perhaps low-income students learn more when high-income students are present; if so, this externality would support a subsidy to the nonneedy, on economic efficiency grounds. More important, possibly, is the desire to avoid the demeaning nature of the higher education subsidy that would exist if the subsidy were available only to those who "passed" a test of financial plight.

Turning to the criterion of flexibility suggests that as among alternative redistributional programs the choice should be made in favor of maximum visibility and recognition as a subsidy.[47] For unless subsidy programs are recognized as such, there may be little likelihood of their being altered or dropped in response to changing circumstances.[48] Visibility of subsidies conflicts directly, however, with the non-demeaning-benefits criterion.

The conflict between the criteria of consumer and taxpayer sovereignty—involving who should decide the use to which benefits from redistributional programs may be put—was alluded to above and need not be belabored here. It is noteworthy, though, that the conflict between these criteria reflects two rather distinct views of "society." The taxpayer-sovereignty criterion implies a view of society not as a unit but as a bifurcated organization consisting of "we"—the "haves"—and "they"—the "have-nots." From this standpoint, income redistribution is not an activity which benefits "society," but rather one that benefits "taxpayers." Normally, everyone decides for himself how to spend his income, subject only to modest legal constraints that apply, however, to everyone. In invoking the taxpayer-sovereignty criterion, however, taxpayers appear to be saying that they should decide not simply to whom income will be transferred but how the funds will be spent by (or for) the recipients.

Granted that the criteria for choosing among redistributional programs are frequently in conflict, the next question is what relative weights should be given to each of the criteria—how much is "society" willing to sacrifice in terms of each criterion in order to obtain more in terms of each of the other criteria? If, for example, a retraining program for the long-term unemployed increased the (present value of) lifetime earnings of trainees, but only by an estimated 95 percent of the program cost, would this be "preferable" to a pure transfer program? If yes, if it is worth a 5-percent loss on investment in order that people can earn their way out of poverty, is it worth a 50-percent loss? The answer obviously depends on value judgments. So far, little research has been done either on what prevailing value judgments are with respect to these multiple goals of social policy, or on what the policy implications are of alternative "tradeoff" rates.[49]

CONCLUSION

The income-redistributional effects of governmental actions pervade most, if not all aspects of governmental economic activity. Some activities are intended to be redistributive (e.g., welfare payment or a negative income tax); other activities may or may not have such an intent but are clearly recognized to have that effect (tax policy). There are, however, many governmental programs that ostensibly have little or nothing to do with redistributional policy, yet they do bring about distributional effects. Economic stabilization policy and resource-allocation policy—ranging from education to highway to flood-control programs—have direct as well as indirect or secondary consequences for the distribution of income. Recognizing the widespread effects of government actions on the income distribution is the first step in learning to anticipate these effects, taking them into account, and deciding how to deal with them.

If government has such widespread effects—some intended, others not—on the income distribution, it is important that an effort be made to establish criteria by which to judge the desirability of alternative means for redistributing income. Thus, the second part of this paper presented six criteria by which all income-redistributional effects of government actions might be assessed. Conflicts among a number of these criteria were considered in the third part of this paper, but, in general, not resolved. The principal point is that for a variety of reasons, people—both taxpayers and program beneficiaries—care not only about how much income is transferred, but about how it is transferred and to whom other than the intended target group it is transferred. Further study of income distributional considerations in the context of government decisionmaking is warranted in order to develop more rational public policy. Needed particularly is consensus on criteria for choosing among programs that have a significant redistributional *effect*—whatever their *intent*—and on the relative importance of each criterion.

NOTES

[1] R. Musgrave, *The Theory of Public Finance* (New York: McGraw-Hill, 1959), ch. 1.

[2] Not all income-redistributional proposals, however, have such a goal. Some may be designed to benefit a geographic region—e.g., the Southwest—or a group felt to be deserving whether or not needy—e.g., war veterans.

[3] For an analysis of the necessary and sufficient conditions for achievement of economic efficiency see J. de V. Graaff, *Theoretical Welfare Economics* (Cambridge: Cambridge University Press, 1957); F. Bator, "The Simple Analytics of Welfare Maximization," *American Economic Review*, March 1957, pp. 22–59; or J. Henderson and R. Quandt, *Microeconomic Theory* (New York: McGraw-Hill Book Company, 1958), chapter 7 ("Welfare Economics").

[4] At the analytic level see W. Baumol, *Welfare Economics and the Theory of the State* (Cambridge: Harvard University Press, 2d edition, 1965), and P. Samuelson, "The Pure Theory of Public Expenditure," *Review of Economics and Statistics*, 36 (Nov. 1954).

[5] It should also be noted that a change in the composition of Government expenditures may alter the amount and distribution of aggregate unemployment in the economy, and this, too, has clear implications for the distribution of income. For further discussion see R. Haveman and J. Krutilla, *Unemployment, Idle Capacity and the Evaluation of Public Expenditures* (Baltimore: Johns Hopkins Press, 1969) and the paper by Haveman in this volume.

[6] For a discussion of this effect in the context of geographic income distributional consequences of water-resource programs, see S. Marglin, *Public Investment Criteria* (Cambridge: MIT Press, 1968), pp. 83–84.

[7] A "benefit principle" of taxation could be defined in various ways and although all would involve beneficiaries paying the total cost of the public service, the cost burden could be shared in various ways. Hence the net effect on the distribution of income might well not be "neutral."

[8] For an examination of this matter in the higher education area see W. L. Hansen and B. A. Weisbrod, "The Distribution of Costs and Direct Benefits of Public Higher Education: The Case of California," *Journal of Human Resources* (Spring 1969), pp. 176–191.

[9] This amounts to stating those elements in a social welfare function that are likely to be affected by the choice of a particular redistributional mechanism.

[10] The usual intention of such mechanisms is to aid some needy group, not to penalize any other group, and so the choice of an aid program normally is considered separately from the decision regarding how to finance the program. Indeed, the financing is customarily from general revenue, no explicit attention being given to the question of which group should pay for a particular income-redistributional program. The distributional effects of alternative tax policies have received considerable attention. See, for example, Musgrave, *op. cit.*, chs. 4, 5, and 8; L. Johansen, *Public Economics* (Chicago: Rand McNally & Co., 1965), ch. 7; and J. Pechman, *Federal Tax Policy* (Washington, D.C.: The Brookings Institution, 1966).

Although the tax and transfer (benefit) structures are often considered separately, they are, to some extent, substitutes. Insofar as the needy are taxed they have more need for transfers. (See V. Tanzi, "Governments' Approaches to Income Redistribution: An International Comparison," *National Tax Journal,* XXI [December 1968], pp. 483–486.)

[11] C. Green, *Negative Taxes and the Poverty Problem* (Washington, D.C.: The Brookings Institution, 1967), pp. 46–50; and J. Vadakin, *Family Allowances* (Miami: University of Miami Press, 1968).

[12] In the context of tax policy the analogous concept is "horizontal equity"—equal taxation of people with equal ability. See R. Musgrave, *op. cit.,* ch. 8.

[13] As Kenneth Boulding put it, discussing the California water plan:

"It would be well to be quite sure
Just who *are* the deserving poor,
Or else the state-supported ditch
May serve the Undeserving Rich."

[14] For an analysis of effects of considering net worth when estimating the prevalence and distribution of poverty, see B. A. Weisbrod and W. Lee Hansen, "An Income-Net Worth Measure of Economic Welfare," *American Economic Review,* December 1968.

[15] This point came out in a discussion with Eugene Smolensky.

[16] See W. Lee Hansen and Burton A. Weisbrod, *Benefits, Costs, and Finance of Public Higher Education* (Chicago: Markham Publishing Co., 1969), especially chapter IV.

[17] Thomas Ribich, *Education and Poverty* (Washington, D.C.: The Brookings Institution, 1968).

[18] For further discussion of appropriate relationships between efficiency and equity in Government decisionmaking see B. A. Weisbrod, "Income Redistribution Effects and Benefit-Cost Analysis," in S. B. Chase, Jr. (ed.), *Problems in Public Expenditure Analysis* (Washington, D.C.: The Brookings Institution, 1968), pp. 177–209. See also the paper by Myrick Freeman in this volume.

[19] Similarly, the favorable (unfavorable) distributional effects of programs undertaken for allocative-efficiency reasons should receive positive (negative) weight.

[20] C. Green, *Negative Taxes and the Poverty Problem, op. cit.,* especially chs. V and VI: C. Green and R. Lampman, "Schemes for Transferring Income to the Poor," *Industrial Relations,* February 1967; J. Tobin, *et. al.,* "Negative Income Taxation—Practicality and Cost," *Yale Law Review,* November 1967; and W. Klein, "Some Basic Problems of Negative Income Taxation," *Wisconsin Law Review,* summer 1966, pp. 1–25.

[21] There would occur shifts in demand through the income effects, of course, but there would occur no substitution effects, given the absence of any initial change in relative prices.

[22] For additional information see H. Watts, "Graduated Work Incentives: An Experiment in Negative Taxation," *American Economic Review, Papers and Proceedings,* May 1969.

[23] C. Green, *op. cit.,* especially p. 119.

[24] T. R. Marmor, "Income Maintenance Alternatives and American Politics," University of Wisconsin, mimeo, n. d. (circa February 1969), p. 3. (Paper presented at the Poverty Seminar of the American Academy of Arts and Sciences, Boston, Mass., May 16, 1969.)

[25] J. F. Handler and Ellen J. Hollingsworth, "How Obnoxious is the 'Obnoxious Means Test'? The Views of AFDC Recipients," University of Wisconsin, Institute for Research on Poverty, Discussion Paper 31–69, January 1969.

[26] See, for example, E. J. Mishan, "A Survey of Welfare Economics, 1939–59," in Mishan, ed., *Welfare Economics* (New York: Random House, 1964), p. 6; A. Bergson, "Consumer Sovereignty and 'Real' Income Distribution," in Bergson, ed., *Essays in Normative Economics* (Cambridge: Cambridge University Press, 1957), ch. I.

[27] An alternative way of viewing this issue is that while consumer sovereignty is accepted generally, a question exists as to who is the "consumer"—the program beneficiary or the taxpayers?

[28] For further analysis see Jerome Rothenberg, *Economic Evaluation of Urban Renewal* (Washington, D.C.: The Brookings Institution, 1967), especially pp. 54–56.

[29] See Burton A. Weisbrod, *Economics of Public Health* (Philadelphia: University of Pennsylvania Press, 1961), especially pp. 18–20.

[30] This general point came out in conversation with W. Lee Hansen.

[31] See his "The Distribution of Benefits from Cotton Price Supports," in Chase, (ed.), *op. cit.*, pp. 223–248; and J. Bonnen, "Distribution of Benefits of Selected Price Support Programs," in *Rural Poverty in the United States,* A Report of the National Advisory Commission on Rural Poverty, USGPO, 1968. See also the paper by Bonnen in this volume.

[32] See Council of Economic Advisers, *Annual Report,* January 1964, ch. 2.

[33] B. A. Weisbrod and W. L. Hansen, "An Income-Net Worth Measure of Economic Welfare," *op. cit.*

[34] Mollie Orshansky, "Recounting the Poor—A Five-Year Review," *Social Security Bulletin,* April 1966.

[35] B. A. Weisbrod and W. L. Hansen, "An Income Net Worth Measure of Economic Welfare," *op. cit.,* table 3.

[36] For further discussion see Edward C. Budd and Daniel B. Radner, "The OBE Size Distribution Series: Methods and Tentative Results for 1964," *American Economic Review, Papers and Proceedings,* May 1969.

[37] For an analysis of the general issue of what constitutes efficient behavior when some of the necessary conditions for efficiency do not hold, see R. Lipsey and K. Lancaster, "The General Theory of Second Best," *Review of Economic Studies,* 24 (December 1956).

[38] M. F. W. Joseph, "The Excess Burden of Indirect Taxation," *Review of Economic Studies,* June 1939, pp. 226–231; and I. M. D. Little, "Direct versus Indirect Taxes," *Economic Journal,* September 1951, pp. 577–584 (also in American Economic Association *Readings in Economics of Taxation*).

[39] For a survey of the debate over direct versus indirect taxation, see D. Walker, "The Direct-Indirect Tax Problems: Fifteen Years of Controversy," *Public Finance,* November 1955, pp. 153–177.

[40] T. Ribich, *op. cit.*

[41] B. A. Weisbrod, "Expenditures on Human Resources: Investment, Income Redistribution, or What?" in Joint Economic Committee, U.S. Congress, *Federal Programs for the Development of Human Resources,* a compendium of papers prepared for the Subcommittee on Economic Progress, vol. I (USGPO, 1968), especially p. 82.

[42] This is apart from the issue of whether the cognitive effectiveness of the program for the target group is influenced by increased heterogeneity of the student body.

[43] Other considerations such as external benefits might have different policy implications.

[44] For further discussion see Alice M. Rivlin, *The Role of the Government in Financing Higher Education* (Washington, D.C.: The Brookings Institution, 1961), especially pp. 144–145.

[45] In 1968 Michigan State University did institute a flexible tuition schedule under which tuition varied somewhat with family income, from a low of $118 per term for students with family income of $11,800, or less, to a high or $168 per term for students with family income of $16,800 or more.

[46] W. L. Hansen and B. A. Weisbrod, *Benefits, Costs, and Finance of Public Higher Education, op. cit.*

[47] In the context of the use of the Federal tax system to provide subsidies a similar point has been made by Stanley Surrey, former Assistant Secretary of the Treasury. See "What Is the Impact of Those Tax Breaks?", in *Business Week,* Feb. 1, 1969, p. 62ff.

[48] James Bonnen, in commenting on the present paper, noted that over the past 8 years the agricultural program mix has shifted away from price supports toward direct payments. This, he points out, is a movement from a not very visible subsidy to an extremely visible one that now constitutes over three billion dollars a year in direct payments. He has speculated as to whether the Kennedy-Johnson Department of Agriculture deliberately shifted the program emphasis so as to place the programs in greater political jeopardy—to exert indirectly some constraining influence that the Department itself was unable to exercise.

[49] See, however, the citations in footnote 18, p. 139.

PART TWO

Institutional Considerations in Effective Expenditure Policy

****

CHAPTER 6

THE ROLE OF INCENTIVES, PENALTIES, AND REWARDS IN ATTAINING EFFECTIVE POLICY

Charles L. Schultze

INTRODUCTION

The traditional theory of public expenditures concerns itself primarily with such questions as the proper role of government, the evaluation of the benefits and costs of public programs, and the optimum allocation of national resources to the various public programs. It deals with *what* ought to be done and *how much* of our resources ought to be devoted to doing it.

In a similar vein, designers of social legislation in the past decade have concentrated primarily on what ends should be sought. Most federal programs are characterized by two features—(1) a *grant-in-aid* of funds to state and local governments or private institutions, conditional upon the submission and approval of (2) a *plan* setting forth the objective for which the funds will be used.

But objectives, plans, and budgets are not synonymous with actions and results. Promises are not performance. The adoption of an urban development plan does not guarantee that urban investment will fit the plan. The establishment of water quality standards does not clean up pollution. The formulation of a model city neighborhood plan will not itself produce a model neighborhood. When a particular public program in health or education or pollution control or urban development must be jointly carried out by a complex governmental structure and a host of private decisionmakers, it becomes crucial that those who execute the program have incentives or inducements to act in directions which are consistent with the objectives of the program.

It is becoming increasingly important to recognize the difference between objectives and plans on the one hand and performance on the other. The great expansion of public spending in recent decades has primarily been devoted to programs which involve the private as well as the public sector of the economy. While programs which produce purely public goods (like national defense) or simple income redistribution (like veter-

Charles L. Schultze is Senior Fellow at the Brookings Institution and Professor of Economics at the University of Maryland.

ans' pensions) are still important, the cutting edge of the recent expansion in government activities involves such matters as urban rehabilitation, control of air and water pollution, the provision of medical services, on-the-job manpower training, the development of depressed areas, and the like—programs in which public actions and decisions cannot alone determine results. Moreover, even where programs are predominantly confined to the public sector—as is the case with elementary and secondary education—the major instrument of federal policy is not direct action but joint action with state and local governments through the grant-in-aid mechanism. To a growing extent, therefore, public program performance depends upon the behavior of a large number of *independent* decisionmakers, public and private. Actions cannot be commanded. There is no hierarchy of officials in a single line of command who can be directed toward a set of predetermined objectives. In such cases the careful specification of plans and objectives by a public agency will not suffice to guarantee effective programs. The program must also be explicitly designed to provide incentives or inducements for the relevant decisionmakers outside the public agency to act in directions which are consistent with program objectives.

Even within the public sector itself, the problem of incentives is taking on growing importance. Social goals have become more ambitious, program objectives more complex. The model cities program is infinitely more difficult to execute than the disbursement of veterans benefits or the management of an agricultural conservation program. Designing, procuring, and operating a strategic nuclear weapons systems is a far cry from buying and maintaining the mounts for a cavalry regiment. Moreover, one of the chief characteristics of recent social legislation is that it seeks to realize national objectives in thousands of diverse communities across the land. A highly centralized managerial system cannot cope with the sheer number and diversity of the day-to-day decisions which have to be made. Decentralization of decisionmaking is not only desirable, it is unavoidable. But decentralized decisions should be compatible with central goals. And that in turn requires a system of rules, organizational structures, performance measures, and penalties and rewards, which induces decentralized decisionmakers in public programs to act in ways consistent with overall program plans and objectives.

For two reasons, therefore, the problem of incentives deserves particular attention in the formulation of public expenditure policy: *first,* because national objectives increasingly depend for their realization on the joint action of many independent decisionmakers, private as well as public; and *second,* because the growing complexity and geographical diversity of public programs requires decentralized decisionmaking within the public sector itself.

Incentives have a role to play in public expenditure policy which goes well beyond the problem of program execution. Incentive considerations should enter into the formulation of public objectives, the design of public programs, and the allocation of budget resources equally as much as in program execution. Or to put the matter another way, the problem of incentives is not a discrete and separate part of public expenditure theory relating to how programs are carried out, but an aspect of social behavior which should be taken into account at every stage of public policy formulation.

The first section of this paper considers the role of incentives at the various stages of public expenditure policy—program design, budget allocation, and program execution. The next part of the paper discusses the various types of incentives which appear to be relevant in formulating public policy. A final section examines some of the theoretical and political problems which arise in applying incentive concepts to public expenditure programs.

THE ROLE OF INCENTIVES AT THE DIFFERENT STAGES OF POLICY FORMULATION

Webster defines the word "incentive" as "something that incites or has a tendency to incite to determination or action"; looking further, we find the word "incite" defined to be: "to induce to exist or occur."

In the case of public programs, considerations of incentives arise when we concern ourselves with the problem of inducing individuals and groups, either public employees or private decisionmakers, to undertake actions which produce results desired by public policy. There are three stages of public expenditure policy to which considerations of incentives apply: program design, program execution, and budget allocation.[1]

Program Design

Many of the federal government's most important expenditure programs involve—or at least ought to involve—a mixture of public and private actions. More specifically, in perhaps the majority of public programs, the public sector is not producing a pure public good, but is attempting to take account of external costs and benefits in the production of private goods. Public programs seek to modify, in quality or quantity, the outcome of private production and investment decisions. Urban development programs, air and water pollution controls, and flood protection are examples. Yet too often, by concentrating solely on the public sector side of a joint public-private problem, public programs produce distinctly inferior solutions.

Flood protection is a case in point. Since the Flood Protection Act of

1936, the federal government has spent some $7 billion on flood protection projects. Expenditures on such projects currently run about $500 million per year with an additional $100 to $150 million per year spent on disaster relief to flood victims. While estimates of national flood damages are very approximate, they exceed $1 billion a year and are increasing. Extensive economic and engineering literature has been developed on the optimum design of flood control projects and on the techniques of benefit-cost measurement for such projects.

National policy toward flood losses has been quite straightforward—build flood protection and prevention works primarily at public expense and assist states, localities, and individuals to recoup against large flood losses. Where it could be shown that potential projects would prevent losses whose value exceeded the cost of the project, then those projects became eligible for federal financing, subject to the overall availability of funds in the Corps of Engineers budget and the normal vicissitudes of pork barrel politics.

But, as a matter of fact, public policy ought not to be expressed solely—or even primarily—in terms of criteria for the construction of public works for flood prevention. Rather it should be formulated in terms of encouraging rational use of flood plain lands. We should be seeking a policy which induces public and private investment in the flood plains only if the advantages of locating there are greater than those of alternative sites by an amount which exceeds the expected value of flood damages or the cost of preventing those damages. The present policy, which concerns itself almost solely with public projects, not only fails to consider the establishment of incentives for economic private investment in flood plain lands, it sets up a series of monetary and political incentives which induce distinctly uneconomic investment decisions.

Once the floor plain is developed, the standard cost-benefit calculation will often show that the construction of flood prevention or protection works is worthwhile in terms of expected damage avoided. However, in all too many cases the preferred alternative would have been a much less intensive development of the flood plain land or no development at all. In other words the differential advantage of the flood plain over the next best alternative is worth less than either the cost of flood protection works or the expected value of damage. Since states, local communities, and individual beneficiaries typically contribute only a fraction of the cost of federal flood protection works (ranging from 5 to 60 percent and averaging 25 percent) there has developed a set of incentives for uneconomic use of flood plain lands. Development occurs in flood plains. Either in response to or in anticipation of floods, strong and often successful pressure is brought to bear for federal flood protection. In many cases, floodproofing of individual buildings would be much cheaper than building flood control public works. But the costs of floodproofing are borne by the individual owner; the cost of public works is not. Once federal works are constructed, further development occurs beyond the protected areas. The resulting encroachment on the flood plain itself raises unexpected flood heights, increases the expected flood damage to prior investments and leads to still further flood protection works. Studies of flood plain use "show that some flood plain encroachment is undertaken in ignorance of the hazard, that some occurs in anticipation of further federal protection, and that some takes place because it is profitable for private owners even though it imposes heavy burdens on society."[2]

In earlier years most flood control projects were justified on the basis of protecting existing developments. More recently, however, an increasing proportion of flood control projects have been justified on the basis of protecting land for future development. Most often the economic and engineering surveys upon which construction authorization is based do not examine alternative sites for the projected development. As a consequence, benefits are calculated on the basis of the absolute value of the site as a location for the potential development, rather than its differential value compared to the next best alternative. This tends to accelerate still further the "cycle of losses, partial protection, further induced (though sub-marginal) development, and more unnecessary losses."[3]

As the Task Force on Federal Flood Control Policy pointed out, an effective approach to national flood damage policy would "alter the price signals received by potential flood plain developers." The full costs of flood plain occupancy would be shifted to prospective occupants through an occupancy charge equal to estimated annual damages plus any external costs which occupancy causes others. These payments would, in turn, be used to compensate those suffering flood plain damages. Flood control works would lower the annual occupancy charges and the costs of the necessary public works would be charged to the beneficiaries, whose annual costs had been reduced.

As initial steps in this direction, the report recommended the careful experimentation and development of a flood risk insurance program, with premiums on future investment in flood plain land related to flood damage risk. Ultimately such insurance would be a requirement for any investor in flood prone lands in order to be eligible for federal loans, loan guarantees, flood protection investment, or other similar assistance. The development of such a program must necessarily be gradual, since premiums seriously out of line with actuarial risk would invite uneconomic location and heavy costs. As a corollary to this recommendation, the report urged a sharply expanded program for determining flood hazards, flood frequency, and unexpected flood damage. Without such information economically meaningful premiums cannot be developed—and, to stress again—an insurance program with a poor premium structure is worse than no program at all. In 1968 the Congress enacted a flood insurance program. While premium rates on existing residential dwellings and small business establishments will be subsidized (up to a specified dollar value limitation) premium rates on all new construction and major improvements will be set to cover actuarial risks.

In addition to flood insurance the task force report recommended the development of a cost-sharing formula for flood control works which would more nearly assign the costs to the beneficiaries. Should an insurance program be developed, with premiums related to risks, the existence of a heavily subsidized means of reducing premiums would continue to generate excessive development in the flood plains. And requiring beneficiaries to pay for the cost of public works would tend to neutralize the present bias against investment in the floodproofing of individual structures.[4] Where flood control projects are justified on grounds of benefits from future development, as opposed to protecting existing investments, the report urges that only *net* locational benefits be taken into account—that is, only the excess value of flood plain location over the next best alternative be taken into account.

The point of this summary of flood control policy is that the problem of incentives must be considered in the initial specification of public policy objectives in those cases where joint private and public action is involved. And joint action is likely to be involved in a high proportion of cases where the basic objective of public policy is to take into account the external benefits or costs which arise in private decisionmaking. An "incentive-oriented" point of view would recognize that present flood control policy is deficient on at least three counts:

> It fails to provide incentives for private decisionmakers to consider flood hazards sufficiently in their investment decisions.
>
> By its lack of user charges, it positively encourages uneconomic investment coupled with political pressure for subsidized flood protection works.
>
> By its lack of user charges, it also creates a false set of incentives to minimize floodproofing and maximize flood protection.

Other examples are numerous in which failure to consider incentives leads to an inferior specification of objectives and inferior program design. In the field of water-pollution control, for example, public policy emphasizes the subsidized construction of waste-treatment plants, dams for low-flow augmentation, and the separation of storm drains from sewers as means of treating pollution once created. But it generally fails to consider means of altering the price signals received by pollutors through the mechanism of user charges and effluent charges. Through such charges, industrial pollutors would be assessed the social and economic cost of pollution, and in many cases would find it profitable to change their internal processes to reduce the amount of pollution they create. In general, it is cheaper to improve the quality of our streams by combination of prevention and treatment than by treatment alone. But because the private sector is primarily responsible for prevention and the public sector for treatment, public policy excessively concentrates on the latter aspect. And to the extent it does deal with the prevention aspect of pollution control, it does so by attempting to enforce, through the police power, a set of water quality standards rather than providing economic incentives to individuals which would induce them, in their own interests, to take action to improve water quality. Again, the question of incentives arises in the specification of objectives and the design of programs—not merely in program execution.

More generally, public policy must often concern itself not with the provision of public goods which can only be handled by the public sector, but with the problem of external costs and benefits in the private sector. In such cases market prices and costs do not reflect "true" social benefits or costs. As a consequence purely private decisions do not produce desirable results. Pollution is a cost to society which the pollutor does not bear. The full costs of flood damages are often not foreseen and even less often borne by those who locate in flood plain lands. As a consequence, public action is needed. But that public action need not be simply the provision of public facilities (waste treatment plants or flood protection works) to offset the economic losses caused by private actions. Rather the objectives of public policy, in such cases, should include a modification of the "signals" given and incentives provided by the marketplace so as to induce private actions consistent with public policy. Excessive concentration upon the purely public part of public policy may result in poorly specified objectives and ineffective programs.

Program Execution

In the 1920s, expenditures of the federal government outside of the traditional functions of defense, post office, veterans' benefits and interest on the debt represented less than 1 percent of GNP. In the budget for fiscal 1969, such expenditures will equal 10 percent of GNP. The federal government today manages large enterprises—the space program, the Atomic Energy Commission, the Forest Service—whose very size and complexity require highly decentralized operations. The establishment of objectives and plans at the top level of the agency concerned does not guarantee that the vast number of decisions which must necessarily be delegated to subordinate officials will result in effective and efficient program execution.

The problem of providing incentives for effective program execution is closely related to the problem of devising measures of performance for subordinate decisionmakers. It is impossible to provide incentives without knowing what to reward and what to penalize. Two major consequences flow from failure to provide performance measures related to program objectives. The first is the growth of detailed regulations which rigidly specify what is "acceptable" behavior by subordinate decisionmakers. Standard contract provisions multiply and are required to be included in all contracts regardless of their suitability to a particular situation. Tables of organization are centrally established and carefully monitored. Elaborate procedures are developed to control the purchase of supplies, the use of long-distance communications, travel, and the like. Since subordinate decisions cannot be controlled by judging them in terms of their effect on output, they are controlled by a rigid specification of inputs.

The second consequence of failure to provide appropriate performance measures is that individuals and institutions often become avid risk averters. Overall success cannot be recognized, but individual "mistakes" can be singled out for punishment. A few examples will help. In 1966 inflationary pressures mounted rapidly in Vietnam. As one means to counteract those pressures, the Agency for International Development launched a commodity-import program, designed to soak up some of the excess purchasing power with American-furnished commodities. Two options were open in running the program:

A. A carefully controlled license program, in which every possible step was taken to insure that import certificates did not fall into the hands of black marketeers or into the hands of the Vietcong. One consequence of such a program would be a mountain of redtape and a very slow trickle of imports into the Vietnamese commodity markets.

B. A less tightly controlled program whose main objective was introducing rapidly a large volume of commodity imports into the country. One early foreseeable consequence of such a program was that a significant proportion of imports would end up with black marketeers and some part with the Vietcong.

Given its overall objective, AID quite properly chose the second course of action. And inevitably, a year later, it found itself subject to sustained and violent attack in the Congress for the easily identifiable consequences of its policy, namely the appearance of AID-financed imports in the hands of black marketeers and small amounts in the possession of the Vietcong. The obvious reaction of program operators to the performance criteria which implicitly underlay this attack is in the future to accept a lower expected value of program accomplishment in exchange for a smaller proportion of "mistakes."

A similar situation commonly arises in the loan programs of the federal government. Many of these programs, rightly or wrongly, have the supposed objective of providing loan capital to small enterprises which are too risky for investment by commercial lenders. The Small Business Administration is a case in point. Measures have not been developed, however, which can be used to judge the performance of various regional loan offices in terms of overall program objectives. Defaulted loans, on the other hand, are easily identified, and a significant default rate is sure to invite congressional questions. Loan officials, therefore, tend to avoid risky loans. As a consequence, far from meeting their original objectives, the programs end up, in many cases, simply in making loans of commercial quality at less than commercial rates.

The problem of providing incentives for effective program execution is even more difficult when the federal government itself does not directly operate the program, but provides grants-in-aid to other governments or to private organizations. The major growth in federal expenditures in recent years has been devoted to complex social programs in such fields as health, education, manpower training, urban development, and the like. These programs deal with problems which, while national in scope, require very particular solutions in thousands of individual communities. The federal government provides the financing and requires the submission of plans which specify the objectives for which the funds are to be used, but it does not have direct responsibility for operating the programs. The current widespread pressure for decentralization and participatory democracy arises, in part at least, from a recognition that highly centralized decisionmaking is virtually impossible in these programs. Yet without meaningful measures of performance and effective incentive systems, is it possible to decentralize decisionmaking while still making progress toward the generally accepted high priority national goals toward whose realization the federal grant programs were originally established? I believe that in selected cases, at least, an incentive approach can help to resolve the national goal versus decentralization dilemma.

Budget Allocation

It is not customary to think of budgetary allocation from the standpoint of incentives. We tend to view the budget allocation process as one in which the government seeks to adjust program levels so that equal marginal returns are realized from the last dollar spent on each program. Massive problems of evaluating benefits and costs confront decisionmakers in trying to approach this ideal result. But in what sense do incentive considerations arise? In two ways, I believe.

In the first place, with few exceptions, the federal budget is developed on a nationwide functional basis—education, health, defense, space, manpower training, and so forth. There is no mechanism, however, by which tradeoffs among alternative federal programs are possible at the local or regional level. A mayor or governor has almost no means of negotiating a tradeoff between a submarginal flood control project and a highly needed hospital; between an urban freeway and a waste treatment plant. Hospital, highway, pollution control, and water resource budgets are decided nationally. This fact has two major consequences:

First, it sets up incentives for local communities and their congressmen to lobby in the Executive Branch and the Congress for almost any project they have a chance of getting. Incentives are established for inefficient political bargaining; the relevant set of tradeoffs has no way of appearing in the bargaining process.

Second, many functional decisions involve both gainers and losers. Water pollution control programs help downstream communities and often hurt upstream. Location of low-income subsidized housing in suburban communities is often viewed by that community as entailing positive costs. Concentration of assistance to depressed areas in potential growth centers is, quite naturally, viewed with some hostility by hinterland counties who receive no immediate help from this approach, but whose poverty may be much greater than the community actually receiving the assistance. As a consequence, losers are often able to veto potentially high priority programs. But considering the entire range of potential federal programs, it may often be possible to compensate losers in one functional program with perfectly appropriate assistance of another kind. Yet so long as budget allocations are made solely on a nationwide functional basis, there is no mechanism by which compensatory tradeoffs can be negotiated in particular cases.

Third, theory tells us that funds should be allocated among various federal programs so that the benefits from the marginal dollar in each program are the same. But many federal programs have objectives which are reached through particular projects in individual communities scattered across the Nation (for example, hospital construction grants, flood control projects, and so forth). In such cases an evaluation of the merits of one program relative to another is much more difficult to make on a national basis than it is in a specific community. The relative desirability of allocating more federal funds to hospital grants, flood control, or to slum rehabilitation can often be determined more reasonably for New York City than it can for the nation as a whole. This is not to say that considerations of national objectives are unimportant in making such a determination. Rather it is to say that, at the margin, allocation of federal funds among various programs can often be done better on a regional or community basis than on a nationwide functional basis.

In short, for certain types of programs, purely functional budgeting sets up political incentives for inferior bargaining, suppresses incentives for a kind of compensatory bargaining which might hold great promise, and fails to provide for the kind of relative benefit comparisons which efficient allocation demands.

For these reasons experimentation with a limited form of *regional budgeting* could be very worthwhile. Tentative functional budgets could be drawn up on a national basis, just as they are now. But in each locality, Governors and mayors could be given the right, up to some limit, to propose reallocations among particular federal aid funds flowing into their own jurisdiction. They might propose, for example, an increase in funds for education and a decrease in highway grants. In effect, the final allocation of federal budgetary funds would arise out of a joint set of considerations—national allocations based on nationwide objectives, modified by reallocations based on conditions and preferences in particular communities. Functional budgeting would be supplemented where appropriate and feasible by regional budgeting. Such an approach has much to recommend it, but it is not without its problems. I shall return to a discussion of those problems, and some suggested means of overcoming them, at a later point in this paper.

Another type of incentive problem in budget allocation arises when major elements of cost are not charged to the decision unit responsible for making decisions which involve those costs. Examples range from major areas of program policy down through detailed management decisions. The U.S. merchant marine is supported with a massive subsidy program on the primary justification that national security demands it. Yet if the costs of this decision were charged to the Defense Department, it is quite likely that defense strategists would opt for a smaller subsidy program and for use of the savings in other defense purposes. Whatever the result, the appropriate program tradeoffs could at least be considered. On a smaller scale, if military personnel are not charged to the budget of the commander of a military installation, he has every incentive to substitute this free good for those other inputs which do enter his budget.

More generally, budgetary structure affects the incentives of decisionmakers. Programs whose costs do not enter the budget of the decisionmaker, being a free good, are easily recommended. Free resources are overused. In other cases desirable programs are blocked because the budgetary structure provides no means by which "losers" in a particular decision can be compensated. As a consequence they have no incentive to agree to a reasonable compromise. In still other cases state and local officials have no incentive to develop and negotiate an effective program for the use of federal assistance, because the excessively functional character of federal budget decisions leaves them no leeway to negotiate transfers among functions.

So far we have examined the role of incentives under a set of classifications based upon the various stages of public policymaking—the specification of objectives, program design, program execution, and budgetary allocation. Further insight can be gained by considering a classification based on the various types of incentive problems which arise in the consideration of public policy.

THE VARIOUS TYPES OF INCENTIVE PROBLEMS

Incentives Designed to Channel Private Actions toward Public Objectives

A. Removing or Modifying Current Incentive Structures Which Lead to Actions with Large Social Costs or Prevent the Achievement of Social Objectives If we review public programs designed to modify private behavior in socially desirable directions, we find that failure to consider the problem of incentives has often led to very ineffective or inefficient solutions. In some cases ineffective solutions have emerged because public policy has attempted to impose on the private decision system detailed plans which require actions running directly counter to those called for by the existing system of private rewards and penalties. Enforcing the plans by use of the police power may often be far less effective than eliminating or modifying the private incentives which run counter to the plan.

In other cases, public programs have specific subsidy structures which themselves set up highly inefficient responses. Approximately the same subsidy objective could be reached with a subsidy designed to encourage efficiency.

Let me cite some examples:

Both the federal government and city governments have struggled for years with the problem of planning urban development. Almost every form of federal assistance to municipalities is conditioned on some kind of a planning requirement—comprehensive plans, functional plans, planning processes, social renewal plans, workable programs, and so on down the litany. But, all too often, the plans are more breached than observed. And in large part this occurs because the system of rewards and penalties at work in connection with urban investment is not merely neutral to but runs precisely counter to the goals and objectives of the plan.

One major aspect of urban development plans is zoning for differential intensity or other differences in use. The purpose may be esthetic, it may be to control development along lines conducive to efficient urban transportation, or it may have other purposes. But the principal characteristic of zoning is that it reduces the potential rent on specific parcels of land below the rent which could be earned without zoning restrictions. Under the most favorable conditions, this characteristic would make zoning hard to enforce. But this problem is substantially increased by the present tax system. The return to investment in physical improvements will not generally vary with zoning changes—the landowner will capture the gains from such changes. And while physical improvements yield an annual return subject to normal tax rates, the potential rewards from securing a change in zoning can be realized as capital gains, and will be taxed at much more favorable rates. As a consequence, the energies and capital of real estate developers are channeled into land speculation and into massive efforts to secure favorable changes in zoning codes. Other things being equal, this kind of activity yields returns which pay less than half the tax securable by investment in physical improvements. Small wonder that "year 2000" plans in most metropolitan areas quickly succumb to the relentless pressure of land developers.

In a similar vein, the owner of slum property hoping for a rise in land prices has every incentive, when faced with a tradeoff between improving his property and extending his holdings of existing property, to favor the latter. Improvements yield a return subject to normal tax rates. The yield from the acquisition of additional property can be taken as capital gains. The availability of capital gains tax treatment on capital gains from the sale of land, shifts the margin of tradeoff between improvements and extension of holdings in favor of the latter.[5]

More generally, the availability of highly favorable tax treatment for those who speculate in land, tends to work counter to most of the objectives contained in urban plans. A change in the tax system would not itself automatically channel urban investment in socially desirable directions—there are a host of other factors which influence such investment. But certainly the system could be made more neutral with respect to planning objectives, rather than being highly counterproductive as it now is.

The system of payment by which hospitals are reimbursed under medicare, medicaid, and most private insurance plans represents another example of an existing incentive system which produces highly undesirable results.

During the past several years, hospital costs have been rising at a highly accelerated rate. In 1967, hospital costs rose by more than 16 percent for the second year in a row. Average per diem hospital costs now approach $60, and have been projected to rise to $100 within 5 years.[6] If means could be found to reduce the rate of increase in hospital costs by only 2 percent per year, the resulting savings would amount to $5 billion annually by 1975. Not only have per diem costs at hospitals been rising, but hospital utilization, in terms of hospital days per thousand population, has also been increasing rapidly. Per capita utilization of hospital services rose by 47 percent over the 1955–65 decade.[7] There is an accumulation of evidence that some part of this rise reflects an excessive use of hospital services relative to patient's needs. If a 25-percent reduction in hospital utilization rates could be effected, without reducing the quality of patient care, an annual savings in medical costs of $7.5 billion could be realized by 1975.[8]

The federal government's medicare and medicaid programs now pay for the hospital care of a significant part of the population. Built into these programs is the concept of fully reimbursing hospitals for the costs associated with medicare and medicaid patients. Through these programs the federal government can have a major impact on hospital costs, both directly and through its influence on the practices of Blue Cross and commercial insurance carriers.

At the present time federal reimbursement formulae undoubtedly contribute to hospital inefficiency. Essentially each hospital is reimbursed by the federal government for the "reasonable costs" of delivering services to patients under medicare and medicaid programs. Payment is matched to the individual costs of each hospital. There are virtually no incentives for efficiency. Any savings from more efficient operations result in lower federal payments; any increased costs are fully passed on. To the extent that larger staffs bring prestige and promotion, there are positive incentives for inefficiency. Moreover, since policies in most hospitals are controlled by the physicians serving it, and since the hospital provides, in effect, a free workshop for those physicians, there are powerful incentives to upgrade the workshop, when the costs are reimbursed, insofar as most patients are concerned, either by government program or private insurance carriers.

All of the evidence indicates that there is substantial room for improving efficiency in the delivery of hospital services. For example, recent data show that average per diem costs in voluntary short term teaching hospitals in New York City ranged from a low of $50 to a high of $87. The range among 42 New York City community hospitals was $34 to $61. Among a group of 12 hospitals carefully chosen for high quality care, costs per patient-day ranged from $46 to $96, after wage scales had been adjusted to a common basis.[9] The American Hospital Association compiled operational data on 431 hospitals of different sizes throughout the nation and found substantial economies of scale: small hospitals produced an average

3.7 laboratory procedures per man-hour, large hospitals averaged 8.9; small hospitals annually served 1,800 patient-days per one administrative employee, large hospitals 4,100; small hospitals produced 3.9 meals per man-hour, large hospitals 5.9.[10] While some of this huge variance in costs among hospitals may indeed be associated with differences in the quality of care, much of it is undoubtedly traceable to differences in efficiency.

A number of schemes have been suggested for "incentive reimbursement" as a technique for reducing hospital costs. Payment might be based on a regional average cost. Hospitals with higher costs than the regional average would have to absorb part of the excess; hospitals with lower costs would be allowed to share part of the savings. Incentives would thus be introduced for each hospital to reduce costs. Over the longer run, hospitals of more than average efficiency would be able to accumulate internal funds for expansion and to demonstrate to lenders that their cash flow could amortize borrowings. Inefficient hospitals could not. An alternative scheme is to reimburse each hospital initially on the basis of its own costs, but to reward it for reducing costs toward the regional average and penalizing it in contrary cases.

Incentive schemes, however, will ultimately prove viable only to the extent we can distinguish change in cost for a constant quality of care from changes in cost associated with changes in quality. We seek a means to reduce hospital costs per unit of output. We do not seek a reduction in per diem costs achieved by lowering the quality of care provided. The National Advisory Commission on Health Manpower has suggested the establishment of peer review panels—groups of physicians, hospital administrators, and other professional personnel who would review the case provided and make judgments with respect to the quality and utilization of services.[11] While this approach appears to have much merit, and may become an indispensable part of any incentive reimbursement scheme, it needs to be backed up by the development of criteria for evaluation purposes. The range of services provided by a hospital are too complex and diverse to be evaluated as a lump, particularly when the evaluation is for the purpose of establishing payment for those services. Rigorous analysis of hospital care directed toward establishing output oriented functions or categories is clearly a prerequisite for the establishment of meaningful evaluation criteria for peer review panels or for any other quality evaluation mechanism. In short, to apply incentive reimbursement, we must first make progress toward measuring the "output" of hospitals.

Other examples of inappropriate or positively harmful incentive systems are numerous. The American merchant marine is a case in point. We spend about $500 million per year to subsidize the American merchant fleet. The justification is twofold: to provide a carrying capacity in case of war and to have a weapon against discrimination by foreign-owned fleets in this highly cartelized business. While the case for subsidy is dubious on both grounds, let us accept its necessity and look at the subsidy system itself. The basic operating subsidy essentially makes up the difference between American and foreign operating costs. Any productivity gains result in lower subsidies—inefficiency leads to higher subsidies. Not only does the overall subsidy remove any incentives for efficiency, its detailed composition discourages the kind of merchant fleet which is most appropriate for the American economy. The subsidy brings each element of American costs in line with foreign costs—labor, repairs, and maintenance, etc. But the *comparative* advantage of American ships lies in higher speed—i.e., American ships' fuel costs are no higher than foreign costs, but labor costs are much higher. Consequently, American ships should be designed for high speed, quick turnaround time, catering to high-value cargo But the subsidy system removes any incentive for pursuing this comparative advantage. To make matters worse, while the subsidy is partly justified as a means of providing a competitive weapon against potential foreign discrimination, our cargo preference laws have resulted in the fact that more than half of the export cargoes carried by U.S. ships are preference cargoes, leaving less than half of our capacity to compete in the world market. Even accepting the need for a subsidy program, we have designed one which is guaranteed to produce decreasing relative efficiency in the American merchant marine compared to its foreign competitors.

We have so far concentrated on the negative aspect of the incentive question; i.e., those situations in which the existing incentive structure produces private actions which run counter to the public interest. But in addition to removing "negative" incentives, public policy can also provide "positive" ones:

B. Providing New Incentives Designed to Channel Private Actions toward Public Purposes Two important examples have already been given of areas in which incentives for private action might be created as a means of achieving quite specific public objectives:

> Mandatory flood insurance, with premiums adjusted to risk, as a means of encouraging economic investment in flood plain lands.
>
> Effluent charges as an efficient means of reducing air and water pollution.

In both of these cases, the necessity for a public program arises from the existence of external costs and benefits in the private market. But the possibility of creating an incentive system which channels private actions toward public goals is not limited to programs which primarily deal with externalities. The massive new federal housing program, passed by the

Congress in 1968, proposes to construct 6 million low-income housing units in the next decade, and to subsidize part of the rental or ownership costs. The primary objective of this program is presumably income redistribution—redistribution through transfers-in-kind, but redistribution nevertheless. (Anthony Downs has eloquently pointed out the host of problems connected with achieving this ambitious goal—problems whose solutions will require massive changes in urban institutions.)[12] Consideration of this program from an incentive standpoint, however, raises questions which go well beyond the matter of income distribution. In particular, the availability of authority to the federal government to contract for large blocs of low-income housing—both sale and rental housing, both multifamily and single unit—may make it possible to test various devices to encourage innovation in the development and construction of low-cost housing. Will the market provided by large-scale multiyear contracts induce new kinds of firms to enter the industry, encourage the development of specialized materials, promote substantial R. & D. expenditures by building materials and construction firms? The Defense Department's proposal for the fast deployment logistics ships (FDL's) was based on a positive answer to these questions in the case of the shipbuilding industry. In the case of housing we do not know how important economies of scale and the security of long-term markets are. But the new program does make it possible to test whether large-scale markets and long-term contracts will provide incentives for significant cost reductions.

Another example of potential "incentive" creation arises in connection with manpower training programs. The federal government in its manpower training programs has begun to shift emphasis away from numerous small-scale, publicly operated institutional training programs, toward subsidizing large-scale on-the-job training programs with private industry. In effect, federal retailing of training programs proved relatively expensive and ineffective; hence the switch toward wholesale operations. The question arises whether incentive type contracts can be developed, in which private industry is automatically driven toward achieving the kind of results desired by public policy. For example, in training the hard-core unemployed one of the major problems is persistence of effort. Absenteeism is high; motivation is often low; accepting work discipline does not come easy; and all of this is sometimes exacerbated by the hostile attitude of existing employees. To the extent that these obstacles to increasing the employability of the hard-core unemployed can be eliminated with enough time on the job, then program benefits (measured by increases in the long-term employability and productivity of trainees) are not linearly related to hours of on-the-job training. Presumably, up to a point at least, the marginal benefit from on-the-job training rises with length of training.

If subsidy contracts do not recognize this fact, but, for example, treat a half year's training for two men as equivalent to a full year for one man, the program will be less effective than it could be. This argues for incentive contracts—analogous to the incentive contracts in military procurement—under which the return to the contractor depends in part on persistence of effort.

In a similar vein, the government should be interested in the "job mix" into which trainees are placed. If a contractor places all of them in menial and unskilled positions and suffers no monetary penalties, his incentive for testing and motivating trainees is reduced. Again, incentive contracts which include as a performance measure the job content of training positions, might well be devised to overcome the added costs of sophisticated testing and training for higher skills.

I have been able to devise no theoretical framework which could be used to help policymakers determine which kinds of public programs and public objectives lend themselves to the development of new incentives for private actions. The examples given simply show that the range of possible applications is quite wide. I can offer nothing more sophisticated than the proposition that if policymakers are continually aware of the importance and potentialities of the incentive approach, applications will suggest themselves in large number.

C. Improvement of Federal User Charge Policy as a Means of More Efficient Resource Utilization User charges are a special aspect of incentive policy. Most of the potential applications are not new to economists. The use of prices as a rationing device, however, often seems alien to the public policymaker.

One of the most dramatic examples is the current agitation over congestion and delays at major air terminals. It is easy to predict that limited facilities will be rationed by congestion, when the prices charged for facilities are either extremely low (as in the case of general aviation) or unrelated to the degree of congestion. I will not pursue this example in detail, except to note that in the case of air traffic, the administrative problems of levying congestion charges are far less than in the more classic case of highways (despite Professor Vickrey's ingenious suggestions for the application of congestion charges to highways).

There is one major area of federal programs in which user charges might well be profitably employed to change current *political* incentives for the better. At the present time, a large part of federal water resource investment is devoted to projects whose major beneficiaries are identifiable, but who pay little if any of the cost of the projects. In the case of navigation projects, there are no charges levied on the barges which use the waterway. Beneficiaries of federal irrigation and flood control projects typically pay only a small fraction of the cost. Moreover, there is little evidence that the benefits are distributed primarily to lower income groups, and much evidence to the contrary. But the availability of substantial subsidized benefits, primarily available to the "establishment" in the affected communities, sharply increases the political pressure for the authorization of marginal projects, and for the maintenance of very liberal benefit-cost criteria (low interest rates, liberal rules for defining and evaluating benefits, and so forth). Adoption of more stringent rules on user charges would probably reduce sharply the political incentive to maintain uneconomic project evaluation criteria and to lobby for very marginal projects.[13]

We have considered, to this point, the problem of publicly instituted incentives for *private* action. The second major type of incentive problem deals with the provision of incentives for *public* decisionmakers.

Incentives for Public Officials Designed to Improve the Effectiveness or Efficiency with Which Public Programs are Executed

In dealing with large scale programs, top level public executives labor under a major handicap compared to the situation facing their counterparts in large business concerns. Large complicated programs must be carried out by a hierarchy of subordinate officials. Decentralization is necessary. But given the lack of any measurable performance criteria for subordinate officials, the top level public executive is often forced to specify in detail the set of permissible and non-permissible actions of his subordinates. This leads both to excessive rigidity and often to poorly conceived program plans, imposed uniformly from the top on a variety of differing situations.

An analysis of this problem, from the standpoint of creating incentives for decentralized operators to pursue public objectives, suggests two ways of attacking this problem:

- providing market competition for public programs.
- imitating market conditions in public programs.

These approaches may not prove viable in many situations but, at least in selected cases, they may prove very useful in improving the design and execution of public programs.

A. Introduce Market Competition into Decisions about the Production of Public Goods The fact that public programs produce public goods does not imply that they need be completely sheltered from the competition of the marketplace.

Public elementary and secondary education is a case in point. In the inner cities of the nation, the public school system is virtually a complete monopoly, with a captive market, since in practical terms the private school alternative is open to few ghetto residents. Not only is the system a monopoly, but it usually tends to be fairly well isolated from control by the community, except as that control is expressed in overall budget limitations.

Much emphasis has been placed in recent years on educational research, and federal funds have begun to flow into this field. But there is little use in inventing new or more effective approaches to compensatory education if there is no incentive in the various school systems to adopt the more promising changes, and to evaluate alternative educational improvements seeking the most effective. Change in established routines and procedures threatens the security of the existing order, introduces uncertainty and tensions, and is inevitably painful on those who are subject to it. Without strong incentives, therefore, a monopolistic structure is unlikely to be very receptive to innovation.

In recent years a number of proposals have been made, designed to introduce a competitive element into the system, and thereby provide incentives for higher performance. These include the radical proposals of Friedman and Jencks which would in effect completely replace the present public school system with a private competitive model financed indirectly through school support grants made to individual parents. A more moderate suggestion has been made by James Coleman under which school districts would contract out, on bids, for specific parts of the public school curriculum—remedial reading, science courses, etc. A similar suggestion, adapted specifically for neighborhood-controlled school boards, has been proposed by Henry Levin.

The literature on this subject is growing rapidly. And I do not intend to try to summarize it. But analysis and exploration of this approach should not be confined just to the elementary and secondary education systems. Decisions about financing higher education—whether through grants and loans to individual students or through aid to institutions of higher learning—should take into account the incentive effects of the decision. And we can go beyond the field of education. There is no reason why the public health facilities for the poor need be solely run by local or state public health agencies. Cannot private institutions (profit or nonprofit) be allowed to bid for a contract to provide such services?

B. Imitate the Market More Fully in Public Programs This category primarily deals with changes in organizational and budgetary structure designed to provide incentives for public officials to see *efficiency* in the administration of governmental programs.

The recommendations of the President's Commission on Postal Organization are principally directed to this end. Creation of a public corporation, with power (subject to review) to set prices and wages, with authority to borrow from the public for capital investment, and with a directive to cover costs with revenues, would, in effect, make the Post Office an analog to a private utility. While this solution represents no panacea, it is far superior to the present arrangement in which there are few incentives for efficiency, and in which the basic variables of managerial control—prices, wages, investment, location of facilities, etc.—are decided by a 535-man "board of directors" primarily on political grounds.

Other examples, of a less dramatic kind, are not hard to find:

- Federal agencies could be charged in their budgets for the full costs of all the resources they use—rent for building space, full costs of employee retirement benefits, interest on capital equipment used in internal operations, etc. At the present time some resources are free and, therefore, either overused or controlled by arbitrary central regulations.
- Charge federal construction agencies interest on funds during the construction period. In evaluating alternative bids on construction projects, agencies now have no incentive to put any value on time. In addition, use of an interest charge might provide incentives to reduce the seasonality of construction, which in turn should help to moderate the rapid increase in hourly wage costs of construction workers.[14]
- Charge federal agencies for services provided by other agencies. The major case in point is the AEC's nuclear weapons production, which is now transferred to the Defense Department at a zero transfer price. While nuclear weapons costs are given shadow prices in the Defense Department's systems analysis, an actual charge to the DOD budget should strengthen the motivation to consider all costs fully in making decisions. Moreover, by providing the DOD with the funds for nuclear weapons and having them contract for production with the AEC, decisionmaking power would be transferred from the producer to the consumer, avoiding the natural tendency of producer-controlled decisions to result in excessive output.

The suggestions made earlier, to charge the defense budget for subsidy programs primarily justified on national security grounds, is an extension of the "full cost" principle enunciated above. Principal examples are the merchant marine subsidy and the commodity stockpiling program. An even more radical extension would be to charge the defense budget for the economic costs of those "protectionist" programs which are justified on national security grounds, but do not show up as budgetary expenditures. Examples would be oil import quotas and some part of the oil depletion allowance. The likelihood of being able to make these changes, of course, is so low that the suggestion should be treated as an interesting application of the basic principle rather than a serious proposal.

C. The Problem of Additivity and Substitutability in Federal Grant-in-aid and Transfer-in-kind Programs A very particular kind of incentive problem arises in the case of federal grant-in-aid programs, which constitute a very large part of recent federal social legislation. Presumably the purpose of the grant is to increase the resources devoted to a particular objective. (If the purpose of the program were to ease State and local overall financial burdens, revenue sharing or some form of tax credit would be much more appropriate.) But, as a matter of fact, little attention is paid to the problem of whether federal grant funds, designed to achieve a particular purpose, add to the resources currently being spent for that purpose by State and local governments or simply substitute for funds that otherwise would have been spent by those governments.

Various "maintenance of effort" provisions have been written into federal grant programs, but we know little about their effectiveness. In some cases, there may be other approaches to maximizing "additivity." Title I of the Elementary and Secondary Education Act, for example, provides funds to *school districts* to be used for increasing the resources devoted to the education of poor children. But the larger and more diverse the income levels in the school district, the more difficult it is to determine the extent to which federal funds have actually increased resources devoted to the purpose of the program. Allocation of federal funds to units smaller than the school district (neighborhood areas, individual high schools with their associated junior and elementary schools, etc.) might help to increase the additivity of federal funds.

But my point is not so much to describe "solutions" as to point to a major problem. To the extent that the federal grant-in-aid system continues to be the major tool of social legislation, we need to do substantial research on the factors which determine additivity and to experiment with various devices to maximize additivity.

A similar problem arises in the case of federal transfers-in-kind to individuals and institutions. To what extent does the transfer-in-kind increase the consumption of the particular good by the recipient, or merely substitute for funds which otherwise would have been spent on that good, thereby freeing up income for other consumption. More accurately expressed, we need to know the extent to which transfers-in-kind change recipients' consumption patterns from what they would have been if the same resources had been transferred through a cash grant.

Evidence seems to suggest that low income housing subsidies and food stamps do increase recipients' consumption of the goods in question beyond what they would have been under cash grants.[15] But there are other cases which are distinctly questionable. The federal government's college housing program is a case in point. Under this program about $300 million in loans, at 3-percent interest, are made to public and private universities for the construction of college housing. For public universities, who have access to tax-exempt bond financing, the value of the interest subsidy is relatively modest, amounting to about $6 to $7 per month for each student housing in the newly constructed facility. Some 45 to 50 percent of the students at publicly supported universities come from families with incomes of $10,000 or more. Of those who board on campus, the proportion from upper income families is probably higher yet. At these income levels, it is hard to believe that a subsidy of $60 to $70 per year has any significant effect on the quantity or quality of education demanded, although it might have some small impact on the number of those who choose to board rather than commute. In the case of public universities, therefore, the transfer-in-kind probably has little effect in raising the consumption of the particular good, and is, in effect, a disguised *cash* subsidy heavily favoring upper income groups.

More generally, federal grant-in-aid and transfer-in-kind programs need to be reviewed in terms of the additivity question, and techniques devised to maximize incentives for grant recipients to use the funds for the purpose intended.

CONCEPTUAL AND POLITICAL PROBLEMS

The first two sections of this paper concerned themselves with describing and classifying the problem of incentives, first, in terms of the various stages of policymaking and second, in terms of the various types of incentive problems. We now turn our attention to several major problems of concept and political feasibility associated with the use of incentives in public programs.

The Definition and Measurement of Output

There is a major danger associated with the introduction of incentive systems into public programs. In the case of a private good, its various characteristics can be evaluated by the market and reflected in a single measure—*price*. Although buyers are not always perfectly rational, and sometimes lack all the relevant information, in most instances market prices are a reasonably good measure, at the margin, of the value of private output. There is usually no such single measure which commensurates all of the various aspects of the output of a public program—indeed that is why it is a public rather than a private output. The measurement of the output of public programs, therefore, is usually extremely complex. Yet, in devising incentive programs, we must know what is the set of outcomes that we wish to induce. If we are not careful, we may end up producing large unwanted side effects. This was the basic problem of early socialist production systems. The manager of a nail factory, whose quota was set in terms of the *number* of nails, and who was rewarded as he made or exceeded his quota, was inevitably driven to producing large numbers of small nails, regardless of market requirements. With production quotas specified as a certain *weight* of nails, the same manager would necessarily concentrate on producing a smaller number of very heavy nails—again, regardless of market demand.

More to the point, examine the problems of measuring output and defining objectives in a few of the incentive systems used as illustrations earlier in this paper. One suggestion was the establishment of incentive reimbursement schemes for Medicare and Medicaid, designed to induce more efficient design and operation of hospitals. Reimbursement on the basis of regional average cost was suggested, with low cost hospitals retaining some part of their "savings" and high cost hospitals being forced to absorb some fraction of excess costs. The discussion pointed out, however, that we are interested in reducing costs *per unit of output,* not in reducing costs through a sharp deterioration in quality of service rendered. Consequently, any incentive reimbursement scheme must be accompanied by some measure of and control over the quality of output produced. I suggested a possible approach: *first,* research directed toward establishing a usable classification of hospital "outputs," and *second,* the use of peer review panels which would rate hospitals on the basis of these classifications, with the rating results incorporated in the reinbursement formula.

Another example is the use of incentive contracts in federal manpower training programs. Without a careful specification of the multiple objectives sought by the program, an incentive contract might well result in producing one kind of output (e.g. retaining trainees for long periods) at the expense of other aspects of output (e.g. training in a useful skill). A mandatory flood insurance program in which premiums were not reasonably adjusted to risk might increase rather than reduce uneconomic investment in the flood plain. A system of effluent charges on water pollutants, not devised to reflect a reasonable approximation of the costs of pollution, would result in either too much or too little effort being devoted to removing pollution and too much or too little industrial relocation. Introducing competition into the public school system (e.g. by allowing specific types of services to be contracted out to private bidders) may produce little of value unless there is some means of evaluating the various bids and some method of measuring performance.

In short, the use of incentive systems puts a premium on the careful specification of objectives and output. This is both an advantage and a disadvantage. An advantage because it forces program designers to be more specific in their statement of objectives and in the relative weights they attach to various aspects of output.[16] A disadvantage, because we often are literally unable, given the present state of knowledge, to specify objectives and assign weights to various aspects of performance with sufficient confidence to warrant the introduction of incentive systems.

What all of this suggests is that the introduction of incentives into public programs calls for two things: *first,* extensive experimental projects, testing various alternative incentive schemes; and *second,* substantially increased research in the area of specifying and measuring output.

Incentives to Institutions and Incentives to Individuals

Many of the examples suggested in this paper, particularly those related to the provision of incentives for *public* action, take the form of incentives to institutions: the inclusion of all relevant costs in agency budgets so they do not have access to "free" resources; incentive reimbursement for hospitals; reorganization of the Post Office, et cetera. But if decisionmakers in these institutions are not themselves judged and "rewarded" on the basis of criteria which are consistent with the incentives provided the institution, then little good will come of incentives to institutions: the inclusion of all relevant costs in the budget of an agency or an installation is to present the decisionmaker with the full costs of his decision. If he is interested in minimizing costs, he will presumably seek the lowest cost resource mix. But if he has no interest in cost minimization, then we should expect no results from the full cost approach.

It has been suggested that incentive reimbursement for most hospitals will accomplish little. Most hospitals are really run by the staff physicians, who are reputed to have little concern for the financial condition of the hospital itself.[17] To the extent this is true, then incentive reimbursement will not be very effective in lowering costs. Introducing competition into the public school system may change performance very little if the individual decisionmakers, who let the contracts and evaluate performance themselves, have no incentives to seek significant changes and improvements in the school system.

In one sense, these considerations suggest the obvious: that incentives for more effective and efficient performance of public programs cannot be considered apart from the structure of motivations, rewards, and penalties which determine the attitudes and actions of the bureaucracy. To the extent that public employees are themselves judged and "rewarded" by criteria which relate to the effectiveness and efficiency rather than to the mere size of the programs under their control, individual and institutional incentives can be made consistent.

Political Problems in Regional Budgeting

In an earlier section of this paper, I pointed out that purely functional planning and budgeting by the federal government provides little or no scope for the consideration of tradeoffs among alternative federal investments or projects at the local level. I then suggested that some form of regional budgeting, as an adjunct to functional budgeting, might serve this purpose, providing a framework within which bargaining about meaningful choices might take place.

As soon as one begins to consider specific means of carrying out this proposal, one major problem emerges. A complete regionalization of the budget allocation process would surely lead to major power struggles among the various states, regions, and cities over the division of the budgetary pie. The current struggle over functional budgetary shares is widely diffused among a constantly changing set of alliances and factions. No congressman or senator need have his entire constituency at stake in any one functional budget decision. The divisiveness of the conflict is muted because of its complexity. But with purely regional budgets, the struggle would be etched in sharp outline, and the regional allocation of a given budget total would be a zero sum game to the participants.

To derive some of the advantages from regional budgets, however, it is not necessary to construct the "pure" model whose consequences were sketched above. There are a number of ways in which a partially regional approach might be grafted onto the existing process:

A. There are in existence at the present time five federally sponsored regional development commissions. The commissions are composed of the governors of the affected states and a federal representative. Except for the Appalachian Regional Commission, the commissions are still in relatively embryonic form. Rather than become vehicles to lobby for "special" federal authorizations and appropriations, the commissions might be organized to participate in the budgetary planning and allocation of those federal projects which have special relevance for the economic development of the region: water resource projects, highways, economic development assistance, pollution control facilities, and so forth. The commissions could draw up several investment budgets—representing alternative overall constraint levels. These recommendations could then be used as guides in the formulation of the relevant nationwide functional budgets.

B. Functional budgets could be formulated, proposed to the Congress, and appropriated as is now done. In turn, for a selected number of investment and project-type programs[18] the relevant agencies could make allocations to major cities, or metropolitan areas.[19] Those functional allocations could be combined into consolidated budgets for each such area. In turn, the mayor (or a council of chief executives in a metropolitan area) could be given authority to reallocate funds, within prescribed limits, among the functional components. Constraints of various kinds could be imposed—for example, certain minimum sums for particular functions. Depending upon the nature of the project involved, the reallocation might be subject to joint approval by the local chief executive and the governor. Individual projects or grants would still have to be approved in terms of the relevant statutory and administrative requirements.

Several facets of this last suggestion deserve mention. First, it would substantially mute the regional battle over "shares," since the determination of those shares would depend on a complex set of functional decisions and a host of separate regional allocations. Second, it would retain in federal hands the authority to approve individual grants as a means of carrying out national objectives in a local context (for example, Model City grants would still be subject to the requirement of neighborhood participation in decisionmaking, hospital grants would be subject to minimum standards and planning requirements, et cetera). Yet, at the same time, it would transfer to state and local hands some additional authority over budget allocation—that is, authority to determine marginal trade-offs. The *composition* of the local budget would be less completely dictated by federal budgetary decisions than is now the case. Finally, it would tend to transfer power from local department bureaucracies to state and local chief executives. Under today's purely functional budgeting, bureaucracy deals with bureaucracy—the Federal Public Health Service with its state counterpart, the Office of Education with state departments of education, and so forth. These relationships, coupled with the rapid growth of categorical federal grant-in-aid programs, have tended to take a large part of the power over budget allocation out of the hands of state and local chief executives. Introducing some elements of regional budgeting into the federal structure might help to strengthen the central authority and planning capability of state and local chief executives, while retaining in federal hands sufficient control over the use of funds to accomplish basic national goals expressed in functional terms. One final point on this matter. Any move toward "regionalizing" parts of the federal budget will surely be vigorously resisted by many members of Congress. Regionalization transfers some of the power over budget allocation from congressional subcommittees to governors and mayors. Decentralization of power from the executive branch to state and local governments is one thing—presumably a good highly to be desired. Decentralization of congressional de facto powers is quite another matter.

I cannot pretend to have thought through the full consequences of budget regionalization. I am sure that as any particular proposal is worked out in detail, important difficulties and problems will be uncovered. But I believe that the basic concept of budget regionalization warrants further exploration, as a means of changing political incentives and motivations in the direction of making better allocation decisions at the local level among alternative federal investment programs.

NOTES

[1] This paper does not, except peripherally, deal with public regulatory policies, where questions of incentives also arise.

[2] *A Unified National Program for Managing Flood Losses,* a report by the Task Force on Federal Flood Control Policy. (Printed by the U.S. Congress, Senate Committee on Public Works, Aug. 10, 1966), p. 11.

[3] *Ibid.,* page 12.

[4] See footnote 13.

[5] The tax treatment of depreciation on buildings complicates matters, but does not invalidate the basic proposition. In fact the particular rules relating to the tax treatment of existing buildings compared to the treatment of major improvements tends to discriminate in favor of the former and against the latter. See Richard E. Slitor, *Tax Approaches to Low Income Housing Problems:* A study prepared for the National Commission on Urban Problems.

[6] *Secretary's Advisory Committee on Hospital Effectiveness, Report.* U.S. Department of Health, Education, and Welfare, 1967, p. 10.

[7] Derived from data in the *Report of the National Advisory Commission on Health Manpower,* U.S. Government Printing Office, November 1967, app. I, table 4. The per capita increase in average daily hospital beds used (11 percent) was combined with the increase in the deflated value of service per patient day to arrive at the 47-percent figure used in the text.

[8] *National Advisory Committee on Health Manpower, Report,* vol. 1, p. 68.

[9] All of these data are cited in vol. I of the *Report of the National Advisory Commission on Health Manpower,* p. 55.

[10] Cited in Herman M. Somers and Anne R. Somers, *Medicare and the Hospitals* (Washington, D.C.: The Brookings Institution, 1967).

[11] *Report, op. cit.,* vol. I, pp. 46–48.

[12] Anthony Downs, "Moving Towards Realistic Housing Goals," in *Agenda for the Nation* (Washington, D.C.: The Brookings Institution, 1968).

[13] I am aware, of course, that where projects have declining average costs, marginal cost pricing rules may dictate low user charges. Yet I am convinced that the resultant shortrun allocational efficiency is often far outweighed by the lack of investment signals and the political incentives for poor project selection that large project subsidies entail.

[14] I owe this suggestion to Professor David Martin of Indiana University.

[15] In the case of food stamps, additivity arises from the fact that recipients are required to purchase the stamps at an aggregate cost which equals what they had previously been spending on food. Barring a black market on stamps, this should guarantee additivity.

[16] The introduction of incentive contracting into DOD and NASA had the side advantage of forcing decisionmakers to make explicit judgments about tradeoffs among various aspects of contractor performance—promptness of delivery, operating characteristics, costs, etc.

[17] Personally, I do not put much store by this argument. Under incentive reimbursement schemes, continually inefficient hospitals will eventually be squeezed out of existence. And to say that those who make hospital decisions are not overly concerned about the financial condition of the hospital does not square with the vigorous efforts of the American Hospital Association to obtain more favorable reimbursement formulas from Medicare and Medicaid.

[18] That is, "project" as opposed to "formula" grants.

[19] Agencies, in effect, make such allocations now, as they approve individual projects or grants. Under the proposed scheme, they would have to "budget" for such allocations in advance.

CHAPTER 7

A MODEL OF PUBLIC DECISIONS ILLUSTRATED BY A WATER POLLUTION POLICY PROBLEM

Robert Dorfman and Henry D. Jacoby

Merely corroborative detail, intended to give artistic verisimilitude to an otherwise bald and unconvincing narrative.

—W. S. Gilbert

INTRODUCTION

Governmental decisions may be approached from either a normative or a descriptive point of view. The normative approach accepts well-defined objectives for governmental undertakings and recommends specific policies and actions for attaining them. It will not be followed here. The descriptive approach accepts the facts of life, including the nature of governmental agencies and the purposes of diverse interest groups in the community, and attempts to provide insight into what will happen in the circumstances. That will be our approach.

Our method will be to construct a mathematical model of a political decision problem. The model will contain room for a great many data, ranging from the technological features of the problem that technical experts have to take into account, to the political objectives and pressures that responsible officials have to evaluate. One of the advantages that we claim for the model, indeed, is that it provides a systematic framework for assembling such diverse data.

From these data the model will produce, mechanically, some predictions about the outcome of the political decision process. These will not be unambiguous predictions like an astronomer's prediction of the moment that an eclipse will take place. Rather, they will take the form of stating a range of likely outcomes of the process, perhaps a fairly wide range but still

This paper is based upon a chapter in Robert Dorfman, Henry D. Jacoby, Harold A. Thomas, Jr., et al., *Models for Water Quality Management,* now in preparation. The work has been financed by grants from Resources for the Future and from the Federal Water Pollution Control Administration. The responsibility for all opinions expressed in this paper lies entirely with the authors.

much more limited than all the decisions that might be conceived of in advance. The power of a scientific theory, it has been said, is measured not by what it asserts but by what it precludes. This theory will preclude a great deal. Within the range of likely outcomes the theory (or model) will provide some valuable information. It will highlight the political alignments that make some of the outcomes more likely than others and will indicate, rather specifically, the changes in the configuration of political influence that will tend to shift the decision from one outcome to another. Furthermore, it will express vividly just how interests oppose and how different decisions affect the welfares of different participants.

Concede, for the moment, that such a model is possible. Whether this is so or not is for the sequel to determine. Then, surely, the practice of politics should take it into account. (Note that we are being normative temporarily.) Any political decision should be made in the light of a realistic assessment of its consequences, which requires a prediction of how things, people, and political bodies will react to it. In the case of water pollution control, for example, the federal government's policies are implemented by the states and by river basin commissions; the states and river basin commissions work through local agencies and authorities, individuals, and business firms. Any decision at the federal level has to be based on a prediction about how the states and basin commissions will respond to it; the states and basin authorities must similarly predict the reactions of subordinate units and of the public at large. Many other programs of federal and state agencies are similarly affected by the responses of other governmental bodies. All legislation that concerns the powers and composition of government agencies is influenced by predictions of how those provisions will influence the behavior of the agency. In short, a predictive model of political behavior can help improve political decisions.

Constructing a predictive model of political decision processes is an ambitious, indeed presumptuous, undertaking. In fact, there is such good reason to believe that it cannot be done that we have construed our main task to be to convince ourselves and the reader that it is possible. Our method of proof is what mathematicians call "constructive." That is, rather than arguing the matter in the abstract we have considered a political decision problem taken from the field of water pollution control (not a real problem, but one that catches the essence of real problems) and have constructed a theoretical model that predicts the outcome of the political decision process in that instance. This construction shows that such a model is a possibility and exhibits its main features. It does not show that this model is a practical tool of political analysis. That showing would be a major research undertaking. In order to show that this political model or any political model is empirically valid it would be necessary to apply it to several real political decisions and to compare its predictions with the observed political behavior. This would be a laborious and expensive task for it would necessitate ascertaining all the physical, technical, economic, and political data that the model requires and then performing elaborate computations. We have not undertaken this mammoth empirical enterprise (and not merely out of laziness). This large task is not worth undertaking unless the analytic model to be tested shows at least fair promise of success. A necessary preliminary to serious empirical testing is trial experimentation under favorable circumstances to see whether the model can be implemented in principle and whether it behaves sensibly. If the model passes the preliminary screening, then it pays to go further with it. This chapter reports on such a preliminary testing of our conceptual model of political decision. To carry out this test we have conceived an artificial basin with a pollution problem, known as the Bow River Valley. It is small, it is simple; but it could exist in the sense that it does not violate any known principles of hydrology, sanitary engineering, economics, or politics. We have populated this valley with a large industrial source of pollution, two moderate-sized cities and a recreation area, and placed it under the jurisdiction of a pollution control commission organized under the Clean Water Restoration Act of 1966. We have provided everyone concerned with such data and information as he might actually have under the circumstances and no more.[1] We have simplified the problem by suppressing much detail that would obscure the essential conflicts and issues that would arise. For example, we have reduced the specification of water quality to a single dimension, namely dissolved oxygen concentration (DO), and we have limited our description of the waste content of the various municipal and industrial effluents to the number of pounds of biochemical oxygen demanding material (BOD) that they carry.[2] In addition, we have limited the powers of the regulatory authority essentially to a single decision, namely, regulation of level of treatment by each polluter. We have ignored hydrologic uncertainty and other probabilistic complications and have made any number of simplifying approximations to facilitate computation. In short, we have loaded the dice heavily in favor of the model, as is perhaps appropriate for a preliminary test. The question is: can this problem be expressed by a formal analytic model, and if so, does the model provide sensible and useful insights?

THE TEST PROBLEM

The situation which we shall use to try out our conceptual scheme is sketched in Figure 1.[3] As can be seen, the Bow River flows generally from north to south. It is a respectable stream with a flow of 800 cfs during the summer months. But it is not a very high quality stream. Because of the residual waste from upstream cities, the river, as it passes under the Gordon

Bridge, has a dissolved oxygen concentration of only 6.8 milligrams per liter (mg/*l*). Without the influence of effluent discharges upstream, one could expect the level of oxygen in the water to be near saturation (8.5 mg/*l* at summer water temperatures).

The northernmost installation in the region under consideration is the Pierce-Hall Cannery. This is a large but somewhat outmoded vegetable cannery with an annual production of slightly over 7 million equivalent cases a year, concentrated in the summer and autumn months. The cannery

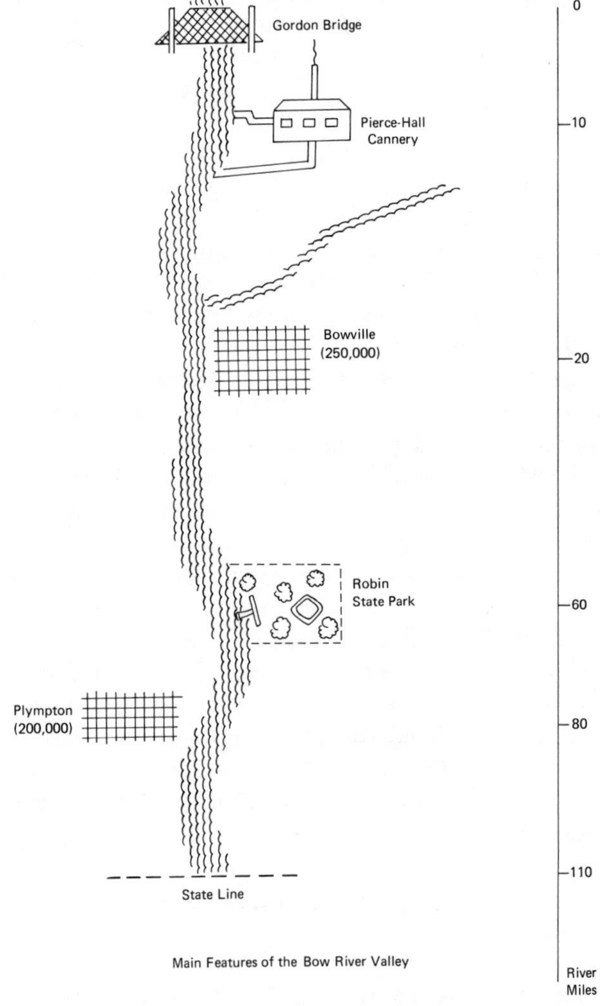

Figure 1
Main Features of the Bow River Valley

adds an ultimate BOD load of about one pound per case to the river, after primary treatment, to which it is already committed. The cannery is not very profitable. Its net operating revenues, allowing for the cost of primary waste treatment, are only about 7.5 percent of stockholders' equity. It employs about 800 workers, many of whom live in Bowville (pop. 250,000), ten miles downstream.

Bowville and the other riparian city, Plympton (pop. 200,000), are both fairly large centers supported by varied light manufacturing and commercial establishments serving the surrounding agricultural region. Both have waterfront parks of which they are proud, and Plympton in particular has some aspirations to being a tourist center because of its proximity to Robin State Park. Both cities discharge their wastes into the river after primary treatment. For simplicity, we shall assume that neither city anticipates that its population or its waste load will grow significantly in the foreseeable future. This simplification will save us from having to forecast growth rates and from having to consider the possibility of "building ahead of demand." In fact, it enables us to neglect all dynamic considerations.

Robin State Park, between Bowville and Plympton, has woodland recreational facilities. All concerned would like to develop its waterfront for boating, fishing, and if at all possible, swimming. The quality of the water does not permit those uses at present. The park is used by the inhabitants of both cities, by the neighboring farm population, and by some tourists and day-trippers from outside the valley. Everyone is agreed that the quality of the water in the neighborhood of the park should be improved.

Thirty miles below Plympton the river crosses a state line and flows out of our ken.

The current quality of the stream at critical points under low-flow conditions is shown in Figure 2. From just below Bowville down to the state line, water quality is very poor during summer droughts. For long stretches the river is anaerobic (i.e., the DO level falls to zero), and it is unfit for recreational or other use. In response to a generally felt need to improve the river, especially near the park, and in response to some pressure from the State Water Commission, the Bow Valley Water Pollution Control Commission has been established, with the editor of the *Bow Valley News* as chairman and membership drawn from the city councils of both cities and including the Deputy State Commissioner of Parks and Recreation.

The commission faces two crucial problems. The first is to determine the quality classification of the river which, for political reasons, must be the same from the Gordon Bridge to the state line.[4] The second problem is

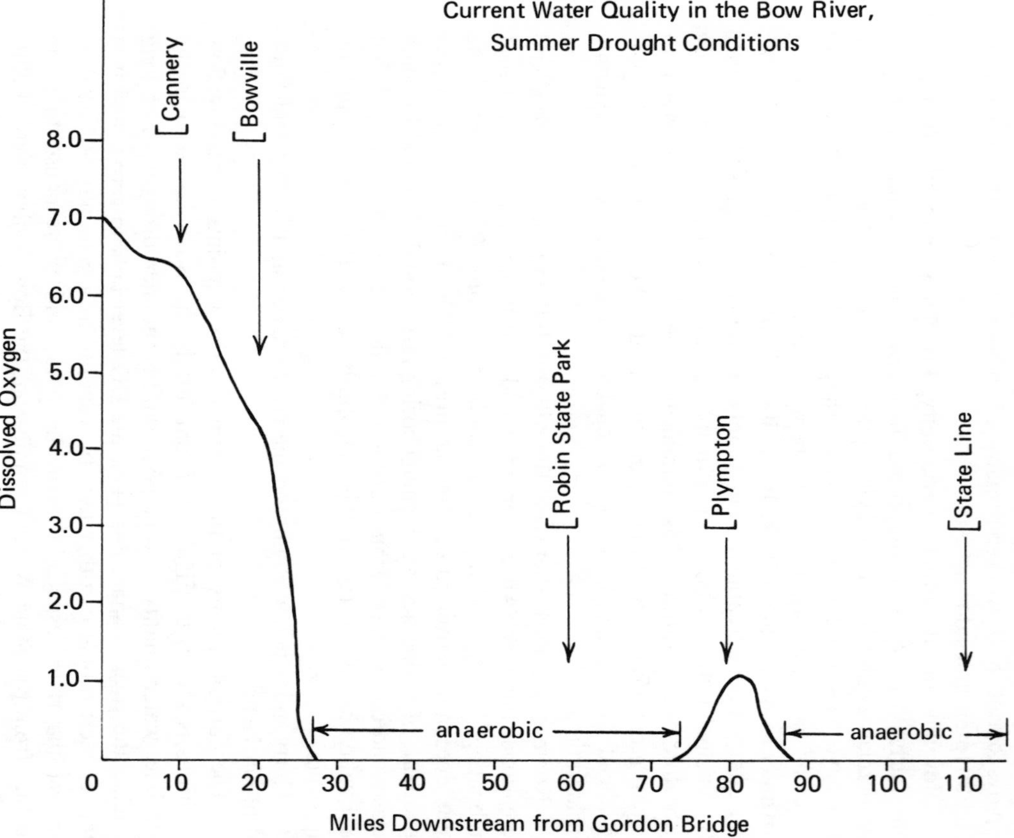

Figure 2. Current Water Quality in the Bow River, Summer Drought Conditions

to decide on the levels of treatment to be required of the three sources of waste within its jurisdiction. The cost of the improvement in quality to each of the polluters is simply the cost of the treatment required of him. Each polluter would therefore like to have a low treatment requirement for himself, but sufficiently high ones for the others to permit the achievement of the quality standards for the stream classification that has been adopted. The standards are expressed entirely in terms of dissolved oxygen levels.

Such are the decisions that we must analyze. But before considering how the commission as a body will act, we must see in more detail how the problem looks from the point of view of each of the interested parties.

The Pierce-Hall Cannery The Pierce-Hall Cannery, located just ten miles upstream from Bowville, is a relatively large installation compared to other plants of this type around the country: over the course of the 180-day canning season the plant handles approximately 40,000 case equivalents per day of a variety of fruits and vegetables. Most years gross sales amount to around $25 million.

In response to mounting public concern for water quality, the plant managers already have identified and incorporated some internal process changes in order to reduce effluent volume and cut back on biological pollutants discharged into the Bow River, and they have installed primary treatment facilities in the form of screening and sedimentation equipment. Even after these changes, however, when the plant is in full operation it discharges a waste stream of approximately 30 million gallons per day (mgd) which carries an ultimate biochemical oxygen demand of 47,600 pounds per day.[5]

In order to reduce these waste flows further, Pierce-Hall would have to install additional treatment facilities, and the plant manager has already obtained preliminary estimates of the cost of different degrees of improvement in effluent quality. These estimates are shown in Table 1.

As the table shows, 30 percent of the BOD in the Pierce-Hall effluent is removed in the firm's primary treatment plant. To accomplish higher levels of BOD removal, the waste stream would be passed through a tank where biological degradation—which in the absence of treatment would occur in the stream itself—can take place under controlled conditions. The degree of purification can be varied over a wide range by proper design of the plant. High degrees of BOD removal are naturally more expensive than low.

From the wide range of possible choices, the engineering consultants to Pierce-Hall have provided two alternative secondary treatment plant designs. The first, referred to rather loosely as a "low-efficiency secondary" plant, would bring the total removal up to 80 percent of the original load. The total cost for the low-efficiency unit would be $13,000 per year as

Table 1

Cost of Additional Waste Treatment at Pierce-Hall Cannery

Type of Treatment	Percent[a] of BOD Removed	Additional Annual Cost ($/yr)	Additional Net Cost to Pierce-Hall ($/yr)	Additional Cost to Pierce-Hall Per % removed ($/yr/%)	Profit After Taxes ($/yr)
Primary (now in place)	30	0	0	0	375,000
Primary *plus* Low Efficiency Secondary	80	13,000	8,000	160	367,000
Primary *plus* High Efficiency Secondary	90	59,000	35,000	2,700	340,000
Primary *plus* High Efficiency Secondary *plus* Tertiary	95	159,000	95,000	12,000	280,000

[a] The figures shown are percentages of the *gross* waste load.

shown in the second column of Table 1. The second design, referred to (again rather loosely) as a "high-efficiency secondary" unit, would accomplish a greater total waste removal, 90 percent. The cost, however, is considerably greater as shown in column two of the table.

If it is necessary to subject the effluent from a high-efficiency plant to still further treatment, there is yet another set of processes, generally referred to as "tertiary treatment," which may be used. In effect, tertiary treatment is any process which reduces the waste contained in the effluent of a secondary unit, by such diverse and expensive methods as holding in stabilization ponds and adding special chemicals. One such design has been provided by Pierce-Hall's consultants. It would remove up to 95 percent of the firm's biochemical wastes. As may be seen in Table 1, tertiary treatment costs considerably more than "secondary" processes.

Of course, the plants shown in Table 1 are only three of an infinite number of alternative designs. The curvilinear cost function in Figure 3 indicates the actual range of alternatives, with additional treatment cost stated as a function of the percentage removal of BOD from the gross waste load. Because the cannery already has primary treatment facilities, the zero point on the cost curve is at the 30 percent removal level. Since the data are so limited, we shall interpolate linearly between the data points provided by the consultants to estimate the cost of levels of removal other than 80, 90, and 95 percent. The resulting piecewise linear cost function is shown as a dashed line in the figure. For example, Figure 3 shows that a plant that brings total BOD removal up to 60 percent of the gross waste load would cost $7,800 per year.[6]

The net cost of waste treatment to Pierce-Hall is lower than this total cost because of the provisions of the corporation income tax code. Pierce-Hall's accountants have estimated that the net cost to the firm would be 6/10 of the total cost, and this latter figure is shown in the third column of the table. Column four presents the same information, expressed in terms of the net cost of each additional percent of waste removed from the plant's effluent. Thus, the figures in column four are the slopes of the piecewise linear cost function as sensed by Pierce-Hall management.

The firm's net operating revenues, after income taxes, are 1.5 percent of gross sales when primary treatment only is employed. This net profit amounts to approximately $375,000 a year, which is equivalent to 7.5 percent of the stockholders' equity. The firm is not a price leader and does not anticipate that it will be able to raise its prices appreciably even if a large increase in treatment costs is imposed. Neither does it know of any changes in its methods of processing that would enable it to reduce its waste load at the current scale of operations. Therefore any increase in treatment costs would have to come out of net profits. The estimated

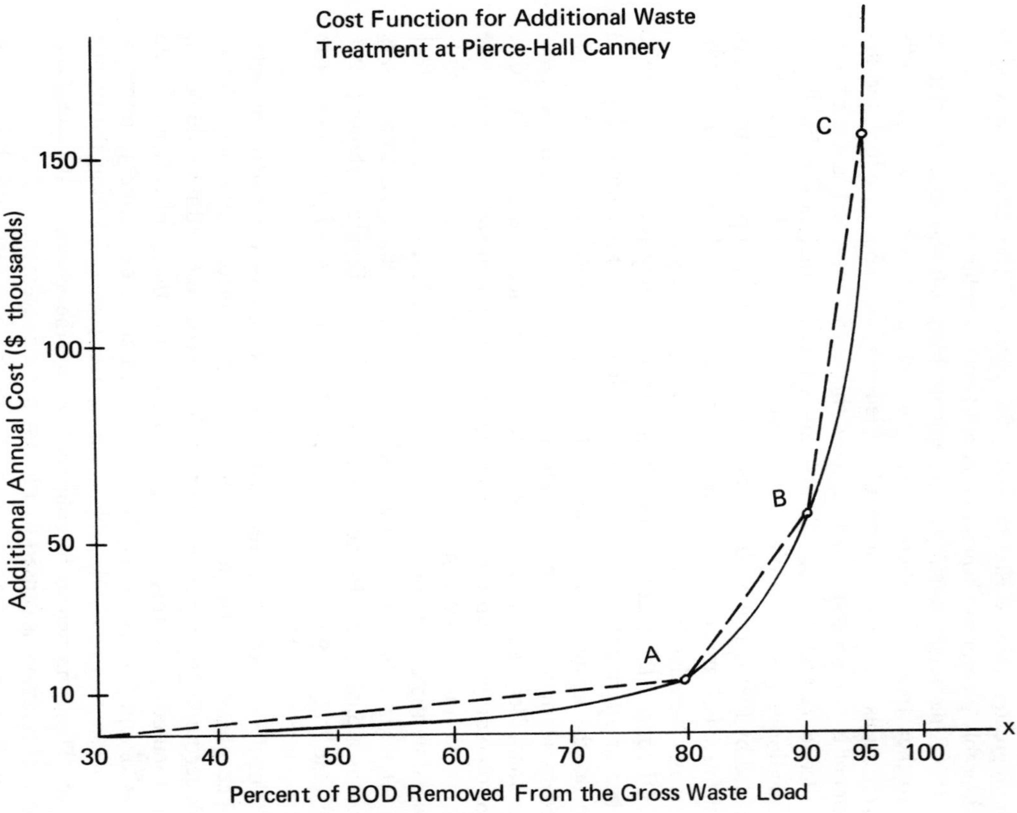

Figure 3
Cost Function for Additional Waste Treatment at Pierce-Hall Cannery

impact of different levels of treatment on net profits is also shown in Table 1. Notice that the effect is appreciable; the highest level of treatment would reduce annual profits by over 25 percent.

On the other hand, the management of Pierce-Hall is not adamantly opposed to improving the quality of the Bow River, even at some cost to themselves. As the major industrial polluter in this reach of the river, they recognize that they have some responsibility to users and inhabitants farther downstream. Besides, many of their employees live in Bowville and make use of Robin Park, so that improvement of the river will enhance the amenities available to the plant's workforce. Finally, the firm has some tentative plans for expanding by constructing a more modern plant on a site near Plympton. The efficiency of the branch plant would be greatly increased if the river near Plympton were of good enough quality to be tapped for washing water, which it is not at present. But the management also keeps in mind that it will not be able to raise the capital necessary for expansion if the return on the present equity falls below about 6 percent.

In short, the position of the Pierce-Hall management is a bit complicated. The prospect of improving the quality of the river is both a threat and an opportunity. They would like to see the river improved but do not feel that they can afford to contribute very much toward bringing improvement about.

Bowville The city of Bowville, ten miles downstream from the cannery, is the second major source of pollution in the valley. The city receives better quality water than her downstream neighbors. According to the data in Figure 2, Bowville escapes the real pollution problems even during severe summer droughts. But the 250,000 inhabitants plus assorted light industries dump a heavy load of wastes into the river. Even after primary treatment, Bowville discharges 123,000 pounds of ultimate BOD into the river on an average summer day. The total volume of effluent discharged is about 51 mgd. This load, added to the cannery wastes, renders the river unsuitable for recreational use farther downstream.

In anticipation of the prospective discussions of pollution management in the valley, the mayor of Bowville requested his public works department to prepare estimates of what it would cost the city to install additional treatment facilities. Like the cannery, cost estimates were made for three different treatment plant designs, each removing a certain percentage of oxygen demanding wastes. These estimates are shown in Table 2.

Bowville would not have to bear the total cost of additional treatment unaided. Under the provisions of the Federal Water Pollution Control Act, Bowville could count on a federal grant in the amount of 50 percent of the construction cost of these facilities, and since capital cost is about half the total cost of waste treatment in this case, the citizens and local industries

Table 2
Cost of Additional Waste Treatment at Bowville

Type of Treatment	Percent[a] of BOD Removed	Additional Annual Cost ($/yr)	Additional Cost to City ($/yr)	Additional Cost to City Per % removed ($/yr/%)	Addition to Property Tax Rate ($/thousand)
Primary (now in place)	30	0	0	0	0
Primary *plus* Low Efficiency Secondary	80	650,000	490,000	9,800	1.17
Primary *plus* High Efficiency Secondary	90	880,000	660,000	17,000	1.58
Primary *plus* High Efficiency Secondary *plus* Tertiary	95	2,520,000	1,890,000	246,000	4.52

[a] The figures shown are percentages of the *gross* waste load.

would have to bear only about 75 percent of the total outlay. The adjusted costs are shown in the third column of Table 2. All these costs are based on the assumption of a twenty-year life of facilities and a 5 percent interest rate. As was true for the cannery, both the total costs of different degrees of waste removal and the net costs to the city can be approximated by segmented linear cost curves of the type shown in Figure 3.

Table 2 shows also the estimated effect of the different levels of treatment on the property tax rate. These data are of particular interest to city officials and taxpayers. It is seen that the adoption of either high or low-efficiency secondary treatment would have only a moderate effect on the property tax rate. (It is now $63.50 per thousand assessed valuation.) Tertiary treatment is far more expensive and the city comptroller has expressed some alarm that it might be adopted. He points out that tax rates are bound to rise in any event, because of recent increases in teachers' and firemen's salaries, and that they are already higher than tax rates in Plympton, which competes with Bowville for new industries.[7]

It appears that Bowville would gain only moderately from improvement in the quality of the Bow River. Bowville waterfront park is already a fine facility, although under extreme drought conditions the beach must be closed to swimming. If the river were cleaned up, these incidents could be avoided. In addition, the entire valley would be made more attractive to tourists and vacationers and, if the improvement were sufficient to permit the development of water-based recreation at Robin State Park, the park would become far more useful to inhabitants of the city. This latter consideration is important. Bowville Waterfront Park is already so overcrowded that some thought has been given to condemning some adjacent warehouses in order to expand it. This would not be necessary if any substantial proportion of the users could be diverted to the state park.

Besides, the *Bow River News* has been running editorials like, "Restore the Bow River!" and, after droughts, "The Shame of Bow River Valley." So there is considerable pressure on Bowville to contribute its share to improving the river, provided that the cost is reasonable.

Plympton The difference between Plympton and Bowville is the difference between upstream and downstream riparian residents everywhere. Bowville has good water in all but the worst drought years; Plympton experiences poor river quality conditions almost every summer. Bowville's wastes degrade the river for most of the distance that concerns us, including the waterfront at Plympton; Plympton's wastes discommode no one, affecting only the quality checkpoint at the southern outlet of the valley. Bowville can improve the quality of the river by subjecting its wastes to a higher level of treatment; Plympton is virtually helpless—it cannot even protect its own waterfront. The stage is set for the classic conflict between upstream and downstream users.

Plympton is slightly smaller than Bowville and generally less affluent. It also has a primary treatment plant. Its effluent volume is 43 mgd, containing after primary treatment 92,400 pounds of ultimate BOD.

Although Plympton has, in fact, little effect on the quality of the river in the region that concerns us, it must expect to bear its share of responsibility for cleaning up the river. Indeed, since the inhabitants of Plympton will be the major direct beneficiaries of improved quality in the river, this city is particularly eager to contribute what it can and put pressure on the more consequential users upstream. The cost data for treatment at Plympton are shown in Table 3, and these also can be expressed as a cost function of the type shown in Figure 3. If you compare these data with the cost table for Bowville, you will see that the dollars-and-cents cost of each level of treatment are lower for Plympton, because it is a smaller city, but the effect on the tax rate is greater. This is because Plympton is a poorer city and the value of taxable property per capita is lower there. Fiscal problems are generally harder for Plympton than for Bowville.

It is true, nevertheless, that Plympton is more eager to participate in a program of river quality improvement than Bowville is. They would like to develop recreational facilities on their own waterfront, which does not now conform to sanitary standards and is occasionally beset by riverine odors. They are more dependent than Bowville on tourism and are closer to the park. For all these reasons, the Plympton Chamber of Commerce is one of the leaders in the movement for improving the river.

Other Interested Parties The cannery and the two cities are the principal defilers of the river and represent the interests of most of the people who are directly concerned. But there are other interests too, which have to be taken into account and which are likely to have considerable influence on any decisions about the river.

First, there is the federal government, which has an expressed interest in protecting and improving the quality of all interstate waters, including the Bow. This national interest is implemented by the Federal Water Pollution Control Administration. The FWPCA administers the grant and incentive programs established under federal water quality legislation, and it can be expected to contribute generously to meeting the costs of increased levels of waste treatment undertaken by the two municipalities. The FWPCA also has some enforcement powers.

The FWPCA's interest in the particular decision taken by the commission is twofold. First, it is responsible for protecting the interests of all users farther downstream, so that it feels compelled to, and is empowered to, insist on a reasonable quality of water at the southern outlet from the

Table 3
Cost of Additional Waste Treatment at Plympton

Type of Treatment	Percent[a] of BOD Removed	Additional Annual Cost ($/yr)	Additional Cost to City ($/yr)	Additional Cost to City Per % removed ($/yr/%)	Addition to Property Tax Rate ($/thousand)
Primary (now in place)	30	0	0	0	0
Primary *plus* Low Efficiency Secondary	80	550,000	410,000	8,200	1.37
Primary *plus* High Efficiency Secondary	90	730,000	550,000	14,000	1.83
Primary *plus* High Efficiency Secondary *plus* Tertiary	95	2,110,000	1,580,000	206,000	5.27

[a] The figures shown are percentages of the *gross* waste load.

valley. Specifically, the FWPCA has required that the river should meet Class C standards (as described below) at the state line. It should be noted that the FWPCA is the only participant with a direct concern for the quality of the water so far south. Second, the FWPCA has a generalized interest in the quality of American streams and in protecting our natural heritage, and thus will share the desires of the inhabitants of Bowville and Plympton for the quality of their waters and for the waterfront potential of the state park. It will, however, be less worried about the effect of increased treatment costs on local tax rates and more concerned with the national economic costs which different plans will imply. On balance, we can expect that the FWPCA will attempt to induce the commission to undertake a combination of stream classification and treatment requirements that will yield the maximum benefit-cost ratio from a national point of view—taking into account the economic cost of abatement measures and the national economic and social benefits of different degrees of improvement in stream quality.

The state government is also concerned, particularly through the State Water and Sanitation Commission, and the State Department of Parks and Recreation. The State Industrial Commission may take a hand, however, if the financial health of the cannery should be jeopardized by any proposal. On balance, the influence of the state agencies can be expected to be similar to that of the FWPCA except that the state will attach more importance to the quality of the water at Robin State Park and less to the quality at the state line.

There are, in addition, a variety of conservation and special interest groups, perhaps typified by a branch of the Izaak Walton League. Although they have little voting power, these groups make their influence felt through all the media of public communications, through any hearings or investigative procedures of the Bow Valley Water Pollution Control Commission, through participation in municipal politics, and even through direct representation on the commission.

All the groups mentioned in this subsection share a more keenly felt concern for the quality and usability of the river than for the cost of achieving high quality. For the purposes of our discussion, we shall lump them together and consider them to be represented adequately by the FWPCA.

Water Quality Standards The first task before the Bow Valley Water Pollution Control Commission is to adopt a stream-use classification for the Bow River between Bowville and the southern outlet at the state line. The State Water and Sanitation Commission has promulgated a set of standards that prescribe the quality of water to be used for different purposes. Once the commission has adopted a use classification, all its subsequent regulations must conform to it; that is, they must be designed to assure water of quality at least as good as that specified in the state standard for water in the use class that has been adopted.

In actual practice stream standards cover many stream characteristics —dissolved oxygen, floating solids, color and turbidity, coliform bacteria, taste and odor, temperature, pH, radioactivity, and others. For simplicity of exposition and analysis, however, we shall pretend that the state standard specifies only one dimension of stream quality, namely instream dissolved oxygen.[8]

The state water standards are accordingly assumed to divide streams into five use classes: A, B, C, D, and U. Class A waters are very nearly in their pristine state—almost unaffected by man. Waters classified U are essentially uninhabitable for fish life, unsuitable for most recreational activities, and offensive to the sight, taste, and smell. Classes B, C, and D identify intermediate conditions of quality, and associated with each is a specified level of stream use. The state standards[9] are specified in Table 4.

These standards must be met under the average minimum consecutive 7-day flow to be expected once in ten years: for the Bow River, this flow is 800 cfs. Under these low-flow conditions, the entire river below Bowville currently is below the quality specified for Class D waters: indeed, as shown in Figure 2, in many parts of the valley the stream goes anaerobic and is occasionally rather unpleasant to be near.

It should be noted that the imposition of defined standards of quality, which is almost inevitable in framing administrative regulations,[10] transforms the decision problem in a fundamental way. In the absence of codified classifications, a DO concentration of 5.1 mg/*l* will be recognized as only imperceptibly safer and more pleasant for swimming than one of 4.9 mg/*l*. But once the higher concentration qualifies the river for a higher use classification, there is all the difference in the world between them—one permits the river to be developed legally for water contact recreation; the other does not.

A fundamental discontinuity is thereby introduced into decisions that impinge on water quality. This will have important consequences for our analysis, as we shall see later.

Waste Discharge and Stream Quality We have been using instream dissolved oxygen as an indicator of water quality and "biochemical oxygen demand," or BOD, as the measure of the pollution content of the effluent of the two cities and the cannery. Improvement in dissolved oxygen concentrations in the river can be obtained in a number of ways—e.g., artificial aerators or flow augmentation—but this example assumes the removal of oxygen demanding material at the waste source as the only management method available.

Table 4
State Water Quality Standards

Use class	Minimum oxygen concentration* (mg/*l*)	Description
A Public water supplies	7	Character uniformly excellent.
B Bathing and contact recreational use	5	Suitable for water contact sports. Acceptable for public water supply with appropriate treatment. Suitable for agriculture, and certain industrial cooling and process uses; excellent fish and wildlife habitat; excellent aesthetic value.
C Boating and non-contact recreation	3.5	Habitat for wildlife and common food and game fishes indigenous to the region; certain industrial cooling and process uses; under some conditions acceptable for public water supply with appropriate treatment. Suitable for irrigation of crops used for consumption after cooking. Good aesthetic value.
D Minimum acceptable	2	Not objectionable; suitable for power, navigation, and certain industrial cooling and process uses.
U Unacceptable	<2	Below Class D standards. Likely to be offensive.

* Standards to be met under the minimum seven-day consecutive flow to be expected once in ten years.

In our model, we shall use the simplest formulation of the relationship between waste loads and stream quality, based on the work of Streeter and Phelps which dates back over forty years.[11] According to the Streeter-Phelps model of stream quality, the effect of discharging BOD into a stream at any point is to reduce the dissolved oxygen in the water at all points downstream by amounts that are directly proportional to the amount of BOD inserted and that depend in a complicated way on the distance from the point of waste discharge to the downstream points and on the hydrology of the stream. The factor of proportionality between waste discharge and quality response will be denoted by d. The value of d depends on where along the river the waste is being discharged and where the water quality is measured. These data will be indicated by subscripts: i for the

Table 5
Dissolved Oxygen Transfer Coefficients, d_{ij}
(Increase in DO at j (mg/l) resulting from decrease of 1000 lbs/day in BOD discharge at i)

Discharge Point (i)	Check Point (j)				
	1 Cannery	2 Bowville	3 Robin Park	4 Plympton	5 State Line
1 Cannery	0.0	0.0461	0.0502	0.0333	0.0159
2 Bowville	—	0.0	0.0585	0.0414	0.0206
4 Plympton	—	—	—	0.0	0.0641
Miles from Gordon Bridge	10	20	60	80	110

point of BOD discharge and j for the quality control point. Specifically, d_{ij} will denote the decrease in dissolved oxygen at point j (in milligrams per liter) caused by an increase of one lb/day in the amount of BOD discharged into point i. For example: at the present time the cannery is discharging 47,600 lb/day of BOD. A pound of waste material dumped at the cannery ($i = 1$) reduces the dissolved oxygen concentration at Bowville ($j = 2$) by .0000461 mg/l because $d_{12} = 0.0000461$. If the load from the cannery were cut by 40,000 lb/day, the concentration of dissolved oxygen at Bowville would increase by 40,000 × .0000461 or 1.84 mg/l. The full set of d_{ij} values for the Bow River is given in Table 5. Furthermore, the effects of different waste sources on downstream quality are additive. For example, if both the cannery and Bowville reduce their waste discharges, then the impact of each reduction on water quality at the park can be calculated in the manner shown in the preceding paragraph, using appropriate values of d_{ij}. The overall quality improvement at the park will be the sum of the influences of the two abatement measures.

MODEL OF THE BOW VALLEY WATER POLLUTION CONTROL COMMISSION

The tedious recital of data in the last section will be recognized as a small-scale replica of the docket of any proceeding concerned with the use and control of public waters. Data and considerations of the sort that we have described are amassed in the form of staff and consultant reports, briefs, submissions, affidavits, transcripts of public hearings, court records, judicial findings, rulings of administrative agencies, and so on. The task of the commission is to digest, assimilate, and ultimately evaluate this mass of data, argument, rhetoric, threat and cajolery dealing with a mixture of technical, economic, legal, demographic, political, aesthetic, moral, and social considerations. We are now concerned with what can be said about the upshot of this task.

One kind of consideration that we have not yet mentioned is precisely what the commission is trying to achieve. If you ask them they will point to the preamble of their charter where they are instructed

> so to regulate and control the use of the Bow River between the Gordon Bridge and the state line, and the discharge of liquid and solid matter of any form whatsoever thereinto, as to assure the highest practicable quality of water between and including the aforementioned points and to confrom to all applicable state and Federal laws and regulations.

That is a vague and high-minded directive, as is the nature of enabling legislation, and needs a great deal of interpretation before it can be used as a guide for either action or analysis. For example, what is meant by "the highest practicable quality of water?" The soundest interpretation of these directions, and the one that we shall adopt, seems to be that the commission is directed to enforce the highest quality of water that can be obtained without imposing undue burdens on anyone. But this interpretation is still vague and in need of further interpretation.

First, what is the "highest quality of water?" Water quality is a multidimensional concept. In a genuine instance, where many characteristics of water are taken into account, there are likely to be measures that will increase the dissolved oxygen concentration at the expense of increasing the amount of phosphates or other plant nutrients in the water. Would such a measure increase or reduce the quality of the water? The Bow River commission is spared this source of perplexity since we have assumed that it pays attention only to dissolved oxygen, but sufficient ambiguity remains. For, different improvement measures will have differential effects on the concentration of dissolved oxygen at different points in the river, and between two measures, one which makes a greater improvement at Plympton and one which makes its major improvement at the state park, it is difficult to say which improves the quality of the river more. Such questions must be decided, somehow, by the commission, and it is not likely that any answer will command the wholehearted assent of all interested parties.

Second, what are "undue burdens?" There is no point in trying to find synonyms for a concept that necessarily incorporates a large ingredient of judgment. Clearly, if a decision requires Pierce-Hall to shut down or to operate at an abnormally low rate of profit, it imposes an undue burden. Or if it requires Bowville to raise its tax rate to a level that is markedly out of line with taxes in Plympton or other competing towns, an undue burden has been imposed. Whether a burden is undue is a matter of judgment, and inherently vague. But the restriction is a genuine limitation on the powers of the commission nevertheless.

In practice the commission's range of discretion is circumscribed even more narrowly than this legal mandate requires. If it is to be effective the commission must secure the willing cooperation of the cities and industries under its jurisdiction; it cannot govern by blunt coercion. This means that it must issue regulations that all concerned will regard as reasonable and fair, and submit to without recourse to law or to higher political authority or to other forms of resistance. In our specific context, this means that the regulations must not endanger the current administrations of Bowville and Plympton if they agree to it, nor can any decision undermine the profitability of the cannery.

We shall refer to all these considerations as "political constraints." However the commission may interpret the objectives set forth vaguely in its charter, it must endeavor to attain them without violating any of the political constraints. In the early stages of consideration it will not be clear whether these constraints impose loose or stringent restrictions on the commission's scope for decision; all interested parties will endeavor to make them appear very stringent. At any rate, the first order of business before the commission is to find some policy that attains a minimum acceptable improvement in the river while respecting all these requirements.

It is highly unlikely that there will be only one such policy. Then a choice must be made among them and, as we have noted, the charter gives only a vague indication as to how this choice is to be made. Within the limits set by the political constraints, therefore, the decision will depend largely on the judgments of the individual commissioners as to where the interests of their constituents lie. These judgments are not likely to coincide. Therefore, the second order of business before the commission is one of pulling, hauling, and compromising to ascertain the decision that best reconciles the interests of all concerned.

Finally, of course, the decision must be technically feasible. If the commission decides to classify the river for Class C use, then it must require all polluters to take whatever measures are needed to bring the river up to this standard.

These, in general terms, are the outlines of the decision problem faced by the commission. This problem must now be formulated more exactly for purposes of further analysis.

Decision Variables, Costs, and Technological Constraints The first step in formulating the commission's problem precisely is to express the decisions open to it in numerical form. The first decision is the use classification of the river. It will be recalled from the description of the water quality standards that the effect of adopting any use class is to prescribe the minimum permissible amount of dissolved oxygen in the river. For example, if Class C use is adopted there must be at least 3.5 mg/*l* of dissolved oxygen in the river at all points. Let us then denote by Q the minimum permissible concentration of dissolved oxygen. Then the commission must, in effect, choose a value of Q, either 7, 5, 3.5, or 2, depending on the use class selected. In order to avoid having to consider the effects of the commission's decisions on users farther downstream, we impose that the dissolved oxygen concentration at the state line shall be 3.5 mg/*l*. This specification is regarded as outside the purview of the commission and will not be considered further.

The only other decisions that the commission has to make concern the level of treatment to be required of each polluter. These, too, can be expressed numerically. Each polluter has a range of possible treatment plant designs from which to choose; as illustrated in Figure 3, the more effective the waste removal, the higher the cost. The commission has to prescribe the degree of removal which each discharger must attain, or in more precise language, the percentage of BOD which must be removed from each of the polluters' waste outflows. These decisions can be expressed numerically as follows. First, assign identifying numbers to the three polluters: 1 will designate the Pierce-Hall Cannery, 2 will designate Bowville, and 4 will designate Plympton (number 3 denotes the state park, and no wastes are generated there). Then, introduce a set of variables, called x_i, where x_i denotes the percentage of BOD removed by polluter i from his effluent. Accordingly, the commission must decide on x_1, the percent removal to be required of the cannery, x_2, the percentage to be removed by Bowville, and x_4, the percentage to be removed by Plympton.

The decision on the x_i simultaneously determines the treatment cost that each polluter has to bear. The relationship is shown clearly in Figure 3. If $x_1 = 85$, the cannery will have to build the plant that lies halfway between points A and B in that figure, which will cost it \$21,500 a year —i.e., ½ (8,000 + 35,000). The simplest way to express mathematically the relationship between percent removal and cost is to introduce some auxiliary variables to represent the percentage of BOD removed in accordance with each segment of the broken-line cost curve. These auxiliary variables will be distinguished by appending a second subscript. In the case of the cannery, x_{11} will denote the percentage of BOD removed by methods along the line-segment from the origin to point A; x_{12} will indicate how far along the segment AB the cannery is required to go, and x_{13} will show how far along the segment BC. Note that x_{11} cannot exceed 50, x_{12} cannot exceed 10, and x_{13} cannot exceed 5. The total amount of BOD removed is simply the amount removed by primary treatment plus the sum of the amounts indicated by the auxiliary variables. In the case of the cannery

$$x_1 = 30 + x_{11} + x_{12} + x_{13}. \tag{1}$$

If $x_1 = 85$, we shall have $x_{11} = 50$, $x_{12} = 5$, and $x_{13} = 0$.

The cost of any level of treatment, x_1, is determined by the corresponding values of the auxiliary variables and the costs of advancing along the line segments, which are given in the fourth column of Table 1. Numerically,

$$\text{Cost of achieving } x_1 = 160x_{11} + 2{,}700x_{12} + 12{,}000x_{13}.$$

For example,

$$\begin{aligned}\text{Cost of achieving 85 percent removal} &= 8{,}000 + 13{,}500 + 0\\ &= 21{,}500,\end{aligned}$$

as we found before by simple interpolation.

The cost of achieving x_2 removal from Bowville's effluent and x_4 from Plympton's, can be computed by using analogous concepts and relationships. An important property of the cost curves is that, in the case of all three polluters, the cost of removing a unit of BOD increases as you move off one of the cost segments to the segment on its right in the diagram.

The commission's decision problem has now been reduced to the selection of four numbers: Q, which determines the use class of the river, and the three x_i $(i = 1, 2, 4)$ which specify the levels of treatment required of all polluters. The decisions about these numbers are not all independent. Once Q has been chosen, the x_i are forced to be high enough so that the level of dissolved oxygen does not fall below Q mg/l at any point in the river. The relationship between the x_i and the concentration of dissolved oxygen at points downstream from polluter i was discussed above in the section on "Waste Discharge and Stream Quality." That analysis led to a set of coefficients, d_{ij}, that give the effect of a unit reduction in the oxygen demanding discharge of polluter i on the dissolved oxygen concentration at any downstream point j. Since the x_i determine the amount of oxygen demanding discharge by polluter i, there is an equation, in which the d_{ij} are the important coefficients, relating the x_i to the dissolved oxygen content of the water at any downstream point j. The x_i have to be chosen so that the dissolved oxygen at all points is at least as great as Q, except that at the state line it must be at least 3.5 mg/l irrespective of Q. There is one such equation for each of the quality checkpoints in the river, designated by $j = 2$ for Bowville, $j = 3$ for Robin State Park, $j = 4$ for Plympton, and $j = 5$ for the state line. A typical equation of this group can be represented in the form:[12]

$$\sum_i d_{ij}L_i(x_i/100 - 0.3) \geq Q - \bar{q}_j. \tag{2}$$

In this equation L_i is the gross BOD load (i.e., before primary treatment) generated by polluter i; d_{ij} is the transport coefficient expressing the effect of his load on point j downstream, and x_i is his percentage removal of BOD from his effluent. The summation on the left-hand side expresses the increase in dissolved oxygen concentration at point j resulting from the waste treatment in excess of primary employed by all polluters.

On the right-hand side, $\bar{q}_j$ is the dissolved oxygen concentration at point j when only primary treatment is used by all polluters. These are the numbers plotted in Figure 2. The right-hand side is then the increase in dissolved oxygen at point j required by the use classification corresponding to Q, and the entire inequality asserts that the x_i must be chosen large enough to achieve the required improvement at point j. There is, as we said, one such equation for each quality checkpoint. These equations typify the technological constraints confronted by the commission.

Political Constraints Once the x_i have been chosen, the increases in treatment costs imposed on the polluters follow as we have seen. The formulas expressing the relationship of removal level to cost (as sensed by the individual polluter) are part of the model. In the sequel we shall frequently denote the cost imposed on polluter i by g_i.

The costs imposed on the FWPCA are somewhat special. In this model the FWPCA plays the role of the custodian of the overall national interest. Therefore, the cost of any pollution-abatement plan as perceived by the FWPCA is the full economic cost of the additional treatment, without any allowance for the effects of tax advantages and federal grants-in-aid. In other words, the FWPCA is taken to react to economic resource costs rather than to budgetary costs.

There are limits on the treatment costs that the commission can realistically impose on the polluters. As was mentioned above, the commission cannot impair Pierce-Hall's earning abilities excessively. This consideration can be expressed in the mathematical model by including a condition such as $g_1 \leq \$50{,}000$, which would prohibit any decision that cost Pierce-Hall more than $50,000 a year.

A different kind of political constraint is illustrated by the role of the FWPCA. The FWPCA, together with associated state agencies, is charged with maintaining the quality of the nation's waterways. It is empowered to enforce minimum standards and, in the case of the Bow River, will not permit it to continue in its present Class U condition. This means that the commission's field of choice of use class is confined to Class D or better, or, in numerical terms to $Q \geq 2$ mg/l.

In this section and the preceding one we have introduced the political and technological constraints that the commission's decision must satisfy. Within the limits set by those constraints the commission will search for the best decision available to it. We now turn to the formulation of that search.

Pareto Admissibility We now envisage the commission in the process of chosing among decisions that meet the technological and political requirements discussed above. This is largely a process of compromise: each commissioner balances in his mind the advantages and drawbacks to his constituents of the decisions that seem within the range of possibility, and argues for the one that he deems most favorable. When the various positions have been aired, he finally agrees to a decision if he feels that it will be acceptable to his constituents and that no more favorable decision to them is obtainable.

Even this very simple and obvious characterization of the deliberations contains important information, for it entails that no decision will be adopted if there is some alternative decision that is just as satisfactory to all interested parties and more satisfactory to some of them. Following the terminology of welfare economics, we call a decision *Pareto admissible* if it is not ruled out by the foregoing criterion, that is, if there does not exist a feasible alternative that is preferred by some interested parties and that is regarded as equally beneficial by all. The commission's decision will almost surely be Pareto admissible, for if an inadmissible decision were proposed someone would point out an alternative that he preferred and that no one would object to. We must therefore consider how the preferences of the commissioners among various possible decisions are determined.

Every decision confers benefits on the participants by prescribing the quality of the water in the river, and imposes costs by requiring certain levels of waste treatment. Each commissioner bases his attitude toward a decision on a mental comparison of the benefits and costs that it entails for the participants with whom he is most concerned, his constituents. The costs, of course, are a matter of dollars and cents. The benefits are not: they accrue largely in the form of amenities and facilities, and the eradication of distasteful conditions. To render the two terms of this balance comparable we (and the commissioners, for that matter) have to assign a monetary magnitude to the extent of the benefits. The natural, and most useful, measure of benefits is "willingness to pay," that is to say, the value of the benefits of any decision to any participant is the greatest amount that he would be willing to pay to obtain them. We shall call the greatest amount that any participant, say participant i, would be willing to pay to obtain any decision his gross benefit from that decision, to be abbreviated GB_i.

This conversion of benefits to a monetary magnitude may seem a little strained. Yet it is done, and has to be done—usually very informally—all the time in the course of arriving at governmental decisions. For example, it would not be at all exceptional to have an exchange like the following at a public hearing on pollution abatement. The Bowville Commissioner of Water and Sanitation is on the stand:

> Q. How much would it cost you to reduce your daily waste load by an additional two percent?
>
> A. About $27,000 a year, I think.
>
> Q. If you did that, we could assure swimmable water at Robin State Park. How would you folks feel about that?
>
> A. I can't answer for the City Council, but I would certainly support that kind of proposal myself.

The commissioner from Bowville has made the monetary comparison and has concluded that swimming facilities at the state park are worth at least $27,000 a year to his city. Further questioning could elicit a more precise estimate.

These gross benefit estimates are part of the basic data on which the commissioner's judgments and the commission's decisions rest. We shall have much more to say about them below. The costs of a decision to participant *i* have already been denoted by g_i. The difference between gross benefits and costs, $GB_i - g_i$, will be called net benefits, or NB_i for short. Net benefits of any decision may be positive, zero, or negative, depending on how the actual costs imposed by the decision compare with the amount that the participant is willing to pay for the corresponding benefit. The net benefits are the crucial quantities that determine how the commissioners, individually and collectively, regard various possible decisions.

These concepts enable us to express some of the considerations we have encountered more formally and quantitatively. First, we have already noted that political considerations place a limit on how disadvantageous a decision can be from the point of view of any participant. The net advantages of a decision to participant *i* are measured by the corresponding value of NB_i. Thus we can express some of the political constraints by requiring that a decision satisfy

$$NB_i \geq b_i,$$

for all participants *i*, where b_i (presumably negative) is an estimate of the smallest net benefit that can be imposed upon *i* without violating the guarantees of due process, or endangering the careers of *i*'s representatives, or otherwise provoking vigorous refusal to cooperate.

Second, we can now express Pareto admissibility in quantitative terms. Call any particular decision X and denote by $NB_i(X)$ the resultant net benefits to participant i. X is then a vector with four components, i.e., $X = [Q, x_1, x_2, x_4]$, specifying the use class of the river and the treatment levels required of the polluters. In this notation, decision X is Pareto admissible if there does not exist any alternative permissible decision, say Y, for which $NB_i(Y) \geq NB_i(X)$ for all participants i with strict inequality holding for some.

We have now formulated the main part of the commission's decision problem mathematically. Suppose, for the moment, that we had estimates of the $NB_i(X)$ for all decisions X within the realm of consideration. It is a purely mathematical task to determine whether any particular decision satisfies the technological constraints typified by equation (2). It is also, now, simply a matter of mathematics to ascertain whether the decision satisfies the political constraints. And finally, as we shall see below, straightforward mathematics can be used to determine whether a decision is Pareto admissible. In short, given the net benefit data and the technological properties of the system we can compute mathematically the range of decisions that are likely candidates for adoption.

Three tasks remain before us: (1) to discuss the estimation of benefits, (2) to indicate how to compute Pareto-admissible decisions from these estimates, and (3) to consider how to evaluate the relative likelihoods of adoption of the different Pareto-admissible decisions.

Valuation of Benefits One way to estimate the values of the benefits anticipated from different decisions is simply to ask representatives of interested parties, as in the colloquy excerpted above. This is an impracticable method for analytic purposes: there are too many questions to ask too many people, and not enough reason to expect thoughtful and candid answers. A better way is to infer from past behavior and other evidence how much the participants have shown themselves to be willing to pay for the advantages that would be offered by the decisions.

Every decision is a package deal, resulting in a bundle of consequences to each participant. For example, if the commission decides on Use Class C then Bowville will benefit in several ways, including, especially, the advantages of improved water at its own waterfront and improved facilities at the state park. To estimate the value of the package, therefore, we separate its components, estimate the value of each of them, and total up these values. The conditions under which this procedure is valid will be discussed below.

The task of estimating the value of a specific improvement to a restricted group of citizens is arduous but not novel. Several methods are well established. One method, especially useful for recreational facilities, is the "user-days" approach. Following this method, to find the value to Bowville residents of an improvement at Robin State Park one begins by estimating the additional use of the park that Bowvillers would make if the improvement were installed. Then, one estimates the value of each day's use of the park by a Bowville resident, and multiplies the two estimates. The record of Bowville's past decisions provides the data for estimating the value of a single user day at a recreational facility. It happens that Bowville's park and recreation budget amounts to $6 per capita. Park department records indicate that the average Bowville resident uses park or recreation facilities about 30 times a year. Thus the city of Bowville is paying $.20 per user-day for its citizens' use of public recreation facilities. This figure, together with a forecast of how Bowvillers will respond to improved water recreation at the park, provides an estimate of the value to Bowville of such an improvement.

Another method for valuing public improvements is the "alternative cost" procedure. This is applicable when the improvement meets a need that will be satisfied by other means if the improvement is not undertaken. In such a case the value of the improvement is the saving that it affords by rendering the alternative expenditure unnecessary. For example, we noted above that if Robin State Park is opened for swimming Bowville will not have to expand its own waterfront park. This would avoid an expenditure estimated at $165,000 a year or, taking an average, each mg/*l* of improvement would save Bowville $33,000 a year.

Estimates of the value of improved water quality have been made from the viewpoints of Bowville and Plympton by these and other methods, and are recorded in Table 6. It will be noted that each city places a value on improvements at its own waterfront and also on improvements at the park. In addition, the value of an improvement, wherever it occurs, depends on whether the water has already attained a quality of 5 mg/*l* of dissolved oxygen, which meets the state standard for water contact use.

The table also contains estimates of the value of unit improvements from the point of view of the FWPCA. The FWPCA is regarded, again, as the custodian of the public interest. Its valuation of the improvement of water quality at Bowville and Plympton is simply a reflection of the values placed by the inhabitants of those cities on the improvement of their own water. Some empirical support for this method of imputation can be found in the federal government's habit of making 50-50 matching grants-in-aid to encourage local improvement. The FWPCA's valuation of improvements at the park is the sum of the valuations of Bowville and Plympton with 50 percent added to allow for the social value of use of the park by local residents who do not live in the two cities and by outsiders.

This table enables us to calculate the benefits of any decision from the

Table 6
Value of Unit Improvements in Water Quality (\$/yr per mg/l)*

Place Improved	Current Water Quality (mg/l)	Value Perceived by Participant		
		Bowville	Plympton	FWPCA
Bowville waterfront	<5	100,000		100,000
	≥ 5	50,000		50,000
Plympton waterfront	<5		75,000	75,000
	≥ 5		25,000	25,000
Park	<5	33,000	30,000	94,500
	≥ 5	17,000	10,000	40,500

* Values valid only for qualities meeting Class D standards or higher.

point of view of each participant, provided that it is valid simply to add up the benefits of the different components of the improvement package. For example, if decision X increases the DO concentration at Bowville (where it is now 4 mg/l) by 2 mg/l and at the park (where it is now virtually zero during summer droughts) by 3 mg/l, then its gross benefits to Bowville are:

$$GB_2(X) = 100{,}000 + 50{,}000 + 3 \times 33{,}000 = 249{,}000.$$

If, in addition, the decision imposes on Bowville treatment costs of \$390,000 a year, the net benefits are

$$NB_2(X) = 249{,}000 - 390{,}000 = -141{,}000.$$

These computations and the ones to be introduced below are facilitated greatly by the fact that both gross benefits and treatment costs are piece-wise linear functions of the decision variables, i.e., the water qualities attained at various points and the treatment levels required. The coefficients of these functions are contained in Table 6 and in the treatment cost tables.

The calculation captures the major measurable benefits of improvement, but there are others. Most importantly, lifting the Bow River out of its current, nearly disgraceful, Class U condition confers a gain on each participant that cannot be evaluated quantitatively. Fortunately we do not have to assign a numerical magnitude to these benefits since they will be enjoyed under all the decisions within the range of possibility, and do not form any basis for choosing among decisions.

But this simple method of deriving gross and net benefits is not inevitably valid. One must ask: are we justified in breaking up the improvement package into its components, attaching a value to each component, adding up, and regarding the total as the value of the entire package? This is an old and classic question in economics. The answer is a qualified affirmative. The value of an entire package to any participant (in the sense of what he would be willing to pay to obtain it) is the sum of the values of its components provided that (1) the components are neither substitutes for nor complementary goods of each other, and (2) the total value of the package, computed in this way, is not a significant proportion of the budget of the participant. We should consider these provisos in order.

For simple summation of the values of improvements at different points to be valid, the benefits from those improvements should not be interrelated. The benefits of improvements at different points would be interrelated if, for example, there were two state parks accessible to Plympton. For then, if a water-based recreational facility were created at one of them the citizens of Plympton would be less willing to contribute to the cost of developing the other. In that case, the value of improvements to one of the parks would depend upon the extent of development of the other; those improvements would be substituable goods as far as Plympton is concerned. Another possibility would be for the quality of fishing at the park to be affected by the quality of water both at Bowville and at the park. Then, if the water were improved at Bowville, it would be more valuable than otherwise to improve the water at the park, because the impact on fishing would be greater. This is an instance of complementarity: improvements of water quality at Bowville would enhance the value of each unit of improvement at the park.

These considerations show that substitutability and complementarity invalidate, in opposite ways, the simple addition of the values of improvements at different points along the river. Whether or not such interactions occur in any instance depends on the circumstances, and particularly on the use that would be made by the participants of the improved water at different points. In the case of the Bow River it appears reasonable to neglect such interactions.

Moreover, if the value of the improvement package is an appreciable proportion of the annual budget of a participant, simple addition of the values of components will not be valid. This is because a participant would not be willing to pay as much for one component of a package if the cost of other components had already strained his budget as he would be willing to pay for it in isolation, without having other costs to bear.[13] This is a serious complication in principle. In our case, expenditures on water quality improvement are only a minor proportion of the total expenditures of any of the participants. We can, as a first approximation, ignore the effect of increasing budgetary drain on willingness to pay for still more improvement, but we shall have to stay alert to the possibilities for error that this approximation may lead to.

On these grounds, we feel justified in adding up the values of the components of an improvement package, with due caution, in order to estimate the value of the entire package to any participant, as we have done.

Finding the Likely Decisions Matters now stand thus: we have expressed the commission's decision numerically (in fact, as a vector with four components) and have found the consequences of any decision to be fairly simple mathematical functions of the decision variables. Now we use these formulations to ascertain the Pareto admissible decisions, for the commission's decision will surely be one of those.

Pareto admissible decisions are found by creating and solving certain auxiliary problems. Suppose we choose any set of positive numbers, to be called w_i, one for each participant in the decision, and use them to form the weighted sum of net benefits,

$$\sum_i w_i NB_i(X).$$

Then if we set ourselves the problem of finding the decision X that makes this sum as large as possible while conforming to all the technological and political constraints, we shall assuredly discover a Pareto admissible decision. For if the solution to this problem, say Decision X, were not Pareto admissible then there would be another decision, say Y, for which $NB_i(Y) \geq NB_i(X)$ for all participants i, with strict inequality for some i, so that

$$\sum_i w_i NB_i(Y) > \sum_i w_i NB_i(X)$$

contradicting the assumption that Decision X solved the auxiliary problem. If the net benefit functions and the constraints are all piecewise-linear or linear, as in this example, this problem can be solved by linear programming. Otherwise more elaborate mathematics will be required.

Every time a set of weights w_i is selected and the corresponding auxiliary problem is solved, a Pareto admissible decision is discovered. A different set of weights is likely to lead to a different decision, more favorable to the participants whose relative weights have been increased. By trying out a number of different sets of weights, we can map the range of Pareto admissible decisions. We can also see how much the relative weights have to be changed in order to move the solution from one decision to another.

We predict, of course, that the ultimate decision will be one or another of the solutions discovered by solving the auxiliary problems with judiciously chosen weights. Just which of those decisions will be chosen we have no sure way of telling—even the members of the commission don't know that until their deliberations are finished—but we can narrow the range of uncertainty further by proper interpretation of the artificial weights just introduced. For they are not actually artificial or arbitrary; they are really measures of political weight or influence.

To see this, suppose that the commission had adopted Decision X, which is a solution to the auxiliary problem with weights w_i. Then the commission has revealed something about the bases of its judgments, namely, that it values benefits to participants 1 and 2 (for instance) in something like the ratio $w_1:w_2$. That is, the commission has shown itself to be willing to reduce the net benefits to participant 1 by \$1 if by so doing it can increase the benefits to participant 2 by $\$w_1/w_2$ or more.

Some of the Pareto admissible decisions will correspond to auxiliary problems with weights that diverge widely from any reasonable estimate of relative political influence. Those decisions can be ruled out; they are too favorable to participants with relatively little political influence, and not favorable enough to powerful participants. The remaining Pareto admissible decisions, those that correspond to auxiliary problems with plausible political weights, are likely candidates for adoption. This theory provides no way for narrowing the prediction beyond this point.

Now we can test the operational feasibility of this approach by applying it to the problem faced by the Bow Valley Water Pollution Control Commission.

PREDICTION OF LIKELY DECISIONS

In the preceding section we showed how to construct a mathematical problem whose solution will be one of the Pareto admissible decisions available to the Bow Valley Water Pollution Control Commission. Specifically, this problem is constructed by assigning political weights, w_i, to the various groups concerned and then finding the decision that maximizes the weighted sum of net benefits, denoted by $\Sigma w_i NB_i(X)$, while satisfying constraints and relationships that describe the technological connection between treatment undertaken and quality achieved, between treatment level and cost incurred, and so on. As we noted, all the relationships are linear or piecewise linear, so that this mathematical problem is a linear programming problem, which is very convenient for computational purposes. It may be necessary in other instances to resort to more complicated mathematical formulations, with consequent increase in the cost of calculation, but such complications would not be justified for our present illustrative purposes.

The linear programming problem that corresponds to our model has been coded for the SDS 940 Time Sharing System.[14]

In this section we shall perform the mathematical analysis of the pollution control commission's decision problem and interpret the results. This is done by setting up and solving a number of auxiliary problems, selecting political weights so as to be able to block out the main outlines of the range of possibilities. These results then serve as a basis for forecasting where within the range the ultimate decision is likely to fall.

In our exploration of Pareto admissible decisions, the auxiliary problem was solved for seventeen different weight allocations. In discussing these weighting schemes, we shall use the notation $w = (w_1, w_2, w_4, w_5)$ to indicate a set of w_i in which Pierce-Hall receives a weight of w_1, Bowville receives w_2, Plympton gets w_4, and the FWPCA receives w_5. As shown in Table 7, our selection of weights ranges from a set that pays exclusive attention to the overall national interest as reflected by the FWPCA,

Table 7
Weight Allocations Used to Explore Possible Decisions

Relative Weight Assigned to			
Pierce-Hall w_1	Bowville w_2	Plympton w_4	FWPCA w_5
0	0	0	1
3	1	3	3
3	3	1	3
3	3	3	1
1	3	3	3
4	1	4	1
1	4	1	4
4	4	1	1
1	1	4	4
1	4	4	1
1	5	3	1
1	3	5	1
1	6	2	1
1	2	6	1
1	1	7	1
1	7	1	1
7	1	1	1

$w = (0, 0, 0, 1)$, to sets that place major emphasis on the profitability of Pierce-Hall, $w = (7, 1, 1, 1)$, on the welfare of Bowville, $w = (1, 7, 1, 1)$, or on the interests of Plympton, $w = (1, 1, 7, 1)$. Intermediate weighting schemes, such as $w = (3, 3, 1, 3)$ and $w = (3, 1, 3, 3)$, place varying degrees of emphasis on the welfares of the two cities. For each set of influence weights there is an appropriate admissible decision available to the commission.

Notice that we have not conducted a systematic search among all possible sets of relative weights in order to exhaust the full range of admissible plans. We do not have any satisfactory method for doing this. Our approach has been to try a relatively small set of alternative weight distributions, chosen in such a way as to cover the plausible range of circumstances. As a result, we probably have failed to detect a number of Pareto admissible decisions that correspond to political weightings that we have not tried. Nevertheless, we believe that we have obtained a fairly accurate depiction of the Pareto admissible choices available to the commission.

Of course, as mentioned earlier the commission is not completely free in its selection of a quality management plan. No matter what the allocation of political weights may be, the range of choice is limited by the requirement, imposed by FWPCA and state regulations, that the river be brought up to at least a Class D standard. To incorporate his externally imposed limitation in the model, Q was set equal to the Class D minimum (2.0 mg/l) for purposes of computation. As will be seen below, this preliminary determination of Q does not prevent the commission from adopting a higher classification in its final decision. Accordingly, in the computations the value of Q corresponding to Class D was inserted in the water quality constraints at Bowville, the state park, and at Plympton; the minimum dissolved oxygen level at the southern outlet of the valley was set at 3.5 mg/l regardless of the value of Q established upstream. With each of the quality constraints set at the proper level, the model could be solved for the seventeen alternative sets of influence weights. The resulting solutions provide the basic set of admissible plans from which we shall draw our prediction of the commission's choice.

In addition to this basic set of decisions, there are other circumstances that are worth investigating. We assume that the commission can choose any stream classification from D on up, but it is possible to imagine situations where such a body might have less flexibility in this choice. For example, political conditions external to the commission might be such that Class D was essentially forbidden, and the choice of stream class limited to C or above. Or the selection might be restricted to Classes B or A, with C ruled out as well. In order to study the influence of this type of political constraint on the commission's range of choice we repeated the calculations two additional times, once with $Q = 3.5$ to identify the decisions admissible if Class C were the minimum allowed, and once with $Q = 5$ to do the same for a Class B minimum.[15]

We also are interested in identifying the management plans that would achieve the different stream quality classifications at the minimum economic cost. In order to determine the "least cost" plan to attain each use class, we solved a revised version of the auxiliary problem, using the (0, 0, 0, 1) weights but ignoring any benefits attached to increased water quality. Because the FWPCA is presumed to take account of the national resource costs of alternative treatment plans, and the (0, 0, 0, 1) weights bring only the federal viewpoint into consideration, each of these solutions yielded the minimum cost plan to meet the requirements of the specified quality class. These plans serve as a basis for estimating the increase in economic cost incurred when the benefit evaluations estimated in Table 6 are taken into account.

The result of the computations under a minimum quality class of D was a set of nine Pareto admissible choices. As will be seen shortly, it often happens that several weight allocations lead to the same decision; seven of our weighting schemes all led to Decision 10, for example. Under a minimum classification of C, the analysis recommended eight admissible choices, and under the requirement of Class B it recommended five. Some plans appeared in more than one of the three sets of computations. The total number of Pareto admissible choices encountered under all the various conditions was fourteen. All are described in Table 8 in terms of the quality class attained and the treatment levels, x_i, assigned to each of the polluters. Each row of the table contains one of the four-component decision vectors, $X = [Q, x_1, x_2, x_4]$, introduced above. For convenience in presenting and interpreting the results, the decisions are numbered in order of their relative attractiveness to Bowville.

The effect of two of the decisions on the quality of the river is shown in Figure 4, which should be contrasted with the existing condition in Figure 2. Both Decisions 5 and 14 are included in the basic set of Pareto admissible choices that results from solving the model with $Q = 2.0$. As the figure shows, Decision 5 fails to achieve 3.5 mg/l at the quality control point located at the state park, and thus is infeasible if the commission is required to attain Class C. Decision 14, which follows from a different set of political influence weights, achieves a higher water quality along almost the entire reach of river, and holds the oxygen concentration above 5.0 mg/l at all quality control points except the state line. If this decision is adopted, the river will be eligible for a B classification.

In the circumstances illustrated by Decision 14, the commission's freedom to select a use classification, within limits, becomes pertinent. Under the political weights that lead to that decision, so much importance is attached to the benefits of high quality that the optimal decision meets the standards for Class B, although the commission was empowered to select a use class as low as D. In these circumstances there are clear advantages to designating the river as Class B. It costs nothing, since this designation will not alter the levels of treatment required of any polluter. The announcement of a high use classification, by obligating the commission to the maintenance of high standards, qualifies the river for all the advantages appertaining thereto, such as public health certification of the

Figure 4

Water Quality in the Bow River Under Alternative Decisions, Summer Drought Conditions

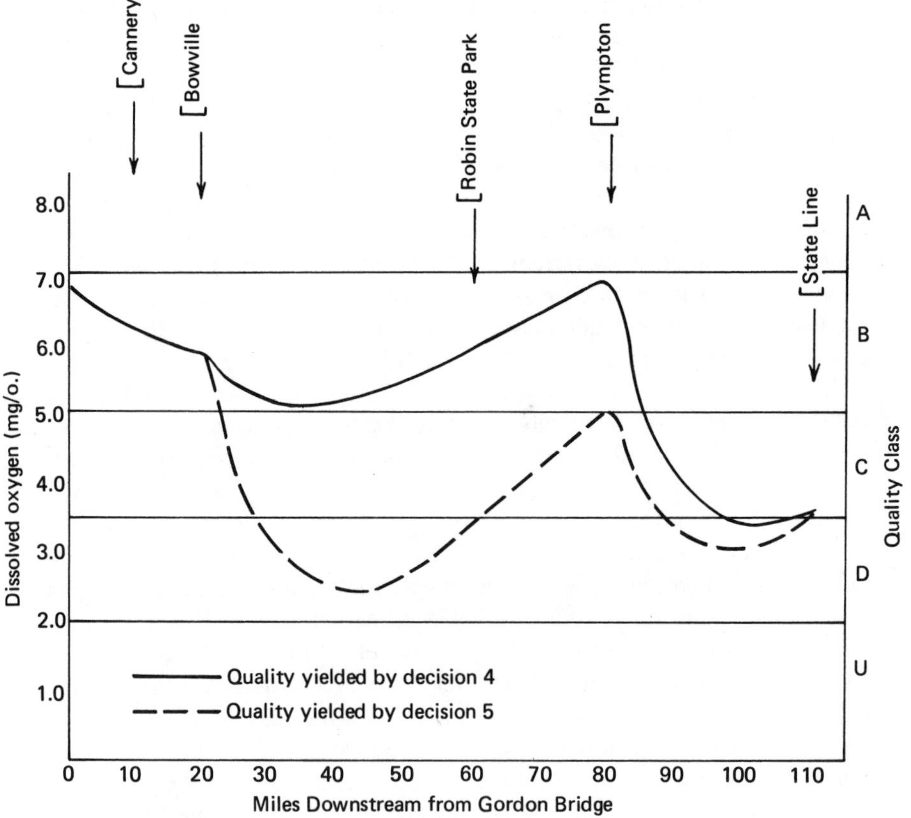

Bow as a swimmable stream. Furthermore, though it might be difficult to enforce expensive levels of treatment that were so high that required quality standards were exceeded by a wide margin, those same levels would be easy to enforce if they were clearly necessitated by the officially adopted classification of the river.

For these reasons, the commission can be relied on to adopt the highest stream use classification that is compatible with the quality levels that result from the other components of its decision. Only this way can it realize the full benefit of the quality levels attained. If Decision 14 is adopted, then the commission will designate the Bow for Class B use. The other use classifications noted in Tables 8, 9, 10 and 11 were derived by similar reasoning.

Table 8 and Figure 4 indicate that there is considerable variation in the individual components of the different quality management plans, depending on the distribution of influence among the participants. Now let us see what political conditions are consistent with each of the admissible choices and compare the economic implications of the alternative outcomes. Table 9 shows the weight allocations that lead to each of the nine decisions that are admissible when the minimum classification the commission may assign is D. The table also shows the quality class actually achieved by each plan and the resultant net costs and benefits to each of the participants.

Table 8
Decisions Recommended by the Analysis

Decision Number	Quality Class Achieved	Treatment Level in Terms of Percentage BOD Removal by		
		Cannery	Bowville	Plympton
1	D	95	50	67
2	D	90	52	67
3	D	80	55	67
4	C	95	65	61
5	D	90	66	61
6	C	90	67	61
7	C	80	70	60
8	B	95	80	54
9	B	94	80	54
10	C	90	80	55
11	B	90	81	54
12	C	80	80	56
13	B	80	85	54
14	B	90	90	51

The net cost figures in Table 9 are straightforward; they are simply the additional outlays required to attain the treatment levels shown in Table 8. The net benefit data, on the other hand, merit further explanation. As mentioned earlier, our benefit estimates do not include all the advantages, achieved under all alternative decisions, associated with lifting the river out of its current Class U status. Therefore, they do not state in absolute terms how much benefit a participant derives from a decision. But if we compare the benefits received by any participant as a result of two different decisions, the unmeasured components of benefits will cancel out, and the difference between two estimates will be a meaningful measure of his comparative gains. That is to say, though $NB_i(X)$ is not a significant indicator of the benefits of decision X to participant i, the difference $NB_i(X) - NB_i(Y)$ does indicate how much better off he is under decision X than under decision Y.[16]

In the table, therefore, we have recorded the net benefits resulting from each choice in comparison with those that would result from one particular decision which is used as an arbitrary base point. For this purpose we use Decision 3, the least-cost plan to achieve Class D waters.

In order to illustrate the interpretation of Table 9, suppose that Bowville's interests are favored by employing the weighting scheme (1, 7, 1, 1). Then the table shows that Decision 1 is appropriate. This same decision is called for if the weight given Bowville's interests is reduced slightly and greater consideration accorded Plympton, as indicated by the weight allocation (1, 6, 2, 1). It will be noted that net benefits for Plympton, the cannery, and the FWPCA are all negative under Decision 1. This result should not be misinterpreted. In particular, it does not mean that all but Bowville will be worse off as a result of plan 1 than if the river were left in its current mediocre state. It only indicates that all but Bowville gain less from Decision 1 than from Decision 3. Other weight allocations, representing varying degrees of concern for the welfares of the four participants, lead to different quality management plans, as shown in the table.

Because the FWPCA is included as a participant in the decision process, it is possible to evaluate alternative plans from a national standpoint. In fact, benefit-cost analysis is a special case of this model in which exclusive weight is given to the representatives of the national interest. Using the (0, 0, 0, 1) weights, the model maximizes the excess of aggregate benefits from a national point of view over aggregate costs, disregarding sectional or specialized interest. Table 9 indicates that Decision 10 is appropriate under these weights, and scanning down the last column in the table it can be seen that this decision yields the greatest total of net benefits as the FWPCA would measure them. Decision 10, then, is the one that would be recommended by a conventional benefit-cost analysis.

Table 9

Decisions Corresponding to Specified Weight Allocations under a Minimum Quality Classification of D

Weight Allocation	Decision Number	Quality Class Achieved	Net Cost ($ thousand/yr)				Net Benefits ($ thousand/yr)			
			Pierce-Hall	Bowville	Plympton	FWPCA	Pierce-Hall	Bowville	Plympton	FWPCA
1711, 1621	1	D	95	201	302	829	−87	72	−3	−61
4411	2	D	35	217	302	750	−27	48	−2	10
L.C.	3	D	8	250	301	746	0	0	0	0
3313, 1531, 1414	5	D	35	349	255	863	−27	−38	160	101
1441, 0001, 3133, 1144, 1351, 1333, 3331	10	C	35	491	204	985	−27	−131	282	147
1261	11	B	35	512	199	1007	−27	−148	292	139
7111	12	C	8	491	214	953	0	−158	255	125
4141	13	B	8	568	198	1034	0	−219	294	97
1171	14	B	35	659	169	1162	−27	−279	348	36

"L.C." denotes least-cost plan for attaining specified quality.

It is also possible to evaluate from a national viewpoint the cost of yielding precedence to local interests. For example, if the cannery's interests are favored, as indicated by the (7, 1, 1, 1) weights, then national representatives would judge the result to involve a loss of $22,000 per year as compared with their preferred plan, for then the national net benefit would be $125,000 from Decision 12 as opposed to $147,000 from Decision 10.

It is also instructive to compare the different decisions with the least-cost plan to achieve Class D, Decision 3. Recall that Decision 3 is the decision that achieves Class D standards at the lowest possible national resource cost.[17] Column 7 of Table 9 shows that the minimum cost is $746,000 per year. When benefits are considered, and the political influence of the participants is taken into account, additional expenditure for waste treatment is warranted. In order to maximize national net benefits, for example, an additional $239,000 in national resource cost is required, as can be seen by comparing Decision 3 with Decision 10.

A striking characteristic of the model is that the same decision may be indicated by a wide variety of different weighting schemes. Decision 10 was recommended in response to seven of the weight allocations that were tried. This phenomenon has already been observed in connection with Decision 1, and there are three separate weight distributions that yield Decision 5. This is a consequence of the usual behavior of linear programming models.[18] For any given set of relative weights, the problem solution is likely to settle on a point where some element of incremental costs or benefits changes. Since there is a limited number of such points,[19] only a limited set of Pareto-admissible decisions will emerge, even though there is an infinite number of possible political weighting schemes.

In some circumstances, this characteristic of linear programming models leads to unrealistic and even ridiculous results. But in other circumstances, and this model is a case in point, it is realistic for the model not to incorporate a finer degree of discrimination than the institutional system that it analyzes is likely to display. In actuality, a commission or other political decision process is likely to focus attention on a few sensible possible decisions, corresponding to actions at which costs or benefits change markedly, and to make its selection from those. In this respect a linear programming model reflects institutional behavior.

The character of the relationships among the interested parties can be seen most clearly by studying some of the data from Table 9 in graphical form. In Figure 5, Bowville's net benefits are plotted against net benefits to Plympton for each of the decisions; cannery net benefits also are noted. By drawing connecting lines between those admissible decision points that have like values of benefits to the cannery, we can trace out a set of

Figure 5

Net Benefits to the Three Polluters
Under Decisions Admissable if the
Minimum Quality Classification is D.

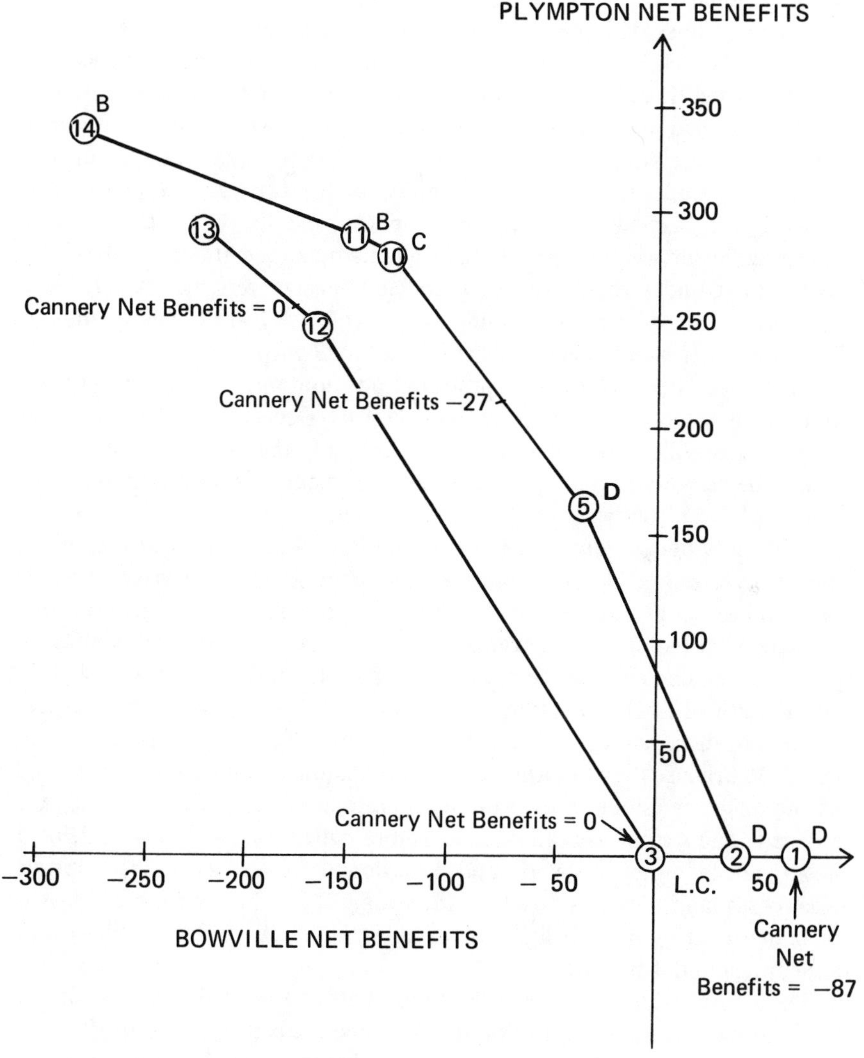

L.C. Indicates Lease Cost Solution

frontiers that indicate the maximum net benefit that can be provided to Plympton, given particular levels of net benefits to Bowville and to Pierce-Hall.[20] Three frontiers are discernible in the figure. The most obvious includes decision points 2, 5, 10, 11, and 14, and involves net benefits to the cannery of −$27,000 per year. A second is made up of Decisions 3, 12, and 13, yielding zero net benefits to the cannery. The third is a frontier in a technical sense, although it consists of a single point defined by Decision 1; cannery benefits are −$87,000 per year.

The conflict of interests among the three polluters is easily seen in Figure 5. The classic upstream-downstream rivalry is evident in the relationship between Bowville and Plympton. Thirteen of our seventeen weight allocations lead to some point on the contour where the Pierce-Hall Cannery is receiving net benefits of −$27,000 per year, and along this contour the tradeoff between the interests of the two cities is particularly clear. There is conflict between the cannery and the two cities as well. Given sufficient weight, Pierce-Hall can maintain the treatment level assigned to it under the least-cost plan, and receive zero net benefit as a consequence. If the cannery dominates, $w = (7, 1, 1, 1)$, it achieves this by Decision 12. If its influence is shared with the downstream city, $w = (4, 1, 4, 1)$, Pierce-Hall maintains its preferred position, but more at the expense of Bowville than of Plympton as indicated by Decision 13. On the other hand, if Bowville dominates, $w = (1, 7, 1, 1)$, the resultant Decision 1 forces the cannery to its highest possible treatment level and imposes a net benefit of −$87,000 per year on Pierce-Hall.

Table 9 and Figure 5 summarize the Pareto-admissible choices when the only restriction on the commission's action is that the river must be brought up to at least Class D. We can prepare similar displays that indicate what happens to the range of choice if external political conditions constrain the choice to some higher use class. If the commission is forbidden the use of D classification, for example, the set of admissible choices changes to those shown in Table 10. Decisions 1, 2, 3, and 5 are no longer available because they fail to meet Class C standards, and they are replaced by three new decisions which were not Pareto admissible when Class D was allowed. The weight allocations that before called for Decisions 1, 2, or 5 now lead to either 4 or 6, and Decision 7 becomes the appropriate least-cost plan.[21] Decisions 10, 11, 12, 13, and 14 yielded waters of Class C or better even when such high classification was not required, and so they appear again in Table 10.

These results are also shown in the top half of Figure 6, which is drawn to the same scale and with reference to the same origin as Figure 5. As a comparison of Figures 5 and 6 will show, the range of choice open to the commission is reduced by the imposition of a higher minimum quality level.

Table 10

Decisions Corresponding to Specified Weight Allocations under a Minimum Quality Classification of C

Weight Allocation	Decision Number	Quality Class Achieved	Net Cost ($ thousand/yr)				Net Benefits ($ thousand/yr)			
			Pierce-Hall	Bowville	Plympton	FWPCA	Pierce-Hall	Bowville	Plympton	FWPCA
1711, 1621	4	C	95	344	251	952	−87	− 21	169	34
4411, 3313, 1414, 1531	6	C	35	360	251	873	−27	− 45	170	105
L.C.	7	C	8	393	249	869	0	− 94	171	94
1441, 0001, 3133, 1144, 1351, 1333, 3331	10	C	35	491	204	985	−27	−131	282	147
1261	11	B	35	512	199	1007	−27	−148	292	139
7111	12	C	8	491	214	953	0	−158	255	125
4141	13	B	8	568	198	1034	0	−219	294	97
1171	14	B	35	659	169	1162	27	−279	348	36

Figure 6

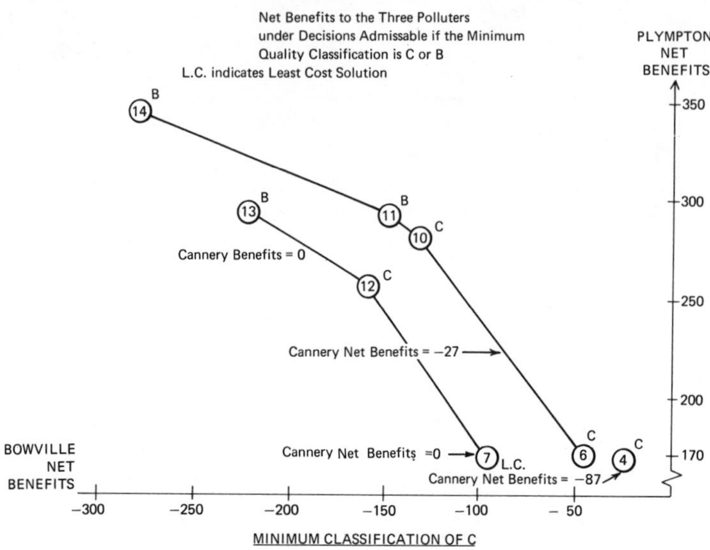

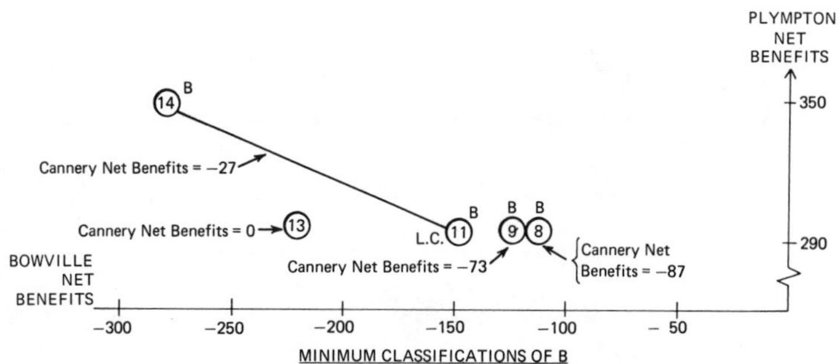

If the commission's discretion is further limited, to the point where it can only consider plans that yield a Class B stream, then the range of choice is even more restricted. Five Pareto admissible decisions that are open to the commission under this condition are presented in Table 11 and in the lower half of Figure 6. Only Decisions 11, 13, and 14 remain from the earlier sets of admissible choices. Most of the weight allocations that formerly led to Decision 10 now result in Decision 11, and 11 also turns out to be the least costly plan that attains Class B. Two new plans previously inadmissible, Decisions 8 and 9, appear as options available to the commission.

Up to this point, we have explored the range of admissible choice and have blocked out the conditions that would lead to the adoption of each of

Table 11

Decisions Corresponding to Specified Weight Allocations under a Minimum Quality Classification of B

Weight Allocation	Decision Number	Quality Class Achieved	Net Cost ($ thousand/yr)				Net Benefits ($ thousand/yr)			
			Pierce-Hall	Bowville	Plympton	FWPCA	Pierce-Hall	Bowville	Plympton	FWPCA
1711, 1621	8	B	95	487	200	1074	−87	−115	292	80
1441, 1531	9	B	81	491	200	1056	−73	−121	292	96
4411, 3313, 0001, 3133, 1144, 1351, 1333, 3331, 1261	11	B	35	512	199	1007	−27	−148	292	139
7111, 4141	13	B	8	568	198	1034	0	−219	294	97
1171	14	B	35	659	169	1162	−27	−279	348	36

the different quality management plans. Now we can apply these results in predicting the outcome of the commission's deliberations. We have already argued that the commission will select one of the Pareto admissible choices discovered using the linear programming model. By supplementing these results with reasonable judgments concerning the influence of each of the participants, we can identify the plans that are most likely to be selected.

Part of the information we need for prediction is available in Table 9. The first column of the table shows the weight allocations that lead to each of the admissible choices under a minimum classification of D, where each set of weights is a shorthand expression for the distribution of political influence among the participants as they impinge upon the commission's decision on the matter at hand. To these data we add our knowledge of the political facts of life in the Bow River Valley. If we can judge some of the weight allocations as more likely to be experienced than others, then we can make similar judgments regarding the decisions they call for.

For example, it seems highly unlikely that the interest of a single industrial firm, such as the Pierce-Hall Cannery, would weigh many times more heavily than those of cities of 200,000 or more population, or that such a firm would be far more influential than the FWPCA in this type of situation. We should, therefore, say that the political condition described by the (7, 1, 1, 1) weights has a very low probability of coming about, and as a consequence that Decision 12 has only a low probability of being adopted.[22]

By the same token, since Bowville and Plympton are roughly the same size, we should not expect one to be able to command a great deal more consideration from the commission than the other. There may be some difference in the political pressures they can bring to bear, but it seems reasonable to place a low probability on any settlement that implies favoring Bowville seven, four, or even three times as much as Plympton. Even this simple political judgment gives us a basis for excluding Decision 1, which implies a willingness to increase Plympton's costs by $3 in order to save Bowville $1, or Decision 2, which similarly overrides Plympton's interests in favor of those of Bowville and the cannery. We also should not expect that Decisions 11, 13, or 14 will be taken, because these are appropriate only if Plympton has a great influence, either alone or in cooperation with the cannery.

That leaves Decisions 5 and 10 as likely candidates for adoption. Decision 5 is called for under more plausible conditions than the plans discussed above. We discovered three different weight allocations that indicate Decision 5; all attribute heavier weight to Bowville than to Plympton. Because Plympton has suffered most among the riparian residents of the valley from the effects of river pollution, and its citizens are greatly concerned with the water quality issue, we should not expect that the downstream city would be dominated by all other interests, $w = (3, 3, 1, 3)$, or by Bowville and the FWPCA, $w = (1, 4, 1, 4)$. On the other hand, it is conceivable that the two cities together would carry a great influence, but that Bowville would come out stronger than Plympton, $w = (1, 5, 3, 1)$, and therefore Decision 5 has some chance of being adopted.

The most likely choice, however, is Decision 10. It seems reasonable to expect that both of the cities will be influential in the commission, but that they will roughly balance each other at points of conflict as indicated by the (1, 4, 4, 1) weights. It is conceivable that the FWPCA might carry weight roughly equivalent to that of each of the cities, $w = (1, 3, 3, 3)$. It is also possible that the cannery would be as influential as the cities, and that the FWPCA would play a lesser role, $w = (3, 3, 3, 1)$. Thus a whole region of weights that give heavy, and roughly equal, influence to the two cities leds to Decision 10. If either city can command an edge on this issue, it is likely to be Plympton, $w = (1, 5, 3, 1)$, simply because the city officials are more concerned with this question than their upstream counterparts, as noted above, and they will work harder in trying to influence the commission.

All together, then, it seems that the probability that the actual distribution of political weight will fall somewhere in the range appropriate to Decision 10 is higher than that for any other admissible decision. On this basis we should predict that the commission will adopt Class C, and that it will bring the river quality up to the required standard by imposing the treatment requirements for Decision 10 shown in Table 8. But Decision 5 is also a real possibility.

Our prediction would not be substantially changed if state and federal regulations were to forbid adoption of Class D. Even with a Class D minimum, the commission is expected to adopt Class C by Decision 10. If the minimum is raised to Class C, this same plan is still the most likely, with Decision 6 a real but less likely possibility.

Under normal circumstances, we should not expect the commission to be forbidden all but the B classification. If a regulatory body is to manage water quality effectively, it cannot have its hands completely tied on the question of use classification, and generally some flexibility is granted by federal and state regulations. Furthermore, in this particular case federal representatives have no incentive to try to enforce a minimum classification of B, for their preferred choice, Decision 10, is not admissible under this restriction. If, for some reason, the commission were restricted to a B classification, the political judgment and reasoning utilized above, when applied to the data in Table 11, would lead to a prediction of Decision 11 as the most likely choice.

The application of the model together with very plausible judgments concerning the balance of political considerations have thus led us to forecast a very restricted range of possible outcomes of the commission's decision process. Of course, this very concrete upshot emerged from the analysis of a single, highly simplified example. Whether equally concrete conclusions can be expected in other instances merits further consideration.

CONCLUSIONS

Appraisal of the Test At the very outset we raised the question of whether a complicated problem of governmental decisionmaking, in which the interests of influential groups were in conflict, could be expressed as a formal model and could be analyzed fruitfully in those terms. This entire discussion has been devoted to casting light on that issue by applying the model to a hypothetical case especially devised for the purpose. In the interests of clarity and economy, the test problem was highly simplified. It did, however, incorporate many of the salient features of real water pollution control problems. There were a variety of hydrologic, technical, social, political, and economic issues to formulate and to worry about. There were deep-seated conflicts of interest among the participants, and no obvious way to make everybody happy. Some of the data were very elusive. Nevertheless the model was implemented, and it produced intelligible results.

The model also provided a useful way to manage the diverse kinds of data that were pertinent to the decision. One especially helpful aspect of the model was its ability to incorporate not only data on aggregate costs and benefits but on costs and benefits as sensed by the individual participants as well. Federal and state tax laws and special grant programs surely have an influence on quality management plans, and the model provided a way to include those considerations in the analysis.

Of necessity, we dealt with information of widely varying quality. Some data—such as how much participants would be willing to pay to be free of occasional noxious odors and how the weight of political influence was distributed among the participants—were not observable at all; some, such as valuations of improved recreational opportunities, could be evaluated only tentatively and with difficulty; the best data, such as costs of waste treatment, were only fragmentary. This is a fair approximation of the situation actually faced by a pollution control commission. One of the advantages of the model was that it provided a way to coordinate such data as were available, and a method of analyzing the way that different assumptions would affect the set of plans likely to be adopted by the commission.

On this last point, our sample results proved highly informative. Even our limited selection of weight allocations allowed us to explore the set of plans that would be adopted under extremes of imbalance in the consideration given to the different participants. We found, of course, that there was conflict among the participants and that, in general, the greater the political weight the individual had the greater were his net benefits. This is no profound discovery; it is only common sense, or perhaps tautology, that as the political influence of any participant grows he will be able to wangle decisions more to his liking at the expense of the others. But the analysis has quantified and sharpened this vague and obvious perception, and has shown concretely how the response to a change in influence is likely to be implemented and how it will effect the welfares of the individual participants.

Our results also provided a framework within which we could utilize reasonable political judgments to arrive at a prediction of the outcome of the decision process. Without performing the analysis, we should not have been able to guess what the different decisions would look like or to foresee which set of political circumstances would favor the adoption of one or another of the Pareto admissible plans. It is not that the analysis can provide any new knowledge of the political situation; on this score we are ultimately limited by the previous experience and political sensitivity that we bring to the problem. But the model results did allow us to combine what judgments we may possess with data on the physical alternatives available and on the relative importance of different aspects of the problem, as viewed by the individual participants in the decision process. As a result, we were able to learn about the physical and economic factors and the political influences that make some outcomes more or less likely than others.

The analysis also taught us something about the commission itself. We have seen how its actions are likely to be influenced if more or less stringent quality requirements are imposed from the outside. In a similar way we could have analyzed the effects of other changes in external conditions. For example, one of the assumptions in our example was that the commission had no authority to tax and to offer grants-in-aid. Our results show, however, that there are circumstances under which such powers would be very useful. Consider the situation that arises if Bowville and the FWPCA carry little influence in the commission so that the (4, 1, 4, 1) weights turn out, in fact, to be appropriate. Table 9 indicates that Decision 13 will be taken under these circumstances. It happens, however, that a shift from 13 to Decision 11 would maintain the same quality class and leave Plympton essentially unaffected, yet the change would save Bowville over $2 for every dollar that it cost the cannery. If fiscal expedients were available, the wasteful Decision 13 would never be adopted: the commission could tax Bowville and use the proceeds to reduce the financial burden on the cannery. In this way the technically efficient Decision 11 could be implemented without imposing any financial hardship, to everybody's benefit. The value of such authority, though it might have been suspected, could not have been established without invoking a model that brings out the economic consequences of the technical peculiarities of the river that make the cannery the strategic site for treating waste.

This finding illustrates that our concept of Pareto admissibility is relative. It depends heavily on the range of decisions that are assumed to be technically and legally practicable. Change those assumptions, and the Pareto admissible set changes correspondingly. Thus the model can be used to estimate the value of changing either the technical possibilities available (by research) or the legal possibilities permissible (by legislation), by comparing the Pareto admissible sets that correspond to alternative assumptions. Among the legal possibilities that merit consideration are the power to tax and make grants, the authority to impose effluent charges, and the authority to operate regional treatment facilities. All of these are issues now being debated earnestly in the several water pollution control commissions that are currently operative.

Applicability of the Model Like any model, this one depends on numerous assumptions and can be applied only to circumstances that correspond fairly well to the assumptions. The fundamental assumption in this model is that a water pollution control commission, like any other government agency, is responsive to the wishes of its constituency. This seems highly reasonable. By being responsive an agency reduces its exposure to complaints, litigation and animosity, builds its reputation for efficiency and fairmindedness, accumulates political support and influence, and fosters cooperative attitudes among the people with whom it must deal. In short, it gains the consent of the governed, which is an essential prerequisite of effective government. In keeping with this assumption we have portrayed the Bow Valley Water Pollution Control Commission as consulting continually with its constituents and as endeavoring to formulate a plan that will be as agreeable to them, individually, as possible. Any government agency or commission that acts according to this simple principle will arrive at one or another of the decisions that we have called Pareto admissible.

The kind of analysis that follows from this assumption stands in contrast to the approach used in much of the literature, which rests on the postulate that government agencies endeavor to achieve some overarching goals which typically are called "the general welfare" or "the national interest." Such an agency, if such there be, would be unresponsive to the sectional or special interests of its constituents. There is much empirical evidence that agencies in fact behave predominantly as we have assumed. See, for example, the work of Matthew Holden [7].

Furthermore, the institutional arrangements that are employed by water pollution control agencies in order to be responsive to their constituents are frequently similar to those used by the Bow Valley Water Pollution Control Commission. This is no coincidence. We have modeled our commission in the image of some established pollution control commissions. The Delaware River Basin Commission (DRBC) is made up of the governors of the four states through which the Delaware flows, plus a representative of the federal government, just as the Bow Valley Water Pollution Control Commission is made up of representatives from the municipalities and industries located along the river. The Ohio River Valley Water Sanitation Commission (ORSANCO) has a similar constitution.

The formal composition of the commission is not essential, however. What is essential is an anxious concern for the interests and responses of the people who are affected by the commission's decisions. Direct representation is one expedient for assuring this concern. A more fundamental expedient is the maintenance of intimate contact with the constituency by both informal consultations and formal conferences and public hearings before any important decision is made. Both the DRBC and the ORSANCO follow such procedures, as does the Bow Valley Water Pollution Control Commission. Indeed, the federal legislation that provides the charter for all the newer commissions requires elaborate consultations. The requirement to conduct public hearings at which all affected "interstate agencies, states, municipalities and industries involved" can present their cases, is stressed repeatedly in the federal laws. Operating practice, so far as we have been able to discern it, sincerely implements these requirements. In these respects the Bow Valley Water Pollution Control Commission appears to be a fair replica of the pollution control agencies now in existence.

A subsidiary assumption that we made was that the constituency of the Bow Valley Water Pollution Control Commission consists entirely of local residents except for a generalized public interest represented by the FWPCA. This characteristic is by no means universal, even in the field of water pollution control. For example, the Water Quality Act of 1965 gave primary responsibility for regulating the use of interstate waters to "State water pollution control agencies," which are simply departments of the state governments. Now the range of interest groups represented on the State Water Commission is quite different from those that we have envisaged the Bow Valley Water Pollution Control Commission as being responsive to. Therefore, if the problems of the Bow Valley were brought before the State Water Commission instead of the Bow Valley Water Pollution Control Commission, the decision might well be affected. It would remain true that in any proceeding before the State commission concerning the regulation of the Bow River, the parties with predominant interest and the ones that would exert the greatest pressure and influence on the decision would be precisely the ones that we have considered. But the political influence weights would be likely to be changed: purely local and sectoral interests would have smaller leverage for asserting their claims, while statewide and national interests would be likely to gain greater recognition. One of the useful applications of the model is to incorporate such variations in the constitution of decisionmaking authorities and to assist in forming judgments about their consequences.

Next, there are a number of specialized assumptions that were made purely to keep the computations simple and tractable. They concern the policy instruments considered, the technical aspects of waste management and water quality, the question of uncertainty, and the problem of growth in municipal and industrial waste loads. We can review each one of these four aspects in turn and give a brief indication of some of the limitations of the sample case we have used.

The first and most important of these simplifying assumptions was the narrow range of discretion permitted the Bow Valley Water Pollution Control Commission. Many actual commissions have a scarcely wider range of authority but, as we noted above, additional powers and privileges can permit superior decisions (in the Pareto admissible sense) and some authorities have them. Additional policy instruments can be incorporated into the model, but only at the cost of some increase in complexity.

By means of a second set of assumptions, we vastly simplified the technological and hydrologic aspects of the problem. In particular, we utilized a highly simplified description of the biochemical composition of municipal and industrial sewage and of the technology of waste treatment. We ignored altogether such waste management methods as manufacturing process change and wastewater recirculation. In addition, we reduced water quality standards to a single dimension, dissolved oxygen, and built our analysis on the simplest available formulation of waste transport and decay. The model can be revised to incorporate more adequate assumptions about these aspects of pollution control, but then the problem solution and interpretation will be more difficult than in our case. For example, in the reformulation it may not be possible to maintain certain convenient mathematical properties (such as linearity) that were built into the Bow Valley example.

A third way we reduced the difficulty of the analysis was by ignoring the unpredictability and variability of streamflows, gross waste loads, treatment plant performance, and all of the other aspects of uncertainty that are vexatious parts of most real decision problems. There are decision models, of course, that incorporate these complications, and they are invariably far more elaborate than ours. To introduce uncertainty in its manifold aspects we should have to modify our model along well-established lines. To have done so in the present application would have been to obscure its main intent, which was to test the feasibility of comprehending both political and technical considerations in a model of a governmental decision process.

In our fourth area of simplification, we evaded dynamical considerations by assuming that neither the towns nor the cannery were expected to grow, and that no new industries were likely to be established along the river. The possibility of growth presents serious analytic difficulties of its own. Any satisfactory method for dealing with them could most likely be built into our model, but we have not allowed our attention to be distracted by this separate, important, and difficult analytic problem.

Finally, we must admit to having ignored two important features of the political decision process. One is the influence of logrolling, pressure politics, and side-payments of all sorts. There are pressures, threats, and inducements that Bowville can use to persuade the cannery to acquiesce in a decision that would otherwise be unacceptable, and vice versa. Even Bowville and Plympton, though their interests in the treatment of the river are almost diametrically opposed, can bargain a bit out in the corridor: if Plympton will moderate her demands for waste treatment, Bowville will be more agreeable in sharing the burden of maintaining the county roads. Such bargaining is an essential part of practical politics. It can shift the outcome of the decision process from one Pareto admissible decision to another. Thus it can influence where in the range of likely outcomes the ultimate decision will come to fall. It reinforces the finding that our prediction is a range rather than a point. But such side bargaining will not push the decision outside the Pareto admissible range.

Our other political simplification is, in principle, more fundamental. We assumed that each of the participants had a firm and immutable evaluation of the consequences of every decision for his own welfare. This assumption was contained in our estimation of the values attached by the participants to increments in water quality at different points in the river, and in our treatment of those evaluations as unchanged throughout the decision process. In fact, a significant feature of any group decision process is the attempt by each participant to persuade the others to alter their psychological evaluations so that they are more in line with his. The representatives of Plympton and the Izaak Walton League will emphasize the benefits to everyone of high quality water throughout the river and, in fact, will urge it as a moral imperative. The representatives of the cannery will point out that the prosperity of the entire basin depends on the economical use of the waste-absorption potential of the river. To the extent that this rhetoric is not in vain it will succeed in causing some of the participants to change their subjective valuations of the importance of improvements in water quality. It will make our Table 6 invalid.

How serious is this difficulty? This is a significant and open question, fundamental to the understanding of the political process. Perusal of the histories of ORSANCO and the DRBC suggests, however, that when specific decisions are being debated most of the rhetoric is ineffectual, that people want at the end much what they wanted at the beginning, and that the operative aspect of the bargaining process is a reconciliation of the pressures that the different interest groups have been able to mobilize.[23]

Comparison with Current Practice The prevalent method for analyzing public policy decisions of the sort dealt with here is benefit-cost analysis. Superficially, benefit-cost analysis applies to the government sector the calculus of profit and loss that is used in business decisions. Its popularity is at least partly a response to the businesslike ethic that prevails in our culture. But its contrast with the approach here advocated is, in fact, more profound than the question of whether the government should follow businesslike practices. It is really a reflection of the most ancient cleavage in the tradition of political philosophy.

One great school of political philosophy views a government as the leader of its people, responsible for defining the goals of its citizens and formulating their social standards, preferably under the wise guidance of a philosopher-king or benevolent despot. The other great school sees the government as the corporate embodiment of its people, serving their communal interests and carrying out their wishes, preferably as expressed in direct (nowadays, participatory) democracy.

Traditionally these two views have been advanced as norms, as expressions of what governments ought to be. But they deserve also to be taken seriously as expressions of how governments actually behave. Examples of both governmental leadership and responsiveness are easy to find. ORSANCO, which provides the best documented experience in the water pollution area thanks to Cleary, was established in response to public demand (i.e., the demand of a few leading private citizens who mobilized widespread support) and went on to exercise a good deal of leadership and initiative of its own. It did so, however, less by pursuing its own goals than by undertaking a series of educational activities that increased its constituents' awareness of the importance of abating the pollution in the Ohio.

We cannot pursue here the rather ill-defined issue of leadership versus responsiveness. In practice, government agencies appear to mix the two in varying proportions, with responsiveness proponderating except for transitory episodes, usually at the highest levels of government.[24]

Benefit-cost analysis is, however, an expression of the leadership role of government. A benefit-cost formula is a tool for evaluating the desirability of different undertakings by the government's standards. This has long been recognized, though not so frequently articulated. For example, one of the chronic condundrums in benefit-cost analysis is the choice of the rate of discount to be used in evaluating deferred benefits and costs. This rate, selected by agency officials or expert consultants, represents the official evaluation of the relative importance of consequences that emerge at different dates. Similarly, the Flood Control Act of 1936 instructs agencies to compute benefit-cost ratios by adding up the benefits and costs of a project "to whomsoever they may accrue." The intent is to maintain neutrality, but the effect is to impose a judgment about the relative social importance of effects upon upstream users and downstream users, rich and poor, farmers and urbanites, and so on. All governmental undertakings redistribute income in some manner, as we have seen in the case of the Bow Valley.[25] Any evaluative formula must incorporate some appraisal of dedistributive consequences, either implicitly or explicitly. A third example of the governmental evaluations built into benefit-cost analyses is provided by the problem of aggregating benefits, and costs, of different kinds. When the beneficial results are priced on economic markets, as is the case with irrigation water and hydroelectric power, the market prices are used. Otherwise prices representing social evaluations have to be found. Outdoor recreation benefits, for example, are frequently valued at $1.50 per user day but some authorities insist that use by comparatively deprived urban dwellers should be assigned higher "merit" values.[26] Clearly, some values have to be used, and any values represent the judgment of the agency that adopts them. Finally, some consequences of government undertakings, which are deemed excessively difficult to evaluate, are simply omitted from benefit-cost calculations. This, too, represents an implicit governmental judgment, and one that has drawn much criticism.[27] In sum, there is no way out of it: a benefit-cost formula incorporates many judgments, implicit and explicit, of the relative importance of the numerous diverse consequences of the undertakings being evaluated. These judgments must be those of the agency doing the evaluation or its superiors in the governmental hierarchy.

In fundamental contrast to the benefit-cost approach, the analysis used here invokes no other evaluations than those of the people affected. It is explicitly noncommittal with respect to the relative importance or influence of the different participants; that is why it does not lead to an unambiguous prediction. It assembles the data from which those people and the agency concerned derive their decisions, but it does not presume that anyone has a formula for global social evaluation. Therefore it does not purport to recommend what should be done, but only to describe how actors in a political process interact to produce a decision.

This analysis cannot be regarded as an alternative, even in principle, to the decisionmaking methods actually used. But it can be of assistance in understanding and even facilitating those methods. Its advantage lies in its ability to sketch quickly and cheaply the range of alternative decisions that is worth considering. In our test case, with the data and a moderately fast computer at hand, between two and three minutes were required to determine the corresponding admissible decision. By varying the assumed data artfully, the main outlines of the entire range of admissible decisions were mapped out with about sixty repetitions of this quick computation.

Of course, the computations that would be required in a practical instance are of an entirely different order of magnitude from those encountered in this simple test. Contemplate any actual river basin. It would contain a half-dozen or more cities and towns, several dozen factories or other points of waste discharge, a mainstream, and a number of tributaries with complicated hydrology. In addition, many among our impressive list of simplifying assumptions would be inappropriate. Policy instruments besides the enforcement of a certain percentage waste removal at the source would be relevant, and a rich variety of alternative technologies of waste management would have to be considered. Our uni-dimensional measure of water quality would be considered inadequate, as would our simple specification of the relationship between waste discharge and stream condition. Provision for future growth in wastes would need to be introduced, along with some appropriate method of dealing with uncertainty. If all these complications were taken into account, the calculations would not only be much larger than those that we have encountered, but would be beyond the capacity of any computer now extant or envisaged.

These complexities, however, do not render mathematical analysis inapplicable. They do necessitate a good deal of simplification of the full richness of reality. Simplifying assumptions would have to be made about waste management options, though probably not as severe as the simplifications that we have indulged in. A water quality index of one or two dimensions would have to be introduced in place of the multidimensional specifications set forth in water quality standards documents. The hydrology would have to be simplified. The number of points of pollution would have to be reduced by consolidating groups of nearby installations into a single synthetic polluter. All these and other simplifications would have to be carried to the point where the calculation became manageable.

The result would be an inevitable loss in accuracy. But this necessity does not invalidate the method, for the relevant standard of accuracy is not some unattainable ideal but the level of accuracy that is attainable by alternative procedures. The truth is that the economic-hydrologic-biologic-political ecology of a live river basin in the full majesty of its intricacy far transcends the capacity of any method of analysis of decisionmaking available to man. All methods of decisionmaking require severe simplifications, as a perusal of the dockets of any water control authority will establish. And, there is reason to believe, the simplifications required for mathematical analysis are less disabling than the simplifications that are conventional in more informal procedures. Only hard experience can determine how practical and helpful mathematical analyses will be in actual instances, but the fact that they must invoke some serious simplifications is not *ipso facto* decisive.

NOTES

* References in brackets may be found at the end of this chapter.

[1] Or, anyway, not much more.

[2] The description of the problem necessarily involves some technical concepts, such as these. Most of them will be explained below.

[3] Professor Harold A. Thomas, Jr. acted as consulting engineer for this study. We are indebted to him for formulating and analyzing the hydrological and engineering aspects of our sample basin.

[4] Quality classifications will be explained more fully below.

[5] In more detailed analyses of biochemical pollution, a distinction is made between first-stage (or carbonaceous) and second-stage (or nitrogenous) BOD. For the purposes of this discussion, however, it is preferable to avoid the additional technical discussion which this more complex specification would require. The original version of this paper [5] did include consideration of the two-stage model of biochemical degradation.

[6] Or from the table: $\frac{60 - 30}{80 - 30}(13{,}000) = \$7{,}800$.

[7] There are many ways for a city to finance waste treatment facilities other than by the property tax as we assume here. Alternative financing methods differ not only in the impact of a particular facility on the city budget and in the distribution of costs among households and business firms; they also affect the total amount of waste to be handled. For example, certain types of sewer fees offer an incentive for industries and commercial establishments to cut back on total waste by means of internal process changes, while financing by the property tax offers no such incentive.

[8] Other pollutants that would be especially important in the sort of situation we are discussing include coliform bacteria (from municipal waste) and nutrients. We assume that the former is taken care of by chlorination (which is relatively cheap). Nutrients will not be discussed explicitly but deserve mention here because they are a source of increasing concern to water quality managers.

[9] Adapted from the Massachustets standards.

[10] Examples range from the definition of Grade A fresh eggs to the occupancy and safety regulations in building and zoning codes.

[11] Only the most casual treatment of the technical aspects of water quality is offered here. A brief introduction to the topic is provided also by Kneese and Bower [8, pp. 13–29]; for details of wastewater engineering see Fair, Geyer, and Okun [6].

[12] The constant 0.3 is subtracted from each x_i since this is the BOD reduction achieved under the basal condition of primary treatment by all polluters.

[13] Note the similarity to the difficulties caused by the income effect of expenditure in the conventional theory of consumer behavior.

[14] A full description of the linear programming model was presented in an appendix to the original version of this paper [5].

[15] Class A ($Q = 7$ mg/l or above) was found to be not attainable given the pollution loads and treatment alternatives that we assumed earlier.

[16] This is a familiar situation. To say that the temperature is 90° doesn't say how hot it is in any absolute sense, but only how hot it is compared with other temperatures all referred to the same arbitrary zero, 32° below the freezing point of water.

[17] In fact, Decision 3 is itself Pareto admissible, though not for any of the weight allocations in the range we have used in this analysis. For example, Decision 3 is the recommended plan under the weights $w = (6.0, 3.0, 0.5, 0.5)$.

[18] For an instructive discussion of the technical peculiarities of linear models see Baumol and Bushnell [2].

[19] In our problem, for example, incremental costs change at the breakpoints of the individual polluters' treatment cost functions. As shown in Table 6, marginal benefits to each of the participants change at DO levels of 5.0 mg/l.

[20] There is another dimension—net benefits to the FWPCA—that is not shown in the figure. The pertinent data are in Table 9.

The connecting lines in Figure 5 are analogous to what economists would call "utility-possibility frontiers." For an elaboration of this device, see F. M. Bator [1].

[21] Decision 7 is Pareto admissible under the weights (6.0, 3.0, 0.5, 0.5), as was Decision 3.

[22] There are many sets of weights besides $w = (7, 1, 1, 1)$ that would recommend Decision 12, though our analysis has not revealed them. In fact, the weight distributions form a continuum; for each Pareto admissible decision discovered by the model there is a range of relative weights within the continuum that would lead to that same decision. The probability that a particular decision will be taken is the probability that the actual distribution of political influence will fall within the range of political weight allocations that lead to that decision. If we were to explore in detail the boundaries of the range of influence weights that recommend Decision 12, we should expect to find that all allocations within the range give the cannery the preponderant influence in determining the outcome.

[23] For an instructive account of the issues faced by ORSANCO and their resolution see Cleary [3].

[24] Truman [12] presents a full-dress analysis of governmental responsiveness.

[25] This problem is discussed more completely by Marglin [11, pp. 67ff.]. Marglin recommends that different values be assigned to different consequences, dependent on the beneficiary. For a full treatment of the theoretical significance of income redistribution see Little [9].

[26] Mack and Myers [10] is a careful analysis of the problem of evaluating recreational benefits from a social point of view. There is much additional literature, some cited by them.

[27] These criticisms are reviewed by Dorfman [4] and elsewhere in the volume in which it appears.

REFERENCES

[1] Bator, F. M., "The Simple Analytics of Welfare Maximization," *American Economic Review, 47* (March 1957), pp. 22–59.

[2] Baumol, W. J. and R. C. Bushnell, "Error Produced by Linearization in Mathematical Programming," *Econometrica, 35* (July–October 1967), pp. 447–471.

[3] Cleary, Edward J., *The ORSANCO Story—Water Quality Management in the Ohio Valley under an Interstate Compact.* Baltimore: Johns Hopkins Press, 1967.

[4] Dorfman, R., "Introduction" in *Measuring Benefits of Government Investments,* R. Dorfman, ed. Washington: The Brookings Institution, 1965, pp. 1–11.

[5] Dorfman R., and H. D. Jacoby, "A Model of Public Decisions Illustrated by a Water Pollution Policy Problem" in *The Analysis and Evaluation of Public Expenditures: The PPB System,* submitted to the Subcommittee on Economy in Government, U.S. Congress, Joint Economic Committee, May 29, 1969.

[6] Fair, G. M., J. C. Geyer, and D. A. Okun, *Water and Wastewater Engineering,* Volume II. New York: John Wiley and Sons, 1968.

[7] Holden, Matthew, Jr., "Political Control as a Bargaining Process: An Essay on Regulatory Decision-Making," pub. no. 9, Cornell University Water Resources Center, October 1966.

[8] Kneese, A. V. and B. T. Bower, *Managing Water Quality: Economics, Technology, Institutions.* Baltimore: Johns Hopkins Press, 1968.

[9] Little, I. M. D., *A Critique of Welfare Economics,* 2d ed. London: Oxford University Press, 1957.

[10] Mack, R. P. and S. Myers, "Outdoor Recreation" in *Measuring Benefits of Government Investments,* R. Dorfman, ed. Washington: The Brookings Institution, 1965, pp. 71–101.

[11] Marglin, S. A., "Objectives of Water Resource Development: A General Statement," *Design of Water-Resource Systems,* Arthur Maass, et al. Cambridge: Harvard University Press, 1962, Chapter 2.

[12] Truman, David B., *The Governmental Process: Political Interests and Public Opinion.* New York: Alfred A. Knopf, 1951.

CHAPTER 8

INSTITUTIONAL OBSTACLES TO REALLOCATING GOVERNMENT EXPENDITURES

Murray L. Weidenbaum

INTRODUCTION

The increased efforts that economists and others have been making in recent years to improve the concepts and procedures for allocating public resources make it especially necessary and desirable to focus greater attention on the obstacles to making these improvements operational. One major set of obstacles to improving public resource allocation is the legal and other institutional constraints that limit the discretion of governmental policymakers.

For example, under present law it is almost futile to perform benefit-cost of similar analyses which may demonstrate that the government obtains a lower return on its investments in highway transportation than in air transportation or some other alternative and, hence, that some shifting of funds might improve economic welfare. The futility arises from the simple fact that the major financial authorizations for highway programs are not contained in the appropriation bills requested by the president and enacted by the Congress, but in the relatively long-term legislation which authorizes the federal-aid highway program. Thus, the Congress cannot, through the budget review and appropriations process, in practice effect a transfer of funds from surface to air transportation by reducing the appropriations for the Bureau of Public Roads and increasing those for the Federal Aviation Agency, two component units of the Department of Transportation.

Similarly, there is no discretion through the budget process to shift funds from an income-maintenance program such as public assistance to aid to education, both functions of the Department of Health, Education,

Murray L. Weidenbaum is Professor of Economics at Washington University in St. Louis. He is currently on leave, serving as an Assistant Secretary of the Treasury for Economic Policy. An earlier version of this analysis appears in M. L. Weidenbaum, "On the Effectiveness of Congressional Control of the Public Purse," *National Tax Journal,* December 1965. The author is indebted to Mr. Suk Tai Suh for assistance in developing the statistical materials used here.

and Welfare—or to any other purpose whether it involves expenditures or tax reduction. This rigidity arises because the expenditures under the public assistance program are in the nature of fixed charges; they are predetermined by statutory formulas governing federal matching of state disbursements for public assistance. Given the permanent statute on the books, the amount that the federal government spends on this income-maintenance activity each year is determined by the pattern of state welfare disbursements. Neither the president nor the Congress can much influence the amount of federal expenditures in this area within the confines of the budget process. Changes in the basic social security legislation would be necessary.

There are many other examples of these institutional obstacles to improving the allocation of public resources, as will be shown later on a more comprehensive basis. The end result of course is that the process of public resource allocation is hardly that deliberate and systematic choice among alternatives that economists try to envision. Rather, it is a fragmented and compartmentalized affair. Many of the key decisions are not made during the budget process or within the budgetary framework at all.

It is an earlier stage of the process which is the effective point of decisionmaking on numerous government spending programs—the enactment of substantive and often permanent legislation. This is the birth stage, and rebirth and growth stages, of a substantial proportion of federal spending. This is the stage where many of the basic policy decisions are made—the nature of farm subsidies, the types of public assistance payments, and the level of highway grants. However, since it is the substantive committees of the Congress which handle enabling or authorizing legislation (e.g. Commerce or Foreign Relations or Public Works), rather than the appropriations committees, cost implications of the new programs often are relegated to secondary consideration or even ignored.

As will be demonstrated below in quantitative terms, the effectiveness of appropriations control over federal government expenditures is far less than it superficially appears to be.[1]

This study of the techniques of governmental budgeting may shed some light on the substantive issues involved in the allocation of government resources. It may help to explain, for example, why the military budget goes through cycles of alternate expansions and contractions, while the expenditures of domestic-civilian activities—notably the social welfare programs—continue to rise almost without interruption. The basic explanation presented here is in terms of the differences in the relative controllability, through the appropriations review process, of the different types of government spending programs.

TYPES OF BUDGET CONTROLLABILITY

This study focuses on the effectiveness of congressional power over the public purse, as measured by the degree to which the presidential budgetary recommendations are subject to substantial modification through the appropriations process. In most cases, the discretion of the executive branch in preparing the budget estimates is also limited by similar institutional obstacles.

The rather narrow definition of controllability of government funding used here needs to be emphasized. The analysis is being made from the viewpoint of annual action by the Congress on the appropriation bills that finance the various government agencies. Given a long enough time span and the support of the Congress as a whole, virtually all federal spending programs are susceptible to modification, if not elimination. If it so wished, the Congress could repeal the substantive, permanent legislation requiring public assistance grants or veterans pensions or farm price supports, or at least modify the statutes to make them more permissive. In time, it could conceivably retire the public debt and thus obviate the need for annual interest payments or at least reduce the size of the debt to be serviced.

Nevertheless, in practice the president and the Congress do not face each year's budget preparation and review cycle with a clean slate; they must take account of large accumulations of legal restraints within which they must operate.

From the viewpoint of appropriations review, there are thus numerous exogenous forces and factors which they must take account of and cannot effectively control: the number of eligible veterans who apply for pensions or compensation, the amount of public assistance payments made by the states and for which they must be partially reimbursed according to prescribed matching formulas, and so forth. The relatively controllable portion of the budget, from this viewpoint, consists of those government spending programs where the determining factors are endogenous to the appropriations process, which may modify them, at least to a considerable extent.

Four categories of exogenous institutional barriers to improving (or at least changing) the allocation of government resources are identified here: trust funds, permanent and indefinite appropriations, fixed charges, and ongoing projects. These categories are not mutually exclusive and thus individual programs have been assigned to them sequentially; that is, all federal government activities operated through trust funds have been assigned to that category, even though the great bulk is financed through permanent and indefinite appropriations. Thus the category of permanent or indefinite appropriations is limited to federal activities not operated through trust funds. Similarly, activities financed under permanent appropriations may be viewed as a fixed charge on the annual budget. Nevertheless, only programs which do not fall within the two categories mentioned previously (trust funds and permanent or indefinite appropriations) are shown as fixed charges. Thus, double counting is avoided.

Trust Funds

The first category of relatively uncontrollable items dealt with here are the so-called trust funds. These vary from the large social insurance type of mechanisms, such as the old-age, survivors', and disability insurance program, to the gift fund for the Library of Congress. The common characteristic of these trust funds which is relevant for the present inquiry is that they are generally financed through permanent appropriations which do not require annual action by the Congress. As stated in one recent budget document:

> "Most trust fund receipts are made available for use by permanent law, without requiring further action by Congress."[2]

Another clear indication of the relative uncontrollability of these trust funds through the budget process is that they generally do not even appear in the annual appropriation bills. In the case of the social insurance funds, the actual level of expenditures is determined by the number of eligible persons who apply for benefits during a given year.

For grants to states for highways, the federal-aid Highway Act of 1954 and amendments to it not only authorize the program but also provide authority to enter into obligations, in this case to commit the federal government to make grants to the states at a later date. This bypassing of the appropriations process is often referred to as "backdoor spending." Technically, however, it is backdoor financing. The actual disbursements of the federal funds to the states require the Congress to enact so-called "appropriations to liquidate contract authorizations." The latter is a mere formality. There is virtually no presidential or congressional discretion over these liquidating appropriations—the government was financially committed at an earlier point, at the time the obligations were incurred.

In the federal budget for the fiscal year 1969, trust funds accounted for $55.1 billion or 27 percent of the total budget authorizations requested for the year.

Permanent and Indefinite Appropriations

In addition to the trust funds, there are numerous permanent appropriations which are contained in budget funds. The largest of these is the permanent and indefinite appropriation for the payment of interest on the national debt: "Such amounts are appropriated as may be necessary to pay the interest each year on the public debt" [31 U.S.C. 711 (2) and 732].

Other permanent accounts cover such items as the appropriations to the Department of Agriculture for removal of surplus farm commodities and to the Department of the Interior for range improvements. Thirty percent of gross customs receipts is automatically available to finance the agriculture program each year, regardless of estimated need or relative desirability *vis-à-vis* the changing mix of public sector activities. One-third of grazing revenues from federal lands are similarly available for range improvement work.

A related category of funding is the "indefinite" appropriations. Although these are contained in the annual appropriation bills, they are in the nature of a blank check good for one year. Indefinite appropriations authorize a goverment agency to spend the sums necessary to meet a given specified requirement. For example, the Post Office Department is financed through an annual indefinite appropriation. So is the retired pay of commissioned officers of the Public Health Service.

In the fiscal 1969 budget, permanent or indefinite appropriations (other than to trust funds) accounted for $20.2 billion or 10 percent of the total budget authorizations requested.

Other Fixed Charges

A third type of budget request which is relatively uncontrollable through the appropriations process is often termed a "fixed charge." These are programs where the level of spending is determined effectively by basic statutes rather than through the review of annual appropriation requests. The largest programs in this category are the appropriations for public assistance and for veterans' compensation and pension payments. The Department of Health, Education, and Welfare makes grants to states to reimburse them for a fixed share of the public assistance payments that they make. Similarly, the Veterans' Administration provides statutorily determined benefits to all qualifying veterans or their widows and children who apply.

Although programs such as these are funded through annual definite appropriations, there is little effective control over the actual level of disbursements. Frequently, the initial appropriations turn out to be too low and supplemental appropriations are subsequently requested and routinely approved. There is considerable incentive for the Congress to appropriate less than the initial amount requested in the budget for these items. Thus, it gains some political benefit for supposedly "cutting" the budget. They then can later and much more quietly vote supplemental funds.

In the fiscal 1969 budget, fixed charges (other than those arising from trust funds and other permanent appropriations) amounted to $19.0 billion or 9 percent of budget requests.

Partially-completed Projects

The final type of relatively uncontrollable budget activity analyzed here is the amount of new funds requested to continue or complete construction and similar long-term projects started with money voted in the budgets of earlier years. The almost unassailable justification for these appropriations is the old question, "What is the value of just half a bridge?" Typically for government agencies with large construction programs, such as the Army Corps of Engineers and the Department of the Interior, each year's budget request is dominated by funds needed for projects begun under prior year budgets.

One indication of this influence of previous commitments is the fact that the Federal Budget for 1969 estimated that $2.4 billion would be spent in that year to carry on construction projects previously begun and for which a total of $28.8 billion already had been spent prior to the budget year. Even though these expenditure figures are not directly comparable to the appropriation or budget authority estimates used in the present study, the contrast between large amounts of what in effect are sunk costs and relatively small increments of additional funding is clear.[3]

The National Aeronautics and Space Administration (NASA) may constitute a special case at the present time. The great bulk of its current expenditures is devoted to completion of Project Apollo, the effort to land a man on the moon prior to 1970. Theoretically, the program can be reduced or stretched out and thus the president or the Congress could reduce the funds requested for Apollo. In practice, there is a very natural reluctance to interfere with the successful completion of an undertaking in which the nation already has invested such sizeable funds (over $15 billion for Apollo during the fiscal years 1959–68 alone).

The data for funds requested to continue or complete ongoing projects, as shown in the tables that follow, are incomplete. In many cases it was not possible from publicly available information to identify the specific long-term projects of many agencies. Thus, the funds shown as relatively controllable are overstated, and the uncontrolled funds understated.

The Department of Defense (military functions) constitutes the major example of this gap in our knowledge and thus no military projects are shown in this category of relative uncontrollable programs. On occasion individual weapon systems have been cancelled after substantial investment of development and production funds. Nevertheless, budget reviewers in both the executive and legislative branches often are reluctant to terminate a large project, even though the changing course of events indicates that the returns may not be as attractive as originally envisioned.

It may be that nonstatutory, implied commitments may be of overriding importance in military budgets from time to time. During the Vietnam War, for example, the Congress has appropriated virtually all of the funds requested in support of that specific and costly military endeavor. Formally, the $30 billion a year request for Vietnam was subject to substantial reduction by the appropriations committee, and is therefore included in the controllable portion of the budget in this analysis; in practice no substantial modifications of the Vietnam estimates were considered by the Congress. However, the Congress did critically review and modify the non-Vietnam portions of the budget of the Department of Defense.[4]

In essence, what is involved here in justifying this military situation, and comparable civil ones, is an implicit incremental benefit-cost analysis: will the returns from the completion of the total project exceed the additional cost to be incurred in completing it? Clearly, many projects midway in the construction state may show incremental benefit-cost ratios substantially in excess of unity, whereas freshly computed total benefit-cost ratios would indicate far less attractive results. There may be substantial political onus attached to abandoning an effort after the investment of substantial public funds. The completion and operation of a public undertaking where the newly determined estimated costs are greater than the estimated benefits is hardly likely to attract great public attention.

ESTIMATES OF RELATIVE BUDGET CONTROLLABILITY

On the basis of the foregoing analysis, Table 1 was prepared in an effort to indicate the relative controllability of the budget requests of the various federal departments and agencies. The data cover all of the recommended budget authority (new obligational authority as well as loan authority) contained in the Federal Budget for the fiscal year 1969. Table 1 includes both budget and trust funds and is based on the unified budget concept, the most comprehensive measure of federal finance available at the present time.

In the aggregate, the trust funds, the ongoing construction projects, and the other permanent and indefinite appropriations and fixed charges account for a major share of the budget—$97.5 billion or 48 percent of the total budget authority requested in the fiscal year 1969. It should be emphasized that where the budget document and available supporting materials did not provide sufficient detail, or where any doubtful cases existed, the items in question were treated as controllable. Hence, there

Table 1

Controllability of Federal Government Budget Requests—Fiscal Year 1969

[In millions of dollars]

Department or agency	Relatively uncontrollable				Relatively controllable	Total
	Trust funds	Permanents, indefinites	Fixed charges	Ongoing projects		
Funds appropriated to the President	1,324				4,819	6,143
Agriculture	68	735	3,831		2,896	7,530
Commerce	134	214			679	1,027
Defense—military	7		2,313		76,796	79,116
Defense—civil	9	4		950	344	1,307
Health, Education, and Welfare	37,670	41	7,456	13	6,190	51,370
Housing and Urban Development	159	1,821	358		3,004	5,342
Interior	97	268		180	312	857
Justice					542	542
Labor	4,095		145		596	4,836
Post Office		920				920
State	12	2			414	428
Transportation	4,703	70	51		1,701	6,525
Treasury	39	15,425			−54	15,410
Civil Service Commission	3,626		42		131	3,799
General Services Administration		1	2		327	330
Railroad Retirement Board	1,064		18			1,082
Veterans' Administration	746	12	4,664		2,368	7,790
NASA	1			2,133	2,235	4,369
Export-Import Bank		608				608
Farm Credit Administration	535					535
All other	773	97	91		896	1,857
Total	55,062	20,218	18,971	3,276	104,196	201,723

Note: Includes requested new obligational authority and loan authority.
Source: Based on data contained in *Budget of the United States Government, Fiscal Year 1969*, and appendix.

may be some significant underestimation of the relatively uncontrollable portion of the budget shown here. As mentioned earlier, there undoubtedly is an underestimate in the ongoing project category.[5]

Variations by Agency and Program

Were the fixed charges and other relatively uncontrollable items distributed proportionally to the size of the budgets of the various government agencies, the interference with the allocation of government resources might be less than is presently the case. However, as shown in Table 2, this is hardly the case. Some agency programs virtually escape the scrutiny of effective annual budgetary review—the Post Office, the Export-Import Bank, the Railroad Retirement Board, the Farm Credit Administration, and the great bulk of the Treasury Department.[6]

At the other end of the controllability spectrum, all or almost the entire annual budgets of the Department of Defense (excluding civil functions such as the Corps of Engineers' construction work), the Departments

Table 2
Relatively Controllable Portions of Agency Budgets—Fiscal Year 1969 Budget Requests

Justice	100
General Service Administration	99
Defense (military)	97
State	97
Funds Appropriated to the President	78
Commerce	66
Housing and Urban Development	56
NASA	51
All other	48
Agriculture	38
Interior	36
Veterans' Administration	30
Defense (civil)	26
Transportation	26
Health, Education, and Welfare	12
Labor	12
Civil Service Commission	3
Post Office	0
Treasury	0
Railroad Retirement Board	0
Export-Import Bank	0
Farm Credit Administration	0
Average for Federal Government	52

Source: Table 1.

of Justice and State, and the General Services Administration are subject to effective control through the annual budget process.

An interesting contrast appears between the two departments with the largest budgets, one military and the other civilian. The Department of Defense—which received most of the funds appropriated for national defense purposes—operates with very few and very small trust funds and other fixed charges. Almost all of its budget is subject to annual scrutiny.[7] In comparison, only one-tenth of the HEW budget can effectively be altered during the annual budget cycle. Most of the funds spent are insulated by permanent and indefinite appropriations and other long-term statutory commitments.

Upon further examination, it can be seen that a relatively small number of large programs account for the bulk of the funds which are relatively immune to effective budgetary control. The following 12 programs of over $1 billion each account for over $85 billion or 88 percent of the portion of the fiscal year 1969 Budget which is here estimated to be "relatively uncontrollable":

	In millions
Social security trust funds	$37,670
Interest on the public debt	15,200
Public assistance	5,765
Veterans' pensions and compensation	4,654
Highway grants to states	4,650
Unemployment insurance	4,095
Civil service retirement payments	3,626
CCC (Farm price supports)	3,362
Military retired pay	2,275
Project Apollo	2,133
Medicare (Treasury contribution)	1,360
Railroad retirement payments	1,064

The Relatively Controllable Portion of the Federal Budget

Table 3 shows the distribution by agency of the relatively controllable portion of the federal budget authorizations requested for the fiscal year 1969. It is apparent that the Department of Defense accounts for the great bulk of the funds where the president and the Congress possess substantial discretion over the amounts initially requested (74 percent). For purposes of comparison, it can be noted that the DOD represents 38 percent of the total federal budget.

A handful of other departments and agencies—Agriculture, HEW, Transportation, NASA, and the Veterans' Administration account for the bulk of the remainder of the relatively controlled portion of the budget.

Table 3
Distribution of Relatively Controllable Budget Requests—Fiscal year 1969 Budget Requests

	Percent
Defense (military)	74
Health, Education, and Welfare	6
Funds Appropriated to the President	5
Agriculture	3
Housing and Urban Development	3
Transportation	2
Veterans' Administration	2
NASA	2
Commerce	1
Labor	1
All other	1
Defense (civil)	*
Interior	*
Justice	*
State	*
Civil Service Commission	*
General Services Administration	*
Post Office	0
Treasury	0
Railroad Retirement Board	0
Export-Import Bank	0
Farm Credit Administration	0
Total	100

* Less than one-half of 1 percent.
Source: Table 1.

REDUCING THE INSTITUTIONAL OBSTACLES

The data presented earlier lead to the rather striking conclusion that the great bulk of the expenditures for the domestic civilian agencies of the federal government is authorized virtually automatically as a result of the basic, continuing commitments previously enacted by the Congress, rather than through the deliberations of the annual budgetary process. Somewhat less conclusively, it appears that the military programs are susceptible to effective budgetary review to a far greater extent.

For most of the nondefense programs, the effective point of control appears to occur not at the time that the appropriations are voted, but at the earlier period where the Congress enacts the basic legislative commitments, that is, the rates of veterans' pensions or social security benefits.

For purposes of analysis, it may be helpful to divide the various uncontrollable items into two categories, "natural" and "artificial" (this attempt at labeling by no means exhausts the possibilities).

The "natural" type of uncontrollable item is exemplified by the permanent, indefinite appropriation for the payment of interest on the public debt. These payments arise directly from the amount and types of public debt issues which are currently outstanding. There is no discretion left at the disbursement phase of the process; the federal government simply must honor its promise to pay the interest on its obligations as it falls due. The natural uncontrollability of this item expense is acknowledged by the Congress in the form of a permanent appropriation to pay interest with no fixed dollar limit.

Similarly, the making of monthly compensation payments to veterans on account of service-connected disabilities is a program which is naturally uncontrollable within the confines of the budget process. The law requires monthly payments to all those certified by VA doctors as possessing a given percentage impairment of earnings. However, in this case the Congress insists on annually reviewing the appropriation for the payment of veterans' pensions and compensation. It is hard to characterize this congressional review as anything other than wheelspinning or having "fun and games" with the budget. Moreover, this exercise in futility diverts executive branch and congressional time and attention to the budget away from the areas where they can significantly alter the results.

In sharp contrast, there are numerous government programs which are artificially uncontrollable as a result of statutory law, but which lend themselves, through changes in substantive legislation, to effective annual budgetary review. For example, under section 32 of the act of August 24, 1935 (U.S.C. 612 C) an amount equal to 30 percent of annual customs receipts is automatically appropriated into a permanent, indefinite special fund for the "removal of surplus agricultural commodities." These amounts bear little relationship to the requirements for such funds. In fact, recent appropriation acts have authorized transfers of funds to the school lunch program and for related activities. Clearly, the amount of funds automatically appropriated exceeds the needs of the basic activity financed by the appropriation.

The annual grants of $50,000 paid to each state and Puerto Rico for A & M colleges similarly are made under a permanent appropriation act. Neither the Bureau of the Budget nor the president nor the Congress has any opportunity to review the annual appropriation request and thus annually redetermine the continued need for or desirability of these payments.

There are numerous other examples. Many permanent indefinite appropriations to the Department of the Interior are tied to a portion of revenues from sales or rentals of government assets and bear little relationship to the current requirements for federal expenditures for the activity to which they are earmarked. Thus, visitor fees at Yellowstone National Park are automatically used to provide educational expenses for dependents of park personnel, while visitor fees at Grand Teton National Park are used automatically as payments to the state of Wyoming, in effect in lieu of taxes.

CONCLUSIONS

Although the analysis of individual government programs presented here is incomplete (partly due to the lack of available data), it is clear that the effectiveness of appropriations control over federal government expenditures is far less than is generally appreciated. The following changes might be considered toward reducing these institutional obstacles to improve the allocation of public resources.

1. *A review of the necessity for the numerous trust funds that have been established* —Some of them—such as those for the financing of social security benefits—appear to somewhat approximate the general notion of funds held in trust. In many other cases—such as the federal-aid highway program—it is hard to make a case for segregating the activity from ordinary budget operations. In that particular case, the program of federal grants to the states did operate out of general revenues until 1954. In good measure, the highway-related excises which are now funneled through the highway trust fund may be viewed more properly as a form of earmarked taxes and treated as a special fund within the regular budget procedure.

2. *A reevaluation of the need for the various permanent and indefinite appropriations* —Some of them may have outlived their usefulness. However, there is no automatic or periodic review of their status and a clean slate examination might be most useful.

3. *A reexamination of the "fixed charges" on the budget* —Some of them might usefully be converted into permanent or indefinite appropriations. In other cases, discretion might be restored to the appropriations committee to determine annually the amount to be voted for the stipulated purpose, in the light of then current conditions and competing requirements. This latter action, of course, would require changing the substantive legislation governing the program.

4. *A focusing of greater attention on "new starts" of construction and other long-term projects* —It is a natural tendency to place greater emphasis in the budgetary review process on the items with the largest price tags. However, as has been shown, most of the appropriation requests in this category of long-term projects are to continue or complete projects already

underway. The point of most effective control is at the outset, prior to the investment of public resources in the project. However, it is precisely at the starting-up stage where the appropriation requests are most modest and thus perhaps more readily approved. A careful weighing of the expected full or long-term costs and benefits is thus extremely important at the outset.[8]

The reduction of these institutional obstacles to maximizing the taxpayers' return on their investment will not of itself result in eliminating relatively low priority and less efficient government activity, but it should make efforts in that direction less difficult.

NOTES

[1] This substantive point is developed more fully in M. L. Weidenbaum, *Federal Budgeting: The Choice of Government Programs* (Washington, D.C.: American Enterprise Institute for Public Policy Research, 1964).

[2] *The Budget of the United States Government for the Fiscal Year Ending June 30, 1965,* Appendix (Washington, D.C.: U.S. Government Printing Office, 1964), p. 898.

[3] *Special Analyses, Budget of the United States, Fiscal Year 1969* (Washington, D.C.: U.S. Government Printing Office, 1968), p. 82.

[4] See U.S. House of Representatives, Committee on Appropriations, *Department of Defense Appropriations for 1969* (Washington, D.C.: U.S. Government Printing Office, 1968).

[5] For what was perhaps the pioneering attempt to analyze the controllability of Federal spending, but limited to the administrative budget, see "Controllability of 1952 Budget Expenditures," in Joint Committee on the Economic Report, U.S. Congress, *January 1951 Economic Report of the President* (Washington, D.C.: U.S. Government Printing Office, 1951), pp. 89–103.

[6] Interfund adjustments complicate the Treasury figures. In practice, the budgets of the operating bureaus are generally subject to effective annual review.

[7] As pointed out earlier, the Congress may be reluctant to exercise this potential control over the military budget during wartime and similar emergency periods.

[8] In recent years, the budget requests for military and selected other areas have been prepared on the basis of "full funding" of proposed projects, that is of appropriating the entire estimated cost of a project at the time it is started. This procedure helps to enable the Congress to ascertain the total cost of a project before the work actually begins. However, water resource projects continue to be an important exception to this desirable change. See *Special Analyses, Budget of the United States, Fiscal Year 1970* (Washington, D.C.: U.S. Government Printing Office, 1969), p. 81.

CHAPTER 9

THE ABSENCE OF KNOWLEDGE OF DISTRIBUTIONAL IMPACTS: AN OBSTACLE TO EFFECTIVE POLICY ANALYSIS AND DECISIONS

James T. Bonnen

INTRODUCTION

The distributional impacts of both public and private decisionmaking increasingly are being questioned. Despite our society's equity commitments, many public programs are administered with little attention to their distributional impact. It should not surprise us then when these programs exhibit perverse distributional consequences. Yet surprised we are at nearly every turn because we almost always fail to collect information on distributional impacts of programs. We do not even really understand the process by which distributional impacts work their way through the society. Without such knowledge we often work at cross purposes, we waste resources, and we fail to attain program objectives.

THE LACK OF KNOWLEDGE AND DATA ON DISTRIBUTIONAL IMPACTS

As one reviews congressional hearings and agency program materials, one is impressed by the lack of knowledge or even raw data on program impact including the distribution of program benefits. It is as if these were impolite if not impolitic questions to raise. We are unlikely to improve this situation, until Congress asks some of the more important distributional questions of those administering the programs. Additional resources will have to be put into more sophisticated data retrieval systems than presently exist. If Congress and the president do not demand this information, it will never exist in any systematic form.

James T. Bonnen is Professor of Agricultural Economics at Michigan State University.

The author wishes to acknowledge the helpful suggestions of William Capron, Lynn Daft, William Easter, Robert Haveman, Gail Steg, and Gene Wunderlich.

Economists have not even done the analysis of distributional issues that is now possible. The PPB system has helped to some extent to bring distributional questions into focus and to establish the relevance of equity issues. However, in a general sense, economists are still shirking the responsibility to move beyond efficiency criterion in their analytic interests.

The Information Necessary to Appraise Distributional Impacts

What do we need if we are to estimate the distributional impacts of public programs and judge their desirability? Look first at the ideal situation. We need to be able to answer the following questions in something like the order in which they are stated.

For benefits:

1. What is the purpose or objective of the public program or legislation, part of which is the question, *who should benefit?*

2. *Who actually benefits,* what groups? It is sometimes not easy to identify beneficiary groups clearly.

3. How much are the *total benefits* of the program? Placing a value on the benefits of many programs is also not an easy analytical proposition.

4. What is the *distribution of program benefits* among beneficiaries?

5. What is the *current distribution of incomes and assets* or other relevant dimensions of welfare among (a) actual beneficiaries and (b) intended or potential beneficiaries?

For costs:

6. *Who should pay the program costs?* Sometimes the nature of the program contains strong implications as to who the burdened should be; other times this is almost an unanswerable question.

7. *Who actually does pay* the cost of the program? Identification of the burdened groups should consider not only the tax structure, but direct price and income effects and the indirect effects of major factor and product substitution caused by the program.

8. What are the *total program costs?* Many times this includes, as it does in question 7, economic and social costs not reflected in federal budget expenditures but market and non-market costs generated through the operation of the program itself. Thus, these are not simple questions.

9. *How are program costs distributed* among the burdened groups?

10. What is the *current distribution of incomes and assets* among (a) the actual burdened groups and (b) the intended or potential burdened groups?

Finally:

11. Integrating the above information, what are *the alternatives* in achieving the same program objective and which alternative is most

efficient; that is, attains the same desired distributional (or other) impact but at a lower cost?

When one can answer all of these questions with some degree of clarity and when this information can be reasonably well integrated, it should be possible to evaluate the distributional impacts of the public program involved. I know of no case in which such an ideal has been obtained to date. Major theoretical as well as data gaps must be filled first. Until then, decision makers will operate with far less information. It should be pointed out, too, that economists as economists cannot answer all of these questions. The normative matter of who should benefit or who should pay involves value judgments which economists may not make as scientists. Of course, if some general statement of norms or objectives can be provided, the economist like any logician can develop certain conditionally normative deductions upon which to base a decision as to who should benefit and who should pay.

It is often not possible to answer with any clarity questions one and six about who should benefit and who should be burdened. The evidence from the legislation or from the program's history may not be that clear. The economist, however, may make a substantial clarifying contribution if he can answer questions two and seven; that is, who actually does benefit and who actually is burdened by the costs of these programs. By injecting positive information of this nature into the policy process one often helps produce a clarification of the objectives.

The economic theory literature most related to these questions is focused on the classical theory of factor shares and national income distribution.[1] Little of it is of value for our needs and even on its own grounds it is an intellectually underdeveloped area today. That which does serve to some extent is the eclectic benefit-cost and public finance literature. We are in need of theoretical and analytical constructs that will allow us to interrelate in a causal manner changes in macro-economic variables, public program impacts, and changes in the economic and social rules of society with the distribution of income and assets, not only for the Nation but for regions, various sociodemographic subsets, and interest groups. This is a tall order, but the needs are more and more urgent and economists must pursue this task.

Economists have spent most of their conceptual and empirical energy on questions three and eight, that is, in attempting to measure the total benefits and the total costs of particular programs. The empirical part of the benefit-cost measurement literature focuses almost exclusively on these questions.

Answering questions four and nine on the distribution of benefits and costs is rarely a simple problem for it varies profoundly with differences in the nature of the program and the variety of funding techniques used. Both funding and program influences are discussed in some detail in the following two sections.

Questions 5 and 10, about the prevailing income and asset distributions among actual or intended beneficiaries and burdened groups, are not independent of the first two questions about who the beneficiaries or burdened groups are or should be. Indeed, collecting data on such very specific incidence groups can be a difficult analytical and data collection problem. Not only are asset distributions generally nonexistent but getting income distributions for specific incidence groups can be extremely difficult, if not impossible, in many cases today. However, it is absolutely necessary to proceed through this stage, for even after you have measured the distribution of program benefits and burdens, it is not possible to judge the welfare or equity impact of the programs until you know the welfare and equity situation of those affected. Burton Weisbrod and W. Lee Hansen have a recent interesting treatment of this problem [27].

In the case of none of the programs that I am aware of, are we in a position today to mesh the information on the distribution of program benefits with really adequate knowledge of the prevailing welfare conditions of the target population. In fact, about the best we are able to do in most of these programs is to identify who the beneficiaries are. In few cases are we able to say how much of the benefits individuals with various characteristics receive. In even fewer cases can this then be matched with a little data on income characteristics of beneficiaries. In almost no case can we match benefits with current asset distributions for the target population. If you do not know what a program is currently doing to a target population you cannot possibly work intelligently and systematically to improve the direction and character of impact. Generally, we do not really know today what we are doing to ourselves in equity. Our state of knowledge is frankly pitiful.

Finally, answers to question 11 on the cost of alternatives to attain a program objective are necessary to provide information on the trade-off between alternative distributional (as well as other) features of a program.

The Effect of Funding Source

The funding of the social insurance programs out of trust fund sources presents a fundamentally different problem from that of a welfare program transferring money income to dependent children out of general funds collected directly from taxpayers. Measuring the distribution of burden presents a different problem if the program is funded from an income tax rather than a sales or property tax. In the situation where the program is funded out of general revenues, one has to assume a cross section of the revenue sources in structuring one's analysis of the distribution of burden.

In many cases where a program involves a product that is eventually sold to consumers (as in the wheat price support program) part of the cost of the transfer of benefits (to farmers) is funded not by taxpayers but by consumers through some device, the cost of which is passed on directly in the price to the consumer. In the case of the wheat program, a certificate payment system produces this consequence. Wheat price supports also result in higher than current free market prices and thus create a direct transfer from consumer to producer. In other cases public laws or programs may affect real wealth transfers directly between groups in the society without use of the market. Other programs are funded in a manner that transfers the incidence of burden over time, classically through the sale of debt. There are other issues that involve substantial spatial differences in the distribution of burden so that one region, in net effect, may be subsidizing another even though both are eligible for the program. Other questions of burden may require measurement of the impact on different income groups and various economic interests. In any case, it is readily seen that the problem of measuring the distribution of burden of program costs can be quite a different analytical problem from one program to another.

The real incidence of burden is not always obvious. Factor and product substitution effects can be very substantial and are rarely included in calculations of program costs. Structural factors intervene. The incidence literature in taxation identifies many situations in which incidence is shifted. Analogous situations arise in measuring the distribution of burden of program costs.

The Effect of Program Differences

The nature of the individual program also has a profound effect on the analytical problem. Expenditure programs are of many different forms. Capital investment programs, particularly of the natural resource development type, have been the primary focus of most of the benefit-cost type of analyses. Some of the most common federal expenditure programs, however, are those that transfer real income. These programs can be quite varied in nature. Some transfer income directly, other provide social services and even others transfer real income in kind, as in the food distribution programs. While equity considerations are not given very high priority in most capital investment programs they tend to be a prime objective of most public expenditure programs that transfer real income directly to some group in society. In any case, some equity considerations are eventually imposed on most direct income transfer programs even if they were not an original consideration in the intent of Congress or of the political interest groups that generated the support to create the program.

Government research and development (R. & D.) expenditures constitute a third type of public expenditure program that has distinctive implications for data needs and analysis. While the immediate beneficiaries of a federally subsidized R. & D. investment may be the initial recipients of the funds, the long run consequences of these programs transform the technologies of society and through technology many of society's social rules. These programs are of singular importance for they cast long shadows into all parts of the society.

Closely related are the regulatory programs and legislation that change the social organizational rules of society. Some of these, such as the antitrust laws, attempt direct manipulation of markets by imposing rules on the structure of markets or on market behavior. Much legislation deals directly with the rules by which society lives. Many of these rules, as for example, the patent and copyright laws, specify criteria that attempt to affect who shall get the initial direct benefit of a new idea or technology.

Finally, there are some additional matters. It is worth noting that the distributional impacts of program changes are likely to be different in the situation where the change in the program involves an expansion than where expenditures are cut. In short, there is a need to analyze distributional impacts at the margin when evaluating programs. The experience of tight budgets over the last several fiscal years has underlined this rather dramatically in some cases. Every economist understands that most changes in prices not only have a price effect but an income effect on both household and firm behavior. Similarly, most income changes have a price effect as well as an income effect. It is well to keep in mind in analyzing public programs that most changes in programs will have both a resource use effect as well as an income redistribution impact. Both will have incentive and disincentive consequences. In short, our responsibility in analyzing public programs does not end with the goal of efficiency and its measurement in a benefit-cost ratio. Indeed, efficiency and equity are intertwined analytically as well as in social policy.[2]

Additional Considerations

Besides gaining command over the distributional impacts of individual programs, Congress and the executive branch must know something more about the aggregated impact of federal programs by regions and for the United States as a whole. That is, we should know the regional effects of individual programs and thus their differential regional impacts, but we need as well to be able to aggregate the various resource development or education or health programs into regional aggregates with distributional knowledge within each region and between regions. We must gain an overview of the plethora of individual programs which presumably add up to some comprehensive whole. There are indications in our development literature and in studies of the social pathologies of this society, such as poverty, that some of our difficulties today arise as a result of systematic long term differentials in the distribution of investments in education, in natural resource development, etc. Before we can avoid these kinds of problems we need to know they exist.

There is, in addition, a need to develop a measurement of the distributional impacts of total federal program expenditures. We need an overview of the national picture of public expenditures and funding with their impact by various distributional characteristics—income, age, sex, family status, degree of urbanization and race, for example. Again some subcategorization such as educational programs, health, manpower, etc., would be useful as well. An interesting, though given the state of the arts a necessarily rather assumption-ridden, approach to this problem has been produced by W. Irwin Gillespie. His general finding is rather striking. His results indicate that for total government expenditures and funding:

> The federal pattern of fiscal incidence generally favors low incomes, burdens high income, and is mainly neutral over a wide middle income but is essentially neutral over both the middle and upper income range. The state and local pattern also favors low income ranges. A comparison of the two patterns controverts the conventional view that the state and local's tax structure is regressive and the federal tax structure progressive; indeed, just the reverse is true, for in net terms the state-local structure grants larger benefits to the lower income range than does the federal [13].

There are several reasons why one might question Gillespie's results but his empirical effort underlines dramatically the very significant conceptual and data needs we face before genuinely satisfactory measurement will be possible. Indeed, one of the conclusions that should be drawn from this and the earlier pioneering effort by Alfred Conrad is that this kind of empirical measurement of public program performance can best be done by the federal government itself or in very close cooperation with the Bureau of the Budget and other immediate sources of internal program data. [23].

Perhaps we need again to repeat the model that was followed in the creation of our national income statistics. Much of the intellectual investment in the primary design of concepts and system was executed by the National Bureau of Economic Research in close conjunction with federal statistical agencies. It was then implemented by the government as a federal system. Certainly the conceptual and data problems are on the same order of difficulty and we are in a similar early stage in developing these numbers for program analysis purposes. Such a system, of course, would be designed to collect data for the full range of program analysis needs including distributional questions.

DISTRIBUTIONAL CONSEQUENCES OF THREE GOVERNMENT PROGRAMS

This nation has a long history of creating public programs at least in major part for equity reasons. Among older examples are the farm programs, Corps of Engineers and Bureau of Reclamation programs, and many of the public assistance or welfare programs; examples from recent years include the poverty programs, the food distribution programs, many of the manpower and some of the education (Title I of ESEA) programs. Much of the current aid to urban areas has a major equity element among its purposes.

Yet the distributional consequences of our equity programs often turn out to be perverse. We seem to manage these programs without much continuing thought to their equity objectives. Equity objectives or standards are rarely spelled out in the legislation. Once enacted equity concerns seem to recede. Measurement of goal attainment is often reduced to gross rules of thumb, smearing and confusing the original legislative intent. The efficiency of administrative organization is substituted for program efficiency as an overriding congressional concern once clientele support develops. In execution this seems eventually to lead to a fuzziness if not outright drift in the purpose of some programs. The PPB system should lead to improvement but until Congress concerns itself with these matters more systematically, programs are likely to develop dynamics of their own, running on in a self-serving contemplation of the use of public wealth for private ends. This should be a source of concern to the Congress.

We know that, in some cases, the distributional characteristics of a program, while perhaps not to begin with, have become over time quite perverse when measured against current equity standards or even the program's original purpose. This would appear to be the case in the instance of the farm programs which were created because farmers as a group were receiving far less for their labor and resources than nonfarm people. Today the program is under criticism because the distribution of program benefits *among* farmers is highly concentrated with a large number of farmers receiving very little and a small number receiving very large payments and price-support benefits.

More commonly, the distributional consequences of a program may have been perverse but we have not really known this with any certainty because it was not obvious and we never bothered to measure it. Investment in higher education, for example, may not, as we tend to assume, provide general upward mobility on the basis of ability rather than wealth.

There is evidence, too, that some natural resource investments such as those made in the West by the Bureau of Reclamation have very perverse, and, one assumes, unintended distributional consequences on the growth of other regions.

Let us look briefly at these three cases as examples of the kind of analysis that can be done in the context of public program analysis for policy decisionmaking. By some standards at least, all exhibit distributional characteristics that are not now being considered adequately in program decisions and design.

The Distribution of Benefits and Costs of Public Higher Education

The belief is fairly general that most youth have access to public higher education on the basis of ability, that education provides an avenue for upward mobility in this society based on ability rather than wealth. Certainly this society holds normative beliefs that suggest that the direct benefits of higher education should be distributed in this manner. What are the facts about the distributional impact of this investment in human resources? W. Lee Hansen and Burton A. Weisbrod have analyzed this question for the State of California [14], [15]. Their work is instructive for its ingenuity, for the kind of distributional analysis that it suggests is possible in human investment programs, and for the kind of surprises that distributional analyses can provide.

The California system of higher education has the general reputation of being one of the most open and accessible and as well financed and with as low tuition as any in the nation. Yet Hansen and Weisbrod's data suggest strongly that the effect of the system is most regressive. The public subsidy as a percent of parents' income rises from 12 percent at $8,800 of income to 41 percent at the $12,000 level of income.[3] The authors find that while the tax structure is slightly regressive the benefit distribution is quite regressive.

This results from several factors. The total subsidy to a student's education averages $4,870 at the University of California, $3,810 in the state college system, and only $1,500 in the junior college system. Since the average family income rises progressively from $7,900 for those who have no children in California public higher education to $12,000 per family with children at the University of California, the effect is to provide the largest educational subsidy to the wealthiest. This is partly the consequence of academic entry requirements since 80 percent of the high school graduates are not eligible to enter the University of California. But that is not the end of it. They go on to state:

> Even more interesting is the fact that the percentage of all students qualifying for the University of California [Table 1, column 1] rises quite dramatically by family income level—from about 10 percent in the lowest bracket (under $4,000) to 40 percent in the highest (over $25,000). Thus, the correlation between high school achievement and family income—and all that it reflects—is startling indeed. This pattern persists as we widen our view to include those eligible for both the university and State colleges [Table 1, column 3]. But a close examination of the differences between the two columns shows that the percentage of those eligible only for the State college system is roughly constant at all income levels; thus, university eligibility requirements account largely for the unequal distribution of opportunity [14].

Hansen and Weisbrod also estimated for California that "the combined state and local tax structure is regressive below $8,000 and is essentially proportional above that level."[4] Thus, they conclude that:

Table 1
Distribution of High School Graduates by Eligibility for Public Higher Education in California, by Type of Education and Family Income
[In percent]

Family income	Percentage distribution of high school graduates by eligibility for—		
	University of California (1)	State colleges (2)	University of California and State colleges (3)
0 to $3,999	10.7	17.3	28.0
$4,000 to $5,999	11.5	14.8	26.3
$6,000 to $7,999	11.9	18.6	30.5
$8,000 to $9,999	16.2	17.0	33.2
$10,000 to $12,499	19.4	17.7	37.1
$12,500 to $14,999	22.5	17.3	39.8
$15,000 to $17,499	27.9	17.5	45.4
$17,500 to $19,999	29.5	15.6	45.1
$20,000 to $24,999	33.3	12.8	46.1
$25,000 and over	40.1	14.2	54.3
Not reported	13.3	14.7	28.0
All	19.6	16.7	36.3

Source: W. Lee Hansen and Burton A. Weisbrod, "Benefits, Cost, and Finance of Public Higher Education" (Chicago: Markham Publishing Co., 1969), ch. IV, table 7.

The general nature of the redistributive effects of the current method of financing public higher education in California is clear. Some low-income people have benefited handsomely from the availability of publicly subsidized higher education. But on the whole, the effect of these subsidies is to promote greater rather than less inequality among people of various social and economic background, by making available substantial subsidies that lower income families are either not eligible for or cannot make use of because of other conditions and constraints associated with their income position. To overcome the effects of the present system would require a substantial overhaul of the pricing system in public higher education, a realignment of the tax structure, and/or a broadening of the eligibility base for public expenditure programs. With respect to the latter alternative eligibility for public subsidies to young people might well be expanded so as to embrace all young people—not only those who go on to college but those who opt for alternative ways of expanding their earning power, such as apprenticeship or on-the-job training, or even investments in businesses. In any case, it is clear that whatever the degree to which our current higher education programs are rooted in the search for equality of opportunity, the results still leave much to be desired [14].

The Distributional Impacts of Water Resource Development

A considerable literature has developed around the problems of constructing benefit-cost ratios for natural resource investment projects. These have mostly concerned water and power development, conservation, and flood prevention projects. In all of this activity little effort has gone into comprehensive attempts to measure the distributional impacts.

There are some recent major exceptions. First of all there is the pioneering study by Robert Haveman which develops and applies a procedure for adjusting the benefit-cost calculation for the income redistribution consequences of the benefit distribution as well as the distribution of the cost of funding Corps of Engineers' projects in the 10 southern States [16]. This adjustment results in a number of (though by no means all) projects with otherwise negative B/C ratios to exhibit positive values. Haveman's analysis suggests (as do some of the Corps hearings) that welfare and equity considerations entered into the political decisions to invest in these projects. The substantial adjustments that result also suggest that distributional analyses should be done for all major natural resource investment projects.

Subsequently, A. Myrick Freeman has applied a similar methodology to six Bureau of Reclamation projects in the West with interesting results on the income distribution impacts[5] [12].

Even more recently in a very different kind of study K. William Easter and Charles W. Howe have explored the interregional redistributive consequences of Bureau of Reclamation water development investment in the

West [17]. Their emphasis is upon the regional transfers that take place. This fascinating study is soon to be published by Resources for the Future.

The issues are complex. Western farmers pay an annual price of from $30 to $135 per acre below the cost of supplying water [24]. And the consequent price of irrigation water is below that which "other potential users are willing to pay although at present not all of the irrigation water could be put to these higher valued uses" [17]. The value added per acre foot of water varies greatly by use, from well under a hundred dollars per acre foot in agriculture, through several hundred dollars in various recreational uses, to thousand of dollars an acre foot in municipal and industrial uses [28, 29]. Most of the water developed in Western reclamation projects goes into agricultural uses despite its lower value product. For economic, legal, and political reasons it is difficult to transfer to other uses later. Thus, major malallocations of resources are developing within agriculture and between agriculture and the nonagriculture sector in the West.

But this is not where the problem ends. Since there exists a chronic overcapacity to produce in agriculture, the issue arises as to whether the development of new irrigation lands has any positive benefit nationally whatever its local value. In addition to which the creation of highly productive irrigated land in the West must (particularly in the face of the existence of excess agricultural capacity and acreage allotments) create, through production substitutions, income losses in other regions. The question is where and what are the welfare implications. Easter and Howe have developed a three region farm production model for several commodities along the general lines suggested by George Tolley [25]. From this they are able to estimate the substitution effects in production and the approximate impact on regional farm production and income. Finally, they also attempt to estimate the cost which reclamation projects add to the annual cost of agricultural programs pointing out the inconsistency between federal programs in which tax monies are used in one case to increase production (reclamation) and in another case to decrease production (farm price supports and acreage allotments).

With the permission of the authors, I have reproduced below tabular materials on cotton production from their three-sector model. The model also provides a similar evaluation for potatoes, vegetables, fruits and nuts, dry edible beans, rice, sugar beets, feed grains, and alfalfa hay. It can be seen in Tables 2 and 3 that under the pressures of excess capacity and a consequent reduction in U.S. acreage allotments, cotton acreage has declined in every area, except the reclamation West where it rose, between 1949 and 1966. Nowhere is the decline as precipitous as in the South where 1964 acreage was less than half that of 1949. The authors conclude that:

Table 2
U.S. Cotton Acreage Harvested by Regions
[In thousands of acres]

Regions[1]	1964	1959	1954	1949	1944
California-Arizona	1,128	1,184	1,318	1,234	401
New Mexico-Nevada	188	192	199	286	104
Total, West[2]	1,316	1,376	1,517	1,520	505
Texas-Oklahoma	6,174	6,728	8,417	11,802	8,070
South Central	4,504	4,542	6,115	9,010	6,915
South Atlantic	1,570	1,598	2,383	3,673	3,074
Total, South[2]	12,248	12,868	16,914	24,485	18,060
North	351	405	427	594	397
Total[2]	13,915	14,649	18,858	26,599	18,962

[1] The South Central includes the States of Alabama, Arkansas, Kentucky, Louisiana, Mississippi, and Tennessee. The South Atlantic includes the States of Florida, Georgia, Maryland, North Carolina, South Carolina, and Virginia. The North includes the States of Illinois and Missouri.

[2] May not add to totals due to rounding.

Source: Charles W. Howe and K. William Easter, "Interbasin Water Transfers—Economic Issues and Impacts," Resources for the Future, Johns Hopkins Press, 1969, ch. IV.

> If cotton were not produced on reclamation land, then 978 thousand bales could be produced in other areas by increasing acreage allotments. To meet this production allotments could be increased by about one million acres since the land coming back into cotton production would be less productive and would yield on the average about one bale per acre while the reclamation land taken out yields almost two bales per acre. Assuming a uniform increase in the allotment based on the 1964 distribution of acreage, the South would harvest about 550 thousand more acres and the North 20 thousand, while in the West (including Texas and Oklahoma) acreage would decline by about 85 thousand acres. The West would be a net loser but the non-reclamation West would have a gain in acreage allotments of approximately 430 thousand acres.
>
> In terms of annual net income for farmers, the South would gain roughly $27.5 million and the North $1 million while the reclamation West would lose $50 million and the non-reclamation West would gain $21.5 million [17].

The authors go on to state that:

> There can be little doubt from the data analyzed that reclamation irrigation has had a significant effect on U.S. agriculture. Increased production on reclamation served land has increased USDA payments, stimulated regional production shifts and reduced non-reclamation farmers' income. Annual commodity program payments were estimated to increase from $20 to $464 per acre of land irrigated by reclamation, varying with the commodity and assumptions concerning relative productivity and the effectiveness of commodity programs. The reclamation impact on crops

Table 3
Cotton Acreage Harvested in 17 Western States
[In thousands of acres]

Region	1964	1959	1954	1949	1944
California-Nevada-Arizona	1,131	1,187	1,320	1,235	401
New Mexico-Texas-Oklahoma	6,359	6,917	8,614	12,087	8,174
Total	7,490	8,104	9,934	13,322	8,575
Reclamation portion[1]	514	504	514	381	145
Nonreclamation	6,976	7,600	9,420	12,941	8,430

[1] In 1964, 360 acres were in California, Arizona, and Nevada while 154 acres were in New Mexico, Texas, and Oklahoma.
Source: See Table 2.

not under the annual commodity programs ranged from the $9 million to $20 million shift in gross farm income for pears to the $350 million estimated shift in farm income for potato farmers. Finally, from 5 million to 17 million acres of cropland have been displaced by the 1944–64 increase in reclamation irrigation. In terms of income foregone this would be a minimum of $50 to $170 million annually.

These impacts of reclamation projects have not been adequately considered in evaluating project feasibility. Therefore, additional research indicating possible procedures for including these costs in the cost-benefit analysis would seem very appropriate. Even if the United States were in a situation of no excess capacity in agriculture (which the numerous land retirement programs help remind us we are not) it does not follow that additional federal irrigation is needed. If additional capacity is desired, the least cost means of increasing capacity should be selected. Ruttan's study indicates that the returns from additional investments in irrigation itself would be greater in regions outside the West. In addition, one should consider investments in drainage, land clearing, the development of new or low cost inputs before deciding on a particular mix of programs to increase agriculture's productive capacity [17].

Both the Hansen-Weisbrod and the Howe-Easter studies are thoughtful and imaginative analyses of distributional questions. While neither produce all of the information implied by the ideal set out earlier here, both provide impressive evidence of perverse distributional impacts in major public programs. Their contribution is substantial for little quantitative knowledge of such impacts previously existed.

The Distribution of Benefits from the Farm Program

The final example involves some analysis the author has done on the distribution of benefits from the farm program. In a general way we have known for some time that this program has a concentrated distribution of benefits. Many agricultural economists, most prominently T. W. Schultz, have long drawn attention to this fact. However, there have not previously been any systematic quantitative measures of the degree of that concentration. Little has been known about distributional differences between commodities and between regions and States within commodities [2]. Nor has there been any comparison of the differential distributional impacts of price supports and the direct payments that have entered into the program as a major factor since 1962.

The farm commodity programs, like any government subsidy program, have two quite different primary effects and potential purposes. The first is to redistribute income from nonfarmers to farmers; the second is to affect resource allocation—to attract to an economic activity more resources than the market mechanism would otherwise pull in. The primary political support that brought the farm commodity programs into existence had as its clear objective the redistribution of income on the premise that farmers were generally poor and that the resources farmers commanded earned far less than the same resources would have earned in the nonfarm sector. Both premises were true in general during the 1920s and 1930s when the farm programs were developed.

The criticisms of the farm program today appear to have their origins in two factors. The program has succeeded beyond anyone's dreams in attaining its objective of supporting total farm income. Secondly, the program's distributional characteristics have been ignored.

A 1967 study by the Department of Agriculture for the Senate Agricultural Committee provides a current insight into the old equity problem i.e., returns to resources in farming chronically running below what the same resources could earn in the nonfarm sector [21]. Four different standards were used for computing a parity income or parity return to resources in farming.[6] Farm programs enacted during the Kennedy and Johnson administration years had, by 1966, provided parity or higher income returns (by all four standards) for the 16 percent of all farmers who had gross sales of $20,000 or more. This group produced more than two-thirds of all agricultural products in 1966. The 16 percent of all farmers in the $10,000 to $20,000 gross sales category in 1966 who produced 18 percent of all output earned 81 to 98 percent of a parity return depending upon the standard used. Thus, at current levels of support, the farm commodity programs have now generated a parity return or better to the most efficient farmers who produce the bulk of our farm products.

The industrialization of agriculture has created a far more highly concentrated industrial structure. Today less than 10 percent of all farmers produce over half of all agricultural output; about half of the farmers produce 95 percent of all the U.S. agricultural output [11]. With few exceptions, farm programs, whether they are credit or conservation or commodity programs, are designed today so that a farmer's access to them is directly related to the size of assets he controls, the amount of land he operates and his volume of output. Under these conditions it perhaps is not surprising that the distribution of farm program benefits is highly concentrated.

Recent work by the author throws considerable light on the distributional characteristics of farm commodity programs [4]. For our purposes this presentation will be limited to a summary of the results. The data presented are in the form of Lorenz curves and Gini concentration ratios. The Lorenz curve tells one what percentage of the farmers received what percentage of the benefits. The Gini concentration ratio measures the degree of concentration of the distribution of benefits—that is, it measures how far a given distribution departs from a completely equal distribution of benefits between all beneficiaries.[7]

From Table 4 it can be seen that all of the commodity programs are fairly highly concentrated, some of them greatly so. Looking down this table you will see that the 40 percent of the smallest farmers (allotment holders) receive much less than a proportionate share of the program benefits even in the case of the programs with the least concentrated distribution of benefits.

Even after considering all the qualifications that go with these numbers, the data suggest very clearly that price supports and acreage allotments are not efficient means for affecting an income redistribution to the smaller low income farmers. Since it is clear from the parity income study that the more efficient farmers are already receiving near parity income or better, it seems an inescapable conclusion that any attempt to solve the low income small farmer problem via price supports would generate huge windfall profits to the more efficient larger scale operators.

The welfare impact of these distributions cannot actually be ascertained fully unless we have a measure of the current distribution of income and assets among beneficiaries for comparison with the distributions of program benefits. Ideally, one would desire to have this not only for the U.S. as a whole for all farmers but one should also have the income and asset distribution of cotton producers for comparison with cotton program benefits, and similarly for all the rest of the programs. Such estimates are not available. The best that is immediately available for this purpose is a measure of the Lorenz curve of the net money incomes of farmers and farm managers estimated for 1963 by David Boyne [5] and for 1964 by Joseph Coffey [7].[8] Boyne's figures are arrayed in Table 4 where they can be compared with similar Lorenz distributions for the various programs. At

Table 4

Distribution of Farm Income and Various Program Benefits: Proportion of Income or Benefits Received by Various Percentiles of Farmer Beneficiaries[1]

	Percent of benefits received by the—						
	Lower 20 percent of farmers	Lower 40 percent of farmers	Lower 60 percent of farmers	Top 40 percent of farmers	Top 20 percent of farmers	Top 5 percent of farmers	Gini concentration ratio
Sugar cane, 1965[2]	1.0	2.9	6.3	93.7	83.1	63.2	0.799
Cotton, 1964[3]	1.8	6.6	15.1	84.9	69.2	41.2	.653
Rice, 1963[3]	1.0	5.5	15.1	84.9	65.3	34.6	.632
Wheat, 1964:							
Price supports	3.4	8.3	20.7	79.3	62.3	30.5	.566
Diversion payments	6.9	14.2	26.4	73.6	57.3	27.9	.480
Total benefits[4]	3.3	8.1	20.4	79.6	62.4	30.5	.569
Feed grains, 1964:							
Price supports	0.5	3.2	15.3	84.7	57.3	24.4	.588
Diversion payments	4.4	16.1	31.8	68.2	46.8	20.7	.405
Total benefits[4]	1.0	4.9	17.3	82.7	56.1	23.9	.565
Peanuts, 1964[3]	3.8	10.9	23.7	76.3	57.2	28.5	.522
Tobacco, 1965[3]	3.9	13.2	26.5	73.5	52.8	24.9	.476
Farmer and farm manager total money income, 1963[5]	3.2	11.7	26.4	73.6	50.5	20.8	.468
Sugar beets, 1965[2]	5.0	14.3	27.0	73.0	50.5	24.4	.456
Agriculture conservation program, 1964:[6]							
All eligibles	7.9	15.8	34.7	65.3	39.2	([7])	.343
Recipients	10.5	22.8	40.3	59.7	36.6	13.8	.271

Source: Except as noted all figures are from a 1968 study by Bonnen [4].

[1] This table presents portions of 2 Lorenz curves relating the cumulated percentage distribution of benefits to the cumulated percent of farmers receiving those benefits. Cols. 1 through 3 summarize this relationship cumulated up from the lower (benefit per farmer) end of the curve, and cols. 4 through 6 summarize the relationship cumulated down from the top (highest benefit per recipient) end of the curve.

[2] For price support benefits plus Government payments.

[3] For price support benefits.

[4] Includes price support payments and wheat certificate payments as well.

[5] David H. Boyne, "Changes in the Income Distribution in Agriculture," *Journal of Farm Economics*, vol. 47, No. 5, December 1965, pp. 1221–1222.

[6] For total program payments. Computed from data in "Frequency Distribution of Farms and Farmland, Agricultural Conservation Program, 1964," ASCS, U.S. Department of Agriculture, January 1966, tables 3 and 8.

[7] Not available.

the level of the lowest 40 percent of farmers only tobacco, sugar beet, and ACP programs have the effect of adding proportionately more program benefits to a farmer's income than he commands as a share of farm income. At the level of the lowest 20 percent of farmers wheat, peanut, tobacco, sugar beet and ACP programs add proportionately more program benefits to a farmer's income than he commands as a share of farm income. Rice, feed grains, cotton and sugar cane all provide to this lowest group of allotment holder less of a share of program benefits than they average as a share of farm income. One is tempted to say that these latter programs are regressive in their income impact in farming, but this is not proved by this crude though relevant comparison. Nor can we argue conclusively that the ACP, sugar beet and tobacco (and possibly peanuts and feed grains) programs have a progressive income impact—even though our data seem to suggest this.

There are too many logical difficulties to bridge. Cotton benefit distributions should be compared with cotton farmer income distributions—not all farm income. Also some regionalization of the farm income distribution is needed to allow for geographic and industry mix differences associated with differences in productivity. One cannot always assume that one is necessarily dealing with the same general set of low incomes, or indeed with low income at all, when one speaks of the lower end of the distribution of benefits from a program. A small allotment may sometimes represent a minor enterprise in a substantial operation. It also should be noted that farm income accounts for a relatively small part of the total income of quite a number of smaller producers [11]. This partially accounts for the very low concentration of total income of farmers from all sources as compared to the high concentration of gross and net incomes from farming operations that can be seen in Table 5.

Thus, the net effect of these programs may be less regressive than the data suggest—or slightly more regressive—but the pattern is clear.

There are a few other conclusions that can be drawn from the distributional data. The programs exhibiting the greatest concentration in the distribution of benefits are indeed extremely concentrated. The U.S. sugar cane program exhibits a Gini ratio of 0.8 and individual states have concentration ratios as high as 0.9 (Hawaii).

Another matter of interest is the evidence of a slow time trend toward greater concentration. This can be seen in Table 4 for those commodities in which data for different years is available.

The Agricultural Conservation Program (ACP) benefits are far more equally distributed than any commodity program. ACP subsidizes various conservation practices, from putting lime on the soil to tiling land and building ponds. It is obviously administered in a manner to assure the largest number of participants. This distributional outcome would seem to have more to do with ACP's political role among the farm programs than with any organizational or technological imperatives of conservation.

It is also worth remarking that the variation in concentration within a a particular commodity program from state to state and region to region can be rather large. These reflect primarily great variations in productivity and yield, and rather substantial differences in the median allotments as well as the relative variation around those medians. See the example of cotton in [4].

Lorenz curve and Gini ratio computations are available by state and region for each commodity benefit stream listed in Table 4. The available data also allow one to compute the distribution of benefits by size of allotment. These may all be seen in the original study [4].

The availability of a benefit distribution with an absolute dimension (acreage allotment size) which is highly correlated with productivity allows one, particularly in the case of cotton, to gain some insight into the potential for conflict between efficiency and equity objectives. Let me quote the conclusions from the author's earlier study of cotton benefit distributions [3].

> The older eastern cotton-growing regions are higher cost areas. In fact, cost per unit of output on efficiently managed cotton farms is reputed to decline sharply, possibly by as much as one-half in some major production areas, as one moves from the Southeast to the West [8]. Historically, since 1935 the Delta and the Southwest have maintained their share of national cotton output (about one-third each), while the share of the Southeast had declined from one-third to less than one-fifth, and the West's share has increased from 4 percent to about 20 percent.
>
> Thus, in effect, cotton acreage has been shifting out of the Southeast and to the West. In efficiency terms this is a movement of allotment rights from an area where yields are about one bale per acre to one where average yields are over two bales. In equity terms it is a movement of allotment rights from smaller, lower-income farmers to farmers operating on a large scale and receiving much higher incomes. An acre of allotment rights in California is worth almost three times (before considering production costs) what it is worth in Georgia. Yet almost 40 percent of all cotton farmers earn their living in the Southeast as compared to about 3 percent in the West. The logic of this suggests that the disparity is so great today that it is probably impossible to attain the welfare objectives in the older eastern cotton areas with price supports of the 1964 program type, except at unacceptably high levels of government-generated intramarginal rents in the West and other producing areas of high productivity.

In the case of wheat and feed grains this study provides an opportunity to observe the consequence of the recent addition of direct payments to the price support system allowing price supports to be dropped approximately to world prices. Economists have long argued that:

> If the avowed purpose is to redistribute income from those with higher incomes to those with lower incomes, then a program that directly provides income or services to the intended beneficiaries is more efficient and more effective than one that raises the demand for some product they, and others, produce [6].

Agricultural economists have also said for years that this would produce a more equitable approach to the income problem in agriculture. However, the concentration of program benefits does not automatically decline when one shifts to a direct payment scheme. As one can see in Table 4, in the case of the feed grain program in 1964, direct payments apparently did reduce slightly the overall concentration of program benefits from that which would have prevailed if there had been only a price support program. However, in the case of wheat the direct diversion payment actually increased the Gini ratio on the total benefit distribution above that for price supports. These differences are probably not significant. If the direct payment distributional system is designed in much the same manner as the price support program, the distributional consequences will be approximately similar.

Since the distribution of government payments are both very visible (unlike price support benefits) and highly concentrated, efforts have been made in Congress in recent years to place a limit on the size of the total payment that a single farmer may receive.

Recently available data on the distribution of total payments in 1967 make it possible to examine the concentration of total government payments and to test the distributional impact of a payment limitation [9]. A total of $3.1 billion in government payments were made in 1967. Eighty percent of this total went to three crops: $932 million to cotton, $865 million to feed grains and $731 million to wheat. The only other commodities with direct payments were sugar and wool which received $70 million and $29 million respectively. All the remaining $439 million went into conservation (ACP, $225 million) and land withdrawal [11].

In Table 5 it can be seen that the distribution of total payments in 1967 was highly concentrated exhibiting a Gini ratio of 0.671. This exceeds the concentration in every commodity benefit distribution in Table 4 except sugar cane. It falls between the concentration exhibited in Table 5 by gross and net farm income in 1967—which is what one might logically expect.

If one assumes a $25,000 limit were imposed on total payments to a single beneficiary in 1967, the concentration of the overall distribution of benefits declines only from a Gini ratio of 0.671 to 0.652 and total payments decline from $3.1 to $2.8 billion. If one assumes a $10,000 limitation, the concentration ratio declines only to 0.623 and total payments decline to $2.6 billion. A $5,000 limitation results in a Gini of .582

Table 5

Distribution of 1967 Government Payments and Farm Income: Proportion Received by Various Percentiles of Farmers[1]

1967	Percent of income received by the—						
	Lower 20 percent of farmers	Lower 40 percent of farmers	Lower 60 percent of farmers	Top 40 percent of farmers	Top 20 percent of farmers	Top 5 percent of farmers	Gini concentration ratio
1967 total government payments:							
With no limitation on size of total payment[2]	1.1	5.7	13.3	86.7	69.0	42.4	0.671
Assuming $25,000 limitation[3]	1.1	6.0	14.1	85.9	67.2	39.0	.652
Assuming $10,000 limitation[3]	1.2	6.5	15.3	84.7	64.4	33.8	.623
Assuming $5,000 Limitation[3]	1.4	7.3	17.1	82.9	60.3	26.1	.582
Various measures of farmer income in 1967:							
Gross receipts from farming[4]	1.6	3.3	10.1	89.9	72.3	40.4	.693
Realized net farm income[5]	4.5	9.0	19.3	80.7	50.0	26.2	.541
Nonfarm income of farmers	25.5	51.0	70.1	29.9	15.6	5.6	.125
Total income of farmers	14.9	29.8	44.5	55.5	37.0	16.0	.211

[1] This table presents portions of 2 Lorenz curves relating the cumulated percentage distribution of benefits to the cumulated percent of farmers receiving those benefits. Columns 1 through 3 summarize this relationship cumulated up from the lower (benefit per farmer) end of the curve, and 4 through 6 summarize the relationship cumulated down from the top (highest benefit per recipient) end of the curve.

[2] Government payments to farmers as actually distributed in 1967. Total payments were $3,100,000,000.

[3] Assumes all 1967 beneficiairies continue to participate in programs and are eligible for payments. Under the $25,000 limit payments would total $2,800,000,000, under the $10,000 limit, $2,600,000,000 and under the $5,000 limit, $2,300,000,000.

[4] Including Government payments and imputed nonmoney income from farm products consumed at home and from the rental value of the farm dwelling.

[5] Net of farm production expenses and changes in farm inventories of livestock and crops.

Sources: Computed from data in "Farm Income Situation," USDA, FIS-211, July 1968, pp. 68–69, except direct payment data which are from the Congressional Record, July 31, 1968.

and a decline in total payments to $2.3 billion. This suggests that even quite low payment limitations are unlikely to have any revolutionary impact on the actual concentration of total payments made under present direct payment eligibility rules. It suggests as a consequence that any decision to limit payments should be based primarily on (1) the politics rather than the economics of equity between farmers, (2) the politics and economics of equity between large payment beneficiaries and taxpayers (the $10,000 limit creates a potential transfer of $0.5 billion), and (3) consideration of the impact of a payment limitation on increased federal budget costs for production control that could result from a decline in program participation by large producers.

Changes in program design such as have occurred since 1961, shifting emphasis from price supports towards direct payments, have considerable effects upon the distribution of the costs of the program also. While no quantitative analysis is attempted here it is clear from the logic of the situation that the cost of the price support operation is borne through the taxes necessary to sustain the storage and control operation, and also through consumers who pay some of the cost through higher market prices. The shift toward direct payments shifts the relative burden away from the consumer and toward the taxpayer. One exception to this is the wheat program where direct payments are generated by a certificate system that is paid eventually by the consumer through the market. The price support approach, in which a higher proportion of the costs are borne by the consumer in the form of food costs, has a far greater impact on the low income consumer than would be the case of direct payments in which the cost is borne primarily by the income tax. Thus, price support-acreage diversion programs can be described as doubly regressive—that is, a major share of the cost is borne by consumers with below average incomes and a major share of the benefit is received by farm producers with above average incomes. While the movement in farm program design toward direct payments has had little impact on the concentration of benefits, it would appear to have shifted the burden of costs from lower to higher income families.

CONCLUSION

This paper has argued that distributional consequences of public decisions have major and increasingly important impacts in our society. We have a long history of public commitment to equity purposes. Yet we know very little about the social processes by which distributional impacts are institutionalized and are filtered through the society. We know even less about how to redesign distributional systems without incurring excessive political and social cost. In fact, we do not at this point even have good descriptions of the distributional impacts or characteristics of our public programs. What little we do know suggests, as in the three cases just presented, that there are many surprising and apparently perverse distributional impacts.

Both the integrity of our many public commitments in equity and our efficiency in the use of tax monies to attain public ends require far greater effort to collect data for program analysis of the distributional impacts of public decisions.

The three cases—higher education expenditures, Bureau of Reclamation investments, and the farm program—contain several lessons. If we do not systematically attempt to collect data and assess distributional impacts, we shall always be surprised by the many unintended consequences of our public decisions. Even if we accept the original objectives of older programs, we fail to attain our ends because we have failed to keep the equity objectives clearly before us. The use of indirect means, such as price supports, is a tricky and uncertain way of attaining equity objectives.

Finally, past decisions made without adequate distributional knowledge now appear (given our objectives) often to lack in economic and social wisdom. But even more importantly, these past decisions cannot now be easily or cheaply reversed. This is particularly true in light of the irrevocable specialized capital investments in the reclamation program and the past farm program benefits that are now capitalized into the cost structure of agriculture. The cost of our past ignorance of distributional impacts is clearly high. There is no need to persist in such error. But we must now collect the data and do the analysis of the distributional impacts that are needed for today's decisions.

NOTES

[1] See the review of literature in [18, 19, 20] and the volume on the theory of income distribution by Weintraub [26]. Also look through the A.E.A. Index of Economic Journals [1]. Note that the classification scheme of the Index contains no major distribution category except for factor shares.

[2] See the paper by Burton Weisbrod in this volume for a development of this point.

[3] See the table on page 136 in the paper by Burton Weisbrod in this volume.

[4] Note this is different from Gillespie's results for the U.S. [13].

[5] See the paper by A. Myrick Freeman in this volume.

[6] A "landlord standard" assumed that the resources were rented and the farmer's labor paid for at nonfarm rates for similar age, sex, and skill levels. A "stockholders standard" assumed sale of farm resources and investment in a cross section of the

Standard and Poor's 500 stock average. Both of these standards were then estimated with and without capital gains.

[7] A Gini ratio of 0 indicates a completely equal distribution between all beneficiaries. A Gini concentration ratio of 1 indicates that one beneficiary received all of the benefits and the other potential beneficiaries none. Thus, as the concentration ratio rises from 0 toward 1 it reflects a greater and greater concentration in the distribution of benefits. For those interested in the nature of the data sources, the methodology, and the limitations of the estimating procedure see pages 461–465 of [4].

[8] One may also compare the program distributions of Table 4 with several income comparisons that have been computed in Table 5 using very different and less satisfactory data.

REFERENCES

[1] American Economic Association, *Index of Economic Articles,* vols. 1–7, Homewood, Ill., Irwin, 1961–1967.

[2] Back, W. B. and John E. Waldrop, Jr., ed., *Regional Studies of Income Distribution,* Louisiana Agricultural Experiment Station and U.S. Department of Agriculture, Baton Rouge, June 1966.

[3] Bonnen, James T., "The Distribution of Benefits from Cotton Price Supports" in Samuel B. Chase Jr., ed., *Problems in Public Expenditure Analysis,* Washington, D.C., The Brookings Institution, 1968, pp. 223–248.

[4] Bonnen, James T., "The Distribution of Benefits from Selected U.S. Farm Programs," *Rural Poverty in the United States: A Report of the President's National Advisory Commission on Rural Poverty,* Washington, D.C., GPO, 1968, pp. 461–505.

[5] Boyne, David H., "Changes in the Income Distribution in Agriculture," *Journal of Farm Economics,* vol. 47, no. 5, December 1965, pp. 1213–1224.

[6] Capron, William M., "Comments" in Samuel B. Chase, Jr., ed., *Problems in Public Expenditure Analysis,* Washington, D.C., The Brookings Institution, 1968, p. 250.

[7] Coffey, Joseph D., "Personal Distribution of Farmers' Income by Source and Region," *American Journal of Agricultural Economics,* vol. 50, no. 5, December 1968, pp. 1383–1396.

[8] *Congressional Record,* vol. 109, pt. 15, 88th Congress, first session (1963), pp. 19796–19798.

[9] *Congressional Record,* vol. 114, no. 135, 90th Congress, second session (1968), p. H7928.

[10] Council of Economic Advisers, *Annual Report of the Council of Economic Advisers,* Washington, D.C., January 1969, pp. 244, 250.

[11] Economic Research Service, U.S. Department of Agriculture, *Farm Income Situation* (FIS-211), July 1968, pp. 64, 68–69.

[12] Freeman, A. Myrick III, "Six Federal Reclamation Projects and the Distribution of Income," *Water Resources Research,* 1967, vol. 3, no. 2.

[13] Gillespie, W. Irwin. "The Effect of Public Expenditures on the Distribution of Income," in Richard A. Musgrave, ed., *Essays in Fiscal Federalism,* Washington, D.C., The Brookings Institution, 1965, pp. 112–183.

[14] Hansen, W. Lee and Burton A. Weisbrod, *Benefits, Costs and Finance of Public Higher Education,* Chicago, Markham Publishing Company, 1969.

[15] Hansen, W. Lee and Burton A. Weisbrod, "The Distribution of Costs and Direct Benefits of Public Higher Education: The Case of California," *Journal of Human Resources,* Spring 1969, pp. 176–191.

[16] Haveman, Robert H., *Water Resource Investment and the Public Interest,* Nashville, Vanderbilt University Press, 1965.

[17] Howe, Charles W. and K. William Easter, *Interbasin Water Transfers—Economic Issues and Impacts,* Resources for the Future, Johns Hopkins University Press, Chapter IV (publication planned for 1969).

[18] Kravis, I. B., *The Structure of Income: Some Quantitative Essays,* Philadelphia, 1962.

[19] Mishan, E. J., "A Survey of Welfare Economics, 1939–1959," in Mishan, ed., *Welfare Economics,* New York, Random House, 1964.

[20] Morgan, James N., Martin H. David, Wilber J. Cohen, and Harvey E. Brazer, *Income and Welfare in the United States,* New York, McGraw Hill, 1962, pp. 15–24.

[21] *Parity Returns Position of Farmers,* Senate Document 44, 90th Congress, first session, August 10, 1967, p. 22.

[22] Pfaff, Martin, *The Transfer Economy: The Relationship Between Unilateral and Bilateral Transfers in the National and World Economy,* The Brookings Institution Economic Studies Seminar (mimeo), Washington, D.C., October 28, 1968, pp. 40–42.

[23] Peacock, Alan T., ed., *Income Redistribution and Social Policy,* London, Jonathan Cape, 1954, pp. 178–267.

[24] Ruttan, Vernon W., *The Economic Demand for Irrigation Acreage,* Baltimore, The Johns Hopkins Press, 1965, p. 49.

[25] Tolley, George S., "Reclamation Influence on the Rest of Agriculture," *Land Economics,* vol. 35, May 1959, pp. 176–180.

[26] Weintraub, Sidney, *An Approach to the Theory of Income Distribution,* Philadelphia, Chilton, 1958.

[27] Weisbrod, Burton A. and W. Lee Hansen, "An Income-Net Worth Approach to Measuring Economic Welfare," *American Economic Review,* vol. 58, no. 5, part 1, December 1968.

[28] Wollman, Nathanial, *The Value of Water in Alternative Uses with Special Application to Water Use in the San Juan and Rio Grande Basins of New Mexico,* Albuquerque, University of New Mexico Press, 1962, p. 31.

[29] Young, Robert A. and William E. Martin, "The Economics of Arizona's Water Problem," *Arizona Review,* vol. 16, no. 3, March 1967, p. 10.

PART THREE

Analytical Problems in Policy Analysis

****

CHAPTER 10

ON THE DISCOUNT RATE FOR PUBLIC PROJECTS

William J. Baumol

SIGNIFICANCE OF THE DISCOUNT RATE

It is generally recognized that the discount rate is a critical datum for the evaluation of any proposed government project. Even where there is little basic disagreement about the investment's prospective costs and benefits, the choice of discount rate figure may make the difference between acceptance and rejection. A project which seems to yield substantial net benefits when evaluated at a 3 percent rate may well appear extremely wasteful if the rate is 5 percent.

Yet, despite the critical nature of this parameter, in some calculations it is assigned a value almost cavalierly, with little attempt to show that the selected figure is not chosen arbitrarily and capriciously. One sometimes encounters discount figures in cost-benefit calculations whose sole justification seems to be that similar figures were used in the past. Of course that can never be an acceptable argument, first because the earlier figure may have had as little justification as the one presently employed and, second, because changing circumstances change the appropriate value of the discount rate.

At stake in the choice of an acceptable discount rate is no less than the allocation of resources between the private and the public sectors of the economy. The discount rate, by indicating what government projects should be undertaken, can determine the proportion of the economy's activity that is operated by governmental agencies, and hence, the proportion that remains in the hands of private enterprise.

Moreover, even given the decision on resource allocation between the private and the public sectors, the choice of discount rate can affect profoundly the type of projects undertaken by government agencies. When the discount rate is low this will encourage highly durable investments, the bulk of whose benefits will become available only in the distant future. Thus, when the economy is beset by urgent and immediate investment needs a relatively high discount rate will tend to be appropriate.

William J. Baumol is Professor of Economics at Princeton University.

With so much at issue it is well worth exploring in some detail the principles that should be employed in arriving at a discount figure, and the rationale that underlies them. This paper undertakes to do so without heavy reliance on the jargon of technical economics.

THE BASIC CRITERION: OPPORTUNITY COST

The observation that the discount rate is the arbiter of the allocation of resources between private and public enterprise is the key to the principles which underlie the choice of an acceptable discount figure. The right discount rate becomes that number which indicates correctly when resources should be transferred from one sector to another.

More specifically, suppose one is considering the construction of a dam which will employ x man-hours of labor, y tons of cement, and z kilowatt hours of electricity. In an economy in which the level of employment is high, if those resources are made available to the government they must be transferred out of the private sector. Just as in the guns versus butter case, each item added to the public sector involves some corresponding reduction in the volume of resources in private hands.[1]

We may now establish a rather obvious criterion to test the desirability of the proposed resource transfer. If the resources in question produce a rate of return in the private sector which society evaluates at r percent, then the resources should be transferred to the public project if that project yields a return greater than r percent. They should be left in private hands if their potential earnings in the proposed government investment is less than r percent. The logic of this criterion is self-evident. It states no more than the minimal dictate of efficiency: Never take resources out of a use where they bring in (say) 9 percent in order to utilize them in a manner which yields only 6 percent!

The standard which has just been described is the concept economists call *opportunity cost*. We have stated, in effect, that the proper criterion on which to judge the desirability of a governmental project, from the point of view of the general welfare, is the value of the opportunities which the private sector must pass by when the resources are withdrawn from that sector. A government project is desirable if and only if the value of the net benefits which it promises exceeds the cost of the lost productive opportunities which that investment causes.

It follows almost immediately that *the correct discount rate for the evaluation of a government project is the percentage rate of return that the resources utilized would otherwise provide in the private sector*. That is, the correct discount rate is the opportunity cost in terms of the potential rate of return in alternative uses on the resources that would be utilized by the project. An example will readily show why this must be so. Suppose these resources are capable of returning our hypothetical 9 percent in the private sector. Consider three proposed government projects: Project *A* which offers an average rate of return of 12 percent, project *B* whose expected return is 9 percent, and project *C* whose anticipated yield is 7 percent. It should be obvious that if we discount the returns of project *C* at the opportunity rate of 9 percent we will end up with a negative net present value figure (i.e., 7 percent discounted at 9 percent comes out to less than the principal invested). If we discount project *B*'s expected returns at 9 percent we will obtain a zero figure for the present value of net benefits (the returns will just cover the cost of the investment). Only project *A*, when discounted at 9 percent, will be assigned a positive net benefit figure. Thus the discount rate calculated at the opportunity rate works just as it should: it passes projects whose yield is greater than its resources could earn in the private sector and turns down projects whose benefits are not equal to the earnings the resources could provide in private hands.

The same illustration also shows immediately how an incorrect choice of discount figure—one not equal to the opportunity rate—can result in decisions harmful to the general welfare. For example, consider two extreme possibilities in terms of our hypothetical figures—a discount rate that is much too high (say, 15 percent) and one that is much too low (say, 5 percent). At the excessive 15 percent figure the usual cost-benefit criterion would reject all three projects, even project *A*. The government would then fail to undertake an investment that clearly represents an efficient use of society's resources. On the other hand, a 5 percent discount rate would, on a cost-benefit criterion, lead to the construction of all three projects. Thus even investment *C* would be undertaken even though it uses resources that should better be left in private hands. For it takes resources from employments in which they return 9 percent and puts them into an occupation in which they bring in only 7 percent, a palpable 2 percent net loss to the community.

The upshot is perfectly clear. Any discount rate that is clearly above or clearly below the opportunity cost rate is indefensible because either of these will lead to decisions that reduce the general welfare. We must turn therefore to an investigation of the opportunity cost rate of resources, for once we have determined this we will have the requisite information for the choice of discount rate to be used in the evaluation of government projects.

REASONS FOR DIFFERENCES IN OPPORTUNITY COSTS

Matters would be relatively simple if any batch of resources withdrawn from the private sector were to incur the same (percentage) opportunity cost as any other batch. If an opportunity cost of *r* percent were to apply throughout the economy, to determine the social discount rate one would simply proceed to estimate this number, *r,* and the resulting figure would then be the discount rate.

Unfortunately, for a variety of reasons, the magnitude of the opportunity cost varies with the source from which a project's resources are obtained. As we will see, resources which might otherwise have been used by a corporation will generally incur a higher opportunity cost than do resources drawn from direct consumer use.

In some sense, differences in opportunity costs of resources taken from different sectors of the economy are all a manifestation of imperfections in the market. In principle, if capital could flow without restriction to any sector of the economy where its earnings would be increased and all returns on capital were to accrue to its investors, resources would be forced by the market process to yield the same rate of return in every use. The standard argument is easily summarized. Suppose in such an economy that there were two industries, one of which returned *k* percent on capital while the other yielded some higher return, say 2*k*. In that case investors would find it profitable to withdraw funds from the first of these industries and put them to work in the second. But the growing scarcity of capital in the first industry would tend to reduce its outputs, raising its prices and (therefore) its rate of return. Similarly, in the second industry the influx of capital would expand production, and force prices and returns downward. This transfer of capital would continue so long as any substantial difference in the two rates of return persisted. The flow of capital would cease only when the rate of return in the first industry had risen sufficiently and that in the second had fallen enough to make the two rates of return equal. At that point, clearly, capital withdrawn from the one sector would have exactly the same rate of return as capital withdrawn from the other—their opportunity cost rates would be identical.

Why does such equalization generally not occur in practice? There are two broad reasons: first, part of the return to capital may not accrue to the investor. A prime example of this is provided by taxation which siphons part of that return off to the government, and since the burden of taxation varies from industry to industry, from the corporate to the noncorporate sector, and so forth, it means that opportunity costs will vary accordingly. A second broad reason for such variation lies in impediments, such as monopoly, to the influx of capital into some productive activities.[2] Specifically, we will consider three broad sources of such divergence because they must be taken into explicit account in the determination of the social rate of discount. These elements are the following: (a) taxes, (b) risk, (c) divergence between private and social benefits (externalities). Let us examine them in turn.

THE ROLE OF TAXES: ANALYSIS

As already indicated, the burden of taxes will vary from industry to industry, from one class of producer to another, depending on its mode of organization—that is, corporation, partnership, or do-it-yourself production by the consumer himself.

However, let us, to begin with, assume for simplicity that there are only two classes of producer: the corporation, which pays a 50 percent corporate income tax, and the private individual who produces certain items for his own use, and who pays no taxes on this production process. Assume also that there are available for sale riskless government bonds offering a rate of return of, say, 5 percent.

In our example, it is easy to determine the opportunity cost of resources withdrawn from the corporate sector. Corporations must yield to their investors an after-tax return of 5 percent. For otherwise investors would be unwilling to provide any funds to the corporations and would instead put all their money into the safe government bonds. But the required after-tax return of 5 percent on corporate capital means that these firms must earn 10 percent on capital *before* payment of the 50 percent corporate profit tax. In other words, the presence of special taxes on the output of this sector means that resources invested in it must produce goods and services valued at a level sufficiently high to yield a 10 percent return. The corporation can then engage only in the production of consumers' or producers' goods whose purchasers value them sufficiently to pay a price that yields a 10 percent return on corporate investment. A withdrawal of resources from the corporation, then, will cause a reduction in output whose opportunity cost in terms of consumer valuation is given by that figure: 10 percent.

Notice in evaluating resources from the corporate sector in this way, it does not matter whether the resources are used by the firm to produce consumers' goods or producers' goods (e.g., machinery). So long as the output in question is supplied by a corporation, the resources used in its manufacture will have a 10 percent opportunity cost. The relevance of this consideration will be clear presently.

Let us turn now to the more difficult problem, the opportunity cost of resources withdrawn from the other productive sector in our imaginary economy, the do-it-yourself consumers.

Since goods produced by consumers for their own use do not provide a rate of return that is measurable directly it is necessary to find some indirect means by which their opportunity cost can be inferred. Fortunately there is a straightforward way in which this can be done. When a consumer voluntarily purchases one of the bonds available in our imaginary economy he is indicating that their 5 percent rate of return compensates him for giving up the use of that money in his do-it-yourself operation. Put another way, if this investment in his own production were worth more than 5 percent to him he would not buy the bond, while if his investment in his own work were worth less than 5 percent to him he would purchase more bonds than he does. Thus without any conscious calculation on his part, a consumer's security purchases reveal something about what the rate of return of investment in the production of goods for his own consumption is worth to him—the opportunity cost incurred when a dollar's worth of resources is prevented from going to him and is transferred to a government investment project.

What about consumers who do not buy any bonds? It follows from the preceding discussion that their opportunity cost must be at least as high and probably higher than it is for bond purchasers.[3] To a man who chooses *not* to purchase bonds at 5 percent, the purpose for which he uses his money must by definition be worth more than 5 percent. This is no less true for a man who fails to purchase bonds because "he cannot afford them." That phrase merely implies that his consumption dollar means a great deal to him—perhaps even survival itself, and is therefore certainly more valuable than 5 percent.

We may summarize by saying that the opportunity cost of present consumption to nonbondholders must be at least as great as the figure for bondholders, and that to bondholders the opportunity cost of resources is indicated by the rate of return on their bondholdings.

In practice, of course, there is a broad spectrum of earnings tax conditions, among which are included the untaxed do-it-yourself productive process and corporate production with its (roughly) 50 percent profits tax. We have seen that the opportunity cost of resources from the untaxed sector (assuming the absence of risk and other such complications) is, roughly, r percent. In the corporation, half of whose earnings are taxed away, the opportunity cost rate is $2r$, where r is the bond rate of interest. Similarly, if the earnings of a partnership in a particular industry were reduced by, say, one-fourth through taxation, that firm would also have to earn enough before taxes to yield r percent after taxes to its investors. This company's pretax rate of return, call it s percent, must then satisfy the relationship

$$s - (1/4)s = r, \text{ that is, } (3/4)s = r \text{ or } s = (4/3)r.$$

This figure, which obviously lies between r and $2r$, will then be the opportunity cost rate for resources withdrawn from a firm paying 1/4 of its earnings in taxes.

NOTES

[1] There is one tradition in the literature that attempts to formulate a distinction between risk and uncertainty based on ability to express the possible variability of outcomes in terms of a probability distribution (Knight [18:225–231]). According to this tradition, when we do not know the specific outcome but do know the probability distribution, we have "risk"; when we do not even know the probability distribution, we have "uncertainty." This distinction has proved to be sterile. Indeed, we cannot in practice act rationally without summarizing our information (or its converse, our uncertainty) in the form of a probability distribution (Savage [28]).

[2] The generalization to multiple future time-periods leads to an equation of the form:

$$V_0 = -i_0 + \frac{q_1}{1 + r_1} + \frac{q_2}{(1 + r_2)(1 + r_1)} + \ldots + \frac{q_T}{(1 + r_T) \ldots (1 + r_2)(1 + r_1)}$$

Here $r_1, r_2 \ldots, r_T$ are successive 1-year interest rates up to the economic horizon T.

[3] The two formulations are strictly equivalent only when projects are independent, in the sense that adoption of any one does not affect the investment required or the returns yielded by any others. There are many possible patterns of interdependence: projects may be mutually exclusive, or one may be prerequisite to another, etc. For interdependent projects, the version (a) of the present-value principle remains valid and thus is the more fundamental conception.

[4] See, for example, the recent review of cost-benefit analysis by Prest and Turvey [26].

[5] Essentially the same point arises in the "social time-preference" argument, which maintains that there is inadequate private provision for the future since only the current generation casts "dollar votes" on the disposition of current resources. Attempts to overcome this supposed distortion by expansion of government investment alone, lead once more to the same sort of difficulty (Hirshleifer [15]). In general, it is necessary to compromise between the objectives sought.

[6] Attention here will be restricted to agencies of the federal government.

[7] The current rates on money loans do reflect, however, the market's state of inflationary expectation. Since price level increases of around 1 to 5 percent per year have been experienced in recent years it is reasonable to infer that the market's estimate of the *real* riskless rate of interest must be somewhat lower than the Treasury's borrowing rate. It follows that if future benefits are calculated at today's prices without allowance for inflation, the current Treasury borrowing rate really is too high to be a riskless rate. However, this result seems to be inadvertent, and not a concession in the direction of use of a risky discount rate.

[8] As in the simple PV rule, the two forms here are equivalent given project independence.

[9] If $\frac{\pi_{1a}}{P_{1a}} = \frac{\pi_{1b}}{P_{1b}}$, then their common ratio equals $\frac{\pi_{1a} + \pi_{1b}}{P_{1a} + P_{1b}} = \frac{1}{P_1}$. Then $\Delta V_0' = -\Delta i_0 + \frac{\Delta q_{1a}(P_{1a}/P_1) + \Delta q_{1b}(P_{1b}/P_1)}{1 + r_1}$. This reduces immediately to the *PCEV*, ΔV_0, upon making the substitution $P_1 = 1/(1 + r_1)$.

[10] This is sometimes described as the condition of "diminishing marginal utility of income."

[11] This condition leads to the r_1^* yielding the correct PCEV in

$$\Delta V_0 = -\Delta i_0 + \frac{\pi_{1a}\,\Delta q_{1a} + \pi_{1b}\,\Delta q_{1b}}{1 + r_1^*}.$$

This equation is the discounting version of equation (4).

[12] This discussion omits the problem of dealing with the corporate income tax, a complication that may be of great practical importance. Its role will be reconsidered below.

[13] This point was made in private correspondence by Peter A. Diamond.

[14] The real yield would be the average of 16 percent gross of tax (8 percent net) yield to pay on equity, and 5 percent to pay on bonds.

[15] On the other hand, it should be mentioned that the *personal* income tax has a partially counterbalancing opposite effect. The returns on risky securities can often be taken in the form of capital gains that benefit from a reduced tax rate.

REFERENCES

[1] K. J. Arrow, "Discounting and Public Investment Criteria," in A. V. Kneese & S. C. Smith, eds., *Water Resources Research* (Johns Hopkins Press, 1966).

[2] J. S. Bain, R. E. Caves, & J. Margolis, *Northern California's Water Industry* (Johns Hopkins Press, 1966).

[3] W. J. Baumol, "On the Social Rate of Discount," *American Economic Review,* v. 58 (Sept. 1968).

[4] H. P. Caulfield, Jr., Statement of Henry P. Caulfield, Jr., Executive Director, Water Resources Council, before Subcommittee on Economy in Government, Joint Economic Committee, *Economic Analysis of Public Investment Decisions: Interest Rate Policy and Discounting Analysis,* 90th Congress, 2nd Session.

[5] P. A. Diamond, "The Role of a Stock Market in a General Equilibrium Model with Technological Uncertainty," *American Economic Review,* v. 57 (Sept. 1967).

[6] R. Dorfman, "Basic Economic and Technologic Concepts: A General Statement," in A. Maass, M. Hufschmidt, R. Dorfman, H. A. Thomas, Jr., S. A. Marglin & G. M. Fair, *Design of Water Resource Systems* (Harvard U. Press, 1962).

[7] O. Eckstein, "Reply by Mr. Eckstein" (to Comments of J. Hirshleifer), in National Bureau of Economic Research, *Public Finances: Needs, Sources, and Utilization* (Princeton U. Press, 1961).

[8] O. Eckstein, Statement of Otto Eckstein before Subcommittee on Economy in Government, Joint Economic Committee, *Economic Analysis of Public Investment Decisions: Interest Rate Policy and Discounting Analysis,* 90th Congress, 2nd Session.

[9] O. Eckstein, *Water Resource Development* (Harvard U. Press, 1958).

[10] M. S. Feldstein, "The Social Time Preference Discount Rate in Cost Benefit Analysis," *Economic Journal,* v. 74 (June 1964).

[11] M. Friedman & L. J. Savage, "The Utility Analysis of Choices Involving Risk," *Journal of Political Economy,* v. 56 (June 1964).

[12] A. Harberger, Remarks before Subcommittee on Economy in Government, Joint Economic Committee, *Economic Analysis of Public Investment Decisions: Interest Rate Policy and Discounting Analysis,* 90th Congress, 2nd Session.

[13] R. H. Haveman, *Water Resource Investment and the Public Interest* (Vanderbilt U. Press, 1965).

[14] J. Hirshleifer, "Investment Decision Under Uncertainty: Applications of the State-Preference Approach," *Quarterly Journal of Economics,* v. 80 (May 1966).

[15] J. Hirshleifer, "Preference Sociale a l'Egard du Temps," *Recherches Economiques de Louvain,* v. 34 (1968).

[16] J. Hirshleifer, J. C. DeHaven, & J. W. Milliman, *Water Supply: Economics, Technology, and Policy* (U. of Chicago Press, 1960).

[17] F. S. Hoffman, Statement before Subcommittee on Economy in Government, Joint Economic Committee, *Economic Analysis of Public Investment Decisions: Interest Rate Policy and Discounting Analysis,* 90th Congress, 2nd Session.

[18] F. H. Knight, *Risk, Uncertainty, and Profit* (Harper & Row, 1965).

[19] J. V. Krutilla & O. Eckstein, *Multipurpose River Development* (Johns Hopkins Press, 1958).

[20] S. A. Marglin, "The Social Rate of Discount and the Optimal Rate of Investment," *Quarterly Journal of Economics,* v. 78 (May 1964).

[21] H. Markowitz, "The Utility of Wealth," *Journal of Political Economy,* v. 60 (April 1952).

[22] A. Marshall, *Principles of Economics,* 8th ed. (London: Macmillan, 1964).

[23] R. N. McKean, *Efficiency in Government Through Systems Analysis* (Wiley, 1958).

[24] F. Modigliani & M. H. Miller, "The Cost of Capital, Corporation Finance, and the Theory of Investment," *American Economic Review,* v. 48. (June 1958).

[25] A. C. Pigou, *The Economics of Welfare,* 4th ed. (New York: Macmillan, 1960).

[26] A. R. Prest & R. Turvey, "Cost-Benefit Analysis: A Survey," *Economic Journal,* v. 75 (Dec. 1965).

[27] P. A. Samuelson, "Principles of Efficiency—Discussion," *American Economic Review,* v. 54 (Papers & Proceedings, May 1964).

[28] L. J. Savage, *The Foundations of Statistics* (Wiley, 1965).

[29] W. F. Sharpe, "Capital Asset Prices: A Theory of Market Equilibrium Under Conditions of Risk," *Journal of Finance,* v. 19 (Sept. 1964).

[30] A. Smith, *The Wealth of Nations* (Modern Library reprint of Cannan edition).

[31] E. B. Staats, Statement of Hon. Elmer B. Staats, Comptroller General of the United States, Joint Economic Committee, Subcommittee on Economy in Government, *Interest Rate Guidelines for Federal Decisionmaking,* 90th Congress, 2nd Session (1968).

[32] W. Vickrey, "Principles of Efficiency—Discussion," *American Economic Review,* v. 54 (Papers & Proceedings, May 1964).

[33] U.S. Congress, Joint Economic Committee, Subcommittee on Economy in Government, *Interest Rate Guidelines for Federal Decisionmaking,* 90th Congress, 2nd Session (1968).

[34] J. A. Stockfisch. Prepared Statement of Jacob A. Stockfisch before Subcommittee on Economy in Government Joint Economic Committee, *The Planning-Programing-Budgeting System: Progress and Potentials,* 90th Congress, 1st Session.

[35] U.S. Congress, Subcommittee on Benefits and Costs of the Federal Inter-Agency River Basin Committee, *Proposed Practices for Economic Analysis of River Basin Projects:* Report to the Federal Inter-Agency River Basin Committee (Washington, D.C., Government Printing Office, May 1950).

[36] U.S. Senate Document No. 97, *Policies, Standards Evaluation and Review of Plans for Use and Development of Water and Related Land Resources,* 87th Congress, 2nd Session.

CHAPTER 12

SHADOW PRICES FOR INCORRECT OR NONEXISTENT MARKET VALUES

Julius Margolis

INTRODUCTION

The State of Israel retaliated for the machine gunning of one plane and the death of a passenger by sending troops across a border and destroying 13 planes. The United Nations judged that the exchange was not appropriate and condemned Israel. Other retaliatory raids have not been condemned —was there an implied judgment that the "price was fair?" Many persons would object in principle to retaliation, a forced exchange of losses, and though most of us would be prepared to state whether a specific retaliatory exchange was reasonable or not we would be very hard-pressed to offer a "scientific" defense of our opinion. The oratory at the Security Council may seem far removed from the more prosaic questions of public expenditures analysis, but agreement about shadow prices is the essence of both problems, that is, the evaluation of exchanges which are not carried out under optimal market conditions. The problem of estimation of shadow prices exists wherever the market is imperfect or nonexistent and of course government services and regulation are instances *par excellence*.

In economic analysis the problem of evaluation of goods or activities is solved for the bulk of cases by market exchanges, where money enters on one side of the exchange. Whenever money is used, we can form a ratio of the amount of the good to the amount of money; the ratio is the price and this can be quoted for all goods and activities. However there are many cases where exchanges occur without money passing hands; where exchanges occur but where they are not freely entered into; where exchanges are so constrained by institutional rules that it would be dubious to infer that the terms were satisfactory; and where imperfections in the conditions of the exchange would lead us to conclude that the price ratios do not reflect appropriate social judgments about values. Each of these cases gives rise to deficiencies in the use of existing price data as the basis of evaluation of inputs or outputs. The enumeration and refined analysis of market

Julius Margolis is Professor of Economics and Director of the Fels Institute at the University of Pennsylvania.

imperfections has reached a high level; unfortunately the analysis of how to replace market numbers is still primitive.

Previous papers in this volume have gone into detail concerning the imperfections of the competitive market which both justify public intervention, and at the same time, make prices inappropriate as measures of social value. I shall focus on the analysis of how governments grope towards assigning price-like values, or shadow prices, to their inputs and outputs. But before dealing directly with this issue there are several general background points about the market which should be discussed. The basic question asked by the analyst when he searches for shadow price is: what would the users of the public output be willing to pay. The analyst tries to simulate a perfect and competitive market for the public output, estimate the price which would have resulted, and accept this as the shadow price. Unfortunately, even if the analyst succeeds in finding this price it is not clear that the government would accept it as sufficient to establish a value. Markets and quasi-markets are one form of social interaction; it is not obvious that other forms of social interaction should be interpreted so as to be consistent with the logic of market exchanges.

MARKET LIMITATIONS

A simulated market is a useful approach so long as the market is the process by which all, or at least the overwhelming number of goods are exchanged. Economics has been subject to attack for its attempts to subject all social activity to the measuring rod of money; though there is much merit to this criticism, fortunately, the economist has persisted in extending his calculus. An aggregate index of the state of social welfare is still beyond our ingenuity but the national income figures which were created to estimate the level of welfare have proven invaluable for a wide variety of purposes, and efforts to extend the concepts to social accounts are likely to bear fruit. But more important for our analysis is the huge area of valued social activity contained in the market sector of the economy and which is *not* directly priced. The costs of goods produced do not necessarily measure the value of resources which could have produced other benefits and the prices paid for goods need not be an appropriate measure of final products received.

Consider the case of production of a marketable commodity. Productivity indices are highly variable among nations; within nations, the range of variation among industries or plants is very great. Certainly, some of this variation can be attributed to variable amounts of consumption which occur in the sphere of production. In some cases, government controls are exercised to encourage this consumption, but in other instances more mysterious processes are at work. It would not be surprising if the government rejected the market price as not properly reflecting these other consumption aspects.

One of the most dramatic expansions of consumption in our society has been the reduction in the workday, workyear, and worklife. If leisure could be considered a commodity, it is likely that its volume has increased more than any other commodity. "As a rough measure of past growth in free time, the employed worker has about 1,200 hours per year more nonworking time than his 1890 counterpart. . . . In addition to a shortened workyear, nonworking years have grown by about nine for a male at birth, with present life and worklife expectations."[1] Over the last half-century, about one-third of the gains from productivity have been taken by increased leisure—a non-marketed consumption good. The point of interest to us is that our society has chosen to take a very large percentage of its potential income in the form of reduced work and thereby reduced money income but increased leisure. It should be pointed out that this reduction has taken place by market choices and through government actions. Numerous legislative actions have limited work at every stage in the production process. It would not be surprising to find comparable losses in productivity elsewhere, which might also be judged as consumption.

I would hazard that a very large part of "inefficiency" in production is attributable to consumption. We know too little about inefficiency but certainly the range of difference in productivity among firms, industries and nations is huge, even in identical facilities. Productivity gains in applying well-known techniques are often in the range of 50 percent and great efforts are often necessary to initiate them.[2]

Why is there a willingness to accept lower productivity? Is it too unreasonable to say that a large part of inefficiency are potential losses which are really acts of consumption, and the resistance to reduce inefficiency is the unwillingness to surrender consumption.

A willingness to accept lower productivity can be viewed in another perspective—a reluctance to change. It should not be surprising that men resist change in work patterns, especially as they grow older. New methods involve learning, an investment. What had been previously the consumption of potential income now becomes an actual investment and with advanced age, the expected value of increased income falls, so that investment becomes less desirable. The adaptation to a new process involves not only setup costs in new equipment and losses of production but also sacrifices in search for information and learning new habits at the expense of old comfortable routines. The organizational changes are often the most difficult to make.

I do not want to belabor the social role of "inefficient" production processes. Not only could it be interpreted as extra-market consumption, but I believe it casts some understanding about the production of public goods. For instance, risk aversion is often stated as a common characteristic of individual decisionmakers and sometimes it is argued that it is sufficient to explain why governments must act in some circumstance. The adoption of this position may mean that the government does not accept the individual's evaluations, as expressed in market prices, as binding; the rejection of this price has led to a lengthy and inconclusive debate. The sorting out of utility payoffs in production and investment has proven to be extremely difficult.

A second source of "inefficiency" which has plagued the analyst of the public sector is the immobility of resources. Inputs do move in response to income differentials, but it is clear that there are strong resistances to move, and these resistances grow with age of residents. Individuals have poor information about alternatives and the full range of social activities in the site of a new residence. A move means a necessity of building up their private social capital in a new place instead of consuming the private social capital already accumulated for the old place. Under these conditions, individual resistance to movement is not surprising.

It is equally not surprising that governments in their provision of public services accept this immobility. Many governments assume regional objectives as significant in shaping the public services. Governments are often not persuaded to abandon a depressed district by demonstrations that the costs of moving a population from a declining region may be less than the extra costs of providing services for depressed and less dense regions. On the contrary, the government may supplement the public services with efforts to encourage the expansion of economic activity to support the inefficiently located public services. The government may be responding to extra-market income and consumption.

There is nothing novel about the preceding remarks; the existence of nonpecuniary advantages and disadvantages is well-known. Unfortunately, knowledge of their existence has not led to an appraisal of its importance. I hazard that it may be very important especially in the sectors where the government operates.

In the preceding illustrations we have stressed private evaluations of market activity which are not readily captured in the market. For these reasons, governments may not respect the market process and values. It is also true that there may be social valuations of the market process which vary drastically from the economists interpretation of prices. These social evaluations may lead to a rejection of market guides. For instance, the economist's interpretation of market activity leads him to distinguish carefully between efficiency and distribution effects. If an entrepreneur discovers a better way to produce a commodity, it may lead to a price reduction. His profits may increase; the profits of his rivals may fall; the consumers will gain. Where we evaluate the desirability of the innovation we just look at the gain of the innovator; the losses of other firms and the gains to the consumer are considered to be offsetting and merely transfers. A well-organized competitive economy is constantly generating these transfers. Governments do not share the indifference of the economist toward these distributional effects.

Compensation is granted in many cases where the losses or damages would be considered transfers. If these were paid by the government as part of a project the benefit-cost calculus would include them in the costs. And yet it may be true that the project might never be authorized unless compensation were paid. It could be said that these payments are necessary to have the project be adopted though they do not reflect the value of any resources used for the project. Those who receive losses may have more political influence than the gainers and thereby be able to affect the political decision, or there may be a social judgment that the losses were incurred because of the government's decision, and it would be improper to allow any sector to have undue losses.

Government policies or programs are often massive in nature. Their effects are dispersed throughout the economy but they have major impacts in very restricted areas. A new bridge may create extreme losses along old traffic arteries; a zoning shift may create millionaires and shatter dreams. "Inequities," are charged; lengthy delays result; designs are altered; the distributional effects are relevant for policy but they will also affect the resource cost of getting the public service supplied. Further, the certainty or uncertainty of compensation as a consequence of a public act will affect how the private sector behaves.

The thrust of these remarks is to cast some doubt on the standard interpretation of the price data available in the market. There are many situations, often characterized as transfers, where government has accepted transfers as costs and thereby has been criticized by economists, but where it may be that the government has been responding to distributional effects. Possibly, a more explicit accounting of these distributional effects might lead to a more effectively designed public program. Shifts in prices always have distributional consequences and we may err in too readily refusing to consider these "nonefficiency" aspects.

Finally, the market and the data it generates is limited in that it relies on a model of individuals as consumers, whereas in reality the purchasing decisionmakers or the job choosing decisionmakers are one or both parents. Children ride in the car bought by the parent. If the parent chooses to balance his journey to work against garden space, the child does not face the same tradeoffs, he can only enjoy or suffer the consequence of the parental decision. In principle the parent considers the family welfare in making his decision. However, we need only look at the divorce rates to make it apparent that harmony in the family is far from universal. Many public services are directed toward the special problems of those who are disenfranchised in the private market. However, market prices reflect the values of the private decisionmakers in the families, not the social units for whom they act. Would mass transportation or neighborhood playgrounds be more numerous if children could spend their "equitable" share?

My intention here is not to discuss the limitations of the market and therefore I will not extend these remarks. I believe it necessary to introduce the points about these limitations because my subsequent comments about shadow prices accept much of the economists views about the value content of market processes and prices. From here on, I will in large measure presume that if the market were not beset by technical imperfections as externalities, indivisibilities, and information costs, relative prices would equal relative costs and therefore relative prices would reasonably reflect relative social values.

SHADOW PRICES: WHOSE SHADOW?

Shadow prices are computed to reflect social values; the estimation procedures assume that social welfare is derived by aggregating individual valuations. In practice, economists have accepted the task of generating support for this view of social welfare. Consistent with this position has been the rejection of the legitimacy of an active role of the political process or administrative structure as formulators of the public interest. The result, which could be anticipated, is a tension between the economic analyst, with his view of the public interest, and the political and administrative decisionmakers who do not share the economists' view of the public interest. Those who accept the authority of administrative officials or political leaders have quite different views of appropriate objective functions and what numbers should be used to evaluate outputs and inputs.

The conflict between the two approaches can be crudely phrased by asking: Who is the client, who is the employer of the economist? The typical answer of the economist is that he is true to the principles of serving the public interest as defined by the profession in their scientific journals i.e. the aggregation of individual preferences. He selects his models and criteria so as to maximize the professional view of the public interest; the economist has selected a client who is neither an employer or decisionmaker. This is a noble perspective, unfortunately the purchasers of the economist's information and advice (the administrative officials or political leaders) are neither persuaded by the economist's insight nor do their incentives impel them to accept the perspective of the national interest as formulated by the economist. For instance, a municipal official, concerned with urban renewal, may assign a benefit to a project if there are net gains to his city while offsetting losses in adjoining cities are of "purely academic" interest. Or, a national transportation agency may assign benefits based upon improved traffic flows, but the agency is not expected to consider the losses elsewhere, for instance, the increase in noise or air pollution. Payoffs to decisionmakers, administrative or political, are not based upon what happens to an index of national welfare, even if it could be constructed, and therefore it is not surprising that evaluatory measures developed in response to an agency's needs are partial and sometimes inconsistent with social welfare.

It may be presumptuous for the economist to insist on the primacy of his imputed prices against the views of the legitimately constituted authorities who employ him. However disrespect for authority was not introduced by our rebellious students; professional bodies have long lobbied to influence policy on the basis of their special competency. In the next section we shall assume the economist's vision of the public interest, despite our reservation that there is an alternative scheme by which to evaluate public outputs and inputs. There are social processes by which public decisions are guided. We have alluded to some, e.g. political bargaining, bureaucratic myopia, professional self-interest; it is likely that outcomes of each process considered independently would be far from socially optimal, but this does not mean that the total set of processes are not optimal. For instance, when we analyze the market system we recognize that a unit may not be at its best position though the economy may be operating optimally. We realize that a firm tries to maximize its profits and that its behavior is socially optimal if the economic system is so organized that it behaves competitively. Is it possible that a similar structure exists among different decision-making systems? Are there conditions of social equilibrium which are related to economic or political equilibrium just as general economic equilibrium is related to the equilibrium of the firm? I am far from convinced that a concept of social equilibrium analogous to economic equilibrium is useful but certainly economic criteria are partial and it would be wise to keep an open mind about more general formulations. Meanwhile we see efforts to extend economic equilibrium concepts to political behavior, but as I said, hereafter I will accept the economist's limited view.

SHADOW PRICES AND INPUT COSTS

The correction of market prices, or the imputation of prices, is done for both inputs and outputs. Most of the controversies deal with outputs though the same conceptual difficulties apply to both cases. In principle inputs are valued in terms of what they could have produced elsewhere and, therefore, we are immediately driven to the valuation of outputs. In practice, it is usually assumed that the market price of the inputs reflects their alternative values and therefore they could be used to measure the value of the inputs. Unfortunately there are a few dramatic cases where this is incorrect, and others where the correctness is disputed.

The most commonly advocated adjustment of an input price is for unemployed labor. Clearly, if labor had no alternative use then it would be incorrect to assign a price to it. This adjustment would make a project less costly and it would affect the design of the project. Of course, it would not be appropriate to assume the labor flow of a project over time would have been unemployed, but the problem of timing often holds for even the fairly shortrun. The time lag between analysis and the initiation of a program may extend for years and therefore current unemployment may not be an appropriate assumption. If one could not assume unemployment for the period of actual use of the resource then the full thrust of this adjustment, the substitution of unemployed labor for other inputs, would be lost.

A second input which may often be incorrectly priced, and too often does not bear an adjustment, is land. A program on public land is usually assessed the cost of the land to the agency rather than the opportunity costs of the land. Therefore a project on public land is "less costly" and would receive preference. The value of public land is often misstated because of the nature of the constraints imposed on government, that is, private alternative uses are rarely considered. Private land is also incorrectly valued, though for a different reason—a consequence of using a shadow price adjustment to evaluate benefits over time from the publicly held land but not applying a similar adjustment to the benefits derivable from the same land, if privately held.

If the government does not accept the market interest rate as a basis of valuing its benefits and costs over time, it adopts a "social rate of discount," typically well below the market rate. In applying this rate the government is in all likelihood grossly underestimating its land costs. For instance, the government might purchase an agricultural area and convert it to recreational use if the recreational benefits exceeded the costs of the land which presumably should equal the agricultural benefits. However, the value of the land would be the sum of the returns to agricultural use capitalized at the market rate of interest, possibly twice the assumed social rate. Therefore it is possible that a project may show a favorable benefit-cost ratio solely due to applying a shadow price—the social rate of discount —in the public sector and not extending the adjustment to the private sector.

The preceding error: the setting of shadow prices for a public discount rate but no adjustment for the private market rate is a general problem. This criticism can be extended to all of the capital inputs used by the public sector. Since their foregone use is market values lost, valued at the market interest rate, they will be underestimated relative to public benefits solely because the use of too low an interest rate.

SHADOW PRICES AND CONSTRAINTS

We mentioned in the preceding section that public land is often incorrectly priced since private alternative use is not considered. This difficulty can be generalized to many parts of the government. Institutional rules are established and then prices are estimated within the confines of the rules. For instance, the value of a water supply to an area may be based upon the cost of supply to that area, but there may be a very low cost supply which is ruled out because of a government policy of dedicating the water to another use. Therefore the assigned value of the water may be grossly overstated from the perspective of the nation. Or, an agency may value its inputs in program A in terms of loss of benefits in program B for which the inputs are substitutes. However there may be a much more productive use in another agency, but the possibilities of transfer of funds may be very meager. For this reason, the evaluation of the worth of inputs may be understated.

A classic example of a set of constraints which may run counter to estimated shadow prices arises from budget allocations in conjunction with some discretionary authority residing with agencies. Funds for an agency are raised through taxes or bonds; they are not a concern of the decision-makers of an agency. The agency has no knowledge of the social costs of these funds, but they are very sensitive to the fact that their actions are very limited by the funds assigned to them. They are told that if there exists unemployment or arbitrarily fixed exchange rates, payments made for labor or imported goods inputs will not reflect their approximate social costs. The central authority might calculate a shadow price and instruct the agencies to use, say, a very low price reflecting that it is in surplus. If the agency were to use this price in its calculations, it would use relatively more labor than otherwise, in sensible agreement with the social evaluation of its labor inputs. But if the agency is subject to a budget limitation, which is usually the case, it would find that it would have spent relatively more on the process using labor, that is, from its perspective, a dollar spent on labor is worth a dollar spent on machines and though it may cost society less for them to use labor they make the same budgetary sacrifice whether labor had been over or underpriced. They will be highly resistant to adopting these shadow prices as operational tools in their choices of design of programs.

ESTIMATION PROCEDURES

The estimation procedures used to assign values to public outputs can be described as efforts to simulate market outcomes. It is assumed that for a variety of technical reasons—externalities, public goods, and so on—the private market must be supplemented by public production and distribution. The essential character of the objective function, according to this view, requires the assignment of prices which would have resulted from market behavior, if there had been some way to overcome the technical limitations which gave rise to public supply and a perfectly competitive market were able to operate. This individualistic view is usually supplemented by a judgment in regard to the distribution of income, a far from trivial departure from consumers sovereignty. The measurement rule used to determine the value of a government output is: estimate what the users of the public product would be willing to pay. Since the products are distributed at zero or low, conventional prices there are no direct measures by which the price can be discovered, and therefore several indirect procedures are used to reveal the price.

The Intermediate Good Approach The most common technique used to evaluate public output is to consider the product as an intermediate good and then to estimate the value of the marginal product of the good in further production, that is, assume the user is a producer and then ask: by how much does the public output increase his income? Illustrations are found in natural and human resources development. Some goods are easily and naturally treated in this fashion. For example, water supply is used for home consumption, but the great bulk of it is consumed in agriculture, power generation and industrial processing. Let us consider agricultural water. Productivity studies of irrigated farms are used to estimate the value of the product of an incremental acre-foot of water; this is the agricultural value of the water. It is assumed that the farmer would pay this amount as a price for the water and therefore the marginal product is identified as the "imputed market price," or "shadow price" of water. The computation of this figure is not a simple task, but beyond these problems there are frequent errors in the application of this approach, even when the product is easily treated as an intermediate good.

In practice we find that the farmer is rarely asked to pay as a price to the government the increment in income attributable to the water—an amount which is interpreted as the price he would be willing to pay. It is usually asserted that the unwillingness to charge this indicates a subsidy to agriculture. While this may be true, it also may be true that the computed shadow price may be far greater than a simulated market price for several reasons.

a. There may be alternative sources of supply and the cost of this supply would put a ceiling on the price that the farmer would pay for the water, for example, ground water pumping costs may be greater than the charged price but below the imputed value. The failure to consider this alternative is a shortcoming of this analysis.

b. The budget studies usually computed an expected value over several years. If the farmer is a risk averter he will assign a lower value to this anticipated income. It might be correct for the government to plan its operations on the basis of average expected values, but then it would have to absorb the risk and sell the water below the price. This problem of individual risk and government preference for expected values has not been studied in reference to the design and management of programs.

c. The computation of incremental productivity usually refers to averages rather than marginals. If the water is supplied at a low or zero price then we know that the user will purchase it to the point where the value of the marginal product would equal price. Since the average value will be greater than the marginal, multiplying the total amount which will be purchased by the average value will greatly overstate the total revenue from selling the product at a market price.

The divergency between average and marginal suggests another ambiguity in the concept of the price the users would be willing to pay. A simulated market price equates demand and supply, it balances off marginal gains and costs. But the price users may be willing to pay for the quantity rather than do without it may be much greater. In principle, the users would be willing to pay a sum equal to the area under the demand curve in order to receive the quantity rather than do without the project. If there are reasonably good alternatives to the public output the demand curve will be highly elastic and the difference between the area under the demand curve and the product of the market-clearing price and quantity would be small. As we shall see, the limiting factor of alternative supply is considered in the estimation of benefits in some cases, but not others.

The above difficulties of estimating the productivity values of public services are small compared to those which arise when we consider services like education and health which have been valued as intermediate goods. For educational output, statistical studies have found a correlation between years of schooling and income. Therefore, it is argued that the earning capacity of an individual has been increased by the additional years of schooling. Further, it is said that the individual should be willing to pay that increment of expected income, less his foregone earnings while he is in school, for the educational services provided him. In practice, of course, an individual would not be expected to make such a payment, but this is attributed to the immature judgment of a student and his lack of capital. But does this relationship between education and income, even if it could be convincingly established, exhaust the reasons for public education or is it even the dominant factor? Clearly, the government is interested in many consequences beyond the income of the person. For instance, will he be a better and more responsible participant in the political process? Will he be a better neighbor? Will he have developed values and insights which will make him a more effective parent? Many more goals for education have been asserted, but all we want to establish here is that governments will find unsatisfactory a rule for the design of educational programs, or for the determination of its scale, which is based only upon the enhancement of an individual's expected income.

In the case of health services, a different set of problems develop. Health is much more of a consumer good than education. Health, as an intermediate product, is valued by the additional working time and increased productivity associated with a reduction in disability. A saved life is valued at the present value of the expected income stream it would have earned. (Some would say that it should be net of the consumption of the saved life and therefore it should be the value of his savings.) Certainly, individuals are concerned about the loss of working time, but pain, discomfort and the fear of incapacity and death may be even more of a basis of willingness to pay to avoid illness. If the health program were designed to maximize benefits measured by income growth, then the diseases of the aged would be ignored and diseases of women would receive relatively little support. Neither individuals nor governments are prepared to accept the enhanced income as the sole basis for determining the private or social benefits of health.

The Cost-Savings Approach A second indirect technique commonly used to estimate what individuals are willing to pay is based upon the cost savings of the public service, that is, the reduction in the costs that individuals would have incurred if the public service were not supplied. This approach is most commonly adopted in the fields of transportation and power. Generally, it is assumed that there is an inelastic demand for the output and, therefore, the public somehow would have managed to transport the goods or to develop energy though the costs would have been much higher. The major sources of savings are private carrier costs in the case of transportation and private generation of energy in the case of power.

The cost-savings approach to benefit measurement faces two problems: the identification of the real alternatives which were saved and the constraints imposed upon policy if the user savings are the basis of evaluation. In the case of transportation, the costs savings are realized by shippers and travelers. An improved highway would reduce the travel time and operating costs of traveling between any two points. Presumably the users of the highways would be willing to pay that difference.

The savings for many public services should be the alternative facilities or programs which would have been provided by the government. Unfortunately, public agencies are notoriously poor in considering alternatives. For instance, an apprenticeship training program may be an alternative to vocational training in a school, but the educational agency is unlikely to consider an inservice program as an interesting or feasible alternative. Importing goods may be an alternative to agricultural expansion, but this is not likely to be considered. Organizations are not active searchers for information about alternatives they are not likely to pursue. It is also true that many of the most feasible alternatives may be those ruled out by legal or administrative constraints and never even considered. For instance, a change in the tax structure may provide a very different set of incentives for private consumption but it might never be considered by an operating agency. As a consequence, estimates of the real costs of alternatives which are saved are notoriously bad, except for the calculation of user savings in some cases.

The assumption of inelastic demand leads to greatly inflated multiplier of overstated benefits. The increased traffic generated by a public project would not have existed at the old cost structure and therefore it would be an error to assume a benefit equal to the unit cost savings of the old traffic multiplied by the augmented new traffic, including the increased flow. This problem becomes very acute when activity shifts among cities or ports in response to slight improvement of facilities. There may be large movements responding to very slight gains in private transportation costs, possibly far below the amount necessary to pay for the capital costs of the facilities.

The limitations of the use of costs of alternative programs as a measure of benefits is reflected in the analytical studies of the PPBS groups. These studies are appropriately labeled as cost-effective rather than cost-benefit analyses. The objectives of the program are usually specified in physical terms and the alternatives where trade-offs are considered as restricted to those under the control of the agency. The narrow view is typified by the label given the function of the military system analysts: the most bang for the money rather than the most national security or social welfare.

The evaluation of public output in terms of costs or savings by users is based upon an assumption that we are to be guided by the efficiency calculation of the individual beneficiaries of the project. Political and administrative leaders resist the policy conclusions drawn from these studies since they see them as restrictive of their freedom to plan the development of the nation. For instance, the benefit-cost calculations might indicate the most efficient transportation network but efficiency has never been a sufficient criterion for governments in their locational policies. It is possible that governments have erred in trying to support their declining regions, to populate their empty places, or to stem the flow of population to their capitals, but the public support of these programs has been great. Though economic arguments of external economies and diseconomies have been used to defend these programs, it is clear that regional objectives have been pursued for their own sakes, with a willingness on the part of the government to sacrifice national income for these benefits.

Cost savings on the part of individuals or agencies need not be the only frame of reference in trying to discover shadow prices. There is an alternative formulation which views the legislature or administration as representatives of the aggregate of citizens. It is argued that unrestrained political bargaining is not optimal but that the addition of appropriate information to the decisionmaking process would lead to optimal outcomes. The first step of the analyst is to design a quantitative measure of the product of the public output. This is not difficult in the case of most commercial, marketable commodities like food, clothing, or machines, but for services like recreation, education, or national defense, an appropriate unit of output is not obvious. The most common measures refer to use of the service rather than their desired qualities; e.g., years of schooling rather than increased productivity, socialization, and so on. The second step is to estimate the real costs of resources necessary to produce the outputs. The above information is equivalent to the marginal rate of transformation between two public services. The decisionmaker is then asked to revise the expenditure levels among the public services—the revision, if the authorities are responsive to the public, would be in the direction of equating the marginal rate of substitution in utilities to the marginal rate of transformation in production. A decisionmaker who seeks to be most effective will welcome this information-structure, but there is a great gap between the decisionmaker's objective function and the social welfare, defined by aggregating individual preferences. In practice, this pattern of information of real costs and benefits for decisionmaking is appropriate to the view of a public interest, defined as a social ordering expressed by the government. The net result of applying this criterion, besides optimal allocation, is the derivation of an appropriate set of shadow prices. These are the relative costs of the different public services when the government has decided that the budget has been optimally allocated. The ratio of marginal costs of two public outputs will be the same as the ratio of their social values, and therefore the marginal costs figures will have the same interpretation we give to competitive market prices.

The Direct Estimation Approach The third major technique of shadow price estimation is to estimate directly the users prices by appeal to market information. This is the most difficult task, but it may prove to be the most fruitful. In many cases there are near substitutes for collective consumption. There is usually a private educational, health, or recreational market; the extensive study of this market may provide the needed price information. The difficulty facing the analyst is that the comparable private commodities are sometimes very different. The characteristics of service of a private medical clinic may be sufficiently similar to a public clinic that the private data may be usable, but the differences between a public park and a private camp are huge and difficult to compare.

Another form of use of market data is more indirect, it relies on the responses of the private sector in gaining access to the free public services. Public services are free, but acess to them may be costly. Parks are free, and since they are desirable men will pay higher rents for sites located close to them. There would be similar shifts in the demand for land because of differential quality of schools, medical facilities, highway systems, and so forth. Households will reveal their preferences by their locational decisions, and further, the revelation will be quantitative. An analysis of the household's costs may provide information about the value they assign to these public services. This form of analysis will require complicated econometric studies, since changes in behavior will be due to many factors and some shifts will be due to the initial changes of the users of the public services rather than to the public services themselves.

SHADOW PRICES AND INCENTIVES

I have alluded to the problem of incentives to public officials, but that brief allusion greatly understates their importance. Shadow prices are useful pieces of information, but unless the decisionmakers benefit by acting on the basis of those prices, little is gained. It is utopian to assume that disinterested scientists will compute the shadow prices and devoted public servants will accept them as binding. When I discussed the use of a low shadow price for unemployed labor I pointed out that since the agency is subject to a budget constraint they are not likely to be receptive to a rule which tells them to treat labor as though it were a free good when it is obvious to them labor inputs place a drain on their limited budget. A similar set of improper incentives is reflected in the continuous battling between highway authorities and conservationists. Public parks provide "free or cheap land" from the perspective of the construction agency and since their budget is limited—the use of public land maximizes the amount of traffic served per dollar of their budget.

The problems of incentives and shadow prices may be of even greater magnitude when we deal with the many decentralized programs initiated by the federal government in the urban areas. The federal government may identify targets and even assign values to outputs but if incentives to local governments are not consistent with these values the federal objectives are not likely to be achieved. For instance, fiscal profitability is of minor concern to the national interest but the payoffs of a project along this dimension often dominate the local design and execution of a program.

The thrust of the above remarks is that the problem of shadow price determination is not simply one of calculation. If shadow prices are to guide behavior then those who must make and implement the decisions require incentives to provide the "correct" information needed for calculation, and to use the prices. Therefore the study of shadow pricing rules opens up the even more difficult study of the optimal structure of government.

NOTES

[1] Juanita M. Kreps, *Lifetime Allocation of Work and Leisure,* Research Report No. 22, Office of Research and Statistics, Social Security Administration, U.S. Department of HEW, 1968, p. 36.

[2] For a survey and interpretation of the many studies, see Harvey Leibenstein, "Allocative Efficiency vs. X-Efficiency," *American Economic Review,* June 1966.

CHAPTER 13

EVALUATING PUBLIC EXPENDITURES UNDER CONDITIONS OF UNEMPLOYMENT

Robert H. Haveman

INTRODUCTION

In the postwar period, the expenditure side of the public sector has been the subject of a substantial amount of analysis. While some of this work developed and refined the theory of public expenditure analysis, other work was aimed at improving the methods for evaluating the economic gains and the costs of alternative expenditure projects. This paper reflects the latter of these two emphases. It presents the reasons why monetary costs fail to reflect real social costs when the economy is experiencing unemployment and excess capacity, and elaborates a method for adjusting monetary costs when such conditions prevail. The implementation of this method eliminates the overstatement of real costs by monetary costs when some of the resources drawn into use by a public expenditure have idleness as their alternative.

I

An essential proposition in public expenditure economics is that, in evaluating the economic worth of a public expenditure, it is the *social* costs and *social* benefits which must be evaluated and not the private (or monetary) costs and private (or monetary) benefits. A second proposition is that, while social and private values may well be identical, they are not likely to be when there is some imperfection in the operation of the market system. Clearly, the existence of unemployed resources represents market system imperfection which would cause these two values to diverge.[1]

If resources in the economy are fully employed, the monetary costs of the labor and capital purchased by a public expenditure are likely to be a good approximation of the value of the things which society would be able to enjoy if the expenditure were not undertaken.[2] This is so because the

Robert H. Haveman is Professor of Economics at Grinnell College. At the time this paper was prepared, he was on leave of absence as Senior Economist of the Subcommittee on Economy in Government of the Joint Economic Committee.

The author wishes to acknowledge the helpful comments of John Krutilla and Jack Knetsch on an earlier draft of this paper.

price paid to resources employed in any enterprise tends to equal the value produced by the resources in that use. When they are hired away from the activity, society is forced to forgo the output which they would have produced.

Consider, for example, a $100 public expenditure which is used to purchase $100 worth of labor and capital. If there were full employment and if the economy were functioning ideally in other respects, these resources would have been used to produce $100 worth of goods and services of some unknown composition which would have been purchased, used, and enjoyed by members of the society. This $100 worth of goods and services, then, is the social cost necessitated by the public expenditure. Stated alternatively, because of the $100 public expenditure, resources of that value are diverted from producing $100 worth of other things and society is forced to forego the opportunity of using and enjoying these particular "other things."

However, when there is not full employment of labor, or when plant capacity is not fully used, some of the resources hired by the public expenditure may not have to be diverted from alternative uses. Some of them may be drawn from the pool of unused or idle labor or capital resources. By definition, these unemployed resources are not producing other things. Consequently, to the extent that otherwise unemployed resources are drawn into use by the public expenditure, the social cost of the expenditure—the value of the alternative uses that would have been made of the required manpower and capital—is less than the market or monetary cost.

II

It is clear that public expenditures made during a period of substantial unemployment would call into use some resources which would otherwise have been unemployed. Not so obvious, however, is the fact that a similar result is likely when the national unemployment rate is quite low. However, this latter proposition—that some resources called into use by the marginal public expenditure would otherwise be idle, even under conditions of relatively full employment—is a point which must not be neglected.

The reason for this effect is the substantial variation of unemployment rates by occupation, by industry, and by region around the national average unemployment rate. If the nation showed a full employment rate of 4 percent and if every occupation in every region showed that same rate of unemployment, a public expenditure would in all likelihood cause 100 percent of the resources which it required to be diverted from other uses. However, if the 4-percent national rate is composed of a 2-percent unemployment rate in some occupations (regions) offset by a 6- to 7-percent unemployment rate in other occupations (regions), it is not likely that all of the labor which is hired by the public expenditure would be diverted from other uses. A part of these resources would be drawn from the high unemployment occupations (regions) in which case the public expenditure would call into use some resources which would otherwise have lain idle. Indeed, in the case in which there is substantial variation of occupational, industrial, and regional unemployment around the national unemployment rate, it is conceivable that the full set of resource demands imposed by the public expenditure might be met by units of labor and capital drawn from the idle pool.

Table 1 shows that, in fact, there is a substantial amount of variation of occupational, industrial, and regional unemployment rates around the national average. The distribution of unemployment rates around the national average is presented for 1960. In that year the national unemployment rate was 5.6 percent. From the data in these distributions, it is clear that it is necessary to know the structure of demands which a public expenditure imposes on the economy in order to determine the extent to which the expenditure does or does not use resources which would otherwise be unemployed.

When this result is related to the opportunity cost logic presented in section I, it becomes clear that much public spending in the postwar period imposed social—or opportunity or real—costs on the society which were less than the monetary costs.[3] Moreover, and more importantly given the unemployment situation in 1970, some spending which occurs during pe-

Table 1

Variation of Occupational, Industrial, and Regional Unemployment Rates Around National Average, 1960

Unemployment rates	Occupational[a]	Industrial[b]	Regional[c]
Below 2.6	4	1	0
2.6 to 3.6	3	2	6
3.6 to 4.6	0	0	8
4.6 to 5.6	2	4	15
5.6 to 6.6	3	4	11
6.6 to 7.6	0	1	7
7.6 to 8.6	1	2	2
8.6 or more	5	2	1

[a] Data for 18 major occupational categories.
[b] Data for 16 major industry categories.
[c] Data for 50 States.

riods of rather full employment may entail the use of resources which would otherwise have been unutilized or underutilized. This would be especially true if the pattern of resource demands imposed by a particular public expenditure emphasized the occupations, industries, and regions which had substantial unemployment even though, overall, the economy was rather fully employed. Again, the use of these resources entails zero opportunity costs.[4] Clearly, the accurate economic evaluation of the social costs of a public expenditure requires a detailed estimate of the pattern of the occupational, industrial, and regional demands imposed by the expenditure and a comparison of these demands with the existing pattern of occupation, industrial, and regional unemployment, *both* when the economy is not fully employed *and* when it is.

III

The first step in evaluating the opportunity costs of a public expenditure is to estimate the pattern of the demands generated by the expenditure for labor, by occupation, for capital, by industry, and for both labor and capital, by region. While the pattern of labor and materials employed directly by the expenditure is not difficult to ascertain, the set of final labor and capital demands imposed after the material inputs are traced through the several rounds of the production process is far more difficult to estimate. Recently, this estimation task has become possible because of the national input-output matrix assembled and published by the Office of Business Economics of the U.S. Department of Commerce[5] and the industry-occupations matrix completed by the Bureau of Labor Statistics of the U.S. Department of Labor.[6] When these empirical matrices are incorporated along with basic estimates of the direct resource demands of a public expenditure into an appropriate computational model, the full catalog of direct and indirect demands placed on factor sources—by occupation, industry, and region—can be estimated.

In one particular model developed for the purpose of estimating the complete pattern of labor and capital demands imposed by a public expenditure, the sequence of computations proceeds as follows:[7] Given the basic data on the direct material, equipment and supply inputs required by an expenditure, the complete pattern of industrial demands is calculated through use of the input-output matrix. Then, on the basis of a set of relationships which grant a preferred status to the region in which the expenditure is undertaken and the geographic location of each industry's capacity, the geographic distribution of these total industrial demands is estimated. Third, by using the industry-occupation matrix, the labor demands imposed on each region because of the industry output demands are estimated, in occupational detail. Fourth, these occupational labor demands generated by purchases of materials, equipment, and supplies—and distributed among the regions—are added to the on-site occupational pattern of labor demands by region. Finally, the pattern of demands imposed on capital are determined by industry and by region by applying appropriate capital-output ratios to the total output demands, by industry, which were estimated in the second step.

By employing this model, the pattern of resource demands can be computed for any public expenditure in 156 occupation, 80 industry, and 10 region detail. Table 2 shows, in substantially consolidated form, the kind of detailed estimate furnished by this model. In that table the pattern of occupational, industrial, and regional demands is shown when a multiple-purpose—including hydroelectric power generation—water development project is constructed in the lower Atlantic States.

In the final column of this table, it is shown that a total gross output of $1,032 per $1,000 of total project cost is generated by the direct purchases of materials, equipment, and supplies required for the project.[8] Of this total gross output demand, 29 percent of it, or $300, is imposed on the lower Atlantic region—the region where the project is assumed to be constructed. In addition, because of the heavy demands which this kind of installation places on durable equipment manufacturing, a substantial set of demands are imposed by the project on the mid-Atlantic and east north central regions where these industries are concentrated. Together, these three regions account for over 70 percent of the total gross output stimulated by the expenditure. That it is the durable goods industries which account for this regionally concentrated result is also seen in the table. Of the total gross output of $1,032, durable goods production accounted for $539, or over 50 percent. Of the $539 of durable goods output, over $320 or 60 percent is produced by the mid-Atlantic and east north central regions.

In the lower portion of Table 2 the labor demands required by the project are shown in occupational detail and by region. Because of the nature of this kind of construction installation, many of the labor demands are required on the construction site. This accounts for the heavy concentration of labor demands in the region in which the project is assumed to be constructed. The lower Atlantic region supplies nearly three-fourths of the total labor demand generated by the project. Consistent with the gross output estimates which demonstrated the concentration of durable goods in the highly industrialized regions, it is seen that those labor demands which the project imposes on other regions are concentrated in the mid-Atlantic and east north central regions and among the craftsman and operatives occupations.

Finally, the substantial disparity in the pattern of industrial and occupational demands generated by various project types should be noted. While all of the project types analyzed in the full study were water resource investments, the anatomy of their industrial, occupational, and regional impacts is far more diverse than is generally recognized. While some project types require very little on-site construction (dredging), others require the installation of huge capital facilities (multipurpose projects). For the 12 project types analyzed, the ratio of labor compensation (direct and indirect) to total project cost ranges from .52 to .72. The range in the ratio of on-site labor cost to total labor cost extended from .25 to .58. The ratio of durable goods demanded to gross material demands extends from .2 to .65. When all of the project types are assumed to be constructed in the lower Atlantic region, the percent of national gross output retained in that region ranges from 24 to 32 percent; the percent of national labor cost retained extends from 69 to 75 percent. Even more radical disparities among project types are noted as detailed industrial or occupational sectors are studied.

IV

Having ascertained the pattern of resource demands imposed by a public expenditure, the next step in evaluating the social costs of these demands is to compare them with the occupational and regional pattern of labor unemployment and the industrial pattern of excess plant capacity. As described above, the monetary costs of a public expenditure represent real opportunity returns foregone at the margin only if all of the resources used have alternative employments. If there is unemployment, however, some labor used is likely to be drawn from the idle pool. This labor has no comparable opportunity cost. Similarly, the opportunity rate of return on otherwise idle capital drawn into use by the expenditure is zero. However, because capital services are largely storeable, depreciation charges are a real cost properly imputed to the expenditure even when otherwise idle industrial capacity is drawn into use.

On this basis, the occupational, industrial, and regional breakdowns of monetary costs can be modified to the extent that the units of labor and capital represented would have been otherwise idle. To estimate the extent to which any labor and capital demand employs otherwise unused resources, it is necessary to trace each unit of labor and capital employed to its source and to inquire concerning its alternative use. In the absence of data necessary to implement this counsel of perfection, the model discussed here assumes that the levels of occupational unemployment (or, in the case of capital, industrial excess capacity) are significant determinants of the proportion of labor drawn from any occupation and region (capital drawn

Table 2

Gross Output by Industry and Total Labor Cost by Occupation in Each of 10 Regions for a $1,000 Public Expenditure on a Multipurpose Water Resource Project Assumed to be Constructed in the Lower Atlantic Region, in Dollars per $1,000 of Expenditure[a]

	New England	Mid-Atlantic	East north-central	West north-central	Southeast	Lower Atlantic	West south-central	Mountain and West Coast	Total
INDUSTRY									
Agriculture, forestry, and fisheries	([b]) (5)	([b]) (6)	1(15)	2(21)	1(16)	([b]) (4)	1(13)	2(21)	8
Mining (including crude petroleum)	([b]) ([c])	4 (5)	4 (5)	4 (6)	2 (4)	35(58)	10(14)	7 (9)	77
Construction	([b]) (2)	1(11)	1(16)	([b]) (3)	([b]) (3)	5(54)	([b]) (4)	([b]) (6)	9
Nondurable goods manufacturing	7 (7)	20(20)	24(23)	5 (5)	10(10)	11(11)	14(14)	11(10)	103
Durable goods manufacture	31 (6)	126(23)	197(37)	27 (5)	29 (6)	49 (9)	25 (5)	56(10)	539
Lumber and wood products	1 (5)	1 (7)	2(12)	([b]) (4)	2(16)	1 (8)	1 (7)	6(40)	13
Stone, clay and glass products	4 (5)	15(19)	19(24)	6 (8)	7(10)	13(17)	5 (6)	9(12)	78
Primary metals industries	6 (4)	37(28)	47(36)	4 (3)	6 (5)	14(11)	3 (3)	14(10)	129
Fabricated metal industries	6 (6)	23(23)	31(31)	6 (6)	8 (8)	12(12)	5 (5)	11(11)	100
Machinery (excluding construction and electrical)	8(10)	22(29)	34(45)	3 (4)	2 (2)	2 (1)	1 (1)	4 (5)	75
Construction machinery	1 (1)	4 (8)	27(52)	4 (7)	1 (3)	2 (3)	9(17)	4 (9)	52
Electrical machinery	5 (8)	19(29)	26(40)	3 (5)	2 (3)	3 (5)	1 (1)	5 (8)	64
Transportation equipment	1 (4)	3(14)	11(52)	1 (4)	1 (5)	1 (7)	1 (3)	2(10)	20
Miscellaneous manufacturing	1(14)	3(45)	1(21)	([b]) (5)	([b]) (3)	([b]) (2)	([b]) (2)	([b]) (7)	7
Transportation and warehousing	1 (2)	6 (8)	8(11)	2 (2)	2 (3)	49(58)	2 (3)	3 (4)	72
Wholesale and retail trade	1 (2)	6 (6)	9 (9)	1 (2)	2 (2)	70(75)	2 (2)	3 (3)	93
Services	4 (3)	14(11)	21(16)	4 (3)	4 (3)	71(54)	6 (5)	7 (6)	131
Total gross output[d e]	45 (4)	177(17)	264(26)	45 (4)	52 (5)	300(29)	61 (6)	89 (8)	1,032

OCCUPATION									
Professional, technical, and kindred	2	6	9	1	1	49	2	3	72
Managers, officials, and proprietors	1	5	8	1	2	43	2	3	66
Clerical, and kindred workers	2	6	9	1	1	22	2	3	46
Salesworkers	([b])	1	1	([b])	1	6	([b])	([b])	10
Craftsmen, foremen, and kindred	3	11	18	3	3	274	3	5	319
Carpenters	([b])	([b])	([b])	([b])	([b])	48	([b])	([b])	49
Cement finishers	([b])	([b])	([b])	([b])	([b])	4	([b])	([b])	4
Iron and metal workers	([b])	([b])	([b])	([b])	([b])	22	([b])	([b])	22
Construction equipment operators	([b])	1	1	([b])	([b])	45	([b])	([b])	48
Other building trades	([b])	1	1	([b])	([b])	37	([b])	([b])	41
Mechanics	([b])	2	3	([b])	([b])	12	([b])	1	18
Labor foremen	1	2	4	1	([b])	48	1	1	58
Other craftsmen, foremen, and kindred	1	5	9	1	1	58	1	2	88
Operatives and kindred workers	4	13	20	3	4	54	3	7	108
Truck and tractor drivers	([b])	2	2	1	([b])	15	1	1	22
Sailors and deckhands	([b])	([b])	([b])	([b])	([b])	([b])	([b])	([b])	([b])
Other operatives and kindred	3	12	17	2	3	39	3	5	86
Service workers	([b])	1	2	([b])	([b])	3	([b])	([b])	7
Laborers	1	3	4	1	1	77	1	1	89
Farmers and farmworkers	([b])	([b])	([b])	([b])	([b])	([b])	([b])	([b])	2
Total labor cost[d] [f]	12 (2)	47 (7)	70(10)	12 (2)	14 (2)	527(73)	13 (2)	24 (4)	719

[a] Percent of row totals stated in parentheses behind the dollar values.
[b] Less than $0.1 but greater than 0.
[c] Less than $0.5 but greater than 0.
[d] Rows may not add because of rounding.
[e] Percent of total gross output stated in parentheses behind regional total gross output figures.
[f] Percent of total labor cost stated in parentheses behind regional total labor cost figures.

from any industry) which would have, in the absence of the expenditure, been idle. For example, this approach treats an increase in the demand for labor at low levels of unemployment as simply shifting workers among jobs without reducing unemployment below the frictional minimum. However, as the rate of unemployment (excess capacity) rises, so too does the probability that the incremental demand will draw otherwise unemployed labor (idle capital) into use. Because accurate knowledge on the pattern of labor and capital market response does not exist, a set of synthetic response functions is employed. These functions relate the probability that a given increment in the demand for labor and capital will be drawn from otherwise unemployed resources to the level of occupational unemployment and industrial excess capacity on the basis of reasonable assumptions concerning market operation.

In Figure 1, the kind of relationships used to estimate the extent to which labor demands are supplied from otherwise unutilized resources in this model are shown.[9] The set of synthetic functions inscribed within the area between the two curves states that the higher the unemployment rate, the greater the proportion of labor from any given occupation which is hired from the idle pool. The region labeled r_f describes the range of unemployment rates at which each of the major occupational categories is said to be fully employed.[10] Full employment for each occupation is defined by

Figure 1

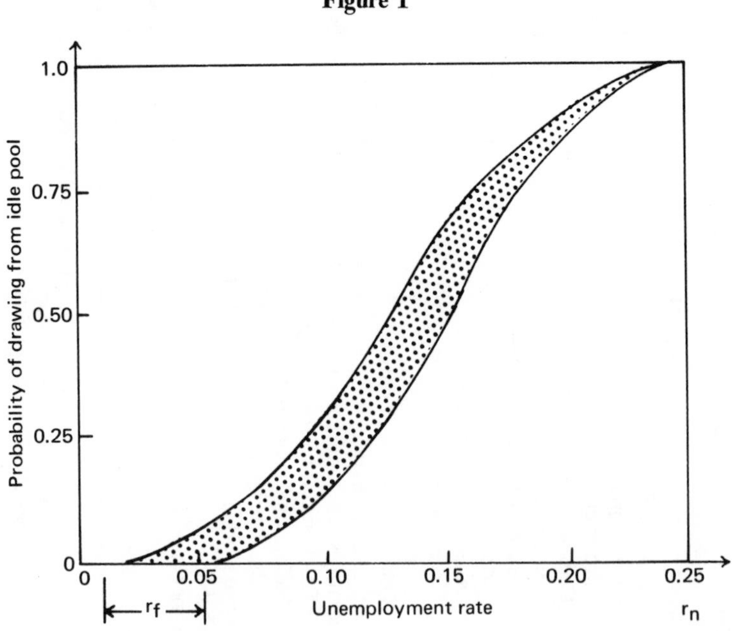

the national unemployment rate experienced by that occupation in 1953—a year with minimum unemployment without undue inflationary stress. The point labeled r_n signifies the rate of unemployment at which an increment of demand would be entirely supplied from otherwise unutilized resources. For the set of relationships included in the shaded area of Figure 1, this unemployment rate is .25, which is the estimated rate of unemployment at the height of the depression of the thirties. It is assumed that under such conditions, increments to the demand for labor and capital are satisfied with no displacement of alternative outputs. The relationships incorporated into the curves which lie in the shaded area are offered as an accurate portrayal of actual labor market behavior.

These relationships (and similar ones for estimating the withdrawal of capital from the idle pool) are used with detailed data on the level of occupational unemployment by region and industrial excess capacity to provide the basis for estimating the real costs of public expenditure. By combining the labor and capital response relationships with detailed evidence on the occupational, industrial, and regional patterns of unemployment, an estimate of the proportion of the labor and capital withdrawn from the idle pool in each pertinent occupation, industry, and region is obtained. By multiplying these percentages by the dollars of monetary cost in each category, the amount of monetary cost which, because of the use of otherwise unemployed resources, is not matched by social cost is estimated. When the monetary costs are adjusted for the idle resource use which is incorporated in them, the remainder represents the true social cost of the public expenditure.[11]

V

In Tables 3 and 4, some estimates of social cost and its relationship to market cost are shown for a sample of public expenditures. These estimates are based on the unemployment conditions experienced in 1960. As noted, the unemployment rate was 5.6 percent in that year. Consequently, the adjustment to market cost required for investments undertaken in that year was substantially greater than for investments undertaken in more recent periods with unemployment levels below 4 percent. In Table 3, the variation in the percentage which social costs form of total *labor* costs is shown for five public expenditure categories in the water resources area. While this data shows the influence of regional unemployment differentials on the degree to which *total* monetary labor cost requires adjustment, the model described above also generates tables which highlight the variation in social cost as a percentage of monetary cost for numerous detailed occupational and industrial categories.

Table 3
Estimate of Social Labor Cost as a Percent of Market Labor Cost for 5 Representative Public Expenditures in 10 Regions of Project Location, 1960

Region	Large earthfill dams	Local flood protection	Medium concrete dams	Large multiple-purpose projects	Dredging
New England	88	82	88	87	83
Mid-Atlantic	80	74	82	81	76
East North Central	90	89	92	92	89
West North Central	87	84	89	89	88
Southeast	93	92	94	94	88
Lower Atlantic	75	65	74	73	73
Kentucky-Tennessee	81	75	81	80	77
West South Central	92	91	93	93	86
Mountain	91	92	93	93	94
West Coast	85	82	86	86	74
Range of percentages	75–93	65–92	74–94	73–94	73–94.0
Median percentage	87.5	83	88	88	84.5

In Table 4, estimates of social cost as a percent of the total *expenditure* are shown for the same public projects constructed in each of the 10 regions, again with unemployment conditions prevailing in 1960. Table 4 demonstrates the substantial variation in the required cost adjustment which exists among project types. It also shows that the variation in adjustment for any single project type as its geographic location changes is even more significant than the variation among project types. In no case does the range for the former variation fail to exceed 15 percentage points. The influence of geographic unemployment on required cost adjustment is clearly seen by comparing the cost adjustments for projects constructed in the high unemployment lower Atlantic region with similar data for project construction in other regions. For every project type, the cost adjustment required for construction in this region is at least 10 percentage points below the median adjustment for all regions.

The results of both Tables 3 and 4 are summarized in Figure 2. The charts shown there display the percentages by which the dollar costs of the selected public expenditures undertaken under economic conditions similar to those of the 1957–64 period—of which 1960 is taken to be typical—would overstate the social costs. The differences vary with the unemployment levels and other economic conditions in the region where a project is located, and also with the amounts, kinds, and origins of labor and materials required for each type of project.

Table 4

Estimate of Total Social Cost as a Percentage of Total Expenditure for 5 Representative Project Types in 10 Regions of Project Location, 1960

Region	Large earthfill dams	Local flood protection	Medium concrete dams	Large multiple-purpose projects	Dredging	Range of percentages	Median percentage
New England	89	84	88	87	84	84–89	86.5
Mid-Atlantic	82	77	84	82	78	77–84	80.5
East North Central	91	90	92	92	90	90–92	91.0
West North Central	88	85	90	89	89	85–90	87.5
Southeast	93	93	94	94	88	88–94	91.5
Lower Atlantic	78	69	77	76	75	69–78	73.5
Kentucky-Tennessee	83	78	83	81	79	78–83	80.5
West South Central	92	92	93	93	87	87–93	90.0
Mountain	92	92	93	93	94	92–94	93.0
West Coast	86	84	87	87	76	76–87	81.5
Range of percentages	78–93	69–93	77–94	76–94	75–94		
Median percentage	88.5	84.5	89	88	85.5		

Figure 2

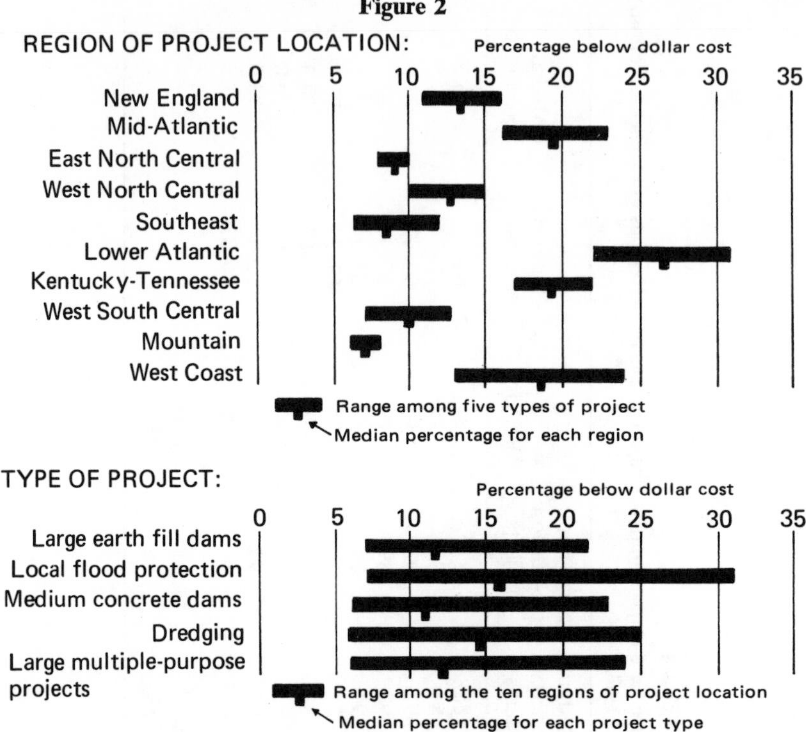

Examination of this data suggest that the social cost of public expenditures for investment projects undertaken in 1960—and by inference from 1957–64—is between 70 and 90 percent of nominal monetary expenditures. The precise percentage depends on the category of expenditure, the region in which it is undertaken, and the nature of the relationship used to relate the rate of idle resources to the proportion of resources demanded by the public expenditure which will be withdrawn from the idle pool.

VI

Given the estimated social costs, the question remains as to the extent to which the "nominal" benefit-cost ratios computed for projects constructed during the slack conditions between 1957–64, for example, or for chronically depressed areas, diverge from the more appropriate "opportunity cost" benefit-cost ratios.

While nominal capital (construction) costs overstate opportunity costs by the magnitude suggested, the effect on the benefit-cost investment criterion will be dampened to the extent that future operating, maintenance, and interim replacement costs occur in a fully employed economy.

It is convenient, although not essential, to assume that investments made under conditions of unemployment do not operate in a less than fully employed economy. With this assumption, the component of annual project costs requiring adjustment will be only the capital charges—that is, the interest and amortization component of annual costs. The required adjustment in annual costs, therefore, will be a function of the ratio of annual operating, maintenance, and interim replacement costs (c) and the capital (or construction) costs (K).

The impact of construction cost adjustment on benefit-cost ratio calculations is shown graphically in Figure 3 on the assumption that only construction costs require adjustment. Here the divergence in the nominal benefit-cost ratio from the true social benefit-cost ratio is analyzed for capital intensities (c/K) of .01 and .10. The upper curve shows the relationship of the social to the nominal benefit-cost ratio at different ratios of social capital costs to total capital costs for a public expenditure in which the annual operating costs (c) are 10 percent of initial construction costs (K). The lower curve shows the same relationship for a more capital-intensive expenditure—one in which annual operating costs are only 1 percent of initial capital costs. From these relationships, it is seen that when social costs for initial project construction are, say, 75 percent of total monetary costs, the nominal benefit-cost ratio for an economically efficient project can be as low as .78:1 if the undertaking is very capital-intensive (say, $c/K = .01$). On the other hand, for a less capital-intensive expenditure

Figure 3

Ratio of Social Capital Costs to Total Market Cost

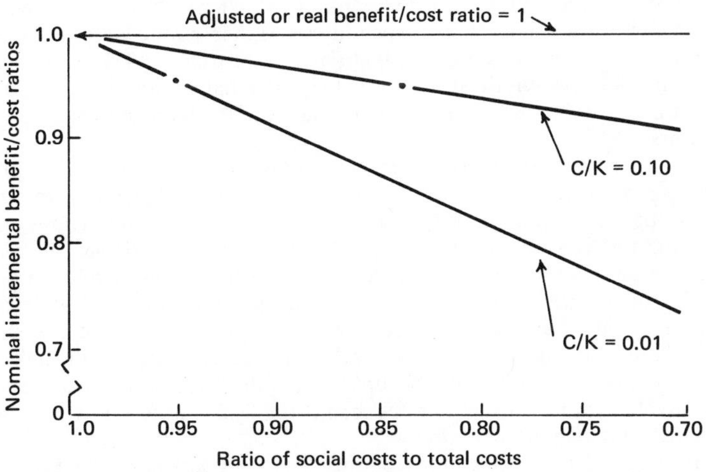

(say, $c/K = .1$), a ratio of social capital costs to total costs of 75 percent would require a nominal benefit-cost ratio of at least .9:1 for the investment to be efficient. On the basis of this evidence, it can be asserted that most proposals for heavy construction projects bearing an unacceptable benefit-cost ratio from .85–.99 when evaluated under full employment assumptions would be deemed efficient under the conditions of unemployment and excess capacity of the sort prevailing in the 1957–64 period.

VII

From the analysis of this paper, it is clear that the level and distribution of unemployed resources in the economy does affect the evaluation of the social cost imposed on the economy by public expenditures. Moreover, the pattern of unemployment and excess capacity should influence the *design, location,* and *priorities* of public investments to be constructed during any time period. While the general proposition which follows from the study is that the monetary cost of public expenditures overstates the true social cost when otherwise unemployed resources are drawn into use by the expenditure, there are a number of more specific conclusions which are corollaries to this general proposition:

- If the national unemployment rate exceeds the frictional minimum or if there is variation of occupational or regional unemployment around a national full employment rate, it is likely that more of all expenditures, public and private, can be justified than would be implied by the efficiency criterion using monetary benefit and cost estimates.
- If either of the idle resource conditions described above exist, the ranking of projects by the standard benefit-cost ratio using social value estimates would differ from the ranking which would occur if monetary estimates were used. Those expenditures, either public or private, which place heavy demands on occupational, industrial, and regional sectors showing idle resource rates above, the frictional minimum would rise in the ranking relative to those which place predominant demands on other sectors.
- If either of the idle resource conditions exist, the design of projects relying on social benefit-cost computations will differ from the design resulting from adoption of the full employment assumption. Those projects placing relatively heavy demands on occupational, industrial, and regional sectors showing high idle resources rates will be oversized relative both to their full employment design and to the scale of projects which place demands on other sectors. Moreover, all expenditures, public and private, which rely on social benefit-cost calculations for design, will make relatively heavier demands on occupations, industries, and regions showing relatively high idle resource rates than if the design criterion were based on the full employment assumption.
- Because of the implications of the above propositions, the problem of

unemployment, regional stagnation, and high unemployment occupations and industries would tend to be eased by use of the social benefit-cost design criterion rather than the market cost design criterion based on the full employment assumption. This is so because unused resources are evaluated at a very low cost in the social benefit-cost criterion. Use of these resources is, consequently, encouraged.

As a word of caution, it should be emphasized that the results of this study should not be taken to imply that every public expenditure project which has been rejected because of an inadequate benefit-cost ratio should be undertaken when the unemployment rate rises above 4 percent. The conclusion to be drawn is that there is an operational framework by which to re-evaluate projects in terms of their opportunity costs when regional or national unemployment rates depart from frictional minima.[12] Moreover, to avoid biasing public expenditures in the direction of a single program, all public investments (including tax cuts) should be similarly analyzed to determine what, if any, differences exist among them.

A second warning concerns the extent of adjustment required in the benefit-cost ratio when otherwise unutilized resources are a part of monetary costs. As seen in the calculations of Table 3 and 4, the level of social costs typically falls only about 10 to 15 percent—at most 25 percent—even when the rate of unemployment is 8 to 9 percent, as it was in a number of regions in 1960. At a time when there is much expectation that the incorporation of "redevelopment benefits" or "secondary benefits" into benefit-cost analysis will lead to the justification of many projects not otherwise meeting the efficiency criterion, this conclusion should be sobering.

Only through substituting social opportunity costs for nominal monetary costs in the expenditure criterion can public decisionmakers isolate expenditures which are both intrinsically economic and substantial employment generators. Through such shadow pricing efforts, more discriminating judgment can be applied to public expenditure policy in general and especially to public expenditure policy in the chronically depressed, high unemployment, and declining areas of the Nation.

NOTES

[1] William J. Baumol, *Welfare Economics and the Theory of the State* (second edition, Cambridge: Harvard University Press, 1967), pp. 135–142. In that volume, Baumol treats unemployment as an external diseconomy requiring a collective remedy outside of the market system.

[2] This, of course, assumes that the market system is operating at its "efficient best" in all other respects.

[3] If an unemployment rate of 5 percent is defined as full employment, 10 of the 21 years since World War II were years with idle productive capacity in excess of this minimum; 15 of the 21 years saw unemployment in excess of the frictional minimum if 4 percent is the full employment rate.

[4] Implicit in this position is the proposition that involuntary leisure has zero benefit to either the unemployed worker or the society.

[5] Morris R. Goldman, Martin L. Marimont, and Beatrice N. Vaccara, "The Inter-Industry Structure of the United States." A Report on the 1958 Input-Output Study, *Survey of Current Business,* 44 (Nov. 1964), 10–29; Norman Frumkin, "Construction Activity in the 1958 Input-Output Study," *Survey of Current Business,* 45 (May 1965), 13–23; National Economics Division Staff, "The Transactions Table of the 1958 Input-Output Study and Revised Direct and Total Requirements Data," *Survey of Current Business,* 45 (Sept. 1965), 33–49.

[6] U.S. Department of Labor, Bureau of Labor Statistics, *Handbook of Methods for Surveys and Studies,* Bulletin No. 1458 (Washington, 1966), Chap. 7, and U.S. Department of Labor, Bureau of Labor Statistics, *Occupational Employment Statistics, Sources and Data,* Report No. 305 (Washington, June 1966).

[7] An elaboration of the details of this model and its use can be found in Robert H. Haveman and John V. Krutilla, *Unemployment, Idle Capacity and the Evaluation of Public Expenditures* (Baltimore: Johns Hopkins Press, 1968).

[8] This $1,032 represents the total gross output, both direct and indirect, generated by the final expenditure. Its size and industrial breakdown was estimated by an input-output calculation. The value of final demand, representing direct purchases of materials, equipment, and supplies, was $514 (out of $1,000 of total project cost). It is this final demand which, through the input-output calculation, generated the $1,032 of total gross output. The portion of the $1,000 of total project cost not represented by direct purchases of materials, equipment, and supplies is largely accounted for by the direct demand for on-site labor.

[9] The area between the two curves is the region within which the response functions, one for every major occupational category, fall. A separate set of functions, not shown here, was used to estimate the proportion of capital demands, by industry, which were satisfied by otherwise idle capacity.

[10] There is a single rate for each occupational category within r_f.

[11] On the basis of this formulation, it is seen that the exercise of adjusting nominal costs for the unemployed labor and idle capital which is used is an example of "shadow pricing."

[12] See Haveman and Krutilla, *op. cit.*

CHAPTER 14

PROJECT DESIGN AND EVALUATION WITH MULTIPLE OBJECTIVES

A. Myrick Freeman, III

INTRODUCTION

In an open, nondictatorial, and rationally governed society all government expenditures are made ultimately in pursuit of a single objective, the improvement of human welfare or well-being in that society. This lofty goal is above dispute. But since we have no direct measure of welfare it is also incapable of giving effective guidance to decisionmakers who are trying to make the most of a limited budget by choosing among alternative expenditure plans.

Decisionmakers must view their expenditures as producing not simply increments to welfare, but many separate kinds of benefits: flood control, education, transportation, cleaner air, more livable cities, et cetera. In these terms there is not one but a multiplicity of objectives which are to be sought with government expenditures. Yet it is inappropriate for decisionmakers to try to maximize the amount of flood control plus the number of students educated, et cetera. We cannot have more flood control *and* more education and more of everything else. It is "either/or." Choices must be made. The identification of multiple objectives in itself does not provide adequate guidance to decisionmakers who must make these choices.

Neither of these views of objectives, the single, all-encompassing welfare goal or the multiple, noncommensurate objectives, can provide any practical basis for allocating limited government budgets among competing programs. The task of this paper is to explore the shape of this dilemma and to examine our progress in finding possible solutions at the practical level.[1]

The progress so far has been substantial, but this is because the easy steps have already been taken. We have developed fairly acceptable techniques for attaching money prices or market values to some kinds of

A. Myrick Freeman, III is Assistant Professor of Economics at Bowdoin College.

The author wishes to express his appreciation to Professors Robert Haveman, Otto Eckstein, Martin McGuire, Thomas Hopkins, and William Shipman for helpful comments and criticisms of an earlier draft of this paper. Of course they bear no responsibility for remaining errors, nor do they necessarily endorse the views in this paper.

benefits from government expenditures. Where this can be done for the principal benefits of a project, the efficiency criterion can be employed. By this criterion projects are evaluated on the basis of the difference between the money values of their benefits and costs. However for some kinds of benefits (and costs), outputs (and inputs), cannot be valued in money terms. Where benefits which are not susceptible to market valuation are important, the efficiency criterion is not adequate to the task of project evaluation. To use the efficiency criterion, one must assume that the unvalued effects of the project, including income redistribution, are not significant or do not matter. Of course in practice this is rarely true; and in principle it is never true.

If valuation techniques could be improved so that all kinds of benefits could receive meaningful price tags, there would be no problem of multiple objectives. Or if some higher order measure of value (welfare?) could be developed, into which all dollar values could be converted, and in terms of which all otherwise noncommensurable benefits could be measured, there would be no problem. In short the multiple objective problem exists because of limitations in our techniques for assigning values; the multiple objective problem is a valuation problem.

This valuation problem cannot really be avoided, at least if choices are to be made on anything but an arbitrary or random basis. In the literature two techniques have been proposed for making choices where there are both benefits which are subject to market valuation and benefits which are not. These will be described below. It will be shown that any choice made using either of these techniques implies a particular set of relative values for the noncomparable benefits. When these techniques are used, choices determine values rather than values determining choices. Thus the problem of valuation cannot really be avoided. My thesis is that since valuation is unavoidable, it is better to confront the choice of values openly and explicitly.

KINDS OF BENEFITS AND COSTS

A *benefit* is anything resulting from the activity of the government which is favorable. To be more specific, a benefit is a government produced economic good, where good is defined broadly to include all things tangible and intangible (e.g. services) which individuals desire. Finally desire is shown by a willingness to pay some amount of money rather than do without the benefit entirely. Similarly *costs* are any unfavorable consequences of government action. To increase one benefit it is necessary to decrease some other benefit (which is a cost) or withdraw more resources from the private sector (which is also a cost). While the remainder of the paper is addressed to the problems of noncommensurate benefits, the same principles and conclusions apply to costs.

Benefits can be further classified according to several attributes. Table 1 lists the several classes of benefits discussed here and provides examples of each. Some benefits are sold by the government. Markets are used to allocate them to those individuals with the highest willingness to pay, or to those who placed the highest valuation on them. If there are no spillover effects, the market price is the value of that benefit. Where there are spillovers or externalities, prices are not equal to values; there is market failure. The external effects must be taken into account in determining the value.

The nonmarketed benefit can be divided into three groups on the basis of two attributes. First the benefits may or may not be measurable in units other than those of the inputs required to produce it. A benefit is measurable if units, standards, and techniques have been developed to indicate and to express the quantity of the benefit and changes in this quantity. National defense is an example of an unmeasurable benefit.[2] Also the benefit may or may not be divisible. Benefits are divisible if one person can have more without simultaneously increasing the amounts going to all other individuals. Nondivisible benefits are usually called public goods.

One class of nonmarketed benefits is divisible and measurable. An example is outdoor recreation which can be measured in user days or particular activities such as wilderness hiking, or flat water boating. This class of benefits could be marketed, but presumably the consequences of marketing are not desirable. For example there could be substantial spillovers or externalities, or as in the case of open access highways, the costs of enforcing the exclusion principle may be considered to be too high.

Table 1

Type of benefit	*Examples*
1. Marketed:	
(*a*) No spillovers	Municipal water.
(*b*) Spillovers	Treatment services for industrial wastes; the services of toll highways.
2. Not marketed:	
(*a*) Divisible and measurable	Public recreation; the services of toll-free highways.
(*b*) Public good and measurable	The distribution of income; public health services; water and air pollution abatement.
(*c*) Public good and nonmeasurable	National defense; the quality of life; basic research.

The nondivisible or public good class of benefits presents a different set of problems. Neither private nor publicly supplied markets would perform satisfactorily since once the benefit was provided to one individual it would be freely available to all. Examples include clean air, clean water, and certain public health services. Some of these benefits are stated in terms of attributes of the economic, political, or social system, for example the degree of equity in the distribution of income.[3] At least these attributes can be measured. In addition there are the nonmeasurable benefits such as aesthetics, cultural or political stability, and other even less specific indicators of the quality of life.[4]

All of the types of benefits described here have value, if by value we mean a willingness to pay some amount of money by individuals. The problem is to discover this value. In the private sector of a market economy there is an outlet for expressing willingness to pay. Values are determined in markets. And where there are no spillover effects or externalities, value or willingness to pay at the margin is equal to the market price.

The basis for valuation of goods in private markets is individual preferences.[5] It is usually accepted that individual preferences should also govern the values placed on things produced by the public sector as well. Since direct expression of willingness to pay for benefits through markets is not possible for individuals, valuation must be based on indirect evidence garnered from observations of market related behavior of individuals.

The art of valuing the benefits of public investments in reclamation, flood control, hydroelectric power, etc. consists of just this. In fact considerable progress has been made in developing acceptable techniques for inferring willingness to pay or value for several types of benefits. These techniques are bound to be improved and extended over time.

Let us define *money valued benefits* as those benefits for which monetary values having a basis in individual preferences are directly observable in markets or can be inferred indirectly from market information.[6]

It is the remaining *unvalued benefits* and costs which constitute the multiple objective problem. Solution of the multiple objective problem requires a two pronged program of:

(*a*) Stepping up efforts in the area of estimating money valued benefits from information on individual preferences and market behavior; and

(*b*) for those types of benefits where this does not seem to be potentially fruitful, developing alternative forms of public investment criteria where noncommensurate benefits and costs are involved.

It is to this latter possibility we now turn.

PUBLIC EXPENDITURE CRITERIA

If there are only money valued benefits and costs from a program, the efficiency criterion is adequate as a public expenditure criterion. It calls for the selection of those projects with positive net benefits (money valued benefits less costs).[7] The criterion also provides rules for finding that design for a particular project which will maximize its net money valued benefits.

The analyst has to estimate the quantities of benefits forthcoming from a project under alternative designs, the quantities of things being used up or reduced, and to utilize available information generated from markets or the market oriented behavior of individuals to determine the prices to be used. The final step is to use the prices to convert the physical measures to values, add them all together, and determine net benefits. The process can be repeated for alternative designs until the best possible design is chosen.[8]

Let there now be some benefits (or costs) from this project which cannot be valued.[9] It must be assumed that they are measurable, although not in dollar terms, and that the amounts of both money valued and unvalued benefits and costs are known. The efficiency criterion, maximum net money valued benefits, is inadequate since some benefits (and cost) are not included in or captured by that criterion. What alternative criteria can be employed? Three approaches to this problem have been offered in the literature.

The first has been advocated by Roland McKean.[10] He suggests that the decisionmakers be provided with a schedule showing the net money valued benefits as well as descriptions of the other benefits (and costs, if appropriate) for each alternative project design that was analyzed. The decisionmaker is to choose that alternative which conforms best to his subjective evaluations or his interpretation of society's preferences for or valuation of money valued benefits vs. other benefits.[11]

Table 2 is a presentation of data on a hypothetical project in the

Table 2

	Net money valued benefits	Measurable unvalued benefits
Project A:		
Design No. 1	$ 9,000	4 units.
Design No. 2	10,000	6 units.
Design No. 3	12,000	5 units.
Design No. 4	13,000	4 units.
Design No. 5	14,000	3 units.

format recommended by McKean. Net money valued benefits have been estimated for each of five alternate designs for the project. In addition the impact of the project on some unvalued benefit has been estimated for each design.[12] Of course this other benefit must be measurable.

The first design is clearly inferior to Nos. 2 and 3, the latter having more of both valued and unvalued benefits. The choice among the remaining designs cannot be made without some knowledge of the relative desirability or valuations of valued and unvalued benefits. McKean's suggestion is to rely on the decisionmaker to make the choice himself. Whichever design is actually chosen will provide a clue as to the relative values of valued and unvalued benefits which are held by the decisionmaker. For example, if he chose No. 3, this implies that one unit of unvalued benefit is worth at least $1,000 since this was the amount of money valued benefit he was willing to forego to obtain the fifth unit. But the value is less than $2,000 since by not choosing Design No. 2 he showed that he was unwilling to sacrifice this much to obtain the sixth unit. If project design can be continuously varied so that any level of net monetary benefit (and its corresponding level of unvalued benefit) can be obtained, the decision maker could choose that design which exactly corresponded with his relative valuations, and the relative valuation would be exactly determined.[13]

In evaluating this approach to the decision problem with noncommensurate benefits, we must question the ability of the decisionmaker to infer the society's valuation for unvalued benefits and to apply it consistently to a number of similar choices over time. In McKean's system the decisionmaker is not encouraged to think in terms of an explicit relative value to be applied to the available data, but rather to rely on his judgment after viewing the range of alternatives. Since each choice implies a relative price or a trade-off ratio between valued and unvalued benefits, the question is whether or not this ratio will be relatively stable over time and over a number of choices. We will return to this question at a later point.

Stephen Marglin has proposed a somewhat different technique for incorporating multiple objectives in a single expression for determining the optimum project design.[14] Briefly he suggests that some minimum level of one benefit be established and that the project be designed to maximize the other benefit subject to meeting the constraint.[15] There is no established rule for deciding which variables are to be constrained and which are to be maximized in the analysis. The choice might be made on the basis of analytical convenience. In the example of Table 2 suppose that the decision has been made that unvalued benefits must be no less than 4 units. Design No. 4 maximizes money valued benefits subject to achieving at least four units of unvalued benefits. The same design would be optimal if valued benefits were constrained to be at least $13,000 and the objective was to maximize unvalued benefits. The interesting thing is that just as in the case of McKean's procedure, any choice of a design implies a certain relative valuation or trade-off ratio between valued and unvalued benefits.[16] The choice of the minimum value for the constrained benefit determines the resulting relative valuation of the two benefits. Once again choice determines values.

Any choice among alternative designs or projects whether made by Marglin's or McKean's procedure logically implies a valuation of one type of benefit in terms of the other. The question is whether choice should be allowed to determine value in this way or should value be determined independently of any particular project analysis and used to make the choice. It seems to me that a good case can be made for encouraging the conscious, deliberate selection of weights by politically responsive decisionmakers. Support for this idea can be found in the economics literature.

Otto Eckstein has argued that economists could make an important contribution to policy making if they would ". . . interpret the desires of the policy people . . . and express them in an analytical form as an objective function," and get on with ". . . the establishment of decision-models which will reveal explicitly what actions will maximize the achievement of specified objectives."[17] Eckstein is referring to those cases where net money valued benefits do not measure all of the favorable effects of an expenditure program. If the preferences of the policy people can be expressed in terms of explicit weights or values of one form of benefit in terms of the other, then the consequences of this particular set of weights for the design and selection of projects can be clearly seen. More importantly, if these consequences are thought to be desirable, then the same set of weights or objective function can be used to achieve a consistent set of decisions concerning all proposed projects. Usually broadening the design and selection criterion to include unvalued benefits will result in the choice of a different design as the optimum. This is true so long as the monetary and nonmonetary benefits are not strictly correlated.[18]

The use of weights in defining an objective function and selecting the optimum project design is illustrated with the example of Table 2. Suppose that decisionmakers conclude that society's relative preferences for valued and unvalued benefits can be approximated by attaching a relative weight of 1,500 to each unit of unvalued benefits. This is equivalent to saying that each unit is worth 1,500 units of money value benefits or $1,500. The object of project design is to maximize the sum of valued benefits plus the assigned monetary value of unvalued benefits. The total benefit or contribution to welfare for each design has been computed. They are given in Table 3.

On the basis of the weighted total of both valued and unvalued benefits, Design No. 3 is the optimum and should be chosen. But this is not surprising since it was shown above in the discussion of McKean's suggestions, that if the decisionmaker chose Design No. 3, this implied that each unit of unvalued benefit was valued at between $1,000 and $2,000. When the procedure is reversed and a value between $1,000 and $2,000 is placed on unvalued benefits, Design No. 3 is the optimum.

In this section we have outlined three approaches to choosing among alternative projects when benefits are not commensurate. These are McKean's discretionary approach, Marglin's minimum target levels approach, and the system of explicit weighting of benefits. We have shown that given the necessity for making choices among alternatives, relative values must be determined. The process of valuation can be implicit and can be obscured behind the preferences of a decisionmaker or the apparent objectivity of a predetermined minimum target. But valuation cannot be avoided. In the first two approaches the valuation is implicit and may vary as decisionmakers make many choices over a period of time. It is also not obvious to the members of the body politic what relative values are actually implied by the set of choices made. Political review is made difficult by the lack of information. If weights are assigned and an explicit objective function is formulated, the valuations are obvious, and the implications of different weights for project design and selection can be worked out. With value made explicit, subject to political review, decisions are more likely to reflect the general preferences of society, and less likely to be influenced by the pressures from special interest groups.[19] Also they are likely to be more consistent over a wider range of choices and a longer period of time.

It should be noted that some economists and political scientists see positive value in failing to define clearly the objectives of programs. This point of view, which might be called the political value of ambiguity, emphasizes decisionmaking as a political process rather than an analytical exercise. For example, Fritz Machlup sees the International Monetary Fund Agreement on supplemental drawing rights (SDR*s*) as resulting from

Table 3

	Weighted total benefits
Design No. 1	$15,000
Design No. 2	19,000
Design No. 3	19,500
Design No. 4	19,000
Design No. 5	18,500

a more or less deliberate fuzziness of language which avoided show downs over some fundamental differences among the negotiators.[20]

THE CHOICE OF WEIGHTS

If one accepts the notion that the systematic assignment of weights or values to unvalued benefits as a guide to choice is to be preferred to the piecemeal, *ex poste* determination of weights as a consequence of choice, there is still the question of how these weights are to be determined. This seems to be largely a political or administrative matter, since by the nature of the problem market oriented information is not adequate to the task.

One approach, first suggested by Eckstein, is to look for clues in the past decisions on resource allocation and taxation.[21] In a study of Corps of Engineers projects, Robert Haveman, following this suggestion, used an explicit set of weights derived from the marginal effective tax rates on personal income to value incomes received by different individuals.[22] And more recently Burton Weisbrod has made imaginative use of expenditure data on water resource projects to solve for the implied weights given to incomes (benefits) to different groups.[23]

The logic of this approach has already been outlined. If a choice concerning any one project implies a set of weights for the several kinds of noncommensurate benefits, similar information from a number of projects with different characteristics should enable the analyst to infer the weights used in different situations. Yet, Haveman and others, myself included, have serious doubts as to the efficacy of using expenditure data to infer the weighting functions. One cause for doubt is that it does not seem reasonable to asssume, as one must, that those ultimately making the decision, Members of Congress, had full knowledge of the magnitude and composition of benefits of all forms when they made their decision. It seems more likely that decisions were actually based on an incomplete understanding of the full range of effects of the project, and also that the decisions were influenced by other considerations such as political advantage and the efforts of special interest groups.[24] Haveman also doubts that the choices made by Congress have exhibited a stable and consistent pattern of weights over time.[25] At issue is not only the stability of congressional choices over time but the internal consistency of the set of choices made in any period of time. In viewing the relative weights given to, for example, money valued benefits and redistribution or equity, has Congress employed the same set of collective values in approving the oil depletion allowance, the various farm price support programs, Upward Bound, and Aid to Dependent Children?

Even if these questions of the congressional history of making informed and consistent choices among alternative packages of noncommensurable benefits could be answered affirmatively, there is still the question of whether the technical conditions will be met for deriving the weights from observed choices. If a stable weighting function exists and all congressional choices have been consistent with it, its properties cannot be inferred from these choices alone. In addition we need to know the terms on which one benefit can be exchanged for another in moving from one alternative design to another. Turning again to the example of Table 2, knowledge that Design No. 3 was chosen was not sufficient to infer the relative weights given to valued and unvalued benefits. We needed to know the amounts of benefits for Designs No. 2 and No. 4 so that we could determine the costs of the fifth and sixth units of unvalued benefits in terms of valued benefits. It is not a common practice for agencies to draw up alternative designs for given projects. Usually they settle on a single design early in the decision process. Choices are usually limited to "yes" or "no" for any one project. The transformation conditions among different types of benefits for alternative designs are not likely to be known nor can they be readily inferred from the data usually available for use in project evaluation.[26]

While the likelihood of extracting information on the social welfare function from observations on expenditures seems to be quite low at present, it has been suggested by Haveman and others that examination of tax information might be fruitful at least for the relative valuations of money valued and redistribution benefits.[27]

For one thing, in contrast to expenditures, the redistributive aspects of tax programs are not complicated by the existence of efficiency gains attributable to the correction of market failures. The redistribution consequences of tax programs are reasonably clear, at least in the case of personal income taxation, and they are given considerable attention in the debate and decision.

However, this approach runs up against the same problem as use of expenditure data, the necessity for knowledge of the transformation conditions before the social welfare function can be inferred from the tax rate schedules. If taxes on incomes and transfer payments to low income persons have any effect on incentives and the supply of effort, and if there are any administrative or deadweight costs to implementing a tax program, the level of aggregate income is not independent of the level and structure of tax and transfer rates. Using the tax system to achieve redistribution benefits may have a cost in terms of lower aggregate income.[28] Unless this cost, i.e. the transformation conditions between money valued and redistribution benefits, is known, the relative weights attached to redistribution benefits, is known, the relative weights attached to redistribution and money valued benefits cannot be inferred from the observed tax system.

An alternative approach to the valuation problem is to provide decisionmakers with specified weighting functions determined after study of the stated objectives of the programs and discussion of the factors which are usually considered in making choices. The decisionmakers could accept or reject any weighting function depending on whether they thought it was representative of their objectives. Weighting functions could be given trial runs on sets of projects already decided upon, using the same information available to planners at the time of the decision. The object would be to see if things would have been different if the weighting function had been used, and if so, would the weighting function have improved the pattern of choice in the eyes of the decisionmakers. An exact reproduction of past decisions would neither be expected nor necessary as a test of the acceptability of the weighting function. The dry run might produce a set of projects which decisionmakers would agree was better than the original set, which would indicate the potential advantage of a more systematic approach to valuation. Or the trial run might select a list of projects thought to be suboptimal by decisionmakers, in which case the weighting function would be rejected as not adequately reflecting policy objectives.

One very interesting application of this approach has been developed by two economists formerly with the Economic Development Administration.[29] They noted that grant-in-aid projects for regions which are administered through EDA are to be approved on the basis of the twin criteria of efficiency and need. The first criterion is reflected in a benefit-cost ratio which captures those benefits which can be valued in monetary terms. The need criterion reflects a concern for obtaining greater equity in the interregional and interpersonal distribution of income. The authors also noted that high unemployment rates and low incomes relative to national averages have been established by Congress as the basis for allocating grant-in-aid funds among applicants.

They then showed how these multiple objectives can be combined explicitly in a single expression which shows the total value placed on a package of noncommensurate benefits. The benefit-cost ratio for each project was weighted by a factor which combined the unemployment and low income situation in that locality into a single measure of need.

This exercise by McGuire and Garn is valuable for two reasons. First, it shows that legislative guidelines stated in nonquantitative terms may be translatable into quantitative counterparts which can be used in a weighting function. Second, it shows that thinking about how decisions are made, what is important, and how the important things are related, may reveal some heretofore unnoticed but quite reasonable ways of relating the quantitative counterparts.

The most vexing problems of multiple objectives revolve around the relationships between money valued benefits and income distribution. The efficiency objective simply adds up all increments to income irrespective of who receives them. One way to express the distribution objective is that increments to income are valued differently depending on who receives them. The two objectives can be combined if a decision can be made concerning the weights to be attached to additional income to different individuals. The total value of a project would be the *weighted sum* of its incomes. Here alternative weighting functions could be presented to decisionmakers along with tables illustrating the implications of the weights so that they could indicate which one most closely corresponded to their judgment of society's relative valuations. In Table 4 seven alternative weighting functions are presented along with the values placed on additions to incomes to persons at various income levels. The first column gives the expressions used to calculate the weights where I is current income. The other four columns show the weights to be attached to \$1 of additional income to individuals with current income of \$1,000, \$10,000, \$100,000, and \$1,000,000 respectively. The weighting functions have been normalized to give a weight of 1 to \$1 of income to persons with \$10,000 current income.

The reader may wish to "play the game" by trying to decide which function comes closest to reflecting his own views as to the weights society should place on increments to income generated by public expenditure. Consider a project the costs of which are covered by personal income taxes. Recall that more than half of all personal tax collections come from individuals with incomes of less than \$10,000. Since some persons' incomes

Table 4

Form of social welfare function: Marginal social welfare (MSW) =	Value placed on 1 extra dollar of income to a man with income of—			
	I = \$1,000	I = \$10,000	I = \$100,000	I = \$1,000,000
(1) $I^{-1.5}$	\$31.62	\$1	\$0.03	\$0.001
(2) $I^{-1.0}$	10.00	1	.10	.01
(3) $I^{-0.5}$	3.16	1	.32	.10
(4) I^{0}	1.00	1	1.00	1.00
(5) $e^{-\left(\frac{I}{10,000}\right)}$	2.46	1	.0001	Nil
(6) $\left(\frac{I}{5,000}+1\right)^{-1}$	2.50	1	.14	.01
(7) $\left(\frac{I}{5,000}+1\right)^{-2}$	6.25	1	.02	.0002

are reduced to pay for the project, would you be indifferent as to whether the benefits accrued to millionaires, persons getting $100,000 a year, or persons with only $1,000? If so then weighting function No. 4 reflects your judgment that redistribution should get no weight in valuing project benefits. If you think that no value should be placed on publicly generated incomes to millionaires, then No. 5 may be for you. And if you think that income to poor ($1,000 per year) persons is at least 30 times more valuable than income to middle class ($10,000) persons, then No. 1 may come closest to reflecting your value judgment.

SOME RECOMMENDATIONS

Our discussion has proceeded heretofore as if there were some Solomon-like decisionmakers who judged all alternatives on the basis of available evidence, and pronounced judgment, after which there was no appeal. It has ignored any of the realities of the political decision process in the federal government. The suggestion that decisionmakers be provided with *a priori* specified welfare and weighting functions and be directed to make future decisions in accordance with these functions should not be interpreted as a prescription for all agencies, or for Congress itself. It is neither feasible nor desirable to adopt such a plan across the board. But I think it is possible to draw from this paper some suggestions which recognize the political and administrative realities, yet can assist in making more rational choices where multiple objectives are concerned.

First let me state what I think two of the important political realities are. Congress is not equipped for, nor is it likely to wish to involve itself in, consideration of a social welfare function or weighting function for particular programs. Also social welfare functions are not likely to be able to play any role in major one-shot decisions such as the shale oil development program, or the antiballistic missile system (thick or thin). This suggests that explorations of social welfare functions are more feasible and more likely in the executive branch and in areas where less is at stake on any one decision and decisions are more repetitive. The above cited work on EDA grant-in-aid programs is a case in point.

My recommendation is that executive agencies be encouraged to spell out the objectives of their own programs in terms of valued and unvalued benefits and to carry out studies similar to the McGuire-Garn work on EDA programs in an attempt to specify acceptable relative valuations for non-commensurate benefits. As their experience and self-awareness grows they should be encouraged to use their valuations as the basis for discretionary decisions. However, there should be continual review by a higher authority both of the weighting functions used and the decisions made. Approval of the Bureau of the Budget should be required before any such weighting system is implemented or is altered. This is necessary to assure that weighting functions and relative valuations are consistent among agencies rather than contradictory. Also it is necessary to curb a natural tendency on the part of agencies to assign relatively high weights to those things that it is best at producing, thus assuring a continued high level of authorizations and appropriations.[30] The Bureau of the Budget should take the initiative in establishing guidelines, and in selecting weighting functions for unvalued benefits produced by several agencies, such as redistribution.[31]

Congress itself could take the initiative when establishing a new program by stating its intent as clearly as possible so that this could be translated into a weighting function by the agency for its use in administering the program.[32]

This effort could parallel present efforts to implement PPBS and cost effectiveness analysis in more executive agencies. These new types of analysis force agencies to state their targets and to look carefully at alternative ways of achieving them. But it also naturally leads the agencies into consideration of the current set of targets itself, and the possibility that the current targets may not be consistent with the agencies' own estimates of the relative values to be placed on achievement of various targets. The implementation of PPBS may make it easier to begin explicit consideration of the implicit valuations placed on unvalued benefits and to gain acceptance of the principle that policy should be determined by one's objectives.

CONCLUSIONS

The main points I have tried to make can be stated very briefly.

1. Choices among different kinds of benefits are unavoidable.

2. There is a one-to-one relationship between choices and relative values for different benefits. If values are known, choices are determined; if choices are made, values are determined.

3. Where values are not generated by market behavior, I have urged the systematic consideration of values in the form of explicit weighting or social welfare functions in order to obtain a consistent set of decisions on projects.

4. We are not likely to be able to infer weighting functions from observed choices among public expenditure programs, both because we cannot be sure that the same weighting function was used to make all the choices included in the sample, and because the required information is not likely to be available.

5. Therefore if weighting functions are to be used, they must be based

on consideration of legislative intent, guidelines established in law and precedent, and ultimately subjective evaluations by politically responsive decisionmakers.

6. The procedures outlined here are most likely to be successful if the initiative comes from executive agencies, and in areas of established programs and repeated decisions, rather than if Congress is deeply involved in the process or if it is first applied to new programs or major one-shot decisions.

NOTES

[1] This paper does not deal with the welfare theoretic basis of public expenditures analysis. For a good introduction and survey of this area see Otto Eckstein, "A Survey of Public Expenditure Criteria," in *Public Finance: Needs, Sources, and Utilization,* Universities-National Bureau Committee on Economic Research (Princeton: Princeton University Press, 1961), pp. 439–504.

[2] The remainder of the paper deals only with measurable benefits. Until a type of benefit can be measured, values cannot be assigned to varying quantities of it. The omission of nonmeasurable benefits from the remaining discussion does not mean that they are unimportant. It does mean that I consider measurement and valuation to be distinctly different processes.

[3] The inclusion of income distribution as a benefit for which individuals are willing to pay calls for explanation. Under plausible assumptions about individuals' utility functions, namely interdependence, it can be shown that individuals can increase their utility by contributing to government enforced tax and transfer systems. See, for example, Harold M. Hochman and James D. Rogers, "Pareto-Optimal Redistribution," *American Economic Review,* LIX, No. 4 (September, 1969), 542–557, Edgar O. Olsen, "A Normative Theory of Transfers," *Public Choice* (Spring, 1969), 39–58, or A. Myrick Freeman, "Income Distribution and Social Choice: A Pragmatic Approach," *Public Choice* (Fall, 1969).

[4] The fourth possible combination of the two attributes, divisible but nonmeasurable, is, I believe, an empty box.

[5] Technically, individual preferences along with income determine demand. Prices and values are determined by the interaction of demand and supply.

[6] I have not used the conventional distinction between efficiency and nonefficiency benefits and costs. In practice "efficiency benefits" has meant money valued benefits as I have defined them; but I think the latter is a more descriptive term. I would prefer to restore efficiency to its more conventional meaning, of getting the most out of what is put in.

[7] If the resources which can be committed to public projects are limited by a political decision, it may not be possible to undertake all those projects with positive net benefits. I assume here that there is no budget constraint so that all opportunities for increasing the total value of output by redirecting resources from private to public uses will be utilized. Also for simplicity I am assuming that all problems of discounting, risk, uncertainty, and measurement can be ignored.

[8] Of course there are mathematical techniques available which greatly simplify the search for an optimum design.

[9] All of the following arguments and conclusions are similar for the cases of unvalued costs. The remainder of the paper will deal with the case of unvalued benefits only.

[10] Roland N. McKean, *Efficiency in Government through Systems Analysis* (New York: John Wiley & Sons, Inc., 1958). See especially pp. 127, 206–208, 240–242. His suggestion has been reformulated to conform with my terminology and framework.

[11] I interpret Arthur Maass' discussion of the political determination of trade-off ratios between efficiency and redistribution as falling in this category. See his "Benefit-Cost Analaysis: Its Relevancy to Public Investment Decisions," *Quarterly Journal of Economics,* LXXIX (May, 1966), pp. 208–226, Maass describes a three-step process wherein the agencies present data on alternative mixes of efficiency and redistribution, the executive proposes one such mix as the optimum, and Congress accepts, rejects, or modifies it. Maass both argues that this is an accurate description of the actual decision process in several instances and urges that this process be adopted in other areas where multiple objectives are involved.

[12] These must be net benefits. If there are associated unvalued costs, they would be displayed in the same way.

[13] The design possibilities can be plotted as a production possibilities curve. The implied relative value is the slope of this curve at the point chosen. But if the production possibilities curve is linear, value is predetermined, and little additional information is revealed by the decision maker's choice of designs. This case is analogous to that of a market with perfectly elastic supply in which price is determined by supply alone.

[14] In Arthur Maass, Maynard M. Hufschmidt, and others, *Design of Water Resource Systems: New Techniques for Relating Economic Objectives, Engineering Analysis, and Governmental Planning* (Cambridge: Harvard University Press, 1962), pp. 62–86.

[15] Where there are "n" groups of noncommensurate benefits, minimum levels must be set for $(n - 1)$ of them and the remaining one benefit maximized subject to these $(n - 1)$ constraints.

[16] In mathematical terms, this is a problem in the calculus of constrained optima. The solution of the problem includes a value for the LaGrangian multiplier which is the marginal cost measured in units of one benefit of obtaining one additional unit of the other benefit.

[17] Otto Eckstein, "A Survey," *op. cit.,* p. 445. His paper also includes an excellent discussion relating his suggestions to conventional welfare economics. Marglin also suggests an assignment of weights, to different forms of benefits or values as an alternative to specifying minimum achievement levels. See Marglin, *op. cit.,* pp. 78–84.

[18] This has been proven in the case where repayment of costs by beneficiaries is required and redistribution is the unvalued benefit. See A. Myrick Freeman, "Income Redistribution and Planning for Public Expenditure," *American Economic Review,* LVII, No. 3 (June, 1967), pp. 495–508.

[19] I am ignoring all of those problems of voting and the political process familiar to both political scientists and economists. I assume that most of the political decisions and choices which are made reflect and are responsive to individuals' preferences, although imperfectly so. It seems that this way of making choices produces reasonably tolerable results, or to put it another way, most people seem to think that the costs of changing the system outweigh any gains in the form of improved decisions.

[20] Fritz Machlup, *Remaking the International Monetary System: The Rio Agreement and Beyond* (Baltimore: Johns Hopkins Press, 1968). See also the paper by Peter Steiner in this volume.

[21] Eckstein, *op. cit.,* pp. 447–448. "He may choose to use a form of the [objective] function that has been implicitly produced by the political process."

[22] R. H. Haveman, *Water Resources Investment and the Public Interest* (Nashville: Vanderbilt University Press, 1965).

[23] B. A. Weisbrod, "Income Redistribution Effects and Benefit-Cost Analysis," in S. B. Chase, ed.,*Problems in Public Expenditure Analysis* (Washington: The Brookings Institution, 1968). See Freeman, "Income Distribution and Social Choice," *op. cit.,* for a discussion of the issues.

[24] See the comments on Weisbrod's paper by Mack and Haveman in *ibid.,* pp. 209–222; and Haveman's "Comment" on the previously cited paper by Maass in the *Quarterly Journal of Economics,* LXXX (November, 1967), pp. 695–699.

[25] He raises this issue in both of the Comments cited in the preceding footnote.

[26] This problem is discussed in greater detail in Freeman, "Income Distribution and Social Choice," *op. cit.*

[27] Haveman's "Comment" on Weisbrod, *op. cit.,* p. 210.

[28] This is a case of an unvalued benefit, redistribution, having a monetary cost.

[29] Martin C. McGuire and Harvey A. Garn, "An Experiment in the Integration of Equity and Efficiency Criteria in Project Selection," (mimeo).

[30] I am indebted to Robert Haveman for emphasizing this point.

[31] This recommendation bears a strong family resemblance to Maass three-step description. See Maass, "Benefit-Cost Analysis," *op. cit.* The main differences are that I think more progress is likely to be made in spelling out objective functions in existing programs and within executive agencies while Maass in his example suggests that Congress plays a larger role and that the procedure is primarily applicable to new programs.

[32] Again see McGuire and Garn, *op. cit.*

PART FOUR

The Planning-Programing-Budgeting System: A Critique and Some Recommendations

****

CHAPTER 15

THE STATUS AND NEXT STEPS FOR PLANNING, PROGRAMING, AND BUDGETING

Jack W. Carlson

PURPOSE AND CHARACTER OF THE PPB SYSTEM

The Planning, Programing, Budgeting System (PPBS) is an approach to decisionmaking designed to make as explicit as possible the costs and consequences of major choices and to encourage the use of this information systematically in the making of public policy. It is an evolutionary change that grows logically out of 50 years of improvement in the techniques of budgeting, accounting, and analysis, in both the government and the private sectors.[1] Normally, such changes work their way into practice slowly, as the logical nature of the development becomes clear. In contrast, with respect to PPBS, starting in 1961 in the Defense Department and in 1965 in 20 other agencies, a deliberate and major effort was started to effect reforms more rapidly. This effort was accompanied by some fanfare and—in retrospect—exaggerated expectations.

The attention focused upon the methods used to implement PPB has obscured somewhat the pressing problems of government decisionmaking and resource allocation that provided the basic rationale for its introduction and, more particularly, for the attempt to achieve change quickly. But, in evaluating PPB, it is important to keep it in the context of these difficulties of decisionmaking in a highly complex governmental apparatus that now oversees the spending of nearly $200 billion through a multitude of large and small decisions made at many levels of authority in an intensely political environment.

These basic problems are:

1. The resources available to the government are obviously limited, and demand for their use always exceeds supply. This dilemma has been exacerbated as more and more people in the society have come to see

Jack W. Carlson is Assistant Director for Program Evaluation of the U.S. Bureau of the Budget. This paper was prepared with the assistance of James V. DeLong of the Office of Program Evaluation.

government financing as not only justifiable but necessary in one area after another. Since few demands for government funds are clearly and completely without merit, the president and his subordinates need techniques for defining objectives and priorities and insuring that public funds are used most effectively in achieving them.

2. The portion of the budget over which the president, the cabinet, or Congress has effective control in any given year is small because the legal and moral commitments made by past decisions are great. Effective government requires that some technique exist to ensure that the small portion of the budget subject to discretion is foreclosed only through deliberate policy choice, not by inadvertence. This requires recognition of the extent to which present decisions, possibly minor at first glance, commit the government to future expenditures.

3. The problems of evaluation and coordination of federal programs are large and intractable. It is easy to overestimate the extent to which we know the results of programs, even in terms of the simplest output measures. Readily available measurement techniques of statistics, social science, or common sense can often supply this information, but it is important that federal agencies have incentives to use these techniques and that a method exist for incorporating their results into the government decisionmaking processes. Without such a link, in an organization as large as the federal government, it is possible to have evaluation occurring that has no impact on existing or potential programs.

4. Because of the size of the government and the uncertainties inherent in the problems with which it deals, the government tends to be sluggish in implementing new ideas. A large number of agencies and persons are involved in any given policy area, and the difficulties of communicating, agreeing to, and implementing policy changes are immense.

5. There are some programs in the federal government which do not pay off because their costs exceed their calculated benefits, or because they do not really assist the intended target groups. The existence of moral or political claims upon society may cause such programs to continue indefinitely. No one would deny that such claims should receive careful consideration, but the government still needs a method of identifying such programs, calculating the cost of meeting the claims, and developing less costly or more effective alternatives.

6. Planning methods devised to meet these difficulties have not been adequate. Too often, there is no link between long-range plans and either the resources which will realistically be available or the likely effect of past decisions on future resource claims. Better links between plans and probable resource availability need to be developed and applied more extensively.

7. Once money is committed in a budget, there are only limited attempts to hold program managers to any predetermined plan to use this money on a time-phased basis with performance tied to resource use. This shortcoming is ameliorated by general or selective oversight techniques used by the Budget Bureau, the Congress, the General Accounting Office, the press, and the public, but there is still a need to develop time-cost-performance measures and to use them.

PPBS helps deal with these problems in a comprehensive way through two closely related changes in the process of making government resource allocation decisions. The first of these is premised on the belief that the expansion of our knowledge in the social and physical sciences and of the sophistication and quantity of data holds great promise for improving specific decisions of the government if, and only if, this knowledge can be brought to bear on problems at the right time and in the right place. Therefore, one thrust of PPBS is to develop and apply this type of knowledge in a meaningful way to major issues as they arise—such as the development and deployment of a major new weapons system, the implementation of a project for exploiting mineral resources, or the creation of a new manpower training program.

In many areas, however, major decision points are not obvious. Resources are committed by accretion over time, with no occasion on which the relationship between limited resources, the universe of need, and the effectiveness of the program receive specific attention. This can result in either overinvestment or underinvestment in a particular area. For example, federal transportation policy decisions might not consider explicitly the possible intermodal tradeoffs available; we have a series of programs to which we add resources independently. Therefore, the second purpose of PPB has been to improve the normal decision process so that questions of comparative costs, benefits, resource inputs, outputs, and effectiveness are routinely raised and comprehensively considered. Even if data or conceptual knowledge are scarce with respect to a particular area of government activity, improvements can be made by developing a decision process that ensures that these crucial questions are not simply ignored. The purpose is to achieve explicitness about objectives and outputs; to aggregate costs and programs according to objectives; to develop alternative methods of accomplishing objectives; to analyze benefits, outputs, and costs at whatever level of sophistication is possible; and to project the extent to which future options are mortgaged by past or present decisions. A key part of this is the development of overviews of program areas that display, insofar as possible, comparative data on related programs.

The two objectives—applying knowledge to specific issues and improving the decision process—are very much intertwined. Nonetheless, they are separable to some extent in both concept and practice, and it is worthwhile to point out the difference. Many debates over PPBS are conducted with one party talking major issues and the other discussing the decisionmaking process and the need for program overviews. In evaluating PPB both must be taken into account.

If these objectives are to be achieved, a formal system is necessary. New methods of approaching problems may evolve slowly without such a system, but a deliberate attempt to increase the rate of change requires one.

The formal system developed for PPBS was based on several premises: First, PPBS would be tied into the budget cycle, partly because this is the only recurring administrative process through which almost all major decisions must pass and partly because it is the government's formal resource allocation process and decision forcing mechanism.[2] Second, the major responsibility for developing PPBS would belong to the agencies. It seemed obvious that no improvement in the decision processes or increase in the quality of information and analysis brought to bear on major issues could be made unless the decisionmakers were interested in the improvement; thus, 98 percent of the staff increases went to the agencies, not the Bureau of the Budget,[3] and, for research in support of PPBS, reliance was placed on agency funds and capabilities. The Budget Bureau did not attempt to create a capacity to do independent research of its own. Third, since many diverse agencies were to be covered, the system established had to be somewhat flexible so as to allow scope for adaptation.

Pursuant to these premises, 26 agencies have established analytic staffs reporting to the agency head or his deputy and some or all of the component parts of the PPB system; a few of these agencies have initiated the development of a PPB system since January 1969.[4] Five formal parts of the PPB system were identified and their use incorporated into the budget process.[5] These were and are program structures, issue letters, program memoranda, special analytic studies, and program and financial plans.[6]

Each of these is intended to fulfill a particular role within the process. To summarize this conception briefly, the functions of these diverse elements are as follows.

Program Structures This is a grouping of agency activities into objective-oriented classifications so that programs with common objectives or common outputs are considered together, along with the cost of each. Programs whose outputs are closely related and are, therefore, substitutes or complements are grouped together in broad categories such as "education." Each category is further subdivided into, for example, "development of basic skills," "development of vocational and occupational skills," etc.

These subcategories are further subdivided into more detailed elements.[7]

The major purpose of the program structure is to make possible better analysis of agency programs by organizing cost and output information so as to include all areas relevant to a problem. It should also produce a number of other benefits, however. The exercise of putting together a program structure is often very useful in that it forces agency personnel to devote explicit attention to the objectives of different agency programs and to their differences and similarities. In itself, this exercise can produce useful insights. In addition, the program structure, if well done, highlights possible tradeoffs and alternatives that might not be considered if an agency examined its programs only in terms of organizational alinements or appropriations categories. Finally, the structure can reveal gaps in agency programs or new alternatives which have not been considered before.

The use of program structures brings to three the main ways of displaying the budget: Appropriations categories for insuring that obligations and expenditures stay within limits (for control); activity categories—by type of activity—for improving the efficient use of each component (for management); and program categories for relating program objectives and the evaluation of outputs in terms of these objectives (for strategic planning).[8]

Issue Letters These are letters from the Budget Director to the agency heads defining the major program issues that should receive attention during the current planning and budgeting cycle.[9] They are the product of negotiations between the Budget Bureau and each agency. The rationale behind the identification of major issues is the need to focus the limited analytic resources on the more important problems, the importance of reaching agreement upon the nature of the problems involved, and the value of analysis which can broaden the range of policy alternatives considered by the agency and the President.

Program Memoranda The program memorandum (PM) for a selected major program category is intended to be a brief document summarizing the decisions made by an agency on major issues in the program category and articulating the reasons for them. It should incorporate the results of any analysis bearing on the issue, identify the alternatives considered and state explicitly the assumptions made in the evaluation.[10]

The requirement of a PM helps insure that decisions are in fact made on the basis of evidence and after consideration of alternatives, that the choices made are deliberate rather than accidental, and that they do in fact represent the decisions of the agency head. Further, PM's are intended to serve as bases of discussion by identifying similarities and differences in the judgments of the bureaus, agencies, and subsequently the Budget Bureau, thus promoting focused, relevant discussion of major problems.

PM's also should show not only current year costs, both direct and indirect, of new projects or programs but also costs in the future as well. Finally, they may serve as a means of policy guidance within an agency.

It has taken some evolution for the concept of the PM to reach this form. Originally, the PM's were envisioned as papers which would, for each major program category, set out objectives of an agency, discuss alternative ways of getting there, and choose the best. The PM's during the first year consisted, for the most part, of objectives stated at a very high level of abstraction, a description of the agency's present programs, and no clear link between them. Since then, in successive bulletins, PM's have been more firmly tied to the actual decisions that must be made on the major issues which an agency faces, and not on the entire group of interrelated programs. PM's are now required to include only highly selective issues—just the major issues in each program category. To give an adequate explanation of its decisions on these issues, of course, an agency must still have a realistic idea of its objectives.

Special Analytic Studies This category of document is extremely broad; it means any piece of work analyzing a particular problem with the object of coming to conclusions that can be used in the policymaking process. Such studies could be economic analyses, sociological evaluations, data collection efforts, development of useful techniques, mathematical models, or almost anything else that is appropriate to the particular issue. Ideally, special studies are done in advance on the major issues that should be covered in the PM's. In practice, of course, the process is seldom that tidy. As a result, there are two basic types of studies: those that analyze—in terms of whatever theory and data are immediately available—questions which must be decided in the course of the current planning and budgeting cycle, and those that develop concepts or information for decisions which must be made in the future.[11]

Program and Financial Plans (PFP's) This document lays out, by program category, and for the next 5 years, the funds committed to various program areas by past decisions and, wherever feasible, projected program outputs for the same period. (It also includes 2 preceding years and thus includes a total of 7 years; for example, the current program and financial plan includes budgetary commitments for fiscal year 1968 through fiscal year 1974 budgets.)

Since the President must recommend his budget to the Congress in terms of the congressionally established appropriations structure, the plan also provides a "crosswalk" which translates program costs classified by objective-oriented category into individual appropriation requests.

The PFP is intended as a bridge to relate annual budget allocations more closely to longer-term plans and priorities, and thus provides a tool for department heads to gain more discretion over future budgets.

The concept of commitment used for the PFP is necessarily rather amorphous. It includes expenditures or appropriations to which the government is committed by law or contract, but it also includes obligations that are logically or morally compelled by past decisions. There is some looseness in defining the concept because of the wide divergence in the areas covered and lack of experience in using it carefully. The basic purpose behind the PFP is to identify the extent to which future budget choices are already foreclosed so that remaining options are identified, and so that future consequences of present decisions are routinely identified and considered during the decision process.[12]

In the case of defense, the 5-year defense program displays the defense forces for 8 future years and estimated costs and manpower by force, type, and major mission for 5 future years. These are total program costs through each of 5 future years as compared to the lower budget levels based on the concept of commitments which are now used by other agencies which develop PFP's. The Defense Department also has a formal planning document prepared by the Joint Chiefs of Staff titled the "Joint Strategic Objective Plan" (JSOP). It arrays a single force over a longer horizon than the 5-year plan but without close ties with resource costs.

CRITERIA AND EVALUATION

From this summary of the objectives of PPBS and the strategy of implementation chosen, a number of criteria of evaluation can be derived. They fall into three general categories of questions.

The first category compares the actual operation of the formal structure with the preconceived ideal. Does it work as envisioned? Do the documents and the process of preparing them have the benefits envisioned? What is the quality of the program structures, issue letters, program memoranda, special analytic studies, and program and financial plans? What basis has been laid for future improvement? What have been the patterns of staffing and education programs?

The second category of questions requires a different review of the same general area of the nature of the process of decisionmaking in the government. Whereas the evaluation of the formal structure necessarily compares what now exists with a preconceived ideal, it is also important to compare what now exists with previous conditions. That is, even if PPB has not done all that was envisioned, what improvements in the decisionmaking process have occurred? Have the objectives of government programs been made more precise? Has there been improvement in the structure, quality, and relevance of information on which resource allocation decisions are based? Is the information an analysis generated in the PPB system actually used by the people making decisions? Have tradeoffs between programs been recognized so that the scope of decisions is better suited to the dimensions of the problems? Have realistic alternative programs been developed and considered during the process?

The third and final category of questions concerns the degree to which analysis has been applied to specific problem areas. What specific decisions of the federal government on important issues during the last 3 years have been influenced by analysis? Would the analysis have been done without the innovation of PPBS?

The Effectiveness of the Formal Structure

Although many benefits are attributable to PPB, the formal structure has been only partially successful.

While the bulk of this subsection is devoted to appraisal of the individual elements of the system, one basic, general difficulty deserves separate mention at the start. This is that PPB has become in large part a different, competitive method of decisionmaking, appended to the traditional channels of budgeting supported by the appropriation accounts and budgeting through the legislative development and clearance process. The intent was to make the budget and legislative channels broader and more effective, but the result in several cases has been otherwise. Each of these processes has data requirements, time schedules, and semi-independent players with only partial overlap and communication.

These three channels exist in varying forms at the bureau level, the agency level, and in the Bureau of the Budget. While some effort has been made to merge them and provide adequate analysis at the key decision points of each, progress is gradual.

Program Structure Twenty-six agencies have developed program structures. These differ widely in quality and utility. Generally, they do represent helpful ways of looking at agency activities for analytic purposes, involvement in their preparation has been educational, and they do tend to highlight programs which should be considered together. In some cases, they have had impact on officials who had not realized the breadth or triviality of agency efforts in particular fields and in pursuit of particular objectives.

Because they have not been the central focus for decisionmaking, they have not always resulted in generation of alternatives and new ideas from the agencies. Final budgets are still resolved primarily by reference to the appropriations structure, although, increasingly, budget reviews are being conducted on the basis of the program structures with the use of a crosswalk to obtain the appropriations structure for submission to the Congress.[13]

There are obvious improvements to be made on many of the structures. Some of them reflect primarily the present organization of an agency and do not represent a serious attempt to think through objectives; others set objectives at too low a level, automatically cutting off major alternatives. Nonetheless, the concept is useful.

For the first time, the fiscal year 1970 budget includes a tabulation of expenditures by agency according to the program structure.[14] Despite the limitations imposed by its level of aggregation and lack of output or benefit measures, the utility of this sort of tabulation seems clear: It raises many questions about the rationale for this particular configuration of Federal expenditures and opens productive lines of inquiry.

Issue Letters The second element, the issues definition process, has presented greater problems. The Bureau has had difficulty in sending the letters to the agencies early enough in the planning and budgeting cycle, in defining the issues with sufficient specificity, and in limiting the number of issues posed in relationship to scarce analytic capability. In the letters for the fiscal year 1970 planning and budget cycle (January through December 1968), for example, about 380 issues were posed to 17 agencies and were sent as late as the end of April.[15] A few of these issues were already under study through earlier informal agreements between agency and BOB staffs.

About one-half of all issues were analyzed. The reasons for unresponsiveness range from insufficient time or analytic capability to reluctance to deal formally with sensitive problems. When analysis has been done, the proportion of analyses that have proven useful ranges from 16 percent in the human resource programs to nearly 90 percent in the community and economic develpment programs. In part, this reflects the greater difficulty in analyzing human resource problems than physical resource problems. It also reflects the shorter history of serious analysis or interest in analysis in the human resource agencies.[16]

The process of explicit identification of major issues has utility independent of the follow-up, of course. It sharpens and focuses the general quality of discussion and debate between the various levels of management within each agency and between the Executive Office of the President and the agencies.[17] It also aids the Budget Bureau in performing its functions during the planning and budgeting cycle.

Program Memoranda The program memoranda (PM's) have been of uneven quality. Most of them have contained useful information, but only about 25 percent could be judged as adequate to excellent. Most of the others have not identified major alternatives, have not concentrated on policy decisions, or have not presented a multiyear strategy directed toward specific objectives and outputs. Many of the PM's tend to be descriptive, verbose, nonanalytic accounts of existing and proposed programs, together with an impassioned plea for funding at the full request. This is not very helpful in making resource allocation decisions, since it is difficult to know if an "urgent necessity" is more important than a "dire national need," a "must expenditure," or a "vital responsibility."

However, PM's have become important sources of program information at all levels in the executive branch because they do give a summary of information related to specific issues within an objective-oriented program category, something that seldom existed before. Where there has been a wide involvement of agency staff in preparing each PM, the broad educational gains for executives and subordinates in itself may have made the exercise worthwhile.

Special Analytic Studies This has been a successful part of the PPB innovation. There is no complete census of the number and results of analytic studies,[18] but good ones have been done and have been inputs into major policy decisions. In some cases, public policy bargaining has been sharpened and needless friction avoided because of revealing analysis. The preferences and judgments of the decisionmaker have been applied more knowingly than would otherwise have been the case.

However, there are great difficulties involved in doing usable public policy analysis. First, analyses aimed at identifying ways to achieve national objectives are greatly constrained by the fact that several tiers of government, often with many agencies in each tier, are involved in federal grant-in-aid programs to state and local governments. Seemingly obvious improvements can be thwarted by the multiplicity of agencies and program managers, each with a de facto veto over change. Analysis concerned with improving institutions for serving the public may have higher payoff than that which merely measures returns from public investment or who benefits or who pays.

Second, some agencies tend to concentrate their limited analytical people upon fairly minor issues involving a few million dollars or a minor social impact. Sometimes the major issues involving hundreds of millions or billions of dollars are left to rather superficial treatment. There is inadequate incentive for program managers or agency heads to analyze their programs because the result may mean the phasing down of their programs.

Therefore, it is not surprising that many federal executives prefer less or no analysis to more analysis.

Third, individual agency studies do not usually encompass the full breadth of program problems when these are related to the activities of several different agencies. For example, additional manpower training objectives can be partly or completely satisfied by programs in the Labor Department, the Office of Economic Opportunity, the Department of Health, Education, and Welfare, the Veterans' Administration, and the Department of Defense. This has been a major shortcoming of the planning and budgeting process to date.

In the author's judgment the quantity of adequate-to-excellent and useful analysis has increased by about 200 percent during the last 4 years. This may mean only that it has gone from five to 15 on a scale that has 100 as maximum, but it still represents considerable progress. Obviously the agency heads who have been slow in building capable analytic and planning staffs suffer most from a paucity of analysis or mediocre analysis.

Program and Financial Plans There have been difficulties with the program and financial plans (PFP's). In the beginning, the agencies were asked for planning figures on how much and in what way they would spend money in the future; the result was a series of lengthy wishlists of what the agencies would like to spend on their programs if no fiscal constraints were imposed. Some agencies showed program increases in all areas of more than 25 percent per year while other agencies showed small increases reflecting a level they thought politically feasible. The lack of consistent constraints on the future availability of public resources made this exercise almost useless.

The definition of the PFP was then changed to include only those future appropriations to which the government is committed by legal or moral obligations resulting from past decisions or required by present decisions. The definition of "commitment" used has to be somewhat amorphous, but this has restricted the utility of the modified PFP's. Each agency used a somewhat different definition of commitment and then imposed an individual standard of resource limitations. Further improvement is necessary in the definition of commitments and uncontrollable expenditures. Much more precision is possible. Currently, many agencies develop the PFP in haste and guess the measure of program output.

The PFP has been useful to a few agencies and to the Budget Bureau. It has helped to provide some perspective on the level of committed public funds in the future, and even a modest improvement in this area represents progress. By knowing this, public executives can exercise more discretion over future budgeting than they would otherwise. It has also been useful for identifying previously unforeseen growth of seemingly uncontrollable expenditures.

Staffing and Education The directions on PPB issued by the Bureau of the Budget instructed the agencies to provide an analytic staff reporting to the Secretary or his immediate subordinate and, in addition, encouraged the creation of analytic staffs located in key bureaus. During 1966 and 1967, the greatest growth in these staffs was at the agency level; between fiscal year 1968 and fiscal year 1969, the greatest growth was in the subordinate organizations.[19]

As of the fiscal 1969 budget year, the total of new positions for PPBS in the federal government was about 825 professionals. Of these, approximately one-third were net additions to agency staffs; the rest came from revision or rechristening of other jobs. There has been no substantial change for fiscal year 1970. However, there are many other personnel who are and should be involved with the PPB process and therefore the equivalent in man years is higher. The yearly expenditure for personnel connected with PPBS is roughly $40 million or about 0.0002 of total federal expenditures. Perhaps the total of in-house and contract services for policy analysis would bring this total to $60 million or 0.0003 of federal expenditures. The Congress has enacted legislation in several program areas which provides that one-half to 1 percent of the program funds should be earmarked for program evaluation.[20] If this were applied to all federal programs, program evaluation funds would climb from about $60 million to $1–2 billion or 17–33 times as high as they are now.

At the same time that agencies created analytic staffs, several educational and training programs were started. These were intended to provide both analysts and analytically-oriented program managers for the future. All of these are now supervised by the Civil Service Commission (CSC) with Bureau participation on policy matters. The most extensive of these has been a 9-month course, the Educational Program in Systematic Analysis, given at several major universities. Currently, these universities are Harvard, Massachusetts Institute of Technology, Stanford, University of California at Irvine, and University of Maryland. So far, 246 career federal employees have attended the program. The CSC also gives a 3-week course in analysis that has been attended by 1,055 people, 2-day orientation sessions that have had an enrollment of 3,350, and a number of other courses in areas relevant to analysis, such as data processing, statistics, mathematics, and cost/benefit and cost/effectiveness workshops.

In addition to the CSC's efforts, the graduate school of the Department of Agriculture and individual agencies have conducted courses in PPB or related subjects, or have developed special orientation or on-the-job training programs. These educational efforts have furnished a large number of the staff members with new skills or valuable orientation. Also, there have been continuing efforts to recruit more qualified personnel from the nation's graduate schools.

Improvements

The above discussion gives a somewhat negative picture of progress to date under PPBS when comparing the actual with the ideal. And, compared with the high hopes and expectations during 1961 in Defense and during 1965 in 20 other agencies, the system has not done as much as anticipated.

Viewed more realistically, from the standpoint of improvements in the process over the pre-PPB situation and the addition of some useful analysis, progress has been significant. Some of these improvements have been discussed in the preceding section on the formal structure. In general, within the agencies and the Executive Office of the President—and also in State and local governments—benefits are observable in several areas.

1. *Definition of objectives*——During the last 4 years, many agencies have undergone at least a partial reappraisal of their functions and missions. The general result has been an increase in the understanding of programs and in the awareness of possible alternatives and limitations that would not have occurred otherwise.

2. *Information*——The quality, relevance, and structure of information being developed by the agencies have improved substantially. There is more solid information on program inputs and outputs, related to objectives, than was true a few years ago. The progress in this area includes the all-important element of structuring information into useful form.

The additional information has been shared with the Congress and the public in various ways and especially through improvements in budget and economic documents and budget justifications. This year, *Part 3* and *Special Analysis R* of the budget are products of the PPB system, and several other special analyses include PPB materials; also, some of the data in the latest *Economic Report* was obtained through the PPB system. Several special reports provide additional information, such as the report on oil shale development, evaluation of the Job Corps, and economic impact of air and water pollution abatement.[21] The justifications of appropriation requests submitted by the agencies have reflected the increase in program information.[22]

3. *Use of analysis in decisionmaking*——As studies are made, they are used increasingly to assist decisionmakers. Some of these are identified below.[23] As indicated above, useful analysis in the domestic agencies has increased by about 200 percent during the last 4 years, and in the Defense Department by a higher percent during the last 8 years.

4. *Evaluation of programs*——The federal government traditionally has not obtained sufficient feedback on the results of its programs. But there is now general agreement that it is important to measure the accomplishments of programs and to obtain information on whether the concepts that underlie each program prove to be useful. PPB has placed emphasis on this, and during the last 4 years the amount and caliber of program evaluation has increased. As more work is done to make the review and evaluation function a routine part of program administration, progress should be faster. It is still true, though, that the evaluation of existing programs is far from complete and receives less emphasis than evaluation of new programs or the redirection of experimental programs.

5. *Management efficiency*——During the last 4 years in a few agencies and 8 years in parts of the Defense Department, some attempts have been made to trace the use of resources and measure them against predetermined program plans. These steps have been useful in indentifying the complexities and difficulties of doing this and also in whetting the appetite to try it on a wider scale.

6. *Wider involvement of officials in the budget process*——One of the standard jokes among BOB officials is that high executives only make policy —they do not worry about budgets. The point, of course, is that no one can hope to make many important policy decisions without concerning himself with the actual allocation of resources, information reflected almost exclusively in the budget. An official who tries to do so will find that he is making policy statements, but, since plans that exclude resource constraints are usually irrelevant, someone else is making the real decisions.[24] Of course, the opposite extreme of annual budgets without plans and priorities to insure more balanced perspective and foresight is also unfortunate.[25] One impact of PPB has been to increase the awareness of agency officials that in many areas the allocation of the agency's resources *is* the policy, and that this does not automatically follow the officials' preferences unless they work at it. The result has been an increasing involvement of top officials in the planning and budgeting process. This is a healthy trend.

7. *Recognition of the legitimacy and necessity of analytic arguments*——When PPBS was initiated, many of the analysts who joined the government were familiar with quantitative analysis of different types. They were aware of its value and also of its possible abuses and limitations, so many of the problems involved were not entirely unexpected. But they were surprised to find that large numbers of people would deny the relevance of analysis to government activities.

This perhaps requires a little explanation. No one was surprised to have it said that analytic treatment of government problems does not tell one everything, or that political factors are important, or that distribution of benefits is often as important as amount, or that analysis in many areas is difficult. All of this could be readily agreed upon. But the idea that anyone would *deny* any utility to rigorous thought, quantitative where possible, about the gains, losses, and resource expenditures involved in a particular course of action was not expected.[26]

There have been many reasons for this type of resistance. Partly, it results from the way in which PPB was sprung rather suddenly upon the entire government. There was also the problem that examples used tended to be drawn from defense, water resources, or other areas where work had been going on for some years; such examples had a degree of real or apparent sophistication that was neither readily attainable nor expected in other agencies. Unfortunately, some analysts overstressed the importance of their own effort relative to that of others, and thereby caused friction with operating officials. Also, there was a fear of replacing a generalist's judgment with the narrower view of an "expert." And there was an element of inertia inherent in large bureaucracies which reduced responsiveness to innovations of any kind.

Over time, some progress has been made in alleviating these difficulties. Instead of resistance to the whole idea of analysis, some recognition is now given that where bargaining is a vital part of any political process, it operates to the benefit of the participants when there exists a better understanding of the costs, benefits, outputs, and beneficiaries of alternative courses of action. That is, there has been a realization that PPB is not a substitute for the bargaining process but an important part of it, and a necessary element in making it work more effectively. There is also a recognition that good judgment is made even better when it can operate with good analysis. The framework of PPB and the systems analysis approach necessary for its use have, to a large extent, achieved legitimacy.

It should be reemphasized that the type of analysis that can be done on most federal programs is a very long way from the sophistication that is the dream of each new graduate student. Government personnel must use whatever tools are available. Sometimes this means very accurate measures are feasible and needed. Other times the analyst must use very rough methods and only partially reliable data to deal with the complex realities which public policies seek to affect, and this may be all that is necessary anyway. The margins of error may be plus 200 percent and minus 50 percent—as in the case of a very useful recent study on air pollution abatement—and still be adequate. One cannot, and should not, attempt to make fine distinctions when only crude data is available; however, at present public officials are often faced with trying to find good, realistic ways of making even crude distinctions. Improvement can and should be emphasized as the use of program evaluation increases.

8. *Comparisons of related programs in several agencies*——Some improvement in ways of displaying related programs in several agencies has occurred. These promise to further the establishment of general priorities by measuring the impact of complementary programs irrespective of organizational lines. For example, the 24 manpower programs found in six agencies, the 21 education programs found in five agencies, and the 16 health programs found in three agencies can be reviewed with related programs irrespective of agency identification.

When the manner and assumptions with which one approaches problems are improved, one insures that the conclusions will be better as well. Recognizing the tradeoffs one can make is only a start, of course; the next step is to devise ways to make them more rationally.

9. *State and local interest*——State and local government officials have shown interest in planning and programing to complement their budgeting process. The federal government has responded by including several projects to assist state and local governments develop their own budget and planning processes and increase the application of systems analysis.[27] Since many federal programs depend heavily on effective state and local action, this is a very important development.

Major Issues

The third question in evaluating PPB is whether one can identify major policy issues where analysis assisted the decisionmakers. The answer is clearly "Yes." There are a number of examples in which the amount of resources and/or the manner of their allocation has been influenced, at least in part, by systematic analysis. Such is the case for the following illustrative list of topics:[28]

- Electricity for gaseous diffusion plants
- Enforcement of civil rights laws
- Allocation of legal resources for anti-trust purposes
- Structure and program of the Institute of Criminal Justice
- Internal Revenue Service audit program
- Oil shale development
- Post Office organization and efficiency
- Atomic Energy Commission cascade improvement program
- Single class priority mail
- Highway safety programs
- Supersonic transport
- Manpower Development Training Act program
- Helium supply
- Heavy metals supply
- Timber management
- Forest roads
- Topographic mapping
- Work experience program
- Saturn V rocket production
- High energy physics
- Water resources
- Air pollution abatement strategies
- Water pollution abatement strategies
- Earth resources technology satellite

USIA media use
Peace Corps volunteer priorities
Collection of customs duties
Fast breeder reactor program
Coast Guard aviation program
GSA motor pools
FAA air traffic control facilities
Infant mortality
Nursing manpower
Disease control
Medical care prices
Vocational rehabilitation
Nuclear rocket R. & D.
Demand for park recreation facilities
Job Corps program
Distribution of National Archives materials
Distribution of Federal visual aid materials
Coast Guard merchant marine safety program
Optimum modes for supplying Federal agencies with equipment, services and supplies
Building space acquisition
Off-shore mineral leasing policies
Veterans' pension rates
Area economic development

This is only a partial list. No attempt was made to canvass the government in an effort to find all possible examples. Other analyses that were useful are not included because of classification problems and other identification problems. In addition, some analyses now underway or newly completed will probably be useful in the future, but the policy decisions have not yet been made.

The role of analysis should not be overstated. In many policy decisions analysis played only a minor role; in other cases not included in the list, analysis was done that played no role at all. This occurred where the relevant decisionmakers were unaware of the analysis; found the analysis was misdirected and did not provide useful information; thought the analysis was more misleading than helpful; were uncomfortable with anything other than their own experienced judgments; or thought the analysis did not include measurements of factors that were most important.

The relationship between the examples above and PPB as a system is unclear. Some of these studies were done strictly within the channel created by the PPB system, others were parallel to it but stimulated by PPBS, and some analytic efforts antedated it. So it is difficult to say which of this work would have been done anyway, which would not have been done, which would have been done more poorly, and which would have been done sometime in the future.

However, the important purpose in initiating PPB was not to initiate a separate system but to improve the quality of public policy decisions. PPB cannot be judged solely by what is accomplished under its formalized mechanisms but by its total impact on the present and future quality of decisions. It has, undeniably, been important in creating a climate more receptive to the use of analysis and more demanding of analysis than existed in the past. If some, or even all, of the response to PPB occurs outside the formal structure necessary to initiate and develop PPB, it should be of little concern.

One of the most difficult questions to answer is whether PPB should have concentrated completely on analysis of individual issues and ignored the concept of PPB as a system of decisionmaking. The argument in favor of this approach is that the requirements of the system may have drained off valuable effort that could have been devoted to actual analysis and evaluation. This issue is especially acute in the light of the comments made here about the value of the documents produced in the system. There is no ready answer.

On balance, though, one is faced with the fact that to increase the use of analysis in government decisionmaking one needs both a supply of relevant analytic work and a demand for it. One of the objectives of PPB as a system is to create this demand. If one were to rely totally upon the supply to create the demand, several problems would arise:

- Under traditional government decision methods, even good analysis might lie fallow if its relevance at a specific decision point is unclear;
- Analyses designed without participation by those who must use the results are much less likely to be relevant to actual decisions;
- The government, not to mention the private sector, already turns out thousands of analyses, evaluations, and studies every year, some of them quite good. Their influence on policy is often negligible. This seems to indicate that more than supply is needed;
- There is no reason to think that the effort that produced poor PM's would have produced good studies. The PM is largely an exercise in asking the right questions; this is only one step—albeit the most important one—in doing good analysis.

For all these reasons, work to increase demand is as important as the attempt to increase the quantity and quality of the supply of analysis.

THE FUTURE OF PPB

At the beginning of this paper, several pressing problems of modern government were mentioned. These problems remain and the PPBS approach represents the best foundation for making substantial improvements. Therefore, it is not surprising that the executive branch still affirms the objectives of the PPB System and wishes to pursue them with vigor.

Improvements are obviously possible and necessary if decisionmakers and the decisionmaking process are to respond to public needs efficiently and effectively. As experience indicates, care should be exercised so as to not oversell the innovations that will be tried this year and next before they are adequately tested. Improvements to the budget and planning process are planned to proceed as follows.

Minimize Changes for the Fiscal Year 1971 Planning and Budgeting Cycle

Until major directions for changes in PPB are identified, changes in general form and substance will be minimized while changes in emphasis will receive attention. This means that the existing directions for the budget and planning cycle, Bulletin No. 68–9, will apply for the fiscal year 1971 cycle. But the emphasis on, for example, the spring preview (June 1969) as the main planning and program evaluation session within the Executive Offices of the President will be increased. The spring preview will include a review of commitments or "uncontrollable" expenditures from past decisions projected for 5 years ahead, of proposed new commitments, of results of major policy analyses, and of program evaluation efforts.

The major components of the PPB system will be used with the following changes in emphasis:

Program Structure While it is important that the program structure reflect objectives and lend itself to analysis of tradeoffs and choices, there is no need to split accounting or appropriation structures or lowest level decisionmaking unit accounts unnecessarily. Beyond this generality, program structure should be designed according to the nature of each agency.

Issue Letters Some changes in emphasis are occurring with the issue letters. First, the issue letters are being sent earlier in the cycle; most of the letters were sent before the end of March this year. Second, the number of Major Policy Issues has been reduced from a number of nearly 400 last year to 75 this year and include primarily, although not exclusively, those that have a budgetary impact of $50 million or more in fiscal year 1971 and/or $500 million during the next 5 years or an equivalent social impact. Third, each issue requiring analysis is developed in full consultation with each agency along with consideration of the resources and time necessary to complete the analyses early enough to be useful in the decisionmaking process. Fourth, before the major policy issue analysis is requested, greater care is given to specifying each issue in a meaningful and rigorous way so as to assure more useful analysis. Fifth, each issue will receive the continuing attention and assistance if necessary of a BOB representative during its analytical phase. Sixth, issues requiring analysis spanning several future years are being developed also. Seventh, issues identification is intended to occur during all phases of the planning cycle; second issue letters have already been sent to some agencies this year. However, the completion of analysis is best accomplished by summer in order to help each agency head decide his fall budget request and for the President to establish his priorities.

Program Memoranda PM's should be used in reporting the results of major program issues—one PM for each program category in which there is at least one issue. The emphasis should be conciseness, precision, and inclusion of only a minimum of descriptive material.

Special Analytic Studies No modifications are anticipated other than better timing of the effort to enhance relevance to the decision process and improvement in quality.

Program and Financial Plans The PFP's should be improved and used more extensively.

Emphasize Agency Role in Planning, Programing, and Budgeting

Realistically, the relationship between the president's Budget Bureau and any government agency must be somewhat schizophrenic. In part, the Bureau appears as the adversary who consistently refuses to give an agency all the resources it would like. At other times, it appears to offer assistance to agencies too burdened with day-to-day problems to develop long-range innovations. There is little prospect that this conflict of roles can or should be completely resolved. Its mere existence, however, reduces the extent to which the Bureau can assure marked improvement in the quality of public policy decisions until each agency's capability is increased. It is only realistic to state that the responsibility for improvement in the planning and budgeting processes must be primarily within the agency.

At present, there is a tendency to think of PPB as a tool primarily for the Budget Bureau. This is not the intention, and should not be the result. Each agency head is responsible to the president and he to the Congress for national policy in his area of public responsibility; PPB should be a tool for the agencies to use in meeting this responsibility. It should be made clear that the Cabinet officers and other agency heads are primarily responsible for its implementation and use.

This emphasis on the role of the agencies will be reflected in several ways during the coming year.

1. As stated, fewer major issues will be requested by the Budget Bureau. Only 75 Major Policy Issues have been specified for analysis so far this year in contrast to about 380 last year. In turn, the agencies are being encouraged to develop additional issue analyses for their own use, and for possible future budget justification.

2. Consultation is occurring between agencies and the executive offices before the limited number of major issues are identified for evaluation and analysis.

3. Some additional agencies are developing components of the PPB

system to fit their needs. Three agencies have already started since January 1969.

4. Each agency has been requested to survey the adequacy of their planning and analytic staffs at the agency level and within each major suborganization. Even in tight budget years, it is a good investment to expand each agency's capability to evaluate how best to achieve their priorities with very limited funds. To assist, the results of the Budget Bureau's 16-agency study of PPB staffs has been shared with each agency that participated.

5. Educational programs and training programs are being continued and expanded to help upgrade skills in analysis and planning. The Educational Program in Systematic Analysis is being further developed to serve the needs of preparing career personnel for evaluating public programs. Universities are being encouraged to design programs to serve the public need for graduates equipped with both the traditional skills of the professions (e.g., law and medicine) and the additional skills useful for evaluating public resource alternatives; Harvard University has initiated such a program leading to masters' and doctors' degrees in public policy, which is one useful approach for satisfying this need. The Civil Service Commission and other organizations are being encouraged to continue upgrading their courses to assist further in planning, analysis, and budgeting.

6. Agencies are being encouraged to hire additional capable analysts when vacancies occur. Even with the current limitations on personnel ceilings, some vacancies occur and qualified people must be recruited. To assist, the Budget Bureau, in cooperation with the agencies, has contacted deans and department heads of most universities with graduate schools requesting them to call to the attention of their graduate students and faculty members the many opportunities for analyzing public resource use; university people have been supplied with the names of the chief planning officer and the personnel officer in each agency.

7. Improved methods for evaluating public policy are being sought and shared with all agencies. This includes development of improved discounting procedures, sensitivity tests for investment risk, better definitions of direct and indirect benefits and reasonable assumptions of socioeconomic variables (e.g., future changes in GNP, population, labor force, etc.).

8. Techniques for increasing agency awareness of the interrelationship of its own programs to similar ones in other agencies are being further developed, and analysis of major policy issues which affect more than one agency are being accomplished.

9. Improvements to the planning and budgeting process are being implemented in a more flexible way so as to recognize each agency's unique characteristics and capability for innovation.

10. Agencies are being encouraged to review their procedures for analyzing legislation to insure that adequate analysis is done before it is recommended to the president and the Congress. The discipline inherent in the planning and budgeting cycle could help provide badly needed analysis in this area.

11. Agencies working to develop social indicators of the need (or lack of need) for particular public programs are being assisted in their efforts. Some agencies have been helpful in laying some groundwork, but what is needed is a cooperative effort among all affected agencies. To assist, a conceptual format for showing data that measures social conditions in conjunction with data that measures the impact of public and private expenditures aimed at improving those social conditions is being developed. For example, data on the current stock of housing, quality measures, and measures showing changes over time are contrasted with expenditures on housing and projections of the time period needed to achieve specified levels of numbers and quality at current rates of improvement.

12. Agencies are being helped to develop a conceptual framework for comparing and evaluating all their programs. With the proper format, the existing data and informed judgments could provide a useful summary of the social impact of federal programs and/or the limits of our knowledge. These program overviews are attempting to provide the following information:

a. The physical goods or services each federal program produces. For example, the Manpower Development Training Act Institutional Training Program is estimated to provide 57,000 man-years of training in fiscal year 1969: the Hill-Burton hospital construction program is estimated to provide 18,618 new hospital beds or the rough equivalent of 2,000 additional patient-years of hospital care; a water project provides acre-feet of water and kilowatt hours of electricity; etc.

b. The cost of each unit of goods or service, both on the average and for small additions. For examples, the average federal cost, based on an average of 18 weeks of training, for MDTA institutional training is about $1,400.

c. The dollar value of the goods or service in the economy, where possible. For example, an estimate has been made from limited data that MDTA institutional trainees can be expected to receive $700 additional yearly income for each of the next 10 years or about $4,700 in present value terms (10-percent discount rate). However, in many cases it is not possible to find suitable market prices, such as for military aircraft.

d. The characteristics of the beneficiaries. For example, the trainee beneficiaries of MDTA institutional training are estimated to be 50 percent Negro, 65 percent from households below the poverty threshold, 40 percent below 21 years of age, 45 percent from central cities of cities over 250,000 people.[29]

Improvements to Planning and Budgeting for the Fiscal Year 1972 Cycle

Between now and September, an evaluation of the present process will be completed. Such an evaluation will benefit from—

The papers submitted to the Joint Economic Committee's Compendium on the PPB system and the subsequent hearings;

Other papers and hearings of the Congress;

The studies of the General Accounting Office concerning staffing in the agencies;

Studies by the Budget Bureau concerning the operation of the PPB process in several agencies and an assessment of the output of the system in terms of improved decisions, documents with useful analytical and descriptive material, and the improved capability to analyze public policy issues in the future;

A major study of potential informational improvements by an outside contractor to the Budget Bureau;

Evaluations of the system by the planning and budgeting officers who have participated in it; and

Evaluations of knowledgeable people in the academic community and other parts of the private sector.

The major changes for the next cycle should be identified by September 1969 and will be implemented shortly thereafter. It is already obvious, for example, that the analysis of policy issues could be greatly improved if policy issues are identified even earlier than was the case for the fiscal year 1971 cycle.

Assist State and Local Governments Improve Their Own Analysis and Planning Processes

In many program areas, federal expenditures are, for all practical purposes, administered by state and local governments. If these funds—$26 billion in fiscal year 1970—are to be used with maximum effectiveness, the capability to analyze and evaluate programs must exist at these levels. Therefore, several projects have been initiated to further this goal. Some of the present projects include—

An experimental program has just been completed under which five city, five county, and five State governments were given grants to implement PPBS;

An experimental BOB-HUD project has been initiated to survey areas of greatest potential improvement in state government planning, programing, and budgeting functions. Two states have been surveyed and HUD has provided some funds to augment State funds to implement the recommendations in areas of greatest possible improvement. Six other states are scheduled for fiscal year 1970.

The development of data showing federal expenditures and socioeconomic data on a geographic basis and analyzing social impact of programs is going forward.

These efforts will continue and be of increasing utility to state and local governments. In return, the federal government will be assured of more effective use of the federally collected funds it passes on to these governments.

NOTES

[1] Prior to 1921, an executive budget did not exist, except for the term of the first two Presidents, Washington and Adams; rather, each department submitted budget requests and received authorizations directly from the Congress. In 1911, the New York Bureau of Municipal Research recommended budgetary classification by function and objects of expenditure and recommended the three functions of budgeting that are embodied in PPBS: Control, management efficiency, and planning. President Taft in 1912, as the result of the Report of the Commission on Economy and Efficiency, submitted to the Congress a model budget based on expenditures by function, by organization, by type of activity, by capital and current expenditures, and by cross classification among each category. The Budget and Accounting Act of 1921 created the Bureau of the Budget in the Treasury Department and created a central executive budget, but the emphasis was on operational control until the budget was taken out of the Treasury Department and placed in the newly established Executive Office of the President in 1939; then the budgetary emphasis shifted to managerial efficiency. This was enhanced by the call for performance budgeting found in the 1949 Hoover Commission. The 1950 Budget and Accounting Act directed improvements in accounting and cost data. Finally, in the 1960s, the third function of the budget was slowly developed: Executive planning. The development of methodology for evaluating public programs has occurred over a long period of time. Some of the more notable sources were in the water resources area during this century and particularly through the 1950s and in the defense area with the long gestation period provided by the RAND Corporation and others since World War II.

See Allen Schick, "The Road to PPB: The Stages of Budget Reform," *Public Administration Review,* 26:4 (December 1966), p. 243; and Charles Schultze, *The Politics and Economics of Public Spending,* pp. 1–17 (Washington, D.C.: The Brookings Institution, 1968).

[2] This in effect was building on 2 previous functions of the budget: (1) Operational control of subordinate units to insure that public funds are spent for only those program objectives specified by law; (2) managerial control to assure efficient use of resources—although stressed timidly. Planning was the additional function tied to the budget. See Arthur Smithies, *The Budgeting Process in the United States* (New York: McGraw-Hill, 1955) for the development of these functions to the 1950s.

[3] Of the 825 professionals assigned specifically to "PPB jobs" within 17 of the agencies with PPB systems, less than 20 are now within the Bureau of the Budget. See Attachment 1 for total staff increases according to basic function.

[4] Attachment 2 lists the agencies subject to PPBS as of May 1969.

[5] See Attachment 3 for the time sequence of the process during a typical budget and planning cycle.

[6] See Bureau of the Budget Bulletin No. 68–9 (Apr. 12, 1968), reproduced in Attachment 4 of U.S. Congress, Joint Economic Committee, *The Analysis and Evaluation of Public Expenditures: The PPB System,* Vol. 2 (Washington, D.C.: U.S. Government Printing Office, 1969). There have been changes in PPB over time as experience accumulated. This paper concentrates on the structure as of the fiscal year 1970 budget cycle and does not attempt to recapitulate the history, although a few changes are mentioned.

[7] See Attachment 5 of U.S. Congress, Joint Economic Committee, *op. cit.,* which contains a comparison of program structures and appropriations structures for one program subcategory. Attachment 10 of U.S. Congress, Joint Economic Committee, *op. cit.* shows the Federal fiscal year 1970 budget according to program structure.

[8] This tripartite division is discussed in Schick, "The Road to PPB: The Stages of Budget Reform," *Public Administration Review,* 26:4 (December 1966), p. 243.

[9] See Attachment 6 of U.S. Congress, Joint Economic Committee, *op. cit.* for an example.

[10] See Attachment 7 of U.S. Congress, Joint Economic Committee, *op. cit.*

[11] See Attachment 8 of U.S. Congress, Joint Economic Committee, *op. cit.* for an example.

[12] See Attachment 9 of U.S. Congress, Joint Economic Committee, *op. cit.* for an example.

[13] Attachment 5 of U.S. Congress, Joint Economic Committee, *op. cit.* shows the relationship of the program structure for part of one agency, HEW, as compared with the appropriation structure. This gives some idea of the scope of the changes involved.

[14] See Attachment 10 of U.S. Congress, Joint Economic Committee, *op. cit.*

[15] Issues in a few agencies are developed without the use of a formal issue letter.

[16] See Attachment 4 for a summary of the major program issues identified and analyzed during 1968.

[17] Charles L. Schultze, former Director of the Budget Bureau, has commented:

"The most frustrating aspect of public life is not the inability to convince others of the merits of a cherished project or policy. Rather, it is the endless hours spent on policy discussions in which the irrelevant issues have not been separated from the relevant, in which ascertainable facts and relationships have not been investigated but are the subject of heated debate, in which consideration of alternatives is impossible because only one proposal has been developed, and, above all, discussions in which nobility of aim is presumed to determine effectiveness of program." Schultze, *op. cit.* n. 1, at 75.

[18] For a partial summary tabulation, see attachment 4.

[19] See Attachment 1.

[20] The following pieces of legislation have such provisions:

1. Public Health Service Act
   a. Sec. 309(c)(2), grants to schools of public health.
   b. Sec. 314(d)(1), formula grants for public health services.
   c. Sec. 314(e), project grants for public health services.
   d. Sec. 797, allied health profession.
   e. Sec. 901(a), regional medical programs.
2. Community Mutual Health Centers Act, sec. 262 [sec. 303(a) of Public Law 90–574].
3. Social Security Act, sec. 513(b), maternal and child health.
4. Juvenile delinquency, sec. 404 of Public Law 90–445.

5. Vocational Rehabilitation Act, sec. 7(e).
6. Education programs, blanket authorization in sec. 402 of Public Law 90–247.
7. Work incentive programs, sec. 441 of the Social Security Act.

The executive branch continues to support the designation of funds for program evaluation.

[21] For a partial list of studies completed during 1966 and 1967, see attachment 12 of U.S. Congress, Joint Economic Committee, *op. cit.*

[22] For an example, see attachment 5, which contains excerpts from the fiscal year 1967 and fiscal year 1970 budget submissions to Congress made on behalf of a particular program; most of the improvement is due to PPB.

[23] See p. 382–83.

[24] The usefulness of some planning by the military services reflected in the Joint Strategic Operations Plan suffers from such a lack of resource constraints.

[25] This was one of the reasons for broadening the traditional budgetary process from operational control and management efficiency to include strategic planning.

[26] This is a paraphrase of the definition of systems analysis contained in "Systems Analysis and the Political Process," by James Schlesinger, *Journal of Law and Economics,* Vol. XI, 1968, p. 281.

[27] See the reports from the experimental project directed by Selma J. Mushkin: "PPB Pilot Project Reports from the Participating 5 States, 5 Counties and 5 Cities," State-Local Finances Project, George Washington University, February 1969.

[28] Some of this analysis has been completed and released in various reports. Other analysis is incomplete but will be completed and released in the future; some analysis will likely remain incomplete because the issue has changed.

[29] For further explanation see statement of Jack W. Carlson before the Subcommittee on Economy in Government of the Joint Economic Committee, on "Guidelines for Estimating the Benefits of Public Expenditures," U.S. Congress, May 12, 1969.

List of Attachments

Attachment 1

STAFF INCREASES FOR PPBS

Number of PPB Positions Shown in the Fiscal Year 1969 Budget[1]

	Added 1966–68	Added 1968–69	Total, 1969
Central staff; analytic:			
Professional	177	21	198
Support	82	6	88
Program monitoring and data handling:			
Professional	105	9	114
Support	46	5	51
Other (including subordinate agencies):			
Professional	428	85	513
Support	159	22	181
Recapitulation:			
Total professional	710	115	825
Total support	287	33	320
Total	997	148	1,145

[1] Represents only 21 agencies. Department of Defense (military), Central Intelligence Agency, Small Business Administration, Civil Service Commission, and Tennessee Valley Authority are excluded.

Attachment 2

AGENCIES WITH PLANNING-PROGRAMING-BUDGETING SYSTEMS AS OF MAY 1969*

Department of Agriculture
Department of Commerce
Department of Defense—Military functions (including civil defense and military assistance)
Department of Defense—Corps of Engineers, civil functions
Department of Health, Education, and Welfare
Department of Housing and Urban Development
Department of the Interior
Department of Justice
Department of Labor
Post Office Department
Department of State (cultural affairs only)
Department of Transportation
Department of the Treasury
Agency for International Development
Atomic Energy Commission
Central Intelligence Agency
Civil Service Commission
General Services Administration
National Aeronautics and Space Administration
National Science Foundation
Office of Economic Opportunity
Peace Corps
Small Business Administration
Tennessee Valley Authority
U.S. Information Agency
Veterans' Administration

* Some other agencies are considering adopting components of the PPB System during 1969.

Attachment 3

THE PPBS PROCESS IN A TYPICAL BUDGET YEAR

Planning and Budgeting Cycle for Fiscal Year 1971 (July 1970-June 1971)

1968 November-February 1969	Identification of major policy issues affecting the fiscal year 1971 budget and/or subsequent budgets, or having major social impact. Issue letters sent by the Director of the Bureau of the Budget to each agency head.
May-June	Results of issue analysis reported to agency heads and then to the Budget Director. Commitments or uncontrollable budget expenditures based on past decisions are identified and projected 5 years ahead along with the identification of proposed additional or new expenditures and the identification of low priority expenditures for the fiscal year 1971 budget.
June-July	Bureau of the Budget holds spring preview of major policy issues and plans for the reorientation of existing programs and/or identification of new low priority programs. The implications of changes in policy and spending levels are projected ahead for 5 years.
August	The Budget Bureau releases tentative guidance by agency and selected programs for each agency to develop final budget requests.
September-October	Final budget and program and financial plan are submitted by each agency to the Bureau of the Budget.
October-November	Budget holds final agency hearings and budget review.
November-December	President decides on the major budget issues.

Attachment 3 (Continued)

1970	
January	Hearings on the budget by various committees of the Congress.
February-June	Presidential budget message transmitted to the Congress.
March-July	Congressional approval of the major items in the fiscal year 1971 budget.
July-June 1971	Fiscal year 1971.

Attachment 4

SUMMARY OF ANALYSIS OF MAJOR PROGRAM ISSUES DURING THE FISCAL YEAR 1970 PLANNING AND BUDGET CYCLE (JANUARY TO DECEMBER 1968)

Major program areas	Major program issues (number)	5-year potential impact on budget (billions)	Issue analysis completed by final budget review		Issue analysis in progress (number)	Issues not analyzed (number)	Percent of completed analysis used in decision process[1]
			Number	Percent of dollars impact			
1. Community and economic development	114	$18	35	37%	40	39	89%
2. Human resources	64	11	25	26	6	33	16
3. Science and technology	42	8	31	61	6	5	70
4. General government	51	6	13	8	13	25	75
Total for domestic programs	271	$43	104	35%	65	102	68%
5. International and national security affairs[2]	109	100	90	85	5	17	89
Total	380	$103	149	44%	80	151	82%

[1] This number represents the percent of the potential dollar impact of all completed analyses that was actually influenced, in major or minor fashion, by the analyses.

[2] The definition of issues and completion is somewhat different for international and national security problems, which are only partially tied to the budget cycle, so the numbers in this row are only roughly comparable to the other four areas.

NOTE: It should be emphasized that this table represents a composite of the subjective judgments of staff members familiar with analysis in the various areas. The process by which it was developed was to ask those staff members to list the issues posed as a part of the FY 1970 cycle and then to appraise each one, on a judgmental basis, in terms of its impact. Thus the data only suggest the relative magnitudes involved. Because of the complexity of the decision process, no attempt was made to assess the marginal impact of analysis, that is, the result that occurred as compared with the result that would have occurred without the analytic work.

Attachment 5

COMPARISON OF FISCAL YEAR 1967 AND FISCAL YEAR 1970 CONGRESSIONAL BUDGET SUBMISSIONS FOR ONE PROGRAM*

Budget Submission for 1967

Relocation and Adult Vocational Training for Indians

Subactivity	1965 amount available	1966 amount available	Fiscal year 1967 estimate	Increase (+) or decrease (−), 1967 compared with 1966		
				Total	Pay cost[1]	Program
(a) Relocation services	$2,797,036	$3,039,000	$3,039,000		$10,000	−$10,000
(b) Adult vocational training	9,320,061	11,473,520	12,145,000	$671,480	21,000	+650,480
Total	12,117,097	14,512,520	15,184,000	671,480	31,000	+640,480

[1] To provide for increased pay cost for fiscal year 1966 positions.

Note: The estimate of $15,184,000 is an increase of $671,480. The increase consists of:

(1) A decrease of $10,000 in relocation services and a decrease of $34,000 in adult vocational training due to program savings resulting from improved manpower utilization and cost reduction actions.

(2) An increase of $10,000 in relocation services and an increase of $21,000 in adult vocational training for increased pay costs.

(3) An increase of $684,000 to provide the full range of adult vocational training services including employment following training for approximately 200 applicants currently awaiting this service.

*** Department of the Interior, Bureau of Indian Affairs. Program Subcategory: Relocation and Adult Vocational Training.**

Program of Work These two programs provide financial assistance to Indians to enable them to become self-sufficient through adequate employment. The relocation services phase of the program provides services and financial assistance to Indians who are prepared to accept immediate employment. The adult vocational training program (Public Law 959) provides training which will lead to self-support. Relocation services will provide service and financial assistance to approximately 1,775 units (4,083 persons). The funds requested for adult vocational training services will provide services and financial assistance to 3,726 units (7,785 persons) in training. Financial assistance and services will also be available for approximately 2,500 units (8,250 persons) in on-the-job training.

Examples of Recent Accomplishments There are approximately 380,000 Indian persons living on or adjacent to reservations for whom the Bureau assumes some responsibility. Opportunities for self-support on or near the reservations are inadequate and the increasing population is faced with the alternative of relocating to areas where opportunities for self-sufficiency are available or remaining partially or wholly dependent upon some form of public assistance. This program assists these people to leave the reservation area and accept employment or training which will qualify them for employment. Since the inception of this program through June 30, 1965, over 89,447 persons will have benefited from either institutional training services, on-the-job training or direct employment assistance. Staff effort by Bureau Offices with the cooperation of the state employment services, employers, and others concerned have made employment opportunities available to meet the needs of Indian people. Realistic counseling and guidance are provided to encourage them to take advantage of these opportunities and they are assisted to adjust to the living and working conditions of the new community.

Budget Submission for 1970

Relocation and Adult Vocational Training for Indians

Subactivity	Fiscal year 1968 amount available	Fiscal year 1969 amount available	Fiscal year 1970 estimate	Increase (+) or decrease (−) 1970 compared with 1969
A. Relocation services	$7,173,448	$8,558,000	$19,026,000	+$10,468,000
B. Adult vocational training	13,614,952	15,818,000	25,000,000	+9,182,000
Total	20,788,400	24,376,000	44,026,000	+19,650,000

A. *Relocation Services.*—Fiscal year 1969, $8,558,000; fiscal year 1970, $19,026,000; increase, $10,468,000. The increase consists of:

Explanation	Increase (+) or decrease (−)		Total program	Total positions
	Amount	Positions		
To provide services and financial assisance to Indians who are preparing to accept employment	+$10,468,000	55	$19,026,000	342

Need for Increase All Americans should have the opportunity to realize their full potential—economic, political, social, and cultural. Indians have the right to expect equality of opportunity with all other Americans. They are entitled to a standard of living equal to that of the country as a whole with freedom of choice to remain in their homeland or opportunity to move to the towns and cities of America. Whatever their choice, they must have adequate job opportunity and be equipped with the necessary skills to qualify for and retain employment.

There are over 600,000 Indians in the United States, over 400,000 of them living on or near reservations. They live in varying degrees of poverty which stem from lack of job opportunities, lack of educational opportunities, underdevelopment of resources and cultural differences. The Indian unemployment rate is about 37 percent—10 times the national average. A large portion of Indian families have incomes that are below the $3,800 poverty level. Without a positive employment assistance program, the problem will worsen as populations increase.

Job need by 1974	
Current unemployment	49,000
Current underemployment	27,000
To employ new entries into labor force (1968–74)	51,400
To raise labor force participation to U.S. rates	4,000
Total jobs needed (1968–74)	131,400

During the past 2 years, initial reservation development studies have been completed for all major reservations to ascertain the income potential and related costs for fully developing each reservation's resources to maximize Indian income and employment. While much can and is being done to increase reservation employment and income opportunities, it will not be possible to provide full employment for a major portion of either the current or future labor force entirely through reservation development programs. If the on-reservation programs are accelerated as proposed in this budget, an additional 49,400 jobs would be provided by 1974. (An increase of 21,800 over what would be accomplished at the 1969 program level.) However, this will fall far short of meeting employment needs as there still would be need for some 82,000 additional jobs. This emphasizes the urgency for providing the Indian people with off-reservation employment opportunity through direct employment assistance and institutional training.

For on- or near-reservation employment, the greatest opportunity is industrial development and development of the institutions of the community. For individuals, the choice is more complex. Many Indian young people will opt to work in their communities for a better way of life. Others, eager to make their way in the competitive larger society, will wish to leave the reservation and fit into the economy as productive workers wherever suitable jobs are available and conditions are conductive to a good life. This second choice, always voluntary, has been made real in the past for over 115,000 Indian people through the employment assistance program.

While motivation of individuals has been a deterrent to a maximum program of relocation in the past, today, as a result of the example of relatives and friends who have left the reservation and as a result of improved job opportunities throughout the Nation, a large backlog of individuals awaits assistance in finding off-reservation jobs, some near home and a majority in the state of origin.

The last Congress recognized this opportunity by increasing the authorization of the adult vocational training program from $15 million to $25 million. Even with the constraints of the current budget, the option of finding off-reservation jobs and job training is so popular with Indians and so viable that the relocation and the adult vocational training programs should be expanded as proposed.

Indian employment goals by 1974 are:

Provide employment opportunity for the estimated 131,400 Indians that will need such assistance.

Reduce unemployment in the present labor force to rate consistent with the national average (currently less than 4 percent).

Increase labor force participation rates from the current 56 percent to the national average rate of 61 percent.

Reduce underemployment by providing full employment opportunity.

Provide job for new labor force entries of young people and returning veterans.

The following table summarizes the additional job opportunities that should result from the increased program levels proposed in the 1970 budget:

	Jobs provided by 1974	
	Without recommended increase	With recommended increase
Additional Indian jobs provided by on-reservation programs	27,600	49,400
Jobs provided by relocation and adult vocational training programs	39,000	70,400
Adjustment for replacement and duplications	−3,000	−13,700
Underemployment and unemployment	67,800	25,300
Net 1968–74 change in underemployment and unemployment	−8,200	−50,700

If reservation programs and relocation and adult vocational training programs were continued at 1969 levels they would not make significant improvements in the Indian employment situation. They would be barely sufficient to keep up with a growing population and to prevent a worsening employment situation. However, under the proposed program, projected employment improvement will be increased 6 times over and above that of the 1969 level program by 1974. Projected income improvement under the program would bring 78 to 95 percent of the trainees above the poverty level of $3,800 for a family of five. In addition, such a program would bring increasing returns as these programs are expanded to increase employment and otherwise lessen economic dependence on the federal government.

Program of Work Direct job placement efforts in urban areas are currently running at the rate of 2,780 annually and will be expanded to 6,530 annually in 1970 with the proposed increase in funding to $19 million. Residential family training which is currently running at a rate of 905 annually will be expanded to 1,280 trainees with the 1970 increase. Expansion of ongoing relocation services programs will require $17.1 million of the total $19 million increase. These programs will, with the addition of the following specific new projects, enable the bureau to increase the fiscal year 1970 relocation services initial placements by about 3,900 or 124 percent over fiscal year 1969 initial placements. The specific new projects are:

(1) Experience has shown that distance to employment centers played a significant role in motivating Indians to relocate. To further alleviate this we propose the establishment of two additional placement centers in cities located near Indian reservations. The cost for these centers will require an increase of $200,000.

(2) The vicious poverty cycle of a particular group of Indians, the

so-called hard-core poor, will deepen unless the residential training program is immediately expanded to offer these individuals an opportunity to better themselves economically. The Roswell Employment Training Center (RETC) was specifically designed for this purpose. RETC facilities will be expanded under the proposed program to accommodate 200 more trainees, bringing it up to full capacity of 500 which yield about 650 graduates annually.

At present, residential training centers, which are extremely popular with the Indian people, since they serve entire families, have a potential service population of approximately 7,700. Many of these are willing to forgo welfare assistance in order to take this training. This expansion of the RETC will require an increase of $1,050,000.

(3) One of the most difficult groups of Indians to serve are the "Solo Parents." These consist of unwed mothers, widows, and divorcees with children who have special problems and need special attention and treatment. A recent survey has been made and it was found that there is an immediate potential of approximately 2,150 applicants in this group. Many of these are now receiving Aid for Dependent Children but would prefer to learn a skill and become gainfully employed. To assist this group, we propose to establish a pilot "Solo Parent" program in one of the larger western cities where training and employment opportunities are good and where individual special problems can be minimized or resolved. This program will require an increase of $300,000. The immediate goal of this project is to develop a program suitable to the training needs of solo parents so that they are able to enter the world of work at a level comparable to other institutional trainees. Project evaluation will enable the BIA to determine the feasibility of a full scale effort aimed at the special problems of solo parents.

(4) $400,000 is included to provide for increased costs for transportation, subsistence en route to the employment and subsistence until the first paycheck is received.

Adult Vocational Training Fiscal year 1969, $15,818,000; fiscal year 1970, $25,000,000; increase $9,182,000. The increase consists of:

Explanation	Increase (+) or decrease (−): Amount	Increase (+) or decrease (−): Positions	Total program	Total positions
To provide training which will lead to self-support	+$9,182,000	41	$25,000,000	321

Need for Increase About 50 percent of the 49,000 unemployed, 27,000 underemployed and most of the 55,000 new entrants into the labor force will require job training, either institutional or on-the-job (OJT), before they can become employed. The increased emphasis being placed upon commercial and industrial development of Indian reservations also requires supportive increases in both institutional vocational training and OJT placements.

Program of Work The proposed fiscal year 1970 program would provide $22.4 million of AVT funds for institutional training; an increase of $8.8 million. This program will assist 9,130 institutional trainees of which 7,175 are new entries and will result in 3,935 initial trainee placements in fiscal year 1970, an 86-percent increase over fiscal year 1969.

The proposed fiscal year 1970 OJT program amounts to $2.6 million of adult vocational training funds, an increase of $0.4 million over fiscal year 1969. This program will serve 3,140 trainees during fiscal year 1970 and of these, 2,140 will be new entries into training. The OJT program will be closely coordinated with the commercial and industrial development program.

Examples of Recent Relocation and Adult Vocational Training Accomplishments A graphic presentation of employment assistance output by activity for fiscal years 1968, 1969, and 1970 is shown in Figure 1. It should be noted that 1969 outputs are depressed due to increased subsistence grants put into effect in fiscal year 1969 thereby raising the per-unit cost of training.

Since the inception of the employment assistance program through June 30, 1968, 31,479 single persons or heads of families were placed directly into employment from which 67,522 persons benefited. During fiscal year 1968 there were 3,172 new entries into institutional vocational training increasing the total serviced since enactment of Public Law 959 to 21,253 entries, 13,538 completions, 5,883 discontinuances with 1,832 still in training at the end of the fiscal year. From this training about 13,905 initial skilled job placements have resulted, benefiting approximately 23,640 persons. On-the-job training placements have totaled 8,082 benefiting 24,245 persons.

The family residential training centers at Madera, Calif., and Roswell, N. Mex. are operated under contract by Philco-Ford Corp. and Thiokol Chemical Corp. respectively. As of June 30, 1968, these centers had accommodated 840 entries of which 158 had completed and 170 had discontinued with 486 families still in training. These centers have become extremely popular with Indian people in the lower education and lower skills group.

The placement services recently initiated in the cities of Tulsa, Oklahoma City, and Minneapolis–St. Paul have resulted in 533 job replacements during fiscal year 1968.

On October 12, 1967, a "Joint Statement of Principles of Cooperation" was entered into with the Bureau of Prisons. The objective being to assist Indian offenders to achieve self-dependence upon their release from confinement through help in acquiring needed skills, changes in attitudes

Figure 1

EMPLOYMENT ASSISTANCE SERVICES BY ACTIVITY FISCAL YEAR 1968 (ACTUAL), 1969 (ESTIMATE), AND 1970 (ESTIMATE) SINGLES AND HEADS OF FAMILY SERVED

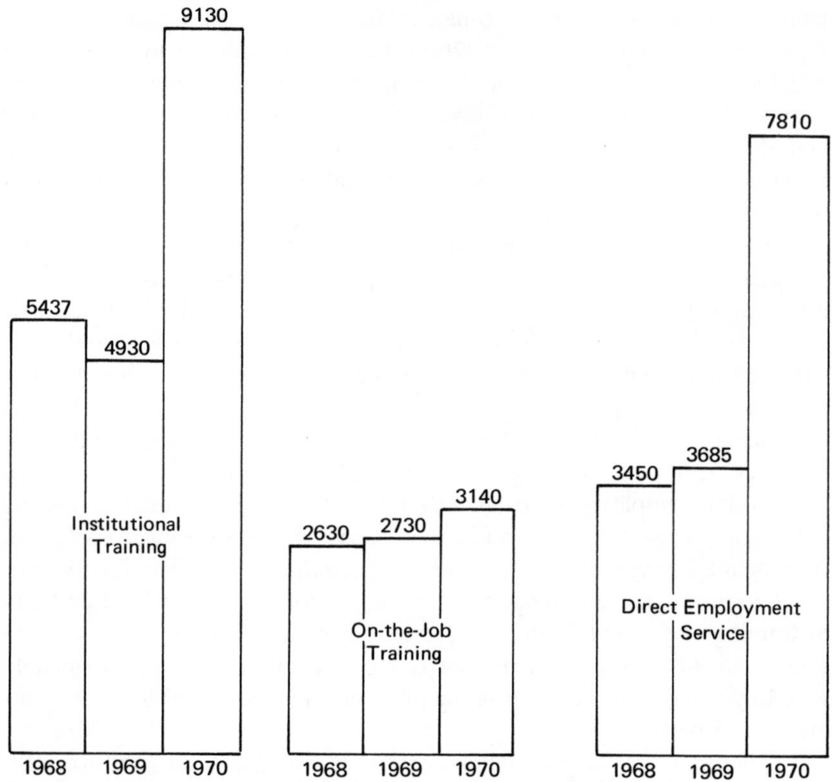

and other resources necessary to adjust acceptably to the community. From October 1967 through June 30, 1968, 61 parolees were assisted. Of these 46 are still in the program and 15 dropped out.

In 1963, 5,108 persons received services in the fields of direct employment, on-the-job training, and institutional training. During 1966 a study was completed of the socioeconomic status of 327 of the 1963 program recipients. The results of that study were published in October 1966 as "A Followup Study of 1963 Recipients of the Services of the Employment Assistance Program, Bureau of Indian Affairs."

As part of ongoing evaluation of employment assistance programs, the Bureau completed another survey of the 1963 recipients of employment assistance. Eighty-five percent of the trainees originally surveyed in 1966 were again interviewed for this 1968 study to determine their present socioeconomic status. Figure 2 illustrates progress of the sample program recipients between 1963 and 1968, as related to the commonly accepted "poverty level" which currently is $3,800 for an average family of five. The progress shown is probably the most important indication of the success of the various employment assistance programs.

Actual average 1966–67 earnings for recipients of all services showed that 186 male recipients were averaging $4,774 per year by 1967 and 93 female recipients were averaging $2,238 for an overall weighted average of $3,929 per year.

Based upon hourly wages being earned in 1968, the average direct employment recipient has a projected annual income of $4,306 and a projected household income of $6,430 (more than head of household employed). The average on-the-job training trainee has a projected annual income of $3,702 and a $7,921 projected household income. The annual income of institutional trainees projects at $4,909 with a household projection of $7,460.

In order to meet training requirements of Indians unable to benefit from either direct placement or conventional training programs, residential family training was initiated by the BIA at Choctaw, Miss., in February 1967. Since then, additional centers have been opened at Madera, Calif., and Roswell, N. Mex. As of December 31, 1968, 1,196 Indian persons have participated in this type of training; 317 have actually completed training and were placed in jobs.

Residential family training has not been in existence long enough to permit extensive evaluation such as that made of adult vocational training and direct employment. However, two preliminary evaluations have been made of the work experience of 120 of the first trainees to complete or partially complete training at the Madera Center.

Madera Employment Training Center: Analysis of Cost to Government

A cost analysis was made of METC graduates and those partially completing training to evaluate the economic benefits that may accrue to the government as a result of the METC program.

The method used in the METC cost analysis was to compare, for the selected group (120 trainees and 69 children), their current status against their status prior to entering the training center, assuming that, if this group had not gone through the training program, their current status would be the same as it was prior to entering the training center. The following cost factors were considered—(1) METC training cost ($389,000), (2) welfare costs, (3) education costs of the children (reservation school costs versus locally administered public schools), (4) health service costs. (Government provides complete health services to reservation Indians.) In addition, the payment of income taxes by gainfully employed graduates of

Figure 2

Percent of 1963 Program Recipients above Poverty Level

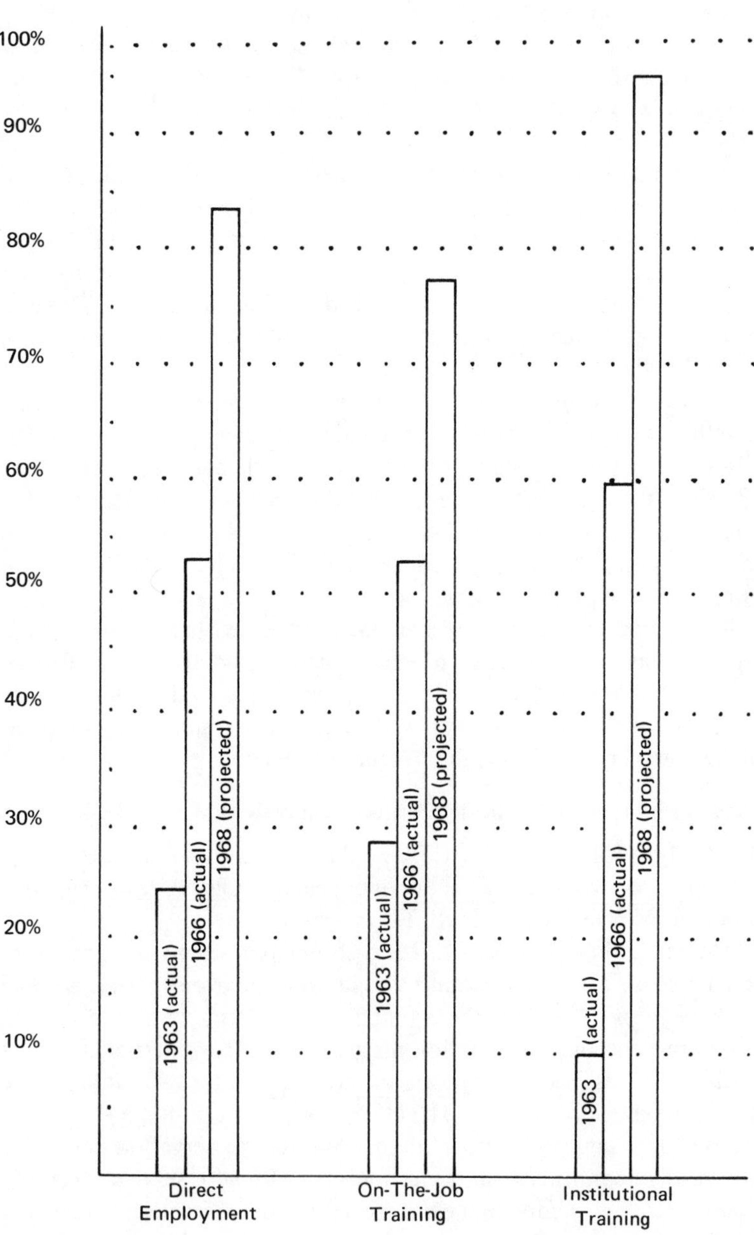

the program was considered as an element which would reduce costs to the government.

Figure 3 illustrates the results of the study. It compares costs of the sample trainees with hypothetical costs assuming they had not undergone training:

Figure 3

Cumulative Cost Comparisons of METC Trainees — With and Without METC

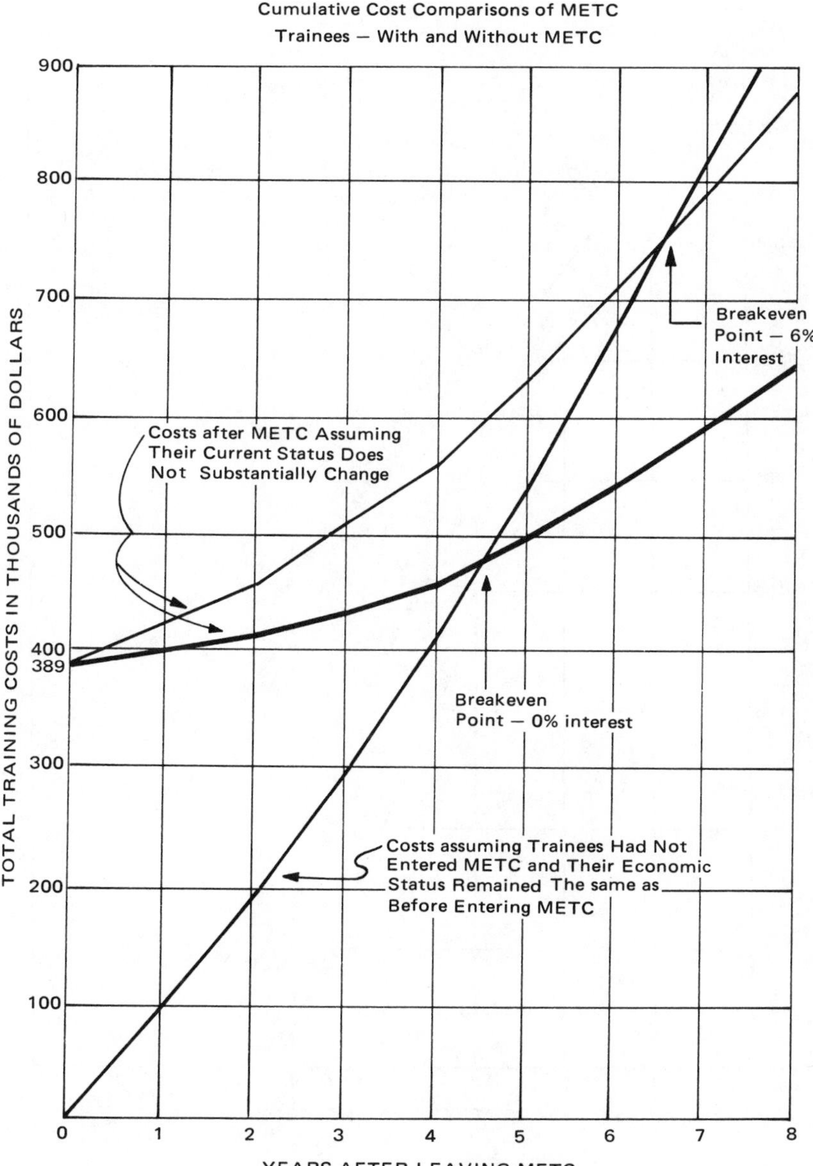

Figure 4

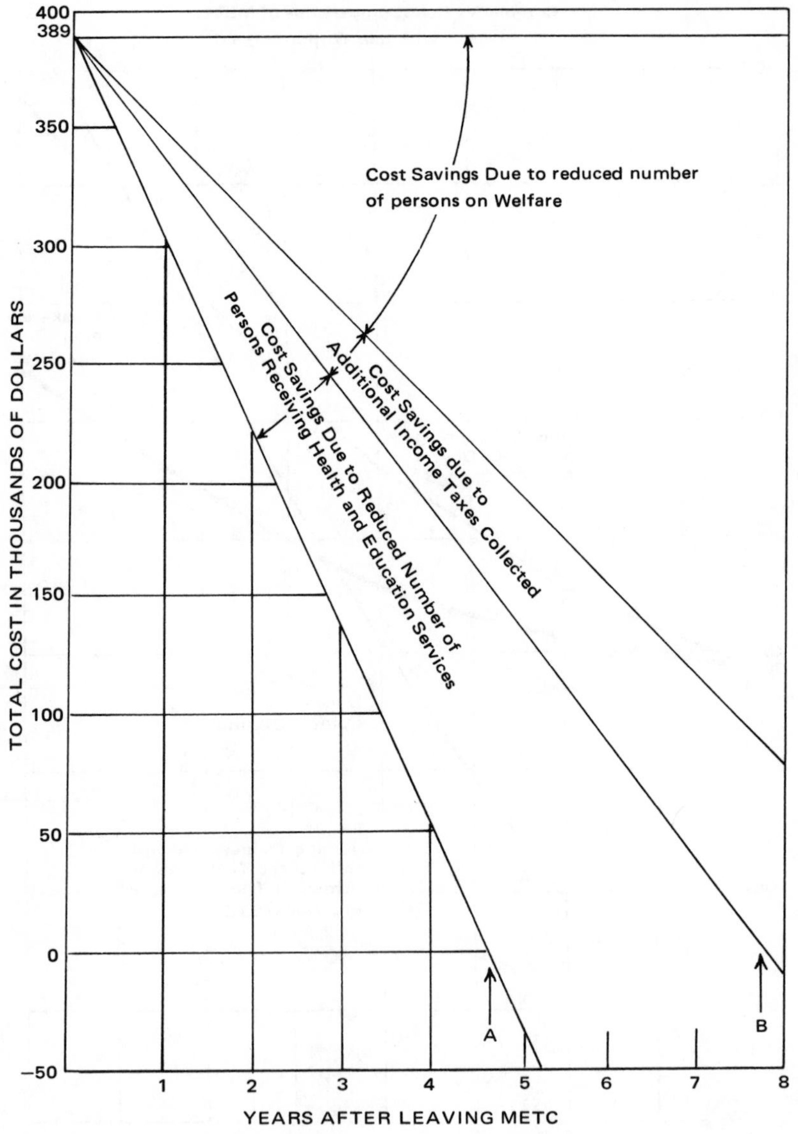
METC TRAINING COSTS LESS WELFARE COSTS REDUCTION, INCOME TAX PAYMENT INCREASE, AND HEALTH AND EDUCATION COST REDUCTIONS
TOTAL COST IN THOUSANDS OF DOLLARS
400
389
350
300
250
200
150
100
50
0
−50
Cost Savings Due to reduced number of persons on Welfare
Cost Savings due to Additional Income Taxes Collected
Cost Savings Due to Reduced Number of Persons Receiving Health and Education Services
A
B
1
2
3
4
5
6
7
8
YEARS AFTER LEAVING METC

Conclusions derived from the cost analysis and illustrated above are:

1. At a 0 percent interest rate the breakeven point is 4.5 years. That is, considering all costs, METC training, welfare, health, and education, the cost to the government after 4.5 years for the METC trainees begins to be less than if they had not received any training.

2. At 6 percent interest the breakeven point is 6.6 years, again considering all costs.

Figure 4 shows the cumulative cost differences between costs with METC training and without METC training assuming no interest charges. It shows that:

1. The government will have obtained benefits equal to its costs 7.7 years after completion of training considering only the immediately realizable cost savings of welfare and negative costs of income taxes. This point is represented at B on the graph.

2. If other costs savings for health and education services are included the breakeven point is 4.5 years (point A). While these savings in health and education costs are not defined as readily as welfare costs or tax payments, they nevertheless do contribute to the economic feasibility of the residential training concept.

METC Cost-Benefit Analysis The METC cost-benefit analysis considered only benefits accruing to the trainee as compared to cost to both the trainee and the government. Using this technique METC training has a benefit-cost ratio of about 3 to 1 assuming a work span of 40 years at the constant wage rate.

The following table on page 412 summarizes the computation of the METC benefit-cost ratio.

Computation of Benefit-Cost Ratio for METC (Per Trainee)

Benefits: Present value of additional annual earnings, per trainee $11,078.00

Prior to METC 45 trainees were employed at an average hourly wage rate of $1.84 or an annual income of $3,800. After METC 57 trainees were employed at an average hourly wage of $2.19 or an annual income of $4,550. Additional annual earnings per trainee =

$$\frac{(4{,}550 \times 57) - (3{,}800 \times 45)}{120} = \$736.25$$

The present value of this amount for 40 years (assuming an average age of trainees is 25 and retirement is at age 65) at a 6% rate of interest is $11,078.

Costs:

Training costs per trainee surveyed 2,806.41

Estimated cost per training "slot" per year is $5,000. Monthly cost per trainee is $417 $\left(\frac{\$5000}{12}\right)$. Average length of training for the 120 trainees surveyed was 6.73 months. Therefore, the average length of training multiplied by the monthly cost yields an average cost per trainee of $2,806.41 (6.73 × $417 = $2,806.41).

Clothing allowance per trainee 94.50

Allowance of $60 per trainee and child; an average of .575 children per trainee.

Foregone earnings per trainee 799.19

Number of trainees working prior to METC times their monthly income times the average length of training divided by the total number of trainees.

$$\frac{45 \times \frac{3{,}800}{12} \times 6.73}{120}$$

Total costs 3,700.10

Benefit-Cost Ratio: $\frac{\$11{,}078}{3{,}700} = 2.994$

CHAPTER 16

PPB, THE AGENCIES AND THE CONGRESS

Senator William Proxmire

THE PPB SYSTEM AND RATIONAL DECISIONMAKING

It is now 4½ years since federal agencies were instructed to develop planning-programing-budgeting systems. During this period there has been great activity in connection with the PPB system and substantial debate concerning its success. Although PPB was a major reform, the concrete of tradition which surrounds the budgetary process has only been cracked. From the outset, it should be emphasized that the PPB system is not a partisan issue. Although initiated by President Johnson, it also is supported by the new administration. As Budget Director Robert Mayo has stated, it is now clear that any administration needs techniques of program evaluation if it is to make effective decisions on resource allocation.

The absence of partisan dispute over the use of PPB points to the recognition by responsible government officials that we must adopt a rational approach to public policy decisions. For, to use PPB to obtain information about the gains and losses to be anticipated from a decision is to demand no more than that the decision be rational. Properly defined, PPB is the most basic and logical planning tool which exists: it provides for the quantitative evaluation of the economic benefits and the economic costs of program alternatives, both now and in the future, in relation to analyses of similar programs.

Any decisionmaker, whether he be the head of a household or the head of a business firm, must rely on the comparison of the gains and costs of his decisions if he is to be successful in achieving his objectives. To ignore the careful consideration of gains and losses is equivalent to saying that he has no objective at all; no goal which he is attempting to achieve. While the objectives of the federal government are less tangible and more

Senator William Proxmire, Democrat from Wisconsin, is Chairman of the Subcommittee on Economy in Government of the Joint Economic Committee. This paper was adapted from a speech given to the Agency Program Planning Officers Group luncheon meeting on Thursday, April 24, 1969 in Washington, D.C.

complex than those of a household or a business firm, they do exist, and analysis should be carried out to determine which of our alternatives will allow us to satisfy these objectives at least cost. I would add that the very effort of attempting to evaluate alternatives is of substantial assistance in determining what our objectives really are.

I have never been able to understand why we are only now getting around to the task of developing such a system of analysis and evaluation. It is even more difficult for me to understand why many official and private groups sometimes object so violently to the application of this logic to public sector choices. Obviously, they themselves demand such information before they buy a new car or trade 15 shares of one common stock for seven shares of another.

The Congressional Budgetary Process

As a U.S. Senator, I also have a strong interest in the potential of PPB for improving decisionmaking in the legislative branch as well as in the executive. This is a very important possibility because, in my view, the legislative resource allocation process is sorely in need of improvement. In a very real sense, the congressional appropriation process is a classic example of an *inexplicit, closed,* and *uninformed* decision process. This does not mean that the executive budgetary process is perfect, or even that it is, in fact, very good on any absolute scale of values. But it is both informed and open compared with the budgetary process which exists in the legislative branch.

In the Congress, with its appropriations committees and subcommittees, there is very little explicit consideration of program objectives or tradeoffs, of alternative means of attaining objectives, or of the benefits and costs of budget proposals this year and in the future. In short, Congress does not really give the budget a meaningful review because it fails to ask the right questions. Perhaps the primary reason for this is the traditional policy of executive branch dealings with the Congress. The Executive Branch comes to Congress with only one budget, with only one set of program proposals, and typically with no quantitative information on the benefits and the costs of even their own proposals. In fact, the only program area in which the Congress is presented with substantive cost-benefit evaluation information is that for water resources development. Since the Flood Control Act of 1936, project proposals in this area have been accompanied by a benefit-cost ratio. This number enables congressmen and senators to get some sense of the economic value of the choices which they are making and of the implicit costs involved when they choose to accept a project with a low benefit-cost ratio despite the fact that one displaying a higher ratio is available. (Even so, the usefulness of these analyses has been impaired by the use of artificially low discount rates in computing the present values of benefits over time. This has made bad projects look far better than they should.)

A second reason why the Congress has performed so badly in the budgetary and appropriations area has to do with the interests of congressmen and senators. Many in the legislative branch have little interest in or patience for careful deliberations on budgetary matters. The careful consideration of alternatives requires much effort and concentrated study of the relative merits and demerits, the costs and the gains, of alternative policy proposals. This is hard and grubby work. Those not used to thinking in such terms find it easier simply to rely on the executive agencies. Unfortunately, these agencies are often more interested in selling their programs, regardless of merit, than in having Congress analyze them.

A final reason for Congress' poor performance in this area is the severe staffing constraints under which the legislative branch operates. Currently, we do not have the staff either to interpret or to evaluate the analysis done by the executive branch were it presented to us, nor does Congress have the staff to do policy analysis of its own. Indeed, in my judgment, this is one of the primary barriers to the ability of the Congress to fulfill its mandate as controller of the public purse. Dr. Jack Carlson, who is Assistant Director of the Bureau of the Budget, stated this well in his testimony before my Subcommittee:

> You [the Congress] have some outstanding people who can provide program evaluation, but very few. I frankly think that Congress is not very well equipped to provide that evaluation.

Nonetheless, even if the interest and the staff existed, there would still be substantial organizational problems to hinder an effective public expenditure decision process. A primary difficulty is the organization and structure of the appropriations committees. In considering appropriations requests from the executive, we in the Congress have organized ourselves into appropriations committees and subcommittees with each subcommittee having control over a particular portion of the budget. The subcommittees consider the executive's proposed budget, deliberate on it, perhaps amend it, and ultimately report out an appropriations bill. The structure of this arrangement is such that the powerful people on the appropriations subcommittees—the chairmen—almost inevitably desire to see the budgets which they oversee rise. They are not interested in careful scrutiny and evaluation of their own budgets. Other budgets should be cut, of course, but everyone knows that defense (or agriculture, or space, or public works, as the case may be) is "absolutely necessary" to the further growth and prosperity of the nation.

I happen to be on the steering committee of the Democratic Party. It is this committee which assigns the Democratic membership to the available committee vacancies. In the deliberations of this committee, there are enormous pressures to place those senators whose states benefit from, say, public works appropriations on either the Senator Interior Committee or the Public Works Subcommittee of the Appropriations Committee. In fact, a senator who is from a state which benefits substantially from these programs is, at least in the short term, rather clearly serving his own best interests and those of at least some of his constituents if he attains a seat on one of these committees. The net result of all of this, however, is that the committee structure develops a built-in bias toward higher budgets. Because the people who serve on each committee have an interest in seeing the budget for which they are responsible increase, they often fail to encourage careful evaluation and analysis of expenditures.

An example of the bias which results from this process is clearly seen by observing the state membership of the Senate Committee on Interior and Insular Affairs. The Democratic members on that committee are from Washington, New Mexico, Nevada, Idaho, Utah, North Dakota, South Dakota, Wisconsin, Montana, and Alaska. The Republican membership is from Colorado, Idaho, Arizona, Wyoming, Oregon, Alaska, and Oklahoma. With the exception of my able colleague, Gaylord Nelson, there is no senator on this committee representing a state east of the Mississippi River. A similar kind of situation holds in the Public Works Subcommittee of the Senate Appropriations Committee. The Democratic membership of this committee represents Louisiana, Georgia, Arkansas, Washington, Florida, Mississippi, Rhode Island, Nevada, West Virginia, and Wyoming. Again, a substantial concentration of senators from those southern and western states which receive major water resource appropriations. Much the same is true with the Republicans on that subcommittee, although I should add that at least two of these are from the eastern states—Maine and New Jersey.

Largely as an outgrowth of this built-in committee bias, the relationships between the staffs of the committees and subcommittees and their counterparts in the executive agencies is hardly one of arms-length dealings. The degree of mutuality of interest between the executive staff and those on legislative branch committees is substantial. I would add that this problem is not peculiar to legislative-executive relationships. The serious colleagiality between Budget Bureau examiners who work on the military budget and their counterparts in the Pentagon has recently been the cause of much concern.

Toward an Improved Appropriation Process

Given the institutional constraints which inhibit change in this situation, is there anything which can be done to improve the congressional budgetmaking process? In my judgment, there are a number of important steps which can be taken. Many of them entail the bringing to bear of additional PPB-type information on the appropriations process. Congressmen and senators who are concerned with national priorities and efficiency in government must have the information and data necessary to raise and debate the right basic questions about program effectiveness and worth.

Building a Capability to Ask the Right Questions: The First Step The most basic and elementary step which the Congress needs to take in improving the appropriation process is to develop a capability to ask the right questions. Whether this means a substantial increase in staff capability or an independent office of economic analysis or an increase in the PPB capability of the General Accounting Office or of the Joint Economic Committee is undetermined. What is clear, however, is that the Congress cannot respond to the demands of the people, cannot establish proper national priorities, cannot improve the quality of its decisions, cannot properly scrutinize the executive budget unless it equips itself to ask the right questions.

The right basic questions are those having to do with the outputs of a program and its inputs and the economic values of each. They are questions concerning the total costs of program decisions, and not just the given year costs. They are questions having to do with the distribution of a program's costs and benefits among the people. We must, for example, determine the economic losses which will be sustained (or gains which will be foregone) if program X is reduced by 10 or 50 percent, or increased by 10 or 50 percent.

The following are a few examples of the kinds of questions which I have in mind:

- What, for example, are the real national security costs of removing Southeast Asia from the primary defense perimeter and what are the budgetary savings from its removal? On the basis of very little evidence and information, I am inclined to say that the costs of removing Southeast Asia may well exceed the value of the budgetary savings which we would experience. However, I cannot make a rational decision on this matter, nor can my colleagues in the Congress, unless we have the best analysis available on the costs and gains of such a policy alternative.

• What would be the national security impact of a 30-percent reduction of total U.S. ground forces, and what would be the budgetary savings from this reduction? An article in the *Congressional Quarterly*[1] claimed that $10 billion could be cut from the defense budget with no loss of national security effectiveness. Over 50 percent of this suggested $10 billion cut was in the area of manpower. The efficiency of the Department of Defense in the handling of manpower policy is very low. Indeed, the national security costs of reducing ground forces by 30 percent may well be zero. In any case, it is evidence—data and information on the costs and gains of that sort of decision—which Congress requires if the level of rationality is to be increased.

• What are the total costs of eliminating a nuclear carrier force with all of its required support from our existing 15-carrier complex? What would be the loss in national security? How much elementary and secondary education could we purchase for the dollar cost of the new carrier?

• What national economic benefits would the nation sacrifice and what national costs would it avoid, if the Trinity River project is not constructed? This project involves the creation of a channel from Dallas-Fort Worth to the Gulf of Mexico. Some observers have argued that it would be cheaper to move Dallas-Fort Worth to the Gulf than to construct this channel.

• What benefits are available from manned space flights that are not available from unmanned flights? What are the incremental costs of manned over unmanned flights? The space agency is now asking us for funds for 10 moon landings and for the exploration of still additional planets. Those planets are going to be there 10 years from now, or even 20 years from now. On what basis can we justify the current expenditure of these funds in view of the other social objectives which we would obtain if these funds were not allocated to the space program? Moreover, some scientists believe that all of the information that we need from space flights can be obtained from unmanned flights, that manned flights are not necessary for this purpose. We need hard analysis of this decision.

• What are the real costs to the American economy of specific protectionist measures that are sought by industry, such as the oil import program? What, in hard economic terms, do similar measures by other countries cost us? Such information is essential for effective bargaining.

• How much do we spend to maintain the military capability to keep open important transportation bottlenecks, such as the Panama Canal, Gibraltar, or the Straits of Malacca? What costs would be incurred if such bottlenecks were not open?

• What is the relationship between resources put into federal criminal investigation, prosecution and judicial activities and the outputs of those activities in terms of cases actually processed? What are the benefits obtainable through federal payments for increasing the number of state and local law enforcement personnel versus those obtainable from increasing the support available to existing personnel? In particular, to what extent are trained police officers now used less than optimally because of a lack of subprofessionals, dictating equipment, vehicles, cameras, or other fairly elementary support items?

• Which policy of preschool education produces greater benefits: a policy which is going to reach all poverty children to at least some extent, or a program of intensive work with fewer children?
• What economic losses will be incurred in the future—in terms of loss of productivity and increased welfare costs—that could be prevented by child nutritional and health care programs? How do the benefits available from such programs compare with the benefits available from further extension of the medicare program? For each type of program, upon whom would the costs and benefits fall or accrue?
• What are the costs and benefits involved in the construction of mass transit systems in cities which do not presently have them? What should be included in our calculation of benefits, and how accurate can we be in our judgments? In the northeastern United States, are the costs of constructing a high-speed ground transit system for intermediate intercity journeys less than those of constructing additional airport capacity?
• What is the likely yield from the government's investment in fast breeder reactor R. & D., and how does it compare with the return that the relevant private sector would demand? Are there possibilities for international cooperation that would avoid the overlap between this work and similar work in other countries?

These are the kinds of questions that Congress needs to ask, and for which responsible executive branch agencies must develop and supply answers. In my judgment, concerned congressmen and senators can reduce much gross waste from our budgets if we can first develop enough information to ask the right questions, and second, have the cooperation of the executive branch in getting answers.

In this same vein, it seems to me that the recent ABM discussion in the Congress is one of the few examples of careful policy analysis by the legislative branch. It is a case in which Congress—the whole Congress—was asking the right questions about the benefits which will be achieved from this decision, about the costs which it will entail. As in good policy analysis, the question of objectives was explicitly discussed and the interrelationships between the program proposal and the attainment of objectives was investigated with some care. It is my belief that with more PPB-type information, the Congress can do this kind of policy analysis on increasing numbers of issues and expenditure proposals.

Gaining Access to Appropriate Data and Analysis: A Second Step In addition to developing the capability to ask the right questions, the Congress needs to be provided with certain basic kinds of PPB-type information on a continuing basis. The executive branch must be asked to develop this information and submit it to the Congress in appropriate form. The Bureau of the Budget must assume the leadership in this effort. Let me describe a few specific kinds of information which are essential to a more open and explicit congressional decision process.

OVERVIEW INFORMATION The first of these items of analysis and data I will call "Overview Information." We need a display of each program in the federal budget and an estimate of its benefit-cost ratio—that is, the efficiency impact of that program. We also need information on the distributional pattern of project outputs by income level, race, and geographic location—its equity impact. This information is often as important to those of us in the legislative branch as is the efficiency information. We can frame good policy only if we have knowledge of who we are helping when we appropriate money and who is bearing the cost. Even though many of these estimates would have to be rough, they would generate a major improvement in the appropriation process by giving Congress a better perspective on the probable impacts of these public expenditures. I urge the agencies to develop this kind of information, and I urge the Bureau of the Budget to collect and supply it to the Congress for individual programs and in summary form. I should note that in recent hearings before my Subcommittee on Economy in Government, Dr. Jack Carlson of the Bureau of the Budget presented us with a sample format for this overview information and some preliminary data. The format is an excellent one. We now need the calculations to be made and the tables completed.

BUDGET PROJECTIONS A second body of information which Congress requires is out-year budget information. For each program, what are the expenditures to which we are committed over the next five years because of decisions which we have already made? For each new program proposal, what are the total 5- or 10-year costs entailed by the decision? An example of what happens when we do not have this kind of information is the Higher Education Act of 1965 (Public Law 89–329). In this legislation, we provided thousands of student scholarships for the first year without really recognizing that to maintain our commitment the funding would have to double in the second year, triple in the third year, and quadruple in the fourth. By keeping the program at its present level, and refusing to honor the implied commitment, we have placed college and university administrators in an impossible position. They now either have to reduce the scholarship aid for the class which entered school last year, or they have to completely eliminate scholarship aid from this source for students currently entering school. If Congress had been oriented towards explicit consideration of the future costs of present decisions I think it would have avoided this bind.

I urge the executive branch to formulate a framework and procedure to develop this out-year budget information across the federal budget and to present it to the Congress. Moreover, I would propose that the president use the out-year budget framework which is developed to convey his budgetary priorities to the Congress. The numbers which he would place in the appropriate slots in this framework would not commit him, and would change over time. However, they would show the level of program outlays for which commitments have already been made as well as the budgetary areas to which the president would like to see uncommitted funds devoted. This would give the Congress an ongoing description of how the president hoped to allocate the federal budget over the next several years and how much discretionary room remains in the budget if existing laws remain unchanged. This would give the Congress a bird's-eye view of the executive's plans and priorities. I would hope that the Bureau of the Budget could play the leadership role in developing this information.

QUANTITATIVE ANALYSIS OF ALTERNATIVES The final type of information which is essential to improvements in Congress' performance of its budgetary function entails the quantitative economic analysis of alternatives. As stated earlier, when the administration comes to Congress with a new program, it typically comes with a single recommendation. If Congress is to effectively carry out its decisionmaking role, it must do more than simply accept or reject an administrative recommendation. The Congress needs to be presented with a number of alternatives which would achieve a given objective. These alternatives should be accompanied by quantitative analyses of the benefits and the costs of each. It is only slightly less than absurd that the Congress is expected to participate meaningfully in the policymaking process when it is not asked to consider alternatives, but only to approve or disapprove or to amend slightly at the margins. This problem is especially severe in the area of defense spending and military budgets. The development of a changed policy on the part of the executive branch in this area will, I suspect, be long in coming. Current policies are rooted in the concrete of both tradition and realistic gamesmanship. Nevertheless, it is something that we should work hard to change.

THE FURTHER DEVELOPMENT OF THE PPB SYSTEM

All of these improvements in PPB in the legislative branch are tied to the further development of the PPB system by the executive.

As is obvious, I am a strong supporter of program analysis. I also think the efforts that have been made recently to strengthen the process are important. In particular, the narrowing of the number of issues which receive special analytic attention was an important step, as is the insistence that these issues deal with the larger budget questions. Hopefully, agencies will be able to respond with more quantitative and more pointed analyses on the reduced list of issues. I also support the goal of increasing the role of agencies in the PPB process.

In my judgment, of high priority in the further development of the PPB system is the issuance by the Bureau of the Budget of a number of guideline documents to insure that economic analysis is consistently applied to public expenditures throughout the federal government. Last year, the Subcommittee on Economy in Government learned of the enormous divergence in the discounting analysis of public investment programs. The interest rates used ranged from zero percent in some programs to 20 percent in others. In testimony before the subcommittee, we learned from recognized economists that the discount rate to be used by public agencies should be at least 8 percent. This would eliminate the economic waste of diverting resources from the private sector, where they are producing at least this return, to the public sector where, if rates of discount lower than this are applied, they will be likely to produce less. As stated earlier, I am well aware that the equity aspects are as important as the efficiency ones. However, one should not think that programs with low rates of return automatically produce equity, because they do not. Nor do I doubt our ability to find programs which meet both criteria.

In a report of the Subcommittee on Economy in Government,[2] we recommended that (1) the Bureau of the Budget should require all agencies to develop and implement consistent and appropriate discounting procedures on all federal investments entailing future costs or benefits; and (2) the Bureau of the Budget, in conjunction with other appropriate government agencies, should immediately undertake a study to estimate the weighted average opportunity-cost of private spending which is displaced when the federal government finances its expenditures. In response to these recommendations, the Bureau of the Budget has developed a guideline document to insure consistency in discounting practices across the federal government. In my judgment, that document represents a major step in the right direction.

On the basis of recent hearings before the Subcommittee on Economy in Government, I judge that federal government practice in benefit estimation is also extremely disparate. The issuance of a guideline document on the procedures for benefit estimation is also necessary. We need to develop a consistent concept of program benefits viewed from a national accounting stance. We need to establish a consistent procedure for handling benefits such as regional effects and secondary impacts, which are not appropriately considered from a national economic viewpoint.

In addition to increasing the role of consistent analysis through the issuance of guideline documents, the executive branch should build explicit procedures for the ongoing evaluation and appraisal of programs into new and experimental social programs. The Congress should require that provision for ongoing evaluation be included in appropriations for these programs. We know little about the kinds of inputs and program structures which will yield the outputs we desire and if we ever hope to generate improvements in programs in the areas of education, health, labor retraining, and so on, we must have followup evaluation. This information must be available to Congress on an ongoing basis as these programs evolve.

Finally, we need a new budget analysis which breaks down and evaluates the economic impact of tax expenditures, as well as direct expenditures. In testimony before the Joint Economic Committee, Joseph Barr, former Secretary of the Treasury, pointed out that the special provisions, exceptions, and deductions in the federal tax structure cause an enormous reallocation of the nation's resources. The volume of these tax expenditures is huge; in some of the functional categories of the federal budget they outweigh direct expenditures. So far we have little analysis of these expenditures; we know very little about the kinds of outputs which they are producing, and the kinds of resource diversions they entail. The federal budget should include information on these items, as well as the information which it currently includes. I call upon the Bureau of the Budget to develop a new budget format to include a description and analysis of both direct and tax expenditures.

NOTES

[1] *Congressional Quarterly,* June 28, 1968.

[2] U.S. Congress, Joint Economic Committee, Subcommittee on Economy in Government, "Economic Analysis of Public Investment Decisions: Interest Rate Policy for Discounting Analysis," September 1969.

CHAPTER 17

PUBLIC EXPENDITURE ANALYSIS AND THE INSTITUTIONS OF THE EXECUTIVE BRANCH

Fred S. Hoffman

INTRODUCTION

The planning, programing, and budgeting (PPB) system, as the name suggests, was conceived as a system of interrelated elements. The system was intended to improve federal decisionmaking about resource allocation in several important ways. The system is designed to:

- Compare the efficiency of alternative ways of carrying on government resource-using or resource-affecting activities, as the market tests the efficiency of private resource-using activities.
- Relate tests of efficiency to the proper objectives of public action (not necessarily the historical or organizational objectives of government agencies).
- Present major issues for decision in a useful way to high officials who have no time to be specialists on even a fraction of the matters they must decide.

To accomplish the desired improvements in governmental decisionmaking, PPB has strived to introduce or strengthen three aids to the making of choices about resource allocations:

Analysis Comparisons of the cost and effectiveness of alternative ways of achieving the objectives of public policy.

Program Budgeting Presentation of the agency budget in a classification system related to the major program choices to be made.

Planning Presentation of information about the future implications of current program choices for cost and effectiveness beyond the budget year.

Analysis, program budgeting, and planning are distinct elements of PPB, and might have been introduced separately. Moreover, their development has proceeded at different rates during the three years since the introduction of PPB, and in response to different stimuli and impediments.

Although analysis, in my view, is at the heart of PPB, I believe that there were good reasons for linking the three elements. The reasons are

Fred S. Hoffman is vice president of Laird Systems, Inc., in Los Angeles, Calif. Until January 1969, he was Assistant Director of the U.S. Bureau of the Budget.

related to the nature of systems analysis and to the nature of decisionmaking in a large organization such as the federal government. The paper first reviews the nature and origin of systems analysis and then turns to the relations among the three elements as they have developed in PPB.

THE ORIGINS OF SYSTEMS ANALYSIS IN NATIONAL SECURITY PLANNING

The PPB system is extending to the other major departments and agencies of the executive branch the approach to resource management developed by Secretary McNamara in the Department of Defense. Systems analysis played a central role in the system that evolved in the Defense Department, and an understanding of its salient characteristics is necessary to understand the PPB system.

Systems analysis is a term whose meaning has been eroded by very wide and diverse usage. The sense of the term most relevant to PPB is the one that describes the approach to national security problems developed during the early 1950s. The approach evolved in response to the planning problems of the early post-World War II period; it was not the result of a grand intellectual design.

Operations analysis in World War II provided the immediate antecedents for systems analysis. The successful application of applied mathematics, physical science, and systematic data collection to tactical problems of increasing complexity, created the presumption that people trained in these activities could contribute to postwar planning. The air force, in 1946, at the urging of Secretary of War for Air Lovett (later to become Secretary of Defense) and under the leadership of Gen. H. H. Arnold, created Project RAND, later to become the RAND Corporation, to bring together people of the sort who had done wartime operations analysis, in order to advise the air force on its research and development activities.

The nature of the problem facing the air force in 1946 was vastly different and more difficult than the wartime operations analysis problems had been. The postwar problem was one of maintaining for an indefinite period, peacetime readiness for combat, rather than conducting ongoing combat operations. After 1946, the problem became one of making decisions that would shape our military forces for many years in the future, subject to the resource constraints encountered in a peacetime economy. This was a far less determinate problem than that of choosing the best search tactics for a destroyer hunting a submarine, or firing tactics for a fighter in pursuit of a bomber.

The indeterminancy of the postwar planning problem was augmented by the postwar technological revolution. In addition to increasing the urgency of national security questions and the cost of providing and maintaining military forces, the flood of new technology so changed the character of prospective conflict that very little past military experience could be considered relevant to the problem of deterring World War III, or of protecting the United States if conflict should come. Under the circumstances, it was necessary to gather such data as might be available from physical science, engineering analysis, and past military operations, and from these, to synthesize by analytic means, predictions and comparisons that would be useful for policy decisions.

The analysis that developed in response to this need could be no respector either of organizational boundaries or of the limits of traditional disciplines. The analysis of air defense could not stop within the limits of a fighter squadron, for fighter aircraft became dependent on information provided by a radar network connected by an elaborate communications system. In the choice of bombers, also, the wide range of alternative bomber designs offered by technology made it necessary to take account of the overseas bases or tanker aircraft needed in larger quantities by the shorter range aircraft, and also of the greater vulnerability to enemy attack involved in operating from overseas bases. And, as the linkages among elements of the problem forced the boundaries of the analysis outward, more and more diverse skills were required in intimate interaction during the course of an analysis.

One important effect of the systems approach is to call into question the narrower, organizationally oriented objectives of many programs. During the 1950s, for example, there was an important reorientation of air defense to take account of the growing importance of protecting the country by deterrence of attack rather than by defeating the attack if it came. Under the conditions of that period, the highest priority tasks of the air defense system became the provision of warning to the strategic bombing forces, permitting them to survive a surprise attack and retaliate. Such reorientations of objectives have generally followed a long series of analyses with steadily widening perspectives. Thus, the neat, logical characterization of analysis as beginning with a clarification of objectives is somewhat misleading.

In reality, systems analysts have more often than not begun by accepting current objectives and later proposed changes in them only after repeated analyses of broadening scope have shown objectives to be in conflict with one another. Certainly, the most fruitful systems analyses have not indulged in argument about objectives for argument's sake, but have been forced to review existing objectives and priorities as inconsistencies among them have appeared or because they proved to be inappropriate under changing conditions. The analytical process is an educational process revealing new objectives and often new means of achieving them.

In summary, then, systems analysis was a response to the complexity of the national security planning problems encountered after World War II. It is not a discipline or a technique, but rather a style for dealing with complex problems of choice. The style is characterized by two salient characteristics:

Explicitness From its origins in the application of scientific method to the analysis of military operations, systems analysis has emphasized explicit treatment of objectives, assumptions of fact, criteria for choice, and above all, the alternatives among which choice is to be made. Explicit statement permits reproducibility of results, and by isolating points of disagreement, permits the policy process to converge to agreement.

Orientation to Decision The scope of the analysis is determined by the scope of the decision. The systems analyst attempts to include all those elements which interact strongly in determining the implications of a choice among the alternatives, regardless of the boundaries of academic disciplines or of bueaucratic organization. Such an approach inevitably calls into question existing objectives from time to time and suggests new policies for inclusion among the set of alternatives. It also calls for consideration of effects that go beyond a 1-year budget period.

THE APPLICABILITY OF SYSTEMS ANALYSIS TO DOMESTIC PROGRAM CHOICES

A Misleading Distinction

Those who question the relevance of the experience in the Department of Defense to the analysis of domestic programs have often done so on the grounds that quantitative analysis is appropriate for programs that are essentially concerned with *things* such as aircraft, missiles, and radar, but that it is not appropriate for programs which deal with *people.*

This distinction is misleading, first of all, because it is not true that domestic programs are concerned entirely with people any more than that national security programs are devoid of such considerations. Deterrence of war, the central concern of national security policy, is a question of how people and governments will react. Analysis has been useful in decision-making about the requirements to maintain deterrence, despite the fact that no one has devised a quantitative, objective measure of deterrence. Similarly, analysis can be useful in allocating resources among programs to combat disease, despite the fact that no way exists to establish a socially accepted dollar value for a human life.

Secondly, domestic programs are far from devoid of questions involving large, expensive, and long-lived items of equipment for capital. Schools, hospitals, dams, air traffic control radars, and highways are all objects of decisionmaking about domestic programs.

There are, nevertheless, real and important distinctions between domestic and national security programs from the point of view of analysis. These differences stem largely, I believe, from differences in the basis for the government's role.

The Basis for the Role of Government in Resource Allocation

Economists call national security a "public good." A public good is one that is either consumed in common or not consumed at all. Either nuclear war is deterred for all of us, or it is deterred for none of us. In the case of a private good, like shoes, for example, if I buy a pair of shoes there is one less pair available for use by everyone else. In the case of national security, my enjoyment of the benefits of peace does not detract from that of others. It is therefore impossible to use a private market mechanism to determine the amount of a public good to be provided. Everyone would sit back and wait for everyone else to pay for his security. The decision about the level of spending on national security must, consequently, be made by government.

Examples of public goods may be found also in domestic programs, although national security is probably the purest and most extreme example of a public good. Education provides an example of a good that has both public and private elements. Individuals want education for themselves and for their children in order to increase the quality of themselves and their earning power. But there are also a variety of public motives for education. In particular, the requirement that a self-governing electorate achieve certain minimal educational standards, establishes education as at least partly a public good and one about which public decisions are, therefore, required.

In the domestic area, there are a number of additional government roles in resources allocation decisions. Since 1946, the government has had a statutory responsibility for the maintenance of full employment. More recently, the maintenance of a suitable growth rate without excessive inflation has become a widely recognized responsibility of government. There are, however, a number of more specific roles for government which bear upon the analysis of government programs.

Dealing with Spillover Effects Spillover effects exist when the consequences of a decision affect not only the individual making the decision, but others as well, and the decisionmaker need not or cannot take into account his effect on others. Spillovers become more important as we live ever closer to our fellow citizens. When John Doe burns leaves with a prevailing wind toward Richard Roe's garden party down the street, a spillover effect exists. The two individuals have conflicting interests if John Doe finds burning leaves preferable to having them removed; but this is not the essence of the problem. Richard Roe may be bothered enough by the smoke to be willing to have the leaves removed, but if there exists no social mechanism which will permit this, the spillover situation is an appropriate subject for governmental action. (In the case of near neighbors there exists a variety of informal mechanisms by which this situation may be resolved; in the more general case, this is not so.)

In the particular example, the government might either subsidize the removal of the leaves until removal is so cheap that John Doe will prefer it to burning, or it might tax their burning. In place of monetary incentives, government often resorts to regulatory action to deal with spillover effect. Each way will induce John Doe to act in a way that takes account of the effect of his actions on others. Less trivial examples than leaf burning are actual environmental pollution, traffic congestion, etc.

The effects that spill over need not always be bad. Examples of beneficial spillovers occur in unpatentable research activities, social welfare programs which not only benefit the individual but reduce the costs to society by making him less of a public charge and less likely to break the law, etc. Spillover effects it can be seen, are closely related to public goods, and like them, require public action.

Making the Distribution of Income and Opportunity More Equal For the last 35 years government has become more and more concerned to increase the equality of income and especially of opportunity, to limit the risks of old age or ill health, and to compensate for the handicaps of poverty, racial discrimination, or disability. There has been a great variety of programs with these objectives, including direct transfers of income, food subsidy programs, social insurance programs, training programs, programs to provide social services, and more recently, medical insurance and assistance.

Managing Publicly Owned Resources As a result of history, political preferences, or economic factors, the government owns a wide variety of resources and provides to the public many different kinds of services. The publicly owned resources range from the electromagnetic frequency spectrum to the highways and federally owned mineral and forest lands. The services provided include such large-scale and diverse activities as the post office, the federal health service establishments, and the FAA's air traffic control facilities. Government is expected to manage its resources and provide the services it is engaged in in an efficient manner. However, there is very rarely, if ever, a market test of the efficiency of the government's activities, and since the government is very often a monopolist, profit-maximizing behavior would not lead to a socially desirable result.

Large-Scale Risk-Bearing and Innovation There are many activities which would be socially desirable but which involve operation on a scale beyond that which is feasible for private enterprise, or that involve risks that are too large for an individual decisionmaker to assume but that may be tolerable when spread over society as a whole. Examples that illustrate both the problems of scale and risk are attempts to stem the decay of central cities (urban renewal requires in addition to the scale and risk-spreading available to government, the exercise of government's power of eminent domain) and attempts to open major new areas of technology such as nuclear power. These activities must be carefully examined and periodically reviewed to insure that they do not merely provide windfalls for private activities that would be undertaken even without government subsidies.

Increasing the Efficiency of Private Markets Government attempts to increase the efficiency of private economic activity in a number of ways, including the strengthening of competition, and the regulation of injurious trade practices. Especially important in this role, however, is the provision of information to labor, businessmen, and consumers, permitting them to behave more efficiently.

Significant Differences between the Analysis of National Security Programs and Domestic Programs

The principal difference between the application of systems analysis to domestic programs and to national security programs is to be found in the differences between the government's role in these two areas. The overriding objective in national security, as discussed above, is the provision of a public good. Most domestic programs of any significance, however, are involved in more than one of the several government roles discussed above. The multiplicity of government's roles in domestic programs is reflected in a multiplicity of objectives for individual programs, greatly complicating the analysis of the program and the comparison among alternatives.

Consider, as an extreme example, programs for the education for the disadvantaged, such as Title I of the Elementary and Secondary Education Act of 1964. Virtually all of the government roles are involved. Like other educational programs, this one is intended to provide the public good of a better educated electorate; it is clearly an attempt to redistribute resources in a way that will equalize the opportunity of the children involved; to the extent that it leads them to become more productive members of the labor force, it will increase the efficiency of private markets; and, to the extent that it results in less dependence on social services and less frequent criminal behavior, reducing the cost of social services and law enforcement, it will realize spillover benefits. Moreover, it is likely that aid furnished to local school districts to improve the education of the disadvantaged partly displaces local resources for that purpose (although such is counter to the intent of the legislation). Therefore, it represents a contribution to a developing role of the federal government not discussed above, that of supporting state and local governments with federal revenues.

Clearly this large program has very complicated objectives. Some of them are joint products, others are in conflict with each other. But whether they are mutually reinforcing or in conflict, the comparison of an alternative way of improving the status of disadvantaged children with the Title I programs, would involve comparisons in many dimensions. Since there is no hope of finding a common unit to measure the public good of a better-educated electorate against the benefits due to redistribution of income or increases in individual productivity, it is highly unlikely that an analysis of alternatives will result in a conclusive preference for one program over another.

This complexity is also encountered in the analysis of national security programs, but to a lesser degree. Although the objectives of national security programs are simpler, there are some respects in which analysis in that area encounters more severe limitations than in the domestic area. Since the predominant objective in national security programs is the provision of a public good, and since a public good cannot be evaluated in the marketplace, it follows that the outputs of national security programs cannot be measured in terms of dollars. Consequently, the Department of Defense has developed cost-effectiveness analysis. Cost is used as a measure of the inputs to the program, but the outputs are measured in physical terms. This means, for example, that one cannot compare the efficiency of resources spent on improving our Strategic Air Command against resources spent on improving our forces for guerrilla war. It also means that analysis must be supplemented by judgment to arrive at the desirable level of spending on national security programs as a whole.

To the extent that government domestic programs are involved in the provision of public goods, or the redistribution of income or opportunity, the same limitations apply. However, many government programs are predominantly concerned with spillover effects, with the provision of marketable goods or services by the government, or with improvements in the efficiency of private markets. In these cases, analysis can aspire to go beyond cost-effectiveness analysis to measure both costs and at least some benefits in dollars. Even in such cases, however, the analysis is limited by a variety of conceptual problems and data gaps.

The lack of sound theory and data with which to analyze most domestic programs points to another difference between systems analysis in the national security and domestic program areas. For over 20 years, the Department of Defense and the military services have spent large sums of money on systems analysis of national security choices. As a result, there exist substantial analytic organizations within the Department of Defense as well as large independent ones outside. Large numbers of highly trained people from many disciplines have for years been working together on the analysis of national security programs. They have developed the data and analytic models needed to evaluate programs. Prior to 1965 this situation was a very rare exception in most domestic agencies. As a result, the newly developing analytic organizations in the domestic agencies must begin with very little in the way of accumulated knowledge or experience in the program areas concerned.

Finally, and in some way perhaps the most pervasive of the differences between the analysis of national security and domestic programs, is the greater political sensitivity of decisions about domestic programs. Although individuals, special interest groups, and sectional interests do sometimes play a role in national security decisions, that role is circumscribed by the overriding common interest in providing the nation's security. In most domestic programs the question of who benefits is much more important. Analysis can shed light on the distribution of the benefits among the beneficiaries, but the resolution of conflicts among individual interests must be done by the political process. In the leaf-burning example above, analysis may reveal that either a tax on leaf burning or a subsidy to leaf removal would be a more efficient solution than allowing the leaf burning to continue, but analysis will not be able to choose between a subsidy for leaf removal, borne by the community at large, or a tax on leaf burning, which will be borne by the man who has to get rid of the leaves. Thus analysis, properly conceived, complements the political process and cannot replace it.

PROGRAM BUDGETING IN PPB

Program budgeting is, of course, a good deal older than either PPB or systems analysis. Students of budgeting assert that the basic ideas have been in evidence since at least the early part of the twentieth century, and the idea received powerful support from the postwar Hoover Commission.

Program budgeting is often described as involving the presentation of budget data in a classification system based on output categories rather than input categories. Sometimes it is described instead as involving categories based on objectives. When the PPB system was introduced, agencies were asked to review their objectives and to devise program categories that were based on the systems of objectives resulting from the review. In particular, in order to free the so-called "program structure" from the traditional budget classification schemes, agencies were instructed to disregard traditional classification systems in developing their program structures.

The attempt to construct program structures that cut across organizational lines and existing appropriations accounts, is closely related to the tendency of systems analysis to ignore predetermined definitions of a problem and follow instead the boundaries of the decision. Thus, it was natural for an alliance to occur between systems analysis and program budgeting. The program budget was to show *all* the costs and outputs relevant to each program decision.

The alliance has, however, resulted in some confusion and excesses in abandoning the older classification systems. To begin, there were some who confused the presentation of costs and outputs in the program budget with the analyses themselves. A program budget does not directly assist in choosing among alternatives, for it shows only the cost of outputs of one specific set of choices. It does not present a comparison among alternative choices, which is the essence of program analysis. The program budget serves instead as a standard reference document displaying the costs and output implication of the approved programs. It also serves as a base for subsequent reviews of the program. Thus the program budget provides the link between the analysis and the budget.

In doing so, however, it imposes significant administrative costs which need to be considered in the design of the program structure. These costs arise because the program structure supplements rather than replaces the older classification systems based on appropriations and organizational lines. So long as the appropriations committees of Congress choose to enact the budget into law in terms of the older appropriations structure, it will be necessary for the executive branch to continue to prepare the budget in those terms. Moreover, apart from the preferences of the appropriations committees, so long as there is divergence between organizational structure and the structure imposed by the analysis of program decisions, it will be necessary to have separate classification systems for planning and for program execution. Execution must, of course, be manageable mainly within organizational boundaries or a reorganization is indicated.

For these reasons, it appears that most agencies will have to develop and maintain at least two distinct classification systems for their activities and must sustain the workloads of doing so. This being the case, divergence between the classification systems should be justifiable on the grounds of contribution to program analysis, and should not be undertaken merely in a spirit of innovation.

PLANNING IN THE PPB SYSTEM

An unsophisticated approach to federal planning would simply attempt to prejudge, in its entirety, the budget for each year of the planning period. Such an approach ignores the uncertainties inherent in planning. It would also raise arguments concerning decisions which need not yet be taken. A more realistic approach to planning treats the projection of programs as having several tiers.

The bottom tier of the planning structure is the projection of the cost and output implications of decisions *already made* or *currently proposed.* A second tier consists of the cost and output implications of those future decisions necessary to achieve *currently approved* goals in *specific* programs, such as the 10-year housing goal adopted by President Johnson. And, finally, it is possible to project the aggregate level of agency budgets by working from the top down, estimating a likely or desirable level of future government expenditure as determined by fiscal policy, and then allocating portions to agencies on the basis of broad priorities. Estimates of the output implications of this tier may not be possible since the program activities will not generally be sufficiently defined.

A multitiered approach is essential to planning in a bureaucratic environment. If upper levels of an organization request plans from subordiate levels without specification of several distinct tiers as indicated above and without imposing future resource constraints, they will get blue-sky estimates. Or, if budget ceilings are imposed, the subordinate levels will often omit some high-priority programs from the plan to bring pressure to bear to restore them and thus to raise the budget.

We might call this response "Portia's Ploy" from its resemblance to the way in which Portia protected her client against Shylock in the *Merchant of Venice*. Shylock, it will be recalled, after proving his case at law, was told to take his pound of flesh—but only flesh and no blood and from the victim's heart—and he was threatened with execution if the victim died. The analog, when the Budget Bureau plays Shylock, is that the agency will all too often offer up that program which is closest to the president's heart in response to a request for their priorities within a budget ceiling. This device plays hob with the development of a decentralized planning process.

In addition to problems like Portia's Ploy, planning must cope with uncertainties about the general state of budget stringency in future years and about future priorities. Because of these problems, attempts to develop *overall* agency and government budget *totals* for a period as long as five years are more valuable for the stimulation derived from the process of developing them than for their reliability as a guide to future activities. Consequently, a planning process that deals only with the total of the three tiers discussed above is likely to intensify bureaucratic bargaining unnecessarily and embarrass an administration that must defend future budget totals with little basis in analysis or fact.

A multitiered approach, on the other hand, offers several useful contributions. The projection of commitments resulting from past or currently contemplated decisions is essential to preserve the future flexibility of the president and to avoid the problem of starting a number of programs which later will not only absorb the resources that might be wanted for future new program starts, but which themselves may be underfunded as a result of failure to take account of the future growth in the resource demands implied by current program decisions. In some cases, the future growth is obvious but is nevertheless not systematically taken into account without a formal planning process. "Commitments" in the sense intended here is a broader term than contractual or statutory commitments. It also embraces commitments that arise as a logical consequence of program decisions. When we buy a hospital or a truck there is no legal commitment to operate it over a period of years, but there is a clear, logical implication that we will do so. In fact, for the government to walk away from a newly built hospital would be a very embarrassing act. Commitment projections offer a way to take such implications into account.

In other cases, the implied commitment may be less obvious but is, nonetheless, real. For example, if the Federal Aviation Agency were to request funding for a new ground control radar system at one or two heavy traffic airports on a demonstration basis, it would be difficult to withhold subsequent installation at other airports with equally heavy traffic. The commitment to install systems at other similar airports implied by the decision to install the first one or two should be considered in deciding whether to proceed at all. The projection is also necessary to test whether the aggregate of currently contemplated decisions will exceed any likely or desirable level of commitment of future resources.

The second tier of projection, comprising the costs and outputs necessary to reach selected future goals, permits the president to espouse high-priority goals, gain public support for them, and provide guidance to the bureaucracy to achieve them in an orderly fashion. Such commitments to major future goals should require the approval of the president in order to avoid the tendency for each agency to rush in with its high-priority programs with the likelihood of overcommitment of resources.

Finally, if the first two tiers of projection are clearly identified.

agencies may usefully be requested to propose an overall plan for the expenditure of likely levels of total budget resources in order to permit them to display their priorities to the president and the Budget Bureau. In my view, however, the political and administrative costs of attempting to arrive at an approved set of government-wide agency budgets for a 5-year period is not worth the cost.

PROBLEMS ENCOUNTERED IN THE INTRODUCTION OF PPB TO DOMESTIC AGENCIES

This section will recapitulate some of the problems mentioned in the discussion above, and also introduce some new ones. The problems are largely related to the differences between PPB in the domestic and the national security areas already discussed. They fall into three main groups:

—The lack of trained and experienced people, conceptual frameworks, and data.
—Bureaucratic problems.
—Problems arising from conflict of individual interest among the public.

The first of these has been adequately discussed above. The other two will be taken up in turn.

Problems Arising out of the Operation of a Bureaucracy

Perhaps the root problem besetting the operation of the PPB system during its first 3 years of operation has been the inability, except in a relatively small number of cases, to state issues for decision in terms of a range of relevant alternatives. Most often, issues will be stated in terms of acceptance or rejection of a specific program proposal. When alternatives are stated they are very often a mere mechanical compliance with the requirement to do so imposed by the Budget Bureau.

An almost classical style for the statement of alternatives has evolved. The alternatives most often will be stated in terms of three possible levels of funding for a given program—zero, quadrupling of the current program level, and a 10-percent increase. It is not terribly difficult to guess which alternatives the agency wants chosen. Issues involving a reorientation of the objectives of the program, or the mix of the programs intended to serve a given purpose are much less frequently encountered.

The absence of realistic, relevant alternatives is related to both the dearth of experienced analysts outside the government and to the way in which a hierarchial bureaucracy like that of the executive branch normally tends to operate. Each level wants to receive alternatives from those below

—and to pass only the preferred course of action to those above. To rely upon a bureaucracy to generate alternatives is to encounter a dilemma.

Most of the operational experience necessary to suggest a practical new approach to the problem is to be found at relatively low levels in the line organizations of the agencies. On the other hand, people at that level may lack the breadth of view as well as the incentives to suggest changes. As one moves toward the peak of the hierarchy, in the White House and the Budget Bureau, the breadth of view increases, and certainly the general level of ability is high, but the familiarity with operational details is missing. Even though the people involved at those levels may have had substantial experience in one or another part of government, their experience is too selective and their exposure not recent enough to afford the kind of familiarity that generates approaches that are both new and practical.

Moreover, the conflict of interest between higher and lower levels of the government, and the resulting bargaining situation, has affected the overall development of PPB. The decision to introduce PPB comprehensively, to all of the major domestic agencies at once, made inevitable the assumption of a major role by the Bureau of the Budget. There were both advantages and disadvantages of this decision and it is not my purpose now to evaluate it in retrospect.

The resulting identification of PPB as a system, of, by, and for the Bureau of the Budget has, however, been a substantial disadvantage in the development of PPB. If, instead, the system had developed in a way that led agency and department heads to identify themselves with the system more, I believe that some of the bureaucratic problems would have been alleviated. It is true, of course, that bargaining occurs not only between departments and the Budget Bureau, but also between the office of the secretary of a department and his bureau chiefs. Nevertheless, the responsibility of a department head is more direct than that of the Budget Bureau and it is possible for him and his staff to provide more continuous, better informed, and more forceful guidance for the activities of his agency.

Bureaucratic bargaining also manifests itself in attempts to make agencies establish priorities. The usual response to a request for a ranking of activities by priority is that all agency activities are vital to the welfare of the country and would not be otherwise undertaken. If a more operational approach is taken, and the agency is given a budget planning figure within which it must make allocation decisions, the response described above as Portia's Ploy is often the result.

Finally, bargaining within the government is not restricted to internal jockeying in the executive. Relations between the executive and the Congress are, of course, also a mixture of cooperative and adversary proceedings. Moreover, whereas the executive is organized, at least roughly, in a hierarchial way, the Congress represents a much more complex set of arrangements of diverse interests and responsibilities.

The problems that have arisen between the Congress and the executive in the development of PPB are correspondingly diverse. They are characterized under three headings; lack of PPB output, lack of congressional access to the existing PPB output, and lack of interest (or actual antipathy) in some quarters of Congress to the things that PPB is striving to do.

Of the outputs of PPB, the Congress probably is and should be most concerned with the alternatives and the comparisons among them that PPB is to generate. Because of separation from the operations of government agencies (even more so than in the case of the White House and the Bureau of the Budget), and because of staff limitations relative to the executive branch, the Congress will probably continue to be dependent upon the information and analyses generated by the executive. The presentation of decisions in terms of choices among relevant alternatives, together with analyses comparing the alternatives and presenting the basis for the choice proposed by the executive, should permit the Congress and its staff to ask more relevant questions, and should provide the data base to make it possible for even a small staff to test the sensitivity of the conclusions reached by the executive to changes in key assumptions. Thus, when PPB has overcome the problems of generating alternatives and of making systematic comparisons among them, it should offer output of high value to the Congress.

There is, however, a further problem, the problem of congressional access. With the exception of data concerning the current budget year, the executive branch has preferred not to release PPB material for either congressional or public examination. The reluctance of large organizations to make explicit the basis for their choices would result in sterilization of PPB material if it were all routinely to be released for scrutiny outside the executive. As it is, the discussion above indicates that it is very difficult to get a high degree of candor even within the executive family.

An answer to this problem may be found in distinguishing the degree of sensitivity of the different kinds of PPB materials. The most sensitive documents of all are the program memorandums which are intended to present, for review by the White House and the Budget Bureau, the choices recommended by the heads of the agencies and departments, together with the basis for those recommendations. Less sensitive are the analytic comparisons among alternatives which often are far short of conclusive with regard to policy choices. Because of the limitations of quantitative analysis, especially in regard to the treatment of conflicts among individual interests, the results of the analytic comparisons will require a considerable mixture of judgment and advocacy before a decision will emerge. But it is precisely in regard to the quantitative analysis that the Congress needs most to rely upon the executive. A possible solution, therefore, would be to continue to treat the program memorandums as documents privileged to the executive, but to make the analytic studies available for public use.

Planning data for future years beyond the budget year has also been a sensitive item of PPB output. So long as the 5-year plan was comprehensive and appeared to commit the executive to decisions which the president had not yet either considered or resolved, the data on costs, outputs, and budget totals for the future years was also considered highly sensitive. If, however, the kind of multitiered planning discussed above is developed and applied, there should be much less sensitivity about making public the commitments implied by decisions already taken by the executive. Moreover, in the case of selected future program goals, the president will have positive reasons for wanting to make them public in order to mobilize public understanding and support.

Conflicts among Individual Interests

Apart from, but related to, the bargaining among the various elements of the government, is the bargaining that goes on to resolve conflicts among the interests of the public. In the example discussed above, it is quite likely that John Doe, the leaf burner, would attempt to resist by political means, any attempt to impose a tax on leaf burning. Richard Roe, on the other hand, the unwilling inhaler of John Doe's smoke, would probably resist an increase in taxes to subsidize the collection of leaves. As indicated above, analysis cannot say whether it is preferable to deal with the spillover effect by a tax or a subsidy. It can, however, say that either would be preferable to a situation in which John Doe goes on burning leaves, and Richard Roe goes on inhaling the smoke. All too often, an impasse is reached because John Doe merely sees the impending tax on leaf burning and Richard Roe sees the tax to support a subsidy on leaf removal and neither is clearly aware of the implication of one course or the other or of the possibility of some compromise that might be acceptable to both.

Analysis cannot be expected to replace the political horse-trading by which many conflicts are resolved in our society. Rather, it has great potential for making that horse-trading a more effective process by clarifying the implications of alternative choices or by generating new and more effective alternatives, and where there is an overriding common interest, by helping to clarify and present the case for that interest.

Another limitation of analysis is its inability to establish, without the aid of the political process, desirable priorities among such broad aggregates as health, education, economic development, conservation, and national security. In order to make analytic comparisons among alternative patterns of resource allocation, it is necessary that costs and outputs of the various activities be comparable. Obviously, there is no unit of measure that will establish the relative benefits of education against those of health or national security. No computer, therefore, will ever produce an allocation of resources among these activities that has any claim to optimality, let alone compelling appeal to the electorate. Choices at this high level of aggregation must be developed on the basis of public preferences that largely find their expression in the political process.

Nevertheless, analysis does have an important role to play in the making of such decisions. All too often, at present, the choice between spending an additional billion dollars on urban transportation as opposed to, say, the education of disadvantaged children, is a choice between putting resources into one black box as opposed to another. For public preferences to find intelligent expression, it is necessary that the public know something about the benefits to be gained from an increment of expenditure on urban transportation and an increment to education. The comparison will still have to be made in the minds of individual citizens and elected officials, but the factual basis for making such a comparison can be greatly improved.

SOME DIRECTIONS FOR THE IMPROVEMENT OF PPB

Greater Involvement by Department and Agency Heads

The interest and attention of the head of each department or agency or of his deputy are crucial to the success of PPB. The prototype of PPB was created by Secretary McNamara who considered the job of managing the resources of the Defense Department as among his prime responsibilities. Other cases where PPB has taken hold almost all show some similar pattern of interest on the part of the agency head or his immediate deputy. Although the president expects his cabinet officers and their immediate subordinates to assist him in many capacities, he must accord high priority to the role of resource manager if government resources are to be used more efficiently. The Bureau of the Budget will continue to have an important role to play in monitoring the development of PPB, but steps should be taken to make PPB responsible to the needs of department and agency heads, and to encourage initiatives on their part in developing the system further. Increasing the ability of the Budget Bureau to do independent analysis can help to stimulate the departments and agencies to improve their own analyses.

More and Better Analysis and Data

If we are to improve our understanding of the program choices open to us, it will be necessary to devote much larger resources on a long-term, continuing basis to efforts to improve our conceptual understanding and to increase and improve the data available. Some significant steps in this direction have already been taken.

In particular, a start has been made on the systematic evaluation of the performance of programs already in existence. In several recent pieces of legislation, the statute contains authorization and direction to the secretary of the agency involved to spend up to 1 percent of the authorized funds on evaluation of the program, either in his own office, in the field organization of the federal department, or (in the case of grant-in-aid programs) at the state and local level. Such provisions should be contained in more legislation, perhaps in all new authorizing legislation, and other methods should be sought to indicate the intent of the Congress to encourage and support program evaluation.

Improvement is also needed in our ability to evaluate new programs that have no existing counterparts. An example of an attempt to do this is the OEO experiment to determine the effects of a negative income tax on such aspects of behavior as labor force participation and consumption patterns. Imaginative, controlled experiments of this sort are essential to improving our ability to design new programs. But it is also essential that both the executive and Congress require more systematic presentation of the implications of proposed new legislation and comparisons with alternative ways to accomplish the desired ends.

Most of all, it is necessary to assemble groups of people who are technically trained in analysis and who have an understanding of the substantive areas which they are to analyze. Because of the twin problems of institutional blinders on those currently involved in operations, and lack of relevant experience on the part of outsiders, a pattern of rotation from analytic positions to operating positions should be developed. Such rotation between program analysis and program operation could occur within government between an agency line organization and the office of the secretary, between line organizations and an expanded program evaluation staff either in the Budget Bureau or elsewhere in the Executive Office of the President, or between government line organizations and private independent research organizations of the sort that have proven useful in the national security area. A start has been made in increasing outside expertise, but much more needs to be done, and the domestic agencies must develop patterns of long-term continuing funding of research like those in the Defense Department. To the extent that the problems encountered are interagency problems, it will be especially necessary to develop groups of analysts either in the Executive Office of the President or outside government.

To help meet the requirements for trained people, government should encourage universities, through graduate fellowships, to develop curricula that combine analytic training and substantive courses in the applied fields of health services, urban transportation, the evaluation of education, and so on.

Increased Accessibility to PPB Material

Although the program memorandums should continue to be privileged documents if they are to be useful at all, analytic studies displaying alternative programs and comparing their costs and benefits should routinely be made available to the Congress and to the public. Such analyses need not and should not attempt to be conclusive and reach definite program recommendations. That can be left to the program memorandums in the executive branch and to the legislative process in Congress. The analyses should, however, provide a common basis in fact for making program choices. In addition, as the executive develops the projection of the commitments implied by decisions that have been made, it should make these projections available, together with the projection of selected programs to realize future goals approved by the president.

The Further Development of Program Budgeting

Since the maintenance and development of program budgets will be superimposed on the requirement to maintain budgets along traditional lines in many cases, the existing program structures should be reviewed to determine whether the added workload is justified by their contribution to the understanding of the agency's program activities. The criterion by which the program structure should be judged should correspond to the lines of definition of the analyses required to assist in making program choices. Other things being equal, ease of translation between program structure and appropriation structure or organizational structure should be considered in reviewing the program structure. Wherever possible, of course, a single, integrated classification system should be devised and proposed for acceptance by the executive and the Congress.

As yet, little has been done to establish a government-wide program structure. In the many areas where departmental responsibilities overlap, the development of departmental program structures that are consistent with one another and that will correspond to the program decisions is necessary to improve our understanding of resource allocation and to provide a common starting point for analyzing subsequent program decisions. A substantial interagency effort, led by the Bureau of the Budget, should be undertaken to develop a government-wide program structure and consistent definitions of costs and outputs in areas where agency programs overlap.

Improving the PPB Process

One of the purposes of PPB is to permit program evaluation to go on continuously during the year rather than under the crisis atmosphere of fall budget review. The schedule for development of PPB material and its submission to the Budget Bureau has been extremely late in each of the three PPB cycles so far completed. In part, this has been the result of changes in the process from year to year, but more fundamentally, it has stemmed from lack of interest on the part of the department heads and unwillingness to commit themselves to decisions in the spring. Greater interest on the part of the secretary will help to alleviate this situation, but it is also necessary to distinguish the analysis preparatory to decisionmaking from the decision itself. The spring review should concentrate on reaching an understanding of the costs and benefits of the alternatives. Formal choices among them by high-level officials should be separated from this process in order to avoid delaying the analytic process. Such choices can be made in the fall if their implications are understood as a result of the spring review.

CHAPTER 18

THE STATUS OF PPB IN FEDERAL AGENCIES: A COMPARATIVE PERSPECTIVE

Keith E. Marvin and Andrew M. Rouse

INTRODUCTION

Much has been written on the purposes of planning-programing-budgeting (PPB), its uses in analyzing areas of public expenditures, the applicability of various analytic techniques, the effect of the PPB process on various public functions and on the federal political and administrative environment. While there has been considerable discussion, little factual knowledge of the organizational impact of PPB on the civil agencies particularly is available.

The PPB system has been used formally in the Defense Department for eight years and in many civil agencies for three years. Enough time has elapsed to examine the systems created by the federal agencies. Such an examination is useful if we are to discern ways of making the system more effective.

The purpose of this paper is to describe the current status of PPB in the federal agencies and the facts which appear to account for this condition. The paper is based on recent surveys of PPB systems conducted independently by the General Accounting Office and by the Bureau of the Budget. These surveys looked at the systems which had been developed from the point of view of agency management. They assumed that management would want analysis of agency policy issues and would want these analyses carried out in a systematic way. Major aims of the surveys were to ascertain if and how managers used analysis in decisionmaking, and the organizational process for documenting and reviewing it.

Keith E. Marvin is Associate Director of the Office of Policy and Special Studies at the General Accounting Office.

Andrew M. Rouse was Director of the Resources Planning Staff at the U.S. Bureau of the Budget.

The authors wish to acknowledge their debt to Herman Galvin of the General Accounting Office and Edwin Harper of the Bureau of the Budget for their help in writing this paper. They would also like to thank Lucy Harper for editing several versions of this paper. The patience of all three, interspersing work on this paper among their other duties, is much appreciated.

The paper first describes what the expectations for the PPB system were. It then explores what was actually created in the agencies. The patterns of development of agency PPB systems and 13 of the factors which appear to have affected the development of these patterns are discussed.

PPB IN CONCEPT

Just what PPB was intended to be has been a source of some misunderstanding. There are those who think that PPB is simply the injection of the analytic techniques associated with modern operations research and systems analysis into the decisionmaking process; they point out that analysis of sorts existed in many bureaus and agencies long before the PPB innovation was ordered. Others say that PPB is a system for decisionmaking; they point out that the men who introduced and supported PPB through the years intended "to develop a coherent and comprehensive system through the imposition of certain formal elements of procedure and requirement for documentation."[1]

Although the introduction of PPB has undoubtedly led to the currency of certain tools of analysis common to the field of operations research and systems analysis, there seems to be little doubt that it was the intention of both President Johnson and the supporters of PPB to develop a systematized approach to decisionmaking and not merely to introduce analytic tools.[2] Early in the literature of PPB, Arthur Smithies suggested that such systems serve as the focus of a *process* of comparison and coordination. He argued that it involved:

(1) Appraisals and comparisons of various government activities in terms of their contributions to objectives;
(2) Determination of how given objectives can be obtained with minimum expenditure of resources;
(3) Projection of government activities over an adequate time horizon;
(4) Comparison of the relative contribution of private and public activities to national objectives; and
(5) Revision of objectives, programs, and budgets in the light of experience and changing circumstances.

"These operations are inherent in any planning, programing and budgetary *process*. Program budgeting involves more explicit recognition of the need to perform them than has been traditional. It also involves the application of new analytical techniques as an aid to the exercise of human judgment on which choices must ultimately rest."[3]

The early proponents of PPB saw planning, programing, and budgeting as interrelated activities, each an aspect of a circular process of decisionmaking; i.e., a new process, not simply the injection of different or new analytic techniques into an already established decisionmaking process.[4]

Three early decisions should be noted since they were aspects of presidential expectation and have indeed affected the development of the system in the government. These, cited by the former Assistant Director of the Bureau of the Budget, Fred S. Hoffman, were:

> (1) Assigning to the Bureau of the Budget the role of leading and monitoring the introduction of PPB in the civil agencies of the government;
> (2) Applying the Defense PPB model as a prototype on which to base expectations for the domestic agencies; and
> (3) Introducing across-the-board PPB in most large civil agencies.[5]

The role of the Bureau of the Budget was expected to be primarily a managerial one. However, the Bureau, because of its need for the outputs of analysis, soon became as much a user as a monitor of the PPB system. The ambiguity of the Bureau's role tended to emphasize PPB as a Bureau tool rather than a tool of agency policymaking. Some agencies which looked to the Bureau for help and guidance found that there was little to be had. The Bureau appeared to be, contrary to expectation, a demander of their output. The decision to assign the Bureau a central role in developing the PPB system left as an unresolved problem the ambiguity inherent in the dual and sometimes conflicting roles of the Bureau in dealing with the PPB implementation in agencies.

The institution of PPB in the civil agencies was expected to produce some of the benefits which had been produced in the Defense Department. There is, however, question about the applicability of the Department of Defense's PPB process as a prototype on which to base expectations for civil agencies. Because the Defense Department's goal is primarily national security, the objectives to be achieved by Defense programs have been reasonably well-defined. On the other hand, most civil agencies have more undefined, varied and multi-dimensional objectives than the Defense Department. Further, the Defense establishment had used policy analysis extensively prior to the formal introduction of PPB and so the technical requirements were not unfamiliar to people in the Department. However, in the civil agencies, with few exceptions, systematic policy analysis was rare.

Finally, the across-the-board introduction of PPB in the civil agencies had at least two important consequences which tended to defeat what was expected of PPB. One was that hundreds of analysts were needed, of which there were almost none, either in the government outside Defense, or the private sector. The result was to spread then existing talent and to literally reclassify as "policy analysts" large numbers of men without the requisite training. Result: analytic studies were extremely variable in quality; almost non-existent in some agencies. Across-the-board implementation created other problems such as the need to articulate rapidly program structures to be used in analysis and output measures.

This, in effect, brought to the surface problems which had been dealt with for years in an intuitive manner. The lack of quantitative measures which are related to program achievement and objectives, for example, became apparent in the process of developing program structures and output values. The fact that many structure and output definition problems remain unsolved creates an impression that PPB has been unsuccessful. In retrospect, it is clear that the expectations of federal agencies exceeded their ability to satisfy.

A complicating environmental aspect is the fact that the executive decisionmaking process has never operated independently of the legislative bodies. Various subcommittees have become deeply involved in monitoring the execution of the programs authorized or funded by legislation which they have formulated. The formal approach of PPB impinged upon the highly variable legislative liaison process. Thus, each agency considered how it could make use of PPB analysis in support of its particular position within its particular legislative environment.

As a result of these factors, agencies, left to their own devices, created a wide variety of systems—none of which has fully satisfied the expectations of its proponents.

PATTERNS OF DEVELOPMENT

The formal elements of the PPB process are well known and are described in detail elsewhere in this collection. For our purposes, note that the definition of program structure, analytic study, program memoranda and program and financial plans have undergone much change from the days of their Defense Department incarnation. Our focus is not on the quality of the elements of PPB but rather on the way their development has been incorporated into the policy decisionmaking apparatus of the agency.

The systems which are emerging in the federal agencies are not uniform.[6] However, agencies can be grouped according to the degree to which they have developed a decisionmaking process which incorporates the elements of PPB as these elements seem to fit the environment, programs, and organizational realities of their agencies.

In placing agencies within these groups, a number of criteria were used. These criteria were:

(1) The use of and attitude toward policy analysis;
(2) The use of planning as an aid in achieving stated goals;
(3) The development of a process by which planning, the analysis of program alternatives, and budgeting is integrated; and
(4) The adequacy of analytic staffs both in number and qualifications.

Each of these may be looked upon as a continuum on which each agency can be placed. Some agencies which conform to one criterion may not conform to another. The groupings of the agencies, therefore, represent the congeries of agency ratings along the various continua.

Five agency groupings are apparent. In one group, analytic activities have evolved toward integration with the PPB process and their outputs have been used by decisionmakers; for example, HEW. Agencies in this group also utilize a planning document which displays future year figures for agency programs geared to agency goals in many areas. The agencies have either formal or informal processes by which the outputs of the PPB staffs are fed into the budget process. That the success of such integration has been sporadic at best reflects the difficulties of adaptation rather than deep seated resistance to the injection of the products of policy analysis into the decisionmaking process.[7]

In a second group, well-developed analytic activities have contributed to decisionmaking and did so long before the advent of PPB. The AEC is an example of an agency in this group. The result is that PPB's contribution in restructuring the decisionmaking process in these agencies has been marginal.

Detailed PPB processes have been developed in the third group of agencies; for example, Interior. With the exception of the work in an occasional bureau, the materials produced through these processes have not been used extensively by decisionmakers. Such agencies have developed one of the aspects of PPB, the process, to a high level, but have not yet succeeded in developing the program analysis and planning aspects which are the heart of the PPB process.[8]

Analysis, most often generated outside the PPB process, has contributed to decisionmaking intermittently in the fourth group; for example, the Post Office Department. In these agencies, the planning and analytic effort has been fragmented by relatively strong bureaus, by separation of the functions in the formal structure, and other disintegrative factors.

In the last group, rudimentary analysis generally has been integrated with the PPB process and used at the program or bureau level, but top level management has used these analyses very irregularly. GSA is an example in this group.

FACTORS CONTRIBUTING TO PATTERNS OF DEVELOPMENT

Many factors have contributed to the emergence of the different agency patterns. Thirteen, in particular, were commonly perceived to have had some impact upon the form which the development of PPB took in federal agencies. These are:

(1) Confusion among analysts and program managers as to whom PPB is intended to serve, the agency or the Bureau of the Budget;
(2) Duplication of effort seemingly required by PPB as distinct from the traditional budgeting process;
(3) The attitude of the relevant congressional committees toward PPB;
(4) Bureau of the Budget attitude and guidance;
(5) The attitude and interest of the agency head;
(6) The qualifications of the man selected to head the central analytic staff;
(7) The qualifications of both the central and bureau level analytic staffs;
(8) The size of the agency analytic staffs;
(9) The age of the agency or its programs;
(10) Formal organization, including both comprehensive procedures for the PPB system and the reporting and role relationships of the analytic functions to policymaking executives;
(11) The susceptibility of the agency's mission to analytic effort, notably the difficulty in designing benefit measures;
(12) The degree of congruity between the PPB program structure and the agency's organization structure; and
(13) The difficulties of developing appropriate data and accounting systems.

Confusion as to Whom PPB Serves

One factor which has had a most important effect upon the pattern of PPB development in the agencies has been diversity in perception as to whom PPB serves. In some agencies, personnel in general and the agency head in particular, have seen PPB as a tool in agency decision making. In other agencies, frequently reflecting the indifference of the agency head, most agency personnel have seen PPB largely as a requirement of the Bureau of the Budget.

In those agencies where PPB is perceived as serving a Bureau need, the PPB innovation has been viewed largely as a budget justification requirement. In other agencies, PPB has increasingly been seen as a system for improving decisions within the agency, but even here there are variations in perspectives. There are some agencies where the tool has been regarded largely as a mechanism serving the agency head, developing information upon which he may make his decisions. In others, the process has been viewed as useful to program and bureau chiefs as well.

These perceptions of agency personnel have had an important impact upon the organization and the working relationships of the PPB function in the agency. In those agencies which see it largely as a BOB tool, more often than not the PPB responsibility has been divided between analytic and process activities; each of these reporting to a different agency official. In many of these agencies, program memoranda and program and financial plans are prepared by units which are responsible for preparing more traditional budget justification materials. Analytic activity, if any, is separately staffed. These activities frequently serve as a staff resource to the agency head working, in most cases, outside the context of the agency's PPB process. On the other hand, in those agencies seeing PPB as an agency tool, it has been integrated under a single official, more often than not the agency head.

A key force in the development of the agency's perception of PPB appears to have been the agency head. In those agencies in which the agency head has been indifferent to the development of PPB and has used the results of analysis intermittently, for advocacy of programs or for organizational control, PPB has usually been seen as a Bureau of the Budget tool. Where the agency head has been either strong in his support or passive in his support, but has recruited strong leadership for the PPB unit, the PPB system has more often been regarded as an agency decisionmaking process.

Duplication of Effort: PPB and Traditional Budgeting

Budget decisionmaking in most agencies is described as a "two-track system," the traditional budget process being one "track" and the PPB system, the other. Associated with each track are different documentation requirements, classifications, and data systems.

The pattern of linkage between the two tracks in the advanced PPB agencies has been different from that in the slower agencies. In the latter, it was hard to find evidence that the two tracks have been functionally relevant to each other; there has existed little interest in or use of the crosswalks which would relate appropriation budget categories to PPB program categories. Budget and PPB units carried on their affairs almost without reference to the work of the other. However, in those agencies where substantial progress has been made, there was general agreement that PPB had made some impact upon budget decisionmaking. In one of these agencies, OEO, the budget function has been absorbed by the PPB unit. In another, HEW, the program and financial plan has been used as a source for internal budget targets at the beginning of each budget season.

In the slower agencies, relationships between the PPB and the budget activities were often strained. Budget units frequently claim difficulty in satisfying the requirements for data of the PPB activity; and that the requirement for PPB documentation represented little more than "make work." It is not surprising that these sentiments still exist if the DOD experience is taken as a model of the manner in which PPB and traditional budgeting interact. After all, the Defense Department started to integrate the program and traditional budgets in the 1950s and this integration has only recently been accomplished.

Congressional Attitude

The attitude of the Congress toward PPB is not entirely clear but whatever it is, it is not uniform. Individual members and committees have expressed a variety of attitudes varying from a desire to obtain direct outputs of PPB, to advocacy, to curiosity, to skepticism. Interest in PPB has been expressed infrequently, suggesting that the Congress, in general, has not considered this innovation in the executive decision process as very important to the legislative bodies. In one case, for example, the chairman of an appropriations subcommittee has expressly prohibited any salary expenditures for PPB personnel in one agency. The agency, not surprisingly, has made little progress toward developing a PPB system or integrating it into agency decisionmaking. Even here a cause/effect relationship is difficult to establish because many of the agency professionals express an anti-PPB bias. Some members of Congress, however, are now asking for the analytic studies and agency plans which the PPB system has produced. This interest, unlike the past indifference, may have an important effect on agency PPB development.

Agencies, regardless of how they have progressed in implementing PPB, claim to have used analytic studies often to generate and support legislative changes. However, there is little evidence of this use to be found in the legislative hearings.

Bureau of the Budget Attitude and Guidance

While officially the Bureau supported PPB, among the Bureau's examining units the attitude has been more ambivalent. In general, even negative Bureau examiner attitudes, in the cases where they were apparent, have not led to noncompliance with requirements, but rather have affected the time and emphasis placed on submission of program memoranda, and program and financial plans. Consequently, examiner attitude had little effect on the patterns which developed.

The Bureau's clearest impact upon the development of the PPB system in the agencies has been through its issuance of formal guidance. Agencies, to varying degrees, have relied upon it as the mechanism to force their bureaus to submit PPB materials and to inject the analytic staffs into agency information flows. In a few agencies which have made relatively little progress toward the injection of systematic analysis into the agency decision process, the Bureau of the Budget's general guidance has been only slightly recast and promulgated as agency procedures. Not unexpectedly, these agencies are also among those that have regarded the PPB system as a Bureau tool.

Agency Head Attitudes

The attitude of the agency head has been the single most important factor in the development of a PPB system and its integration with the agency decisionmaking system.

Where agency heads have supported analytic effort, agencies have made substantial progress toward the integration of the PPB system and the decisionmaking process. Agency head support is most clearly evidenced by requests for and use of analytic studies. In all of the advanced agencies, the agency head has used the PPB outputs for policy decisionmaking as well as subsequent advocacy of his position. Several of the agency heads also have used PPB outputs to assist them in coping with agency biases and occasionally in reviewing program performance.

Where agency heads have been indifferent toward the development of systematic analysis and planning processes, agencies have made less substantial progress. In most of these agencies, there are instances of the sporadic use of policy analysis. More often than not, however, the examples reflect *ad hoc* requests for analysis to be used for advocating new programs. These studies are generally produced outside the framework of the PPB process.

Three reasons often cited for agency head indifference were: wide experience in the agency's program area; professional background which leaned toward bargaining or argument as issue resolving techniques; and finally, strong agency constituencies whose interests would not be served by the kind of policy analysis contemplated by the PPB system.

Qualifications of the Heads of Central Analytic Staff

The successes of those agencies which have made progress toward the development of PPB have been attributed to the quality of leadership of the central analytic staff. There appear to be some attributes which all of these men have in common. First, they were generally acknowledged to have strong analytic skills. While, in some cases, there was little evidence of strong managerial competence in their backgrounds, they were all known as aggressive men, interested in developing systematic analysis as part of the decisionmaking process. Finally, each of them, early in their tenure, undertook one or more studies which were intended to demonstrate the value of systematic analysis to their agencies.

There are similarly qualified analytic staff heads in agencies which have made relatively little progress. The difference appears to lie in the attitude of the agency head. Where a strong staff chief has been indifferently supported but not hampered, he seems to have been able to operate effectively. On the other hand, where a strong staff head has been unsupported, where the agency head either has not reviewed analytic results, and/or has not had the analytic shop reporting directly to him, the staff chief has had little impact. Similarly, in agencies having interested agency heads, but comparatively unqualified central analytic staff heads, the staff heads have had little impact. Consequently, a qualified central analytic staff head appears to be necessary to the development of a useful PPB system, although such a staff head is not sufficient to guarantee progress in the face of a nonsupportive agency head.

Qualification of Staffs

Table 1 summarizes personnel data on approximately 800 analysts in 16 domestic agencies. Included are data on the education, training, and work experience of members of staff identified as spending most of their time on special analytic studies, writing program memoranda and program and financial plans.

The advanced agencies have staffs which have had more formal education, more recently acquired training, have spent fewer years in the agency, and have had broader experience than the staffs in the less advanced agencies. The central staffs of the agencies which have made progress differ from their bureau staffs in the same ways.

It is interesting to note that in the less advanced agencies, the differences in the characteristics of the central and bureau staffs vary in much

TABLE 1

Background of Analytic Staffs,[1] Bureau Compared to Central Analytic Staffs,[2] 16 Selected Domestic Agencies

	Education and training						Work experience							
	Years of formal education		Recent highest degree (years)		Percent staff quantitative major		Percent staff PPB training		Percent staff quantitative experience		Percent staff broad experience		Average years present agency	
	Central[3]	Bureau[4]	Central[3]	Bureau[4]	Central[3]	Bureau[4]	Central[3]	Bureau[4]	Central[3]	Bureau[4]	Central[3]	Bureau[4]	Central[3]	Bureau[4]
Average for 3 agencies making progress toward use of analysis and planning in decisionmaking	18.4	17.5	8.6	16.1	47.9	53.6	18.6	24.4	28.1	23.8	56.8	21.4	2.8	7.9
Average for 16 agencies	17.7	16.8	13.4	13.9	47.9	39.5	25.4	27.7	37.8	23.9	35.9	19.3	6.5	8.3

[1] These data are derived from analysis of personnel data supplied by agencies on professionals identified as analysts meeting the following definition: professional involved most of the time (more than 50 percent in carrying out special analytic studies associated with issues generated within the PPB system and/or writing program memoranda and program and financial plans.

[2] Office of Economic Opportunity, U.S. Department of Agriculture, Department of Health, Education, and Welfare, Veterans Administration, General Services Administration, Atomic Energy Commission, Corps of Engineers, Department of Labor, Treasury Department, National Aeronautics and Space Administration, Justice Department, Post Office Department, Department of Housing and Urban Development, Department of Transportation, Department of Commerce.

[3] Central analytic staff.

[4] Agency bureau staffs as a group.

the same way as for the agencies which have made progress. While there are differences between the central and bureau staffs in the recency of degrees, for example, in general the qualifications of central staffs of the slower agencies appear to bear a similar relationship to bureau staffs as do the central and bureau staffs in the more advanced agencies.

In short, the advanced agencies have better qualified staffs, but central staffs are, in general, better qualified than bureau staffs in these agencies. Central staffs in both advanced and slower agencies bear similar relationships to their respective bureau staffs.

Staff Size

PPB staff size is difficult to ascertain. First, the PPB staffs cannot, in all cases, be considered incremental, required solely for PPB. Some of the analytic and planning responsibilities of the PPB staffs were performed prior to the implementation of the formal PPB system and would continue in its absence.

Second, identifying the PPB analysts was another kind of problem encountered in assessing the personnel resources involved in PPB. Different definitions were used in the Bureau and GAO surveys. These generated different responses by the agencies. Given the differences in definition, however, the responses were compatible. Third, part of the difficulty also lies in the fact that the agencies themselves are not clear on who is and who is not a PPB analyst.

With these caveats, there are about 1,600 full-time PPB employees in the 21 agencies surveyed by GAO.[10] Another 2,100 employees spend part time on PPB for an additional full-time equivalent of about 900 full-time PPB employees. The grand totals are 2,500 full-time equivalent employees allocated to the planning, programing, and budgeting functions.

The impact of the sufficiency or insufficiency of staff size upon the development of the agency's PPB system is also difficult to assess. Several agencies which have made very little progress—HUD, for example—are understaffed, but so is HEW which has made significant progress.[11] AEC is understaffed but is one of the agencies which has a well-developed analytic process. These inferences suggest that the *total* agency staff size has not had a great impact upon the agency's development of PPB unless the staffs are so small as to be a mere nod toward a policy analysis function.

The size of the central staff, however, seems to have been of some significance. In all of the agencies which have made substantial progress, the central staff has at least sufficient staff to provide an important analytic capability.

Age of Agency or Agency Programs

New programs and old bureaucrats are often mentioned as major roadblocks to the development of PPB.

Pressures for the establishment of program apparatus for new programs have made the deliberate approach of the PPB process appear an undesirable burden to top program officials. Consequently, agencies with new programs, such as EDA or HUD, frequently have not developed a PPB process with the same speed as they have developed their program apparatus.

The argument is often made that in older bureaus well-developed procedures and entrenched bureaucracies make it very difficult to change the decisionmaking process, a fact which accounts for the slow development of PPB in such organizations.

There are good examples which support both the "new program" and "old bureaucrat" arguments and equally good examples which demonstrate the opposite of each proposition. However, it does appear that in older bureaus, the pattern developed for the implementation of PPB tended to emphasize process, and the few analyses prepared have relied heavily upon less complex techniques. Agencies with very new programs did not develop analytic processes at the same pace as they geared up the new programs.

Formal Organization

The Bureau's PPB instructions to the agencies have provided very general guidance, allowing for agency adaptation of the PPB system to its own needs and peculiarities.

In almost all agencies, even those with well-established analytic and planning activities, the day-to-day responsibility for the PPB function has been assigned to newly created units at both the central and bureau levels. The structure of these units and the formality and detail of the PPB procedures established vary widely from agency to agency. Twelve formal organization patterns in fact have emerged among the 16 domestic agencies studied.[12]

Those agencies making substantial progress have a very similar formal organization pattern. They each have:

(1) Integrated reporting relationships for both the analytic and process elements of PPB;
(2) The responsible unit reports to the agency head;
(3) The agency head formally reviews the analytic studies and the program memoranda, injecting the results of analytic effort into agency policymaking; and

(4) The agency has promulgated detailed procedures, often down to field units, dealing with required inputs for the planning and analytic process.[13]

The formal organization of agencies which have made less progress may have some of the above characteristics but they tend also to have one or more of the following:

(1) Split reporting relationships for analytic and process activities;
(2) Responsible units report to assistant secretaries;
(3) Absence of detailed procedures; and
(4) Intermittent or no review of analytic output by agency head.

While much has been said about reducing conflict between budget and PPB units in agencies by the combination of the two, this has occurred in only two agencies—DOT (very recently) and OEO. The formal arrangement differs in each and in both cases, results are still completely speculative.

Susceptibility to Analytic Effort

Some argue that wide variation in mission makes for varying degrees of difficulty in applying PPB. Nothing inherent in the subject content of any agency's program mix should impede PPB analysis, although organizational lines may do so.

Frequently heard is the complaint that output/benefit definition is not possible for many programs. While such measurements are difficult to define in many program areas, some of both advanced and slower agencies have yielded to the temptation of using intermediate outputs in place of program benefits. This avoided wrestling with benefit definition, the role of secondary benefits, and like problems, but it does so at substantial cost to program evaluation capability. The factor, in short, does not appear to have affected the *pattern* of development of PPB in the agencies, although it has been used as justification for the slow rate of progress made by many agencies.

Program Structure

Whether existing program structures aid or impede analytic effort is often discussed. One reason for this is the importance attached to structure in Bureau of the Budget guidance. Another is the implication for government-wide planning and analysis, a subject which elicits strong feelings.

A good structure should ease the analysis of agency activities directed to the same or similar objectives. However, analytically sound structures will not insure progress in integrating analysis into policy decisionmaking. Similarly, analytically inept structures do not make success impossible.

There does appear to be a relationship between the progress of PPB and structure. The slower developing systems are frequently characterized by program structures which resemble agency organization structure. What seems to follow from this is that the PPB analyses and displays become collections of supporting information for the particular means employed by the organization, without due consideration of alternatives whose adoption might require changes in entrenched activities or even more shattering, involve administration outside of the organization.

Appropriate Data and Accounting Systems

Fundamental to analysis is credible cost and output data. However, few agencies have systems which produce the timely, routinized cost and output information appropriately classified for use in analysis.

The least difficult to get are costs expended in the aggregate for various time periods. More difficult is obtaining reliable information about the achievements of the programs, that is, quantitative outputs for given periods of time. Therefore, it is also difficult to determine unit costs of the services or other achievements of the programs.

The problem of finding usable quantitative measures of achievement for many programs has been discussed briefly above. The special requirements for data for this purpose have frequently been misunderstood. These needs have not been integrated into the routine accounting procedures, although there are currently some significant projects underway, for example, in the Department of Labor, which have this as one of their objectives.

Some of the impediments to developing appropriate data systems stem from the fact that organizational lines and program structures do not coincide. The requirement for accounting on a program basis is superimposed across organizational accounting requirements. The practical difficulties in accounting for costs of all kinds under such circumstances has led to the use of estimation and statistical allocation methods which are seen as an imposition but have been prepared on an "as required basis" in almost all agencies.

Generally, agencies have depended on *ad hoc* data collection for their analytic studies. Some analysts in both advanced and less advanced agencies have become inventive, creating personal data files and ingenious data constructs to substitute for regular reports on costs, intermediate outputs and the benefits resulting from agency expenditures.

This creativity has been required particularly in agencies having programs in the form of formula grants to states and localities. In these agencies, neither cost nor output data is identified by the formal systems in the detail required to relate it to specific objectives within the broad statutory categories. Various studies are underway which may ameliorate these data systems problems.[14]

CONCLUSIONS

None of the factors discussed, taken alone, cause the patterns of development of PPB in federal agencies. Many of them in combination make up the fact of an agency's adaptation to PPB. Which seem to have had the greatest impact upon PPB development? The authors find that five factors appear in each agency that has made substantial progress toward the development of PPB systems for policy decisionmaking. These are:

(1) The active support, both formal and informal, of the agency head. He evidences support by asking for, using, and talking about analytic studies; and by encouraging the systematic production of these studies and the action documents based on them;
(2) Leadership of the central analytic unit by an executive with recognized analytic experience, managerial skills, and an aggressive interest in developing a systematic process for the production and use of analysis in his agency;
(3) A general perception in the agency that PPB is essentially an agency decisionmaking tool rather than a Bureau of the Budget requirement;
(4) Qualified agency staffs; and
(5) Sufficient agency staffs, particularly in the central analytic unit.

In addition, the more successful agencies have evidenced a tolerance of the differences between the analytic and budget processes, permitting effective interaction of the two tracks at appropriate points during the year. That these are frequently not formal interactions only emphasizes the fact that policymaking and systematic planning and analysis are still loosely connected.

NOTES

[1] *A Progress Report on PPB in the Federal Government,* a paper prepared for the Committee for Economic Development by Fred S. Hoffman, former Assistant Director of the Bureau of the Budget, Washington, D.C., Oct. 10, 1968.

[2] While President Johnson launched PPB and gave it strong initial support, his interest in more recent years appeared casual. For example, subsequent to the presidential memo of Aug. 25, 1965, which announced PPB to the civil agencies, only one further official presidential paper, other than several paragraphs in the budget messages for fiscal years 1968, 1969, and 1970, evidence presidential concern for the status of the implementation of PPB in the civil agencies. This was a presidential memorandum of Nov. 17, 1966, on government-wide PPBS. While this memo

required quarterly reports by the Budget Director on the implementation of PPB in agencies, such reports, to the best of the authors' knowledge, were neither submitted nor asked for.

[3] Arthur Smithies, "Conceptual Framework for the Program Budget" in *Program Budgeting,* David Novick, ed. (Washington, D.C.: U.S. Government Printing Office, 1965), p. 5.

[4] Charles Hitch, *Decision Making for Defense,* H. Rowan Gaither Lectures in Systems Science, University of California, 1965. David Novick, *A New Approach to the Military Budget,* RM–1759, RAND Corporation, June 1956. Arthur Smithies, *op. cit.,* note 3.

[5] *Op. cit.,* note 1.

[6] Sixteen agencies in particular were covered. They are: USDA, HEW, OEO, Corps of Engineers, AEC, GSA, Interior, VA, Treasury, Labor, Commerce, Justice, NASA, DOT, POD, and HUD.

[7] The authors conducted over 400 interviews. In only a small number of these was any objection raised to the purposes or value of analysis in policymaking. More often expressed, particularly by nonanalysts, was resentment at being uninformed and unconsulted. Also expressed were misgivings about too hasty use of "theoretical" analytic results unsupported by existing data.

[8] Process as used in this paper refers to the procedures, the system for producing PM's and PFP's primarily. This is distinguished from analysis; i.e., substantive studies of programs and issues.

[9] There are undoubtedly others. Some of these have been suggested by other commentators on PPB in the federal government. However, the 13 covered here were those most often mentioned in the GAO and BOB surveys upon which this paper is based.

[10] The agencies surveyed by the GAO include the following: Post Office, Commerce, Treasury, GSA, VA, NASA, DOD, AEC, DOT, Corps of Engineers, HEW, Labor, HUD, OEO, NSF, USDA, Interior, USIA, State, AID, and Peace Corps.

[11] The sufficiency of staff size was estimated by using the DOD Office of Systems Analysis as a standard for central staffs, and a generous workload capacity estimate to establish a range within which the total agency staff size should fall.

[12] Agencies with PPB systems not included are DOD, USIA, AID, Peace Corps, SBA, and NSF.

[13] It should be pointed out that the extent to which procedures are formalized and detailed should correspond to the extent to which PPB responsibilities have been decentralized within the agency. Where staffs are small and centralized, as in many regulatory agencies, the need does not appear pressing.

[14] Examples of efforts to improve the information systems of agencies are:

Agency	*Study or experimental system*
Post office	Postal Source Data System.
DOT	Transportation Information Program.
Labor	Touche, Ross, Bailey & Smart study on accounting and management information systems.
Commerce	Study with Technical Analysis Division of Bureau of Standards to improve Department information system.
HEW	Lindsley, Noble & Associates study on accounting systems

CHAPTER 19

RESCUING POLICY ANALYSIS FROM PPBS

Aaron Wildavsky

INTRODUCTION

Everyone knows that the nation needs better policy analysis. Each area one investigates shows how little is known compared to what is necessary in order to devise adequate policies. In some organizations there are no ways at all of determining the effectiveness of existing programs; organizational survival must be the sole criterion of merit. It is often not possible to determine whether the simplest objectives have been met. If there is a demand for information, the cry goes out that what the organization does cannot be measured. Should anyone attempt to tie the organization down to any measure of productivity, the claim is made that there is no truth in numbers. Oftentimes this is another way of saying, "Mind your own business." Sometimes the line taken is that the work is so subtle that it resists any tests. On other occasions the point is made that only those learned in esoteric arts can properly understand what the organization does, and they can barely communicate to the uninitiated. There are men so convinced of the ultimate righteousness of their cause that they cannot imagine why anyone would wish to know how well they are doing in handling our common difficulties. Their activities are literally priceless; vulgar notions of cost and benefit do not apply to them.

Aaron Wildavsky is a Professor of Political Science at the University of California at Berkeley and is associated with the Center for Planning and Development Research there.

This paper supplements the author's recent studies. It is meant to be read in conjunction with these other works. Thus, he has felt no need to describe the traditional budgetary practices covered in *The Politics of the Budgetary Process* (Boston: Little, Brown, 1964) or modern modes of "efficiency" analysis beyond the account in "The Political Economy of Efficiency," *Public Administration Review,* Vol. XXVI, No. 4, December 1966, pp. 292–310. Nor has he sought to set forth fully his ideas on desirable budgetary reform as found in "Toward a Radical Incrementalism" (Washington, D.C.: American Enterprise Institute for Public Policy Research, December 1965), also, in *Congress: The First Branch of Government* (Washington, D.C.: American Enterprise Institute for Public Policy Research, 1966), pp. 115–165.

Thanks are due Arnold Meltsner, a graduate student in the Department of Political Science, for his critical comments and the benefit of his experience with Defense budgets. The author also wishes to thank Robert Biller, Yehezkel Dror, Todd LaPorte, Frederick C. Mosher, and Nelson Polsby for helpful comments and Peter Dahl who made useful stylistic suggestions, but reserves all the blame for himself.

Anyone who has weathered this routine comes to value policy analysis. The very idea that there should be some identifiable objectives and that attention should be paid to whether these are achieved seems a great step forward. Devising alternative ways of handling problems and considering the future costs of each solution appear creative in comparison to more haphazard approaches. Yet policy analysis with its emphasis upon originality, imagination, and foresight, cannot be simply described. It is equivalent to what Robert N. Anthony has called strategic planning: ". . . the process of deciding on objectives of the organization, on changes in these objectives, on the resources used to attain these objectives. . . . It connotes big plans, important plans, plans with major consequences."[1] Policy analysis is similar to a broadly conceived version of systems analysis.[2] Yehezkel Dror has pointed up the boundaries that separate a narrow study from one with larger policy concerns. In policy analysis—

> 1. Much attention would be paid to the political aspects of public decisionmaking and public policymaking (instead of ignoring or condescendingly regarding political aspects). . . .
> 2. A broad conception of decisionmaking and policymaking would be involved (instead of viewing all decisionmaking as mainly a resource allocation). . . .
> 3. A main emphasis would be on creativity and search for new policy alternatives, with explicit attention to encouragement of innovative thinking. . . .
> 4. There would be extensive reliance on . . . qualitative methods. . . .
> 5. There would be much more emphasis on futuristic thinking. . . .
> 6. The approach would be looser and less rigid, but nevertheless systematic, one which would recognize the complexity of means-ends interdependence, the multiplicity of relevant criteria of decision, and the partial and tentative nature of every analysis. . . .[3]

Policy analysis aims at providing information that contributes to making an agency politically and socially relevant. Policies are goals, objectives, and missions that guide the agency. Analysis evaluates and sifts alternative means and ends in the elusive pursuit of policy recommendations. By getting out of the firehouse environment of day-to-day administration, policy analysis seeks knowledge and opportunities for coping with an uncertain future. Because policy analysis is not concerned with projecting the *status quo,* but with tracing out the consequences of innovative ideas, it is a variant of planning. Complementing the agency's decision process, policy analysis is a tool of social change.

In view of its concern with creativity, it is not surprising that policy analysis is still largely an art form; there are no precise rules about how to do it. The policy analyst seeks to reduce obscurantism by being explicit about problems and solutions, resources and results. The purpose of policy analysis is not to eliminate advocacy but to raise the level of argument among contending interests. If poor people want greater benefits from the government, the answer to their problems may not lie initially in policy analysis but in political organization. Once they have organized themselves, they may want to undertake policy analysis in order to crystallize their own objectives or merely to compete with the analyses put forth by others. The end result, hopefully, would be a higher quality debate and perhaps eventually public choice among better known alternatives.

A belief in the desirability of policy analysis—the sustained application of intelligence and knowledge to social problems—is not enough to insure its success, no more than to want to do good is sufficient to accomplish noble purposes. If grandiose claims are made, if heavy burdens are placed on officials without adequate compensation, if the needs of agency heads are given scant consideration, they will not desire policy analysis. It is clear that those who introduced the PPB system into the federal government in one fell swoop did not undertake a policy analysis on how to introduce policy analysis into the federal government.

In a paper called "The Political Economy of Efficiency,"[4] written just as PPBS was begun in national government, I argued that it would run up against serious difficulties. There is still no reason to change a single word of what I said then. Indeed, its difficulties have been so overwhelming that there is grave danger that policy analysis will be rejected along with its particular manifestation in PPBS. In this essay I shall assess the damage that the planning-programing-budgeting system has done to the prospects of encouraging policy analysis in American national government. Then I would like to suggest some ways of enabling policy analysis to thrive and prosper.

WHY DEFENSE WAS A BAD MODEL

A quick way of seeing what went wrong with PPBS is to examine the preconditions for the use of this approach in the Defense Department, from which it was exported throughout the federal government. The immediate origins of PPBS are to be found in The RAND Corporation,[5] where, after World War II, a talented group of analysts devoted years of effort to understanding problems of defense policy. It took five years to come up with the first useful ideas. Thus the first requisite of program budgeting in defense was a small group of talented people who had spent years developing insights into the special problems of defense strategy and logistics. The second requisite was a common terminology, an accepted collection of analytical approaches, and the beginnings of theoretical statements to guide policy analysis. When Secretary of Defense Robert McNamara came into office, he did not have to search for men of talent nor did he have to wait for a body of knowledge to be created. These requisites already existed in some degree. What was then necessary was his ability to understand and to use analytical studies. Thus the third requisite of program budgeting is top leadership that understands policy analysis and is determined to get it and make use of it.

The fourth requisite was the existence of planning and planners. Planning was well accepted at the various levels of the Defense Department with the variety of joint service plans, long-range requirement plans, logistical plans, and more. Military and civilian decisionmakers believed in planning, in coping with uncertainty and in specifying some consequences of policy decisions. The problem as the originators of PPBS saw it was to introduce cost considerations into planning; they wanted to stop blue-sky planning and to integrate planning and budgeting. They wanted to use the program budget to bridge the gap between military planners, who cared about requirements but not about resources, and budget people, who were narrowly concerned with financial costs but not necessarily with effective policies.

Policy analysis is expensive in terms of time, talent, and money. It requires a high degree of creativity in order to imagine new policies and to test them out without requiring actual experience. Policy analysis calls for the creation of systems in which elements are linked to one another and to operational indicators so that costs and effectiveness of alternatives may be systematically compared. There is no way of knowing in advance whether the analysis will prove intellectually satisfying and politically feasible. Policy analysis is facilitated when: (a) goals are easily specified, (b) a large margin of error is allowable, and (c) the cost of the contemplated policy makes large expenditures on analysis worthwhile. That part of defense policy dealing with choices among alternative weapons systems was ideally suited for policy analysis. Since the cost of intercontinental missiles or other weapons systems ran into the billions of dollars, it was easy to justify spending millions on analysis.[6] The potential effectiveness of weapons like intercontinental missiles could be contemplated so long as one was willing to accept large margins of error. It is not unusual for analysts to assume extreme cases of damage and vulnerability in a context in which the desire for reducing risk is very great. Hence a goal like assuring sufficient destructive power such that no enemy strike could prevent devastation of one's country may be fuzzy without being unusable. If one accepts a procedure of imagining that possible enemies were to throw three times as much megatonnage as intelligence estimates suggest they have, he need not be overly troubled by doubts about the underlying theory. If one is willing to pay the cost of compensating against the worst, lack of knowledge will not matter so much. The point is not that this is an undesirable analytic procedure, but that the extreme cases were allowed to determine the outcomes.

INERTIA

The introduction of new procedures that result in new policies is not easy. Inertia is always a problem. Members of the organization and its clientele groups have vested interests in the policies of the past. Efforts at persuasion must be huge and persistent. But there are conditions that facilitate change. One of these is a rising level of appropriations. If change means that things must be taken away from people in the organization without giving them anything in return, greater resistance may be expected. The ability to replace old rewards with larger new ones helps reduce resistance to change. The fact that defense appropriations were increasing at a fast rate made life much easier for Mr. McNamara. The expected objections of clientele groups, for example, were muted by the fact that defense contractors had lots of work, even if it was not exactly what they expected. Rapid organizational growth may also improve the possibilities for change. The sheer increase in organizational size means that many new people can be hired who are not tied to the old ways. And speedy promotion may help convince members that the recommended changes are desirable.

The deeper change goes into the bowels of the organization, the more difficult it is to achieve. The more change can be limited to central management, the greater the possibility for carrying it out. The changes introduced in the Defense Department did not, for the most part, require acceptance at the lower levels. Consider a proposed change in the organization of fighting units that would drastically reduce the traditional heavy support facilities for ground forces. Such a change is not easily manipulated from Washington. But the choice of one weapons system over another is much more amenable to central control. The kinds of problems for which program budgeting was most useful also turned out to be problems that could be dealt with largely at the top of the organization. The program budget group that Mr. McNamara established had to fight with generals in Washington, but not with master sergeants in supply. Anyone who knows the army knows what battle they would rather be engaged in fighting.

The ability of an organization to secure rapid change depends, of course, on the degree of its autonomy from the environment. I have argued elsewhere[7] that the President of the United States has much more control over America's foreign policy than over its domestic policy. In almost any area of domestic policy there is a well-entrenched structure of interests. In foreign and defense policy, excluding such essentially internal concerns as the National Guard, the territory within the American political system is not nearly so well defended; there are far fewer political fortifications, mines, and boobytraps.

PERSONNEL

Experienced personnel may be a barrier to change. They know something about the consequences of what they are doing. They may have tried a variety of alternatives and can point to reasons why each one will not work. If I may recall my low-level Army experience (I entered as a private first class and was never once demoted), the usual reply to a question about the efficacy of present practice was, "Have you ever been in combat, son?" But the most dramatic changes introduced in the Pentagon had to do with questions of avoiding or limiting nuclear war, in which no one had a claim to experience and in which the basic purpose of analysis is to make certain that we do not have to learn from experience. If the system fails, the game is over. And since McNamara's men possessed a body of doctrines on defense policy, they had an enormous advantage over the regular military who were for a long time unable to defend themselves properly in the new field.[8]

The new policy analysts did not accept the currency of military experience. In their view, naked judgment was not a satisfactory answer to why a policy should be adopted. The Army might know the firepower of an infantry division, but firepower was not "effectiveness." Competition among the services for appropriations, however, was favorable to PPBS. There was a defense budget that covered virtually all of the Department's subject matter. There were defense missions in which trade-offs could be made between the services. Resources could actually be diverted if the analysis "proved" a particular service was right. Programs could easily be developed because of the facile identification of program with weapons systems and force units. Once the military learned the jargon, they were willing to play the game for an extra division or carrier. So long as dollar losses in one program were more than made up by gains in another, the pain of policy analysis was considerably eased.

The favorable conditions for the limited use of program budgeting in the Department of Defense do not exist in most domestic agencies. There are no large groups of talented policy analysts expert in agency problems outside the federal government. These nonexistent men cannot, therefore, be made available to the agencies. (The time has passed when eighth-rate systems engineers in aerospace industries are expected to solve basic social problems overnight.) Most agencies had few planners and even less experience in planning. There is no body of knowledge waiting to be applied to policy areas such as welfare and crime. A basic reason for wanting more policy analysis is to help create knowledge where little now exists. There are only a few agencies in which top managers want systematic policy analysis and are able to understand quantitative studies. Goals are not easily specified for most domestic agencies. Nor do they usually have handy equivalents for programs like expensive weapons systems. What Thomas Schelling has so pungently observed about the Department of State—it does not control a large part of the budget devoted to foreign policy—is true for the domestic departments and their lack of coverage as well.[9]

Except for a few individual programs like the proposals for income supplements or assessing the desirability of a supersonic transport, the cost of most domestic policies does not rise into the billions of dollars. Congress and interested publics are not disposed to allow large margins of error. Instead of increasing, the availability of federal funds began declining soon after the introduction of program budgeting. A higher level of conflict was inevitable, especially since the acceptance of proposed changes required the acquiescence of all sorts of people and institutions in the far-flung reaches of the agencies. Social workers, city officials, police chiefs, welfare mothers, field officers, and numerous others were involved in the policies. Program budgeting on the domestic side takes place in a context in which there is both less autonomy from the environment and a great deal more firsthand experience by subordinates. On these grounds alone no one should have been surprised that program budgeting in the domestic agencies did not proceed as rapidly or with as much ostensible success as in the Defense Department.[10]

NO ONE CAN DO PPBS

In past writings I argued that program budgeting would run up against severe political difficulties. While most of these arguments have been conceded, I have been told that in a better world, without the vulgar intrusion of political factors (such as the consent of the governed), PPBS would perform its wonders as advertised. Now it is clear that for the narrow purpose of predicting why program budgeting would not work there was no need to mention political problems at all. It would have been sufficient to say that the wholesale introduction of PPBS presented insuperable difficulties of calculation. All the obstacles previously mentioned, such as lack of talent, theory, and data, may be summed up in a single statement: *no one knows how to do program budgeting.* Another way of putting it would be to say that many know what program budgeting should be like in general, but no one knows what it should be in any particular case. Program budgeting cannot be stated in operational terms. There is no agreement on what the words mean, let alone an ability to show another person what should be done. The reason for the difficulty is that telling an agency to adopt program budgeting means telling it to find better policies and there is no formula for doing that. One can (and should) talk about measuring effectiveness, estimating costs, and comparing alternatives, but that is a far cry from being able to take the creative leap towards formulating a better policy.

Pattern of Events

On the basis of numerous discussions with would-be practitioners of program budgeting at the federal level, I think I can describe the usual pattern of events. The instructions come down from the Bureau of the Budget. You must have a program budget. Agency personnel hit the panic button. They just do not know how to do what they have been asked to do. They turn, if they can, to the pitifully small band of refugees from the Pentagon who have come to light the way. But these Defense intellectuals do not know much about the policy area in which they are working. That takes time. Yet something must quickly come out of all this. So they produce a vast amount of inchoate information characterized by premature quantification of irrelevant items. Neither the agency head nor the examiners in the Bureau of the Budget can comprehend the material submitted to them. Its very bulk inhibits understanding. It is useless to the Director of the Budget in making his decisions. In an effort to be helpful, the program analysis unit at the Budget Bureau says something like, "Nice try, fellows; we appreciate all that effort. But you have not quite got the idea of program budgeting yet. Remember, you must clarify goals, define objectives, relate these to quantitative indicators, project costs into the future. Please send a new submission based on this understanding."

Another furious effort takes place. They do it in Defense, so it must be possible. Incredible amounts of overtime are put in. Ultimately, under severe time pressure, even more data is accumulated. No one will be able to say that agency personnel did not try hard. The new presentation makes a little more sense to some people and a little less to others. It just does not hang together as a presentation of agency policies. There are more encouraging words from the Budget Bureau and another sermon about specifying alternative ways of meeting agency objectives, though not, of course, taking the old objectives for granted. By this time agency personnel are desperate. "We would love to do it," they say, "but we cannot figure out the right way. You experts in the Budget Bureau should show us how to do it." Silence. The word from on high is that the Bureau of the Budget does not interfere with agency operations; it is the agency's task to set up its own budget. After a while, cynicism reigns supreme.

PPBS must be tremendously inefficient. It resembles nothing so much as a Rube Goldberg apparatus in which the operations performed bear little relation to the output achieved. The data inputs into PPBS are huge and its policy output is tiny. All over the federal government the story is the same: if you ask what good PPBS has done, those who have something favorable to say invariably cite the same one or two policy analyses. At one time I began to wonder if the oil shale study[11] in the Interior Department and the maternal and child health care program[12] in Health, Education, and Welfare were all that had ever come out of the programing effort.

The orders to expand PPBS did not say, "Let us do more policy analysis than we have in the past." What it said was, "Let us make believe we can do policy analysis on everything." Instead of focusing attention on areas of policy amenable to study, the PPBS apparatus requires information on *all* agency policies.

Program Structure

The fixation on program structure is the most pernicious aspect of PPBS. Once PPBS is adopted, it becomes necessary to have a program structure that provides a complete list of organization objectives and supplies information on the attainment of each one. In the absence of analytic studies for all or even a large part of an agency's operations, the structure turns out to be a sham that piles up meaningless data under vague categories.[13] It hides rather than clarifies. It suggests comparisons among categories for which there is no factual or analytical basis. Examination of a department's program structure convinces everyone acquainted with it that policy analysis is just another bad way of masquerading behind old confusions. A mere recitation of some program categories from the Department of Agriculture —"Communities of Tomorrow," "Science in the Service of Man," "Expanding Dimensions for Living"—makes the point better than any comment.

Even if the agency head does understand a data reduction summarization of the program budget, he still cannot use the structure to make decisions, because it is too hard to adjust the elaborate apparatus. Although the system dredges up information under numerous headings, it says next to nothing about the impact of one program on another. There is data but no causal analysis. Hence the agency head is at once oversupplied with masses of numbers and undersupplied with propositions about the impact of any action he might undertake. He cannot tell, because no one knows, what the marginal change he is considering would mean for the rest of his operation. Incremental changes at the Bureau of the Budget at the agency level are made in terms of the old budget categories. Since the program structure is meant to be part of the budget, however, it must be taken as a statement of current policy and it necessarily emerges as a product of organizational compromise. The program structure, therefore, does not embody a focus on central policy concerns. More likely, it is a haphazard arrangement that reflects the desire to manipulate external support and to pursue internal power aspirations. Being neither program nor budget, program structure is useless. It is the Potemkin Village of modern administration. The fact that generating bits of random data for the program structure takes valuable time away from more constructive concerns also harms policy analysis. The whole point of policy analysis is to show that what had been done intuitively in the past may be done better through sustained application of intelligence. The adoption of meaningless program structures, and their perversion into slogans for supporting existing policies, does not—to say the least—advance the cause of policy analysis.

Gorham Testimony

I do not mean to suggest that the introduction of PPBS has not led to some accomplishments. Before we consider the significance of these accomplishments, however, it is essential that we understand what PPBS has manifestly *not* done. One could hardly have a better witness on this subject than William Gorham, formerly Assistant Secretary (Program Coordination), Department of Health, Education, and Welfare, and now head of the Urban Institute, who is widely acknowledged to be an outstanding practitioner of program budgeting.

At the highest level of generality, it is clear that PPBS does not help in making choices between vast national goals such as health and defense, nor is PPBS useful in making tradeoffs between more closely related areas of policy such as health, education, and welfare. In his testimony before the Joint Economic Committee, Gorham put the matter bluntly:

> Let me hasten to point out that we have not attempted any grandiose cost-benefit analysis designed to reveal whether the total benefits from an additional million dollars spent on health programs would be higher or lower than that from an additional million spent on education or welfare. If I was ever naive enough to think this sort of analysis possible, I no longer am. The benefits of health, education, and welfare programs are diverse and often intangible. They affect different age groups and different regions of the population over different periods of time. No amount of analysis is going to tell us whether the nation benefits more from sending a

> slum child to preschool, providing medical care to an old man, or enabling a disabled housewife to resume her normal activities. The "grand decisions"—how much health, how much education, how much welfare, and which groups in the population shall benefit—are questions of value judgments and politics. The analyst cannot make much contribution to their resolution.[14]

It turns out that it is extremely difficult to get consensus on goals within a single area of policy. As a result, the policy analysts attempt to find objectives that are more clearly operational and more widely acceptable. Gorham speaks with the voice of experience when he says:

> Let me give you an example. Education. What we want our kids to be as a result of going to school is the level of objective which is the proper and the broadest one. But we want our children to be different sorts of people. We want them to be capable of different sorts of things. We have, in other words, a plurality of opinions about what we want our schools to turn out. So you drop down a level and you talk about objectives in terms of educational attainment—years of school completed and certain objective measures of quality. Here you move in education from sort of fuzzy, but very important, objectives about what it is that you want the schools to be doing, to the more concrete, less controversial, more easily to get agreed upon objectives having to do with such things as educational attainment, percentage of children going to college, etc.
>
> I think the same thing is true in health and in social services, that at the very highest level objective, where in theory you would really like to say something, the difficulty of getting and finding a national consensus is so great that you drop down to something which is more easily and readily accepted as objectives.[15]

What can actually be done, according to Gorham, are analytic studies of narrowly defined areas of policy. "The less grand decisions," Gorham testified, "those among alternative programs with the same or similar objectives within health—can be substantially illuminated by good analysis. It is this type of analysis which we have undertaken at the Department of Health, Education, and Welfare."[16] Gorham gives as examples disease control programs and improvements in the health of children. If this type of project analysis is what can be done under PPBS, a serious question is raised: Why go through all the rigamarole in order to accomplish a few discrete studies of important problems?

A 5-year budget conceived in the hodgepodge terms of the program structure serves no purpose.[17] Since actual budget decisions are made in terms of the old categories and policy analysis may take place outside of the program structure, there is no need to institutionalize empty labels. If a policy analysis has been completed, there is no reason why it cannot be submitted as part of the justification of estimates to the Bureau of the Budget and to Congress. For the few program memoranda that an agency might submit, changes could be detailed in terms of traditional budget categories. Problems of program structure would be turned over to the agency's policy analysts who would experiment with different ways of lending intellectual coherence to the agency's programs. There would be no need to foist the latest failure on a skeptical world. Nor would there be battles over the costs of altering a program structure that has achieved, if not a common framework, at least the virtue of familiarity. The difference is that stability of categories in the traditional budget has real value for control[18] while the embodiment of contradictions in the program structure violates its essential purpose.

Incentives for Policy Analysis

PPBS discredits policy analysis. To collect vast amounts of random data is hardly a serious analysis of public policy. The conclusion is obvious. The shotgun marriage between policy analysis and budgeting should be annulled. Attempts to describe the total agency program in program memoranda should be abandoned. It is hard enough to do a good job of policy analysis, as most agency people now realize, without having to meet arbitrary and fixed deadlines imposed by the budget process. I have proposed that policy analysis would be facilitated by abolishing the annual budget cycle. One of the great weaknesses of governmental policymaking is that policies are formulated a good two years before funds become available. Given the difficulties of devising policies in the first place, the timelag wreaks havoc with the best analysis. Since no one seems disposed to consider this alternative seriously, I mention it merely in passing as a change that would fit in with what has been suggested.

There is no way of telling whether an analysis will be successful. There is, therefore, no point in insisting that half-baked analyses be submitted every year because of a misguided desire to cover the entire agency program. The Budget Bureau itself has recently recognized the difficulty by requiring agencies to present extensive memoranda only when major policy issues have been identified. It is easier and more honest just to take the program structure out of the budget.

The thrust of the argument thus far, however, forces us to confront a major difficulty. Policy analysis and budgeting were presumably connected in order to see that high quality analysis did not languish in limbo but was translated into action through the critical budget process. Removing policy analysis from the annual budget cycle might increase its intellectual content at the expense of its practical impact. While formal program structures should go—PPBS actually inhibits the prospects for obtaining good analysis that is worth translating into public policy—they should be replaced with a strong incentive to make policy analysis count in yearly budgetary decisions. I am therefore proposing a substitute for PPBS that maintains whatever incentive it provided for introducing the results of policy analysis into the real world without encouraging the debilitating effects.

The submission of program memoranda supported by policy analysis should be made a requirement for major dollar changes in an agency's budget. The Bureau of the Budget should insist that this requirement be met by every agency. Agency heads, therefore, would have to require it of subunits. The sequence could operate as follows:

1. Secretary of agency and top policy analysts review major issues and legislation and set up a study menu for several years. Additions and deletions are made periodically.

2. Policy analysts set up studies which take anywhere from 6 to 24 months.

3. As a study is completed for a major issue area, it is submitted to the Secretary of the agency for review and approval.

4. If approved, the implications of the study's recommendations are translated into budgetary terms for submission as a program memorandum in support of the agency's fiscal year budget.

No one imagines that a mechanical requirement would in and of itself compel serious consideration of policy matters. No procedure should be reified as if it had a life of its own apart from the people who must implement it. This conclusion is as true for my suggestion as for PPBS. We must therefore consider ways and means of increasing the demand for and supply of policy analysis.

INCREASING DEMAND AND SUPPLY

The first requirement of effective policy analysis is that top management want it. No matter how trite this criterion sounds, it has often been violated, as Frederick C. Mosher's splendid study of program budgeting in foreign affairs reveals.[19] The inevitable difficulties of shaking loose information and breaking up old habits will prove to be insuperable obstacles without steady support from high agency officials. If they do not want it, the best thing to do is concentrate efforts in another agency. Placing the best people in a few agencies also makes it more likely that a critical mass of talent will be able to achieve a creative response to emerging policy problems.

Policy analysis should be geared to the direct requirements of top management. This means that analysis should be limited to a few major issues. Since there will only be a few studies every year, the Secretary should have time to consider and understand each one. The analytical staff should be flexible enough to work on his priority interests. Consequently, one of the arguments by which program budgeting has been oversold has to be abandoned. Policy analysis will not normally identify programs of low priority. Top management is not interested in them. They would receive no benefit from getting supporters of these programs angry at them. Instead, agency heads want to know how to deal with emergent problems. Practitioners of policy analysis understand these considerations quite well. Harry Shooshan, Deputy Under Secretary for Programs, Department of the Interior, presents a perceptive analysis:

> . . . We have tried to more heavily relate our PPB work and our analytical work to the new program thrusts, and major issues, not because it is easier to talk about new programs, but rather, there is a good question of judgment, on how much time one should spend on ongoing programs that are pretty well set. So you restate its mission and you put it in PPB wrapping and what have you really accomplished?
>
> There are going to be new program proposals, new thrusts of doing something in certain areas. Let's relate our analyses to that and get the alternatives documented as well as we can for the decisionmakers. So it is a combination of on the one hand it being difficult to identify low priorities in a manner that really means something and on the other hand, it is the fact of what have we really accomplished by simply putting old programs in new wrappings when new programs really should get the emphasis right now in terms of what are the decisions now before, in my case, the Secretary of the Interior, in terms of what should he know before he makes decisions relative to where he is attempting to go. If I can relate PPB to the decision on his desk today and the near future, I can sell him and in turn, our own Department on the contribution that we can make.[20]

The implications of Shooshan's point go beyond making policy analysis more desirable by having it meet the needs of top management. The subjects for policy analysis ought to be chosen precisely for their critical-fluid-emergent character. These are the places where society is hurting. These are the areas in which there are opportunities for marginal gains. Indeed, a major role for top management is scanning the political horizon for targets of opportunity. Yet the characteristics of these new problems run counter to the criteria for selection that PPBS currently enforces, since they are identified by ambiguity concerning goals, lack of data upon which to project accurate estimates of costs and consequences, and pervasive uncertainty concerning the range of possible changes in program.

There would be a much larger demand for policy analysis if it were supplied in ways that would meet the needs of high-level officials. Let us consider the example of the president of the United States. He can certainly use policy analysis to help make better decisions. Substantial policy studies would give him and his staff leverage against the bureaucracy. Knowledge is power. Indeed, command of a particular field would enable presidents to exert greater control over the agenda for public decision and would give them advantages in competition with all sorts of rivals. Presidents could use perhaps a dozen major policy studies per year of their most immediate concerns. If even a few of these turn out well, the president may be motivated to make use of them. Contrast this with the present inundation of the Executive Office by endless streams of program "books," summaries, and memoranda that nobody ever looks at.

What is true of the president is also true for important executives in the agencies. Policy-oriented executives will want to get better analysis. Executives wishing to increase their resource base will be interested in independent sources of information and advice. Those who would exert power need objectives to fight for. It is neither fashionable nor efficient to appear to seek power for its own sake. In polite society the drive is masked and given a noble face when it can be attached to grand policy concerns that bring benefits to others as well as to power seekers. The way to gain the attention of leaders is not to flood them with trivia but to provide examples of the best kind of work that can be done. The last years of the Johnson administration witnessed a proliferation of secret commissions to recommend new policies. The department secretary often became just another special pleader. If they have any interest in curbing this development, secretaries may find that producing their own policy analyses allows them to say that outside intervention is not the only or the best way to generate new policies.

CONGRESSIONAL DEMAND

If strategically located congressmen demanded more policy analysis, there is little doubt that we could get it. What can be done to make them want more of it? The answer does not lie in surrounding them with large staffs so that they lose their manifestly political functions and become more like bureaucrats. Nor does the answer lie in telling congressmen to keep away from small administrative questions in favor of larger policy concerns. For many congressmen get into the larger questions only by feeling their way through the smaller details. A threat to deprive congressmen of the traditional line-item appropriations data through which they exert their control of agency affairs also does not appear to be a good way of making congressmen desire policy analysis.

Policy analysis must be made relevant to what congressmen want. Some legislators desire to sponsor new policies and they are one clientele for analysis. For other congressmen, however, policy is a bargainable product that emerges from their interactions with their fellows. These members must be appealed to in a different way. They often have a sense of institutional loyalty and pride. They know that Congress is a rare institution in this world—a legislative body that actually has some control over public policy. They are aware that the development of new knowledge and new techniques may freeze them out of many of the more serious decisions. Policy analysis should be proposed to these men as an enhancement of the power of Congress as an institution. The purpose of analysis would be, in its simplest form, to enable congressmen to ask good questions and to evaluate answers. Oftentimes it is hardest for a layman to recognize the significant questions implicit in an area of policy. Are there other and better questions to be asked, other and better policies to be pursued?

A Congress that takes seriously its policy role should be encouraged to contract for policy analysis that would stress different views of what the critical questions are in a particular area of policy. Each major committee or subcommittee should be encouraged to hire a man trained in policy analysis for a limited period, perhaps two years. His task would be to solicit policy studies, evaluate presentations made by government agencies, and keep congressmen informed about what are considered the important questions. In the past, chairmen have not always paid attention to the quality of committee staffs. Following the lead of the Joint Economic Committee, seminars might be held for a couple of weeks before each session. At these seminars discussions would take place between agency personnel, committee staff, and the academics or other experts who have produced the latest policy analysis. If all went well, congressmen would emerge with a better idea of the range of issues and of somewhat different ways of tackling the problems, and the policy analysts would emerge with a better grasp of the priorities of these legislators.

SUPPLIERS OF POLICY ANALYSIS

Thus far we have dealt solely with the incentive structure of the consumers who ought to want policy analysis—agency heads, presidents, congressmen. Little has been said about the incentive structure of the suppliers who ought to provide it—analysts, consultants, academics. Our premise has been that the supply of policy analysis would be a function of the demand. Now, the relationships between supply and demand have long been troublesome in economics because it is so difficult to sort out the mutual interactions. Upon being asked whether demand created supply or supply created demand, the great economist Marshall was reported to have said that it was like asking which blade of the scissors cuts the paper. There is no doubt, however, that changes in the conditions and quality of supply would have important effects on the demand for policy analysis.

Disengaging policy analysis from PPBS would help build the supply of policy analysis by:

1. Decreasing the rewards for mindless quantification for its own sake. There would be no requests from the Bureau of the Budget for such information and no premium for supplying it.

2. Increasing the rewards for analysts who might try the risky business of tackling a major policy problem that was obviously not going to be considered because everyone was too busy playing with the program structure. Gresham's Law operates here: programed work drives out unprogramed activity, make-work drives out analysis.

One way of increasing the supply of policy analysis would be to improve the training of people who work directly in the various areas of policy. Instead of taking people trained in policy analysis and having them learn about a particular policy area, the people in that area would be capable of doing policy analysis. Three-day or 3-month courses will not do for that purpose. A year, and possibly two years, would be required. Since it is unlikely that the best people can be made available for so long a period, it is necessary to think in terms of education at an earlier period in their lives. There is a great need for schools of public policy in which technical training is combined with broader views of the social context of public policy. Although no one knows how to teach "creativity," it is possible to expose students to the range of subjects out of which a creative approach to public policy could come.

Another way of increasing the supply of policy analysis would be to locate it in an organizational context in which it has prestige and its practitioners are given time to do good work. Having the policy analysis unit report directly to the secretary or agency head would show that it is meant to be taken seriously.[21] But then it is bound to get involved in day-to-day concerns of the agency head, thus creating a classic dilemma.

TACTICS

The effective use of a policy analysis unit cannot be specified in advance for all agencies. There are certain tensions in its functions that may be mitigated on a case-by-case basis but cannot be resolved once and for all. Serious policy analysis requires months, if not years, of effort. A unit that spends its time solely on substantial policy analysis would soon find itself isolated from the operational concerns of the agency. There would be inordinate temptations on the part of its members to go where the action is. Before long, the policy unit might become more immediately relevant at the expense of its long term impact. The frantic nature of day-to-day emergencies drives out the necessary time and quiet for serious study and reflection. What can be done? One tactic is for the policy unit to consider itself an educational as well as an action group. Its task should be to encourage analysis on the part of other elements of the organization. It should undertake nothing it can get sub-units to do. The role of the policy unit would then be one of advising sub-units and evaluating their output.

A second tactic would be to contract out for studies that are expected to take the longest period of time. The third tactic is the most difficult, because it calls for a balancing act. Immediate usefulness to top management may be secured by working on problems with short lead times while attempting to retain perhaps half of the available time for genuine policy analysis. To the degree that serious policy analysis enters into the life of the organization and proves its worth, it will be easier to justify its requirements in terms of release from everyday concerns. Yet the demand for services of the analysts is certain to increase. Failures in policy analysis, on the other hand, are likely to give the personnel involved more time for reflection than they would prefer. Like headquarters-field relationships, line and staff responsibilities, and functional versus hierarchical command, the problems of the policy unit are inherent in its situation and can only be temporarily resolved.

These comments on incentives for increasing the supply and demand for policy analysis are plainly inadequate. They are meant merely to suggest that there is a problem and to indicate how one might go about resolving it. We do not really know how to make policy analysis fit in with the career requirements of congressmen, nor can we contribute much beside proverbial wisdom to the structure and operation of policy analysis units. There are, however, opportunities for learning that have not yet been used. One of the benefits flowing from the experience with PPBS is that it has thrown up a small number of policy analyses that practitioners consider to be good. We need to know what makes some live in the world and others remain unused. Aside from an impressive manuscript by Clay Thomas Whitehead,[22] however, in which two recent policy analyses in defense are studied, there has been no effort to determine what this experience has to teach us. Despite the confident talk about policy analysis (here and elsewhere), a great deal of work remains to be done on what is considered good and why. The pioneering work by Charles E. Lindblom should not be wrongly interpreted as being antianalysis, but as a seminal effort to understand what we do when we try to grapple with social problems.

REEXAMINATION

Critical aspects of policy analysis need to be reexamined. The field cries out for a study of coordination as profound and subtle as Martin Landau's essay on "Redundancy."[23] That most elemental problem of political theory —the proper role of the government versus that of the individual—should be subject to a radical critique.[24] The fact that cost-benefit analysis began with water resource projects in which the contribution to national income was the key question has guided thought away from other areas of policy for which this criterion would be inappropriate. There are policies for which the willingness of citizens to support the activity should help determine the outcome. There are other policies in which presently unquantifiable benefits, like pleasure in seeing others better off or reduction of anxiety following a visible decrease in social hostility, should be controlling. Although social invention is incredibly difficult, the way is open for new concepts of the role of government to liberate our thoughts and guide our actions.

In many ways the times are propitious for policy analysis. The New Deal era of legislation has ended and has not yet been replaced by a stable structure of issues. People do not know where they stand today in the same way they knew how they felt about Medicare or private versus public electric power. The old welfare state policies have disenchanted former supporters as well as further enraged their opponents. Men have worked for 20 years to get massive education bills through Congress only to discover that the results have not lived up to their expectations; it takes a lot more to improve education for the deprived than anyone had thought. There is now a receptivity to new ideas that did not exist a decade ago. There is a willingness to consider new policies and try new ways. Whether or not there is sufficient creativity in us to devise better policies remains to be seen. If we are serious about improving public policy, we will go beyond the fashionable pretense of PPBS to show others what the best policy analysis can achieve.

NOTES

[1] Robert N. Anthony, *Planning and Control Systems: A Framework for Analysis* (Boston: Harvard University Press, 1965), p. 16.

[2] Aaron Wildavsky, "The Political Economy of Efficiency," *Public Administration Review,* Vol. XXVI, No. 4, December 1966, pp. 298–302.

[3] Yehezkel Dror, "Policy Analysts: A New Professional Role in Government Service," *Public Administration Review,* Vol. XXVII, No. 3, September 1967, pp. 200–201. See also Dror's major work, *Public Policy-Making Reexamined* (San Francisco: Chandler, 1968).

[4] Wildavsky, *op. cit.*

[5] See David Novick, "Origin and History of Program Budgeting," The RAND Corporation, October 1966, p. 3427.

[6] I once tried to interest a graduate student who had experience with defense

problems in doing research in the city of Oakland. He asked the size of Oakland's budget. "$50 million," I said. "Why, in the Air Force we used to round to that figure," was his reply.

[7] Aaron Wildavsky, "The Two Presidencies," *Trans-action,* Vol. IV, No. 2, December 1966, pp. 7–14.

[8] For further argument along these lines see the author's article, "The Practical Consequences of the Theoretical Study of Defense Policy," *Public Administration Review,* Vol. XXV, No. 1, March 1965, pp. 90–103.

[9] Thomas C. Schelling, "PPBS and Foreign Affairs," memorandum prepared at the request of the Subcommittee on National Security and International Operations of the Committee on Government Operations, U.S. Senate, 90th Cong., first sess., 1968.

[10] Dr. Alain Enthoven, who played a leading role in introducing systems analysis to the Defense Department, has observed that: "The major changes in strategy, the step-up in production of Minutemen and Polaris and the build-up in our non-nuclear forces including the increase in the Army, the tactical air forces, and the air lift . . . were being phased in at the same time that PPBS was being phased in. . . . We speeded up the Polaris and Minuteman programs because we believed that it was terribly important to have an invulnerable retaliatory force. We built up the Army Land Force because we believed it was necessary to have more land forces for limited non-nuclear wars. We speeded up the development of anti-guerrilla forces or special forces because we believed that was necessary for counter-insurgency. Those things would have happened with or without PPBS. PPBS does not make the strategy. Subcommittee on National Security and International Operations of the Committee on Government Operations, U.S. Senate, *Hearings, Planning-Programing-Budgeting,* 90th Cong., first sess., pt. 2, Sept. 27 and Oct. 18, 1967, p. 141.

[11] *Prospects for Oil Shale Development* (Washington, D.C.: Department of the Interior, May 1968).

[12] The study is presented in Committee on Government Operations, *op. cit.,* pp. 10–45.

[13] Similar difficulties under similar conditions evidently occur in the business world. It is worth citing Anthony's comments: "Strategic planning [that is, policy analysis] is essentially *irregular.* Problems, opportunities, and 'bright ideas' do not arise according to some set timetable; they have to be dealt with whenever they happen to be perceived. . . . Failure to appreciate the distinction between regular and irregular processes can result in trouble of the following type. A company with a well-developed budgeting process decides to formalize its strategic planning. It prepares a set of forms and accompanying procedures, and has the operating units submit their long-range plans on these forms on one certain date each year. The plans are then supposed to be reviewed and approved in a meeting similar to a budget review meeting. Such a procedure does not work. . . . There simply is not time enough in an annual review meeting for a careful consideration of a whole batch of strategic proposals. . . . It is important that next year's operating budget be examined and approved as an entity so as to insure that the several pieces are consonant with one another. . . . Except for very general checklists of essential considerations, the strategic planning process follows no prescribed format or timetable. Each problem is sufficiently different from other problems so that each must be approached differently." *Planning and Control Systems, op. cit.,* pp. 38–39.

[14] Joint Economic Committee, Congress of the United States, Hearings, *The Planning-Programing-Budgeting System: Progress and Potentials,* 90th Cong., first sess., September 1967, p. 5.

[15] *Ibid.,* pp. 80–81. One might think that a way out of the dilemma could be had by adopting a number of goals for an area of policy. When Committee Chairman William Proxmire suggested that more goals should be specified, Gorham replied, "I would like to be the one to give the first goal. The first one in is always in the best shape. The more goals you have, essentially the less useful any one is, because the conflict among them becomes so sharp" (p. 83).

[16] *Ibid.*, p. 6.

[17] Anthony again supplies a useful comparison from private firms that makes a similar point: "An increasing number of businesses make profit and balance sheet projections for several years ahead, a process which has come to be known by the name 'long-range planning.' . . . A 5-year plan usually is a projection of the costs and revenues that are anticipated under policies and programs *already approved,* rather than a device for consideration of, and decision on, new policies and programs. The 5-year plan reflects strategic decisions already taken; it is not the essence of the process of making new decisions. . . . In some companies, the so-called 5-year plan is nothing more than a mechanical extrapolation of current data, with no reflection of management decisions and judgment; such as exercise is virtually worthless." *Planning and Control Systems, op. cit.,* pp. 57–58.

[18] An excellent discussion of different purposes of budgeting and stages of budgetary development is found in Allen Schick, "The Road to PPB: The Stages of Budget Reform," *Public Administration Review,* Vol. XXVI, No. 4, December 1966, pp. 243–258.

[19] Frederick C. Mosher, "Program Budgeting in Foreign Affairs: Some Reflections," memorandum prepared at the request of the Subcommittee on National Security and International Operations of the Committee on Government Operations, U.S. Senate, 90th Cong., second sess., 1968.

[20] Hearings, *The Planning-Programing-Budgeting System: Progress and Potentials, op. cit.,* pp. 77–78.

[21] When Charles Hitch was controller of the Defense Department, the policy analysis unit reported directly to him, as did the budget unit. One reported result is that the policy unit was able to do its work without being drawn into the daily concerns of the budget men. When policy analysis (called systems analysis) was given separate status, with its own assistant secretary, there was apparently a much greater tendency for its members to insist upon control of immediate budgetary decisions. Hence the distinction between longer-run policy analysis and shorter-run budgeting tended to be obscured. It would be interesting to know whether the participants saw it in this way. Optimal placement of a policy analysis unit is bound to be a source of difficulty and a subject of controversy.

[22] Clay Thomas Whitehead, "Uses and Abuses of Systems Analysis," The RAND Corporation, September 1967.

[23] See Martin Landau, "Redundancy," *Public Administration Review,* Vol. XXIX, No. 4, July/August 1969.

[24] For a fine example of original thought on this question, see Paul Feldman, "Benefits and the Role of Government in a Market Economy," Institute for Defense Analysis, Research Paper, February 1968, p. 477. See also the paper by Feldman in U.S. Congress, Joint Economics Committee, *The Analysis and Evaluation of Public Expenditures: The PPB System, op. cit.,* Vol. 3, pp. 865–885, for an elaboration of this argument.

PART FIVE

Policy Analysis in Federal Programs: Some Lessons and Next Steps

****

CHAPTER 20

THE PLANNING, PROGRAMING, AND BUDGETING SYSTEM IN THE DEPARTMENT OF DEFENSE: AN OVERVIEW FROM EXPERIENCE

Alain C. Enthoven and K. Wayne Smith

The purpose of this paper is to discuss briefly the essential ideas behind the Planning, Programing, and Budgeting System (PPBS) in the Department of Defense (DoD), the changes and improvements it has brought in the management of the department from 1961 to the present (January, 1969), some problem areas, and some possible next steps in extending and improving the system.

THE ESSENTIALS OF PPBS

In developing the defense program, the job of the Secretary of Defense is to insure that the interests of the nation take precedence over the special institutional interests of the military services, the defense contractors, the project managers, the scientists, the localities, and the other groups that make up or depend on the Defense Department. PPBS was developed and implemented in DoD in the early 1960s in order to give the Secretary the information and management tools he needed to shape defense programs in the national interest. The fundamental idea behind PPBS is decisionmaking based on explicit criteria of the national interest as opposed to decisionmaking by compromise among various institutional and parochial interests. The main purpose of PPBS is to develop publicly defensible criteria, openly and thoroughly debated by all interested parties, that can be used by

Alain C. Enthoven is vice president of Litton Industries and a consultant to the RAND Corporation. Until January, 1969, he was Assistant Secretary of Defense (Systems Analysis). K. Wayne Smith is a member of the staff of the RAND Corporation and a former Special Assistant to the Assistant Secretary of Defense (Systems Analysis).

Any views expressed in this paper are those of the authors. They should not be interpreted as reflecting the views of the RAND Corporation or any of its governmental or private research sponsors.

the Secretary of Defense as measures of the national need and adequacy of defense programs.

Initially such criteria may be, indeed probably will be, very crude. But one has to start somewhere, and the value of even a rough statement of such criteria is that it generates a debate on better ways of defining the national interest in defense programs. The Secretary of Defense can tell his critics, "if you don't accept these criteria, please come up with better ones."

If the Secretary is to shape defense programs in the national interest, he must also be able to choose from among a number of alternatives. By alternative, we mean a balanced, feasible solution to the problem, not a strawman chosen to make an alternative preferred by the originating staff look better by comparison. Choosing among real alternatives, is the only way the Secretary of Defense can effectively translate his judgments about national security matters into policy. The explicit consideration of alternatives at the top decision level is the second basic idea underlying PPBS.

Some might say that the Secretary of Defense has always considered alternatives. For example, because the Joint Chiefs of Staff (JCS) regularly recommend forces costing roughly 25 percent to 35 percent more than the defense budget the president believes the nation should provide, there is always implicitly one set of alternatives—the Joint Chiefs' force levels (and implied budget) and the Administration's budget and (implied force levels). But the Joint Chiefs' force recommendations have not been developed in the light of an explicit awareness of their costs, and the pre-1961 defense budget ceilings were not explicitly tied to a military strategy and force plan. Thus, each of these alternatives was based on a consideration of only part of the relevant factors. PPBS seeks to insure that the Secretary can judge several alternatives in which strategies, forces, and costs have been considered together. Thus, he and the president can choose a defense budget in full awareness of its implications for the military posture and in light of information on whether extra spending would bring military benefits which justify the sacrifice of other competing public programs.

This search for alternatives, and their explicit consideration by the top level managers in DoD, is a vital part of the defense decisionmaking process. Given the nature of the issues involved, the huge costs, the judgments that must be made, and the uncertainties inherent in any defense program decision, it is not enough for the Secretary of Defense to consider only a single staff solution, no matter how well-reasoned it may be. Yet, prior to the development of PPBS in DoD, presenting realistic alternatives to the Secretary was the exception rather than the rule.

A third basic idea underlying PPBS is considering needs and costs together. In DoD this means identifying the costs of accomplishing major military missions such as strategic retaliation, strategic mobility, and anti-submarine warfare rather than merely identifying costs by object classes of expenditure, such as personnel, operations and maintenance, procurement, and the like.

Military needs and costs must be considered together. Ends and means interact. What is worth trying to do depends in large part on how much it costs to do it. If an Administration is not willing to meet the costs implied by its foreign policy objectives, then it should revise its objectives to bring them into line with the budgets it is willing to provide. Otherwise, the consequence will be an imbalance between objectives and forces and, in all probability, an imbalance among programs designed to support the actual forces. In other words, strategy decisions and budget decisions cannot be sensibly separated. PPBS explicitly recognizes this fact.

Many critics resent the intrusion of cost considerations into the choice of military forces. We frequently heard charges of "overemphasis on cost." But the fact is that our total resources are inevitably limited by other needs in our society, so that the way to get the most effective total defense program is to put each dollar where it will add the most to total effectiveness. If cost is ignored in program design, the result will be a less effective total program.

A fourth major idea of PPBS is that of a forward force and financial plan, i.e., a plan which projects into the future the foreseeable implications of current decisions. Such a plan is not meant to be an inflexible blueprint for the future. Rather, it is a projection of the implications of past decisions, a set of official planning assumptions, and a point of departure in the continuing search for improvements. Having such a plan forces the decisionmaker to look into the future to the time when today's decisions will have their most important effects and to judge programs versus needs in the light of their consequences over time. If a decisionmaker insists on seeing costs over a period of years, proponents of new programs find it harder to conceal the future cost implications of decisions made today, and thereby drive the "thin edge of the budget wedge" into the program.

The practical result of the ideas of tying together needs and costs and of having a forward force and financial plan is the FYDP or Five Year Defense Plan, one of the basic management tools in DoD which makes PPBS work. Developed in 1961 and constantly refined since then, the FYDP is a series of force tables which show an 8-year projection of forces and a 5-year projection of costs displayed in mission-oriented programs. The FYDP not only ties together force and financial planning but provides a vehicle for insuring that the process of changing the approved program is orderly and that the changes are accurately recorded. The FYDP is also the official source of planning assumptions. It is an authoritative record of what the Secretary of Defense has tentatively approved for purposes of force and financial planning. In other words, all interested parties within DoD know how many and what kinds of divisions, squadrons, ships, etc. have been authorized and how many men and how much money it will take to support them. By clearly relating forces to their costs and to the defense budget, the FYDP gives financial planning within DoD the same output orientation as force planning.

This is a major improvement over the pre-1961 system. At that time there was an almost complete gap between force planning, which was long range, expressed in terms of combat units and performed mainly by military planners in the Joint Staff and the services; and financial planning, which was short range, expressed in terms of objects of expenditure, and performed mainly by civilians in the Comptroller organization. Given this situation, it is not surprising that there were serious imbalances in the defense posture—divisions without equipment and ammunition or the airlift to move them, aircraft without spare parts, and so on.

With the FYDP, there is a common planning base in the literally hundreds of separate agencies and offices in DoD. The left hand can know what the right hand does and plans to do. Logistic planners can see how many and what kinds of divisions are planned and budget for ammunition accordingly. Each service can see what is planned for the other and thus better determine what forces are needed for common missions. The air force, for example, can see how large an army is projected and plan its airlift capability accordingly. Furthermore, with a common set of planning assumptions, the wastefulness associated with starting or continuing a great many individual service projects which will all do the same job can be and has been reduced. By providing this common planning base and tying together forces and costs by major mission areas over time, the FYDP has contributed significantly to the acquisition of more balanced and better-supported forces.

The very characteristics of effective management tools such as the FYDP have led to much of the political opposition to PPBS. Since the FYDP does constitute an official record of program decisions and tentative planning assumptions, it requires the Secretary explicitly to make controversial decisions. This is quite a different procedure from the pre-1961 method of simply setting a 1-year budget ceiling, without nailing down choices between competing programs. One-year ceilings usually led to starting and continuing more and larger programs than the budget could adequately finance since the long term financial implications of decisions were not explicitly considered, and competing claims for resources did not have to be met head on. This, in turn, led the services to hold onto their prestige items (divisions, wings, and ships) at the expense of less glamorous—but essential—support items, causing a progressive deterioration in the real effectiveness and combat readiness of the forces. In the short run, however, a simple budget ceiling generates much less political heat than a system which requires explicit, long-range program decisions. (It also creates better relations with the military. It is much easier to accept, "I'm sorry, but there just isn't enough money in the budget for your program," than "In my judgment, your program isn't worth the extra money.")

A fifth important idea of PPBS is the active use of an analytical staff at the top policymaking levels and the regular use of analysis as an aid to judgment. Most large organizations, governmental or otherwise, have some kind of analytical or planning staff somewhere in the organizational structure. Most often, these staff groups are little more than "window dressing." They are not active contributors to the decisionmaking process. They do not report directly to the top decisionmakers nor do they receive frequent guidance from them as to what studies to undertake for what reasons. More often than not, they do studies that are not read on subjects that are not important. Their continued existence depends on remaining non-controversial and most of them excel in this regard.

But in DoD the active use of an analytical staff at the top policymaking levels has been from the beginning a key element of PPBS. The staff we are referring to, of course, is the Systems Analysis Office.

A 1961 organizational chart of the DoD would show the JCS as the principal advisers to the Secretary of Defense on military strategy and forces; the director of defense research and engineering as the principal adviser on research and engineering matters; the comptroller on financial matters; the assistant secretary for international security affairs on foreign policy matters; and so on down the list. Each adviser was concerned primarily with his own specialty rather than with the defense program in its entirety. The Secretary of Defense was expected to integrate all of this specialized advice and to do so without staff assistance. The Systems Analysis Office was established to gather and analyze information relevant to forces and other major requirements from these different areas and to help the Secretary of Defense fit the pieces together. In other words, it integrated the cost, effectiveness, and requirements data and the recommendations of the services and JCS in such a way that the Secretary could understand what capabilities he was buying, at what cost, and how they related to overall defense needs. It regularly provided the Secretary with the staff assistance necessary to identify and analyze alternative levels and mixes of forces so that his choices were not limited to those proposed by the services and the JCS.

The Systems Analysis Office reported directly to the Secretary of Defense and undertook studies directly at his request. These studies were then formally reviewed by all interested parties and, upon completion of the review, formed a major input to the decisionmaking process. The purpose of such studies was not primarily to determine the "best" solution, even given a certain set of assumptions. Rather, their purpose was to sort out which assumptions were important and show how they affected the outcome, so that judgment could be focused on the really crucial issues. In short, the purpose of analysis as used in DoD between 1961 and 1968 was to illuminate and inform judgment, not to replace it.

A final basic idea of PPBS is that analysis should be open and explicit. That is, each analysis should be made available to all interested parties so that they can see what assumptions were used and so they can retrace the steps leading to the conclusions. Open and explicit analysis is our best protection against persistence in error and against reaching conclusions on the basis of hidden or rigged assumptions. It also helps to build confidence in the results of an analysis. All calculations, assumptions, empirical data, and judgments should be described in an analysis in such a way that they can be checked, tested, debated, discussed, and possibly refuted. Adversary proceedings are the best stimulant to analytical progress. More importantly, analyses *should* be tested, checked, and debated by all interested parties. Analyses should not be believed simply because they are analyses. It is the method—not the authority—of analysis that is important.

The analysis and debate of issues within DoD has been carried on in a variety of ways. Between 1961 and 1968 one key vehicle was the Draft Presidential Memorandum (DPM). A series of these memorandums, each addressing a major functional area, was prepared annually by the Office of the Secretary of Defense (OSD). Each DPM was initially prepared based on the guidance given by the Secretary and using the latest available DoD analyses, intelligence information, and service and JCS recommendations. Each DPM (called a "For Comment" draft at this stage) expressed not only the Secretary's initial, tentative decisions, but his reasons for those decisions. The services and the JCS were then asked formally to comment on each DPM, beginning a process of debate and interaction which lasted most of the year, and which generated innumerable special studies and additional memoranda. In short, every interested party not only had his say but had an opportunity to say it several times.

Another key vehicle for structuring debate was the Development Concept Paper (DCP). The DCPs, which did not become a regular procedure until late in 1967, represented an attempt to document the performance, cost, and schedule estimates, as well as the technical risks, which were the basis for a decision to start or continue a major development program. Each interested party was required to concur in these estimates or state explicitly his objections. The goal was not to insist on completely accurate cost and schedule estimates but rather to combat tendencies to grossly overstate expected performance and grossly understate costs and risks merely to get a project underway.

The DCPs also provided thresholds in these estimates which, if exceeded, would call for a review of the project by the Secretary of Defense. Estimates in a DCP were then periodically updated, and the new estimates compared with the original ones, so that the Secretary could see if expectations were being realized and if the reasons for continuing the project were still valid. If there were conflicting ideas about the potential usefulness of a proposed new weapon system, the DCPs helped bring those disagreements out into the open for further debate and discussion.

One of the most significant achievements of PPBS in DoD has been the stimulation of intense but orderly debate over relevant program issues, not just over arbitrary allocations of budget ceilings. Indeed, in a very meaningful practical sense, PPBS is a set of ground rules for constructive debate. This aspect of the system is especially interesting, in view of the charges that it has "shut off discussion" and "frozen the military out of decisions." In fact, one of the most successful aspects of PPBS has been the focusing of the inevitable conflict and debate within DoD onto a much more constructive and objective level than before.

Open and explicit analysis, reviewed and commented on by all interested parties, is fundamental to the workings of PPBS in the Pentagon. Through such vehicles as the DPMs and DCPs the analyses underlying the Secretary's decisions were circulated for comment and review by all interested parties. These comments went directly to the Secretary. The procedures were designed so that the Secretary would hear all sides, so that no one had a monopoly on the information going to him. They helped to insure that all important assumptions were made explicit, that all interested parties were given "due process," and that all opinions were fully considered.

Decisionmaking based on explicit criteria of the national interest, the consideration of real alternatives, evaluating needs and costs together, a forward force and financial plan, the active use of an analytical staff at the top policymaking level and the regular use of analysis as an aid to judgment, the concept of open and explicit analysis—these are the fundamental ideas upon which PPBS was developed and has operated in DoD. As we have seen, these ideas are clearly reflected in the principal management tools that have made PPBS work—the FYDP, the DPMs, the DCPs, and the Systems Analysis Office. They are also reflected in the procedures established for debate and review. But it is these underlying ideas and not the specific tools or procedures that are fundamental. There is nothing easy or mechanical about PPBS. It is not a closed, rigid, or perfected system. In its broadest sense, it is an approach to management—an approach that, we believe, has helped to channel the initiative, drive, imagination, dedication, hard work and judgment of the civilian and military leaders in DoD along more rational and objective lines.

PPBS has provided the Secretary of Defense more useful information and meaningful alternatives than he had before. It has provided an effective framework for making and carrying out major program decisions in an informed and orderly way. By unifying programing and budgeting, it has closed the "gap" between force and financial planning. By providing an official force plan, it has given the planners and analysts in the whole department a firm foundation for their planning and a solid point of departure for their analyses. It has led to a major improvement in the quality and relevance of debate over requirements. Under PPBS, the idea of open and explicit analysis, reviewed and commented on by all interested parties has been widely accepted. The systematic search for real alternatives to prevent the Secretary from being the prisoner of a single staff solution has become the rule rather than the exception. The consideration of requirements on an overall mission basis, rather than on the basis of a single service, has led to the elimination of much unnecessary duplication in research and development projects. Most importantly, PPBS has helped to give the Secretary of Defense the information and analyses to see what the major alternatives are from a department-wide point of view and to help him make a reasoned choice among them. It has given him a way to structure debate over defense issues along objective lines. In an organization as large and diverse as the Department of Defense, where many issues are highly emotional, where the "facts" are hard to pin down, and where parochial and institutional interests constantly compete with the national interest, these are not small accomplishments.

SOME PROBLEM AREAS

PPBS as it now exists is a good foundation on which to build, but it is by no means complete. Indeed, one of the more desirable aspects of the system is that it has helped to identify additional areas where improvements are needed. Four such problem areas are: (1) the quality and usefulness of analyses; (2) the lack of good cost estimates and test data on new equipment; (3) the lack of an adequate theory of requirements in many important areas; and (4) inadequate economic discipline in the services.

While some of the study effort on defense programs has been excellent, much has been relatively poor. Ideally, the large-scale study effort within the services, the Joint Staff, and the major contract study organizations should provide a base of knowledge which can be drawn on when specific program decisions are being considered. Yet, while hundreds or possibly thousands of studies are turned out each year, few of them are of any real use for decisions at the Secretary of Defense level. For example, the number of major studies of total U.S. requirements for tactical air forces done by the services and contract study organizations over the last five years must number in the dozens. Many involved large study groups and complex computer models. All came up with recommendations and conclusions. None shed much light on the subject. In fact, what few confident conclusions that can be drawn on the subject have come from the development of much simpler analyses and measures, mostly by the OSD staff.

This is not necessarily a criticism of the individuals participating in these studies, many of whom are highly capable. Nor do we believe that the problems addressed by these studies are so complex that they can never be understood. In part the problem stems from the fact that nearly all such studies are oriented to near-term program decisions. Few ever attempt any "basic research" on underlying areas where data and knowledge are lacking. Most studies have fairly short deadlines and specific terms of reference. Normally, the study group is neither capable of—nor authorized to—investigate and question basic data supplied by other agencies, such as data on intelligence or technical performance.

Another important aspect of this problem area and one that also helps to explain the poor quality of many analyses is the inherent bias toward the specialist's view over that of the generalist's. The defense establishment includes many men who are pushing their own programs very hard and who see the whole defense of the United States as being tied up with their own programs. They are often personally affronted and publicly outraged if their program is cut back a little. There are too few people in DoD who appreciate the problem of getting a total defense program that makes sense. The military and civilian participants in this process must learn to take a larger view and recognize that the perspective that is appropriate for a project officer is not one that is appropriate for someone who is participating in the development of the total national defense program.

It might be noted in this regard that PPBS is on the side of the generalists. One of its main purposes is to translate the specific technical criteria of the specialists into terms that are meaningful to the generalist. For example, while probabilities of damage that different nuclear forces could achieve against various lists of targets are sufficient for the specialist, they are very difficult for a generalist to interpret and judge. By translating these into, say, the number of Soviets and Americans that would survive a nuclear war, they are more easily grasped. PPBS has gone a long way in helping to organize information along these lines, as a perusal of the Secretary of Defense's annual presentations to Congress since 1961 will show. But a more widespread awareness is needed in DoD that the whole takes priority over the individual parts.

One line of attack for improving the quality of studies is for the

Secretary of Defense to insist on better studies. However, upgrading is not easy to accomplish even for studies done in OSD. And the vast majority of studies are not done by OSD but by the service staffs or contract study organizations. The Secretary's insistence has proven to be a feeble counterweight within the service staffs to that of more immediate superiors, the pressures for using assumptions that put service proposals in a more favorable light, the frequent turnover of personnel assigned to service staffs, and the deficient training in modern analytical techniques of most such staff members.

A more productive way of getting better studies from the services has been for the Systems Analysis Office to do a pilot study in a particularly sensitive area and then send it to the services for comment and review. The zeal with which service staffs can uncover errors in such studies and come up with better ways to approach the problem is impressive.

A second and related problem area is the lack of relevant and reliable test data for equipment, particularly under conditions approximating actual combat. Many of the major program decisions in DoD concern the introduction of new equipment. Realistic estimates of performance must be available if the choices made are to be good ones. Indeed, the problem of reliable performance estimates has become more significant in the last ten years as complex electronic systems have become the key elements in the effectiveness of many new weapons systems.

Much more needs to be done to insure that reliable and accurate performance information on new weapons is obtained. Frequently, the only performance data available on a new system come from the contractors who are developing or producing it, or the officers who are managing the project. Granting the best intentions, it is not surprising that estimates from these sources are frequently too optimistic.

Along this line, too little emphasis has been placed on the use of prototypes for testing. Even where prototypes have been developed, the time allotted for testing has frequently been too short to do the job thoroughly. Yet very few systems are really so urgent as to warrant a production decision before being fully tested.

A third major problem area is the incompleteness of the theory of requirements for some major components of the defense program. In some areas, particularly strategic nuclear forces and strategic mobility forces, requirements have been thoroughly analyzed. While considerable disagreements remain over what assumptions are most likely to be valid, no one argues that an important assumption is missing or that the results of the calculations based on these assumptions are inaccurate. In other areas, however, progress toward developing good requirements analysis is just beginning. In the areas of tactical air forces, anti-submarine warfare, and land forces, for example, simple indicators of force capability have just recently been developed. These indicators hold promise of greatly improving the analysis of requirements in these areas but much more work remains to be done before any high confidence statements of how much is enough can be made.

In still other important areas, communications and intelligence programs for example, we are quite far from having any satisfactory principles for determining aggregate requirements. Given the large sums of money that are spent in these areas it is imperative that more progress be made toward understanding explicitly what these resources are buying.

A final problem area concerns the lack of adequate financial discipline by the services themselves; in other words, the reluctance of the services to set priorities and make hard choices. General Eisenhower's remarks of a decade ago describing this problem are still appropriate:

> Words like "essential" and "indispensable" and "absolute minimum" become the common coin of the realm, and they are spent with wild abandon. One military man will argue hotly for a given number of aircraft as the "absolute minimum," and others will earnestly advocate the "indispensable" needs for ships, tanks, rockets, guided missiles, or artillery, all totaled in numbers that are always called "minimum." All such views are argued with vigor and tenacity, but obviously all cannot be right.

The way PPBS has operated thus far, the services and the JCS have been able to propose specific programs (such as a new aircraft or tank or ship) generally without explicit consideration of the impact on the overall service budget or on the overall defense budget. It is possible, for instance, for the navy to argue for more nuclear-powered aircraft carriers, and have the other Joint Chiefs support this recommendation, without having to specify whether the total defense budget should thus be increased (with appropriate reasoning and evidence to support that conclusion), or whether the greater cost of nuclear carriers should be paid for by a reduction in the total number of carriers. In fact, if nuclear carriers are really more "effective," then their advantages should permit a corresponding reduction somewhere else, possibly in the total number of navy ships. The current system does not force the navy or the JCS to address this fundamental question. The result is that choices are not faced up to by the services and the JCS, since they have the option of avoiding choice by simply adding all "requirements" together.

Given this situation, the burden of choice rests almost entirely on the Secretary of Defense and his staff. We believe too much of the burden of proof has been on the Secretary of Defense and his staff for not accepting service proposals and not enough of the burden has been on the services and the JCS for proving that their new programs should be added to the defense budget rather than being substituted for an existing program. Since the analysis of complex defense issues is almost never clear cut and "provable," one way or the other, the pressure on the Secretary for continuous budget increases is very great.

Similarly, although PPBS has meant a large improvement over what went before, current procedures still favor the procurement of costly new weapons systems just because they have been developed, without adequate knowledge of whether they are the best way of doing a given job. The fact that a new device has been invented is not a sufficient reason to increase the total cost and capability of our armed forces. The rate of new inventions is simply not a good indicator of need. However, since it is almost always possible to develop a set of assumptions that, in isolation, will "prove" the worth of any new military device, it is extremely difficult to make a convincing case against introducing and producing a new system. (This is made doubly difficult because of the lack of reliable test and experience data, discussed above.) The result is that the national interest, in terms of resources spent unwisely, sometimes suffers. The services themselves suffer because the claims made for many new systems often are not realized in the field, while the maintenance and support problems are even greater and more costly than predicted.

One reason for the increases in the cost and complexity of U.S. forces is that the numbers of major force units (such as divisions and wings and ships) have been largely treated as being inflexible. These units are the most widely known aspect of the services' structure and the number of such units has remained relatively fixed for some years. The pressure for increased capabilities and increased budgets has therefore been manifested mainly through introducing more expensive equipment, communications, support, and the like. The cost to buy and operate an A-6 navy attack bomber is much more than that of an A-1, for example, so that the replacement of A-1s with A-6s means a major cost (and performance) increase, even though the nominal force structure in terms of wings remains constant. This trend has not only increased substantially the overall defense budget, but has inhibited service incentives to develop simple, low-cost equipment which often could be introduced in larger numbers and possibly with far greater effectiveness per dollar.

The problem of how to provide incentives for the services to face up to hard choices and get the most capability for the money they spend is a difficult one that does not lend itself to simple solution. Part of the answer lies in creating a political environment which demands that they do face up. Part lies in building up the "case law" of equal-cost and equal-effectiveness trades for new weapons systems; in limited use of budgetary guidance as a prod in this direction; and in continued efforts by the Secretary of Defense to have the services separate, in their proposals, issues of force level and force mix. In any event, a service which lets its costs go up disproportionately should not be "rewarded" by simply having its budget increased.

POSSIBLE NEXT STEPS

These problems are not the result of poor choices in how PPBS has been set up and operated to date; each of them was a serious problem in DoD management before PPBS. They do, however, represent possibilities for further improvements in defense management which are enhanced by having reached the current "state of the art." Actions taken to meet these problem areas should be viewed as extensions and improvements in PPBS as it now stands, not as alternatives to it.

Some possible next steps which, in our judgment, appear promising are discussed below.

First, a more formal procedure is needed for a periodic review of strategy and force alternatives that are broader than those considered for the current year budget alone. The last such broad review was conducted in 1961–62 and resulted in the shift from the policy of "massive retaliation" to that of "flexible response." The broad outlines of this policy have continued until today. Such a review is not necessary or even desirable every year. (It would result in chaos if basic policy changes were made and attempted to be implemented every year.) At the same time, unless one believes that important circumstances change only every four or eight years, a more regular procedure than a change in administrations is needed to get a thorough review of broad alternatives.

The foundation provided by PPBS and the methods and tools which have been developed to put the system into operation would be invaluable to such a review. Ideally, this review would describe for each of several alternative postures the types of military contingencies the force would be capable of meeting, the risks involved, and the costs. The domestic and foreign political implications and the economic impact on the rest of the U.S. budget would also be explicitly considered. Other means of meeting our broad foreign policy objectives, such as economic aid, technical assistance, training and educational programs, would be considered and compared with military options, before a military program and budget were decided upon. To be meaningful, this process should culminate in setting a target for defense spending over several years, a target which could then be used internally in DoD as a guide when making specific program decisions. Such a procedure would seem to fit in fairly well with the renewed emphasis on the National Security Council by President Nixon.

A second desirable change would be to reorient the analytical effort which supports PPBS. With respect to DoD, at least, certain points which bear on this problem have become very clear. To begin with, too many study groups spend far too little effort attempting to define the problem they are working on and to develop a logical way of relating data to it. The design phase of a study is usually by far the toughest and most critical. It may require a lot of preliminary estimating and rough trials; it may take up a significant portion of the total time spent on a study. It also often takes an iron will to carry out, because there is little to show bosses who are anxious to see results. It is essential, however, that the design phase be done well. There is little to be gained from charging off to gather data and make detailed calculations until one knows what is really needed and understands how the parts of the problem fit together.

In addition, far too many defense studies are becoming so complex that they are almost impossible for anyone except (and sometimes including) the authors to understand. The most compelling reason to make analyses understandable is that it increases the probability that decisionmakers will use them. We all recognize that decisionmakers usually add judgment to the facts they consider. This is as it should be; analysis is the servant of judgment, not a replacement for it. However, in most cases where the decisionmaker doesn't personally understand at least the basic logic of the analysis, he must not only add judgment but is forced to rely on it entirely. Given the importance of defense decisions and the enormous costs they involve, few would argue that this is a desirable situation.

The complex mathematical and computerized methods of analysis are useful in their place. They have proved to be very helpful in analyzing problems such as strategic nuclear exchanges or worldwide mobility requirements. It would be wrong not to use them on such problems. It would be equally wrong, however, to try to use them on some problems where they do not work, especially on problems where their use requires data that cannot be obtained. The emphasis should be on the definition and solution of problems by whatever tools are well-suited to them rather than on the application of complex analytical tools for its own sake.

Most of the really important contributions made by the Systems Analysis Office in DoD between 1961 and 1968 were based on the simplest tools of analysis. For example, the tool that finally cut through the maze regarding conventional force ratios in Europe was a simple cost analysis which showed we could buy (at U.S. prices) three Soviet-type division forces for the price of one of ours, and therefore either a simple comparison of the number of divisions was either not a valid measure of relative military power or we were buying the wrong kind of division. The tool that finally stopped the charge that U.S. tactical air capability was being reduced because the total inventory in 1961 was larger than that projected for, say 1968, was a simple payload index which showed that the payload (i.e., the number of tons of bombs that the force could deliver over a representative combat sortie) had doubled between 1961 and 1968. Cost analyses and payload indices are far from the complex analytical tools normally discussed in the literature on analytical methods.

Another related point concerns the fact that too few studies in a given mission area (for example, NATO, anti-submarine warfare, or tactical air forces) are done on the basis of a consistent set of assumptions. A great deal of the work of the Systems Analysis Office has consisted of trying to enforce the use of a consistent set of assumptions, so that we did not end up buying one weapon system on the basis of a set of assumptions particularly favorable to it and another on a different set particularly favorable to it. What is needed is to look at several consistent sets of assumptions that can be applied to competing weapon systems in order to build a balanced posture that will be effective under a broad range of alternatives. Reaching this goal is doubtful so long as each new study starts with its own particular set of assumptions.

Lastly, as we discussed earlier, much of the basic input data that is being used in these studies, particularly in studies of general purpose forces, is suspect. Most of this data is supplied by sources which cannot be considered totally objective. Moreover, not enough research on underlying areas (ordinance effectiveness, target acquisition, the impact of tactics and training, etc.) that bear on most of these studies has been done. Basic data on intelligence and technical performance are too frequently accepted without being questioned. Renewed efforts are needed to develop systematic and objective input data.

Over the years the Systems Analysis Office developed a number of practical rules for how to go about analyzing and planning the defense program. Three of these rules which are particularly pertinent to the problem of reorienting the analytical effort which supports PPBS are discussed below. We believe these rules have useful application in other areas as well.

The first rule might be called "McNamara's First Law of Analysis," that is, "always start by looking at the grand totals." Whatever problem you are studying, back off and look at it in the overall context. Don't start with a small piece and work up—look at the total first and then break it down into its parts. For example, if cost is the issue, look at total system cost over the useful life of the system, not just this year's procurement costs. When analyzing a new strategic missile, start by looking at the total strategic forces. When considering nuclear attack submarines, look at the total anti-submarine warfare force which includes carriers, patrol aircraft, destroyers, sonars, and so on.

One of the most striking things about this rule is how few people understand and act upon it, and how many people behave on the opposite principle. One of the main reasons that overall program decisionmaking in the Pentagon is so controversial is that so many people are concerned exclusively with a small piece of the total. Not only do they not see the total context in which decisions must be made, they tend to be skeptical that broad questions of force levels and mix can ever really be understood and answered. This is understandable, but it must be balanced by men with an opposing point of view—men who want the overall totals to make sense.

A second practical rule of analysis is best summarized by one of the mottos of the Systems Analysis Office: "It is better to be roughly right than precisely wrong." One must resist the temptation to concentrate on pinpoint accuracy on a part of the problem rather than approximate accuracy on the total problem. The ability to recognize, make judgments about, and be comfortable with roughly right information is a most valuable but scarce talent. It is the opposite of the habit of suspending judgment until measurements are precise and until "all the facts are in." In most important policy issues, all the facts will never be in, and in the meantime decisions have to be made with the best information available.

The third such rule is to recognize that policy analysis is not primarily a search for the "best" solution. Generally speaking, there is no "best" solution to complex matters of policy choice. There are only better solutions and worse solutions. Identifying and avoiding bad solutions is a sufficiently ambitious goal for most analyses. For example, in evaluating the decision to deploy a full-scale, anti-ballistic missile (ABM) defense, the important thing is not to design a mix of ABM and air defense systems that is optimum under some single set of assumptions. Rather, the important thing is identifying major facts such as: (1) a full-scale ABM system would be ineffective in saving our cities if the Soviets were to react to our deployment by deploying penetration aids, multiple warheads, and more offensive forces of their own, and (2) a full-scale ABM system would be ineffective in saving lives after a full-scale Soviet attack if we were to deploy it without a large civil defense (fallout shelter) program. Identifying such facts helps the civilian and military leaders in DoD to apply their judgment where it counts.

Finally, one of the most significant contributions of PPBS in the Defense Department has been toward integrating related things in an intelligible way. We believe an extension of the same ideas would improve the integration of our overall national security programs and operations.

PPBS has already contributed to this kind of integration by tying together within DoD things that were previously treated separately; for example, strategic retaliatory forces, airlift and sealift forces, and the like. But there is a problem at the next level up, at the broader level where national security policy and operations come together. Vietnam shows this problem quite clearly. Examples abound of instances where we have destroyed with the left hand what we were building up with the right. For instance, one of our basic goals in South Vietnam is to establish strong armed forces and an honest civil service. Yet the heavy deployment of American forces has contributed directly to the great inflation which has eroded the economic position of both the South Vietnamese officer corps and civil servants, making them more susceptible to corruption and disunity.

Various ideas—such as consolidated country programing, putting the ambassador in charge of all U.S. programs in an area, program budgeting by country or region, etc.—have been proposed for how to move in this direction, but none have received much more than lip-service thus far. One of the great challenges and unsolved problems in the national security field remains that of developing a way to integrate effectively all the U.S. operations and programs affecting national security in overseas areas. We believe an imaginative and vigorous extension of the ideas underlying PPBS at the national policymaking level offers one promising way of meeting this challenge.

CHAPTER 21

THE PLANNING, PROGRAMING, AND BUDGETING SYSTEM IN THE DEPARTMENT OF HEALTH, EDUCATION, AND WELFARE: SOME LESSONS FROM EXPERIENCE

Alice M. Rivlin

INTRODUCTION

In this paper, I take the opportunity to look back on an operation in which I have been, until recently, deeply immersed. I have just left the Department of Health, Education, and Welfare after three years of working to implement the planning, programming, budgeting system. This is a good chance to set down briefly my own thoughts on what was accomplished, what the difficulties were, and what could be done better or differently in the future.

To implement the PPB system, Secretary John W. Gardner established a new office under an assistant secretary for program coordination (later and more aptly called planning and evaluation). I suspect he would have done this even without the impetus of the president's directive on PPBS. A new secretary trying to understand and manage the vast, sprawling Department of Health, Education, and Welfare clearly needed a staff of his own to analyze where the department's resources were going, what was being accomplished, and how the job could be done better.

We conceived of our mission as that of helping the secretary make better—or at least more informed—decisions about the allocation of resources among the many programs and possible programs of the depart-

Alice M. Rivlin is Senior Fellow at The Brookings Institution. Until March 1969, she was Assistant Secretary for Planning and Evaluation, Department of Health, Education, and Welfare.

The views expressed are the author's own, and do not purport to be those of The Brookings Institution or the Department of Health, Education, and Welfare.

ment. These decisions would be reflected primarily in the department's budget and legislative program.

We proceeded on six assumptions:

1. Decisions will be better if you know what you are trying to do—if objectives are stated and resources devoted to the accomplishment of a particular objective are grouped together.
2. Decisions will be better if information is available on how resources are presently being used—by major objectives, ways in which objectives are being carried out, types of people being served, and so forth.
3. Decisions will be better if the effectiveness of present programs is evaluated.
4. Decisions will be better if alternative ways of accomplishing objectives are considered and analyzed.
5. It makes sense to plan ahead—to decide first what the department should be doing several years in the future, and then what immediate legislative and budgetary changes are needed to move in the desired direction.
6. It is good to be systematic about decisionmaking—to follow an explicit procedure for reviewing long-range plans periodically in the light of new information, evaluation and analysis, and translating changes of plans into budgetary and legislative consequences.

We worked on all six of these premises at once. What follows is a brief attempt to describe what we did and what we learned from the experience.

PROGRAM BUDGET AND INFORMATION SYSTEM

The Secretary of HEW now has some new tools which he did not have 3 years ago. He has a program budget and information system which enable him to get a better grasp of what HEW does and where the money goes than he could get from the budget in appropriations terms.

Making up a program budget involves identifying the major objectives and subobjectives of the department to which resources are devoted. In a complex operation like HEW, where many programs have multiple objectives, there is certainly no unique way of organizing a program budget. We tried several ways and did not find an ideal one. Our first attempt at a program budget was organized under three major objectives of department activity: (1) "human investment"—improving the earning capacity and ability to function of individuals and families, (2) providing income and other benefits to individuals and families, and (3) institutional and community development. These three categories cut across the organizational lines of the department. Manpower training programs managed in various parts of the department, for example, were grouped together in category (1) while construction programs of various sorts were put together in category (3). This crosscutting was useful for some purposes, but not for others. It made it difficult, for example, to look at education as a whole and see the relationship between department programs to provide services for children and those for training the teachers needed to provide those services. To facilitate looking at these questions, we moved in the next program budget to the more conventional major objectives of (1) improving health, (2) improving education, (3) income maintenance, and (4) social and rehabilitative services.

The program information system sorts out department funds not only by program objectives, but also by population group served, type of activity, method of finance, and so forth. Using the information system, the secretary can see, for example, what portion of the department's resources go for health; within health, how much is for the development of health resources; and within health resources, how much is for the training of physicians. He can see who is helped by HEW programs—how much goes to the old, the young, the poor. He can see what means are used to further objectives—how much for construction, how much for research. He can see how much goes to the states in formula grants, and how much in the form of project grants. He can also see how all these proportions have changed over the last several years.

These are important questions, and the answers do not leap out of the appropriations budget. Some of these questions had, of course, been asked before by secretaries or by members of Congress, and estimates of the answers had been painstakingly put together, but now the secretary has ready access to this kind of information on a regular basis.

In my opinion, the greatest impact of the program information system has been in facilitating some simple calculations at high levels of aggregation. My favorite example is Secretary Cohen's astonishment at a table showing that most of the department's recent budget increases had been devoted to older people and relatively little to children. Why the father of Medicare should have been surprised at this, I do not know, but he was; and he immediately began talking about a new emphasis on programs for children.

Granted that a program budget can provide useful information to decisionmakers and new ways of looking at programs, how useful is a program budget as a decision tool? Our HEW experience indicates, I think, that a program budget is a useful *planning* tool, but at the moment of budget decisionmaking the program budget cannot be substituted for the appropriations budget. Both are necessary. Let me explain this.

HEW operates under several hundred legislative authorities and separate appropriations categories. Sensible planning necessitates organizing these activities in terms of major objectives and subobjectives of the department and deciding on the relative emphasis to be given to these various objectives and subobjectives. For example, planning for health has to involve such questions as these: What should the department be doing to improve the access of individuals to medical care by providing them the means of paying for such care? How much effort should the department be making to increase the supply of medical services by training doctors or building hospitals, or other means? To what extent should the department be investing in future medical discoveries rather than present provision of services? On the education side, planning for the department must involve questions such as these: Should the department expand its aid to elementary and secondary education at a more rapid rate than its aid to higher education? Should it increase the proportion of resources devoted to improving the education of the poor rather than that of the whole population? How much emphasis should be put on finding new methods and approaches to education as opposed to increasing resources going into the present system?

Obviously a program budget cannot answer these questions, but it is a useful framework for laying out the choices so that decisions can be made about them. Once these major decisions are made, however, they cannot automatically be translated into a budget to be sent to the president and the Congress. Each of the several hundred programs operated by HEW has unique characteristics. It has a legislative history and an authorization level. It is handled by a particular committee or subcommittee whose chairman may have definite views. It may have a strong lobby supporting it or gunning for it. It may be administered by states or localities or other non-federal institutions. All of these particular characteristics or programs are relevant to a decision to translate a program budget decision into budgetary and legislative terms. For example, a secretary of HEW may decide to increase the resources devoted to experimenting with new methods in education. Once he has decided that, however, he is confronted with where to put the money. Should he use Title III of the Elementary and Secondary Education Act, which is largely controlled by the states? Should he use the regional laboratories under Title IV of the same act which are administered in an entirely different way and have different strengths and weaknesses? Should he ask for a new authorization and run the risk that a committee which has shown itself reluctant to fund new programs will deny him the funds? No matter how useful the program budget proves, as a way of organizing information and as a planning tool, the final decisions on the budget must be made in appropriations terms and in the light of all of these complicated considerations which, though they may not be desirable, are facts of life for a secretary of Health, Education, and Welfare.

The answer to the question "Have decisions been made in program budget terms in HEW?" is both "Yes" and "No." Since the advent of PPB, major decisions have been made in program budget terms—decisions to emphasize health services for the poor, family planning, education research and innovation, efforts to help welfare recipients become self-supporting, etc. The process of translating these major decisions into appropriations terms, however, necessitates continuous walking back and forth between the two sets of budget categories. At some points in the decision process the program budget formulation was extremely helpful to the decisionmakers, especially, I think, in the health area where it facilitated joint consideration of health programs administered in several different agencies. At other points the program budget seemed to make decisions more complicated because a particular appropriation was either buried in a larger total or split among several program categories. For example, Title I of the Elementary and Secondary Education Act is primarily an education program, but provides some funds for health services for disadvantaged children. An estimate of the health expenditures from Title I showed up in the program budget under "health." At the moment of decision on "how much for Title I?" it was necessary to add the two pieces together and make a decision on Title I as an entity.

I see no simple solution to this problem, although simplification of the HEW appropriations structure would help. Both kinds of budgets are necessary to good decisionmaking, and HEW executives simply have to be adroit at considering decisions both in program and in appropriations terms, and translating back and forth frequently.

EVALUATION: MEASUREMENT OF PROGRAM ACCOMPLISHMENT

The second result of PPB in HEW has been a new emphasis on evaluation of what programs actually do. The first step was to collect information on a regular basis about the "outputs" of programs. The secretary now has available in the program information system a continuing series of measures of the "outputs" of individual programs—hospital beds constructed, teachers trained, patients served, persons participating in basic literacy programs, etc. In some cases it was almost impossible to find a meaningful output measure for a program. "Number of research projects supported," for example, is not an interesting statistic. Yet, it is the only readily available measure of output of a research program. At best, these output measures are rough guides to what the program is buying, and can be useful in showing the secretary what he would give up if he shifted money from one program to another. For example, how many nurses does one give up to train a psychiatrist, or how many teachers could be trained for the price of a hospital bed? These statistics are better than no information on what the program is buying, but they do not throw much light on what is actually being accomplished. They do not tell the secretary what the program is contributing to the health or education or welfare of the nation.

Evaluating the effectiveness of most HEW programs is difficult—not because the people who run them are incompetent or falsify the information, but for at least three more basic reasons. First, it is usually far from obvious what one would *like* to have happen—what the measure of success of the program should be. For example, Title I of the Elementary and Secondary Education Act gives money to school districts to improve the education of disadvantaged children. Should we look for a measure of success of this program in the test scores of these children, in their dropout rates, in their future ability to hold a job, or in some measure of their attitude toward themselves and their environment? Second, most HEW programs are designed to help individuals function better. Their success can only be gauged by following the individuals over some considerable period of time to find out what actually happened to them. Followup is expensive even if done on a sample basis. Third, it is difficult to disentangle the effects of HEW programs from all the other things which affect the health, education, and welfare of individuals. If infant mortality drops in a particular locality, it may be the result of a prenatal care program, or better nutrition, or higher incomes, or a lower birth rate, or a combination of all of these things. In some cases, control groups and sophisticated statistical techniques can help sort out these various factors; in some cases, they cannot.

Can a government agency be expected to evaluate its own programs? In particular, should program managers be expected to participate in evaluation? Can they be objective about their own programs?

Before trying to answer these questions, I think it is important to distinguish two kinds of evaluation. The first (and the one in which Congress seems to be most interested) is overall evaluation of the accomplishment of a program. It is the attempt to answer the question: To what extent is a program meeting its objectives? It amounts to giving a grade—often a pass or a fail grade—to a program as a whole. For example, one might want to know how many additional doctors have been trained as a result of a program of aid to medical schools, how many welfare recipients have become self-supporting as a result of training and day-care programs, or what has happened to the incidence of measles as a result of the measles vaccine program.

While program managers must cooperate in providing the information necessary for these overall evaluations, it is too much to expect them to carry out the evaluation themselves. No one wants to admit failure. In order to insure objectivity, it is necessary to have the information analyzed and judgments made by someone not directly responsible for the execution of the program—perhaps someone outside the government altogether.

For many important HEW programs, however, I think this kind of overall pass-or-fail evaluation is next to impossible. For example, it is not really possible to answer the question, What is Title I of the Elementary and Secondary Education Act accomplishing? Title I provides only a small part of the resources used to educate disadvantaged children, and school itself is only one of the influences (and probably not the most important one) on the performance of these children. If a national testing program showed an increase in the test scores of disadvantaged children, everyone would be happy, but it certainly would not be clear what proportion of this increase, if any, should be attributed to Title I. A negative finding—no change in the tested performance of poor children—might suggest that Title I money was being wasted, but would not prove that nothing could be done through the schools to help these children. Title I funds (as well as other education resources) are spent in many different ways in different localities presumably with varying degrees of effectiveness. The really interesting problem for the evaluator is not to figure out what the average effectiveness of the program is, but to identify the kinds of education projects which are successful with low income children so they can be replicated and expanded.

This second kind of evaluation—that designed to identify successful ways of spending money for a particular objective and to improve the average effectiveness of a program—should be of tremendous importance to a program manager who wants to do a good job. It should have his full support and participation. The manager of a manpower training program should have a strong interest in discovering which types of training projects are most successful. The manager of a family planning program should have a strong interest in discovering which ways of delivering family planning services are the most effective. In the long run, I think this kind of evaluation is of more importance to the wise use of government resources than is the overall pass-or-fail type.

Evaluation—of both types—is still in its infancy in HEW. The planning and evaluation staff has succeeded in getting some funds authorized for evaluation in various legislation and in some cases in getting the funds appropriated. We worked with the staffs of several of the HEW agencies—most notably with the Office of Education—to design evaluation plans, and we funded a number of pilot evaluations. But designing sound evaluation techniques and collecting, processing, and interpreting the information takes time and expert staff resources. These resources are not presently available in HEW, nor is it easy to find them outside the government. To do a good job on evaluation, it will be necessary to recruit a staff of competent people who can work closely with managers of major programs to define what kinds of information are needed, to design a system for collecting this information, and make sure that it does get collected and analyzed.

ANALYSIS OF ALTERNATIVE COURSES OF ACTION

Systematic analysis of alternative ways of reaching objectives is the heart and soul of PPB. A good analysis specifies an agreed-on objective or set of objectives, outlines alternative ways of reaching these objectives, and brings together as much information as possible about the costs, benefits, advantages, and disadvantages of each. The analyst uses the results of program evaluation and goes beyond them to try to estimate the effectiveness of new programs. In a sense he is an evaluator of programs which do not exist yet.

Analysis of alternatives is, of course, not a new idea. Studies of program alternatives of various sorts have been done in different parts of HEW for years. What was new in the last three years was the existence of a staff of economists and other analysts in the Office of the Secretary which was specifically devoted to studying the major options open to the secretary with respect to budget and legislation. Perhaps even more important was the presence of an assistant secretary in budgetary and legislative decision meetings whose job it was to see that relevant analysis was considered at the decision moment. By way of illustration, let me describe briefly two recent analyses carried out by the planning and evaluation staff at HEW which should be of considerable interest to the Congress and the general public as well as to the executive branch.

The first is a study of higher education undertaken at the request of President Johnson, and released by Secretary Cohen just before he left office.[1] In this study we made an attempt to specify the various objectives which the federal government has in supporting higher education—objectives such as improving access to higher education on the part of all students, improving the quality of higher education by increasing the resources available to institutions, and preserving diversity and autonomy in American higher education. The study examines the available information on the degree of equality of access to higher education on the part of students from different income levels, documenting the fact that students from low-income families have relatively low chances of going to college even if they have high ability. A student of good college potential, scoring in the top two-fifths on high school achievement tests, is more than twice as likely to enter college if he comes from a family in the top quarter of the income distribution than if he comes from one in the bottom quarter.[2] The study also examines available information on the financial health of higher education and the relative strength of public and private institutions. One interesting and somewhat surprising finding of this part of the study was the widening gap in resources per student available in public and private institutions, with *private* institutions enjoying a more rapid increase. Between 1959–60 and 1965–66 the study found:

> "There was a marked disparity in the rates of increase in revenues per student in public and private institutions, with public institutions' revenues per student increasing 4.0 percent annually while the comparable rate of increase for private institutions was 8.1 percent."[3]

An attempt was made to lay out the major options available to the federal government in support of higher education—the student-aid through loans, grants, the work study-program, and institutional aid of a variety of types—and to evaluate the advantages and disadvantages of these various alternatives as ways of furthering the particular federal objectives. The report contained a set of recommendations, but these may well be of less importance than the analysis itself.

A second analysis which I would like to discuss briefly concerns major alternatives to the present welfare system.[4] Estimates were made of the number of people who would probably still be in poverty five years from now if present welfare programs were continued, and of the cost of such continuation. It was estimated that the cost of present welfare programs would rise from about $3.7 billion in 1969 to perhaps $6.2 billion by 1974, but that poverty would not disappear in this period:

> ". . . poor households will still number some 8.8 million by 1974, compared to 10.8 million in 1966, even if we are successful in maintaining a high rate of employment and economic growth."[5]

An attempt was made to analyze major alternatives to continuation of the present welfare system. The alternatives considered included a childen's allowance and a negative income tax-type program which would give aid to the working poor as well as those aided by present welfare programs. The various alternatives were evaluated with respect to cost, coverage, contribution to closing the poverty gap, savings to the states, and their effects on incentives to work, incentives to establish separate households, incentives to move from low to high income states, and other factors.

Analytical effort in HEW has been hampered by two main factors—lack of staff and lack of information. Studies of the sort just described take many man-months of effort. The present staff of analysts under the assistant secretary for planning and evaluation can handle only a small number of studies a year, and must choose the three or four issues which seem likely to be of importance in upcoming budgetary or legislative decisions, perhaps leaving aside issues of more basic long-run importance. Better use could be made of analysts in universities, foundations, and elsewhere if funds were available to finance more outside studies.

The second difficulty (that of lack of information) is more basic. Indeed, it may be that the most important result of the PPB effort in HEW so far has been the discovery of how little is really known, either about the status of the nation's health, education, and welfare, or about what to do to change it. A recent report of the department prepared in the Office of Planning and Evaluation, attempted to measure the nation's progress toward certain widely accepted social goals.[6] The study was an attempt to see what could be said about such questions as: What is the state of the nation's health? Are we getting healthier? Are we better educated? Are we winning the war on poverty? If nothing else, the volume served to illustrate the thinnesss of social statistics and how little is really known about the state of the nation even with respect to such apparently measurable factors as physical health and intellectual capacity.

The child health study, which has been discussed by Dr. Wholey, is a good example of an analysis which uncovered more questions than it answered.[7] I remember being astonished when we first started the study that doctors could produce no evidence that children who saw doctors regularly were healthier than children who did not. They all believed it (and I do, too), but they did not have any statistics to prove it. I was equally astonished to find that educators have little or no evidence that children who get more expensive education (newer buildings, higher paid teachers, more teachers, etc.) learn more than children who get less expensive education. They believe it (and so do I), but the available statistics do not prove it, nor does presently available information give any solid clues about what kinds of schools are best, or whether particular educational methods are more effective than others.

Analysis, experimentation, and evaluation must proceed together if we are to make progress in providing decisionmakers with good bases for decisions in health, education, and welfare. Serious effort on the evaluation of federal programs would give the analyst more data. Additional analyses will also provide a better idea of where the gaps in information are and what kind of statistics should be collected.

THE FIVE–YEAR PLAN

The major objectives of the Department of Health, Education, and Welfare —improving health and education and eliminating poverty—all take time and are highly interrelated. Successful compensatory education, manpower training programs, and provision of health services would reduce the need for income maintenance in the future or, conversely, provision of income to large numbers of poor persons through a new kind of income maintenance system might reduce the need for special services in health and education. Moreover, most of the programs of the department involve the provision of services by skilled manpower or in highly specialized facilities. It would not be possible to provide good quality pre-school education or pediatric care for all children next year. Neither the facilities nor the trained people exist. For all of these reasons, planning ahead in the health, education, and welfare area is essential to realistic decisionmaking.

Probably the most important thing about the HEW 5-year plan is that it exists. For the first time at the secretary's level a real effort has been made to look at the department as a whole, to address alternatives and priorities, and to lay out at least a tentative program for 5 years into the future.

The present HEW 5-year program and financial plan is a plan only in this sense: it shows how assumed budget totals would be allocated by objectives and sub-objectives in the future in order to reflect presently conceived priorities. It shows how an increased emphasis on such priorities as reducing welfare rolls, educating disadvantaged children, and providing health services for the poor would be reflected in future HEW program budgets.

Some elements of the HEW plan are only projections. In the income maintenance area, for example, the HEW plan is not a plan at all. It is simply a projection of the future costs of present income maintenance programs. A great deal of work was done on alternative income maintenance programs (as noted above, these were transmitted to the Bureau of the Budget in a program memorandum), but the last administration did not commit itself to the choice of a particular alternative to present income maintenance program.

Only a few segments of the HEW plan are real plans in the sense that they show how specific objectives could be reached over a multi-year period. Planning for the work incentive program (WIN) is the best example. A plan was designed which, it was thought, would result in removing a specific number of people from the welfare rolls by 1975 through provision of training, day care, and other services.

Ideally, the HEW plan should state performance goals—elimination of poverty, elimination of specific diseases, reduction of infant mortality to specified levels, availability of health services to all persons, raising average reading scores of poor children to given levels, etc.—and show how these goals are to be accomplished. Right now, it is not possible to lay out this kind of plan because in most instances we cannot yet specify the connection between money expended and results achieved. It is not now possible, for example, to make any estimate of how much it would cost to raise the reading levels of poor children to the national average, or how one would go about it.

The process of putting together the plan revealed dramatically how little is known about the connection between expending money and specific accomplishments. If nothing else, producing the plan provided a strong case for increases in systematic experimentation, evaluation, and analysis so that more informed planning can be done in the future.

The Bureau of the Budget, after initially requiring a comprehensive multi-year program and financial plan backed away from this requirement. Present Bureau of the Budget instructions require the department to submit estimates of the future costs of present decisions, but specifically do not require laying out the implications of future decisions. For HEW, this change in signals was equivalent to rejection of planning on the part of the Bureau of the Budget. Only a few HEW programs—those involving construction or multi-year research projects—have built-in future costs. Most HEW programs involve services to people and can be run at various levels depending on the number of people one has the resources to serve. Hence, a plan which reflects only future implications of present decisions is really not a plan at all.

I think it was a mistake for the Bureau of the Budget to back away from forward planning. Indeed, HEW ignored the backing away and submitted a full program and financial plan as required by original PPB directives. Presumably, the Bureau of the Budget changed its mind because of the fear that it might prove embarrassing to the administration to have plans laid out in advance which might reveal or seem to reveal a hidden strategy or cause unwarranted criticism of tentative plans on which decision had not yet been made. These risks are real, but I suspect that as planners become more sophisticated and better able to specify the connections between goals and expenditures, the obvious advantages of planning ahead begin to outweigh the disadvantages. Indeed, Congress itself may some day require the administration to submit multi-year plans in addition to single year budgets.

THE PLANNING CYCLE: EXPERIMENTS IN SYSTEMATIC DECISIONMAKING

Evaluation, analysis, and program budget categories are all useful tools, but the moment of truth is the decision. The real point of PPBS is to establish a process for bringing the relevant tools to bear at the right moment so that decisions are made in the light of maximum information about present and future consequences of alternative courses of action.

Until the advent of PPB, budgets in HEW had been made by building on the previous year's base and adding additional funds where administration priorities, congressional interest, or the bargaining power of program managers dictated. New legislation was handled separately, usually after the budget was put to bed, and with little explicit consideration of trade-offs between funding old programs and adding new ones.

What we tried to do in implementing the PPBS idea was to institute a regular process in which (1) the secretary and his principal advisers sat down together to consider major alternative ways of using department resources over the next several years; (2) decisions were made in the spring or early summer about the major directions in which the department wanted to move; (3) these major long-run decisions were translated into budgetary and legislative decisions in the fall.

There have been two full budget and legislative cycles at HEW since the implementation of PPBS. We tried out the new procedure first in the formulation of the fiscal year 1968 budget and 1969 legislative program. We began the process of getting a fiscal year 1968 budget by having the secretary ask the constituent agencies of the department to examine the missions of their agencies and their priorities for the future, and to submit a program budget for the fiscal year 1973 indicating how they would allocate resources to achieve objectives for that year. Each of the constituent agencies was given a high and a low planning figure for fiscal year 1973. When the agencies' plans for that year were submitted, the secretary's planning and evaluation staff analyzed them, suggested alternatives, and presented the secretary with a series of decision memoranda outlining major long-run options, and giving as much analysis as possible of the advantages and disadvantages of each, together with indications of positions taken by the constituent agencies and by members of his own staff and the reasons therefor. After considerable back and forth discussion, the secretary made decisions on program objectives for fiscal year 1973. These were then transmitted back to the agencies with instructions that they develop a plan for moving from the present to those 1973 objectives (i.e., fill in the intervening years) making their fiscal year 1968 budget consistent with this plan. When the budgets were submitted, they were reviewed in the Office of the Secretary to make sure they were indeed consistent with the 1973 objectives—that programs scheduled to receive increased emphasis by 1973 had indeed been increased in the budget, and those scheduled for decreased emphasis had been cut back or held level. In other words, the plan provided a rough set of guidelines for accepting or rejecting agency budget requests.

In formulating the fiscal year 1969 budget, a similar procedure was used except that, since the department now had a plan for the years 1968 through 1973, the agencies were asked to start with that plan, extend it through fiscal year 1974 and submit revisions consistent with new information or new priorities. As in the previous year, the revised agency plans were worked over by the planning and evaluation staff, alternatives were suggested, and secretarial decisions sought so that guidance could be prepared for formulation of fiscal year 1969 budgets and 1970 legislative proposals.

What we were trying to achieve in the planning cycle in both of these years was an orderly process in which the secretary was able to make major decisions early enough in the year to allow the staff work necessary to translate these decisions into budgets and legislative proposals. In both years, however, we ran into considerable difficulties in obtaining early decisions on major matters (the second year happened to be an election year and the last year of a lame-duck administration, which made planning more than usually difficult). There were at least three reasons for the difficulty. First, the secretary himself was reluctant to make major decisions early in the year, and was always eager to hold open as many options as possible. Second, much of the initiative on new legislation came not from the department itself but from the White House. The White House procedure was to organize legislative task forces in August or September to report about the first of November with major legislative proposals for consideration by the president. This procedure interfered with early decisionmaking in the department. Third, the procedure we were using depended on the constituent agencies making the first move. They were required to submit plans or revisions of plans for reaction by the secretary and his staff. Since the agencies tended to drag their feet and turn their plans in far after the deadline, the time available for analysis by the secretary's staff was short, and secretarial decisions tended to occur later in the year than desirable. The result was that major decisions on the long-range plan were delayed until August and September and tended to be overtaken by the shorter range budget decisions which had to be made at the same time.

I do not think there is any complete solution to this problem. Being human, federal executives will tend (where possible), to avoid commitments, to preserve their options, and to put off major decisions as long as possible. However, the planning cycle procedure in HEW could be altered so as to facilitate earlier decisionmaking. One way to do this would be to shift the initiative to the Office of the Secretary which would issue specific guidance on major program emphasis for the agencies to follow in formulating their plans. This would take the secretary's office out of the position of reacting to the agencies and put the agencies in the position of reacting to the Office of the Secretary. This would make it more difficult for the agencies to slow down the whole process by coming in late with plans. Such a procedure presupposes a capable and knowledgeable staff both in the agencies and in the Office of the Secretary.

SOME CONCLUSIONS FROM EXPERIENCE

Anyone who thought that PPBS was a magic formula to make the allocation of federal resources easy had better think again. There is no magic formula because these decisions are inherently difficult. They are difficult, first, because they are made in the face of great uncertainty and, second, because the outcomes affect different groups of people importantly and differently. Far from making the decisions easier, the PPB system has undoubtedly made decisionmakers more aware than ever before of how hard the decisions they have to make really are.

In the defense area, uncertainty is the dominant difficulty. Good analysis of the costs and effectiveness of alternative U.S. actions is highly useful, but it can only reduce the uncertainties by a small percentage. A tremendous amount of guesswork about enemy motivations and intentions is still necessary. There is little room for experiment. Decisions are not made in small, discrete steps but tend to be of the all-or-nothing variety, and the cost of making a mistake is great.

In the domestic area, the uncertainty surrounding decisions *need* not be so great, although at present it probably is. It would be possible to run domestic programs as a continuous series of experiments—to try different things, to evaluate the results, to expand those that work well, and cut back on those that do not. Good evaluation systems will certainly not be quick or easy, but they can be used to make programs far more effective than they are now, not just at the federal level but at all levels of government. The potentiality of PPBS for reducing the uncertainty surrounding decisions seems to me far greater in the domestic than in the defense area.

The other difficulty—the differential impact of decisions on people—is, however, far more obvious and troublesome in the domestic than in foreign area. Defense decisions result in some people being better protected or bearing a heavier burden than others, but these differential effects are not nearly so obvious as in domestic programs. In domestic programs of direct service to particular types of people, everyone knows who the immediate beneficiaries are. A good PBB system can illuminate these distributional decisions, but cannot make them any easier. Indeed, assembling and publicizing information on who is helped by particular government programs may intensify political conflict.

I view PPBS as a commonsense approach to decisionmaking. The terminology may well change—and probably should—but I fail to see how a secretary of Health, Education, and Welfare who wants to do a good job can get along without planning ahead, evaluating the effectiveness of programs, analyzing alternatives carefully, and making decisions in an orderly way in the light of maximum information. It does not matter what he chooses to call it, but he badly needs the basic tools of PPBS.

The progress made in the department in the last 3 years is clearly a start toward improved decisionmaking, but it is only a start. More attention needs to be paid to evaluation, and more resources need to be devoted to building up a continuous flow of useful information on the effectiveness of programs. Far more resources need to be devoted to good analysis, especially to understanding the complicated interactions between federal programs and what happens in the state, local, and private sectors. Better ways need to be found within the department for focusing attention on major long-run decisions, and considering budgetary and legislative options at the same time. Above all, the secretary himself has to use the system. If he wants good analysis, he will get it. If he wants good information, he will get it. If he wants to make decisions in an orderly way, considering all important options carefully and systematically, he will, with patience, be able to do so.

NOTES

[1] U.S. Department of Health, Education, and Welfare, *Toward a Long-Range Plan for Federal Financial Support for Higher Education,* Washington, D.C., 1969. Estimates are for the 1960 high school graduating class.

[2] *Ibid.,* p. 5.

[3] *Ibid.,* p. 11.

[4] U.S. Department of Health, Education, and Welfare, Office of the Assistant Secretary (Planning and Evaluation), *Program Memorandum on Income Maintenance and Social and Rehabilitation Services Programs of DHEW,* November 1968, pp. III.1–III.20.

[5] *Ibid.,* p. III.1.

[6] U.S. Department of Health, Education, and Welfare, *Toward A Social Report,* Washington, D.C., January 1969.

[7] See Joseph Wholey, "The Absence of Program Evaluation as an Obstacle to Effective Public Expenditure Policy: A Case Study of Child Health Care Programs" in U.S. Congress, Joint Economic Committee, *The Analysis and Evaluation of Public Expenditures: The PPB System, op. cit.,* vol. 1, pp. 451–472.

CHAPTER 22

PROBLEMS OF RESOURCE ALLOCATION IN HEALTH

Robert N. Grosse

INTRODUCTION

At this stage of our knowledge about how to improve resource allocations within the field of health, it is much easier to discuss problems than to point out solutions.

Approaches to better resource allocation decisions require insight into who participates in the allocating process, what the resources are, the groups to which we allocate and the accomplishments of differing allocations.

Allocations take place in the "market"—either the conventional one of money bidding for goods and services, or that of political forces and coalitions, or most usually some combination of the two. Rather than address the awesome challenge of explaining how resources are allocated throughout the entire health area—I would like to narrow my comments to problems of resource allocation on the part of a governmental or quasi-public agency which has control over allocating some of the resources at stake. Such agencies function within economic and political marketplaces, and must take the existing operations of these markets into account, but they may also be concerned with improving the allocation process itself.

In particular, this paper discusses some of the informational requirements involved in improving the allocation process, and describes approaches taken by analysts in the Department of Health, Education, and Welfare to develop information, analyses, and a planning system.

Resource allocation decisions usually appear as allocations among "programs," but that is probably too neutral a term to convey much meaning.

Clearly, we allocate among organizations. Governmental budget and legislative decisions do this, and voluntary groups such as community chests and welfare federations do. We allocate among institutions—hospi-

Robert N. Grosse is Professor of Health Planning at The School of Public Health of the University of Michigan.

tals, medical schools, research institutions, nursing homes, neighborhood centers, third party insurers.

We also allocate among beneficiary or target populations such as Indians, Negroes, whites, the poor, the middle class, the retarded, veterans, etc.

We allocate among professions—or between professionals and target populations, so much to psychiatrists, to other physicians, to nurses, to social workers, to professors, and to the individuals requiring the services of these different professional groups.

We allocate among locations—central city versus suburban versus rural, North as against South, Texas as against Massachusetts.

We also allocate over time, investing in building hospitals and nursing homes, training nurses and doctors, and biomedical research and development, as opposed to purchasing current services.

In another sense of time, we allocate among generations—such as children, working age, aged.

We also allocate among health problems such as diseases: tuberculosis, syphilis, mental illness, cancer, etc.; among approaches to disease control: research, prevention, and treatment; between approaches: categorical versus comprehensive programs.

Although I have touched on only a few examples, even thinking about targets for allocation introduces complexities. Learning how we have been allocating is hard, and deciding what to do may seem impossible. It is easier to select one facet, such as multiple sclerosis, underfed children in Texas, or cancer care, and develop tactics to secure more money for it than to determine the economic and political strategies for solving allocation problems—who or what gets less when some get more.

What is it that's allocated? We usually think of money—and that's a meaningful and convenient measure, but we recognize that scarcity of resources in physical terms sometimes may be more constraining and thus more significant—number of physicians and their time, availability of facilities for the mentally retarded, transplantable organs, kidney dialysis units, and personnel. Among the things we are allocating may be life and death.

Nevertheless resources are allocated every day in any complex organization. But the problem which faces us is to make "better" allocation decisions. It seems reasonable that a better understanding and measurement of the costs (what is given up) and the effects (what is accomplished) of various possible courses of action will improve allocation decisions. The search for a clearer identification of what we are really trying to accomplish and how we are going about it has led to more systematic thinking about objectives and classification, information and analysis systems.

These ideas—few of them novel—are surfacing as aids in resource allocation decisions at a time when the health planning field itself is under great stimulation. This stimulation is being caused by increasing interest in health services on the part of the American people, evidenced by the growth of personal and governmental health expenditures, increasing concern over mounting costs and prices, and moves on the part of the federal government to require and support planning and decisionmaking at state, regional, area, and community levels.[1] Some hope that planning can work may also come from the assumption that the systematic techniques of systems engineering, operations research, cost-effectiveness analysis, and program budgeting make the task more feasible.

How do we proceed to better understanding? The first step would be to structure the significant elements of our health system. There are many approaches to this—let me discuss one that has been meaningful to me.

We start with identifying problems—health situations which need improvement and where intervention or change may be useful. This involves an assessment of our population and its subsets in terms of health status and access to health services. It also involves examining environmental hazards and social forces which threaten to affect adversely the normal development or health of our people.

Second, what are the current and potential activities that are or might be addressed to these problems—and we need to know not just the what of them, but also the who and the how—who manages and carries them out, with what instrumentalities, how are they organized, and who benefits? These include the delivery of personal health services, environmental control, consumer education, and programs to affect social factors related to mental health.

Third, we need to know what stock of assets are needed for health activities—knowledge, technology, manpower, and facilities. What do we have, how are these stocks added to, and how are they organized into desired activities?

In addition, we need to understand how resources are or could be financed, the effects of various financing mechanisms, and the barriers between consumers and services—financial and social.

We need evaluations to understand what programs accomplish—how the delivery of services affects health; how environmental control programs affect the ambient world; and at what costs?

All of these form a system of interdependencies or interrelationships. For example, through the political and budgetary process resources are allocated which, in turn, provide services or goods that benefit certain sectors or groups in our country. The process, furthermore, appears to be somewhat circular in that we have what students of cybernetics would call a "feedback" effect. One of our problems in resource allocation is that we are never sure whether the feedback will be positive or negative. Will the beneficiaries of a policy alternative feel that they are actually getting benefits? I suppose that in Los Angeles if we were able to implement a program which would suddenly get rid of smog, most citizens would be quite pleased and we would expect to get a positive feedback to continue or increase our program. On the other hand, many health programs are not so visible, or it may take several generations for us to be able to discern their impact (for example, biomedical research activities).

Finally, we also need to understand the political environment in which we work.[2] We must be able not only to identify where it makes sense to intervene, i.e., where political and economic costs can be minimized, but also to appreciate the broader policy concerns which set the context for our activities.

Analysis of major policy areas like health is not just a mechanical exercise of mathematics; we have to consider qualitative factors as well which may affect the outcome of our studies. Indeed, sometimes this is all we have to work with. Knowing the number of beds in a hospital or the beds' utilization rate is only a rough index of capacity and not a measure of the quality of care. Similarly, there are tradeoffs between health services and education for improving the communication flow between patient and doctor; such tradeoffs may actually involve value conflicts where we cannot measure the benefits of education and health in the same terms and in these situations the judgment of political decisionmakers is required to resolve the conflict.

Now I would like to be more explicit and give some content to terms like better resource allocation.

Improving the allocation of health resources does not necessarily mean saving money or cutting budgets. In fact, in order to make improvements sometimes we have to spend more. What is meant is getting more out of the resources such as money, time, doctors, drugs, nurses, etc., which are involved in health activities. As we are all aware, the country needs more physician and nursing services. But our problem is not just how much more; we are also concerned with the distribution of these scarce resources. We want to find ways to increase the productivity of the doctor, but we also want to make sure that all segments of our nation are able to receive medical care when they require it. Thus, when we talk about improving or maximising the use of our scarce health resources, we can mean many things and what we mean exactly is a function of the analysis or problem under consideration.

Actually the annual cycle of the budget process establishes the context of resources allocation decisions in the public sector. We often talk about the budget as a plan. When we make budget decisions we are setting priorities for the attainment of various goals either by adding, cutting back, or modifying programs. There is some truth to the saying that budget decisions are program decisions. But the saying is also misleading because the relation of the budget to current and future programs is frequently obscure and uncertain. The budgetary categories are frequently either administrative organizations such as government bureaus or resource inputs such as construction or personnel. To determine the "program" for alleviating mental retardation, for example, one must analyze in some depth the programs of a score of bureaus in several different agencies. Further, most often neither the impact on future years beyond those for which we are budgeting, nor the program objectives within whose context the budget has been formed are made explicit. Somehow we must attempt to reduce the uncertainty of dealing with the future; we have to plan even if most plans have to be continually revised.

To talk about uncertainty reduction is relatively easy but to do something about it is quite different. Health is a rapidly changing policy area. The technology of delivering medical services, the list of our health priorities and goals, and even the definition of what we mean by health—all are in flux. But the fact of a dynamic social and physical environment argues for more knowledge, for more analysis and understanding. For example, we have to know how well we have been doing with our current programs. In a complex organization, it is not unusual not even to be aware of just what these programs are, let alone to have some technique for evaluating them. Most studies of actual decisionmaking find that the problem solver starts looking for alternatives somewhere around the neighborhood of the present alternative. It is not just that planners or problem solvers are myopic; we also have our own resource problems. There are costs of getting additional information and there is also a scarcity of trained analysts. But in spite of these limitations, one of the signal contributions of planning and analysis is to extend the range of search, to seek out and develop new, imaginative, and hopefully better, alternatives.

This we attempt to do by developing a "model" or a framework to analyze the particular health system or subsystem. Such a model explicitly takes into account the same informational needs which I have mentioned. It abstracts the relevant features of the various institutions that are germane to the particular health problem which we are examining. This process of system definition sets the stage for our work by limiting the problem to which we pay attention. We have to delimit or arbitrarily set boundaries around the problem. Thus, one aspect of system definition or model construction is to define boundaries. Another aspect of system definition is to develop some understanding of the relationships which exist among the elements of the system. To do this we have to find out not only that a particular health agency exists, but also what aspects of it are related to the other variables in our analysis. The notion of interdependencies and the ability to specify functional relations is what we mean when we talk about a system.

Although in making resource allocations we may find it an analytical convenience to talk as if there is such an animal as a health system, in fact, the system that we know about is fragmented. We tend to be analyzers rather than synthesizers. This is the result of the fact that we, as health planners, are usually concerned with specific agencies of more or less specified jurisdictions. No single agency, public or private, makes authoritative resource allocations for the totality of the nation's health. Thus, there are many actors who provide inputs into the nation's health decision process.

It would be a misperception to view analytical tools such as cost-effectiveness studies or planning activities such as program-budgeting as centralizing decisionmaking or compelling the creation of the health system qua system. What these tools are and what they are used for is very much a function of the particular organizational context in which they are set. The point is that making resource allocations for the total field of health is not an appropriate description of what analysts do. We are always involved with some chunk or aspect of health as pollution, or the problem of the aging, and with the particular organizations which deal with each problem.

In addition to the fact that many agencies are involved in the field of health, we also cannot expect any single agency head to make all its decisions on everything, for every budgetary cycle. Even if you assume that a particular agency functions like a pyramid with a single policy or decisionmaker at the top (which most agencies do not, in practice), this "omniscient" individual cannot possibly have the time nor capacity to look at everything. The planning staff has to be selective. And one interesting problem is just what criteria they will use in making their selections. Obviously the planner could ask the decisionmaker but sometimes the latter may not know what he wants. Or, if he does, then this just shifts the problem to finding out the selection criteria of the decisionmaker. One could anticipate that the decisionmaker might want to be able to make choices on the highly "visible" programs of the agency. An index of visibility may be a high dollar commitment or high resource type program.

Or the program may be low in the resources assigned to it but still be very politically visible because of the existence of a small and active constituency or clientele. Another likely criteria would be to present choices concerned with omissions or gaps in the health system. Where are the areas of policy in which the particular health agency ought to be involved? This is not particularly simple to answer in any comprehensive fashion. But when a significant area appears to a planner to have been overlooked, there is a high probability that he will select the area for further attention. In addition to feasibility and omissions, the policy preference of the planner, himself, undoubtedly influences his criteria of selection.

In other words, the line between analyst and decisionmaker is somewhat blurred. The planner or analyst is involved in what Herbert Simon once called uncertainty absorption. He structures the decisions or choice situation by selecting certain problems and alternatives, and planners and users of planning output ought to be aware of this. Because we do have so many people involved in the health field, because we do have to cut our information and time costs, because no single decisionmaker even attempts to consider everything, and because planners themselves tend to also be selective, I sometimes think "comprehensive health planning" may be a contradiction in terms.

The use of planning and analytical tools, however, does make a great deal of sense when we view it within its organizational context. Therefore, it would be useful to discuss how program budgeting interacts with the use of tools like cost-benefit or cost-effectiveness analysis to improve the quality of organizational decisionmaking or resource allocation.

Program budgeting is one management tool which assists in health planning. It has two central features: (1) A framework designed to show the resource allocations which are made to problems, beneficiary groups, organizations; what activities and resource developments are being funded; and what results are anticipated from each; and (2) a multiyear program designed to reflect in these same terms what we are moving toward in the future.

A major aspect of the program budget is the structuring of the health system—of the part which the organization engaged in planning affects. And it should be set in such a fashion that it relates to the broader health system.

The program budget I have described has a structure too complex (in that it has numerous dimensions) to be laid out as a simple laundry list. It is a management information system which can be called upon to tell us what we are doing in each area of interest.

If an area of interest is one of disease control, we must be able to pull together all of the principal actions directed against the particular problem

—from state and regional programs, from projects, from research and training.

If we are interested in a target population, we must be able to pull programs affecting that population out from programs which may be aimed at disease control, financing of services, comprehensive care, and environmental protection.

When we have this capability, we have a framework for better planning. What is then *best* to do will not spring forth as did Athena from the head of Zeus. If all the programs could be related to a single dimensional output on whose virtues and validity we could all agree, the problem of allocating resources would be much simplified. But we know this is not so. Outputs of health programs have numerous dimensions—changes in morbidity, mortality, disability, services, contamination, etc., and these outputs apply to different components of our people.

For this reason, cost-effectiveness analyses cannot tell us the preferred mix of programs to be included in our program budget. Rather, the analyses are aimed at one or another set of problems—air pollution, kidney disease, child health, delivery of services to the poor. They explore the costs and accomplishment of alternative approaches to these narrower problems.

When we have information on costs and benefits we can not only indicate the preferred alternative for each problem, but also have some additional information by which to improve the total allocation. This addition is simply more insight into what we get for what we pay out.

The program budget is a means of noting what we are doing in an organized fashion—with emphasis on objectives and accomplishments—rather than on the organization or line item inputs of conventional budgets. It may serve to give better insight into what we are doing, give us inspiration for useful change, and form a record for program decisions. It is neither a planning process nor a means of discovering better plans. Rather, its categories should serve as useful organization and communication devices for program decision.

The actual process of planning—the ingredients to be reflected in the program budget—are the analyses and the priority decisions. By analyses I refer to work addressed to designing and evaluating strategies for the solution of problems. Generally, analyses would be conducted in the framework of cost-effectiveness comparisons of alternatives, but in many cases the formal approaches are unsuitable, although use of analytical perspectives is helpful.

Formal measurement of costs and outputs may be of little help in cases where we are trying to select preferred methods of affecting the behavior of institutions; for example, hospital behavior, formation of group practices, or consumer education. We may have a measurable idea that certain behavior would make things better; i.e., resources better utilized, more people taken care of. Our preferred program is to figure what mix of incentives and regulations may induce the desired behavior. While in concept we may believe or hope that the desired effects are thus produced at minimum cost, our program's effects and measures are obscure. For example, if we want hospitals to become community oriented, or to work with other facilities, we may argue and even prove how this would happen, but what we pay them to do is to become concerned—to move in certain directions. How much it costs society and what will happen depends on what institutions respond, how they perceive themselves and their community, etc.

For example, with regard to air pollution, we can study program alternatives which reduce contaminants at minimum cost within an airshed, paying attention to location of emitters, meteorological conditions, and end-stage costs, etc. But the government program is designed to move in this direction by providing incentives or penalties. We are rarely certain of the response.

When we have made our analyses, we have more confidence that we have examined alternatives and investigated the relationship to objectives, that we have weighed the responses of society and the costs to society and to our own resources.

We can now begin the process of developing programs in each area of interest and forming mixes of these. But resources are scarce and we cannot buy all that we want. We must negotiate with other actors in the organization and in the broader social and political environment. Even though we may think we have identified a preferred economic solution, it may have to be modified in order to be implemented by the legislative and administrative process.

The program structure provides a cognitive map, a frame of reference to consider alternatives using cost-benefit analysis. Similarly when we have identified by analysis an alternative that we may have high expectations of being implemented, we will adjust the program structure to reflect this. Thus program budgeting and cost-benefit analysis interact. They are both different parts of the resource allocation process, but they are also intimately related. Problems of resource allocation are an intrinsic part of both of these activities.

The most recent and most comprehensive attempt to apply quantitative methods to the allocation of resources to health problems was introduced in the federal government under the title of the "Planning-Programming-Budgeting System." This approach was first generally used in government by the Department of Defense beginning in the spring of 1961.[3] In August of 1965 the President ordered all principal agencies of government to adopt similar systems. The new Secretary of Health, Education, and Welfare, John Gardner, took this charge seriously, creating a new office to develop and implement the system, that of the Assistant Secretary for Program Coordination (later called Planning and Evaluation).

While the broad goal of the PPB system was to improve decisionmaking, especially budgetary decisions, those concerned had different ideas as to what its specific objectives and procedures ought to be. Some were most concerned to develop better insights into program objectives so that the Secretary and his agency heads and program managers would better understand program interrelationships and complementaries. Others believed the most important step was the delineation of long-range needs and goals. The Bureau of the Budget was asking for detailed 5-year plans and analytical bases for all budget decisions.

Program administrators feared not only that the volume of paperwork would increase, but also that program decisions might be made on improper bases, i.e., on narrow economic or quantitative grounds, and by individuals lacking in an understanding of the programs and the issues at stake. Budget and executive officers in the various agencies saw a potential dilution of their responsibilities and authority.

After a period of experimentation in 1966, a system was developed at HEW which was used in calendar year 1967 as the basis for the fiscal year 1969 budget. It is this system and its problems which I will discuss in the remainder of this paper.

But first, it may be useful to outline some of the difficulties with the earlier budgetary system.

Historically, budgets tend to be formed "from the bottom up." The cycle commenced with a call for a preliminary budget from the Office of the Secretary with no guidelines as to scale or priorities. Agency heads, in turn, passed the call along to their bureaus, and the bureaus to their divisions, etc. It was usually assumed that existing budget levels were an inviolate base, not needing reexamination. The budget process focused on upward changes. The import of proposed legislation was not considered, but was channeled into a separate legislative proposal process, with little interaction between it and the formulation of the budget. The planning horizon was the budget year, with little longer range planning. Appropriation categories are, for the most part, coincident with administrative organizations, and little attention was paid to competing or complementary programs.

The general philosophy of program managers has been that the social problems their programs are addressing are so vast, and the resources allocated to these worthy objectives so miniscule, that their objective in the formation of budgets is the tactical one of increasing these resources. The effects of programs have not been evaluated in systematic fashion, and alternatives to present approaches remain largely unexplored, especially in the context of budgeting for "existing legislation."

It was not surprising, then, to find that budget proposals usually took the form of asking for increases in almost every program. Bases for these increases were either the ability to grow and satisfy more social needs, or the growing demand for federal grants on the part of potential recipients. Workload increases, annualization of past midyear increases, and price rises also were considered.

Higher echelon reviews usually consisted of concern with whether the rates of growth were feasible and salable, whether the administrators of the programs were capable, and with giving visibility to commitments of the administration as evidenced by recent legislative programs. Questions about interactions or effectiveness of programs were infrequently asked, and more rarely answered. Attention was paid, of course, to congressional desires and the power of constituencies.

Despite its lack of quantitative analysis and long-range strategy, on a tactical level the system had worked quite well. Budgets had increased, doubling about every five years, and scores of new programs had been created by the Congress. But problems loomed on the horizon: the multiplicity of new programs threatened management understanding of what was going on, and it seemed unlikely that the rapid pace of budget increase would be sustained. Problems of imbalance in programs could no longer be resolved by expansion. Choices would have to be made.

Much hope was held by some in developing a system similar to that which appeared to work so well in the Department of Defense. Of course, skeptics were quick to point out that social programs dealt with people, not military equipment, and that quantitative analysis was irrelevant to problems so irrational as protecting and improving the health of the American people.

There were and are difficulties in transferring the Defense approaches, but the nature of the product was only one, and possibly not the most significant. In national security, the federal government has almost total responsibility, and controls most of the resources. In health, federal expenditures accounted for only 16 percent of the total outlays in 1966. Even of these, HEW doesn't operate many of its own programs. Most of the funds go out in the form of grants-in-aid to state and local governments, universities, school districts, hospitals, and nonprofit agencies. Of its fiscal year 1969 budget, 94 percent were in the form of such grants-in-aid. HEW itself operates the Indian Health Program, the Food and Drug Administration, and relatively small intramural research programs. So the problems to be analyzed are largely affected by funds other than federal and administered by others as well. There are a multiplicity of factors: 7,000 hospitals, 3,000 counties, hundreds of universities, several hundred thousand medical doctors, 50 states, etc.

Compounding the confusion is the all too obvious fact that we know little about the cause and effect relationship in social areas. We don't know how federal programs influence the operating institutions, we don't know the effects of most health services on health status, or what forms of health delivery systems produce better results than others. We lack models, coefficients, and data.

The first step toward improving budgetary decisionmaking in a huge, complicated organization like HEW was to provide comprehensible information about the current allocation of resources and a mechanism for showing how future changes in programs would affect this allocation. As a start one should be able to answer such questions as: What share of the Department's resources is going into health programs? What share is directed toward improving the lives of the poor? What share is directed at assisting old people, and how many people are affected? What share of the Department's budget is devoted to research and is the share growing or declining?

None of these questions can be answered easily by looking at the conventional budget of the Department. Health programs appear in several different agencies. The Public Health Service, the Social and Rehabilitation Service, the Social Security Administration, the Food and Durg Administration, the Administration on Aging and the Office of Education all have significant health programs. Activities such as research and training are often buried in other programs. The groups affected by programs are not identified in a conventional budget; nor are measures of output or accomplishment (classrooms built, patients treated, students supported) readily available.

For these reasons the Department developed a new information system which serves both as a classification system and as a planning tool.[4] Under this system an individual Department program is classified in a number of different ways—by objective, by the target group in the population at which it is directed, by type of financing (project grants, loans, etc.), by activities used in carrying out the program (construction, training, etc.). The result is a flexible information system which can be used to answer a great many questions quickly and easily and to give a clearer picture of how the Department's dollars are being used.

Along with the dollar information, measures of output of programs in nondollar terms are being developed. At present these outputs are largely limited to measures of initial impact of programs (square feet constructed, children enrolled, persons rehabilitated). Eventually we may be able to provide measures of more ultimate benefits of programs (cases cured, students graduated, individuals rescued from poverty) which will aid in evaluating the effectiveness of programs in meeting their goals.

About each of the programs, then, there are a number of questions. What is it for? What does it accomplish? Who is being helped? How is it being carried out? How much does it cost? Who carries it out in the federal government and elsewhere? How is it funded? These questions lead to the development of a program information structure.

Figure 1 gives some insight into the way in which the structure arrays the programs. On the left-hand stub, are the names of possible program objectives or purposes such as the provision of medical care, consumer protection, development of basic skills, income maintenance, social services, and the like. To answer the question of how, programs are subdivided into activities, a sampling of these is listed, innovation, the training of personnel, the delivery of beneficial services, the construction of facilities. For each we are interested also in for whom are you doing it—the target population. So in this three-dimensional diagram we also look at what is being done, for example, for the handicapped, the aged, and migrants.

A particular program, say facilities for medical care of the handicapped, may appear simply as a cell in the structure. And its program manager asked, "I filled out these forms and all I see is I'm in a box and it doesn't help me to decide anything at all." He's probably right.

What we're interested in, of course, is building insight into what takes

Figure 1

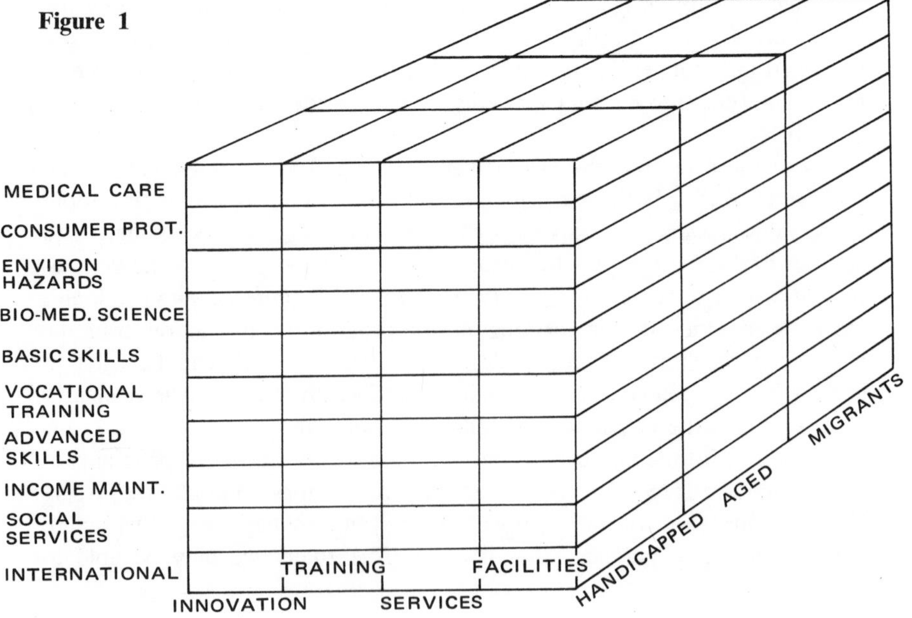

place. We can add other activities to this cell which was concerned with building of facilities for the medical care of the handicapped and we can pick up the rest of the medical care activities for the handicapped and get some more understanding as to whether or not they are reasonably in balance for what we are trying to do. We can go further and pick up what we are doing in the area of medical care for the various target groups. Another way of looking at it is to ask the question of what are we doing for a particular target group in all programs.

Illustrated in Table 1, for example, is a way program information can

Table 1

Target Group: Children and Youth—Income Under $5,000 (Age 0–21)

EDUCATION PROGRAMS

Improving the education of the disadvantaged

- Educationally Deprived Children (ESEA Title I)
- National Teacher Corps
- Educational Opportunity Grants (HEA Title IV–A)
- Educational Talent Contracts (HEA Title IV–A)
- College Work Study Grants (HEA IV–C)
- Vocational Work Study Grants (HEA IV–C)

HEALTH PROGRAMS

Health problem classification

- Child Development
- Crippled Children
- School and Pre-School Children
- Maternity and Infant Care
- Maternal and Child Health
- Comprehensive Maternal and Child Care
- Early Case Finding and Treatment

General health care programs

- Hospital Care
- Physicians
- Dental Services
- Nurse Services
- Home Health Services
- Out Patient

SOCIAL SERVICES PROGRAMS

Individual and family services

- Day Care
- Foster Care
- Other Child Welfare Services

Strengthening resources and organization of social services institutions

- Juvenile Delinquency

INCOME MAINTENANCE PROGRAMS

Other individual and family support

- Aid to Families with Dependent Children

be classified. For a target group—children and youth of low-income families—we can identify these programs—the educational programs, the specific health programs which are aimed at children with respect to child development, crippled children, early case finding and treatment, various social services and money payments, as well. We can begin to look at programs from the point of view of the recipients of the benefits of these programs.

If the first step toward rational decisionmaking is a good information system, the second is a strong capability for analyzing the consequences of alternative courses of action. In the past 2 years HEW has undertaken a series of analytical studies of existing health programs and possible alternatives.

One of the first analytical studies of the PPB era at HEW was a study of disease control programs.[5] Considerable work had been done during the last ten years in estimating the economic costs of particular diseases. Among the best known of these are Rashi Fein's *Economics of Mental Illness,*[6] Burton Weisbrod's *Economics of Public Health*[7] in which he estimated the costs of cancer, tuberculosis, and poliomyelitis, Herbert Klarman's paper on syphilis control programs,[8] and Dorothy Rice's studies covering the international classification of diseases.[9] A generation earlier Dublin and Lotka's classic explored the impact of disease and disability and their relation to changes in earning power.[10] The economic implications of disability were, of course, a matter of central interest in the area of workmen's compensation insurance.[11] It was not surprising, then, that when systematic quantitative analysis of government programs and policies began to spread from defense to civilian applications, one of the first analytical studies was a study of disease control programs.

The basic concept of the study was a simple one. HEW supports (or could support) a number of categorical disease control programs, whose objectives are to save lives or to prevent disability by controlling specific diseases. The study was an attempt to answer the question: If additional money were to be allocated to disease control programs, which programs would show the highest payoff in terms of lives saved and disability prevented per dollar spent? The study defines "disease" liberally. Motor vehicle accidents were included along with tuberculosis, syphilis, cancer, and arthritis.

I'm talking here not about research, but where a technology exists and the problem is whether to put the same, more, or less federal funds behind these control programs to support activities in hospitals, states, and communities. The question we address is where should we allocate the resources available for this purpose.

Table 2 illustrates the approach to one set of diseases, cancer. We

Table 2
Cancer Control Program: 1968–72

	Uterine-cervix	Breast	Head and neck	Colon-rectum
Grant costs (in thousands)	\$97,750	\$17,750	\$13,250	\$13,300
Number of examinations (in thousands)	9,363	2,280	609	662
Cost per examination	\$10.44	\$7.79	\$21.76	\$20.10
Examinations per case found	87.50	167.30	620.20	496.00
Cancer cases found	107,045	13,628	982	1,334
Cost per case found	\$913	\$1,302	\$13,493	\$9,970
Cancer deaths averted	44,084	2,936	303	288
Cost per death averted	\$2,217	\$6,046	\$43,729	\$46,181

looked at cancer of the uterine cervix, breast, head and neck and colon-rectum. We estimated cost per examination, and the probable number of examinations that would be required for each case found. From this was derived the number of cases that would be found for an expenditure level, and estimates of the cost per case found. An estimate was made of the number of deaths that could be averted by the treatment following the detection of the cancers and then we calculated the cost per death averted which ranged from about \$2,200 in the case of cervical cancer up to \$40,000 to \$45,000 in the case of head and neck and colon-rectum cancer.

On the vertical axis of Figure 2 we have plotted the program costs; this includes the cost of the treatment in addition to the federal detection program. On the horizontal axis estimates of deaths averted are ordered by increase in cost per death averted in each program. Segments of the curve identified to each disease cover the extent of the program which it was estimated could be mounted in the years 1968–72 before running into sharply increasing costs. In concept, the cervical cancer curve is cut off where costs become higher than the breast cancer program, etc. From this analysis one might say that if there is only available \$50 million, cervical cancer should get all the funds. If we have \$115 million, then breast cancer control programs look quite competitive. Head and neck and colon-rectum cancer detection program as major control programs did not look attractive when viewed in this context. The analysts recommended that they concentrate on research and development.

The same kind of analysis was performed for each of the five programs studied (Figure 3). There seemed to be a very high potential payoff for certain educational programs in motor vehicle injury prevention trying to persuade people to use seatbelts, not to walk in front of a car, and so on.

Figure 2

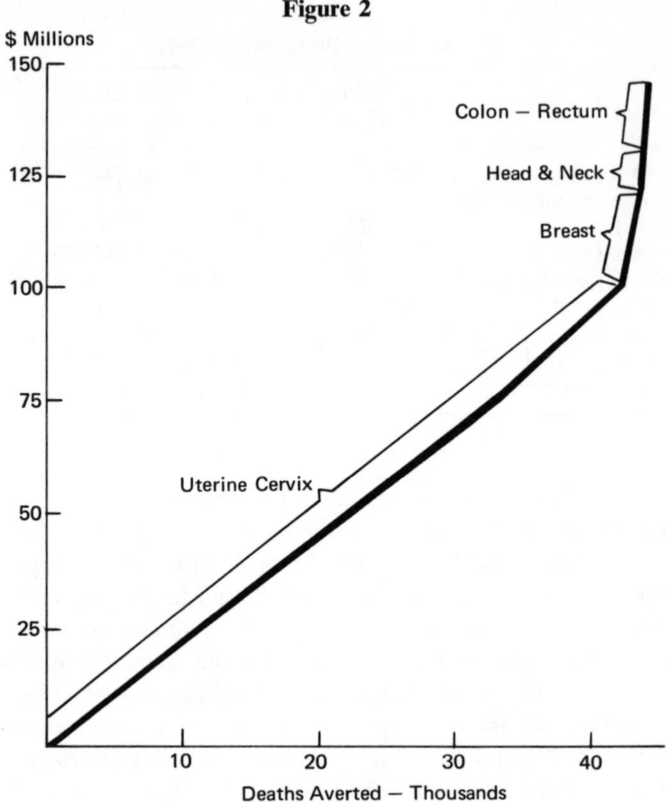

Figure 3

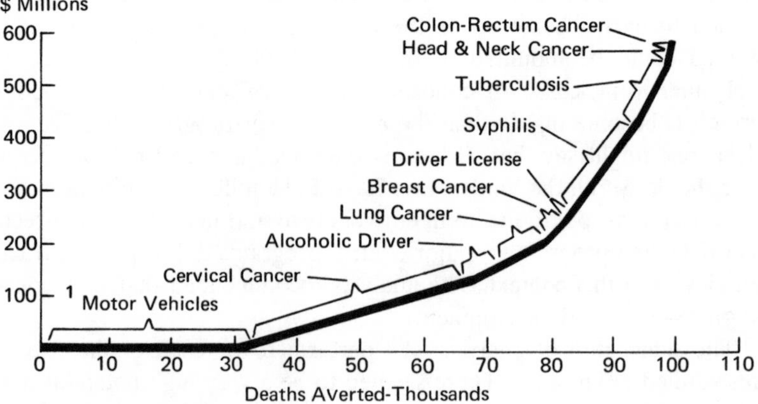

1/ Seat Belt, Restraint
Pedestrian Injury

Figure 4

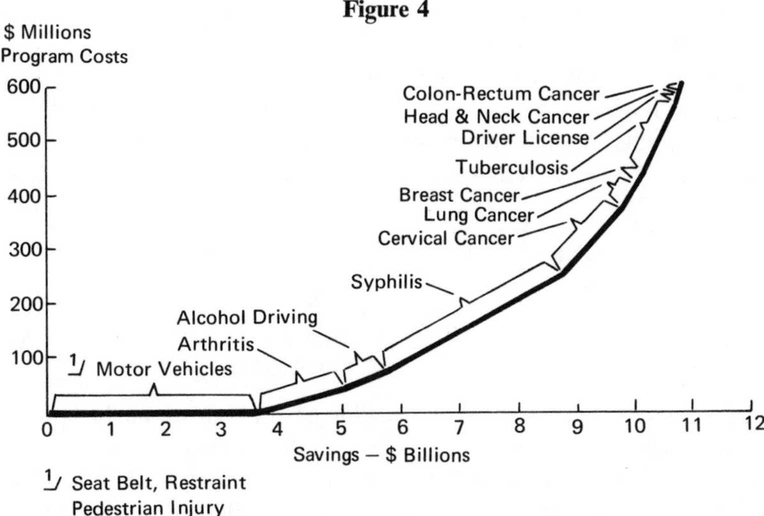

And then as we move up this curve, again ordered by cost of averting death we begin adding the others. This particular criterion, deaths averted, was not completely satisfactory. The number of fatalities attributed to arthritis were negligible. Secondly, there is the question, did it matter who died? Did it matter whether it was a 30-year-old mother or a 40-year-old father of a family or a 75-year-old grandfather? In Figure 4, dollar savings summing avoided medical treatments and a crude estimate of the average (discounted) lifetime earnings saved are plotted as a variable in place of deaths averted. There are two changes in results: cervical cancer and syphilis control programs change places in priority order, and we are able to introduce the arthritis program.

Allocations of resources to programs are developed from such analyses by using information such as this and the preceding charts as an additional insight to give an additional feel for what were relatively high-priority and what were relatively low-priority programs, and then to feed these insights into the decisionmaking process which also considers existing commitments, the political situation, feasible changes in the rates of spending, the ability to get people moving on programs, and so on.

These studies were not greeted with universal acclaim. Criticisms focused on a number of problems. First, with almost no exception the conclusions were based on average relationships. That is, the total benefits were divided by the total costs. There was little evidence of what the actual impact of increasing or decreasing programs by small amounts might be. If we actually believed the average ratios to be valid at the margin, ought we not put all our funds into the program with the highest benefit-cost or deaths averted per dollar ratios?

Let me illustrate with a hypothetical example how such marginal information might be used to determine the preferred mix of disease control programs. Assume that we can determine, as in the following tables, the number of lives saved by different expenditures on disease A and disease B:

Disease A		*Disease B*	
Expenditures	*Lives saved*	*Expenditures*	*Lives saved*
$500,000	360	$500,000	200
$1,000,000	465	$1,000,000	270

If we only knew the effect of spending $1 million, we might opt for a program where all our money was spent on controlling disease A, as we could save 465 lives instead of 270 if we spent it all on disease B. Similarly, if we only knew the effects of programs of a half million dollars, we would probably prefer A, as we'd save 360 rather than only 200 lives.

But if we knew the results for expenditures of both half a million and 1 million dollars in each program, we would quickly see that spending half our money in each program was better than putting it all in one assuming we have $1 million available:

Our calculations would be:

Expenditures			*Lives saved*
$1,000,000 on A			465
$1,000,000 on B			270
$1,000,000	$500,000 on A	360	560
	$500,000 on B	200	

But suppose we had still more discrete data, as in the following tables which give us the effect of each hundred thousand dollars spent on each control program:

Disease A		*Disease B*	
Expenditures	*Lives saved*	*Expenditures*	*Lives saved*
$100,000	100	$100,000	50
$200,000	180	$200,000	50
$300,000	250	$300,000	135
$400,000	310	$400,000	170
$500,000	360	$500,000	200
$600,000	400	$600,000	225
$700,000	430	$700,000	240
$800,000	450	$800,000	255
$900,000	460	$900,000	265
$1,000,000	465	$1,000,000	270

We could then spend the million dollars even more effectively:

Expenditures	*Lives saved*
$600,000 on A	400
$400,000 on B	170
$1,000,000	570

The lack of marginal data resulted from both a lack of such data for most programs, together with a lack of economic sophistication on the part of the Public Health Service analysts who performed the studies. Despite the theoretical shortcomings, the results were useful when applied with some common sense.

Practical obstacles of existing commitments made it almost impossible to recommend *reductions* in any program. So the decisions dealt with the allocation of modest increments.

In the case of oral and colon-rectum cancers, the average cost per death averted seemed so high that the Department recommended emphasis on research and development, rather than a control program to demonstrate and extend current technology.

In cervical cancer, investigation indicated a sizable number of hospitals in low socioeconomic areas without detection programs which would be willing to establish these if supported by federal funds. The unit costs of increasing the number of hospitals seemed to be the same as that of those already in the program. Shifting the approach to reach out for additional women in the community would increase costs per examination, but not so high as to change the relative position of this program. At most, it raised costs to about those of the breast cancer control program.

Despite the seeming high potential payoff of some of the motor vehicle programs, there was considerable uncertainty about the success. As a consequence, recommendations were for small programs with a large emphasis on evaluation for use in future decisions. The same philosophy was applied to the arthritis program.

What resulted then, was a setting of priorities for additional funding, based on the analytical results, judgment about their reliability, and practical considerations.

A second type of criticism of the analysis described above was concerned with the criteria, especially the calculation of benefits.[11a] They were considered inadequate in that they paid attention to economic productivity alone, and omitted other considerations. In particular, they were thought to discriminate against the old who might be past employment years, and women whose earning were relatively low. It was also feared that the logic, if vigorously pursued, would penalize not only health programs for the aged such as the newly launched medicare, but also programs aimed at assisting the poor whose relative earning power is low by definition.

In actual practice in the programs studied, these concerns were only hypothetical. The programs for cervical and breast cancer looked to be good despite their being for women. As for the poor, most of the programs considered, especially cervical cancer, syphilis, and tuberculosis were aimed primarily at them, and projects were usually located to serve low income residents.

Another type of objection was raised not against the technique of analysis, but against its being done at all. Choices among diseases to be controlled and concern with costs of saving lives can be viewed as contrary to physicians' attitudes in the care of an individual patient. Yet, such decisions are made, analysis or no. Prior decisions on allocations to various health problems rested upon a combination of perception of the magnitude of the problem and the political strength organized to secure funding, e.g., the National Tuberculosis Association.

The disease control cost-benefit analyses suggest that additional considerations are very relevant. Given scarce resources (and if they are not, there is no allocation problem), one ought to estimate the costs of achieving improvements in health. If we can save more lives by applying resources to a small (in numbers affected) problem than a large one, we ought to consider doing so.

A somewhat separate issue is that of the disease control approach to personal health. This is too large an issue to deal with in this paper, but it may make more sense to develop programs of delivering comprehensive health care, including preventive services, than to maintain categorical disease programs.

The following year a number of additional control studies were performed. One of the most interesting and important was on kidney diseases.[12] This analysis was launched at a time when the public was becoming conscious of a new technique, the artificial kidney (chronic dialysis), which could preserve the life and productivity of individuals who would otherwise die of end-stage kidney disease. About 50,000 persons a year do so die. It is estimated that about 7,500 of these were "suited" by criteria of age, temperament, and the absence of other damaging illnesses for dialysis treatment. The national capacity could handle only about 900, who would remain on intermittent dialysis the rest of their lives. About 90 percent would survive from one year to the next. The operating cost of dialysis treatment in hospitals was estimated at about $15,000 per patient per year. A home treatment approach might reduce this to about $5,000 per year.

The federal government was under great pressure to expand the national capacity, which was limited not only by the large money costs, but

Figure 5

SCHEMATIC OF TRANSPLANT AND DIALYSIS PATIENTS

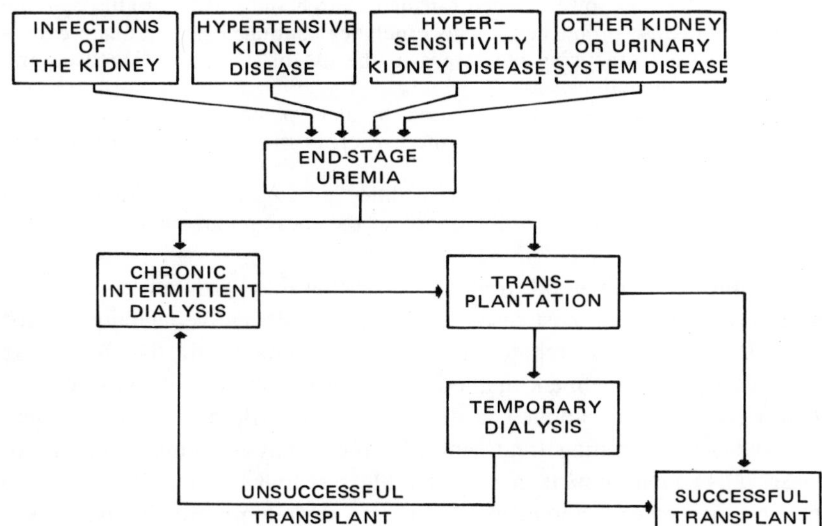

also by shortages of trained personnel and supplies of blood. Indeed, at the same time as this analysis was being performed, an advisory group to the U.S. Bureau of the Budget was studying the problem of end-stage kidney disease. This group came in with the recommendation for a massive national dialysis program.[13]

The HEW program analysis was somewhat more broadly charged, and took a more systems oriented approach. It concerned itself not only about the 7,500 annual candidates for dialysis, but also about the other 40,000 or so who would suffer the end-stage disease, but were unsuited to dialysis. If some way could be found to reduce the numbers falling into the pool of end-stage patients, perhaps a larger number of people could be helped. Figure 5 illustrates the classes of kidney diseases leading to end-stage disease. If these could be better prevented or treated we might keep down the number of patients requiring dialysis or transplantation.

The analysis group, therefore, examined a number of mechanisms or program components. Among these were:

1. Expanded use of existing preventive techniques.
2. Expanded use of existing diagnostic techniques.
3. Expanded use of existing treatments, including chronic dialysis, kidney transplantation and conservative management (drugs, diets, etc.).

4. Laboratory and clinical research to produce new preventive, diagnostic, therapeutic and rehabilitative methods.

5. Increased specialized scientific medical and paramedical training to provide the manpower needed for the research and treatment attack on the kidney disease problem. This also includes continued postgraduate education to train practicing physicians in the use of the latest diagnostic and treatment modalities.

6. Increased public education to alert potential victims of kidney disease to seek medical help at the earliest possible emergence of warning signs.

7. Provision of specialized facilities not currently in existence which are essential for the execution of any of the above programs.

It must be understood from the outset that these program components are interdependent in most cases. For example, preventive techniques exist that need further research to make them maximally effective for broad application. New treatment methods are useless if existing diagnostic techniques are not being applied in medical practice. Because of the present inadequacies of existing treatments, be they dialysis, transplantation, or conservative management, a considerable research effort is called for to increase their efficacy and economy to make them more broadly useful.

Time does not permit a detailed description of the analysis. Costs were estimated for relevant public and private expenditures for the nationwide treatment of kidney disease. The latter includes cost of physician care, hospital care, nursing home care, and other professional services for diagnosis and therapy of kidney diseases, as well as the cost of drugs and net insurance costs. In addition, the cost was estimated for ongoing research efforts, for demonstration, screening and detection programs, for education and training efforts, and for that portion of the cost of construction of hospital and medical facilities which can be prorated to the use of patients with kidney disease.

Based on the substantive information obtained and statistical and economic data collected, estimates were made of the benefits to be gained by different approaches to the solution or amelioration of the overall national kidney disease problem at different expenditure levels of HEW funds.

Several different funding levels were assumed, and estimates were made assuming both the current state-of-art and an expected advanced state-of-art in 1975.

Each program consisted of a hypothetical situation where a specific level of HEW program funding was divided among a rational mix of program components (screening, diagnosis and treatment, research, training, etc.) based on the particular characteristics of the specific disease group involved, and was applied to specifically involved or particularly vulnerable groups or, as the case may be, to the entire population. The benefits accruable from these programs were estimated and stated in terms of overall reduction of mortality, prevalence, and morbidity due to kidney disease.

Benefit indices were quantified in terms of the reduction in annual mortality, the reduction in annual morbidity (number of sick days per year), and in terms of the disease prevalence in the total population due to the specific type of kidney disorder analyzed, which would accrue thanks to the impact of the various program components—such as research advances, disease prevention and improved treatment.

The analysis group avoided estimates of the impact on economic productivity in their results, although such calculations have been made independently.[14]

The HEW study concluded that concentration in future programs merely on the treatment of end-stage kidney disease is not likely to solve the problem of annual deaths due to irreversible uremia unless unlimited funds are available for an indefinite continuation of such a program. Thus, steps must be taken to decrease the number of people who enter the irreversible fatal stage each year by a systematic prevention or treatment of the primary kidney diseases which initiate their progressive downhill course. It is obvious from the analyses in the three major kidney disease groups—infectious, hypersensitive, and hypertensive—that the otherwise inevitable annual reservoir of patients with irreversible kidney failure can be diminished considerably through vigorous programs activated to deal with each of these groups. The application of relatively minor funds in the group of infectious kidney diseases to stimulate systematic screening of high-risk groups followed by diagnosis and treatment, even within the current state-of-the-art and without awaiting additional advances due to ongoing or future research, can bring about a significant future reduction in the number of end-stage patients. Continued and expanded research activities will be necessary to increase the percentage of patients ultimately benefited by this approach.

In the area of hypersensitivity diseases involving the kidney there appears to be no promising mode of attack in sight except for the launching of a systematic research effort intended to increase our knowledge of the disease mechanisms involved. Here, the sooner this effort is started the greater the likelihood of a reduction of the number of end-stage victims in the near future. The promise for benefits to be derived from this type of research effort is such that it should not be postponed—particularly since any new effective treatment or prevention modality would produce major benefits in the entire field of hypersensitivity diseases, such as rheumatic heart disease, rheumatoid arthritis, and others.

In the group of hypertensive diseases of the kidney an immediate start, within the current state-of-the-art, of screening, diagnosis and treatment can begin to diminish the number of patients who will eventually require end-stage treatment because of their progressive renal involvement. Simultaneous research efforts are likely to make this particular portion of the overall program more effective as time goes by, in the same fashion in which the new antihypertensive drugs developed during the last 10 years have succeeded in decreasing by about 50 percent the mortality due to malignant hypertension.

Thus, a meaningful federal program to reduce the annual mortality due to kidney disease and aimed at a general reduction of the prevalence of the various kidney diseases must perforce be a multifactorial one which brings into play all of the program components—research, prevention, treatment and education—available in our arsenal. An optimally proportioned mix of these program components must be present to yield maximum benefits in overall number of lives saved. This last concept includes not only deaths avoided today but deaths to be prevented in the years to come. Needless to say, such a total program, to be meaningful and productive, must be aimed at all three major primary kidney diseases, as well as at end-stage kidney failure.

Figure 6 shows a hypothetical program mix that might come from such conclusions. Note the early emphasis on research to affect the state-

Figure 6

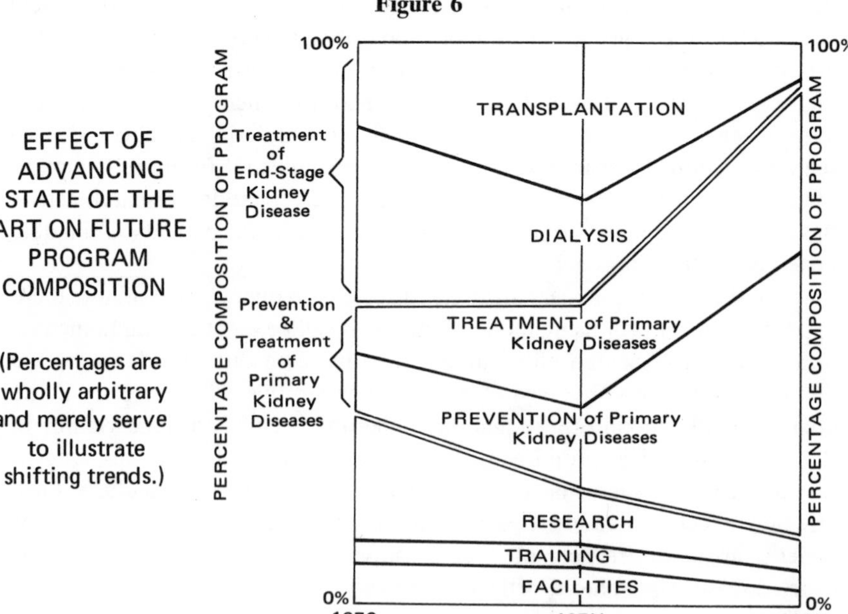

of-the-art, and the growth in allocations to the prevention and treatment of primary kidney diseases as relative allocations to dialysis are diminished.

In 1966, HEW also did a rather different type of analysis in the field of health: a study of alternative ways of improving the health of children.[15] The President had focused public attention on the problem of child health and expressed a desire to introduce new legislation in this field. The HEW study was an attempt to assess the state of health of the nation's children (to what extent the children have correctable health problems and in what groups in the population were the problems concentrated) and to estimate the cost and effectiveness of various kinds of programs to improve the health of children.

This study proved more difficult than anticipated. Hard information on the state of health of children is hard to come by. Surprisingly, estimates of improvement in health attributable to medical care are almost nonexistent. It is not easy to demonstrate statistically that children who see doctors regularly are healthier than children who do not.

In regard to maternal and child care programs the stated goal was to make needed maternal and child health services available and accessible to all, in particular to all expectant mothers and children in health depressed areas. Health depressed areas could be characterized as areas with excessive infant mortality rates. There is no universal index of good or bad health among children. Two measurable areas were selected—mortality and the prevalence of chronic handicapping conditions. Over a dozen possible programs aimed at reducing these were examined. In Table 3, three selected programs addressed to the problem of coverage of maternal and child health are illustrated, two of them comprehensive programs of care to expectant mothers and children. This table shows the annual effects of spending the same amount of money, $10 million a year, in different ways. The analysts examined comprehensive care programs covering up to age eighteen and up to age five with estimates based on the best assumptions derived from the literature and advisers on the probabilities of prevention of maternal deaths, premature deaths, infant deaths, and mental retardation, and handicapping conditions prevented or corrected by age eighteen. They also looked at a program of early case finding and assured treatment which focused on children at ages four and again every other year until they were nine. Expending the same amounts, where you put the money yields different results. With respect to reduction of infant mortality, several other programs had higher payoffs than these. For example, a program of intensive care units for high-risk newborns was estimated to reduce annually 367 deaths if we put all our money in that basket—it would cost about $27 thousand per infant death prevented. The programs shown cost about four times that, but they do other good things too.

The HEW analysts also looked at programs with a given amount of

Table 3
Yearly Effects per $10,000,000 Expended in Health Depressed Areas

	Comprehensive programs to age—		Case finding of treatment
	18	5	0, 1, 3, 5, 7, 9
Maternal deaths prevented	1.6	3	
Premature births prevented	100–250	200–485	
Infant deaths prevented	40–60	85–120	
Mental retardation prevented	5–7	7–14	
Handicaps prevented or corrected by age 18:			
Vision problems:			
All	350	195	3,470
Amblyopia	60	119	1,140
Hearing loss:			
All	90	70	7,290
Binaural	6	5	60
Other physical handicaps	200	63	1,470

money (Table 4) aimed at reducing the number of children who will have decayed and unfilled teeth by age 18. Fluoridation programs in communities which do not possess this, will, for the same amount of money, give us close to 300,000 fewer children in this condition, compared to 18,000 or 44,000 fewer in other programs noted. Fluoridation looks like a very attractive program. It was so attractive that it could be inferred that a program as cheap as this is not being inhibited by lack of financial support by the federal government; there are other factors at work.

One other program, additional funds on family planning, looked like a very good way not only to reduce the number of infant deaths, but also the rate of infant mortality in high-risk communities.

Despite the information difficulties, several conclusions emerged clearly from the study. Two of these conclusions resulted in new legislation being requested from Congress. First, it seemed clear that a program of early casefindings and treatment of handicapping conditions would have

Table 4
Reduction in Number of 18-year-olds with Decayed and Unfilled Teeth per $10,000,000 Expended in Health Depressed Areas

Fluoridation	294,000
Comprehensive dental care without fluoridation	18,000
Comprehensive dental care with fluoridation	44,000

considerable payoff. It was also clear that if the large number of children who do not now have access to good medical care were to be provided with pediatric services, an acute shortage of doctors would be precipitated. Ways have to be found to use medical manpower more efficiently. The Social Security Amendments of 1967 include provision for programs of early casefinding and treatment of defects and chronic conditions in children, and for research and demonstration programs in the training and use of physician assistants.

These condensed discussions of some of HEW's applications of cost-benefit analysis to disease-control programs illustrate both the usefulness and limitations of such analyses for decisionmaking.[16] Issues are sharpened, and quantitative estimates are developed to reduce the decisionmakers' uncertainty about costs and effects. Nevertheless, the multiplicity of dimensions of output, and their basic incommensurabilities both with costs and the outputs of other claimants for public expenditure, still requires the use of value judgments and political consensus.

Prior to the introduction of the planning-programing-and-budgeting system, long-range planning in HEW was sporadic and generally not Departmentwide. No mechanisms existed for focusing attention on longer range objectives, deciding which types of programs should be given highest priority over the next several years, and then drawing up a budget consistent with those objectives and priorities.

In 1967 and 1968, the Department experimented with a new procedure for making budget decisions in the context of a long-range plan.

The procedure involves several steps. First, very early in the calendar year the planning and evaluation staff drew up a list of significant issues which would have to be addressed in formulating the budget and legislative program. This list of issues was discussed within the Office of the Secretary, with the operating agencies, and with the Bureau of the Budget. Decisions were made as to which of these issues seemed likely to be illuminated by analytical work, and studies of many of them were initiated.

The second step in 1967 was the development of a set of tentative Departmental objectives for 1973. The operating agencies were asked to formulate their objectives for 1973 in program terms. The Secretary gave each agency two ceilings for 1973—a "low" which implied continued budget stringency, and a "high" which implied somewhat greater availability of funds. Each of them was asked to answer the question: How would you allocate these sums in 1973 among existing programs or new programs which could be developed between now and then?

The agencies took this assignment seriously, despite the difficulties of forcing busy administrators to take the time away from daily crises to think five years into the future. The 1973 objectives which the agencies sent back to the Secretary reflected considerable thought and effort on the part of agency heads and their bureau chiefs.

The agency 1973 objectives were reviewed by the Secretary and his staff and a set of Departmental objectives for 1973 was formulated.

In both the agency plans and those of the Department, the tentative results of analyses were considered. For example, the study of the delivery of health services to the poor made recommendations which involved policy decisions with respect to the coverage of the medicaid program, the training of physician assistants and family health advisers, reorganization of delivery systems (especially those dealing with ambulatory care), hospital-community links, and comprehensive care versus categorical control programs. The Departmental objectives, reflecting the Secretary's judgment about priorities for 1973, were then transmitted back to the operating agencies as guidance for formulating their fiscal year 1969 budget submissions and fiscal year 1969–73 suggested program and financial plan, and legislative program. These were reviewed for conformance to Department objectives, and a Department program and financial plan (1969–73), fiscal year 1969 budget and framework for legislative proposals were then developed and transmitted to the Bureau of the Budget.

The HEW system has proven of some use. A better understanding of the health programs of the Department and their interrelationships have been achieved. This was true not only at the Office of the Secretary, but also at the Bureau of the Budget. The primitive analyses have assisted the dialog on budget and legislative programs. The 5-year planning system has enabled the Secretary and his staff to control the processes somewhat more by testing budget and legislative proposals against the Secretary's program and financial plan.

Problems, of course, remain. One of the greatest is inadequate program evaluation.[17] Very little is really known of the impact of programs. Partly this is because of the complications in sorting out federal funding impacts from all the others. Partly it is because health effects take considerable time to become evident. But a large measure of the reason is that it has not been a matter of high interest to program managers. This is beginning to change. New health legislation increasingly contains authorization of a portion of the funds for evaluation. For example, Public Law 90–174, the Partnership for Health amendments of 1967, contains wording affecting formula grants to the States, project grants, and training and demonstration grants in the following manner:

> . . . such portion of the appropriations for grants under this subsection as the Secretary may determine, but not exceeding 1 percentum thereof, shall be available to the Secretary for evaluation (directly or by grants or contracts) of the program authorized by this subsection.

Under the direction of the Office of the Secretary, agencies are developing evaluation plans which may lead to significant gains in information for policy decisions.

NOTES

[1] Public Law 89–749 establishes planning requirements for State Health Planning Councils, State Health Planning Agencies, Areawide Health Planning Councils, and State Health Authorities and/or State Mental Health Authorities. Public Law 89–239 supports planning by Regional Medical Programs and Regional Advisory Groups. Public Law 88–443 required planning activities by State Hill-Burton Agencies and State Advisory Councils. Public Law 88–164, title II, provided grants to designated State agencies and State Advisory Councils for planning community mental health centers. Public Law 88–164, title I, part C did the same for planning mental retardation facilities. Public Law 89–272, title II provides money to designated state or interstate agencies for planning solid waste disposal activities. Public Law 90–148 provides planning funds to Air Pollution Control Agencies and to Interstate Air Quality Agencies or Commissions. The Social Security Act, as amended, title V, parts 1 and 2 provides for the state plans by State Health Agencies, State Crippled Children's Agencies or State Health Departments of programs for maternal and child health. Title XIX of the act requires state plans for Medicaid. The Vocational Rehabilitation Act, as amended, section 4(a)(2)(B) provides for Comprehensive Statewide Planning for Vocational Rehabilitation Services.

[2] For some interesting discussion on the interactions between systems analysis and politics see:

Charles Schultze, *The Politics and Economics of Public Spending,* The Brookings Institution, 1969; William N. Capron, "The Impact of Analysis on Bargaining in Government," delivered to a meeting of the American Political Science Association, Sept. 1966; James R. Schlesinger, *Systems Analysis and the Political Process,* the RAND Corp., June 1967; Ralph Sanders, "Systems Analysis and the Political Process," *Perspectives in Defense Management,* Dec. 1968; and Aaron Wildavsky, "The Political Economy of Efficiency: Cost-Benefit Analysis, Systems Analysis and Program Budgeting," *Public Administration Review,* Dec. 1966.

Specifically in the health area, see, for example:

Henrik L. Blum and Alvin R. Leonard, *Public Administration—A Public Health Viewpoint,* The Macmillan Company, 1963; Ralph W. Conant, *The Politics of Community Health,* report of the Community Action Studies project, National Commission on Community Health Services, Public Affairs Press, 1968; J. Enoch Powell, *A New Look at Medicine and Politics,* Pitman Medical Publishing Co., 1966; and Eugene Feingold, *Medicares Policy and Politics,* Chandler Publishing Co., 1966.

[3] For descriptions of the Department of Defense experience see:

Charles J. Hitch, *Decisionmaking for Defense,* University of California Press, 1965, and Stephen Enke, editor, *Defense Management,* Prentice-Hall, 1967.

[4] U.S. Department of Health, Education, and Welfare, Office of the Assistant Secretary (planning and evaluation), *Planning-Programing-Budgeting: Guidance for Program and Financial Plan,* revised February 1968.

[5] U.S. Department of Health, Education, and Welfare, Office of the Assistant Secretary for Program Coordination: *Motor Vehicle Injury Prevention Program,*

August 1966; *Arthritis,* Sept. 1966; *Selected Disease Control Programs,* September 1966; and *Cancer,* October 1966.

[6] Rashi Fein, *Economics of Mental Illness,* Basic Books, Inc., New York, 1958. For later study using a new conceptual framework resulting in cost estimates almost 10 times higher see Ronald Conley, Margaret Cromwell, and Mildred Arrill. "An Approach to Measuring the Cost of Mental Illness," *American Journal of Psychiatry,* December 1967, pp. 63–70.

[7] Burton A. Weisbrod, *Economics of Public Health: Measuring the Economic Impact of Diseases,* University of Pennsylvania Press, Philadelphia, 1961.

[8] Herbert E. Klarman, "Syphilis Control Programs," *Measuring Benefits of Government Investments,* edited by Robert Dorfman, The Brookings Institution, Washington, D.C., 1965, pp. 367–410.

[9] Dorothy P. Rice, *Estimating the Cost of Illness,* Public Health Service Publication 947–6, Washington, D.C., May 1966; Jacob Cohen, "Routine Morbidity Statistics as a Tool for Defining Public Health Priorities," *Israel Journal of Medical Sciences,* May 1965, pp. 457–460, estimated the weighted impact of 25 mass diseases on deaths, loss of life years under 65, hospitalization, days of hospitalization and cases in Workers' Sick Fund.

[10] Louis I. Dublin and Alfred J. Latka, *The Money Value of a Man,* Ronald Press, New York, 1930.

[11] See, for example, Earl F. Cheit, *Inquiry and Recovery in the Course of Employment,* John Wiley, New York and London, 1961.

[11a] For discussion of some of these issues see Dorothy P. Rice, "Measurement and Application of Illness Costs," *Public Health Reports,* February 1969, pp. 95–101; T. C. Schelling, "The Life You Save May Be Your Own," *Problems in Public Expenditure Analysis,* edited by Samuel B. Chase, Jr., The Brookings Institution, 1968, pp. 127–176; and Pan American Health Organization, *Health Planning: Problems of Concept and Method,* Scientific Publication No. 111, April 1965, esp. pp. 4–6.

[12] U.S. Department of Health, Education, and Welfare, Office of the Assistant Secretary (Planning and Evaluation), *Kidney Disease,* December 1967.

[13] The Bureau of the Budget convened an expert Committee on Chronic Kidney Disease. See *Report* by this committee, Carl W. Gottschalk, chairman, Washington, September 1967. Herbert E. Klarman, John O'S. Francis, and Gerald D. Rosenthal, "Cost Effectiveness Analysis Applied to the Treatment of Chronic Renal Disease," *Medical Care,* vol. VI, No. 1, January–February 1968, pp. 48–54, analyzed the committee's data to explore what is the best mix of center dialysis, home dialysis, and kidney transplantations. The authors restricted their beneficiaries to those in end-stage kidney disease, and concluded that transplantation is economically the most effective way to increase life expectancy of persons with chronic kidney disease, although they recognize the factors that constrain the expansion of transplantation capability.

[14] Jerome B. Hallan and Benjamin S. H. Harris, III, "The Economic Cost of End-Stage Uremia," *Inquiry,* volume V, No. 4, December 1968, pp. 20–25, and J. B. Hallan, B. S. H. Harris, III, and A. V. Alhadeff, *The Economic Costs of Kidney Disease,* Research Triangle Institute, North Carolina, 1967.

[15] U.S. Dept. of Health, Education, and Welfare, Office of the Assistant Secretary for Program Coordination, *Maternal and Child Health Care Programs,* October 1966.

[16] Other studies included U.S. Dept. of Health, Education, and Welfare, Office of the Assistant Secretary (Planning and Evaluation): *Delivery of Health Services for the Poor,* December 1967; *An Economic Analysis of the Control of Sulphur Oxides Air Pollution,* December 1967; *Nursing Manpower Programs,* March 1968; Public Health Service, Bureau of Health Services, *Recommendations and Summary: Program Analysis of Health Care Facilities.*

[17] A useful reference to the existing literature on evaluation is Willy De Dyndt and Karen B. Ross, *Evaluation of Health Programs—An Annotated Bibliography,* Systems Research Project, University of Minnesota, comment series No. 8–9(9).

CHAPTER 23

EDUCATION PROGRAM ANALYSIS AT HEW

John E. Brandl

INTRODUCTION

There are three characteristics of an ideal program budgeting system: (1) a management information framework for keeping track of information and fostering intelligent, timely decisions; (2) good analysis; and (3) bureaucratic and institutional structures incorporating incentives for socially productive activity.

This paper reports on program budgeting for education decisionmaking at the Department of Health, Education, and Welfare, where some progress has been made on desiderata (1) and (2), but little on (3). Only the first two will be discussed here.

I. MANAGEMENT SYSTEM

The Uses of Information

There is a tendency for those engaged in program analysis in the domestic agencies of the federal government to compare themselves with (or be compared by others with) the systems analysis and programing operations of the Department of Defense, if only because the Defense Department pioneered in these endeavors. But comparing soon becomes contrasting; the differences start to appear as soon as one asks what kinds of decisions are made and what kinds of information should be collected and funneled to decisionmakers in the department. HEW is basically a conduit of funds from the federal government to the states and localities which run programs and spend money. Whereas the secretary of defense operates what has been

John Brandl is Director, School of Public Affairs, University of Minnesota. At the time this paper was prepared, he was Deputy Assistant Secretary for Education Planning at the Department of Health, Education, and Welfare.

The author thanks Worth Bateman, Robert Hartman and Alice Rivlin who may recognize some of their ideas in this paper; the paper, however, contains the author's views, for which neither his friends nor the Department of Health, Education, and Welfare should be blamed.

called the third largest Socialist organization in the world, and can actually (if he wants to), direct men and materiel around from one day to the next, the secretary of HEW can almost only make big decisions. He can reorient programs by affecting legislation or by requesting a reallocation of his next year's budget,[1] but he does not have control over the ultimate realization of most programs for which his department provides planning, advice, funds, and guidelines. Even more than the secretary of defense, the secretary of HEW ought to be sheltered from minutiae. This paper is concerned with program budgeting and secretarial decisionmaking, so that the great bulk of the enormous amounts of information collected, classified, printed, and distributed in the department is not of relevance here.

The Program Budget: Equity and Efficiency

To facilitate understanding and control of a department's activities, a program budget system involves first the development of a set of program categories; a supposed advantage is that these categories present information on "outputs" of programs—information which is often more meaningful than the "input" categories of traditional line item budgeting.[2]

HEW is concerned to reallocate resources within this society, and to improve the quality of certain activities; that is, with both equity and efficiency matters. But the questions, "who gets what?" and "what effect does it have?" can be answered in a variety of ways. The first question is the easier of the two and can be answered descriptively. But no single type of breakdown, whether by income class, race, geography, or age, can wholly summarize the population to whom the programs are directed. The department has, however, fashioned a set of program distinctions which are useful in showing how money is spent. At the most general level, we use program categories organized roughly along chronological lines as follows: development of basic skills; development of vocational and occupational skills; development of advanced academic and professional skills; library and community development; general research; and general support.

These categories are then subdivided into programs for the general population and those for the handicapped or disadvantaged. They are also displayed according to the type of operation involved—operational aid, student aid, personnel training, innovation or research. These levels of distinction enable us to make some decisions based on what we know about the general nature of the categories, populations, and activities, but they do not contribute directly to answering the second and more difficult question of how effective the various programs are. This is partly because of disagreement about what the programs are effective *at,* and partly because of technical measurement problems. These difficulties are taken up in the paragraphs immediately following and again in the second part of this paper.

The Program Memorandum: Inherent Conflicts

Key elements of the federal government's program budgeting system are the annual program memorandums from the departments to the Bureau of the Budget for each major area of activity of the government. Ideally, each of these documents assesses progress toward attaining the objectives represented by the program categories, lays out a multiyear plan for meeting the objectives, and indicates how the department's budget fits into and contributes to the plan. But no single set of program categories adequately expresses all that a department is interested in. It should be clear that writing a program memorandum is not a straightforward process, but the difficulties are not simply in finding categories for filing information. The main difficulty is that no single set of preferences determines the makeup of the plan and the budget. Programs whose purposes conflict with each other appear side by side. Plans and (especially) budgets are made up over a long period of time by large numbers of people often not in communication with each other and having different sets of preferences.

Some people involved in the process might argue that the federal government's role in education is to foster equality of opportunity (an equity argument), others that it should develop new and innovative educational approaches (on public good grounds), and some would say that it should strive for excellence in education throughout the nation's school system (supposedly a federal function because of the beneficial externalities arising from education). There is no assurance that the plan and budget which result from the bureaucratic haggling are compatible with *any* self-consistent set of preferences or weighting of the several objectives,[3] and certainly no guarantee that they will represent the desires of any single individual or group involved in the process. Indeed, a decisionmaker may not wish to issue a program memorandum which is *too* explicit as to objectives and preferences—hoping to assuage several competing constituencies.[4] So, in agencies where this sort of fencing takes place, it may not be possible to produce a program memorandum that makes an integral whole out of all the programs of a department. There is something basically naive about the idea of a program memorandum which is supposed to make sense out of the conglomerate of a department's programs; but perhaps the attempt to be open and explicit in such a document has the merit of sharpening preferences—and maybe of narrowing differences of opinion.

The System: Suggestions for Change[5]

Despite the difficulties outlined above, HEW operates a fairly orderly planning-budgeting cycle at least partly in program budget terms. The 5-year plan projects programs and their costs and outputs. The program budget is sophisticatedly computerized to permit translation back and forth to the line-item budget. Presentable program memorandums are published annually for each of the areas of health, education and income maintenance-social services.

Nevertheless, we have not yet been able to avoid perennial chaotic rushes in September and October to produce numbers to comply with the inexorable schedule of the Bureau of the Budget. Planning and budgeting get jumbled in the fall every year. The main planning documents, the program memorandums, tend to appear each year only *after* the budget has been completed. Alternatives are not always given sufficient attention; conflicting items appear in the same budget. Some suggestions which might improve on this situation are the following:

1. More secretarial initiative in the planning cycle.
   Tentative decisions could be made by the secretary early in the planning cycle (i.e., in the spring of each year) on the guiding objectives and major thrusts of the department's programs. His office could communicate these decisions to the department's constituent agencies in the form of a written rationale and a statement of its implications for specific major programs over the next several years.
2. Fit the budget to the plan.
   After the agencies have received tentative guidance from the secretary, an orderly mechanism would be needed whereby they could appeal for changes. (E.g., a request for change could be submitted to the Office of the Secretary, where the appeal would be considered by two or more parts of his office, and the conflicting views, together with recommendations, presented to him for decision.) In this way the tentative plan would evolve throughout the summer and fall. Eventually, the first year of the plan would become the following year's budget. Legislative proposals could be handled in a similar way.

The advantages of this approach are clear. It would avoid the fall pileup. Alternatives would be given systematic attention. Programs would be more apt to reflect a set of rational objectives. The budget would have something to do with the plan.

But the drawbacks of such an approach are also clear. By definition, imposing consistency, order, and rationale involves centralizing decision-making, which has its problems. Also candor, explicitness, openness, may be politically counter-productive if they mean alienating constituents. Another desirable change is:

3. Get the Bureau of the Budget to cooperate in the planning-budgeting process.

> At present the Bureau encourages the development of a program budget and the analysis of alternative courses of action. It is also eager to receive written rationale for decisions made within the department. But it gives little indication of making its own decisions in the program budget framework; it is highly secretive and uncommunicative about whatever work it produces that influences its decisions; and at budget time it tends to accept arguments for cutting programs but not for expanding them. In sum, the Bureau seems not to practice what it preaches about program budgeting.

II. ANALYSIS

The foregoing plea for orderliness in planning can hardly depend on the argument that neatness for its own sake is a good thing. Its justification is, rather, that in a respectable planning-budgeting system, *analysis of alternatives* gets done—on time—and gets a hearing. Analysis, not order is the *sine qua non.* By analysis I mean asking "what is it that we are trying to do?" (determining objectives), "how can we do it?" (planning and budgeting), and finally "how are we doing? can we do better?" (evaluation).

The Focus of Current Analysis

Without agreement on objectives (as discussed in section I) it is hard to get past the first of the above questions. I conclude[6] that the federal government's and HEW's (in particular) responsibilities in education are twofold: (1) to foster equality of opportunity by assisting in the education of the disadvantaged of this society; (2) to improve education for all by sponsoring research and evaluation activities which benefit the entire country but would not be undertaken by other individuals, groups or governments. These two objectives indicate a rough rationale for allocation of education resources by HEW which follows: We do not know very much about how to affect the educational lives of disadvantaged youngsters, but at least we can orient federal funds into programs which reach them. Meanwhile we should foster innovations and new approaches. Despite its embarrassing simplicity, this approach can keep a lot of planners busy planning changes because many programs contributing little to these objectives are now funded by the federal government. For example, the executive branch has tended to want more money for Title I ESEA and to request less than Congress appropriated for aid to federally impacted areas. Assistance under the former is more closely correlated with income than it is under the latter.

To the extent that redistribution of resources from better-off individuals and governmental jurisdictions to worse-off is itself an objective, evaluation consists of determining who gets what. And indeed our programing system now contains much information of this sort. The further, tougher question of whether poor children not only receive attention but benefit by it has to do with the very nature of the federal-state system and in particular with the way in which the federal government expends funds through HEW. Categorical grant programs (which constitute the bulk of HEW's appropriations) are targeted to particular problem areas, with federal guidelines defining precisely the purposes for which the money can be spent. A pure revenue-sharing or bloc-grant program would be simply redistributive (from better-off governmental jurisdictions and people to the worse-off). Many existing categorical HEW programs have redistributive effects while having as their main purpose the application of funds to a particular problem area. Evaluation of such programs is bound to be frustrating, since an evaluator or program analyst at the federal level will want to try to relate program inputs to outputs (are children doing better at school?). But the nature of the programs makes this difficult and America's decentralized school system resists (actively and passively) national evaluation. Whether federal money is distributed with or without strings, that is, whether by categorical or by bloc grants, the funds are not contingent on performance, and do not come with a built-in incentive to produce. And local school districts do different things with the money precisely because they *want* to. Different American school boards do have different values and preferences about what they would like to have schoolchildren accomplish—frustrating though that may be to federal bureaucrats who would like to be able to say more about how well our nation is doing educationally. So federal education planners and evaluators are stuck with "evaluating" mostly where money goes, rather than how well it does when it gets there. (As we will see, another reason for this is that the analytical difficulties of relating inputs to outputs in education are horrendous.)

Still another factor contributing to this state of affairs in the past, at least as far as higher education is concerned,[7] is the implicit conviction that educators knew what they were doing. Recently, two major studies of higher education have been completed—one inside the government and one outside.[8] In neither was there an attempt to determine how to improve higher education or even to describe what happens at that educational level. Both were concerned not with the quality of higher education, but with the manner and extent to which the federal government should contribute assistance. The conclusions of the two studies were similar—the federal government should contribute more to higher education, and since resources are scarce, the funds should be oriented to students rather than to institutions, since in that way the students who need the money can be given it (whereas assistance to institutions is presumably spread over rich and poor students alike). The question asked and answered implicitly assumed that education should be left to the educators—with government providing *financial* assistance, but not assessment or evaluation.

So analytical and evaluative efforts at HEW (which it should be noted, are still in their infancy) have been devoted largely to redistributive rather than effectiveness questions.[9]

Shortcomings of Existing Analytical Techniques

The typical evaluative effort to get at the question of effectiveness in education proceeds as follows: Collect information on an "output" measure—any output measure—such as achievement scores of schoolchildren, and relate that output or dependent variable (through a linear regression) to a host of "input" variables—school characteristics as well as attributes of the child and his parents. This approach grows out of economists' attempts to estimate "production functions" for firms. But the economist has two advantages over the education evaluator:

(1) Economics provides a theoretical rationale (growing out of the profit maximizing hypothesis) for arguing that the relationship which he finds will be efficient—that it will indicate the lowest-cost way of achieving any particular level of output. Since we do not know what school administrators are maximizing, the economists' approach can only yield a description of current practice in education, not necessarily any insight into how to do things better.

(2) The profit maximization hypothesis simplifies statistical or econometric analysis. Whatever school administrators are maximizing—or the American public(s) wants schools to do—it is more complicated than a single measure can show.[10] To carry over the economists' approach might then involve attempting to maximize an amalgam of achievement measures, attitudinal measures, and whatever else is relevant, subject to the *set* of production functions—one for each of the output measures of interest.[11] To the author's knowledge, no one has yet attempted to do this for education.

It is not as though traditional methods are hopeless, however.[12] There are some cases where one approach to an education problem appears to be so much more effective—even on the basis of rudimentary uniequational analysis—as to provide grounds for implementing the approach. For example, Henry Levin (following the typical pattern) has run linear regressions of student verbal score on a host of variables representing student, environment, and teacher characteristics, in an effort to determine what advice could be given to persons hiring teachers.[13] In particular, he compared the relationships between teacher verbal score and teacher experience with student verbal score. He found that to accomplish a given increase in measured student achievement "for Negroes, it appears that obtaining teachers with higher verbal scores is about one-fifth as costly as obtaining more teacher experience, and for white students the verbal score route is 10 times as efficient."[14] The strong and interesting implication of this is that hiring bright teachers might be more effective and/or less costly than hiring experienced ones.

Political Implications of Analysis

The academically hallowed distinction between analysts and decisionmakers is often not useful in government. One reason for this is that analysis itself has political implications. What a department requests from the Congress, how it requests it and how it is spent—these are all related. To admit publicly that a particular program of a department is doing poorly, may be to invite cuts in that program—and others. The economist or program analyst likes to talk of trade-offs—of the (to him) obvious fact that if one wants more of one thing he must have less of something else. In fact though, an agency head may get a larger budget to work with by declaring that he needs an increment of X and an increment of Y. It is not lost on agency or department heads that evaluation of programs can have adverse effects on budgets. And a decision not to evaluate a program, or to downplay negative results of evaluations can be rationalized not only for this reason, but also by arguing that other programs of other departments, which are "obviously" a waste have not been evaluated. Why then should this program—which has great potential—be jeopardized?

There are other ways in which analysis can have political implications. The two recent studies of higher education referred to above are political phenomena by their very existence and the prestige of the individuals associated with producing them. By ignoring in the main the question of the effectiveness of higher education they may contribute to the difficulties of convincing people that it is important to ask effectiveness questions. Politically, the studies—both of which recommend a surge in federal assistance to higher education—could lead to a new federal emphasis on higher education. But this would be at a time when, if there is an educational crisis it is in urban elementary and secondary schools. It may be that a countervailing force to higher education is needed in the form of a large visible study of precollege education in the United States.

What Might Be Done Next

This has been a gloomy recital. I have intentionally concentrated on difficulties and shortcomings because they need airing, but in the confidence that observers of the practice of program analysis in Washington already recognize that progress at HEW has been encouraging and the process helpful to the department.

This paper closes with a commercial for an approach to improving this country's knowledge of how education happens.

We now see that the evaluation of existing programs is intimately related to the development of new approaches. Several educational models have emerged, some of which have shown promising results in particular cases. Development and evaluation merge in implementing and observing these models as applied in actual schools.

Particular federal programs are difficult to evaluate since they are just a small part of the enormous American education system. We now have neither sufficient educational theory nor powerful enough statistical techniques to separate—and determine the relative importance of—the various factors influencing a child's educational progress. The typical evaluative effort drastically oversimplifies the real world, but even if it did not, it would only describe current educational practice; it would not reveal the most effective way to use our educational resources. The meager evaluative results we do have, for example on federally assisted compensatory education programs for disadvantaged children, suggest that although some youngsters are being helped, the average student's performance may not be improving—and even where results are hopeful it is difficult to specify what it is that makes the difference.

This is not a simple matter of a social scientist wishing the real world were less complicated. What I am saying is that the present state of the relevant social and statistical sciences is such that in the absence of large scale, scrupulously controlled, educational experiments we are not going to be able to identify productive approaches to compensatory education. In the moon race, America had the luxury of being allowed to succeed through brute expensive force. We are not allowing ourselves that luxury in education, where $100 million increments to operational programs are a drop in a $50 billion bucket. But $100 million could support a lot of demonstration and model schools, a lot of experimentation and development in education.

NOTES

[1] He has very little authority to reprogram funds from one category to another within the budget appropriated by the Congress.

[2] Here and elsewhere in this paper words and ideas are borrowed from the *Program Memorandum on Education Programs of the Department of Health, Education, and Welfare* (Washington, D.C.; Office of the Secretary of Health, Education, and Welfare, Dec. 1, 1968). This document was prepared by the author and his staff.

[3] For examples of grant-in-aid formulas the implications of which are apparently incompatible even with the intentions of their designers, see, "On Budget Allocation in Government Agencies," *Review of Social Economy,* March 1967, by this author.

[4] It may also be that the lack of any single set of preferences governing the determination of the optimal set of programs for a department contributes to a "more is better" approach, which will seize any opportunity to expand a department's programs since someone important probably favors it.

[5] What follows requires some basic knowledge of the federal budgeting calendar. In HEW, preliminary plans for the fiscal 1970 (starting July 1, 1969) budget began in the spring of 1968; by October several alternative budgets had been drawn up; in October the department's budget went to the Bureau of the Budget which made several more changes in it; in December it was practically completed. The president (Johnson) submitted it to Congress in January 1969. If past practice holds, the Congress will not make its appropriations until the fall of 1969, i.e., until after the fiscal year has begun.

[6] The first person singular is used here because what follows is the author's personal opinion about what the federal government's responsibilities in education should be.

[7] For elementary and secondary education, America's long and solid history of dissatisfaction with the quality of its schools has been matched by its insistence that the federal government not stipulate how they might be improved. See Richard Hofstadter, *Anti-Intellectualism in American Life* (New York: Random House, 1963), part V.

[8] See *Toward a Long-Range Plan for Federal Financial Support for Higher Education*—A Report to the President, U.S. Department of Health, Education, and Welfare, Assistant Secretary for Planning and Evaluation, January 1969; and *Quality and Equality: New Levels of Federal Responsibility for Higher Education*—A special report and recommendations by the Carnegie Commission on Higher Education, December 1968.

[9] Exceptions to this statement include some unpublished work of George Mayeske and Harry Piccariello of the Office of Education. Both are attempting to relate inputs and outputs in elementary and secondary education. See also Joseph Froomkin, *et al., Students and Buildings: An Analysis of Selected Federal Programs for Higher Education* (Washington, D.C.: U.S. Government Printing Office, 1968).

[10] Cf. my "Comment on Estimating Education Production Functions" in *Studies of Income and Wealth,* vol. 35 (New York: National Bureau of Economic Research, 1969).

[11] This approach has been attempted empirically in economics, most often for

macroeconomic problems. See Henri Theil, *Optimal Decision Rules for Government and Industry* (Chicago: Rand McNally & Co., 1964).

[12] Samuel Bowles has written an elegant description and critique of current practice in estimating the relationship between inputs and outputs in education. See "Toward an Educational Production Function" in *Proceedings of a Conference on Research in Income and Wealth* (New York: National Bureau of Economic Research, 1969).

[13] "Cost-Effectiveness Analysis and Educational Policy—Profusion, Confusion, Promise," (mimeo), School of Education, Stanford University, Stanford, Calif., December 1966.

[14] *Ibid.*, p. 12.

ADDENDUM

[*This is very much a personal statement written after leaving government —in the comfort of hindsight and the calm of academia.*]

The above paper was written in January 1969, that is, just before the change of administrations in Washington. For a variety of reasons the new Administration fostered the attempt to implement the recommendations made in the paper. This addendum is a brief account of the carrying out of the recommendations and the lessons learned in the process.

Procedurally, the paper recommended more secretarial initiative, fitting the budget to the plan, and inducing the Bureau of the Budget to cooperate with the planning-programing-budgeting activities of the department. Substantively, the paper argued for accepting equalization of opportunity and improved educational practice as the objectives of the federal government in education. Large-scale experimentation was said to be the best way to identify more effective educational approaches.

Shortly after the inauguration, Secretary Robert Finch appointed a small task force to help him devise a new budget for fiscal year 1970. The outcome was a drastically reoriented budget, one devised at the secretarial level and reflecting two main thrusts: concentration of federal education funds on disadvantaged students; and increased research and experimentation to improve the educational process. The $3.2 billion budget submitted to the Congress was considerably ($400 million) smaller than the 1969 appropriation, but actually allocated *more* money both to disadvantaged students and to research and experimentation. Thereupon the secretary elected to conduct the next round of planning and budgeting (for the 1971 and future budgets) in similar fashion and to set up a small task force with unusually broad bureaucratic powers to do so.

Thus, soon after taking office, Secretary Finch had institutionalized a planning-budgeting process involving secretarial initiative and direction and had produced a budget explicitly reflecting a set of controversial objectives. By fall of 1970 the new system had yielded a program memorandum, five year plan, and 1971 budget. *Relative* emphases in these documents derived from the above considerations, but the *absolute* level of the Administration's budget was held below the 1969 level for four reasons: (1) realization that the ambitious proposed welfare reform could easily sop up whatever additional money that could be garnered for HEW in the years ahead; (2) confidence that revenue sharing (i.e., return of some federal income tax revenues to the states) would be operating on a large scale within a few years—which funds could be expected to be used for education; (3) the conviction, or rather the hunch, that the American educational system would not use increased funds effectively; and (4) the fear of inflation. The attempt to reorient priorities while cutting the total budget led the Administration to an historic confrontation with the Congress in January, 1970 (of which more below).

SOME IMPLICATIONS AND LESSONS

Centralization

An ambitious *centralized* planning-budgeting operation came into being. This demoralized large parts of the bureaucracy which quite clearly felt estranged from the new Administration and its henchmen. Centralized management of the details of a planning-budgeting mechanism of the size needed to produce a $3 billion-plus budget also diverted the attention of the secretarial staff from the few major issues they should have been worrying about. Administration and power seem to have an insidious attraction.

The Relevance of Power

The more centralized planning-budgeting process permitted the reflection of the *values* of the secretary and his staff in the plan and budget; but it is not clear how productive that was, since little *analysis* was available to bolster the arguments for change. So, it is frustrating to exist in an unwieldy, obstinate bureaucracy; but streamlining the bureaucracy has little value *per se.* It is also frustrating to be able to act, to plan, to decide, to implement—when little basis exists for knowing what to do.

Executive-legislative Interchange

Program-budgeteers, systems analysts, economists seem to have a penchant for ignoring the politics as opposed to the "substance" of public policy. This tendency may have contributed to the timid, inadequately funded and staffed, ineffective approach used by the Administration in selling its budget to the Congress. Openly stating objectives, or at any rate proposing budgets obviously reflecting a few values at the expense of others, draws the wrath of those hurt in the process. Reorienting priorities while cutting the budget antagonized educational interest groups, many of which joined together in an awesomely powerful lobbying effort to prevent not only the budget cutting but also the only new program (for a system of experimental schools) offered by the Administration. It is very important that the Congress be involved in the planning-budgeting process, but it is almost never done. What is later perceived as a politically motivated but inscrutably clever plan (as in the case of the president ultimately vetoing the 1970 HEW appropriations bill) often is only the result of bungled Congressional liaison.

The Inertia of Bureaucracies

It is one thing to declare policy and something else to see that it is carried out. This paper began with the statement that one of the three characteristics of a good bureaucratic system is "bureaucratic and institutional structures incorporating incentives for socially productive activity." This feature received no attention in the paper, but is receiving some now at HEW. Decentralizing governmental activity, building evaluation into programs, greater use of market and other innovative incentive structures—these are all being attempted now. After seeing the problems that remain after implementing a smoothly functioning planning-budgeting system, the need for bureaucratic reform becomes all the more evident.

CHAPTER 24

ECONOMIC ANALYSIS IN NATURAL RESOURCE PROGRAMS

Jack L. Knetsch

INTRODUCTION

The public expenditure category encompassing natural resources spending derives its importance not only by virtue of the large sums of funds devoted to it, but also because of the large market and nonmarket economic values associated with natural resource development activities.

It is also the case that explicit analysis of the consequences of public actions has probably the most successful history in the natural resources area. Such analysis has without doubt proven to be of immense usefulness in improving public expenditure decisionmaking by directing resources toward efficient uses and eliminating some of the most inefficient. This has particularly been the case in the more traditional natural resources activities such as water development projects to provide flood control, hydropower, navigation, and irrigation.

Whatever problems remain, the demonstrated utility of formal specification of project effects cannot be minimized. Further, the application of analyses and development of techniques and methodology in the natural resources field can provide valuable insights into the issues and policies in other expenditure areas where such techniques have not been as rigorously applied.

It is not the intent here to catalog the myriad problems relating to natural resources, nor to tabulate the successes and failures of applying program planning and budgeting systems and benefit-cost analyses to natural resource expenditures. Instead, the aim is to focus on a few of the items which appear to be germane to efforts to improve public expenditure decisions in natural resources programs, especially as related to relevant information and decision tools. More specifically, the discussion will deal with: (1) some notions about the changing concerns of natural resources programs; (2) a sketch of how analytical guides for public expenditures bear a resemblance to the way markets allocate resources, and how there

Jack L. Knetsch is Director of the Natural Resources Policy Center and Professor of Economics at The George Washington University.

may be gains in a greater use of market incentives to set priorities in public provision of resource services; (3) the weakness of much demand information and the consequent effects on rationalizing expenditure decisions; (4) an outline of some problems posed by the increasingly important values associated with natural resources which are largely beyond present means to quantify; and (5) a caveat concerning the varied viewpoints of the results of natural resource programs and the assessment of their effects.

ALTERED CONCERNS FOR RESOURCES POLICY

While expenditure analysis, particularly in the form of benefit-cost analysis, has shown merit in many natural resource areas, the potential for more extensive and serious analysis is even greater. In natural resources, the focus of analysis has been on traditional development activities—construction of dams for irrigation and levees for alleviating flooding, for example. While marked improvements can be made in these areas, others, often involving large values and rapidly changing demands, are becoming of equal or even of more pressing importance. Attention is increasingly called for in analyzing areas where public awareness and activity has, until recently, lagged—such as environmental quality and the provision of more outdoor recreational opportunities to larger numbers of urban residents.

The newer areas of concern in natural resources are far ranging, not limited to resources as traditionally defined, and involve issues often differing from a straightforward federal investment in construction projects. These include, for example, the large and growing demands for recreational opportunities, municipal and industrial water supplies, waste disposal, pollution control and other environmental concerns, preservation of complex ecosystems, and the minimization of dangers from pesticides. In all of these, each growing in importance, indications are that the issues will involve more than a simple federal expenditure to provide the various resource services. Such expenditures will no doubt remain important, but increasingly more attention will be given to other institutional arrangements where traditional benefit-cost analysis will need to be cast in other roles and a greater use made of other explicit decision criteria.

Evidence of change, and a significant opportunity for program budgeting and benefit-cost analysis, is provided by the growth of state and regional expenditures on natural resource projects. Much of this is directly tied to federal activity and programs, but there is little doubt that the trend of state and local involvement will continue, especially as meaningful state and regional planning activities increase.

Further, in many of the new areas of concern in natural resources, public involvement and spending will include areas in which the consequences and values are difficult to measure; for wilderness preservation, for example. Also, many of the concerns involve, quite apart from projects and their direct effects, questions of spillover or external effects, such as air or water pollution and the impacts of urban sewer and water decisions. In other areas natural resource programs encounter questions of serious uncertainties, as for example in programs of oceanography and desalination.

Another set of issues, which is becoming increasingly important, encompasses the uses of natural resources in urban and metropolitan areas. The traditional rural bias in natural resource development activities, and in the natural resource literature, is beginning to yield to concern for the real problems of making urban areas more habitable. Natural resource-related programs and projects can deal not only with questions of providing open spaces and water and sewer services, but also with shaping the type of urban development that takes place, and providing more attractive and healthful environments. It is becoming clear that, although now largely ignored, the principles of economics as applied in other natural resource situations are applicable to metropolitan resource problems. The application may not be as straighforward as, for example, in problems of river basin development. Urban planning decisions usually take place incrementally with each contemplated change or addition influenced by the presence of large fixed assets such as piping systems and treatment plants, rather than in a context of relatively undeveloped river basins. Characteristically, urban activities are also carried out with the existence of many involved agencies, each of which has its own geographic and/or service jurisdiction.

MARKET INDICATORS AND ANALYTICAL ANALYSIS

Most public activity in the natural resource field takes place because of a rejection of the outcome of private market decisions. There may well be good and sufficient reason for such judgment.

Public provision of natural resources services has usually meant that we lose the restraints and incentives provided by a market, substituting instead public decisions to set policies, to design plans and programs, and to allocate resources. Benefit-cost analysis and program budgeting, as well as other devices, have usefulness for these public decisions as substitutes for market indicators.

Even though the public provision of natural resources services does not often use market prices to allocate resources, national economic efficiency objectives remain the announced primary goal of most such programs. It is usually failures of various kinds in the private markets that provide the main rationale for public involvement to assure a greater efficiency in the use of resources. While keeping national efficiency objectives in project and program expenditures, public policies have enlarged the purposes to be served to include concern for other national objectives such as income redistribution. In some cases such redistributions are disguised in the language of efficiency, although the usual policy of not expecting beneficiaries to pay the costs of providing the services would often run counter to this.

Putting allocation decisions into a system that is expected to accomplish most of the same objectives of the market, but without the incentives and restraints provided by that institution, imposes considerable strain on the methods of determining which choices best serve the public interest. Benefit-cost analysis and other techniques are an immense aid, and a greater use of better analysis can more nearly assure better choices, but they are not a complete substitute.

The current provision of natural resource development activities and services has been alleged to have built-in biases, since interest groups surrounding proposals to undertake certain types of natural resource development projects often systematically favor such decisions.[1] These biases stem in large part from the disassociation of the incidence of benefits from that of the cost of the projects, and further from the fact that the magnitude of the gain to those individuals favoring the project is large relative to the magnitude of the loss falling on individual taxpayers. It is also generally conceded that the law under which most agencies operate, together with clientele interests which are often aided by elected officials, nearly assures that a fairly narrow range of alternatives are considered.[2]

The need, it would seem, is to adhere strictly to improved analytical devices to insure that decisions are more nearly consistent with national welfare and do not sacrifice this for the welfare of individual regions or groups. This need for rigorous analysis to offset demands for projects is increased with most present cost-sharing policies that favor low non-federal contributions, making these attractive expenditures for local areas. The need is still more the case because of the organization of most resource development agencies, which encourage many decisions to be made in regional offices. There is, of course, much to be gained with such decentralization and the opportunities for familiarization with local problems. However, part of this gain is offset by the strong tendency for regional officials to identify themselves with local interests and consequently promote projects of sometimes questionable desirability to the nation.

The absence of any (or any realistic), fair-cost sharing, particularly when this absence serves little other purpose, places a great burden on objective analysis. A disequilibrium between supply and demand is imposed by greatly underpricing the outputs of resource development projects, giving rise to a large demand relative to limited availability or supply of such projects brought about by constrained budgets. A public agency is, therefore, dependent upon a substitute mechanism and is called on to parallel the allocation objectives of the market where limited goods with numerous applications are allocated, but where demand far exceeds the supply.[3]

Even if the private market is not used to make allocation decisions, it may still be possible sometimes to use the market mechanism to allocate resources and thus still achieve gains of efficiency inherent in private market transactions. An example may illustrate both the difficulties and burdens placed on analysis and also the possibilities which may remain for using the market to allocate natural resource activities even though these are publicly provided. Such a situation exists in the current problem involving the selection of ports to take advantage of possible significant economies to large cargo vessels and tankers.[4]

If present ports are to accommodate large ships, the facilities will need to be improved dramatically, principally by dredging very deep ship channels. In most, if not all cases, this can be done only at very large cost, probably dictating that choices for initial improvement will need to be made among alternative locations. If alternatives to port improvement are not deemed appropriate, and costs are not borne by the beneficiaries, the ports selected will reap a large windfall benefit.

Consistent with goals and objectives of our economy, the port offering the greatest economic advantage should logically be improved to accommodate the new ships. The selection can be based on careful planning considerations and detailed benefit-cost analysis. While this can result in the most appropriate, that is the most efficient, selection, it places a great burden on planners and their techniques and furthermore encourages other noneconomic and other nonrelevant considerations which may mitigate against the best solution. Even if the best selection is made, the issue of economic equity or fairness remains in that the beneficiaries do not bear much of the cost.

It would seem that these problems may be resolved by basing the selection on market preference, such as might be given by an open-bidding scheme involving the potential recipients. Each port community desiring port improvement could compete with the others by pledging payment from the local area to the national government. The payment would, of course, reflect both the anticipated gain or benefit which each community would receive from the improvement as well as the relative cost that would need to be incurred. In this way, the port which stands to gain the greatest net benefit from the improvement would also be able to bid the highest price.

The criterion of selection among the ports could be that which minimizes the difference between the actual cost of port improvement and the bid received from the city. As the cost of the construction of the port would be reflected in this criterion, a great incentive is provided for the port to be located in the area in which the greatest increase in national economic benefits is achieved. A port requiring more costly improvements would need to reflect far greater benefits in its bid before it could successfully compete with ports where the cost of improvement is less.

The benefits of the bid approach are that national economic welfare considerations are more nearly assured than by alternative means and that the economic equity or fairness problem is far better handled because the beneficiaries receiving the gains would bear more substantial portions of the costs.

While the example of the port improvement is merely illustrative, other opportunities for improving allocation and establishing development priorities may be provided by the wider use of market indicators. Pricing water in water-deficient regions is surely another case.[5] Gains in the efficiency of natural resource services provision in this country could no doubt be greatly enhanced by a closer association of benefits received and costs incurred by the beneficiaries of public programs and projects. I would agree with the observation of Fox and Herfindahl that:

> "If the direct beneficiaries were required to pay for the services they receive, political support for projects would more accurately reflect their social value. Probably no other single measure would contribute more to the attainment of efficiency in satisfying demands for water services and in decisions such as location that are presently distorted by subsidized prices."[6]

DEMAND INFORMATION

In spite of the significant progress that has been made in the application of formal analysis to investment policy and management choices in natural resources, a major limitation continues to be the inadequacy of information relating to the demands for natural resource services. This remains the case even in those areas of natural resources development, such as water, where analyses have met with the most success.

Demand information is immensely important as a guide for planning and carrying out natural resource programs. However, all too often the meagerness of meaningful available data and the interpretations made of them give rise to assessments which—when converted into decisions—have needlessly all but guaranteed results that are far from satisfactory.

A primary weakness stems from the predominantly single-purpose nature of demand studies in the natural resources field. Demand studies commonly precede investment projects and programs, but are nearly always an assessment of the demand for a single means of accomplishing an objective or providing a service. Thus an assessment of reservoir recreation demand is made rather than that for water related recreation or outdoor recreation; demands for low-flow augmentation are estimated with little attention given to the myriad of substitute measures for quality control; and demands for future acreages of timber become invariant national needs rather than some among other demands to be considered for these resources.

Without making relevant comparisons, alternative means of obtaining objectives and goals are often overlooked, and alternative uses of resources are seldom realistically examined and compared. Consequently, a great deal of uneconomic development may well take place. The procedures tend to assure a minimum of attention to a search for alternative ways of dealing with problems. Examples of attention to but a small segment of the range of choice abound, for instance, in the area of seeking efficient means for dealing with water pollution or ways of providing recreation opportunities. These alternatives are seldom examined when the planning mechanism is based on single-purpose demand projections.

There are often important trade-offs which can be made in attaining various natural resource related purposes. There may, for example, be ranges of substitutions that can be made in coping with outdoor recreation demands—substitutions that could result in more economical use of resources. Developing utility rights-of-ways, or flood plain areas for recreation in urban areas is, for example, often a better alternative than development of a single large unitary park area in the region. There are likewise alternative means for dealing with problems of air and water pollution.[7]

All too often single-purpose projections are made to legitimatize increases in the current means of providing a resource service. This is reinforced by interpretation of demand data which almost invariably show that more of the program in question is needed. This outcome tends to become locked into the planning procedure as a result of the constraints on the demand studies which are undertaken. Much of this particular difficulty stems from the single purpose or interest advocacy built into the agency structure that deals with natural resources problems. Single agencies usually provide only a single or but a narrow range of means for dealing with problems, and consequently single-purpose demand studies result which combine both poor data and information with the narrowness of interests of the agency and lead to poor investment planning. Surely, the enthusiasm for providing reservoir-based water recreation is an instance of this.

The problems resulting from the single-purpose nature of most demand assessments are compounded by the naive and mechanical nature of most demand projections. For example, open space, recreation, sewer and water supply planning all make extensive use of nearly invariant standards of one sort or another, usually stated in terms of acres, gallons, or other physical unit per capita.[8] Typically, demand projections are made by estimating current and future populations, the current and future use rates for this population, with the increased use rate multiplied by the increased population taken to be the future demand. Such procedures effectively foreclose many of the options that should be open in planning our environment. Few degrees of freedom remain after given use rates are applied as coefficients to given population projections and a minimum cost engineering solution applied.

Too often the myth persists that we are able to multiply population figures by use rates, call it demand, and use the figures to justify doing just about anything we care to in the name of satisfying a "need." Although such number manipulation does occur, it is economic and planning nonsense to treat the resulting magnitudes seriously as guides for improving the provision of natural resource services.

The commonly followed procedure has the apparent advantages of appearing correct, with some of the appropriate terms used; it is straightforward and can be easily institutionalized; and it almost invariably yields large numbers. The reality seems to be, however, that the procedures give erroneous planning guides; are largely a waste of effort that preempts the opportunity to undertake more useful studies; and that many alternative ways of dealing with the problem are effectively blocked.

Too many of the factors which are in reality variable, are assumed to be fixed. Consequently, many of the decisions which we may want to make in dealing with problems of natural resources are all but ruled out of possible consideration before the planning effort really begins. These procedures not only force us into continuing the kind of provisions we have made in the past, but effectively ignore the alternative means for dealing with the problem. Further, by making critical decisions on these supposed standards and needs, planners implicitly have little choice at the end point when there is maximum information—the procedures are rigged to avoid the decisions we most want to make.

The use of such mechanical projections is particularly pervasive in the provision of urban services. They are also common in river basin plans that are intended to take account of a range of water related services. In supposedly comprehensive outdoor recreation plans future recreation activities continue to be projected, almost totally ignoring many of the most important recreational and environmental demands of large segments of the population. Many demand studies are, on the whole, of little value and some are of negative value. Most of the profusion of comprehensive plans and demand appraisals, which abound in the natural resources area, are little more than collections of single-purpose assessments, with a minimum of attention given to the relationships among them or to demands not included.

To do any sort of reasonable planning in many of the resource areas it is simply not enough to know that the demand for the services is increasing. There is usually sufficient evidence to make this kind of growth abundantly clear to all. The important question is, what is to be done about it. For this we need to know far more about the nature of the various kinds of demands. Further, we need to establish far better links between the results of improved demand studies and the investment, management, and policy decisions implied by them. For example, if we knew how use of alternative recreation areas, by number and by population segment, would respond to varied investment opportunities—that is, if we knew more about the demand—we could presumably choose a more appropriate mix of recreation expenditures, one that would more nearly meet all of the objectives of such programs. Public bodies—at national, state, and local levels—and private individuals need to have the nature of demand for activities and facilities defined in such a way that rational policy and investment decisions can be made.

Demand in natural resources activities has often been used in a somewhat special and, in terms of planning and guidance, fairly misleading way. One example has certainly been provided by the planning efforts in the various river basin plans. Ambiguity enters principally at two points.

The first is that the basic premise of a price-quantity relationship which lies behind the concepts of demand and supply is ignored. This effectively rules out a great deal of flexibility in dealing with various demands; for many of our seemingly unlimited demands for certain resource services are largely just a function of unrealistic pricing and repayment policies.

A further persistent difficulty in demand analysis has been a continued confusion between demand and use or consumption. Use rates are dependent upon both supply and demand factors—that is, the result of prevailing supply and demand conditions. For example, outdoor recreation participation or attendance is determined or influenced by both demand and the availability of supply. The data commonly referred to as demand are rather consumption figures, simply the use of given existing facilities with existing prices.

We should expect that the availability of opportunities has as much to do with certain kinds of natural resource use rates as does demand. This is more than a simple semantic problem. It can cause severe difficulty in dealing with ways to meet the demand. Improper accounting of supply consideration leads, for example, to the assumption that people demand only increasing quantities of what they now have and therefore can perpetuate present imbalances in certain kinds of resource provision. This is very much the case, for instance, in some forms of outdoor recreation. Some areas of the country show far greater population participation rates for given activities, and if this is taken as a demand statement without consideration of the availability of opportunities it could lead to decisions to build even more facilities in areas most adequately served rather than attempting to provide opportunities in deficient areas. Thus as facilities are developed and used, new studies report that more of the same should be built in these same places. Nearly any project or investment may then be "justified," and investment decisions can be severely warped. An equally serious error is that we may miss completely many important demands for important natural resource products and values.

Without an explicit account taken of the effect of availability of natural resource supplies on the amount or level of use that we observe, these studies can direct planning efforts to wrong conclusions or to irrelevancies and blunt plans and investment policies. Most demand surveys and studies do not provide any means of determining how resource use will respond to changes in supply—and that after all is the portion on which guidance is needed. As Professor Wantrup has warned:

> "Existing projections of land and water use are neither conceptually nor empirically identical with projections of land and water demand. In the first place, use projections do not separate demand and supply conceptually nor statistically. If demand is to serve as a principle of orientation for public land and water policy—that is to help in planning on the supply side—problems of demand and supply need to be separated conceptually and in empirical investigation, variables pertaining to demand must be differentiated from those pertaining to supply."[9]

NONMARKET VALUES AND MEASUREMENT

Analysis—program planning, budgeting, and benefit-cost—is essentially an aid in determining efficient allocation and investment of public funds. Comparison of alternative means of achieving given ends is an integral part of such analyses. While a great deal of success has been achieved in certain areas of public expenditure, certain shortcomings remain with respect to others. In many cases the principles for determining gains and losses have not been correct nor defined in as meaningful terms as might be possible. In others the estimates have remained poor.

The problems in the natural resources field have been particularly acute with respect to the management of resources yielding products or gains which have thus far not been susceptible to measurement. Among the difficulties posed by such incommensurables is a danger that the focus in many resource programs may be prejudiced in favor of those products which are more quantifiable at the expense of those which may be as meaningful but less easily measured. Problems both of measurement of value and of making provision for their inclusion in natural resource development considerations are posed in these cases.

In certain instances the market can be used to advantage to aid allocation decisions and overcome some inequities as well. One example is a suggestion to deal with the problem of airport noise and the deleterious effect on urban residential areas.[10] Homeowners suffer losses from noise created by airplanes, and as the courts have been a poor resort for relief to homeowners, the market has been advanced as a mechanism for both quantification of the effect and redress for losses sustained. It was suggested that actual loss to the value of property suffered by homeowners as a result of the location under flight paths of urban airports, fall not on the homeowner but on the airport and air passengers. This could be accomplished by a system of payments from the beneficiaries of air travel to those suffering losses. While compensating losers, such a scheme would provide incentives for better locations of facilities and less noisy operations.

One of the more common means for dealing with the measurement problem is to estimate those effects that lend themselves to quantification and to submit an exhibit of the best definition of other effects, either separately or as a direct portion of project formulation and justification. There is a danger that even though such effects are called to attention, they may receive little weight in comparison to project effects for which more readily calculable values are exhibited. An opposite danger is, of course, that basically unsound projects may be justified on the grounds of "overriding social benefits." There is considerable opportunity in this procedure to substitute vague opinion for fact, and sufficient examples exist to raise serious questions regarding such judgments. Indeed, the current response to some of the nation's concern with urban problems, poverty, and regional development, has provided handy crutches for supporting natural resource development projects which may be of marginal or no value in dealing with these issues. Opinions of project formulators on the impact of various natural resource development projects and activities on distantly related national issues, though well intended, carry the serious possibility of being highly biased and an excuse for justifying basically unsound projects.

While direct and adequate quantification of the full values associated with many resource uses is currently not feasible, some principals can still be applied directly to the question of relative values in certain cases. Current procedures in some instances, for example, introduce a systematic bias for given types of development, notably in the recreation and environmental fields. Such a predilection arises in connection with the use of Supplement 1 to Senate Document 97 to determine the values of alternative forms of outdoor recreation.[11]

The procedure currently in use by federal agencies essentially take the recreation benefit to be the product of the total number of recreation days estimated to occur at a site, multiplied by an unvarying unit recreation-day value of from $.50 to $1.50 per day for most forms of recreation or from $2 to $6 for specialized forms.

The major difficulty is that this procedure is simply inadequate to reflect major differences in the economic value of alternative recreation opportunities or alternative development of recreation resources. The efficiency criteria for evaluation of the benefits of recreation afforded by alternative development of natural resources is given by the willingness of users to pay for the alternative opportunity rather than do without it and is measured by the area under the appropriate demand curve. The concept of willingness to pay measured by the area under the demand curve provides value data comparable to other price values in the economy and in terms of economic efficiency is an appropriate guide for social choice.

Current practice of benefit analysis deviates significantly from this principal imparting a severe bias in evaluation of alternative kinds of recreation development. This is particularly the case where, for example, comparisons are made between development of flat water recreation as opposed to maintenance of free-flowing streams or in cases of mass use versus wilderness use of recreation areas. The point is that the criterion outlined in Supplement 1 to Senate Document 97 does not allow for the vast differences that exist in the shapes of the appropriate demand curves which reflect the differences in willingness to pay on the part of users for different kinds of recreational opportunity.

When the same or even similar unit values are used to estimate the value of recreation development alternatives the official procedure is effectively rigged, for the greatest value among the alternatives must be shown to be associated with the greatest number of people attracted. The evaluation simply reduces to a head count (which is itself usually a poor estimate), whereas quite a different result may be obtained when using the willingness to pay measure based on varying shaped demand curves.

The benefits of alternatives depend upon the shape of the relevant demand curves and cannot accurately be estimated in ignorance of the shape. It may be the case, as has been demonstrated by economists, market researchers, and merchants in many cases, that the demand curves for some forms of recreation are likely to be very flat (elastic over much of its range) especially if many ready substitutes are available, and for other forms of recreation, particularly those without substitutes, demand curves are likely to be far more vertical (inelastic over much of its range).[12] The implication for evaluating alternatives is that forms of recreatation which attract smaller numbers of people than other forms may still have an economic value that may even exceed that associated with recreation that caters to larger total numbers of participants. Official methods for evaluating recreation benefits currently in use are simply incapable of indicating this important difference. A more realistic examination of the relative economic values must go beyond the total number of visits that can be expected from the alternatives and examine the likely elasticities or slopes of the demand curves associated with each type of use.

Using basic economic principles, some realistic speculation can be made about the situation surrounding, for example, flat water and free-flowing stream alternatives. If it is established that the recreational opportunities provided by the free-flowing alternatives are relatively unique and rare, that is, that they have few close substitutes, then we can expect that even though the total numbers of visitors making use of this resource for recreational purposes may be quite small, the total value may be relatively large for this number of visitors; alternatively, if substitutes are available for the flat water alternative the opposite would be true. Even though the total visitor use of an area may be numerically greater under a flat water alternative this alone does not insure that the total benefits are greater. Indeed, there is strong reason to suggest that the relative difference in elasticities of the demand curves may often more than compensate for the possible greater use.

It may also be the case in such instances that great differential exists in the changes in demands for each other time. There is, for example, considerable reason to expect that shifts in the demand for more remote forms of recreation may be taking place at a differentially greater rate than for other forms. If such is the case, then resources useful for more esoteric pursuits would take on relatively greater value.

These problems of measurement and of how resource services are to be provided are particularly acute in problems of the quality of the natural environment. Such issues are commanding increasing attention because of a heightening awareness of the values involved. Examples of the concerns include increasing use of pesticides; air and water pollution; landscape deterioration; lack of open areas, particularly in older parts of metropolitan regions; and destruction of scenic amenities and estuarine areas.

Marked changes in our society have established new values and patterns for use of natural resources. Complete protection of natural biological communities as well as open space for active outdoor recreation have taken on new importance. An awareness of environmental problems is reflected in general public support for legislation and programs to dedicate wilderness, attack water pollution, develop recreation areas, and reduce taxes on farmland to relieve urban spread. Some support emanates from a concern for health, but much more can be traced simply to the desire to live, work, and play in pleasant surroundings. The result of the changes in our society and in our environment where technological, economic, political, and social changes have all had an accelerating effect has been a rapidly increasing awareness of environmental amenities, their destruction, lack of availability, and a consequent increase in the demands for them.

Most of these environmental goods are not marketed and have no retail price, but they are just as much economic goods because of their scarcity and value as those regularly produced, purchased, and consumed in our economy. As with market goods, the values attached to better environments—pleasant urban and agricultural landscapes, undisturbed bogs, mass recreation beaches—are related to demand and supply.

While the economic values of different uses of important natural resources change, it is not clear that our usual reliance on the market and other institutions is very effective in bringing about corresponding changes in resource use. Environmental quality values are very real, but our society seems poorly prepared to inject these values into the social and economic calculus in ways which are effective in resolving the conflicts of divergent interests centering on these values. There are many reasons for this, principally those relating to externalities, or spillover effects, of resource use and to the nonmarket nature of most of these demands.[13]

Current efforts to deal with these problems have not all been particularly rewarding. Reliance primarily on such devices as total government purchase in the case of certain types of land areas, zoning to prohibit nonconforming uses, and administrative edicts to prohibit certain types of activities, have a certain number of disadvantages which lead to far less in social payoff than may be obtained from other alternatives. It is in areas such as these that analytical aids will find both difficulties and potentials.

Realistic approaches to many environmental problems take into account the relative supply and demand for the resource products and the incidence of gains and losses resulting from alternative responses. Far more information needs to be developed on causes and effects of activities relating to varying aspects of the quality of the natural environment. Public involvement would seem to call for actions differing from traditional resource development roles to a range of programs and policies, and to administrative devices ranging from tax adjustments, installation of public utilities, effluent charges, subsidies and partial purchases to outright acquisition of fee simple titles. There is, in other words, a range of incentives and restraints which can be utilized to encourage resource utilization which more closely approximates the social optimum.

THE VIEWPOINT OF BENEFIT MEASURES

A persistent problem in the rationalization of public expenditures in the natural resources field stems from the varied objectives of the different interests surrounding natural resource expenditures. A primary reason for this is that the cost and gains of contemplated actions are perceived differently depending on the viewpoint of the individual involved.

Each individual and each community reacts very much in accord with the gains and losses as they themselves contemplate them. Questions of projects being in the interest of the general public are often secondary to affected individuals if losers are not compensated nor gainers required to make payment.[14]

There may indeed be important divergencies between social costs and benefits and those which fall on a single individual. These discrepencies between the interests of individuals or groups and those of the nation as a whole can pose limitations on the implementation of natural resource development activities and often place burdens on the analysis of the desirability of such activities. Those who suffer losses as a result of resource development activities have every reason to object to such activities unless adequately compensated. Similarly, gainers who achieve benefit without payment have every reason to favor projects whether the projects are in the national interest or not.

A similar divergence of interest, together with renewed enthusiasm to use natural resource development activities to aid in the solution of a range of social problems, has brought the issue of secondary benefits to renewed importance. This interest has been further stimulated by increases in the discount rate applicable to federal water resource development projects. The general assumption among resource development agencies and most economists has been that, to the extent that the primary objective of these expenditures is national economic efficiency, by and large secondary impacts associated with development activities are simply transfers of economic activity from one part of the economy to another, and therefore cancel out in terms of the national accounts. To be sure, an individual region stands to gain a great deal from such economic activity generated as a direct result of a project undertaking. However, the entire economy is not likely to gain at all or possibly only to a very slight extent. While direct evidence is not complete, it overwhelmingly appears that the great bulk of the secondary impacts are gains which are only regional benefits that "wash out" from a national point of view because of the loss of benefits elsewhere. There may well be reason to secure information on such impacts, but these cannot be construed as national gains. To include them or to associate them with other projected gains from an investment is to seriously blunt the basic choice rationalizing purpose of benefit-cost analysis.

Certain so-called secondary benefits may well represent a form of legitimate benefit to the national economy. For such gains to accrue, however, special circumstances need to be satisfied, such as increased efficiency as a result of economies in a region or employment of previously unemployed and immobile resources. Even when such conditions prevail, there is reason to suggest that the proportion of secondary benefits which are in fact national efficiency gains, is very small.[15]

It has often been proposed that secondary benefits, even if only regional gains, ought to be counted because the goal of national economic efficiency is only one of those to be pursued by programs of natural resource development. Others, such as income redistribution and balanced regional growth, are also of concern. Therefore, in the interest of dealing with chronically depressed areas, unemployment and "other social objectives" pressures have increased for other water resource agencies to propose counting secondary impacts or "redevelopment benefits" in project justifications. In the main, such calculations impose gross harm to the objective of increasing national economic well-being. While not denying the relevance of other goals, it appears to be highly questionable whether in fact most natural resource development projects contribute significantly to them, or whether they are efficient means for society to go about dealing with them. Lacking much meaningful evidence in support of the efficiency of such projects to aid in the attainment of these other goals, and the competing demands on public expenditures, it would appear that the possibilities for grossly misallocating resources are large.

CONCLUDING COMMENTS

In general, the role of explicit analysis of the effects of public expenditures in natural resources programs has been impressive. There has been sharp criticism of many of the applications. However, much of this can be expected when analysis has been made as explicit as it has, for example, in determining the costs and benefits of water development expenditures.

There is need for improvement in present applications, but probably even more desirable is the extention of analysis to other natural resources programs and expenditures. This is particularly the case with areas of increasing concern that may well involve ever greater spending.

The information flow is far from that needed—with perhaps as much to be gained from redirecting current efforts as initiating new ones. Though not all nor even many value questions can be completely settled, more careful analysis and dependence on adherence to fairly rigid investment and allocation guides appears to remain immensely useful in the natural resources area.

NOTES

[1] Emery N. Castle, "Conceptual Issues in the Conduct of Regional Research on the Economics of Water," in *Opportunities for Regional Research on Water Resources Problems* (Iowa City, Iowa: Agriculture Law Center, 1968).

[2] Robert K. Davis, *The Range of Choice in Water Management* (Baltimore: Johns Hopkins Press, 1968). Interests of the development agencies are sometimes indicated, for example, in such things as the award of the Army's outstanding civilian service award for, "recognition of sustained and outstanding contributions to the expansion and improvement of the inland waterways system." National Waterways Conference, Inc., *Newsletter,* Jan. 24, 1969.

[3] Robert O. Tillman, "Emergence of Black-Market Bureaucracy: Administration Development in the New States," *Public Administration Review,* September/October 1968.

[4] An informative summary of many of the facets of such port developments is contained in, U.S. Army Corps of Engineers, *Harbor and Port Development, A Problem and An Opportunity,* July 1968.

[5] Joe S. Bain, Richard E. Caves, and Julius Margolis, *Northern California's Water Industry* (Baltimore: Johns Hopkins Press, 1966).

[6] Irving K. Fox and Orris C. Herfindahl, "Attainment of Efficiency in Satisfying Demands for Water Resources," *American Economic Review, Papers and Proceedings,* May 1964, p. 205.

[7] John Haldi, "Applications of Program Budgeting to Environmental Problems," in Morris E. Garnsey and James R. Hibbs (eds.), *Social Sciences and the Environment* (Boulder: University of Colorado Press, 1967).

[8] This reaches some extreme with at least one instance of a planning study that sets out the number of acres of historic sites to be provided per population unit.

[9] S. V. Ciriacy-Wantrup, "Conceptual Problems in Projecting the Demand for Land and Water." Land Economics Institute, *Modern Land Policy* (Urbana: University of Illinois Press, 1960), pp. 41–68.

[10] Charles M. Haar, "Airport Noise and the Suburban Dweller: A Proposed Solution," *The Appraisal Journal,* October 1968.

[11] *Policys, Standards and Procedures in the Formulation, Evaluation, and Review of Plans for Use in Development of Water and Related Land Resources,* 87th Congress, 2d sess., Senate Document 97, approved May 1962; *Evaluation Standards for Primary Outdoor Recreation Benefits,* Supplement Number 1, June 1964.

[12] See any standard economics text, for example, Donald S. Watson, *Price Theory and Its Uses,* 2nd Ed. (Boston: Houghton-Mifflin Co., 1968), p. 46.

[13] See for example: John V. Krutilla, "Conservation Reconsidered," *American Economic Review,* September 1967; Jack L. Knetsch, "Economic Aspects of Environmental Pollution," *Journal of Farm Economics,* December 1966; Henry Jarrett (ed.), *Environmental Quality in a Growing Economy* (Baltimore: Johns Hopkins Press, 1966).

[14] Roland N. McKean, "Costs and Benefits from Different Viewpoints," in Howard G. Schaller (ed.), *Public Expenditure Decisions in the Urban Community* (Resources for the Future, Inc., Washington, D.C., 1963).

[15] Evidence on the impact of unemployment is contained in Robert H. Haveman and John V. Krutilla, *Unemployment, Idle Capacity and the Evaluation of Public Expenditures* (Baltimore: Johns Hopkins Press, 1968).

CHAPTER 25

PROSPECTS FOR PPB AT AEC

Milton F. Searl

INTRODUCTION

In the following pages an attempt is made to examine the current status of PPB and related analytic techniques at the Atomic Energy Commission (AEC), the planning and analysis underlying some current atomic energy programs, and the steps that might be taken to further the application of the PPB system to the nation's atomic energy program.

The material should be considered in a specific framework—namely, that of the PPB system and more specifically the economic analysis requirements of that system. There are clearly valid considerations that cannot always be factored into economic analysis which should also enter into public expenditure decisions.

The discussion is centered on the economic aspects although the PPB system encompasses much more than economic analysis. An economic focus appears most appropriate for this compendium and, furthermore, the budget and planning aspects of PPB at AEC generally appear to be either in a reasonably satisfactory state or evolving in a satisfactory manner.

AEC budgeting has been along program lines for many years and adaption to PPB system requirements was not difficult. Planning along program lines had also made some progress at AEC prior to the inauguration of PPB systems. The section 202 hearings (state of the industry) which the 1954 Atomic Energy Act required, as well as other hearings held by the Joint Committee on Atomic Energy, encouraged AEC to lay out at least nominal plans for many of its programs. Perhaps the best known planning effort is the commission's 1962 report to the president on civilian nuclear power. In recent years extensive planning has been carried on by AEC, particularly in connection with the programs of the Production Division and the Division of Reactor Development and Technology. These efforts will be described in more detail subsequently.

Milton F. Searl is Technical Assistant at the Office of Science and Technology in the Executive Office of the President. He was formerly Chief Economist at the Atomic Energy Commission.

The author bears sole responsibility for the views expressed herein. They do not necessarily represent the views of AEC or any other organization or individual.

A convenient place to begin an analysis of the role of PPB system and economic analysis in the atomic energy program is with consideration of the Atomic Energy Act and the institutional arrangements controlling its application. The failures, successes, problems, and potential of the system in the atomic energy field can be better comprehended in such a framework.

The Atomic Energy Act of 1954, as amended, declares it to be the policy of the United States that—

> "(*a*) the development, use, and control of atomic energy shall be directed so as to make the maximum contribution to the general welfare, subject at all times to the paramount objective of making the maximum contribution to the common defense and security; and
>
> "(*b*) the development, use, and control of atomic energy shall be directed so as to promote world peace, improve the general welfare, increase the standard of living, and strengthen free competition in private enterprise." (Sec. 1. Declaration.)

It is further stated to be the purpose of the act to effectuate the above policies by providing for—

> "(*a*) a program of conducting, assisting, and fostering research and development in order to encourage maximum scientific and industrial progress;
>
> . . .
>
> "(*d*) a program to encourage widespread participation in the development and utilization of atomic energy for peaceful purposes to the maximum extent consistent with the common defense and security and with the health and safety of the public;
>
> "(*e*) a program of international cooperation to promote the common defense and security and to make available to cooperating nations the benefits of peaceful applications of atomic energy as widely as expanding technology and considerations of the common defense and security will permit." (Sec. 3. Purpose.)

There is little in the above-quoted portions, or elsewhere in the act, which can be interpreted as calling for an economically efficient approach to the development of atomic energy. The emphasis on the nonmilitary aspects of the atomic energy program is on promotion of atomic energy, scientific progress, and use of atomic energy as a vehicle for furthering world peace and development.

It is hard to argue that the emphasis in the act should have been other than it was in 1954. The potential of the atom was clearly great, although perhaps poorly understood, and facts were not available as to costs of development or as to benefits that would have permitted meaningful analysis. The decision to embark on the major development effort required to harness the atom was not based on detailed economic analysis but rather on the fact that the potential benefits were so large that the beginning effort was clearly justified.

The responsibilities for scientific research placed on AEC by the act are a second factor complicating economic analysis of atomic energy programs. The economic framework for a valid analysis of basic research efforts is still in its infancy. However, even for basic research efforts, where benefits are very uncertain, cost-effectiveness techniques can still be applied in analysis of the relationship of project scheduling to funding levels.

Projects and programs which contain a modest basic research content, some applied research, and a substantial development component present particular problems of analysis.

A third factor complicating the application of economic analysis to atomic energy activities is the military origin of the atomic energy program. This is not so much a result of AEC's responsibilities under the Atomic Energy Act, as were the previously discussed promotional and scientific aspects, as it is an historical accident. Many of AEC's key personnel were associated with the early military programs. For years the overriding priority of the national atomic energy program was the production of weapons and weapon materials. The primary object was regarded as "getting the job done," with economic niceties being of secondary importance. Some of this philosophy, supported by the statutory mandate to promote atomic power, still carries over into current activities, and it has been argued that without this managerial attitude some of the applications of atomic energy would not have achieved their present status. Nevertheless, the fact that the atomic program has become of age suggests that the PPB program does have application to its future funding, as AEC itself has come to recognize.

The institutional framework within which the Atomic Energy Act is carried out, and on which the PPB system has been superimposed, is perhaps even more fundamental to the role of PPB and economics in the atomic energy program than the act itself. Consequently, it is appropriate to describe this framework.

AEC is managed by five commissioners appointed by the president and confirmed by the Senate. The commissioners are men of stature, generally selected from the scientific, academic, and legal communities. At times a member of the industrial community is also included.

The staff is headed by a general manager, who is assisted by a deputy general manager, an assistant general manager, and assistant general managers for various areas of commission activity. Operating divisions, mainly organized along program lines, report to each assistant general manager. Basic program responsibility resides in the operating divisions. In addition, the controller and the general counsel have special responsibilities to the commission as well as heading their respective offices. (The director of regulation also reports separately to the commission.) There are also nonoperating divisions with special responsibilities, such as the Divisions of Operations Analysis and Forecasting (which does little PPB work) and the Division of Plans and Reports (which assists with PPB system planning activities).

AEC programs are for the most part carried out through operations offices, national laboratories, and industrial contractors, all with specific program interests.

In the national laboratories, the operations offices, contractor organizations, and elsewhere, there are highly competent scientists and engineers with a national stature in and sometimes beyond their professions and, therefore, entitled to be heard on policy matters—all of which complicates application of the PPB system.

On the congressional side, AEC operations are reviewed by the Joint Committee on Atomic Energy (JCAE). The JCAE is a very effective committee which takes a close and constructive interest in the work of AEC.

Finally, there are community and industrial interests with a stake in AEC programs and which naturally seek to influence commission activities.

In this complex of decision points the introduction of a new decision-assisting tool—PPB economic analysis—presents obvious difficulties. A fundamental difficulty, of course, is that the basic facts on costs and benefits are not readily available because most AEC programs deal with research and development activities in which future costs and benefits contain large margins for dispute. Few decisions have been based on economic analysis, as opposed to cost, budget, and engineering analysis, and some of the analysis has been in efforts to provide economic backup for previously established program plans.

The formulation of program plans and the conduct of detailed studies at AEC are basically the responsibility of the program divisions. However, AEC has established the position of assistant to the general manager for program analysis to guide and help the divisions in conducting analysis. The assistant for program analysis has three analysts working with him.

Budget aspects of PPB are handled by budget officers in each division who work closely with the controller's office on the budget for each program. The Division of Plans and Reports works with the program divisions in preparing the planning documents required by the PPB system.

Economic analysis of division programs may be carried out by the division itself, by contractors specifically employed for given project, or by contractors with a continuing relationship with the division. Most program divisions contain few practicing economists. One economist works for the assistant to the general manager for program analysis. Consequently, the bulk of the economic analysis is carried out by scientific and engineering personnel.

The Division of Production and the Division of Reactor Development and Technology, the two divisions with the largest civilian-oriented programs, carry on extensive analytic efforts. The Division of Reactor Development tends to use outside contractors with an extensive knowledge of the technical details of AEC reactor programs for analysis of its program.

The Divisions of Production and Military Application have established their own contractor-operated "think tanks," partially staffed by technical people from various production division operating sites on a temporary (1- or 2-year) assignment basis, and partially by permanent staff. They also use some outside contractors.

It would appear that the advent of PPB has strengthened the technical analytic capability of AEC, or at least organized and provided better direction for it. On the other hand, it does not appear to have done much to increase the use of economic analysis in the formulation of program plans.

At various times, AEC has expressed objection to or at least concern about the application of economic analysis, and particularly rate of return, benefit-cost, and cost-effectiveness measures, to its programs on the following grounds:

1. The preference of many economists for high-productivity projects; for example, those with a social rate of return of more than 5 percent;

2. The long-term nature of some of AEC's programs, which means that benefits to society are long delayed, and which delay tends to reduce the productivity of the programs as measured by the rate of return;

3. The failure of analysts to give adequate weight to the intangible or external social and economic benefits of AEC programs;

4. The failure of the analysis to consider the benefits of early versus deferred investment in an inflationary economy;

5. The omission of possible tax benefits to the Government in evaluation of the merit of AEC programs;

6. The lack of confidence by some people outside AEC that there will be benefits from new technological developments even if such benefits are currently unforeseeable; and

7. The lack of confidence at AEC in the validity of applying cost-effectiveness analysis and similar techniques to "basic research" programs.

Presumably the merit, or lack thereof, of the above items falls within the province of other authors in this compendium, so no attempt is made to resolve the issues here.

It may be appropriate to make explicit where this paper considers economic analysis to start and stop. Herein, economics is not considered to cover subjects such as purchasing, contracting, employee relations or the manner in which facilities are operated. Economic analysis frequently assumes that all these things are being done efficiently so that, given the specific plans and programs, there is no more efficient way of doing things. In technical terms, we are on the production opportunity frontier—output cannot be increased without more resources. Of course, we know that in general all through the economy opportunities for increasing economic efficiency exist, but the items cited are frequently the dividing line between economics and other disciplines.

The economic issues rather center around the plans and programs and whether AEC's, the government's, and/or the nation's resources could be better allocated within and between programs to increase benefits to society. It is not, of course, the economist's function to specify society's goals, but rather, once these goals are specified, to use the science of economics to allocate scarce resources among competing ends in order to maximize the achievement of the ends.

Having perhaps to some extent explained AEC's attitude toward economic analysis and the complications of economic analysis of atomic energy programs, the next task is to review the economic aspects of some of AEC's programs involving substantial expenditure of public funds. As a prelude to this task, it is desirable to recognize a basic conflict between economics and engineering. This stems from the difference between engineering (or technical) efficiency and economic efficiency. In general, a plant, device, or technology which is optimum from the standpoint of technical efficiency is nonoptimum from an economic standpoint (e.g., the powerplant with the highest efficiency—best heat rate—is not the lowest cost power producer). This difference between what is technically "best" and what is economically optimum tends to carry over into the design and conduct of research and development programs. Scientists and engineers tend to design high quality research and engineering programs and ones with lots of backup against possible R. & D. uncertainties. Such a program tends to push past the point of diminishing returns from a strict economic standpoint and thus to be criticized by economists.

PLANNING AND ANALYSIS IN SPECIFIC AEC PROGRAMS

No attempt is made to cover all AEC programs in the following discussion. Selection is based on the author's knowledge of specific program efforts, availability of public information on the various programs, and attempts to keep the paper within reasonable limits. In general, no discussion of military or militarily oriented programs is included since these rapidly run into classification problems.

CENTRAL STATION NUCLEAR POWER PROGRAM

This is one of AEC's major programs and is administered primarily by the Division of Reactor Development and Technology. Total reactor development costs for this program in fiscal 1968, including construction and allocation of appropriate supporting activities, appear to have been about $250 million. Program plans call for a substantial increase in the level of funding in the next 5 or 6 years. Aggregate future government expenditures for power reactor development, including general support, safety, R. & D. and fuel, could conceivably reach $7 billion to $10 billion, if various technically interesting and potentially economic concepts which are still under consideration were more fully explored.

From a practical standpoint, the central station power reactor development program appears to be at its first goal—the demonstration of economic nuclear power. Now that nuclear power has come of age, and in view of the large expenditures contemplated to develop the breeder reactor and other advanced types, it is timely to assess whether economic analysis cannot play a large and more constructive role in decisionmaking. The Joint Committee on Atomic Energy, in its report of May 1966 on the fiscal year 1967 authorization legislation, suggested an updating of AEC's reactor development plans. A number of volumes presenting parts of such an updating have been published by AEC, including "The 1967 Supplement to the 1962 Report to the President." As yet no comprehensive overall reactor development plan to guide future expenditures has been made available.

The comprehensive plan should afford a role for economic analysis in further refining or redefining AEC's reactor development objectives and laying out AEC's strategy for achieving those objectives.

The problem is not that the president or Congress will approve AEC's spending $7 to $10 billion on the reactor program without careful review. Rather, the problem is that looking at the program on a year by year, or even several-years-at-a-time basis, it is difficult to exercise meaningful control. It is often hard to abandon unpromising concepts or make new starts without an overall plan that would provide the framework for doing so.

A typical situation is the availability of two or more competing reactor concepts, any of which could be expected to serve the purpose of generating low cost electricity equally well and on about the same time scale. In the absence of overall economic criteria for the reactor program, there is little basis for AEC to choose among them so there is pressure to continue both. Yet, only in some cases will benefits be large enough and the uncertainties great enough to warrant pursuing more than one.

BREEDER REACTOR PROGRAM

The main emphasis in AEC's central station nuclear power program is currently on the breeder reactor program. A plan for AEC's mainline breeder effort, the liquid metal fast breeder reactor (LMFBR), is contained in the "Liquid Metal Fast Beeder Reactor Program Plan, Volume 1—Overall Plan (WASH 1101)." The volume does not give cost estimates for implementing the plan, but it appears that total breeder reactor development costs, including the LMFBR, could cost from one-half to two-thirds of total future estimated central station nuclear power reactor development costs. There is a need for the LMFBR plan to be integrated into an overall breeder reactor plan and this, in turn, made a consistent part of the previously suggested overall plan for all central station nuclear power development.

AEC is developing an economic analysis of its breeder reactor development plans. Such a plan needs to be concerned with the pace and scope of breeder development and the establishment of a competitive manufacturing industry.

The successful development of breeder reactors has always been the main vision of the nuclear power program. Breeder reactors will make available the full potential of uranium and uranium is sufficiently abundant in the earth's crust that with breeders, our ability to supply mankind's energy needs for thousands of years is assured. Breeder reactors can banish the fear which has haunted scientists for much of this century; namely, that our increasingly energy dependent civilization would eventually grind to a halt due to the exhaustion of energy resources.

It appears that this objective is now virtually at hand. Present breeder technology, or at least that to be developed by present programs within the next few years, seems to assure that the world will have available essentially unlimited amounts of energy. This fact seems to have gone largely unnoticed in the excitement over the nation's dramatic commitment to light water reactors. (This paragraph assumes that there will be no problem with radioactive waste disposal.)

The basic goal of the breeder development program now appears to be to reduce the cost of power from breeder reactors to the point where breeders are commercially viable and, perhaps, to reduce the cost of power well below the 4 to 5 mills per kilowatt-hour commonly used as the cost (to investor-owned utilities) of generating power from the best nuclear and fossil plants today.

The task of reducing the cost of power from breeder reactors to "more reasonable" levels is largely an engineering one—albeit a difficult and expensive one, requiring perhaps $3 billion or more in additional government expenditures and substantial expenditures by the private sector.

The fact that the breeder reactor program that is still ahead of us is essentially an engineering development program aimed at reducing the cost of production of an established commodity, electricity, which can be produced by other means seems to make it a natural for economic analysis within the PPB system framework.

PACE OF THE BREEDER PROGRAM

AEC's LMFBR program plan, referenced above (but, not yet, approved by the president), calls for initial criticality of the first commercial plant in 1986 and initial criticality of two more plants before 1990. Considering the time span involved, an acceleration of the program is probably possible and, conversely, the program could be operated at a level designed for a later introduction date. Additional benefits from lower than otherwise electricity generating costs should result from earlier introduction of breeders.

The behavior of R. & D. costs and benefits with a change in program pace are unclear, and the rates of return for both earlier and later introduction dates needs to be calculated. AEC has drafted a liquid metal fast breeder study and may have finalized, and perhaps published it, by the time this paper is published. The LMFBR plan and study represent a major PPB effort.

SCOPE OF THE BREEDER PROGRAM

The main questions regarding the scope of the breeder program involve the number of breeder designs on which AEC should be working and how far AEC should seek to develop breeders before withdrawing from development work and allowing industry to finance further development.

AEC apparently has a very high degree of confidence that costs of the LMFBR can be substantially reduced to the point where it can generate power on a utility system for about 4 mills per kilowatt-hour by 1990 (constant dollars). The LMFBR apparently has potential for further cost reductions below 4 mills, with operating experience and continued development beyond that date.

The public expenditure decisions that the nation faces in connection with the scope of the program are concerned with the number of alternative breeder concepts which AEC should pursue, given expectations for the LMFBR. Such decisions can be aided by economic analysis which can be readily undertaken, given whatever distribution of likelihoods AEC assigns to the achievement of various generating costs at specific dates with the LMFBR.

Breeder reactors using the thorium-uranium-233 fuel cycle are conceptually feasible as well as breeders using the uranium-plutonium cycle, such as the LMFBR system, which is currently AEC's mainline breeder effort. Arguments for the thorium-uranium-233 breeder system center around its possibly favorable economic features, uranium conservation, and thorium availability.

AEC has chosen to make the uranium-plutonium system its mainline effort and has considerable confidence in the success of the system. There is sufficient uranium to fuel breeders for many centuries. From an economic standpoint, therefore, it is questionable if the added costs of developing the thorium system can be justified, even if in the long run it has lower costs in commercial operation. At any rate, such studies should be a part of the decisionmaking process.

Although, thorium is estimated to be somewhat more abundant than uranium, this is irrelevant from the economic standpoint unless its use results in net economic benefits to society when R. & D. costs are included in the evaluation.[1]

NUCLEAR DESALTING

The possibility of making large supplies of clean, fresh water available to water short or arid areas of the world is one that captures the public imagination, perhaps even more than the prospects of large supplies of low-cost energy. However, the two are not necessarily separate. The achievement of desalting goals by the route being pursued by AEC requires large amounts of low-cost energy.

The desalting program is a joint program between the Atomic Energy Commission, the Department of Interior, and various utility systems. An international cooperative program is also carried out in the desalting field.

Atomic Energy Commission costs for desalting applications were approximately $3 million in 1968. Government costs for proposed demonstration plants would involve much larger expenditures.

The first question is whether the energy for desalting should be supplied by fossil fuel or nuclear power. It is doubtful if any general answer can be given to this question, particularly in the United States, where nuclear power and fossil fuel are frequently quite competitive. Each project needs to be analyzed on its own merits.

The question of nuclear versus fossil fuel becomes even more controversial abroad. Many areas in the Middle East and North Africa which need water have prolific oil production and are flaring or reinjecting natural gas. The marginal cost to the country of using this oil or gas appears to be quite low. Such comparisons on a national basis must, of course, be based not on the market price of the fuel but rather on the net cost to the government after considering the tax and other revenue which it gets from each unit of production. This may mean 5 to 10 cents per million British thermal unit oil and gas costs and minimum foreign exchange requirements.

Determination of the relative amounts of water and power to be produced in a dual-purpose plant, and the allocation of costs between water and power, is an area in which it seems there is a need for application of economics to desalting. Given an unambiguous economic objective for the plant, there are perfectly straightforward mathematical economics techniques for optimizing this objective.

In fact, it is possible to apply either product transformation and isorevenue curve or marginal benefit and marginal cost theory. Although this may sound a little complicated, it is likely to be easier and is more accurate than the empirical methods frequently used. Although there seems to be some reluctance to deal with demand, isorevenue, and marginal revenue curves, no strictly economic optimization is possible without them or equivalent concepts.

It needs to be emphasized that allocation of true joint costs is not needed to determine the project economic optimum, including the amounts of each product to be produced and prices. Furthermore, attempted allocation is likely to be confusing and, if improperly done, to force the project off the economic optimum. If cost allocation of true joint costs is required for accounting purposes, it can be best done by working back from price and quantity data. The economic conditions which determine project optimum also effectively determine the appropriate allocation of costs (i.e., the unique allocation which is consistent with the optimization, the acceptance of any other allocation being inconsistent with project optimization).

GASEOUS DIFFUSION PLANT CAPITAL EXPENDITURES

A major public expenditure question which has been raised is whether the large capital expenditures required to enrich uranium for the electric utility market should be made by the government, private industry, or some combination thereof.

Uranium is currently enriched (in the isotope uranium 235) in three gaseous diffusion plants operated for the Atomic Energy Commission by industrial contractors. AEC is planning a cascade (gaseous diffusion) plant improvement program which can be expected to cost about $500 million through fiscal year 1977 and is considering a follow-on power uprating program costing perhaps $150 million. Furthermore, AEC has estimated that construction commitments for new enrichment facilities, probably running into billions of dollars, will need to be made starting in the mid-1970s. (The level of construction costs, the status of enriching technology, and the size of the market in the late 1970s and early 1980s make more precise estimates difficult.)

It goes without saying that PPBS techniques have wide application to evaluating and scheduling gaseous diffusion plant capital expenditures, and such techniques are being used by AEC for programing plant improvement.

GASEOUS DIFFUSION PLANT OPERATION

For many years the government's gaseous diffusion plants were operated at high levels to enrich uranium for government programs. In recent years, government military requirements have been much less than plant capacity and operations have been sharply cut back. However, AEC projections indicate that the full capacity of the plants will be needed by the mid-1970s, primarily to supply electric utility markets for enriched uranium. Furthermore, projected requirements substantially exceed diffusion plant capacity in the late 1970s. Consequently, AEC has embarked on a campaign to preproduce enriched uranium and thereby take advantage of the favorable characteristics of the diffusion plant marginal cost curves and to defer the time at which new plants (or major expansions) are required.

Although a preproduction program is rather clearly desirable, there are economic questions as to the proper extent of preproduction.

Very extensive analysis of the question of the proper preproduction level has been undertaken by AEC. The basic underlying concept of this analysis is that of equal discounted incremental cost. This principle indicates that units should be preproduced each year up to the point where the out-of-pocket cost of such production, plus interest and other holding costs on preproduction, will just equal the minimum future production cost by a feasible alternative. This, of course, requires establishing future sales prices, which in this case are derived from estimates of the cost of additional capacity to be built about 1980.

Although the basic procedure for determining preproduction levels seems sound, questions have been raised about many of the parameters going into the actual calculations and, consequently, the results. A primary question is the appropriate rate for discounting. AEC prefers a 5 percent discount rate with risk analysis. This results in higher production levels than would result from use of a higher discount rate.

Since this program clearly involves market and other uncertainties, attempts have been made to compute the optimum strategy for preproduction under such uncertainty, given the appropriate basic discount rate, but there is not yet general agreement on such calculations.

FURTHER IMPLEMENTATION OF PPBS AT AEC

AEC has largely met the formal requirements of the PPB System. It submits plans and budgets as required and provides special analytic studies. Organizationally, it has established the position of assistant to the general manager for program analysis (assistant and three analysts—one an economist) to help the divisions in conducting program analysis.

However, AEC has not, by and large, made the economic tools and techniques of PPBS an integral part of its decisionmaking process. This is not surprising, considering AEC's scientific, engineering and military orientation.

Any substantial further progress in the use of economic analysis by AEC is unlikely to come except as the result of outside stimulus, such as the trend in government toward increased use of economic techniques.

It is tempting to suggest that AEC be induced to establish a division of economics or some high level economic group to foster and improve economic analysis at AEC. However, until the AEC becomes convinced that economic analysis can be helpful to it in its decisionmaking and funding problems, no form of staff organization is likely to make its mark. In fact, it is not clear that at present economists could even be readily found for such a group. AEC has difficulty recruiting economists and even the young economists who join AEC's intern program soon drift into personnel, contract or similar work, or move on to other agencies.

There are several things which could be done rather easily and would probably improve the quality of the economic analysis of atomic energy programs. One is to require that AEC promptly publish cost-benefit analyses and special analytic studies which it makes. There are, of course, cases where prompt publication of studies is precluded for policy reasons. Even there I would urge in most cases that the studies be published as soon as possible after the policy decision.

Exposing these studies to public view would provide the public and Congress with an opportunity to judge for themselves the merits of the programs. And there is increasing interest in and competence to evaluate the costs and benefits of atomic energy programs at universities and non-profit institutions. There is no reason why the government should not have the benefit of the reviews of atomic energy studies which these groups would make. Such outside review and criticism would almost certainly gradually increase the quality of economic analysis carried out in the commission.

Perhaps the least painful and most productive method of obtaining better analysis of the benefits of government programs would be to separate responsibility for the estimation of the costs from responsibility for the measurement of the benefits. This would more closely approach our traditional market system, where the producer offers his goods and customers place a value on them. In many cases, there is no special capability in an individual agency to measure the benefits resulting from its programs. Manpower must be diverted from the agency's main function to scout other agencies for needed "market" data or to develop it. Because of lack of adequate experience in evaluating benefits, it is also quite possible that errors will be made and benefits may be underestimated as well as overestimated. However, the natural tendency of an analyst to view with some favor his agency's programs may result in a consistent bias toward overestimation.

The idea of separating benefit-cost and related analytic work from the operating agencies is not, of course, original. It has been proposed by others and further research on it is being done. What I have suggested here for AEC's work is a less drastic step and one that could be implemented more quickly. It could be a transition step on the way to the more complete separation proposed by others. It does not appear that separation of the estimation of the technical characteristics of the technology and of the research and development costs of achieving those characteristics is presently feasible in AEC's case. I doubt if there is enough independent technical know-how to make these estimates. Lack of widespread technical know-how outside of AEC and the nuclear industry should not, of course, preclude legitimate questioning of AEC's estimates where they appear to differ from other available data or to be inconsistent with other AEC studies. On the benefit side, there is probably greater capability outside of AEC (and the AEC contractor complex), as far as methodological know-how, experience, and background information availability are concerned, and less chance of bias creeping into the results. AEC might, of course, still desire to make its own estimate of benefits for comparative purposes.

On the methodological side, various improvements are possible, although some studies are better in this respect than others.

In view of differences of opinion over the appropriate discount rate to be used in analysis, it might be desirable to abandon the direct application of specified discount rates in AEC analysis. Instead, from the raw (undiscounted) data, the discount rate which will make the benefit-cost ratio equal to one (or other desired value) should be calculated; i.e., the internal rate of return should be found. This technique is being increasingly used outside of government, chiefly because the results are easier for management to understand—i.e., for most people it is more meaningful to measure the productivity of an investment by stating that it is earning 8 percent than that it has a 2:1 benefit-cost ratio at 5 percent.

Analyses for programs where costs are shared by industry, or where industry is carrying on a program of its own, should incorporate the best possible estimates of industry expenditures in the analysis. It is possible that in some programs both industry and government judge the programs to have a favorable rate of return because both assume *full* national benefits in their calculations but only *their* part of the costs. This could result in carrying out programs which are not economically justified from a national economic interest standpoint. In other cases, failure to take account of industry efforts could result in overestimating the cost of the government development program and thus understating the benefit-cost ratio.

Studies involving estimates of future consumption of goods or services should pay more attention to the concept of demand instead of fixing on "requirements," which are assumed to be independent of price. While demand for many commodities may be inelastic, there appear to be relatively few for which demand is independent of price.

Analysis of alternatives which arrive at rates of return (or other productivity measures, including benefit-cost ratios) should be carried to the point of choosing between the alternatives as far as the economic criteria are concerned. At least some AEC studies terminate the analysis by listing the rates of return (or benefit-cost ratios). In general, under a fixed budget constraint—government, agency, or program—it is not possible to pick the economic optimum without further analysis. For example, a 14 percent rate of return on an investment is better from an overall productivity standpoint than a 15 percent rate of return on one-half as much investment and 10 percent on the other half. There are accepted, mathematically valid methods of carrying the analysis of investment productivity to its optimum value and these should be used. It is relatively easy to do when the basic computations are being made, but somewhat more difficult for another analyst without the basic data to do later.

There is a need, at least on a total basis, if not on a project basis, of finding some method of evaluating the benefits of basic research and also determining the value of "spinoff benefits" from such research. Chairman Seaborg of AEC has recognized this need. In a recent talk, he noted:

> "One of the big problems in establishing a growth rate for basic research, like it or not, is determining the economic value of a discovery. This is tending to become a basic need in the physical and biological

> sciences, perhaps also in the social sciences, and to a lesser extent in the arts and humanities. . . .
>
> ". . . the problem of quantifying the value of "spinoff" from basic research is not trivial. I look forward to the time when some group of economists, perhaps supported by a grant from the National Science Foundation, makes a breakthrough in establishing realistic criteria in this field."[2]

It might be appropriate for AEC to take the lead or at least carry on economic research aimed at quantifying the value of discoveries and of collateral benefits of development work. Such an effort might receive better cooperation from the scientific community, if so sponsored, and there would be a greater likelihood of scientific values being properly reflected in the study than if undertaken independently by economists.

AEC might also pioneer work in the application of cost-effectiveness techniques to the scheduling of research, and particularly applied research, in view of its strong scientific interests. Even where the benefits are unknown, as in the high-energy physics program, but can be assumed to be a fixed amount or vary in some known way, the costs of realizing those benefits can be incurred in various ways and according to varying time patterns, some of which will be more cost effective than others. And the lowest undiscounted cost is not necessarily optimum, so simply minimizing project costs does not suffice.

Along a similar line, it would appear worth some AEC effort to attempt quantification of various external benefits which are frequently emphasized qualitatively. In view of the phenomenal ability of science to measure the elusive in physics, biology, et cetera, it is hardly satisfactory to maintain that many of the much more tangible externalities in economics and the social sciences are immeasurable.

To the extent that it has not already been done, reviews of the reliability of AEC initial estimates of project costs and benefits and of changes in estimates over time should be made. The results of such review should help correct the planning process and indicate any systematic bias and/or methodological deficiencies in the analysis. Such an assessment should probably be carried out by an independent group rather than the agency.

Regardless of what new measures are taken, continued BOB interest in better PPB analysis is a prerequisite for further progress. Congressional interest in the continuance and improvement of PPB is, of course, vital to success of the system.

NOTES

[1] Dr. Paul MacAvoy, of the Massachusetts Institute of Technology, has carried out some pioneer research work in possible breeder reactor development strategies under a grant from Resources for the Future, Inc. This work involves program scope, among other things. This work is described in "Economic Strategy for Developing Nuclear Breeder Reactors" by Paul W. MacAvoy, M.I.T. Press, 1969.

[2] The Government-University Partnership in Graduate Education—AEC press release S–50–68, Dec. 4, 1968.